E–Business Managerial Aspects, Solutions and Case Studies

Maria Manuela Cruz–Cunha
Polytechnic Institute of Cavado and Ave, Portugal

Joao Varajão
University of Trás-os-Montes e Alto Douro, Portugal

BUSINESS SCIENCE REFERENCE

Hershey · New York

Senior Editorial Director:	Kristin Klinger
Director of Book Publications:	Julia Mosemann
Editorial Director:	Lindsay Johnston
Acquisitions Editor:	Erika Carter
Development Editor:	David DeRicco
Production Coordinator:	Jamie Snavely
Typesetters:	Keith Glazewski & Natalie Pronio
Cover Design:	Nick Newcomer

Published in the United States of America by
Business Science Reference (an imprint of IGI Global)
701 E. Chocolate Avenue
Hershey PA 17033
Tel: 717-533-8845
Fax: 717-533-8661
E-mail: cust@igi-global.com
Web site: http://www.igi-global.com/reference

Library of Congress Cataloging-in-Publication Data

E-business managerial aspects, solutions and case studies / Maria Manuela
Cruz-Cunha and Joao Varajão, editors.
      p. cm.
 Includes bibliographical references and index.
 Summary: "This book provides a discussion of the managerial aspects,
solutions and case studies related to e-business, disseminating current
achievements and practical solutions and applications"--Provided by publisher.
  ISBN 978-1-60960-463-9 (hbk.) -- ISBN 978-1-60960-465-3 (ebook) 1. Small
business--Information technology. 2. Electronic commerce--Management. I.
Cruz-Cunha, Maria Manuela, 1964- II. Varajão, Joao, 1972- III. Title.

 HD2341.E223 2011
 658.8'72--dc22

2010025544

British Cataloguing in Publication Data
A Cataloguing in Publication record for this book is available from the British Library.

All work contributed to this book is new, previously-unpublished material. The views expressed in this book are those of the authors, but not necessarily of the publisher.

Table of Contents

Section 1
Managerial Issues

Detailed Table of Contents

Section 1
Managerial Issues

In the eight chapters of Section 1, the reader will contact with strategies, most of them concerned with SME, to enhance enterprise competitiveness by adopting and exploring the potential of e-Business.

The adoption of E-Business by SMEs is a critical issue for economic development. More than 90% of world companies are SMEs and E-Business is widely recognized as a critical source of competitive advantage. Thus, it is important to understand why SMEs are lagging behind large firms in terms of E-Business adoption and assimilation. This chapter will attempt to search for explanations through a comprehensive analysis of main topics in terms of E-Business implementation, strategies and policy. It is believed that the inadequacy of existing E-Business adoption incentives and theoretical models may be due to SME specificity. Empirical evidence shows that SMEs have erratic behaviors in terms of ICT investment and need external support to integrate E-Business in the overall strategy of the firm.

Many SMEs have used e-business models for enhancing their competitiveness. As the needs of SMEs grow, however, so does e-business/ IT strategic alignment. Although some techniques have been proposed in literature to find and evaluate business/ IT strategic alignment, they largely suffer from lack of objectivity and integration. The chapter proposes a practical lightweight interview-based method that permits to align e-business and IT strategies and to obtain investment priorities per software development process and area, towards improvements on service quality and business profitability. This method incorporates goal modeling and the Strategic Alignment Modeling techniques to address the growing needs of SMEs, to avoid inconsistencies and to increase confidence in compiled data and modeling results.

Chapter 3

George Velegrakis, IDEC S.A., Greece
João Varajão, Centro ALGORITMI / UTAD, Portugal
Leonel Morgado, GECAD / UTAD, Portugal
Caroline Dominguez, UTAD, Portugal
Clara Rodrigues, IPBeja (Instituto Politécnico de Beja), Portugal
Dalila Coelho, IPBeja (Instituto Politécnico de Beja), Portugal
Aura Haidimoschi, Camera de Comert si Industrie a Municipiului Bucuresti (CCIB), Romania
Chiara Sancin, Dida Network, Italy
Gerhard Doppler, bit media e-Learning solution GmbH & Co KG, Austria
Hillevi Koivusalo, Hyria koulutus Oy, Finland
Erja Lakanen, Hyria koulutus Oy, Finland

In a dynamic and competitive world, understanding the knowledge, skills and competences that managers of SMEs require is an important endeavor, to ensure that both academic and business training institutions offer well formed programs/courses and curricula. Several studies, conducted by academic researchers and business associations around the world, focused on identifying managers' skills and competences, but there is not an overall perspective on today's requirements of European SME managers. To help overcome this problem, the authors have conducted a study in six European countries through a literature review and several interviews with business associations' executives. The result is a list of 34 competences, which we organized in four categories: personal; team management; business; and technical. These competences are presented and discussed in this chapter, and the findings enable a better understanding of the profile of SME managers and may help in the design of new training programs to fulfill the identified needs.

Chapter 4

Ciara Heavin, University College Cork, Ireland
Frederic Adam, University College Cork, Ireland

Preparing for change is an issue for companies large and small. However, there remains a dearth of empirical evidence that highlight how software SMEs operationalise their approach to knowledge management (KM) as a means of preparing themselves for the future. For an SME, the first step is to take stock of the types of knowledge that are valuable, where it is stored and how it is used. In addition, consideration must be given to knowledge activities, the constituent parts, of a company's KM approach. By doing this, the organization can identify where its strengths lie in terms of the type and extent to which knowledge is managed through acquisition, codification, storage, maintenance, transfer and creation activities. This chapter identifies occurrences of these knowledge activities as a means of assessing an SME's approach to KM with a view to better facilitating an organization's ability to be increasingly flexible in the face of a changing environment.

Agility is an essential feature for SMEs and this chapter intends to examine if and how business processes, as currently understood, are able to promote it. Over the last years a number of viewpoints have emerged which exerted great influence on the design of notations and languages for business processes: the major of them can be referred to as the centralized viewpoint, the role viewpoint, the conversational viewpoint, the case viewpoint and the cooperative one. These viewpoints provide different levels of agility and then beneficial results can be expected from their integration, which is the purpose of the proof-of-concept notation, AgileBPN, presented in this chapter. In AgileBPN, business processes are organized around conversations and role processes (encompassing the tasks pertaining to a given role); shared artifacts are represented as cooperative objects. The notation is illustrated with the help of an example referring to a business process meant to handle applications in a certain organization.

Chapter 6

E-procurement transactions in Business to Business (B2B) environment showed a constant and positive trend in the last years. The most popular methodologies to support these tools are all related to dedicated protocols able to facilitate the agreements among customers and suppliers. This chapter proposes a Multi Agent Architecture integrated with several multi-attribute auction mechanisms specifically designed to support the e-procurement processes. Moreover, differently from other cases proposed in literature, the suppliers' proposal formulation is strongly influenced by their production plans. A simulative environment has been developed in order to evaluate different performances: the customer and suppliers' utilities, the profit distribution among the involved agents and the time necessary to reach an agreement. The mentioned approaches are compared with a negotiation process. The simulation results highlight the weakness and strength points of each auction protocol and why they can be considered as a relevant tool in B2B environments.

The contemporary world is full of innovations, causing both good and bad consequences, including the essential problem of well-being of co-workers. Most troubles of this kind cannot be resolved with measures of the usual management and/or economic theory that have caused these troubles. Therefore, the question is raised: what could be done about the well-being of co-workers, if principles and measures of innovative business, social responsibility, and requisite holism were used in synergy. The electronic business plays a central role in the economy, facilitating the exchange of information, goods, services, and payments, being an innovation causing changes influencing well-being. On one hand the e-business raises productivity and competitiveness, on the other hand it negatively effects well-being of co-workers in all organizations, including SMEs. Most humans tend to prefer their established routine, not change, including innovation. The chapter introduces well-being and its benefits, and discusses the connection between well-being and e-business and both positive and negative effects of this connection.

Even though the energy sector has relied much on the known sources, the production process has gone through some notable changes due to inherent challenges and developments in knowledge management and technology use. The Offshore oil & gas production industry today, at least in the North Sea, is at a cross-road where the traditional operational concepts are seriously challenged due to various risk factors and commercial uncertainties. Subsequently, 'Integrated eOperations' (IO) was adapted as the business solution for a sustainable future seeking major benefits by major players in the sector. SMEs encounter various technical and operational challenges to cope with the mass scale dynamic change process. In order to utilize IO for commercial advantage, SMEs are in the process of exploring various interface solutions today. With respect to the ongoing developments and the scopes of IO, 'Collaborative business interfacing' that is discussed in this chapter is to enable the SMEs to be 'smarter together' to capitalize on the potentials of IO through a strategic capability acquisition process.

Section 2
Applications, Surveys and Case Studies

The second section of this book, includes eight chapters traducing experiences, best practices, case studies and surveys related to the potential of IT in general and e-Business, e-Commerce, e-Procurement in particular, in enterprises' competitiveness.

Based on empirical evidence gained by a telephone survey of 375 SMEs, this chapter uses logistical regressions as a means of identifying the potential for relationships between three variables - industry sector, firm size (as measured by employment), and age of firm - as they influence ICT ownership, ICT use and ICT benefits. Such inter-relationships can then be used to identify networked trading practice and proclivity. Data was gathered for firms on the basis of four industrial sectors ('Media', 'Logistics', 'Internet Services' and 'Food Processing') in a region encompassing West London and adjacent counties. Logistical regressions suggest that possession, application and the benefits derived from ICT can be explained on the basis of single and multiple variables or as the result of none, and are individuated as either 'just sector', 'just size', 'sector and size', 'sector and age', 'sector, size and age' or 'no variable'.

Innovative organizations are moving away from discrete linear value chains towards open innovation models such as networks. SMEs recognize that in order to survive they must be equipped with the relevant competencies required to design, develop and deploy innovative solutions that meet the needs of the end user. More and more small firms are collaborating with each other in order to create value added products and access new markets. However, the task of working in a collaborative network is not easy, and there are very few support structures and systems available to guide successful knowledge sharing and collaboration. This chapter explores the fundamental concepts of collaborative networks and knowledge sharing, synthesizes and presents some of the challenges faced by SMEs and identifies some critical success factors that should be considered to help overcome the barriers identified.

Chapter 11

The chapter presents a research carried out within business-to-business (B2B) electronic markets, with the purpose of asserting the major blocks needed to be covered by an e-purchasing tool in order to be successful. Another goal is to identify how this e-purchasing tool allows buyers (firms) to practice Strategic Sourcing. After an enlarged literature review on E-Sourcing Electronic Platforms (ESEP) and e-purchasing markets, the authors defined a methodological framework and construct a case study. Their strategy was to use one case study, and using the data collected in a survey recently conducted by Vortal (Portuguese firm that owns several B2B platforms in different electronic markets).

Search Engine Marketing (SEM) is one of the most effective online advertising channels which let companies efficiently acquire new and reactivate existing customers at low acquisition costs. In this chapter, authors briefly review the scientific literature on SEM with respect to managerial decision problems along the levers of SEM, mainly bid optimization, keyword selection, and adCopy creation. Based on a case study they discuss challenges of SEM campaigns operated by SME. After briefly describing the technical requirements for effectively controlling SEM campaigns we focus on keyword selection and how to address the long tail issue in SEM. A/B-Tests are shown to be an appropriate measure for optimizing the combination of ad copies and landing pages. Finally they discuss bid optimization at a keyword level taking into account spill-over effects between keywords.

Chapter 13

    Marjorie Luísa Biehl, Unisinos University, Brazil
    Brandon Link, Unisinos University, Brazil
    Adolfo Alberto Vanti, Unisinos University, Brazil
    Gustavo Schneider, Unisinos University, Brazil

A competitive market gives the organizations a constant update on the management process of their businesses and allows the creation of new ways to take competitive advantage. Retail businesses need to identify the value perceived by customers as a strategic source of value generation. This chapter presents a competitive value generation methodology by identifying the most important values perceived by customers of a Volkswagen Car Dealer. As a result, the study obtained a proposal for value generation by setting the strategic variables referent credibility/reliability.

Chapter 14

    Bwalya Kelvin Joseph, University of Botswana, Botswana

E-Commerce, and recently mobile commerce has shown a lot of potential for development in the Southern African Development Community (SADC) bloc given the growth in e-adoption of the region. Partly, this has been attributed to sound policies and initiatives thereby creating an enabling environment for e-Commerce to thrive. However, there are also challenges that are being faced on an everyday basis concerning e-Commerce business and how this impacts the SME sector. This chapter aims to present these challenges and recommend on what should be done in order to consolidate and move forward the adoption of e-Commerce applications in the SADC region. It looks at exploratory studies of e-Commerce penetration specifically from four SADC member countries. In Africa, other than e-Commerce, there has been a transition where businesses are now done using m-Commerce. This chapter also reviews the growth of this new business model, and further looks at Africa's infrastructure preparedness and looks at mobile phone subscription rates, level of trust in these business models, and the general value that this kind of business undertaking brings.

Guided by the authors' theory of the Conservation of Information (COI), which holds that the transformation pairs of information uncertainty between time and frequency remain constant (or alternately uncertainty for geospatial position and spatial frequency), the chapter describes a case study on an international corporation based in Taiwan to demonstrate COI factors associated with the challenges and successes in the adoptions of e-business by the firm and by small and medium size enterprises in general

The chapter reports a study undertaken to determine to what extent organizational size, organizational complexity, and organizational social ties impacted the creation of an organizational Web page and its relative time of adoption among the organizational members of the chamber of commerce in a small city in Minnesota. The research utilized a cross-sectional design, with data being gathered via a self-administered mail survey, where a total of 173 surveys were completed. Two independent variables were statistically significant in predicting whether an organization would have a Web page: (1) organizational size measured by the number of paid employees; and (2) organizational complexity indexed by the number of unique job descriptions, physical locations in Minnesota, and physical locations in other states. The results of this research provide practical information to formal organizations considering the adoption of an organizational Web page.

Preface

ABOUT THE SUBJECT

Electronic business (eBusiness) certainly is not exclusive for large enterprises. It propels productivity and competitiveness, being sophisticated systems like e-Marketplaces accessible both for both buyers and sellers. So eBusiness represents a great potential and opens opportunities to foster competitiveness.

Electronic business plays a central goal in the economy, facilitating the exchange of information, goods, services and payments. This topic is gaining an increasingly relevant strategic impact on global business and the world economy, and organizations of all sort are undergoing hard investments (in cost and effort) in search of the rewarding benefits of efficiency and effectiveness that this range of solutions promise. But as we all know this is not an easy task it is not only a matter of financial investment. It is much more, as the book will show.

Responsiveness, flexibility, agility and business alignment are requirements of competitiveness that enterprises search for. And we hope that the solutions, tools and case studies presented and discussed in this book can contribute to highlight new ways to identify opportunities and improve managerial practice.

The book project was born under the intention to collect the most recent developments on the organizational, technological and legal dimensions of electronic business, discuss its potential applications. This objective was met, due to the high adhesion of contributors and the quality and complementarity of the manuscripts proposed that allowed a comprehensive whole, addressing all the aspects initially previewed.

ORGANIZATION OF THE BOOK

This book is a compilation of 16 contributions to the discussion of the managerial aspects, solutions and case studies related with e-Business, in order to disseminate current achievements and practical solutions and applications.

These 16 chapters are written by a group of 45 authors that include many internationally renowned and experienced researchers and specialists in the e-Business field and a set of younger authors, showing a promising potential for research and development. Contributions came from all over the world and integrate contributions from academe, research institutions and industry, representing a good and comprehensive representation of the state-of-the-art approaches and developments that address the several dimensions of this fast evolutionary thematic.

"E-Business Managerial Aspects, Solutions and Case Studies" is organized in two sections:

- Section 1: *"Managerial Issues"* puts the reader in contact with strategies, most of them concerned with SME, to enhance enterprise competitiveness by adopting and exploring the potential of e-Business.
- "Section 2: *"Applications, Surveys and Case Studies"*, traduces experiences, best practices, case studies and surveys related to the potential of IT in general and e-Business, e-Commerce, e-Procurement in particular, in enterprises' (specially SME) competitiveness.

In the eight chapters of Section 1 *"Managerial Issues"*, the reader will contact with strategies, most of them concerned with SME, to enhance enterprise competitiveness by adopting and exploring the potential of e-Business.

The adoption of E-Business by SMEs is a critical issue for economic development. More than 90% of world companies are SMEs and E-Business is widely recognized as a critical source of competitive advantage. Thus, it is important to understand why SMEs are lagging behind large firms in terms of E-Business adoption and assimilation. In Chapter 1, *"SMEs and E-Business: Implementation, Strategies and Policy"*, Ferreira looks for explanations through a comprehensive analysis of main topics in terms of E-Business implementation, strategies and policy. It is believed that the inadequacy of existing E-Business adoption incentives and theoretical models may be due to SME specificity. Empirical evidence shows that SMEs have erratic behaviors in terms of ICT investment and need external support to integrate E-Business in the overall strategy of the firm.

SMEs grow requires e-business/ IT strategic alignment. Although some techniques have been proposed in literature to find and evaluate business/ IT strategic alignment, they largely suffer from lack of objectivity and integration. In *"Strategic E-Business/ IT Alignment for SME Competitiveness"*, Escofet, Rodríguez-Fórtiz, Garrido and Chung propose a practical lightweight interview-based method that permits to align e-business and IT strategies and to obtain investment priorities per software development process and area, towards improvements on service quality and business profitability. This method incorporates goal modeling and the Strategic Alignment Modeling techniques to address the growing needs of SMEs, to avoid inconsistencies and to increase confidence in compiled data and modeling results.

In a dynamic and competitive world, understanding the knowledge, skills and competences that managers of SMEs require is an important endeavor, to ensure that both academic and business training institutions offer well formed programs/courses and curricula. Several studies, conducted by academic researchers and business associations focused on identifying managers' skills and competences, but there is not an overall perspective on today's requirements of European SME managers. To help overcome this problem, the authors have conducted a study in six European countries through a literature review and several interviews with business associations' executives. The result is a list of 34 competences, organized in four categories: personal; team management; business; and technical. These competences are presented and discussed in Chapter 3, *"SME Managers' Required Entrepreneurship and Business Competences"*, and the findings enable a better understanding of the profile of SME managers and may help in the design of new training programs to fulfill the identified needs.

Preparing for change is an issue for companies large and small; however, there remains a dearth of empirical evidence on how software SMEs operationalise their approach to knowledge management (KM). For an SME, the first step is to take stock of the types of knowledge that are valuable, where it is stored and how it is used. In addition, consideration must be given to knowledge activities, the constituent parts, of a company's KM approach. By doing this, the organization can identify where its strengths lie in terms of the type and extent to which knowledge is managed through acquisition, codification, storage, maintenance, transfer and creation activities. In *"Preparing for Change: Leveraging Knowledge Activities to Enhance Organisational Preparedness in the Case of an Irish Software SME"*, Heavin and Adam identify occurrences of these knowledge activities as a means of assessing an SME's approach to KM with a view to better facilitating an organization's ability to be increasingly flexible in the face of a changing environment.

Agility is an essential feature for SMEs and in *"Business Agility and Process Agility: How Do They Relate to Each Other?"*, Bruno examines if and how business processes, as currently understood, are able to promote it. Over the last years a number of viewpoints have emerged which exerted great influence on the design of notations and languages for business processes: the major of them can be referred to as the centralized viewpoint, the role viewpoint, the conversational viewpoint, the case viewpoint and the cooperative one. These viewpoints provide different levels of agility and then beneficial results can be expected from their integration, which is the purpose of the proof-of-concept notation, AgileBPN. In AgileBPN, business processes are organized around conversations and role processes (encompassing the tasks pertaining to a given role); shared artifacts are represented as cooperative objects. The notation is illustrated with the help of an example referring to a business process meant to handle applications in a organization.

E-procurement transactions in Business to Business (B2B) environment showed a constant and positive trend in the last years. The most popular methodologies to support these tools are all related to dedicated protocols able to facilitate the agreements among customers and suppliers. *"e-Procurement Process: Negotiation and Auction Approaches for SMEs"*, by Renna and Argoneto, propose a Multi Agent Architecture integrated with several multi-attribute auction mechanisms specifically designed to support the e-procurement processes. Moreover, differently from other cases proposed in literature, the suppliers' proposal formulation is strongly influenced by their production plans. A simulative environment has been developed in order to evaluate different performances: the customer and suppliers' utilities, the profit distribution among the involved agents and the time necessary to reach an agreement. The mentioned approaches are compared with a negotiation process. The simulation results highlight the weakness and strength points of each auction protocol and why they can be considered as a relevant tool in B2B environments.

The contemporary world is full of innovations, causing both good and bad consequences, including the essential problem of well-being of co-workers. Most troubles of this kind cannot be resolved with measures of the usual management and/or economic theory that have caused these troubles. Therefore, what could be done about the well-being of co-workers, if principles and measures of innovative business, social responsibility, and requisite holism were used in synergy. E-Business plays a central role in the economy, facilitating the exchange of information, goods, services, and payments, being an innovation causing changes influencing well-being. On one hand the e-business raises productivity and competitiveness, on the other hand it negatively effects well-being of co-workers in all organizations, including SMEs. Most humans tend to prefer their established routine, not change, including innovation. In *"Well-Being and E-Business as an Influential Innovation"*, Žižek, Mulej and Treven discuss the connection between well-being and e-business and both positive and negative effects of this connection.

Even though the energy sector has relied much on the known sources, the production process has gone through some notable changes due to inherent challenges and developments in knowledge management and technology use. The Offshore oil & gas production industry today, at least in the North Sea, is at a cross-road where the traditional operational concepts are seriously challenged due to various risk factors and commercial uncertainties. Subsequently, 'Integrated eOperations' (IO) was adapted as the business solution for a sustainable future seeking major benefits by major players in the sector. SMEs encounter various technical and operational challenges to cope with the mass scale dynamic change process. In order to utilize IO for commercial advantage, SMEs are in the process of exploring various interface solutions today. With respect to the ongoing developments and the scopes of IO, 'Collaborative business interfacing' that is discussed by Liyanage in "Copying with Dynamic change: Collaborative Business interfacing for SMEs under Intergated eOperations", is to enable the SMEs to be 'smarter together' to capitalize on the potentials of IO through a strategic capability acquisition process.

The second section of this book, Section 2 "*Applications, Surveys and Case Studies*" includes eight chapters traducing experiences, best practices, case studies and surveys related to the potential of IT in general and e-Business, e-Commerce, e-Procurement in particular, in enterprises' competitiveness.

Based on empirical evidence gained by a telephone survey of 375 SMEs, the authors Clear, Woods and Dickson of "*SME Adoption and Use of ICT for Networked Trading Purposes: The Influence of Sector, Size and Age of Firm*" used logistical regressions as a means of identifying the potential for relationships between three variables - industry sector, firm size, and age of firm - as they influence ICT ownership, ICT use and ICT benefits. Such inter-relationships can then be used to identify networked trading practice and proclivity. Data was gathered for firms on the basis of four industrial sectors ('Media', 'Logistics', 'Internet Services' and 'Food Processing') in a region encompassing West London and adjacent counties. Logistical regressions suggest that possession, application and the benefits derived from ICT can be explained on the basis of single and multiple variables or as the result of none, and are individuated as either 'just sector', 'just size', 'sector and size', 'sector and age', 'sector, size and age' or 'no variable'.

Innovative organizations are moving away from discrete linear value chains towards open innovation models such as networks. SMEs recognize that they must be equipped with the relevant competencies required to design, develop and deploy innovative solutions that meet the needs of the end user. More and more small firms are collaborating with each other in order to create value added products and access new markets. However, the task of working in a collaborative network is not easy, and there are very few support structures and systems available to guide successful knowledge sharing and collaboration. In "*Collaborative Networks: Challenges for SMEs*", Cormican explores the fundamental concepts of collaborative networks and knowledge sharing, synthesizes and presents some of the challenges faced by SMEs and identifies some critical success factors that should be considered to help overcome the barriers identified.

Chapter 11, "*E-Sourcing Electronic Platforms in Real Business*" by Sampaio and Figueiredo, presents a research carried out within business-to-business (B2B) electronic markets, with the purpose of asserting the major blocks needed to be covered by an e-purchasing tool in order to be successful. Another goal is to identify how this e-purchasing tool allows buyers (firms) to practice Strategic Sourcing. After an enlarged literature review on E-Sourcing Electronic Platforms (ESEP) and e-purchasing markets, the authors defined a methodological framework and construct a case study. Their strategy was to use one case study, and using the data collected in a survey recently conducted by Vortal (Portuguese firm that owns several B2B platforms in different electronic markets).

Search Engine Marketing (SEM) is one of the most effective online advertising channels which let companies efficiently acquire new and reactivate existing customers at low acquisition costs. In "*Search Engine Marketing in Small and Medium Companies: Status Quo and Perspectives*", Alby and Funk review xx

the scientific literature on SEM with respect to managerial decision problems along the levers of SEM, mainly bid optimization, keyword selection, and adCopy creation. Based on a case study they discuss challenges of SEM campaigns operated by SME. After briefly describing the technical requirements for effectively controlling SEM campaigns we focus on keyword selection and how to address the long tail issue in SEM. A/B-Tests are shown to be an appropriate measure for optimizing the combination of ad copies and landing pages. Finally they discuss bid optimization at a keyword level taking into account spill-over effects between keywords.

A competitive market gives the organizations a constant update on the management process of their businesses and allows the creation of new ways to take competitive advantage. Retail businesses need to identify the value perceived by customers as a strategic source of value generation. Chapter 13, *"Competitive Advantage through Customer Relationship: The Case of an Automobile Dealership"* by Biehl, Link, Vanti and Schneider, present a competitive value generation methodology by identifying the most important values perceived by customers of a Volkswagen Car Dealer. As a result, the study obtained a proposal for value generation by setting the strategic variables referent credibility/reliability.

E-Commerce, and recently mobile commerce has shown a lot of potential for development in the Southern African Development Community (SADC) bloc given the growth in e-adoption of the region. Partly, this has been attributed to sound policies and initiatives; however, there are also challenges that are being faced on an everyday basis concerning e-Commerce business and how this impacts the SME sector. Kelvin, in *"E-Commerce Penetration in the SADC Region: Consolidating and Moving Forward"*, presents these challenges and recommend on what should be done in order to consolidate and move forward the adoption of e-Commerce applications in the SADC region. It looks at exploratory studies of e-Commerce penetration specifically from four SADC member countries. This chapter also reviews the growth of e-Commerce and m-Commerce, and further looks at Africa's infrastructure preparedness and looks at mobile phone subscription rates, level of trust in these business models, and the general value that this kind of business undertaking brings.

Guided by the authors' theory of the Conservation of Information (COI), which holds that the transformation pairs of information uncertainty between time and frequency remain constant (or alternately uncertainty for geospatial position and spatial frequency), in *"Conservation of Information and E-Business Success and Challenges: A Case Study"* Tung, Kung, D. Lawless, Sofge and W. Lawless describe a case study on an international corporation based in Taiwan to demonstrate COI factors associated with the challenges and successes in the adoptions of e-business by the firm and by small and medium size enterprises in general.

In Chapter 16, *"The Diffusion of Internet Technology in Rural Minnesota: An Empirical Study"*, Jones and Stover report a study undertaken to determine to what extent organizational size, organizational complexity, and organizational social ties impacted the creation of an organizational Web page and its relative time of adoption. The research utilized a cross-sectional design, with data being gathered via a self-administered mail survey, where a total of 173 surveys were completed. Two independent variables were statistically significant in predicting whether an organization would have a Web page: (1) organizational size measured by the number of paid employees; and (2) organizational complexity indexed by the number of unique job descriptions, physical locations in Minnesota, and physical locations in other states. The results of this research provide practical information to formal organizations considering the adoption of an organizational Web page.

EXPECTATIONS

Along this 16 chapters, the reader is faced with the discussions and confirmation of the relevance and impact of this hot topic on enterprises (and in particular SME) competitiveness; its role in the support of new organizational models (networked, collaborative, virtual, knowledge-based, ubiquitous); discussion of drivers and barriers to e-Business development; and the presentation of state-of-the-art enabling technologies.

The book provides researchers, scholars, professionals with some of the most advanced research developments, solutions and discussions of e-Business managerial aspects, solutions and case studies. This way, is expected to be read by academics (teachers, researchers and students of several graduate and postgraduate courses) and by professionals of Information Technology, IT managers and responsible, Marketing experts, Enterprise managers (including top level managers), and also technology solutions developers.

Maria Manuela Cruz-Cunha
Polytechnic Institute of Cavado and Ave, Portugal

Joao Varajão
University of Trás-os-Montes e Alto Douro, Portugal

Acknowledgment

Editing a book is a quite hard but compensating and enriching task, as it involves a set of different activities like contacts with authors and reviewers, discussion and exchange of ideas and experiences, process management, organization and integration of contents, and many other, with the permanent objective of creating a book that meets the public expectations. And this task cannot be accomplished without a great help and support from many sources. As editors we would like to acknowledge the help, support and believe of all who made possible this creation.

First of all, the edition of this book would not have been possible without the ongoing professional support of the team of professionals of IGI Global. We are grateful to Dr. Mehdi Khosrow-Pour and to Mrs. Jan Travers, Managing Director, for the opportunity and belief in this project. A very very special mention of gratitude is due to Mrs. Christine Bufton, Assistant Development Editor, and to Mr. Dave DeRicco and Ms. Myla Harty, Editorial Assistants, for their professional support and friendly words of advisory, encouragement and prompt guidance. We also address our recognition and appreciation to all the staff at IGI Global, whose contributions throughout the process of production and making this book available all over the world was invaluable.

We are grateful to all the authors, for their insights and excellent contributions to this book. Also we are grateful the authors who simultaneously served as referees for chapters written by other authors, as well as to the external referees, for their insights, valuable contributions, prompt collaboration and constructive comments. Thank you all, authors and reviewers, you made this book! The communication and exchange of views within this truly global group of recognized individualities from the scientific domain and from industry was an enriching and exciting experience!

We are also grateful to all who accede to contribute to this project, some of them with high quality chapter proposals, but unfortunately, due to several constraints could not have seen their work published.

Thank you.

Maria Manuela Cruz-Cunha
Polytechnic Institute of Cavado and Ave, Portugal

Joao Varajão
University of Trás-os-Montes e Alto Douro, Portugal

Section 1
Managerial Issues

Chapter 1
SMEs and E-Business:
Implementation, Strategies and Policy

Mário Pedro Leite de Almeida Ferreira
Universidade Católica Portuguesa, Portugal

ABSTRACT

The adoption of E-Business by SMEs is a critical issue for economic development. More than 90% of world companies are SMEs and E-Business is widely recognized as a critical source of competitive advantage. Thus, it is important to understand why SMEs are lagging behind large firms in terms of E-Business adoption and assimilation. This chapter will attempt to search for explanations through a comprehensive analysis of main topics in terms of E-Business implementation, strategies and policy. It is believed that the inadequacy of existing E-Business adoption incentives and theoretical models may be due to SME specificity, as these companies are conditioned among other by resource availability and high CEOs/owners' dependency. Empirical evidence shows that SMEs have erratic behaviors in terms of Information and Communications Technology (ICT) investment and need external support to integrate E-Business in the overall strategy of the firm.

INTRODUCTION

The ICT capacity to create competitive advantage for firms is now more relevant than ever. In the early days of the Internet, ICT was seen as the key to change consumption behavior and gain competitive advantage, and several firms decided to adopt a high commitment to online technologies. Despite the failure of many, as they just assumed that ICT alone was enough to drive business, there were some that managed to capture solid first-mover advantages. The insertion of ICT was very important to make internal procedures more efficient and to improve communications with all stakeholders. Today, firms that managed to implement ICT in an appropriate manner are among the high performers of the 2008/09 financial crisis.

SMEs can also benefit from E-Business adoption, but they seem to lag behind large firms due to very specific reasons. SMEs have a high level of

DOI: 10.4018/978-1-60960-463-9.ch001

flexibility to adapt to a fast changing environment and can use the Internet to advertise and sell in global markets. However, SMEs have low rates of ICT adoption and mainly ICT assimilation. In most cases, they are still at the initial stage of E-Business adoption with a stand alone website used for marketing purposes, an email address to answer questions and for most transactions, they still use phone and fax. Despite the infinite range of potential combinations and benefits, it seems that SMEs have difficulties in recognizing added value from ICT.

In this context, the chapter focuses on E-Business adoption by SMEs. It is important to understand why assimilation rates are low and why public policies are not working. Emphasis will be given to the specificity of SMEs and to their strategic options in terms of E-Business adoption. SMEs, due to their size and organizational structure and culture, may face different challenges from those affecting large companies. If this is the case, then new solutions should be found, both in the private and public sector.

This chapter attempts to provide a comprehensive and analytical view of all issues relating to the relationship between SMEs and E-Business. The view adopted will go beyond mere description and will focus on discussing existing theory, models and practices, while searching for new insights. The objectives of this chapter are fourfold: characterize E-Business adoption by SMEs, assess the factors that condition E-Business adoption and assimilation, discuss the main strategic issues faced by SMEs and review existing governmental policies.

BACKGROUND

An accurate overview of the importance of E-Business for SMEs must start from a clear understanding of these two realities. Even though the concepts of E-Business and SMEs are used intensively in academia and business, there is still discordance about their true meaning and economic relevance. In most manuscripts, these terms are used interchangeably and choices are determined by national statistics, specific research goals and data collection limitations. This diversity can be a source of misunderstanding in a chapter that attempts to compare different authors, studies and national realities. Consequently, in order to have an objective approach to this topic, two types of explanations are required. First, it is important to understand the relevance of SMEs and E-Business in today's world and how they can relate to each other. Second, it is useful to know their true meaning and define the particular concepts that are going to be used during the chapter.

SMEs

SMEs are a significant component of any national economy and therefore it is important to understand how their competitiveness can be enhanced through innovation, namely E-Business technologies. According to Schmiemann (2008), SMEs represent 99,8% of 20 million EU-27 firms, accounting for 67% of non-financial jobs and 57,6% of non-financial added value. Their role in terms of economic development and social sustainability is crucial for most countries. Consequently, governments are aware that improvements in terms of SME competitiveness can bring substantial benefits to national economies and attempt to influence innovation adoption rates. At this level, the widespread adoption of E-Business technologies by firms is among the top priorities of governments.

Despite their economic relevance, there is no universal definition of SME that is widely acknowledged (Mutula and Brakel, 2006). Definitions vary significantly by country or economic area and they may include several criteria (MacGregor and Vrazalic, 2008): financial measurements (assets and turnover), non-financial measurements (staff levels and other) and qualitative components. Among the enormous disparity found, there are two main criteria that tend to be widely used across countries: employment and total assets. The former is normally the main quantitative reference used by national statistic agencies to distinguish between large companies and SMEs. However, there is also international divergence about a common threshold. In order to be considered a SME, the number of employees a firm must have is less than: 250 for the EU, 300 for South Korea, 100 for Turkey, 200 for Australia, 150 for Malaysia and 100 for Botswana.

The above does not mean that it is not possible to have international comparisons in terms of SMEs. Several studies have shown that, despite disparities in quantitative criteria, SMEs across different countries tend to display similar organizational, cultural and strategic characteristics that are unique. These aspects are more qualitative, but nevertheless provide ground to create a wider homogeneous perspective in the analysis of these firms worldwide. An extensive analysis of existing literature by Ongori (2009) and MacGregor and Vrazalic (2008) led to the identification of eleven common qualitative characteristics of SMEs across nations. From these, aspects such as lack of trained staff, high failure rate, short range management perspective, short product range, owner dependence, and informal and inadequate planning are critical to characterize this type of firms.

Considering the above, there is support to adopt a broad international definition of SME during this chapter. The concept of SME adopted will not be based on a single quantitative criterion, but rather on a qualitative view of this type of firms that focus on its unique organizational features. Despite national differences in quantitative criteria, there are reasons to believe that international similarities in terms of qualitative features are more important. Consequently, SMEs will be directly compared across countries with conclusions and lessons from a specific national reality being considered as valid benchmarks.

E-Business and SMEs

E-Business is considered as an important factor to create competitive advantage for SMEs, however, its implementation must always be carefully assessed. It is a proven fact that most SME's can gain competitive advantage through the use of ICT, as more than 70% consider that ICT helped business in one or more competitive areas (Maguire et al., 2007). However, the adoption of E-Business should not be an end in itself and a magic solution for all SMEs problems. Instead, it should be a means to an end with the end being business performance (Raymond et al., 2005; Taylor and Murphy, 2004), namely: improved marketing and sales practices (one to one) and better relationships with distributors. If E-Business cannot deliver better business performance for a particular firm, then it should not be considered.

There are several applications of E-Business technologies with a positive impact on firm performance. The table below from Raymond et al. (2005) presents a sample of the business functions that changed the most with the introduction of E-Business technologies, in this particular case: the Internet and the Web. The results are from a survey of 108 CEOs of Canadian SMEs.

Despite existing studies about the overall impact of E-Business, few are still known about its impact on SMEs. For large firms, the impact of E-Business is well documented and the existing approaches and business models tend to be widely accepted. At the SME level, perspectives are not straightforward, as each SME has a different E-Business profile. This diversity increases research complexity and at present, there is still not enough empirical evidence about the impact of E-Business in SMEs, namely in terms of growth or global expansion (Raymond et al., 2005)

E-Business as a concept or definition is affected by its complexity. E-Business is defined by Chaffey (2004), as the introduction of electronic networks in the management of information within a company and with external stakeholders. It is a

Table 1. Business functions that use Internet and the Web (Raymond et al., 2005)

Business functions for which the Internet and the Web are used n=108	% of SMEs
Communications / Informational use (e-communication)	**% of SMEs**
Promote the firm	82
Promote products and service	70
Develop in-house communication	67
Interact with customers in order to improve products and services	56
Business Intelligence use (E-Business Intelligence)	**% of SMEs**
Prospect for new clients nationally	58
Prospect for new clients abroad	50
Develop competitive intelligence	40
Transactional / Collaborative use	**% of SMEs**
Sell products/services (e-commerce)	32
Interact with business partners' R&D and marketing departments in order to develop products and service (e-collaboration)	30

global concept that goes beyond the mere adoption of technology, i.e., e-commerce, website or ICT investment. E-Business involves significant changes to firm structure and strategy to allow for the integration of electronic networks in the business model. In practical terms, this concept is hard to model and quantify and therefore tends to be used in a broad interchangeable approach, sometimes being considered as E-commerce, Internet usage or simply ICT investment (see tables 1 and 2). Most of these simplifications are due to lack of appropriate data, knowledge and research about the actual business reality of companies using E-Business. In these cases, proxies must be used and simple indicators become first choices for most authors.

The problem with using proxies to assess E-Business usage by SMEs is precision loss. Existing studies show that basic quantitative measures tend to produce biased estimates that overstate E-Business impact in SMEs. The use of simple proxies provides indicators in terms of ICT adoption and implementation. These are easy to quantify and widely available, but only assess the visible part of E-Business, i.e., the top of the iceberg. In order to uncover the assimilation of ICT in the firm's business model (the bottom of the iceberg), qualitative aspects should also be considered. The main problem at this level is the

Table 2. Main reasons for ICT investments made recently – 378 SMEs (Harindranath et al., 2008)

Increase operational efficiency	Improve communication with suppliers	Enhance customer service	Keep up with competitors	Enhance collaborative ventures	Increase staff satisfaction	Customer requests
83%	25%	45%	34%	23%	33%	19%

scarcity of indicators and data. As qualitative aspects relate to the breadth and depth of use (Dholakia and Kshetri, 2004) of ICT technology, complex indicators and expensive data collection methodologies are required.

In this chapter, E-Business will be handled in an interchangeable, generic, but also focused perspective, considering both ICT adoption and assimilation. Due to the lack of precise E-Business indicators, the approach used in this chapter will not be driven by simple adoption issues, using one or two simple statistical indicators. Instead, it will attempt to focus on the assessment of ICT assimilation levels through the complementary use of both basic and complex indicators. Indicators' diversity will be privileged in order to achieve an in-depth view of E-Business in SMEs.

E-BUSINESS ADOPTION BY SMEs

On a basic generic view, it is possible to observe similarities between SMEs and large companies in terms of E-Business adoption. For both (figure 1), adoption rates are increasing overtime and ICT use tends to decrease as the complexity of business function increases. According to Taylor

and Murphy (2004), even though online activity among SMEs is quite high, online sales volumes are quite low representing less than 10% of firms' total revenue.

The similarity between large companies and SMEs is also observed in terms of digital divide. Digital divide is an issue that affects the adoption of E-Business by large companies and SMEs across the world. In terms of Internet purchasing and selling for all firms by industry in 2008 (OECD, 2008), there is a significant disparity between developed and developing economies. Developed OECD countries (Australia, Netherlands, New Zealand, Norway and the UK) present averages of approximately 30% and 50%, for Internet buying and selling, respectively. On the other hand, developing economies, namely Slovak Republic, Mexico, Greece and Hungary feature very low levels of uptake (around 10% in average). This disparity is evidence of a positive correlation between economic development and E-Business uptake that can be observed both in terms of large companies and SMEs. If not properly handled, the digital divide may work as a means to keep or enlarge the development gap between countries.

Figure 1. Survey on ICT in enterprises (European Commission, 2009)

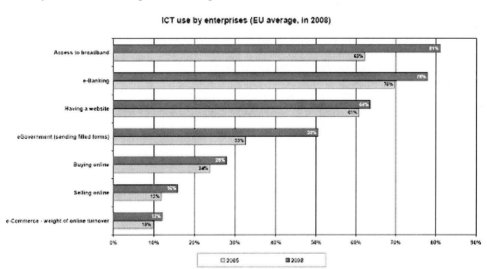

In general, SMEs have different profiles in terms of E-Business adoption when compared to large companies. Despite the recognized value of E-Business to create competitive advantage, few are the SMEs that are actually assimilating this technology in terms of business structure and strategy. Empirical evidence shows that E-Business uptake is slower than in large companies and that most SMEs do not proceed beyond initial stages in terms of adoption. According to Locket and Brown (2003), connectivity goals in the UK are achieved and surpassed, but E-Business implementation is very low among SMEs. Email and Web hosting services are the most used by SME's. Nevertheless, there is little or no engagement in higher complex applications such as e-marketplaces, supply chains or inter-organisational collaborative networks (figure 2). In Malaysia, 75% of SMEs surveyed by Hua et al. (2007) did not adopt E-commerce. From an estimated target of 1 million SMEs in the UK, only 490000 were trading online in 2002. The few exceptions found are associated with technology intensive sectors, such as motor or aerospace industries.

SMEs also tend to lag behind large companies in the use of E-Business to enhance knowledge management. A peculiar feature of SMEs is that they tend to present a discontinuous adoption of ICT and E-Business. Contrarily to large companies, SMEs tend to use their ICT applications independently rather than in an integrated manner. They tend not to take advantage of methodologies developed for large firms, namely: ERP, supply chain management and CRM in order to create explicit knowledge (Maguire et al., 2007). Instead, they use different ICT applications to perform very specific tasks. Overall, this strategy restricts ICT and E-Business potential, because it creates a significant barrier for the implementation of knowledge integration mechanisms (Maguire and Koh, 2004)

Empirical evidence of the independent use of ICT applications comes from two different countries: New Zealand and UK (West Midlands). In the former, according to Ramsey and McCole (2005), the majority of firms had no integration between internal key systems and Internet applications. From those having integration, 34.2% were service and product databases, 27.1% were customer databases and 20% were accounting systems. In the latter, results were similar to New Zealand. 2021 surveys conducted in West Midlands (WMRO, 2009) show a low level of E-Business assimilation. Even though 90.5% of

Figure 2. Survey on ICT in enterprises (European Commission, 2009)

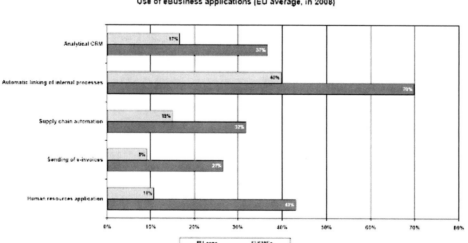

SMEs have a broadband connection and 54.4% have a website, only 24.8% plan internal resourcing and scheduling, only 15.8% have electronic stock control and monitoring systems, and only 19% have CRM (Customer Relationship Management). The results are even more dramatic from a marketing point of view, when 70% of SMEs update their website on a monthly or larger time window (44% on ad-hoc basis). For these companies, online services, such as: product availability check (15.6%), automatic reorder of supplies (8%), electronic payment of goods (13.4%), order progress tracking (8.1%) and technical support (18.7%) have a residual use.

The ad-hoc ICT investment profile of SMEs implies that an assessment of E-Business adoption must preferably go beyond a generic approach and focus on firm specificity. It seems that each firm presents a unique E-Business profile that tends to be determined by specific features. Therefore, observing firms in a generic manner may be too restrictive leading to biased indicators that do not consider SME heterogeneity. In order to understand the rationale of SMEs, it is probably better to segment firms according to variables such as size, technology intensity or sector. For instance, empirical evidence for sectorial diversity in E-Business adoption can be found in the case of West Midlands (WMRO, 2009). In 2021 surveys conducted in 2008, it was found that 62,4% of SMEs engaged in some form of E-Business. However, adoption rates ranged from 100% of Finance and Public administration to 41% in hotels and restaurants.

Overall, SMEs display specific E-Business adoption patterns. When compared to large companies, they tend to have lower adoption rates, avoid complex applications, insert technology in discontinuous ways and tend not to integrate technology across departments. Their ad-hoc approach to ICT produces a significant diversity in terms of solutions, leading to high complexity in terms of analysis.

FACTORS AFFECTING E-BUSINESS ADOPTION AND ASSIMILATION

Benefits from E-Business Adoption (Perceptions and Reality)

International studies show consensus around the main benefits that SMEs derive from E-Business adoption and implementation. In most of these studies, the majority of benefits for SMEs are similar to those that apply to large companies. According to Wagner et al. (2003), European Commission (2009) and Harindranath et al. (2008), the main benefits associated with E-Business are increases in operational efficiency and improved customer service. Harindranath et al. (2008) present the following as the main reasons for ICT investments made by SMEs in the UK.

From table 2 and figure 3, it is possible to observe that productivity gains (cost reductions) tend to be more important than market orientation. The surveys show that SMEs are more cost than market driven when it comes to ICT. This reflects the importance of E-Business to redesign the supply-chain with new purchasing techniques (reverse auctions), disintermediation and re-intermediation. The full integration of procurement, production and logistics is the source of substantial cost reductions. At the marketing level, and despite CEOs' lack of awareness, there are also gains to be obtained. E-Business can lead to better communications, global markets, one to one interaction, CRM (Customer Relationship Management) and development of new products and services. However, when it comes to investment decisions, firms may have difficulties in recognizing the real value of market benefits and seem to favor short-term cost reductions instead of long-term market gains.

Empirical evidence confirms difficulties with benefit recognition. Results from a survey of companies in the EU-27 (figure 3) show two facts: the level of benefit recognition by SME is quite low and generally there is a lower level of recog-

Figure 3. Survey on ICT in enterprises (European Commission, 2009)

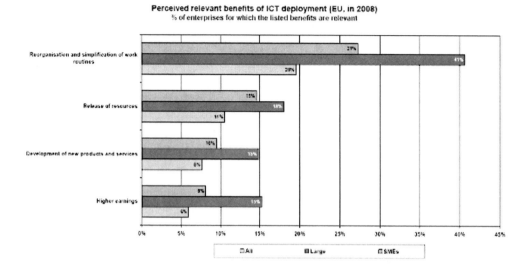

nition among SMEs than among large companies. From the three studies conducted (Wagner et al., 2003; European Commission, 2009; Harindranath et al., 2008), few were the benefits that surpassed or reached the 50% mark. Similarly, the empirical studies conducted in other countries showed that even though benefits are recognized by SMEs, there is a still a low degree of awareness about their real potential for the individual firm. For instance, a study conducted in New Zealand shows than from 7 proposed benefits assessed on a 5 point Likert scale, only one was actually significant for SMEs (Ramsey and McCole, 2005). Aspects such as increased customer base, sales, cost savings or profits were not deemed relevant for firms. Only effective advertising and brand building reached significance, reflecting the fact that companies were still at very early stages in terms of E-Business implementation.

On a theoretical level, a comprehensive list of E-Business benefits was compiled by Windrum and Berranger (2002) including among others: wider access to external resources and expertise, the development of new business models, more opportunities for strategic alliances involving SMEs and the reduction of entry barriers for new

entrants. Regarding the latter, E-Business technology is cheap, widely available and can be used in an extensive manner by any type of company. New entrants may even have an advantage as they do not have switch costs associated with old technology.

Determinants of E-Business Adoption and Implementation

There are internal and external factors conditioning E-Business adoption at the firm level. Internal factors relate mainly to available resources, staff qualifications and CEO profile. At the external level, the sector and the macroeconomic environment are the two principal forces driving adoption. Additional competition or globalization can place pressure on SMEs to be more efficient and use E-Business technologies.

Macroeconomic Environment

The macroeconomic environment plays an important role towards the adoption and assimilation of E-Business by SMEs. The main environmental factors that condition E-Business uptake by SMEs are: globalization, governments and technology.

Globalization is an important determinant of E-Business adoption, because the increasing abolition of trade barriers and lower transport costs have opened new markets and brought more competition for SMEs. The emergence of a global consumer that is online, travels frequently and compares different offers creates an extra challenge for firms. Firms are no longer doing business in protected local markets. They are facing international competition even they are only selling to local markets. In order to survive, SMEs must become more efficient and grow, using among others E-Business technologies.

Governments also have a key role in promoting the implementation of E-Business by SMEs. Government influence normally occurs at three levels. First governments support SME investment on E-Business technologies through specific programs or agencies. Second, government legislation, either national or European, is more demanding in particular areas, e.g., quality or hygiene, and this creates the need to use ICT technologies at the firm level (Harindranath et al., 2008). Third, the increasing implementation of e-government worldwide pushes B2G (Business to Government) communications into electronic platforms, affecting all firms, including SMEs.

The technological revolution of the last three decades also created favorable conditions for the adoption of E-Business. Improvements in computer performance, digital storing and electronic networks have led to smaller units, better performance, faster communication and lower prices. Nowadays, ICT technology is widely available for personal and business use, allowing for the creation of virtual networks and marketplaces (Internet) where companies can advertise and sell their products or services. At present, any type of firm can easily invest in better ICT, spending less than they would some years ago.

Sector

The business sector is an important factor conditioning the uptake of E-Business by SMEs. According to MacGregor and Vrazalic (2008), the business sector is referred as a determinant of E-Business adoption by several authors. Furthermore, available empirical evidence shows that there are significant divergences in E-Business adoption across sectors. Love et al. (2005) show that companies from different sectors have very diverse levels of ICT investment. Also, data for ERP usage in Europe (figure 4) shows that there is a high sectorial disparity among SMEs. Companies in sectors such as chemical and steel make a more intensive use of ERP when compared to retail or transport.

According to Cross (2000) and Adshead (2001), SMEs are forced to adopt E-Business because of three main fears that relate to sector conditions. They are afraid of losing competitive position

Figure 4. Percentage of companies with an ERP system by sector and size (European Commission, 2008)

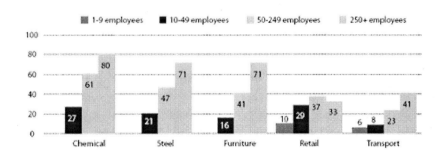

(market share), losing partners that are moving online (supply chain link or collaboration agreement) and being left behind, especially in terms of brand and image. Not having an E-Business may be counterproductive in terms of image for particular sectors (high-tech).

Competitive pressure within the industry or sector is an important motivation towards ICT adoption (Baldwin et al., 2004). Even though intense competition increases uncertainty about the consequences of innovation, it also makes firms more prone to accept innovation. At this level, ICT technologies play an important role as they allow faster access to better information. Therefore, they are important to allow for better decision making that can strengthen performance and ensure survival (Hwang et al., 2004).

Supply-chains are also a critical determinant of E-Business adoption in a sector (Windrum and Berranger, 2002). Customers and suppliers that rely on ICT solutions force others to follow. For instance, by using a "hub and spoke model", large companies compel SMEs to adopt specific ICT solutions. In this case, the ability to bring suppliers and customers into E-Business platforms is positively correlated with the hub company's market power.

Besides supply-chains, there are also other significant factors such a technology and product life cycle. High-tech industries and new sectors (products/services) tend to be more prone to use E-Business. These are sectors that are capital and R&D intensive, therefore they deal with high volumes of information that must be efficiently managed and processed.

Additionally, Windrum and Berranger (2002) also consider the importance of external economies of scale. At this level, there are two main aspects being considered: agglomeration economies and localization economies. The former considers that ICT innovation within a region is determined by a concentration of resources, namely knowledge. Thus, firms are agglomerated to increase innovation potential. The latter relates to spill-over effects and consider that regional clusters create specialized advantages for firms in terms of ICT technology. Location is critical to ensure that benefits are appropriated fast.

Internal Factors

Internal firm factors are important when trying to explain the adoption of E-Business technologies by SMEs. For instance, at the E-commerce level, firm size, age, level of ICT expertise and market focus can have a primal role. There is a positive correlation between E-Commerce adoption and three of the above variables, namely, size, market focus and level of ICT expertise. This relates to the fact that larger SMEs (more resources) with wider market focus (more customer information and competition) and higher levels of ICT expertise tend to have a higher propensity to adopt E-Commerce. Regarding business age, there is a negative relationship as older established businesses are less prone to any type of change. According to an extensive literature review conducted by MacGregor and Vrazalic (2008), it is possible to find several authors that corroborate the significance of the above features.

On a wider view of E-Business that goes beyond E-Commerce there are other relevant features that emerge. In the case of New Zealand (Ramsey and McCole, 2005), four factors were deemed relevant towards influencing SMEs investment decisions in terms of ICT. One of these factors was firms' awareness of environmental forces, as firms that are more aware of external forces tend to have a higher adoption of ICT. Another was the level of staff skills, as learning and capabilities of human resources can condition the adoption of ICT. In third place, there is geographical coverage of service, as a larger geographic coverage tends to motivate the use of ICT. Contrarily, local services tend to rely on face to face communication as potential clients can visit the physical office. Finally, there is the issue of managerial mind-sets, as conservative managers tend not to adopt

ICT (Jeon et al., 2006). The knowledge level and the attitude of the firm's key decision maker are very important. Non-adopters are content with traditional ways of conducting business and do not change their approach, unless there is a reduction in ignorance or fear levels due to increased security, trust and regulation.

On E-Business assimilation, the arguments used are more complex and relate to strategic and structural issues. Raymond et al. (2005) conclude that there are two factors that must be considered at this level: networking intensity and strategic orientation. Regarding the former, the greater the firm's networking intensity, the greater its assimilation of E-Business, because there is a greater need to communicate effectively with all partners. Regarding the latter, the more aggressive the firm's strategic orientation, the greater its need to assimilate E-Business technologies. Entrepreneurial strategies that aim at market growth need technological leadership (competitive advantage). With growth, firm and environmental complexity increase and the communication technology must be upgraded.

Barriers

On a comprehensive view of existing barriers to E-Business adoption and assimilation, there are several factors that can be considered relevant, according to Yap et al. (1992). These factors are organized in three particular categories: organizational characteristics, organizational action and internal and external expertise.

In terms of organizational characteristics, the main barriers considered are: size, ICT qualifications of staff, financial resources and time. In terms of size, SMEs have less complex organizational structures and smaller volumes of information to be communicated and stored. Therefore, they have smaller needs than large companies for E-Business technology. Regarding the ICT qualifications of staff, they tend to be low and are kept at that level, due to low investment in training. Managerial

perceptions are responsible for this state of affairs. CEOs perceive ICT training as a costly and risky investment due to search costs, as there are many private and public initiatives to choose from, and turnover costs, as there is a high chance of losing better qualified staff to other organizations. In terms of financial resources, the main problem is scarcity. SMEs have a higher exposure to cash flow problems and are charged higher interest rates by Banks. This leads to sub-optimal decisions in terms of ICT investment. Finally, regarding time, SMEs have flat organizational structures and rely on multi-task management. There is little time to upgrade competences, knowledge and to adopt long-term strategic planning. This is not compatible with ICT investments as they require time to mature.

In terms of organisational action, SMEs are in the hands of the CEO/owner, therefore the CEO is a key player in the implementation of ICT investments (DeLone, 1988; Yap et al., 1992). The barriers affecting CEOs in terms of ICT investments are time availability and knowledge. In the former case, CEOs are driven by operational rather than strategic issues (Zheng et al., 2004), therefore they have little time available to consider ICT investments. In the latter, CEOs in SMEs tend to have low qualifications, therefore they are unaware of ICT potential, do not consider products/services and/or internal procedures that are ICT prone and have a perception of high initial set-up costs and on-going costs associated with ICT investment (Taylor and Murphy, 2004).

Regarding internal and external expertise, it is important to consider the role of private consultants and social networks. In terms of the former, the main problem is the inability to afford to employ private consultants/analysts (Soriano et al., 2002). Regarding the latter, the issue is to select the right networks as they can be a means to build trust in the adoption of new ICT solutions.

Existing studies consider that the main barriers to the adoption and implementation of E-Business are related to resources and CEO qualifications.

The small size of firms reduces its bargaining power and access to resources, mainly financial and specialized human resources. Simultaneously, the low qualification of CEOs makes them less aware of the actual potential of E-Business and more reluctant to invest (investments lack relevance). The importance of these facts can be observed in several studies.

Evidence from Egypt, Sri Lanka and Malaysia points at low awareness and education level as the main factors contributing to low E-Commerce adoption by SMEs (Hua et al., 2008). The negative impact of this fact is in reinforced by cultural barriers in particular countries, namely Malaysia, Sri Lanka and India where shopping is a face to face social experience.

Ongori (2009) in a study conducted in Botswana (Likert scale questionnaire) found three major barriers to ICT adoption. Firstly, SMEs limitation in terms of funds, reported by 84% of firms. Secondly, lack of internal and external manpower, reported by 77% of firms. Thirdly, lack of awareness of ICT benefits, reported by 73% of firms.

This pattern of barriers is not specific to developing economies. Developed economies also tend to present the same type of barriers. Evidence from Sweden, Australia and the UK confirm this fact. In Sweden and Australia high costs and low awareness are also significant barriers to E-Commerce. Most interviewees consider that their products are unsuitable for online selling and that they do not perceive any advantage from using E-Commerce (Hua et al., 2008). In the case of West Midlands, and according to a WMRO (2009) report, lack of relevance was a crucial E-Business adoption barrier achieving a score of 80% in 2021 surveys applied to SMEs. Lack of relevance was followed distantly by aspects such as lack of skills (17,8%) and cost issues (9,2%).

The lack of qualification and vision of the CEO is a critical issue. The answers of CEOs in West Midlands (WMRO, 2009) are compelling evidence: 88% of those that do not adopt E-Business say that nothing will make them invest in the near future. CEOs are entrenched into old ways of conducting business and do not consider changes that are outside their knowledge.

Overall, there seems to be a certain level of widespread ignorance among CEOs of SMEs that leads to the creation of certain myths. Empirical evidence based on surveys answered by CEOs reveals that there are specific fears and believes associated with E-Business investments. These are mostly due to lack of awareness about E-Business potential. Among the more common fears and believes reported by CEOs, there are five that tend to be more frequently mentioned. First, some firms serve very small local market niches and do not require ICT (Taylor and Murphy, 2004). Second, there may be serious losses in terms of security and privacy when adopting E-Business (Taylor and Murphy, 2004). Third, the benefits of ICT are hard to identify and quantify (Zheng et al., 2004). Fourth, if SMEs adopt E-Business technologies, they will lose their personal touch and the corresponding intimate knowledge of the customer. (Zheng et al., 2004). Fifth, electronic trading makes SMEs more transparent and more vulnerable to critical information loss (Zheng et al., 2004).

STRATEGIC ISSUES IN E-BUSINESS ADOPTION BY SMEs

Existing Strategies

According to Maguire et al. (2007), SMEs have a clear advantage over large firms in terms of ICT investment. The low level of E-Business adoption by SMEs allows a higher degree of flexibility towards future investments in technology. Contrarily to large companies, they are not constrained by high involvement in major ICT projects. Therefore, SMEs are more able to take advantage of the latest technology.

In most cases, the above does not necessarily translate into an advantage as the implementation of E-Business is a complex task for most SMEs. According to Maguire et al. (2007), in order to be effective, the ICT strategy should be built in conjunction with the overall business strategy. However, few SMEs follow that perspective in terms of the actual implementation. SMEs tend to display a reactive posture towards E-Business adoption. E-Business adoption involves a risky (Adshead, 2001) medium to long-term investment and most SMEs do not possess the required conditions to endure that process. Therefore, many SMEs take a non-strategic approach to E-Business. They invest in parts of technology without embedding it in the organizational structure and culture. They basically set up a website and wait for something to happen (Wagner et al., 2003)

In this context, most SMEs fail to recognize the real potential of E-Business and restrict their investments. According to Harindranath et al. (2008), the main strategic mistake of CEOs is to simply focus on driving down costs instead of focusing on creating added value (Pavic et al., 2007). The former leads to ad-hoc investment choices in which the firm attempts to respond in a reactive way to competition or external requirements. However, this approach leaves aside the possibility of exploring the full potential of new technologies. In most cases, this occurs because CEOs are unaware of the full potential of these technologies. Besides restricting future profit and growth potential, a reactive strategy in terms of E-Business tends to create different cells of technology overtime that in later stages may be very difficult to synchronize and coordinate.

Overall, the existing strategies of SMEs towards E-Business adoption are characterized by five aspects according to Zheng et al. (2004). First, few SMEs have a E-Business strategy or plan for further e-adoption. Second, they use ICT locally in separate systems and are generally happy with the benefits. Third, they have an ad-hoc method of investing in ICT and focus on short time horizons,

being reluctant to make investments that yield vague or unsustainable future benefits. Fourth, SMEs regard ICT as discrete tools and consider that in most cases are too expensive or esoteric to be evaluated. Fifth, SMEs regard E-Business changes as incremental and never as business wide revamps.

CEO Decision Making

E-Business investments are complex and risky decision for CEOs of SMEs. The timing of implementation (Windrum and Berranger, 2002) is a crucial choice for any firm and tends to be dependent on specific features, such as, sector, geographic coverage and others. Due to shortage of financial resources, CEOs cannot afford mistakes. Therefore, they struggle to find the right timing for investments to be made. If they invest too early, there is a high potential for failure as consumers/suppliers are not prepared and return will be low. If they invest too late, they lose first mover advantage and fall behind competitors in terms of market share and return. In some cases, missing the right timing may lead companies into agonizing situations from which they may not be able to recover.

In order to determine if E-Business investments should be made and when, an objective discussion of specific issues must occur at the firm level. This involves asking important questions that must be answered by management, external consultants or social networks before proceeding into the investment stage. Five issues must be considered at this level; the relevancy of ICT for the firm, the degree of CEO commitment to growth, the style of ICT investment (reactive or proactive), the CEO level of ICT knowledge and skills, and the firm's power over the business environment.

The strategy followed by SMEs will always tend to be highly dependent on the CEOs vision and ambition. The answers to the above questions are mainly provided by the CEO and are important to define the overall strategy of the firm in terms of ICT. This occurs, because the decision processes within SMEs are highly idiosyncratic and owner led. This concentration of SME power on a single person accentuates the specificity of firm strategies. In this scenario, it is reasonable to expect that different electronic solutions will be appropriate for different strategies (Van Weele, 2002) and this further enhances the uniqueness of SMEs.

E-Business Adoption Models

In terms of modeling the strategic choices in terms of E-Business adoption, there are four models deemed relevant. These models will be explained below and are: the stages model, the ICT-induced business reconfiguration model, the transporter model, and the improvisional model.

The stages model offers four options for E-Business implementation (Windrum and Berranger, 2002; Chaffey, 2004) by any firm. Implementation is thought to progress through several stages and evolves as a business recognizes additional benefits (Zheng et al., 2004) in the next stage. Each additional stage involves a higher complexity in terms of ICT adoption and assimilation. The four stages considered in the model are: email, Web-presence, E-commerce and E-Business.

Similarly, the ICT – induced business reconfiguration model (Venkatraman, 1991) presents five possible stages for firms in terms of E-Business implementation. These stages are defined according to two variables: the range of potential benefits that firms can obtain from E-Business and the degree of business transformation that firms must undergo to invest in E-Business. The two initial stages report to evolutionary transformations at the firm level whereas last three refer to revolutionary changes. The stages are ordered (top to bottom – table 3) by increasing levels of positive correlation between potential benefits and business transformation.

Table 3. Stages in ICT-induced business reconfiguration model (Venkatraman, 1991)

Stage	Type of change
Localized exploitation (1)	Evolution
Internal integration (2)	Evolution
Business process design (3)	Revolution
Business network redesign (4)	Revolution
Business scope redefinition (5)	Revolution

Despite small differences, the two models referred above display important similarities. The main difference between models occurs in terms of firm categorization. The stages model is more technology-driven whereas the ICT-induced model is more business-driven. Regarding similarities, they can be observed in terms of perspectives and design inspiration. Both models (stages and ICT-induced) adopt a developmental perspective, considering that firms evolve in a sequential learning manner through stages, and they were largely influenced by the patterns of E-Business adoption in large firms.

The stages proposed in the two previous models (stages and ICT-induced) are disputed by some authors. For them, it is important to add to these stages another valid stage called the no implementation. This is due to the fact that being ICT free may be a rational option for very specific firms.

The transporter model is proposed by Levy and Powell (2003). This simple model divides SMEs ICT profiles into four static categories (brochureware, business opportunity, business support and business development) according to the level of expected business growth and business value of the Internet. The actual placement of firm allows for an assessment of the importance of competition and owner's knowledge of ICT value. Thus, this model offers a simple diagnostic framework that can be used for guidance in ICT utilization or further investment.

The improvisional model in the adoption of ICT is proposed to explain why firms do not follow original implementation plans (Marasini et al., 2008). The basic argument behind this model is that practical experience with new technologies and experimentation are critical for firms and make them change their implementation plan in a discontinuous and discrete manner. This approach is inline with the theory proposed by Orlikowski and Hofman (1997) that states that SME CEOs improvise to align technology, organisational context and the change model. Therefore, firms are too specific to be categorized. Additionally, formal learning (training) tends to be disregarded when compared to informal learning via experimentation (trial and error), networking and other.

Strategic Assessment

Regarding the above models Zheng et al. (2004) and Beckinsale et al. (2006) consider that SMEs are unlikely to follow developmental models, either a stage or an ICT-induced model. SMEs strategy in terms of E-Business adoption and implementation is different from the one followed by large companies. Adoption by SMEs tends to be fragmented, unplanned and driven by CEO enthusiasm. Even when considered as an imperative, adoption tends to focus on operational support and transactions processing. It is not taken as an integrating process, but rather as an instrumental solution for a very specific area in an organization.

Zheng et al. (2004) believe that the improvisional model is more adapted to SMEs strategy. The above evidence supports that fact. The SME is a dynamic organization that tends to respond in erratic and unplanned manners to different stimuli. Model simplifications, such as the transporter model, fail to capture the broadness involved in these decisions, as they simplify diverse SMEs into a single 2x2 static matrix. SMEs need to experiment and learn in a sequential manner. This is a complex procedure that reflects the entrepreneurial and informal nature of SMEs, creating a high propensity to adopt unexpected implementation strategies. Thus, SMEs are too specific to be categorized.

In this context, Zheng et al. (2004) propose a cautious, wait and see approach for SMEs instead of the ambitious ICT investment plans of large companies. This approach relies on three main aspects that should be considered by SMEs. First, SMEs should be cautious and match existing investment opportunities to their actual risk profile. Incremental learning and trial and error should be privileged before proceeding with high investments. Second, investments should always consider contingency plans. There should be no blind acceptance of "one-fits-all" policies. When investing on a new E-Business solution, full commitment should be avoided and there should be always back up plans. Third, only solutions that show financial value should be considered. A cost-benefit analysis should be conducted for each specific investment and only those showing added value should be considered.

Similarly, Afuah (2001) also believes that contingency is important and considers that firms should have dynamic boundaries to thrive in the face of technological change. Technological changes, such as the Internet, create a high level of uncertainty, but do not necessarily imply changes in the marketplace. In this context, the adoption of contingent/incremental strategies provides the required flexibility to determine which competences can ultimately be the source of competitive advantage. As each firm is very specific, there is no appropriate strategic benchmark that can be used from the start. Consequently, it takes time to assess the full impact of the Internet in terms of B2B (Business to Business), supply-chains (Pandya and Dholakia, 2002) and inter-firm relationships (Jap, 2000).

POLICY IMPLICATIONS AND RECOMMENDATIONS

Existing Policies

The existing governmental policies to foster E-Business adoption seem to suffer from strategic myopia. The important role of SMEs in terms of economic activity and the acknowledged relevance of E-Business as a competitive tool, prompted governments to adopt a proactive attitude towards the promotion of E-Business for SMEs. Their rationale was that generic support should be enough to lead to a rapid uptake of ICT technology by SMEs. However, this approach was careless, because it relied too much on the enthusiasm that surrounded the positive impact of E-Business on large companies. Thus, government support forgot about SME specificity and translated into naïve technical fixes and "one-fits-all" solutions.

The biggest mistake of most governments was thinking that E-Business was more about technology than strategy (Feindt et al., 2004). The "all ICT good, no ICT bad" approach which worked for large companies did not produce significant results among SMEs. Overall, basic government policies promoting generic support led to very low E-Business assimilation rates in SMEs. This was mainly due to the fact that CEOs did not manage to recognize the added value of E-Business through generic support mechanisms. Instead, CEOs relied on formal and informal networks to invest in ICT, neglecting publicly funded initiatives (Anderson and Boocock, 2002). Networks can provide tailor-made advice which inserts E-Business in the global strategy of the firm; something that governments cannot achieve with generic policies. Taylor and Murphy (2004) consider that governments should have a more realistic view of how firms operate avoiding generic support mechanisms which are technology driven and profiled for large companies.

Other critical defaults associated with governmental support were poor promotional campaigns and implementation defaults. According to empirical evidence collected by Harindranath et al. (2008), most of SMEs surveyed had very little or no knowledge of public incentives designed to help them (268 out of 378 never used). Furthermore, some of the firms that used these incentives did not report a happy experience. Programs devised

for SMEs could not avoid the typical defaults of governmental agencies. Too much bureaucracy and cumbersome processes were main issues raised by CEOs.

According to Beckinsale et al. (2006), governments act at a very initial stage and create a very small impact on SMEs strategy. At the E-Business level, governments tend to act in three generic ways. First, they create policy guidelines and websites that provide information about opportunities. Second, they fund advisors to encourage SMEs to take the first steps in terms of Internet usage. Third, they use EU funds to develop projects that promote advice and training for SMEs. Overall, the governmental approach tends to be very shallow.

As expected, the practical results of these policies are quite insignificant (Beckinsale et al., 2006). In the UK, none of the firms interviewed knew of central government schemes to support E-Business adoption and none used the UK Online (a government-supported network) facilities. According to Harindranath et al. (2008), only 4% of companies reported having used governmental agencies as external information sources towards ICT decisions. The main driver of change in SMEs is the owner or CEO followed closely by consultants, friends and family and ICT suppliers. 50% of firms investing in ICT used external consultants, 37% friends and family (networks), 35% ICT vendors and 8% used professional independent sources (Harindranath et al., 2008).

Despite drawbacks, it is considered that the role of local agencies is more important than the role of the government. There is evidence that local project support and suppliers are more instrumental in adoption strategies than direct government intervention (Beckinsale et al., 2006). According to Wagner et al. (2003), Local Enterprise Agencies, due to their close rapport with firms, are more appropriate for general support than governments or governmental agencies. However, defaults still arise at the local agency level, as they have a short-term view, lack internal skills and competences, and have little understanding of SMEs needs. Regarding the latter, agencies, similarly to governments, do not support firms beyond the initial start-up stage. They stop providing continuous assistance and monitoring when the company reaches complex levels of implementation both internally and externally.

Recommendations for Policy Making

At present, governments should forget about implementation and focus on developing effective strategies to build awareness (Marasini et al., 2008). In order to assist SMEs that do not respond to ICT initiatives it is important to demonstrate benefits. According to Ramsey and McCole (2005), the main responsible for low E-Business adoption in New Zealand were the negative mindsets of CEOs. Most of these negative mindsets were determined not by informed perspectives but by ignorance about E-Business potential. At this level, public policy can provide an important contribution, by raising awareness and provide initial support to those that need it. Raising awareness is crucial and Jeon et al. (2006) reiterates the importance of these policy lines for South Korea. The actual implementation of E-Business should be left in the hands of private stakeholders (ICT suppliers, consultants, other), as these are the ones that have the required competencies to provide a tailor-made solution that effectively inserts ICT technologies in the firms' strategy.

The public approach to ICT support should change from generic to specific. According to Zheng et al. (2004), advice to SMEs should be business model specific. Otherwise few CEO's will be able to understand the real potential of E-Business for the firm. CEO's in SME's are time restricted and channel most of their energies to short-term planning. Therefore they have little time for strategic thinking and require tailor-made support that accurately responds to their change needs. For a strategic policy to be effective, it should take into account the following factors: age of owner, qualifications of staff, attitude to

growth. Generic approaches to technology or theoretical statements about the market would not be enough to change CEO's perceptions or to make them better informed towards strategic changes.

Beckinsale et al. (2006) consider also that governments should no longer try to do everything themselves. They should cooperate with suppliers and consultants to create better solutions for SMEs, leading to closer rapports with firms through tailor-made advice and assistance. These solutions may involve among other: grants for SMEs accessed through local suppliers and the development of networks between suppliers and government agencies to assist Internet adoption.

Despite its misuse in the past, generic public policy can also be relevant if properly directed. There are three lines of action that can produce promising results. First, e-government should be a priority, creating role model and stakeholder pressure in the value-chain. Strong e-government policies (e-taxing, e-justice, e-health, e-science and others) can act as an incentive for SMEs to change their information systems and become more receptive to ICT. This would be an important step on an epidemic model of diffusion (Ramsey and McCole, 2005) that is widely used to explain E-Business adoption. Second, there should be an improvement of the quality of human resources, namely CEO's, through education and qualification. Third, there should be an effort towards the provision of national high-tech ICT infrastructure (mobile and fixed broadband) helping E-Business adoption efforts. As stated by Pavic et al. (2007), page 327, "… it is not possible to create the knowledge economy without the knowledge society."

Finally, an important role should also be given to the creation of entrepreneurial networks. According to Marasini et al. (2008) informal learning (individual and group) play a vital role in the successful implementation of new technology in SMEs. Consequently, better learning can be obtained through CoP (communities of practice – groups that share similar practices (explicit and tacit) Wenger and Lave (1991)) than through formal training. At this level, governments can have an important role by promoting the development of this type of communities.

Best Practices Example: eBSN (European E-Business Support Network)

The eBSN is an EU policy initiative established in 2003 to promote the adoption and implementation of E-Business by companies, including SMEs (Eleftheriadou, 2008). It is a network that aims at promoting policy coordination and learning across different Member States. Besides analyzing the evolution of E-Business policies, the eBSN also allows for the international exchange of spillover effects.

From the policies adopted by Member States, eBSN has identified three important policy lines for promoting E-Business in SMEs at present and in the near future (Eleftheriadou, 2008). First, customized support for SMEs through the hiring of private E-Business consultants. So far, these have been successful measures adopted by some Member States (eAskel program in Finland), as consultants allow for a high level of customization of IT solutions making them more appealing to SMEs. Second, sector specific E-Business policies for SMEs in order to support the participation of SMEs in global digital supply chains. At this level, data exchange harmonization (TIC-PME 2010 in France), cross-border pilot projects (Construction IT Alliance eXchange (CITAX) in Ireland) and successful stories from peers are playing a significant role in driving E-Business adoption. Third, cross-border cross-sectoral policies aimed at international companies dealing with different industries. As a new trend in policy, the first evidence comes from developed European Economies that are trying to promote structured electronic data exchange through features such as: e-ordering, e-invoicing, e-payment and others. Nevertheless, there is still much to be done at this level, namely the coordination of intra-sectorial with cross-sectorial policies.

Overall, the case of eBSN illustrates most of the theoretical recommendations proposed in this chapter. The hiring of private consultants is clearly a step towards specific and collaborative approaches, as solutions for SMEs are tailor made and cooperation with private companies or individuals is privileged. The sectorial policies are also a step towards raising CEO awareness and the creation of entrepreneurial innovation networks. Pilot projects and the dissemination of successful stories from peers are important tools to instill CEOs into adopting a proactive view towards E-Business. These measures can also lead to a higher level of networking between players belonging to the same sector.

CONCLUSION

The adoption of E-Business by SMEs is not homogeneous and raises critical strategic issues. When compared to large companies, SMEs under perform in all indicators. Adoption rates tend to change significantly with sector features (value-chain, technology intensity, competition) and internal firms conditions (size, age, ICT expertise, market focus). Furthermore, SMEs have high initial adoption rates that do not materialize into relevant assimilation levels. This portrays the fact that most companies lack awareness of the full potential of E-Business and focus on driving costs down instead of creating added value.

The specific nature of SMEs was a feature that emerged as significant along the chapter and that should continue to characterize future trends in terms of E-Business adoption. SMEs depend strongly on the CEO personality, qualifications and vision. This reliance on a single person combined with limited resources is the source of erratic and ad-hoc investment strategies in terms of E-Business. Some SMEs do not even invest, as CEOs lack awareness of the potential benefits that E-Business can deliver. Others embark in experimental approaches to E-Business applying independent pieces of technology to different departments. The few that evolve into complex and integrated E-Business applications are normally pushed to do so by competitors or value chain partners. The disparity is clear and should continue to dominate further research into this topic, leading to a wide range of options both in terms of public policy and theoretical approaches.

At the strategic level, SMEs should adopt contingent models in terms of E-Business investments. As E-Business learning tends to be firm specific, there are no magic solutions or technical fixes that can be easily adopted by SMEs. Instead each firm must embark on an individual learning process, based on experimentation and trial and error. In such a process, full commitment strategies should be avoided (Afuah, 2001; Zheng et al., 2004) due to their high level of risk.

In terms of public policy, the conclusion is that governmental approaches must change. Existing incentives tend to be too generic to produce any positive effect on SMEs' investment policies. Governments act at very early adoption stages and only provide basic support in terms of technology. Most of the incentives were designed for large companies based on the assumption that E-Business is more about technology than strategy. When applied to SMEs, these incentives did not work. Thus, the actual state of affairs must be changed through five lines of action. First, incentives should be used to build awareness among CEOs. Second, there should be a generic to specific change in terms of perspective, inserting technology in the strategic decision making process of the firm. Third, private stakeholders should be included in incentives, thus allowing for a higher level of policy customization. Fourth, the creation of entrepreneurial networks should be promoted to allow for a better diffusion of knowledge, namely CoP (Communities of Practice). Fifth, generic policies should focus only on public needs in terms of national ICT infrastructure, education and e-government adoption.

REFERENCES

Adshead, A. (2001). The E-Supply Chain is Only as Strong as Its Weakest Link. *Computer Weekly*, *2*, 42–46.

Afuah, A. (2001). Dynamic Boundaries of the Firm: Are Firms Better Off Being Vertically Integrated in the Face of a Technological Change? *Academy of Management Journal*, *44*(6), 1211–1228. doi:10.2307/3069397

Anderson, V., & Boocock, G. (2002). Small Firms and Internationalisation: Learning to Manage and Managing to Learn. *Human Resource Management Journal*, *12*(3), 5–24. doi:10.1111/j.1748-8583.2002.tb00068.x

Baldwin, J., Sabourin, D., & Smith, D. (2004). Firm Performance in the Canadian Food Processing Sector: The Interaction Between ICT, Advanced Technology Use and Human Resource Competencies. In OECD (Ed.), *The Economic Impact of ICT, Measurement, Evidence and Implications* (pp. 153-181), OECD, Paris.

Beckinsale, M., Levy, M., & Powell, P. (2006). Exploring Internet Adoption Drivers in SMEs. *Electronic Markets*, *16*(4), 361–370. doi:10.1080/10196780600999841

Chaffey, D. (2004). *E-Business and E-Commerce Management* (2nd ed.). Upper Saddle River, NJ: Prentice-Hall.

Cross, G. (2000). How E-Business is Transforming Supply Chain Management. *The Journal of Business Strategy*, *21*(2), 36–43. doi:10.1108/eb040073

DeLone, W. (1988). Determinants of Success for Computer Usage in Small Business. *Management Information Systems Quarterly*, *12*(1), 51–61. doi:10.2307/248803

Dholakia, R., & Kshetri, N. (2004). Factors Impacting the Adoption of Internet Among SMEs. *Small Business Economics*, *23*(3), 311–322. doi:10.1023/B:SBEJ.0000032036.90353.1f

Eleftheriadou, D. (2008). *Small and Medium-Sized Entreprises Hold the Key to European Competitiveness: How to Help Them Innovate Through ICT and E-Business*. The Global Information Technology Report, World Economic Forum.

European Commission. (2008). *The European E-Business Report 2008: The Impact of ICT and E-Business on Firms, Sectors and the Economy.* 6th Synthesis Report of the Sectoral E-Business Watch. Retrieved September 2, 2009 from http://www.ebusiness-watch.org.

European Commission. (2009). *Europe's Digital Competitiveness Report*. Annual Information Society Report – Volume 1, European Union. Retrieved September 9, 2009 from http://eur-lex.europa.eu.

Feindt, S., Jeffcoate, J., & Chappel, C. (2001). Identifying Success Factors for Rapid Growth in SME E-Commerce. *Small Business Economics, 19*, 51–62. doi:10.1023/A:1016165825476

Harindranath, G., Dyerson, R., & Barnes, D. (2008). ICT Adoption and Use in UK SMEs: A Failure of Initiatives? *Electronic Journal Information Systems Evaluation, 11*(2), 91–96.

Hua, S., Rajesh, M., & Theng, L. (2008). *Barriers to the Adoption of E-Commerce Among Small and Medium-Sized Entreprises: A Study on the Non-Adopters in Malaysia*. Working paper presented at the 3rd International Colloquium on Business & Management (ICBM) held in Bangkok. Retrieved November, 9, 2009, from http://icbm.bangkok.googlepages.com/ICBM.2008.Sim.Chia.Hua.RP.pdf.

Hwang, H., Ku, C., Yen, D., & Cheng, C. (2004). Critical Factors Influencing the Adoption of Data Warehouse Technology: A Study of the Banking Industry in Taiwan. *Decision Support Systems, 37*(1), 1–21. doi:10.1016/S0167-9236(02)00191-4

Jap, S. (2000). The Relationship-Technology Interface: A Path to Competitive Advantage. In Boase, T., & Ganeshan, R. (Eds.), *New Directions in Supply Chain Management: Technology, Strategy and Implementation* (pp. 3–23). New York: American Management Association.

Jeon, B., Han, K., & Lee, M. (2006). Determining Factors for the Adoption of E-Business: The Case of SMEs in Korea. *Applied Economics, 38*, 1905–1916. doi:10.1080/00036840500427262

Levy, M., & Powell, P. (2003). Exploring SME Internet Adoption: Towards a Contingent Model. *Electronic Markets, 13*(2), 173–181. doi:10.1080/1019678032000067163

Locket, N., & Brown, D. (2003). *Innovations Affecting SMEs and E-Business with Reference to Strategic Networks, Aggregation and Intermediaries*. Lancaster University Managament School – Working Paper. Retrieved September 10, 2009 from http://www.lums.lancs.ac.uk

Love, P., Irani, Z., Standing, C., Lin, C., & Burn, J. (2005). The Enigma of Evaluation: Benefits, Costs and Risks of IT in Australian Small Medium-Sized Enterprises. *Information & Management, 42*(7), 947–964. doi:10.1016/j.im.2004.10.004

MacGregor, R., & Vrazalic, L. (2008). *SMEs and Electronic Commerce: An Overview of Our Current Knowledge*. Hershey, PA: IGI Global. Retrieved September 10, 2009 from http://www.igi-global.com

Maguire, S., & Koh, S. (2004). Identifying the Adoption of E-Business and Knowledge Management within SMEs. *Journal of Small Business and Enterprise Development, 11*(3), 338–348. doi:10.1108/14626000410551591

Maguire, S., Koh, S., & Magrys, A. (2007). The Adoption of E-Business and Knowledge Management in SMEs. *Benchmarking: An International Journal, 14*(1), 37–58. doi:10.1108/14635770710730928

Marasini, R., Ions, K., & Ahmad, M. (2008). Assessment of E-Business Adoption in SMEs: A Study of Manufacturing Industry in the UK North East Region. *Journal of Manufacturing Technology Management*, *19*(5), 627–644. doi:10.1108/17410380810877294

Mutula, S., & Brakel, P. (2006). E-readiness of SMEs in the ICT Sector in Botswana with Respect to Information Access. *The Electronic Library*, *24*(3), 402–417. doi:10.1108/02640470610671240

OECD. (2008). *Internet Selling and Purchasing by Industry (2), 2008*. OECD Key ICT Indicators in Excel table format. Retrieved November, 30, 2009 from http://www.oecd.org/dataoecd/20/22/34083121.xls.

Ongori, H. (2009). Role of Information Communication Technologies Adoption in SMEs: Evidence from Botswana. *Research Journal of Information Technology*, *1*(2), 79–85. doi:10.3923/rjit.2009.79.85

Orlikowski, W., & Hofman, J. (1997). An Improvisational Model of Change Management: The Case of Groupware Technologies. *Sloan Management Review*, *38*(2), 11–21.

Pandya, A., & Dholakia, N. (2002). *B2C Crash as an Innovation Failure: Organization Learning from the Dotcom Debris*. Working paper, University of Chicago. Retrieved April 24, 2002 from http://ritim.eba.uri.edu/wp2003/pdf_format/JECO-B2C-Innovation-Failure-v01.pdf

Pavic, S., Koh, S., Simpson, M., & Padmore, J. (2007). Could E-Business Create a Competitive Advantage in UK SMEs? *Benchmarking: An International Journal*, *14*(3), 320–351. doi:10.1108/14635770710753112

Ramsey, E., & McCole, P. (2005). E-Business in Professional SMEs: The Case of New Zealand. *Journal of Small Business and Enterprise Development*, *12*(4), 528–544. doi:10.1108/14626000510628207

Raymond, L., Bergeron, F., & Blili, S. (2005). The Assimilation of E-Business in Manufacturing SMEs: Determinants and Effects on Growth and Internationalization. *Electronic Markets*, *15*(2), 106–118. doi:10.1080/10196780500083761

Schmiemann, M. (2008). *Enterprises by Size Class – Overview of SMEs in the EU*. Eurostat. Retrieved September 10, 2009 from http://epp.eurostat.ec.europa.eu.

Soriano, D., Roig, S., Sanchis, J., & Torcal, R. (2002). The Role of Consultants in SMEs. *International Small Business Journal*, *20*(1), 95–103. doi:10.1177/0266242602201007

Taylor, M., & Murphy, A. (2004). SMEs and E-Business. *Journal of Small Business and Enterprise Development*, *11*(3), 280–289. doi:10.1108/14626000410551546

VanWeele, A. (2002). *Purchasing and Supply Chain Management – Analysis, Planning and Practice*. London: Thomson Learning.

Venkatraman, N. (1991). ICT-Induced Business Reconfiguration. In Scott Morton, M. (Ed.), *The Corporation of the 1990s. Information Technology and Organizational Transformation* (pp. 122–157). Oxford, UK: Oxford University Press.

Wagner, B., Fillis, I., & Johansson, U. (2003). E-Business and E-Supply in Small and Medium Sized Businesses. *Supply Chain Management: An International Journal*, *8*(4), 343–354. doi:10.1108/13598540310490107

Wenger, E., & Lave, J. (1991). *Situated Learning: Legitimate Peripheral Participation*. Cambridge, UK: Cambridge University Press.

Windrum, P., & Berranger, P. (2002). The Adoption of E-Business Technology by SMEs. *Merit Infonomics Research Memorandum Series*. Retrieved August 12, 2009 from http://meritbbs.unimaas.nl.

WMRO. (2009). *E-Business Adoption in the West Midlands – 2008*. Birmingham, UK: West Midlands Research Observatory.

Yap, C., Soh, C., & Raman, K. (1992). Information Systems Success Factors in Small Businesses. *Ómega. International Journal of Management Science, 20*(5), 597–609.

Zheng, J., Caldwell, N., Harland, C., Powell, P., Woerndl, M., & Xu, S. (2004). Small Firms and E-Business: Cautiousness, Contingency and Cost-Benefit. *Journal of Purchasing and Supply Management, 10*, 27–39. doi:10.1016/j.pursup.2003.11.004

Chapter 2
Strategic E–Business/ IT Alignment for SME Competitiveness

Eduardo Escofet
University of Holguín, Cuba

María José Rodríguez-Fórtiz
University of Granada, Spain

José Luis Garrido
University of Granada, Spain

Lawrence Chung
University of Texas at Dallas, USA

ABSTRACT

Many small and medium enterprises (SMEs) have used e-business models for enhancing their competitiveness. As the needs of SMEs grow, however, so does e-business/ IT strategic alignment. Although some techniques have been proposed in literature to find and evaluate business/ IT strategic alignment, they largely suffer from lack of objectivity and integration. In this chapter, the authors propose a practical lightweight interview-based method that permits us to align e-business and IT strategies and to obtain investment priorities per software development process and area, towards improvements on service quality and business profitability. This method incorporates goal modeling and the Strategic Alignment Modeling techniques to address the growing needs of SMEs, to avoid inconsistencies and to increase confidence in compiled data and modeling results.

INTRODUCTION

Small and Medium Enterprises (SMEs) are key engines of major economies, but usually constrained by tight budgets, lack of skilled personnel, tough competition from other SMEs and large enterprises, and certain state policies and laws. Accordingly, SMEs have sought after a good means improve SMEs' competitiveness, in particular, in e-business.

DOI: 10.4018/978-1-60960-463-9.ch002

The success and performance of an SME inevitably is affected by its competitive edge over whatever business offers similar products and services. Successful enterprises always take into account competitiveness as an essential intrinsic feature of business success, especially for small and medium-sized enterprises where being competitive is a key issue to survive and guarantee a long-term evolution.

Importantly, competitiveness is almost always considered synonymous with the quality and achievement of an SME's strategies and objectives, together with its productivity and ability for designing and producing and market products and services superior to those offered by the SME's competitors. Competitive, of course, is also, at least partially, the result of relationships between firms and local business environment, while at the same time being dependent on social and economic objectives synergy and influenced by factors from external environment (Porter & Ketels, 2003).

A critical step for an SME to achieve a competitive edge is to adopt, where advisable, a good e-business model which captures the vision of a SME in consideration of the needs of its customers who will ultimately cause the success, of lack thereof, the SME. This becomes especially important when SMEs are reluctant to adopt e-business solutions, failing to see the value of such solutions.

Business today is under increasing pressure to improve performance, and success largely depends on a company's ability to re-invent itself to adapt to changing circumstances. So, it is necessary a close cooperation exists between business and IT functions within a company, in a manner to enable the company to adaptable convert strategic business goals into effective IT solutions (Corbett & Molloy, 2000).

Not surprisingly, lots of research has been done on the issue of strategic alignment. A key observation from such research is that the empirical findings indeed support the hypothesis that those organizations that successfully align their business strategies with their IT strategies will outperform those that do not. A good alignment leads to a more focused and strategic use of IT, which, in turn, leads to increased performance (Chang & Reich, 2007).

While taking into consideration the particular constraints that most SMEs are faced with, we need to provide a cost-effective way to help business managers, engineers and stakeholders in general with the adoption of an e-business model. *But, how do we systematically address, and hopefully achieve, strategic e-business/ IT alignment?*

The main objective of this research is to provide a practical and lightweight interview-based method to help with aligning high level business concerns with IT strategic ones, using simple, yet useful, techniques and models, while deploying some best practices. It is a process as a whole to create a propitious scenario for a safe adoption of an e-business model.

The chapter is structured starting with a brief background on forces and factors that affect SME e-business adoption and success, focusing on business strategies and strategic barriers as key issues to tackle. Next, it is presented with e-business/ IT alignment as an effective tool to tackle some of those issues. For such alignment, a practical, lightweight, cost-effective, interview-based method is organized in terms of four main steps:

- *The interview core process*: A very well known technique for data gathering from stakeholders.
- *The application of the Delphi method*: A proved method to increase data quality and reach consensus. These two first steps go together for the whole process.
- *The goal modeling and alignment*: This is the main step, using the Strategic Model Alignment (SAM), the goal modeling technique and some best practices for the e-business/ IT alignment by comparison.
- *The application of Quality Function Deployment (QFD)*: A commonly-used

technique to implement quality improvement processes in heterogeneous production and services environments.

After the conclusion and reference parts, this chapter also provides an extensive and highly recommended additional reading material to dig deeper into e-business and IT alignment subjects, and into the techniques used in the method.

BACKGROUND

Most of the rules of industry competition apply to SMEs competitiveness. There are several studies about this topic: "The Five Forces That Shape Industry Competition" (Porter, 2008) is considered one of the primary sources. Roughly noting these forces:

- *Threat of new entrants*: it usually brings new capacities and expectations, with successful strategies they shake markets and raise necessary investments.
- *Threat of substitute products or services*: functionally replaces an existing product or service; there is a big threat on substitutes because sometimes they are overlooked and their impact diminishes overall profitability.
- *Bargaining power of suppliers*: powerful suppliers can extinct profitability out by charging higher prices or limiting the quality of services, especially if they are very concentrated.
- *Bargaining power of buyers*: powerful customers can force down prices, demand better quality and more services increasing industry costs.
- *Rivalry among existing competitors*: although rivalry is a driving force in business, it could be harmful for industry profitability if it is just based on price competition or on enterprises wanting leadership at any cost.

Although the above mentioned forces also create opportunities, if an SME is unaware of the inevitable changes and the market evolution, they could be lethal for its business. SMEs strategy should consider these opportunities and threats for long-run profitability.

There are several identifiable factors that affect industry-shaping forces, but they are not considered forces by themselves (Porter, 2008):

- Industry growth rate,
- Technology and innovation,
- Government, and
- Complementary products and services.

In the specific case of e-business driven SMEs, technology and innovation appear as defining forces because of the role that information technology (IT) plays on every e-business.

There is a shallow SME market influence on most of these forces and factors but, they are determinant for SME today´s success and future profitability. Adapting to industry-shaping forces and factors and playing with these tendencies is essential to guarantee the dynamic adaptability and the strategic evolution of the SME business.

Strategic alignment involves two basic concepts, namely enterprise strategy and IT strategy. The enterprise strategy is the long-term development plan of an enterprise, it focuses on the strategic goal of enterprises and considers the balances and aligns among the different levels in the enterprises in three aspects: directions and goals, environment restraint and policies, plans and the target system. IT strategy focuses on the plan, management and application of the internal and external information resource of the enterprise as far as the expectation and goal of the organization is concerned, thus to standardize the internal management of the organization, enhance the working efficiency and the customer satisfaction degree, and finally obtain the competitive advantages for the enterprises (Xiang, Wu & Hu, 2008).

SMEs whose business and e-business strategies are aligned should be less vulnerable to changes in their business environment and to internal inefficiencies. They should also perform better as the Internet and web-based technologies provide the systems and support the processes required to successfully implement their business strategy, focused on the development of networks, products and markets. The high level of alignment between the SME's e-business capabilities and its business strategy demonstrates that the use of the Internet and web-based technologies and applications is targeted on its competitive needs and its strategic priorities, and thus allows it to increase its performance (Raymond & Bergeron, 2008).

Hence, developing a strategy to fit SME business, taking into account the above mentioned forces and factors, is a key issue for SME competitiveness. Quality of Service (QoS), holistic quality policies, closed customer relationships and a dynamic observance of user needs should be integrated in this strategy, always considering tight budgets and real market and industry niches.

Strategic Factors that Affect E-Business

For SMEs to adopt e-business strategies and tools, benefits must outweigh the investment and maintenance costs. Commercial considerations and potential returns drive adoption. Some barriers are clearly identified: lack of strategic thinking, availability of information technology (IT) competencies within the firm, and availability and cost of appropriate interoperable small-firm systems, network infrastructure and the Internet-related support services. Lack of reliable trust and redress systems and cross-country legal and regulatory differences also impede cross-border transactions (Vickery, Sakai, Lee & Sim, 2004).

SMEs not using the Internet cite ROI and cost as the primary inhibitors; those using the Internet cite the lack of an e-business strategy as the key barrier; and those who are attempting to implement more sophisticated e-business solutions, such as transactional capabilities, cite security as the key impediment (Ivis, 2001). Endogenous factors explain many adoptions and rejections of e-business solutions. The most important factors (Arbore & Ordanini, 2009; Esteves, 2006) are:

- The level of financial resources able to affect any investment decision.
- The managerial culture; influencing propensity to innovate.
- The organizational readiness; which is relevant for the integration of new technologies.
- Business complexity; with direct influence on business benefit opportunities.

These factors directly impact the SME strategy planning and roadmap, creating and influencing E-Business adoption barriers.

While adopting E-Business technologies, we face a clearly identifiable obstacle: lack of strategic thinking. This impediment is present at all business levels, in particular at the IT level. Aligning E-Business and IT strategies is a way of addressing the lack of strategic thinking and also of positively tackling other barriers such as troubles with developing an E-Business roadmap and the lack of management commitment. Consequently, strategic alignment means the strategic fit between the position of an organization in the competitive product-market arena and the design of an appropriate administrative and technical structure to support its execution. This is a continuous and dynamic process (Henderson & Venkatraman, 1999).

E-BUSINESS AND IT STRATEGIC ALIGNMENT

The E-Business/ IT strategic alignment is an essential step for architectural, structural and new technological adoption decisions. Several problems emerge in this process:

- Interviews to business and IT managers have a high level of incoherence, due to poor skills on new technologies and raw knowledge of on-line business models.
- Applied questionnaires contribute with a high level of subjectivity to the alignment process.
- IT investment priorities are not clear; this is a key element for the success of the E-Business adoption.

We can find several studies about the E-Business/business/ IT alignment subject (Al-Hakim & Memmola, 2009; Baina, Ansias, Petit & Castiaux, 2008; Becker, Prikladnicki & Audy, 2008; Henderson & Venkatraman, 1999; Halleux, Ludovic & Andersson, 2008), but they show lack of integration, obviate priorities on investment and specific features of E-Business model, or usually forget the human-subjective aspect of each alignment process.

It is also important to take into account the development of e-business capabilities in the organization; they may come in four main forms:

- E-communication, referring to the promotion of the firm, its products and services (Turban, Lee, King & Chung, 2006).
- E-intelligence wherein the nature and scope of information now available on the Internet allow the firm to scan its technological, commercial and competitive environment in search of ways and means to improve its operations and decision making, and seek new product-market opportunities (Hill & Scott, 2004).

- E-commerce is of a transactional nature. It concerns the buying and selling of goods and services through the Internet and web-based technologies (Rayport & Jaworski, 2003).
- E-collaboration, that consists of integrating and sharing, through the Internet or Extranets, information on the extended value chain linking the firm with its upstream and downstream business partners. This allows stakeholders within the same industry or network organization that share the same objectives to collaborate in the design, development, production and management of products and services at different stages of their life-cycle (Cassivi, Lefebvre, Lefebvre & Léger, 2004).

Herein, we propose an interview-based lightweight method. Method "lightness" is a cost-effective solution for SMEs E-Business adoption and planning. All these aspects create a more propitious scenario to improve competitiveness through "safe" and reliable E-Business adoption. This is a method used to reduce incoherence in the interviewing process, to improve consolidation results and to reach consensus.

The method consists of four steps (Figure 1). It starts with the preparation of the interview questionnaires, and then applying the Delphi method (Linstone & Turoff, 2002). Next, we apply the goal modeling approach and the Strategic Alignment Model (SAM) relationship identification by comparison, the objective is to reduce subjectivity on the compiled information and to guarantee strategic E-Business/ IT alignment.

Eventually, we relate identified goals with processes and process areas (for example, identified from a CMMI application) using Quality Function Deployment (QFD) to align strategic goals and IT processes in an organization (Becker et al., 2008), and to determine investment priorities in IT processes and process areas.

The proposal of this method is illustrated using an example (Escofet, Rodríguez, Garrido & Chung, 2009) consisting of the fictitious case of *ebooks2go.ws* portal. Similar to other portals like *freebookspot.in* or *dbebooks.biz*, it receives thousands of hits everyday and permits to search for e-books and e-zines from the Internet content providers such as *megaupload.com* or *rapidshare.com*. Its website offers well known typical basic services for this kind of business: simple searching and scrolling features, registration and authentication forms, content descriptors, external content links, and front page pictures when available. Its main business is based on advertisement links, usually from *Google Ads* or sites alike, with all of these attributes organized across a plain web interface.

The four steps to be applied are explained in detail in the next subsections.

Interview Core Process

The proposal is interview-based and model-oriented, so the first thing to guarantee is the accuracy of the questionnaires and the reliability of the resulting data. We would reach this previous achievement if experts in questionnaires and interviews focus their attention on objectives through the whole interviewing process. It is of paramount importance to be considered in the following refinement process for strategic goal modeling. The interviewing process should involve business managers, IT managers, stakeholders and end users, in order to have a whole understanding of the needs and capacities.

A deeper discussion about elicitation requirements is beyond the scope of this chapter, but we encourage people interested in gathering methods to study other materials about questionnaire preparation and interview planning (Esposito, 2002; Frary, 1996). Besides, we need other methods to reduce incoherence and to reach consensus. We recommend a study on elicitation techniques ad-

Figure 1. Steps of the interview-based lightweight method

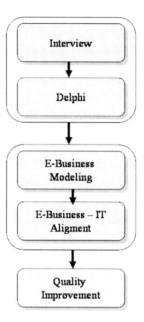

equacy (Carrizo, Dieste & Juristo, 2008) to better grip effectiveness of these methods.

While applying E-Business model taxonomies by Rappa's (Rappa, 2004), Weill & Vitale's (Weill & Vitale, 2001) and Afuah's (Afuah & Tucci, 2003), we have found that this E-Business model should be classified into the Advertising and the Intermediary groups, thus clarifying some of its features and attributes. The identification of E-Business models is important in order to increase the accuracy of the proposed method and to consider the specifics of each model in the processes of questionnaires preparation, interviewing and information consolidation.

A thorough analysis of the answers to the questionnaires should be done in order to attain a better understanding of real e-business needs, end users and stakeholders' preoccupations, business managers' opportunities outlook and IT managers identified IT capacities. In our example, the Business Manager had mentioned and highlighted in his interview that he wanted to increase the amount of clients and the profits without increase the investment. Otherwise, the IT Manager interview shows that his main objective is to offer an automatic customer service and an efficient indexing to the books.

The interview process should be integrated with other elicitation techniques and improvement procedures with a holistic point of view, in order to attain better data quality and reach consensus between stakeholders, that is why we briefly decompose the Delphi method, a very well know technique for a practical solution to this problem, in the next section, looking for a cost-effective interview process that minimizes interview rounds, re-interviewing and pretesting. This is a key concern of SMEs in order to increase productivity and to determine if the e-business model fits user needs and business requirements.

Applying Delphi

Applying questionnaires and interviews usually produce heterogeneous and inexact data that should be compared and verified to increase information accuracy. The Delphi method is intended to reduce incoherence, increment objectivity on subjects and data stability, and help attain consensus. Before applying this method, it is essential to determine the objectives to achieve, to ensure the questions in the questionnaires conform to the objectives and to monitor the way surveys and interviews emerge. Here, the whole process has to be centered on the strategies of e-business and IT.

The selection of the interviewed subjects and the sample size are always connected with the importance of the results of the interview process, the available resources (sometimes scarce for a SME) and the accuracy needed. We suggest that the following summarized steps should be applied to an interview-based process:

- Conformation of a Delphi team to supervise the entire project
- Selection and clustering of the informants (usually informants are experts in the research area)

- First round of Delphi's questionnaires application
- Test questionnaires for proper terminology
- Transmission of the first round questionnaires to the jury members
- Analysis of the first round answers
- Preparation of the second round of questionnaires
- Transmission of the second round of questionnaires to jury members
- Analysis of the second round answers (iterate through the three previous steps, including this one, to increase results stability), and
- Preparation of a conclusion report by the analysis team.

The characteristics of the traditional Delphi technique are anonymity, iteration, feedback and consensus. In Delphi projects one of the main goals used to be consistency, but data quality is a more proper concept today. While many Delphi studies are focused on purely forecasting or consensus issues, a Delphi variant, called Argument Delphi (AD) also concentrates on production of relevant arguments (Ryynänen, Karvonen & Kässi, 2008) knowledge-orienting the whole process.

There are some variants, some researchers using Delphi usually apply it in four rounds or iterations (Hsu & Sandford, 2007) but this is not mandatory, overlooking too much details, those rounds or iterations consist of:

- Applying Delphi with an open-ended questionnaire. After receiving subjects' responses, researchers need to convert the collected information into a well-structured questionnaire.
- Participants receive a second questionnaire (the structured one from the first iteration) and are asked to review the items summarized by the researchers based on the information provided in the first round. Priorities, rankings and agreements (dis-

agreements) are usually identified in this round.

- Participants receive a questionnaire that includes the items and ratings summarized by the researchers in the previous round and are asked to revise his/ her judgments. This is an opportunity to make further clarifications of both the information and their judgments of the relative importance of the items.
- Participants receive a list of remaining items, their ratings, minority opinions, and items achieving consensus are distributed to the panelists. This round provides a final (or not, depending on the level of consensus researchers are looking for) opportunity for participants to revise their judgments.

There is a strong feedback process in Delphi that allows and encourages the selected Delphi participants to reevaluate their initial judgments about the information provided in previous iterations. The results of previous iterations regarding specific statements and/ or items can change or be modified by individual panel members in later iterations based on their ability to review and assess the comments and feedback provided by the other Delphi panelists (Hsu & Sandford, 2007).

A deeper discussion on the Delphi method, especially on its associated statistical techniques, is beyond the scope of this chapter, but we encourage the reader to take a look at some theoretical and practical studies (Hsu & Sandford, 2007; Linstone & Turoff, 2002; Paul, 2008; Rayens & Hahn, 2000; Yousuf, 2007) used in our research. It is important to reduce interviewing noise in consideration of E-Business model features and attributes (Lehtonen & Pahkinen, 2004).

As a result of this step, we have detected and eliminated most of the incoherence from the interviews to Business and IT managers and the rest of the stakeholders, inferring new requirements and relationships between requirements, and obtaining

a filtered subset of features, in particular, useful requirements for subsequent modeling. As example, we have detected that there is a requirement of the managers which is incoherent with the rest of the requirements: the Business Manager must invest in IT Technology because the way of serving the client requests will change. From now on, some tasks such as the client subscription, book selling, etc, will be managed automatically by means of a new Web. Additional requirements also arise in our example after Delphi method is applied, for instance, nobody talked about security in the interviews but now the experts recommend to consider authentication mechanisms and encrypted communications to guaranty system protection and data security respectively.

Creating Models and Aligning

We use visually-oriented goal modeling to reduce subjectivity in the compiled information and to enhance strategic E-business and IT alignment (Baina et al., 2008; Bleistein, Aurum, Cox & Ray, 2004; Lamsweerde, 2001; Vara & Sánchez, 2007). After that, it is essential to establish the relationship between the goal model and the relationships in Venkatraman´s Strategic Alignment Model by comparison. Four perspectives can be identified in SAM (Henderson & Venkatraman, 1999) as follows:

- **Strategy Execution:** this perspective corresponds to the classical, hierarchical view of strategic management. It considers the business strategy as the driver of both organizational design choices and the logic of the IT infrastructure. Top Management formulates the strategy; IT Management is only considered as strategy implementer.
- **Technology Potential:** this perspective also views the business strategy as the driver. However it involves the formulation of an IT strategy to support the chosen business strategy and the corresponding

specification of the required IT infrastructure and processes. The top management should provide the technology vision to articulate the logic and choices pertaining to IT strategy that would best support the chosen business strategy. The role of the IT manager should be that of the technology architect. He designs and implements efficiently and effectively the required IT infrastructure that is consistent with the external component of IT strategy.

- **Competitive Potential:** this alignment perspective is concerned with the exploitation of emerging IT capabilities to: impact new products and services, influence the key attributes of strategy, as well as develop new forms of relationships. Unlike the two previous perspectives, which considered business strategy as given, this perspective allows the modification of business strategy via emerging IT capabilities.

- **Service Level:** this alignment perspective focuses on how to build world class IT organization within an organization. In this perspective, the role of business strategy is indirect. This perspective is often considered as necessary, but not sufficient, to ensure the effective use of IT resources and to be responsive to the growing and fast changing demands of the end-user population.

Note that businesses with a large and dominant presence of the first perspective also present several barriers to E-business adoption. Businesses with a dominant presence of the fourth perspective are usually technology-driven, hardly meeting user needs. A reasonable combination of perspectives with a large presence of the second and third perspectives is greatly recommended; otherwise some alignment and adoption problems exist and must be addressed.

In this case, to reduce subjectivity on the interview/Delphi process, to model goals and to align E-business and IT strategies, we partially used previous proposals (Baina et al., 2008; Bleinstein et al., 2004). It permits to establish an adequate formalization of both strategies alignment, with the difference that we start from consistent information resulting from the application of data elicitation techniques. It permits us more accuracy in modeling and to determine actual perspectives in the strategic alignment model (Henderson & Venkatraman, 1999).

Increasing accuracy in modeling E-business/ IT strategies is not easy if managers and experts don´t follow standards, so we use Weill & Vitale´s and Rappa´s taxonomies to classify the E-business model of the organization; beginning with this classification it is easier to identify fundamental features and attributes of E-business models.

Goal modeling is an important part of the requirements engineering, we encourage to dig notation and formalisms foundations in several studies about goal modeling and goal-oriented requirements engineering (GORE) (Anwer & Ikram, 2006; Chung, Nixon, Yu & Mylopulos, 2000; Lamsweerde, 2001; Lamsweerde, 2004; Halleux et al., 2008) used in our research. The following two subsections address the specific activities to formalize and model compiled interview results looking for the desired strategic alignment.

E-Business Modeling

In this step, we started from the compiled interview results after the Delphi method application and extrapolated E-business and IT strategies to goal modeling. Goal models are used in the earliest phases of business and information systems design, where they help in clarifying interests, intentions, and strategies of different stakeholders answering to the "why" of the business. Business models give a high level view of the activities taking place in and between organizations by identifying agents, resources and the exchange of resources between the agents (Halleux et al., 2008).

As a result of the compiled information obtained from previous steps, we established that the main business goal is to increase profits through the growth of its user base (cloud in Figure 1). Because *ebooks2go.ws* revenue comes from the advertisement it shows, the main concerns according to the interviewing results are increasing on-line ad number that is related to three important aspects: clicks on ads by visiting users, the time of these users spent on searching for e-books and e-zines, and the site registered user base increment, as shown at the second level in Figure 2.

An important E-business gauge is the report from content provider businesses, which includes important data about the origin of a downloading, service level agreement (SLA) satisfaction and current content indexing levels of the site.

After these steps, we have our goal models, as in Figure 2 with E-business strategy and in Figure 3 with IT strategy. These models show relationships, dependencies and refinements of E-business and IT objectives, using one of the prominent goal modeling methodologies (Lamsweerde, 2001; Lamsweerde, 2004). It is a best practice to check identified goals against the results from the interview & Delphi process in order to

avoid possible stakeholder needs and business requirements misalignments.

In Figure 3 we can see some of the identified IT goals, most of them with a cause-effect relation with E-business goals, and also important technology-related goals such as: Automatic Customer Service and Efficient and effective indexing mechanism, both at the second level in Figure 2, which assure the appropriateness of the IT infrastructure to properly achieve high level strategic goals.

Aligning by Comparison

After obtaining the goal models, we establish a comparison between the identifiable elements in order to build the strategic alignment model (SAM). This stage is largely based on the modeler´s skills and expertise, using the reviewed technical literature and our own experience, and some recommended best practices. This stage establishes semantic relations between all pairs of elements (E-business element, IT element), while classifying relationships according to Venkatraman´s perspectives taxonomy and determining cause-effect relations where you can easily find orientation by

Figure 2. E-business strategy

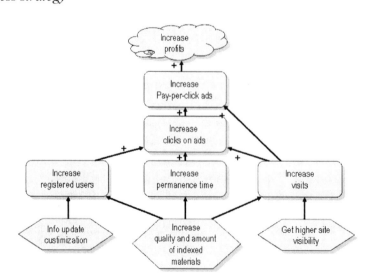

Figure 3. IT strategy

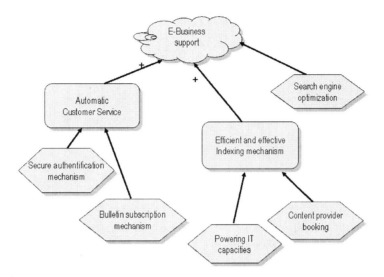

examining element precedence in the compiled results of the interviewing process.

At this moment the Strategic Alignment Model can be implemented. Three types of alignments are identified according to Venkatraman´s perspectives taxonomy:

a. The main soft-goal of Increase profits will demand constant support from IT managers, developers and technologies.
b. The creation of an Automatic customer service defines a publish/subscribe customer relationship management (CRM) style, incrementing the possibility of the creation of a faithful users base.
c, d. An efficient and effective indexing mechanism permeates all systems but specifically help to increase user permanence time and

visits, improving E-business services without big E-business strategy changes.

From Table 1, we derive a Henderson & Venkatraman´s model, as shown in figure 4.

Quality Function Deployment

From the previous step, we obtained the strategic E-business and IT alignment. To further increase the quality of this process and results, we apply QFD. This is a tool to implement quality improvement processes in heterogeneous production and services environments. We used it to establish priorities in investment decisions.

We take the House of Quality matrix (HoQ) to relate E-business goals with the necessary IT elements. Then an initial weight is assigned to

Table 1. Comparison of the e-business/ IT strategies

	IT Element	Orientation	Business Element
a	E-Business support	←	Increase profits
b	Automatic customer service	→	Increase registered users
c	Efficient and effective indexing mechanism	→	Increase permanence time
d	Efficient and effective indexing mechanism	→	Increase visits

Figure 4. Strategic alignment model

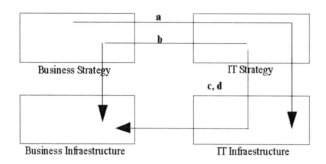

each E-business and IT element, where weights are obtained from the compiled information from informants, in the first two steps of the method (Becker et al., 2008; Denney, 2005; Jayaswal & Patton, 2006). The same process is repeated to assign weights and initial priorities to HoQ, as well as relation levels between E-business elements and IT elements, usually between 0 and 9. The first HoQ is in Figure 5. To adjust priorities we calculate new adjusted priorities using the formula:

*Adjusted Priority = IT Element Initial Priority *
∑ E-Business Goal Initial Priority * Perceived Weight*

This is a columnar calculus and, for every column, we obtain real investment priority for IT elements and actions in order to better fulfill E-Business goals and increase return on investment (ROI).

The same process is applied to a second HoQ to relate tactical E-business goals with problem causes, and in a third HoQ to relate tactical E-business goals and the IT process areas attained from a level 2 Capability Maturity Model Integration (CMMI) process (Kulpa & Johnson, 2008; Mutafelija & Stromberg, 2009).

As a result of these calculations and adjustments, we obtained important numbers. For example, in Figure 4, in the first column of numbers: 5, 4.5 and 8 are the weights indicating initial priorities of E-business goals for business managers, end users and stakeholders (directly from the interviewing process); and in the first row

Figure 5. House of Quality

		Initial priority	IT Elements (actions)	
			Automatic Customer Service	Efficient and effective Indexing mechanism
Initial priority			35	50
E-Business Goals	Increase registered users	5	9	3
	Increase permanence time	4,5	1	3
	Increase visits	8	3	9
Adjusted priority			2572,5	5025

of numbers: 35 and 50 are the initial priorities of IT actions or elements according to IT managers replies. Numbers in the center of the matrix: 9, 1, 3, 3, 3, 9 express the expected cause-effect relation between IT actions and E-business goals as shown in Table 1. Finally, in the last row, we attained the results of the application of the preceding formula expressing the adjusted priorities for IT actions. From this step of our method, some improvements related are obtained:

- Best accuracy in IT actions priorities.
- Secure a better ROI according to main E-business goals.
- Prioritize some processes and IT process areas.

FUTURE RESEARCH DIRECTIONS

Future work includes assessing, and improving the effectiveness of the interviews, in relation to other elicitation procedures, in particular goal-oriented techniques by use of constrain metrics and the generation of new best practices for the aligning process in order to help the practical adopters. Another line of future research concerns a more systematic use of the Delphi method, applying statistical methods to increase data quality, and data mining to identify patterns in order to forecast stakeholder needs and to better adapt to the e-business changing environment.

CONCLUSION

In this chapter, we have identified key forces and factors that influence SMEs competitiveness, and, accordingly, the derived E-business adoption barriers from the strategical point of view. To address these barriers, we have described an interview-based method, using simple, yet useful, techniques and procedures, while deploying some best practices. This method is intended to help with aligning high level business concerns with IT strategic concerns, utilizing goal modeling refinement and comparison.

The application of this method is intended to consolidate more accurate and useful information, through the strategic E-business and IT alignment, and to reduce the interviewing process subjectivity, through goal modeling and SAM visual formalisms. Additionally, we obtained a sketch of prioritization for IT elements and actions in order to increase ROI and to fulfill E-business goals and end user needs.

ACKNOWLEDGMENT

We would like to thank the cooperation of the Ministry of Foreign Affairs of Spain (AECID), project TIN2008-05995/TSI of the Ministry of Education and Science of Spain and the International Association for Development of the Information Society (IADIS).

REFERENCES

Afuah, A., & Tucci, C. L. (2003). *Internet business models and strategies* (2 Ed.). New York: McGraw Hill.

Al-Hakim, L., & Memmola, M. (Eds.). (2009). *Business web strategy: Design, alignment, and application*. Hershey, PA: IGI Global.

Anwer, S., & Ikram, N. (2006, December 6). *Goal oriented requirement engineering: A critical study of techniques.* Paper presented at the XIII Asia Pacific Software Engineering Conference (APSEC'06), Bangalore, India.

Arbore, A., & Ordanini, A. (2009). Environmental drivers of e-business strategies among SMEs. In Lee, I. (Ed.), *Electronic Business: Concepts, methodologies, tools, and applications* (*Vol. I*, pp. 185–196). Hershey, PA: IGI Global.

Baina, S., Ansias, P.-Y., Petit, M., & Castiaux, A. (2008, June 16). *Strategic business/ IT alignment using goal models.* Paper presented at the Third International Workshop on Business/ IT Alignment and Interoperability, BUSITAL'08, Montpellier, France.

Becker, A. L., Prikladnicki, R., & Audy, J. L. N. (2008, May 13). *Strategic alignment of software process improvement programs using QFD.* Paper presented at the BIPI'08, Leipzig, Germany.

Bleistein, S. J., Aurum, A., Cox, K., & Ray, P. K. (2004). Strategy-oriented alignment in requirements engineering: Linking business strategy to requirements of e-business systems using the SOARE approach. *Journal of Research and Practice in Information Technology, 36*(4), 259–276.

Carrizo, D., Dieste, O., & Juristo, N. (2008, September 12). *Study of elicitation techniques adequacy.* Paper presented at the 11th Workshop on Requirement Engineering, Barcelona, Spain.

Cassivi, L., Lefebvre, E., Lefebvre, L. A., & Léger, P.-M. (2004). The impact of e-collaboration tools on firms' performance. *International Journal of Logistics Management, 15*(1), 91–110. doi:10.1108/09574090410700257

Chan, Y. E., & Reich, B. H. (2007). IT alignment: what have we learned? *Journal of Information Technology* (22), 297–315. doi: 10.1057/palgrave. jit.2000109

Chung, L., Nixon, B. A., Yu, E., & Mylopulos, J. (2000). *Non-functional requirements in software engineering.* Norwell, MA: Kluwer Academic Publishers.

Corbett, O., & Molloy, O. (2000). *Alignment of business and IT strategies* (p. 13). Galway, Ireland: National University of Ireland, Galway.

Denney, R. (2005). *Succeeding with use cases working smart to deliver quality.* Upper Saddle River, NJ: Addison Wesley Professional.

Escofet, E., Rodríguez, M. J., Garrido, J. L., & Chung, L. (2009). Strategic alignment as a way of addressing the barriers to e-business adoption. In S. Krishnamurthy (Ed.), *Proceedings of the 6th IADIS International Conference E-Commerce* (pp. 27-34). Algarve, Portugal: IADIS Press.

Esposito, J. L. (2002, November 14). *A framework relating questionnaire design and evaluation processes to sources of measurement error.* Paper presented at the International Conference on Questionnaire Development, Evaluation, and Testing Methods, Charleston, SC.

Esteves, J. (2006, July 6). *Establishing the relationship between enterprise systems benefits, business complexity, and business alignment in SMEs.* Paper presented at the European and Mediterranean Conference on Information Systems (EMCIS'2006), Costa Blanca, Alicante, Spain.

Frary, R. B. (1996). *A brief guide to questionnaire development.* Washington, DC: ERICAE Clearinghouse on Assessment and Evaluation.

Haag, S., Raja, M. K., & Schkade, L. L. (1996). Quality function deployment usage in software development. *Communications of the ACM, 39*(1), 41–49. doi:10.1145/234173.234178

Halleux, P., Ludovic, M., & Andersson, B. (2008, June 16). *A method to support the alignment of business models and goal models.* Paper presented at the Third International Workshop on Business/ IT Alignment and Interoperability, BUSITAL'08, Montpellier, France.

Henderson, J. C., & Venkatraman, N. (1999). Strategic alignment: Leveraging information technology for transforming organizations. *IBM Systems Journal, 38*(2), 472–484. doi:10.1147/ SJ.1999.5387096

Hill, J., & Scott, T. (2004). A consideration of the roles of business intelligence and e-business in management and marketing decision making in knowledge-based and high-tech start-ups. *Qualitative Market Research: An International Journal, 7*(1), 48–57. doi:10.1108/13522750410512877

Hsu, C.-C., & Sandford, B. A. (2007). The Delphi technique: Making sense of consensus. *Practical Assessment. Research Evaluation, 12*(10), 1–8.

Ivis, M. (2001). *Analysis of barriers impeding e-business adoption among Canadian SMEs* (pp. 1–9). Ottawa, Canada: Canadian Chamber of Commerce.

Jayaswal, B. K., & Patton, P. C. (2006). *Design for trustworthy software: Tools, techniques, and methodology of developing robust software.* Upper Saddle River, NJ: Prentice Hall.

Kulpa, M. K., & Johnson, K. A. (2008). *Interpreting the CMMI: A process improvement approach* (2 Ed.). Boca Raton, FL: Auerbach Publications.

Lamsweerde, A. v. (2001, August 27). *Goaloriented requirements engineering: A guided tour.* Paper presented at the 5th IEEE International Symposium on Requirements Engineering, Toronto, Canada.

Lamsweerde, A. v. (2004, September 6). *Goaloriented requirements engineering: A roundtrip from research to practice.* Paper presented at the 12th IEEE International Requirements Engineering Conference, Kyoto, Japan.

Lehtonen, R., & Pahkinen, E. (2004). *Practical methods for design and analysis of complex surveys* (2 Ed.). Hoboken, NJ: John Wiley & Sons.

Linstone, H. A., & Turoff, M. (2002). *The Delphi method techniques and applications.* Reading, MA: Addison Wesley.

Mutafelija, B., & Stromberg, H. (2009). *Process improvement with CMMI v1.2 and ISO standards.* Boca Raton, FL: Auerbach Publications.

Paul, C. L. (2008). A modified Delphi approach to a new card sorting methodology. *Journal of Usability Studies, 4*(1), 7–30.

Porter, M. E. (2008). The five competitive forces that shape strategy. *Harvard Business Review, 86*(1), 78–93.

Porter, M. E., & Ketels, C. (2003). *UK competitiveness: Moving to the next stage Economic Papers.* ESRC.

Rappa, M. A. (2004). The utility business model and the future of computing services. *IBM Systems Journal, 43*(1), 32–42. doi:10.1147/sj.431.0032

Rayens, M. K., & Hahn, E. J. (2000). Building consensus using the policy Delphi method. *Policy, Politics & Nursing Practice, 1*(4), 308–315. doi:10.1177/152715440000100409

Raymond, L., & Bergeron, F. (2008). Enabling the business strategy of SMEs through e-business capabilities: A strategic alignment perspective. *Industrial Management & Data Systems, 108*(5), 577–595. .doi:10.1108/02635570810876723

Rayport, J. F., & Jaworski, B. J. (2003). *Introduction to e-commerce* (2 Ed.). New York: McGraw Hill.

Ryynänen, V. J., Karvonen, M., & Kässi, T. (2008). The Delphi method as a tool for analysing technology evolution: Case open source thin computing. *Proceedings of the 2008 IEEE ICMIT* (pp. 1476-1481): IEEE.

Turban, E., Lee, J. K., Lee, J. K., & Chung, M. (2006). *Electronic commerce: A managerial perspective* (4 Ed.). Upper Saddle River, NJ: Prentice Hall.

Vara, J. L. D. l., & Sánchez, J. (2007, June 11). *Business process-driven requirements engineering: A goal-based approach.* Paper presented at the 8th Workshop on Business Process Modeling, Development, and Support (BPMDS'07), Trondheim, Norway.

Vickery, G., Sakai, K., Lee, I., & Sim, H. (2004). *ICT, e-business and SMEs* (No. DSTI/IND/PME (2004)7). Paris, France: Organisation for Economic Co-operation and Development.

Weill, P., & Vitale, M. R. (2001). *Place to space: Migrating to ebusiness models*. Boston, MA: Harvard Business School Press.

Xiang, Y., Wu, X., & Hu, B. (2008). A Strategic Alignment Method Based on Demand Classification of Information Technology *IEEE Symposium on Advanced Management of Information for Globalized Enterprises* (pp. 1-10). Tianjin, China: IEEE.

Yousuf, M. I. (2007). Using experts' opinions through Delphi technique. *Practical Assessment. Research Evaluation, 12*(4), 1–8.

Al-Qirim, N. A. Y. (Ed.). (2004). *Electronic commerce in small to medium-sized enterprises: Frameworks, issues, and implications*. Hershey, PA: Idea Group Publishing.

Bharati, P., & Chaudhury, A. (2006, July 6). *Small and medium enterprises' (SMES') adoption of technology along the value chain*. Paper presented at the European and Mediterranean Conference on Information Systems (EMCIS) 2006, Costa Blanca, Alicante, Spain.

Brown, E. J., & Yarberry, W. A. (2009). *The effective CIO: How to achieve outstanding success through strategic alignment, financial management, and IT governance*. Boca Raton, FL: Auerbach Publications.

Bush, M., & Dunaway, D. (2005). *CMMI assessments: Motivating positive change*. Upper Saddle River, NJ: Addison Wesley Professional.

Carneiro, L., Alves, A., Carneiro, D., Held, H., Wolf, C., Macey, J., et al. (2001). Methodology for the implementation of e-business solutions in SME's. In B. Stanford-Smith & E. Chiozza (Eds.), *E-work and e-commerce: Novel solutions and practices for a global networked economy* (Vol. 1, pp. 106-112). Amsterdam, the Netherland: IOS Press.

Cassidy, A. (2002). *A practical guide to planning for e-business success: How to e-enable your enterprise*. Boca Raton, FL: CRC Press.

Chia Hua, S., Jashua Rajesh, M., & Bee Theng, L. (2008, November 17). *Barriers to the adoption of e-commerce among small and medium sized enterprises: A study on the non-adopters in Malaysia*. Paper presented at the 2nd International Colloquium on Business and Management, Bangkok, Thailand.

Chitura, T., Mupemhi, S., Dube, T., & Bolongkikit, J. (2008). Barriers to electronic commerce adoption in small and medium enterprises: A critical literature review. *Journal of Internet Banking and Commerce, 13*(2), 1–13.

Chong, S. (2005). Determinants of satisfaction of electronic commerce implementation: Some evidence from the small- and medium-sized enterprises. In D. Bartmann, F. Rajola, J. Kallinikos, D. Avison, R. Winter, P. Ein-Dor, J. Becker, F. Bodendorf & C. Weinhardt (Eds.), *Proceedings of the 13th European Conference on Information Systems: Information Systems in a Rapidly Changing Economy*. Regensburg, Germany: Institute for Management of Information Systems University of Regensburg.

Chrissis, M. B., Konrad, M., & Shrum, S. (2003). *CMMI: Guidelines for process integration and product improvement*. Boston, MA: Addison Wesley.

Corbitt, B. J., & Al-Qirim, N. A. Y. (Eds.). (2004). *E-business, government and small and medium-size enterprises: Opportunities and challenges*. Hershey, PA: Idea Group Publishing.

Cragg, P., Tagliavini, M., & Mills, A. (2007, December 5). *Evaluating the alignment of IT with business processes in SMEs*. Paper presented at the 18th Australasian Conference on Information Systems, Toowoomba, Australia.

Currie, W. L. (Ed.). (2004). *Value creation from e-business models*. Burlington, MA: Elsevier.

Deek, F. P., McHugh, J. A. M., & Eljabiri, O. M. (2005). *Strategic software engineering: An interdisciplinary approach*. Boca Raton, FL: Auerbach Publications. doi:10.1201/9781420031119

Gionis, G., Mouzakitis, S., Janner, T., Schroth, C., Koussouris, S., & Askounis, D. (2007). Implementing next generation e-business platforms for heterogeneous SME environments. In T. Papatheodorou & D. Christodoulakis (Eds.), *Current Trends in Informatics - 11th Panhellenic Conference in Informatics* (Vol. B, pp. 531-540). Patras, Greece: New Technologies Publications.

Gutierrez, A., Nawazish, A., Orozco, J., Serrano, A., & Yazdouni, H. (2007, August 9). *Comparing alignment factors in SMEs and large organizations: A planning integration perspective*. Paper presented at the Americas Conference of Information Systems, Keystone, CO.

Gutierrez, A., Orozco, J., & Serrano, A. (2008, June 9). *Developing a taxonomy for the understanding of business and it alignment paradigms and tools*. Paper presented at the Sixteenth European Conference on Information Systems, Galway, Ireland.

Gutierrez, A., Orozco, J., Serrano, A., & Serrano, A. (2006, July 6). *Using tactical and operational factors to assess strategic alignment: An SME study*. Paper presented at the European and Mediterranean Conference on Information Systems (EMCIS) 2006, Costa Blanca, Alicante, Spain.

Gutierrez, A., & Serrano, A. (2008). Assessing strategic, tactical and operational alignment factors for SMEs: Alignment across the organisation's value chain. *International Journal of Value Change Management, 2*(1), 33–56. .doi:10.1504/IJVCM.2008.016117

Harrington, H. J. (1991). *Business process improvement: The breakthrough strategy for total quality, productivity, and competitiveness*. New York: McGraw Hill.

Hornby, G., Goulding, P., & Poon, S. (2002). Perceptions of export barriers and cultural issues: The SME e-commerce experience. *Journal of Electronic Commerce Research, 3*(4), 213–226.

Hoyle, C., & Chen, W. (2007). *Next generation QFD: Decision-based product attribute function deployment*. Paper presented at the International Conference on Engineering Design, Paris, France.

Hudson, M., Smart, A., & Bourne, M. (2001). Theory and practice in SME performance measurement systems. *International Journal of Operations & Production Management, 21*(8), 1096–1115. doi:10.1108/EUM0000000005587

Jeon, B. N., Han, K. S., & Lee, M. J. (2006). Determining factors for the adoption of e-business: The case of SMEs in Korea. *Applied Economics, 38*(16), 1905–1916. doi:10.1080/00036840500427262

Jouirou, N., & Kalika. (2004, August 5). *Strategic alignment: A performance tool (An empirical study of SMEs)* Paper presented at the Proceedings of the Tenth Americas Conference on Information Systems, New York, NY.

Kendall, J., Tung, L., Chua, K., Ng, C., & Tan, M. (2001). Electronic commerce adoption by SMEs in Singapore. *Annual Hawaii International Conference on System Sciences, 7*, 7037-7046. doi: doi.ieeecomputersociety.org/10.1109/HICSS.2001.927068

Kyobe, M. (2008). The influence of strategy-making types on IT alignment in SMEs. *Journal of Systems and Information Technology, 10*(1), 22–38. .doi:10.1108/13287260810876876

Lee, I. (2007). *E-business innovation and process management*. Hershey, PA: Cybertech Publishing.

Lee, I. (Ed.). (2009). *Electronic business: Concepts, methodologies, tools, and applications (Vol. 1-4)*. Hershey, PA: IGI Global.

Lee, I. (Ed.). (2009). *Emergent strategies for e-business processes, services, and implications: Advancing corporate frameworks*. Hershey, PA: IGI Global.

Levy, M., Powell, P., & Worrall, L. (2005). Strategic intent and e-business in SMEs: Enablers and inhibitors. *Information Resources Management Journal, 18*(4), 1–20.

Lientz, B. P., & Larssen, L. (2004). *Manage IT as a business: How to achieve alignment and add value to the company*. Burlington, MA: Elsevier.

Luftman, J. N. (Ed.). (1996). *Competing in the information age: Strategic alignment in practice*. New York: Oxford University Press.

McKeen, J. D., & Smith, H. A. (2003). *Making IT happen: Critical issues in IT management*. West Sussex, England: John Wiley & Sons Ltd.

Milis, K., Fairchild, A., Smits, M., & Ribbers, P. (2008, May 25). *The I-FIT model: Developing a tool to detect potential alignment problems*. Paper presented at the European and Mediterranean Conference on Information Systems (EMCIS'2008), Dubai, UAE.

Nájera, J. J. (2006, July 6). *The effect of information technology management capability on firm competitiveness*. Paper presented at the European and Mediterranean Conference on Information Systems (EMCIS) 2006, Costa Blanca, Alicante, Spain.

Oktaba, H., & Piattini, M. (Eds.). (2008). *Software process improvement for small and medium enterprises: Techniques and case studies*. Hershey, PA: IGI Global.

Payne, J. E. (2005). *E-commerce readiness for SMEs in developing countries: A guide for development professionals* (p. 38). Washington, D.C: LearnLink.

Poel, M., & Bodea, G. (2008). *The policy mix for e-business use by SMEs: Inspiration from Denmark, Finland and other countries (No. 35569)*. Delft, the Netherlands: TNO.

Renner, T., Vetter, M., Scheiding, F., Remotti, L. A., & Cavallini, S. (2008). *ebusiness guide for SMEs: ebusiness software and services in the European market*. Stuttgart, Germany: European Commission.

Rouibah, K., Khalil, O., & Hassanien, A. E. (Eds.). (2009). *Emerging markets and e-commerce in developing economies*. Hershey, PA: IGI Global.

Shi, N. S., & Murthy, V. K. (Eds.). (2003). *Architectural issues of web-enabled electronic business*. Hershey, PA: Idea Group Publishing.

Shimizu, T., Carvalho, M. M. d., & Laurindo, F. J. B. (2006). *Strategic alignment process and decision support systems: Theory and case studies*. Hershey, PA: IRM Press.

Shin, N. (2005). *Strategies for generating e-business returns on investment*. Hershey, PA: Idea Group Publishing.

Soares, A. L., Carneiro, L. M., & Carneiro, D. (2002, July 20). *Making effective the introduction of e-business in SME: A reference model approach*. Paper presented at the E-manufacturing: business paradigms and supporting technologies: 18th International Conference on CAD/CAM, Robotics, and Factories of the Future (CARs & FOF), Porto, Portugal.

Soto-Acosta, P., & Meroño-Cerdan, A. L. (2007, June 24). *E-business value creation from the RBV of the firm*. Paper presented at the European and Mediterranean Conference on Information Systems (EMCIS'2007), Valencia, Spain.

Sounderpand, J., & Sinha, T. (Eds.). (2007). *E-business process management: Technologies and solutions*. Hershey, PA: Idea Group Publishing.

Sun, Y. (2008). *Business-oriented software process improvement based on CMM and CMMI using QFD*. Doctoral Dissertation, Missouri University of Science and Technology, Rolla, MU.

Svirskas, A., & Roberts, B. (2005, February 23). *Distributed e-business architecture for SME communities - requirements and solutions for Request Based Virtual organisations*. Paper presented at the IADIS International Conference Web Based Communities 2005, Algarve, Portugal.

Van Grembergen, W., & De Haes, S. (Eds.). (2009). *Enterprise governance of information technology: achieving strategic alignment and value*. New York: Springer Verlag.

Chapter 3
SME Managers' Required Entrepreneurship and Business Competences

George Velegrakis
IDEC S.A., Greece

João Varajão
Centro ALGORITMI / UTAD, Portugal

Leonel Morgado
GECAD / UTAD, Portugal

Caroline Dominguez
UTAD, Portugal

Clara Rodrigues
IPBeja (Instituto Politécnico de Beja), Portugal

Dalila Coelho
IPBeja (Instituto Politécnico de Beja), Portugal

Aura Haidimoschi
Camera de Comert si Industrie a Municipiului Bucuresti (CCIB), Romania

Chiara Sancin
Dida Network, Italy

Gerhard Doppler
bit media e-Learning solution GmbH & Co KG, Austria

Hillevi Koivusalo
Hyria koulutus Oy, Finland

Erja Lakanen
Hyria koulutus Oy, Finland

ABSTRACT

In a dynamic and competitive world, understanding the knowledge, skills and competences that managers of small and medium enterprises (SMEs) require is an important endeavour, to ensure that both academic and business training institutions offer well formed programs/courses and curricula. Several studies, conducted by academic researchers and business associations around the world, focused on identifying managers' skills and competences, but there isn't an overall perspective on today's requirements of European SME managers. This is a critical aspect because managers' competences strongly influence enterprises' competitiveness and, therefore, the economic competitiveness of countries themselves. To

DOI: 10.4018/978-1-60960-463-9.ch003

help overcome this problem, the authors conducted a study in six European countries through a literature review and several interviews with business associations' executives. The result is a list of 34 competences, which the authors organized in four categories: personal; team management; business; and technical. These competences are presented and discussed in this chapter and show that an SME manager should be well prepared in a rich set of complementary areas to perform her/his job. The findings enable a better understanding of the profile of SME managers from the point of view of required competences, and may help in the design of new training programs to fulfil the identified needs.

INTRODUCTION

SMEs' economic context is inherently unstable: great economic expansion cycles are followed by significant retraction ones. Therefore, companies must pay permanent attention to changes and be ready to act in a very dynamic way.

As a top leader within a company, a manager is the architect and central engine of the company's ability for competitive development. She/He must combine a diversified set of competences to lead the company towards the right direction.

This article presents a Framework of SMEs' competences, resulting from a study conducted in Austria, Finland, Greece, Italy, Portugal, and Romania with the objective of identifying which competences SME managers must develop.

Having an important role to play in this context, universities and professional training institutions may find in this Framework a useful instrument to prepare their training offer.

The first section of this chapter presents the results of recent studies on this matter. The section methodology highlights the research process used in our study. In the main section, a framework of competences for SME managers is presented. Finally, the chapter ends up presenting some opportunities for future development of this study.

BACKGROUND

Across the 27 member states of the European Union (EU), there are about 19.6 million small and medium-sized enterprises (SME) in the non-financial business economy, with up to 250 employees, representing 99.8% of all businesses and 67.1% of the non-financial business economy workforce – about 85 million jobs (Schmiemann, 2008).

Between 2002 and 2007, the number of SMEs has increased by over 2 million, the number of large enterprise by only 2,000. Most that new firms are created in the service sector and are micro enterprises (Audretsch, van der Horst, Kwaak, & Thurik, 2009).

To support the growth and development of existing SMEs and promote the creation of new SMEs, the European Commission (EC) adopted in June 2008 the 'Small Business Act' for Europe, reflecting the EC political will to recognize the central role of SMEs in the EU economy, by providing a comprehensive SME policy framework for the EU and its Member States (EC, 2008).

Yet, in spite of the important role played by such firms in the European economy, there is a lack of specific training for people heading and/or managing SMEs, and the training that is available "tends to serve either start-ups or medium sized firms" (NJM European, 2000). Furthermore, training for heads of SMEs should be different from training for employees: heads of SMEs "exhibit activist and pragmatist learning styles, prefer learning by doing and favour problem-centred approaches that offer flexibility" (id., p. 3).

To clarify how we employ the notion of "competence" in the context of this article, we present some of the current dictionary definitions. From the Grande Dicionário da Língua Portuguesa[1] (Machado, 1981), "competence" is defined as the ability of an individual to assess a problematic situation and find an adequate solution to it. Therefore she/he must have a number of qualities like aptitude to analyze and find out the right solution to a problem, knowledge, and experience related to the situation. The definition of the Dicionário da Língua Portuguesa Contemporânea[2] (Verbo, 2001) goes further and refers that competence should be understood as a set of theoretical or empirical knowledge or as a number of necessary qualifications that a person must have and master in order to achieve a certain goal. In the new Oxford Dictionary of English (Pearsall, 2001), the word "competence" takes a more practical meaning, as the ability of a person, in a determined sphere of knowledge, to perform an action efficiently and successfully. Finally, the Longman Dictionary of English Language and Culture (Longman, 1992) reinforces the previous ideas and relates to "competence" the ability to do what is required.

From these different definitions, the sense we give to "competence" in this article is the following: aptitude, ability or set of theoretical or practical knowledge necessary to achieve a certain purpose.

METHODOLOGY

To identify a group of rich, consistent, and coherent competencies necessary for today's SME managers, the research followed a systematic process, as shown in Figure 1.

The first activity consisted in performing a brainstorming session with 11 participants from the six European countries involved in the study (Austria, Finland, Greece, Italy, Portugal, and Romania) including business consultants, business training professionals, and academics. Each country formed a workgroup to develop and support research activities from then on. This session produced the master directives for future activities.

In the second activity – literature review – each workgroup in its country had the responsibility of identifying existing studies on SME managers' competences. The systematic analysis of several works (BCC, 2008; HRAKK, 2009; Pichler, 2009) (Audretsch et al., 2009; DIDA, 2009; Klen, Pereira-Klen, & Gesser, 2009; Pais, 2003; Tampere, 2006) resulted in a first draft of competences organized in a first database with more than an hundred entries.

This activity was followed up by the elimination of redundancies and inconsistencies resulting in a considerable reduction of the database ending up in a list of 29 competences.

The third activity in the investigation process – interviews – was performed by each workgroup in each country. It consisted in identifying business associations whose activities were directed to support SMEs. Interviews were then conducted with their representatives (SME managers, executive officers or members of employers' branches) by different means (mail, telephone or in person) in a semi-structured format. Their opinions on the previously-elaborated list of competences were assembled, allowing to evaluate the consistency of the first version of the Framework and to complement it with new information.

Finally, the last activity – validation – was performed. It consisted in confirmation by each

Figure 1. Research process

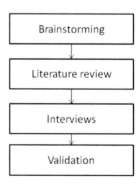

workgroup representative on whether she/he agreed with all the competencies identified until then and whether she/he considered them relevant and meaningful in his/her own country. This final activity included a last meeting with all participants of each country in order to assess the consistency/ coherence of the formulation/definition of the identified competences.

This activity produced the final version of the Framework, which we present next.

COMPETENCES OF AN SME MANAGER

An SME manager needs a large set of competences in order to meet the different challenges of his activity. Considering the number and diversity of these competences, we found it useful to organize them in an *ad hoc* fashion, according to their general nature. Figure 2 presents this framework, which organizes SME manager competences in four categories: personal; technical non-financial; business & financial; and leadership.

In this context, personal aspects are all competences related to the manager's personality that are vital in order to manage an enterprise effectively. Team management aspects are all the competences that are needed in order to create and lead a team and make full use of each team member's capacities. Technical aspects are all competences that help the manager to fulfil everyday tasks and functions in the enterprise. Finally, business & finance aspects are all competences that allow a manager to deal with the basic financial and business tasks of the enterprise.

Table 1 presents the elements of each category of the Framework

Description of the Competencies

Attitude towards uncertainty and risk: Having the emotional framework to enable oneself to resist and overcome difficulties and failures, and a vision focused on a future positive result.

Innovative spirit: Having a tendency to discover new ways of doing things, and a mindset towards the development and implementation of original products, processes etc.

Fulfilment of tasks and goals: Ability to have a focus on achieving goals, objectives, requirements, needs or desires that the manager defined for himself/herself.

Self-confidence: Ability to believe in one's personal competences and abilities to perform successfully.

Figure 2. SME manager's entrepreneurship and business competences' framework

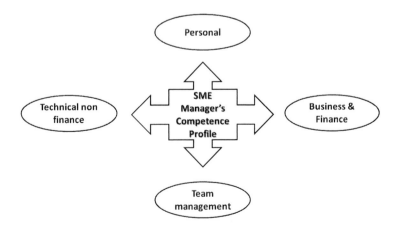

Table 1. SME manager's entrepreneurship competences

Category	Competence
Personal	Attitude towards uncertainty and risk Innovative spirit Fulfilment of tasks and goals Self-confidence Communication skills Ability to discover new opportunities Conceptual ability
Team management	Negotiation and decision-making Time management for one's own work and the team's work Communication to the team of very clear expectations of performance Regular supply of feedback to the team on its performance Full use of the capacities and knowledge of the team Promote mutual confidence Develop autonomy of a group Raise awareness of collective responsibility Ability to build and lead a team (leadership spirit)
Technical non finance	Ability for project management Ability to create and provide Strategic/Tactical/ Operational plans Management of human resources from an organizational perspective (allocation/attribution of tasks) Management of other resources (non-human) Awareness of corporate social responsibility Knowledge of the administrative/bureaucratic process for founding a company Knowledge of the legal requirements for business Knowledge of the most important legal forms of business ownership Process analysis and change management
Business & Finance	Knowledge of general business conditions and functions Knowledge of what to think about when deciding whether to found a business or not Knowledge of foreign trade and international trade relations Distinguish the financial issues between different company sectors (manufacturing/ services) Management of the different performance functions within an enterprise Understanding of different forms of financing (self-financing, external financing) Basic sales-planning skills Knowledge of accountancy and taxes Ability to plan and control: direct costs, overhead costs, cost prices, gross and net sales price, and earnings/profits

Communication skills: Ability to share clearly and effectively thoughts with others, including discussions/arguments.

Ability to discover new opportunities: Ability to identify clearly the business environment, its changes, and opportunities for success.

Conceptual ability: Ability for holistic abstract thinking about dependencies, connections & cause-effect relationships, and for understanding them.

Negotiation and decision-making: Goal-oriented and consistent ability to make common resolutions and conclude negotiations and effective persuasion of others.

Time management for one's own work and the team's work: Ability to plan and organise time for oneself and for the teams: work time, task delegation, priorities.

Communication of very clear expectations of performance: Ability to set clear objectives for others and assessing results logically and effectively.

Regular supply to the team of feedback on its performance: Ability to communicate clear performance expectations to individuals and to the group, set common goals, share information, and provide constant feedback in meetings and/ or informally.

Full use of the capacities and knowledge of the team: Ability to analyse individual potential and performance, define a participated personal development process, and conduct task assignment and work organisation according to competences and development of goals, knowledge, and management processes.

Promote mutual confidence: Ability to define clear structures of roles, responsibilities & incentives, supporting group goals and incentives, discouraging power coalitions, promoting mutual understanding of needs, potentials & expectations, and promoting shared values and goals.

Develop autonomy of a group: Ability to encourage joint decision-making, sharing information, providing encouragement, empowering/

support group thinking, and problem-solving; and to promote shared values and exercise indirect influence.

Raise awareness of collective responsibility: Ability to express positive expectations on group ability and performance, providing feedback and positive/negative encouragement to group behaviour and performance, and encouraging expression of ideas/opinions to solve problems.

Ability to build and lead a team (leadership spirit): Ability to inspire and provide examples, promote and lead change, contribute and cooperate towards common goals, support individuals in their potential and performance, and stimulate enthusiasm.

Ability for project management: Ability for accomplishment of project objectives, including creating clear and attainable project objectives, building project requirements, and managing the triple constraint set of projects: costs, time, and scope.

Ability to create and provide Strategic/Tactical/Operational plans: Ability to create the company strategy, setting priorities, allocating human and financial resources, and defining responsibilities and instruments for evaluating results.

Management of human resources from an organizational perspective (allocation/attribution of tasks): Ability to perform recruitment, make job descriptions, conduct job evaluation/performance assessment, training, career management and motivation, and set a salary strategy.

Management of other resources (non-human): Ability to use with maximum efficiency company resources (non-human) in order to attain planned objectives.

Awareness of corporate social responsibility: Awareness of responsibility for the impact of company's activities on the environment, consumers, employees, communities, stakeholders, and all other members of the public sphere.

Knowledge of the administrative/bureaucratic process for founding a company: Knowl-edge at the level of a strategic overview of common questions faced when founding a company: what for, for whom, with what funding, with whom, where, and for what price.

Knowledge of the legal requirements for business: Knowledge at a basic level of the laws and regulations regarding employees, social insurance, company processes and goods, import, export, taxes, environmental issues, international affairs etc.

Knowledge of the most important legal forms of business ownership: Knowledge of the advantages, disadvantages, operational impacts and accounting issues in order to choose the best suiting legal form for a business situation.

Process analysis and change management: Ability to understand work methods and how they change, and how this change can be actively managed and facilitated.

Knowledge of general business conditions and functions: Knowledge of concepts such as business cycle, market organisation, use of money resources, and role and functions of government in business.

Knowledge of what to think about when deciding whether to found a business or not: Ability to set strategic goals, a planning phase, a formation phase, an implementation phase, and the knowledge of the motivation for starting up a business, of what the advantages of self-employment are and of what individual requirements should be met.

Knowledge of foreign trade and international trade relations: Knowledge at a basic level of the regulations in the European Union and bilateral regulations with other countries; and knowledge about strengths, weaknesses, opportunities, and threats in other regions of the world.

Distinguish the financial issues between different company sectors (manufacturing/services): Knowledge about (and having the ability to understand) the legal, managerial, and financial differences between manufacturing and services companies, and being able to implement the best options for one's enterprise.

Management of the different performance functions within an enterprise: Ability to manage and conceptualize Research & Development, Procurement, Production, Sales, Financing and Investments, and General Management, as well of other functions.

Understanding of different forms of financing (self-financing, external financing): Knowledge about the different forms of financing and the different implications for companies (e.g. costs, accountability, leasing, business angels, venture capital, etc.).

Basic sales-planning skills: Ability to layout out a sales plan, including market forecasting, product lifecycle management, sales strategies definition, etc.

Knowledge of accountancy and taxes: Knowledge of general concepts, including accountancy rules, taxes to be paid or collected (e.g. VAT), etc.

Ability to plan and control: direct costs, overhead costs, cost prices, gross and net sales price, and earnings/profits: Ability to use financial instruments to enable cost control and profit management.

CONCLUSION AND FUTURE WORK

Through a systematic process of research, it was possible to identify a diversified set of competences that SME managers must develop to tackle today's business challenges. These came from a varied set of sources, which in turn developed their content using diverse methods, and such a global perspective was not available before. The framework presented here highlights four fundamental areas of competences: personal; technical non-financial; business & financial; and leadership. Subsequent work will consist in conducting a survey to collect the opinion of SME managers on the relative importance they attribute to each

of these competences, and whether they personally feel they need training on any of them, so that educational agents may start formatting their training supply to meet the more pressing needs of both current managers or of people that intend to become managers.

REFERENCES

Audretsch, D., van der Horst, R., Kwaak, T., & Thurik, R. (2009). *First Section of the Annual Report on EU Small and Medium-sized Enterprises: European Commission*. Directorate General Enterprise and Industry, EIM.

BCC. (2008). *Annual Report on the SME sector in Romania*. Bucharest: Bucharest Chamber of Commerce Publications.

DIDA. (2009). *Description of the Italian entrepreneurs*. Rome: DIDA Publications.

EC. (2008). *Communication from the Commission to the Council, the European Parliament, the European Economic and Social Committee and the Committee of the Region*s - "Think Small First" - A "Small Business Act" for Europe (Vol. {SEC(2008) 2101} {SEC(2008) 2102}): European Commission Directorate-General for Enterprise.

NJM European. (2000). *A Study and Analysis of Management Training~Techniques for the Heads of SMEs, particularly Using the Information and Communication Technologies (ICTs): Report for the Directorate-General for Enterprise of the European Commission* under contract DGENT 99/C/A3/31 S12.128934

HRAKK. (2009). *Description of the main contents of the Finnish entrepreneurs*. Hyvinkaa: HRAKK Publications.

Klen, E., Pereira-Klen, A., & Gesser, C. (2009). Towards the sustainability of virtual organisation Management. In *APENDICE XII – ARTIGO ANEXO AO QUESTIONARIO VALIDACAO ETAPA 2*.

Longman. (1992). *Longman of English Language and Culture*. New York: Longman Dictionaries.

Machado, J. (1981). *Grande Dicionário da Língua Portuguesa* (Machado, J., Ed.). *Vol. 1*). Amigos do Livro.

Pais, C. (2003). *As representações da Liderança Eficaz no contexto empresarial do Norte de Portugal. Dissertação de Mestrado em Psicologia Social e das Organizações*. Porto: Universidade Fernando Pessoa.

Pearsall, J. (2001). *Oxford Dictionary of English* (Pearsall, J., Ed.). Oxford, UK: Oxford University Press.

Pichler, *J.(2009)*. SME-Specific "Profiles", Strategic Potentials And Attitudes Toward Internationalization In The Enlarged EU.

Schmiemann, M. (2008). *Enterprises by size class - overview of SMEs in the EU*. Luxembourg: Office for Official Publications of the European Communities.

Tampere. (2006). *Finnish Survey on Collegiate Entrepreneurship*. Tampere University of Technology

Verbo. (2001). *Dicionário da Língua Portuguesa Contemporânea da Academia das Ciências de Lisboa* (Vol. 1): Verbo.

ENDNOTES

[1] Meaning "Large Dictionary of the Portuguese Language."

[2] Meaning "Dictionary of the Contemporary Portuguese Language."

Chapter 4

Preparing for Change:
Leveraging Knowledge Activities to Enhance Organisational Preparedness in the Case of an Irish Software SME

Ciara Heavin
University College Cork, Ireland

Frederic Adam
University College Cork, Ireland

ABSTRACT

In the current climate, preparing for change is an issue for companies large and small. However, there remains a dearth of empirical evidence that highlight how software Small to Medium Sized Enterprises (SMEs) operationalise their approach to knowledge management (KM) as a means of preparing themselves for the future. For an SME, the first step is to take stock of the types of knowledge that are valuable to the business, where it is stored and how it is used. In addition, consideration must be given to knowledge activities (KA), the constituent parts, of a company's KM approach. By doing this, the organisation can identify where its strengths lie in terms of the type and extent to which knowledge is managed through acquisition, codification, storage, maintenance, transfer and creation activities. Using a qualitative analysis approach in a single case study, this chapter identifies occurrences of these knowledge activities as a means of assessing an SME's approach to KM with a view to better facilitating an organisation's ability to be increasingly flexible in the face of a changing environment.

INTRODUCTION

As the number of SMEs continues to grow through challenging economic times, where entrepreneur-

ship is increasingly encouraged, the importance of understanding how smaller organisations manage what they know has become imperative to their survival. SMEs by their very nature differ from multinational enterprises (MNEs); therefore an SME's KM approach differs to that implemented

DOI: 10.4018/978-1-60960-463-9.ch004

by larger organisations. While some argue that knowledge may be successfully managed in a smaller firm, it is evident that a more formalised approach to KM to access the right knowledge at the right time e.g. to compensate for the loss of a knowledge worker or 'to avoid reinventing the wheel' when designing new products or services, or during software development for instance, allows the firm to better prepare themselves to deal with opportunities and threats as they arise. Although extant research draws on KM studies in large organizations, it is important to realise that the issues faced by SMEs are not scaled down versions of large business experiences (Welsh and White, 1981; Sparrow, 2000). By their nature SMEs experience *"resource poverty"* (Welsh and White, 1981, p18) such as lack of time, financial and human resources (Welsh and White, 1981; Lee and Oakes, 1995; OECD, 2002). Kraaijenbrink *et al.* (2006) concur with this view, arguing that it is not the size of a SME that makes them different from large organisations; it is the lack of economies of scale. As a result, marginal changes in the organisation's environment have a greater impact on smaller organisations in comparison to their larger counterparts (Welsh and White, 1981).

The objective of this chapter is to explore the KA of a software SME, HelpRead Ltd. This chapter is structured as follows. Firstly, existing literature is investigated to establish and classify KA. The research approach leveraged in this study is presented and a background to the HelpRead Ltd. case is then considered. Subsequently, using the classification of KA, the case is examined in terms of the knowledge types and activities leveraged by this firm to support their knowledge requirements. Finally, this chapter illustrates how this company manages important knowledge and highlights where the firm could improve its ability to prepare for changes that may occur both inside and outside the organisation.

MANAGING KNOWLEDGE IN SMEs

While data and information are considered in terms of being static, knowledge is defined as having characteristics of movement (Barthelme *et al.*, 1998); of being *"information in action"* (O'Dell and Grayson, 1998, p5). According to Davenport and Prusak (1998, p6) *"one of the reasons that we find knowledge valuable is that it is close-and closer than data or information- to action"*. From this perspective, it is improvements in the availability and quality of organisational knowledge which leads to improved actions/decisions taken by the organisation. *"We can use it to make wiser decisions about strategy, competitors, customers, distribution channels, and product and service life cycles"* (Davenport and Prusak, 1998, p6). The complex task of managing organisational knowledge in and of itself is a significant endeavour; accordingly it is imperative that this is broken down into its constituent parts or activities. Like many areas of knowledge management, the consideration of actions or activities that result in knowledge management is well contested amongst researchers. Previous researchers (Choo, 1996; Holsapple and Whinston, 1987; Huber, 1990; Kraaijenbrink *et al.*, 2006; Nonaka, 1991; Pentland, 1995; Szulanski, 1994; Holsapple and Joshi, 2004 and Wiig, 1993) use different terms to describe similar knowledge activities (KA). Many of these definitions share common verbs such as storing, creating and applying knowledge in an organisational context. This research takes a balanced view of knowledge activities, discounting the activities proposed by Leonard-Barton (1995), as they have a sole technical focus. In addition, Nonaka's (1991) knowledge activities are directly related to knowledge creation and are integrated into a single *creation* activity. For the purpose of this research a knowledge activity is defined as *"transactions or manipulations of knowledge where the knowledge is the object not the result"* (Kraaijenbrink *et al.*, 2006, p23). Based on extant research, a refined set of six KA is presented in

Figure 1. An organisation's knowledge activities

Knowledge Activity (KA)	Definition
Acquire	Identify and capture knowledge from source to a company. Sources include written form, physical objects, people, courses, cooperation between source and recipient, and outsourcing
Codify	Assess the value of knowledge, distil, refine and assemble into comprehensive format
Store	Store knowledge in an artefact e.g. system, document
Maintain	Update on continuous basis, as a result of additional acquisition activities
Transfer	Identify receiver, organize channel of communication and send
Create	New knowledge cultivated through knowledge transfer. Acquisition activities come into play as new knowledge is acquired

Figure 1. These encompass the key activities experienced when contemplating an organisation's KM approach. The literature proposes many KA labels, for the purpose of this study Figure 1 provides a cohesive set of KA. These activities are described in the following sections.

Acquire

From Huber's (1991, p90) perspective *"Knowledge acquisition is the process by which knowledge is obtained"*. Kraaijenbrink *et al.* (2006) define knowledge acquisition as knowledge transferred from a source to a company through six sub processes:

1. Written form may transfer codifiable knowledge;
2. Physical objects may transfer embedded knowledge e.g. reverse engineering competitor products;
3. People hired to the organization provide knowledge to the organization;
4. Cooperation between source and recipient can enable knowledge acquisition;
5. Courses provide knowledge through oral and visual communication;
6. Outsourcing may facilitate knowledge acquisition where no expertise is currently available inside the organisation

Codify

Knowledge codification converts the generated knowledge into accessible and applicable formats (Davenport and Prusak, 1998). Combine, internalise or absorb are alternative verbs that may be used to describe this activity. Knowledge codification is concerned with the capture, representation and storage of knowledge in computerised knowledge bases (Nevo *et al.*, 2007). It is a way in which knowledge can be categorised. Hansen *et al.*'s (1999) codification strategy supports the use of knowledge repositories e.g. documentation and more specifically technology i.e. databases to store organisational knowledge.

Store

According to Alavi and Leidner (2001, p127) knowledge storage *"involves obtaining the knowledge from organisational members and/or external sources, coding and indexing the knowledge (for later retrieval) and capturing it"*. The key to storing organizational knowledge is that the members must be able to anticipate the future needs of the organisation in order for the most valuable knowledge to be stored (Huber, 1991).

Maintain

The maintenance of knowledge stores is essential to the continued progression of an organisation's ability to learn. Holsapple and Singh (2004) refer to knowledge control to describe the provision of quantity and quality knowledge as a significant KA. They advocate that knowledge should be accurate, consistent (have validity), relevant and important (have utility). Accordingly, Anderson Consulting (1996) acknowledged the need for control over their knowledge repository to ensure useful, fresh and high quality knowledge, *"it would have be more than a dumping ground of documents"* (Holsapple and Singh, 2004, p239).

Transfer

Knowledge transfer is established through person-to-person or system-to-person interaction (Joe and Yoong, 2004). This supports Hansen *et al.*'s (1999) personalization strategy. From Figure 1, it is evident that knowledge transfer occurs inside and outside the organisation. Thus, an organisation may transfer knowledge or receive it from outside the organisation, which is knowledge acquisition.

Create

Figure 1 shows that knowledge creation involves developing new content or replacing existing content within the organization's tacit and explicit knowledge (Pentland, 1995). While it may be argued that new knowledge may be created through formalized mechanisms e.g. surveys and research and development (Kayworth and Leidner, 2004) others propose that the creation of new knowledge should not be a formalised process but one which is socially constructed and occurs over time through human networks (Brown and Duguid, 2000; Fahey and Prusak, 1998).

The six KA described in the above paragraphs are used in this chapter to elicit and analyse an organisation's approach to KM.

IDENTIFYING KNOWLEDGE ACTIVITIES

This study pursued a qualitative analytical approach applied to a single case study (Ägerfalk and Fitzgerald, 2008). The case was selected using purposeful sampling (Patton, 1990); the nature of innovative software products developed by the firm meant that this case displayed a wealth of KA from the outset. As the objective of this chapter was to explore the KA of a small software development firm, the focus of the study was on the two core business processes of sales and software development. Based on Knoke's (1994) selection strategies, the positional method was utilised to uncover key players; the sales and technical managers were identified and other respondents were selected based on their reputations. Six respondents in total were interviewed; each interview was approximately one hour in duration. Interviews were taped and transcribed. An interview guide was utilised to direct these semi-structured interviews. The exploratory nature of the study coupled with the *"thick transcripts"* (Miles and Huberman, 1994, p56) meant that qualitative analysis could be conducted through the use of coding techniques (Ägerfalk and Fitzgerald, 2008). Each interview was coded based on the seed categories; presented as KA in Figure 1. The KA for HelpRead Ltd. were collated based on each individual memo generated at the level of the interview. An alias was used to protect the privacy of the case company.

The HelpRead Ltd Case Study

HelpRead Ltd. was established in 1996 with approximately sixteen employees, producing assistive software to support persons with physical disabilities. It has gradually moved into producing software for learning difficulties. From 2003 the company has experienced significant growth, doubling in size to fifty-one employees in 2005. In 2003 the company focused solely on the education market, they have since increased their offering to the eGovernment and the ePublishing market space; this has resulted in almost doubling the company's gross annual revenue. HelpRead currently have headquarters in Northern Ireland and a US headquarters in Boston with regional sales staff across the Unites States. Twelve employees work in the US, one of whom was interviewed as part of study. Increased focus on new markets has diverted senior management attention away from core software development activities at headquarters. This has created the need for a new middle management role of development manager in the team. It also means that the team no longer relies on daily guidance from the Technical Director (TD). The heightened focus on ISO9001:2000 certification has resulted in more rigorous software testing processes and changes to the way project documentation is managed. The complexity of the software product offering means that a deep understanding of customer requirements is essential to build a useful product.

Knowledge Activity at HelpRead Ltd.

Instances of knowledge activities were systematically identified for the six categories of activity identified in Figure 1 in the case study organisation. In total, 113 instances of 10 knowledge types were identified at HelpRead Ltd., a breakdown of this is presented in Figure 2 where the left column represents the count of knowledge while right column indicates knowledge identified in terms of percentage.

Figure 2 illustrates that as a software producer, HelpRead is largely focused on software development and project knowledge, with the focus on these knowledge types at approximately 55 percent of all knowledge observed in the

organisation. Increased demand on the organisation, as they enter bigger markets offering a larger product portfolio, means that project-related knowledge has become increasingly important. Notwithstanding the focus on software development, the value of external knowledge resources for the acquisition of product, learning disability and customer knowledge at 26 percent, informing additional features and new product development at HelpRead, is significant. This knowledge focus highlights the company's tightly aligned customer-product strategy. Sales knowledge is typically well defined, in terms of dealing with existing customer details, orders and contact reminders. As sales and environment knowledge are closely linked, the HelpRead sales team actively scans the external environment for knowledge that may affect them. In Figure 2, employee knowledge represents the independent training opportunities provided by the organisation. By its nature, employee knowledge is embedded in the other knowledge types identified in the organisation. Company knowledge identified in Figure 2 is strategic in nature, focusing on performance information or the company *'vital statistics'* for both the UK and US.

Leveraging Figure 2, the subsequent sections present the knowledge activities identified at HelpRead, these are grouped by knowledge type. Eighty two KA were identified leveraging 113 instances of knowledge type. This occurs as a single knowledge activity can leverage multiple knowledge types. Each of the knowledge activities are numbered in the tables, these are referenced in the text to ensure all knowledge activities are considered.

Acquiring Knowledge

Figure 3 lists *17 knowledge acquisition* activities identified at HelpRead using *6 different types of knowledge*. The focus on product knowledge acquisition is evident from Figure 3, reflecting the need for a software SME to gather external exper-

Figure 2. Knowledge types at HelpRead Ltd.

Knowledge Type	Percentage (n=113)	
Software Development (38)	34%	
Project (23)	20%	55%
Technical (1)	1%	
Product (19)	17%	
Learning Disability (2)	2%	26%
Customer (8)	7%	
Sales (9)	8%	
Environmental (4)	3.5%	11.5%
Employee (5)	4%	
Company (4)	3.5%	
Total	100%	

Figure 3. Knowledge Acquisition at HelpRead

Types of Knowledge	Knowledge Activity	Instances of Knowledge Activity
Product	1. Carry out questionnaires to acquire customer feedback	Conduct surveys to inform new product releases and existing product shortfalls
	2. Gather software development bugs from customer	Gather Customer feedback to support desk and sales people
	3. Elicit New Product/Features ideas from customers	Customers are encouraged to send emails outlining suggestions for additional functionality or new products
	4. Conduct focus groups	Conduct focus group with two groups: individual customers and resellers as a mean of initiating new product development
	5. Elicit Feedback from certification body	Acquire informal feedback by telephone from Lionbridge
	6. Technical support conduct site visits	Gather software deployment issues through technical support face to face meeting with the customer
	7. Elicit customer and reseller feedback from market	Gather knowledge on market competition from loyal customers and resellers
	8. Conduct workshops on competitor products	Analyse competitor products facilitates new product development
Software development/ Employee	9. Conduct employee training programmes to acquire new software development knowledge	Five training days a year to acquire new technical expertise
Software development	10. Conduct explorative programming driven from initial requirements specifications	Acquire software development expertise through trial and error programming to evaluate whether something can be done
Software development/ sales / employee	11. Carry out training need analysis	Elicit the expertise of each new hire and understanding where training may be required in the future
Software development/ sales	12. Focus on attracting experienced employees to the organisation	Explicitly focus on attracting and hiring smart people
Product/ Customer	13. Sales team conduct site visits	Gather new customer knowledge through face-to-face sales meetings with customers
Customer	14. Research potential markets	Carry out ad hoc research on potential markets
	15. Scan customer websites	Browse through potential customer websites to acquire customer knowledge
Learning disability/ Employee	16. Using external assistive technology expert to train employees	Acquire new expertise through external experts all employees are aware of customer needs
Employee	17. Undertake personal development training schemes	Gather employees knowledge through courses, develop and broaden their wider skills sets to enhance creativity and innovative thinking

tise that they do not possess inside the company. In addition, it emphasises HelpRead's customer oriented, new product development strategy.

In order to further organise and present the KA in Figure 3, they are grouped into three sub-sections representing customer, employee and other knowledge sources. These sub-sections characterise knowledge sources that SMEs typically do not have the resources to generate inside the organisation.

- Knowledge Acquisition through Customers and Resellers

Figure 3 provides evidence that HelpRead actively encourage their customers to provide product feedback on a regular basis through email, questionnaires and telephone conversations (1). All customers have the facility to log any product issues (2) on the company website and, if serious deployment issues arise, the dedicated technical support person makes a site visit (6). Doing these activities enables HelpRead to broaden their knowledge of the implementation considerations required to deploy their software products in diverse environments. The Sales Director (SD) noted that it is during these sales oriented site visits that customers provide feedback on the software, deployment issues, support services and suggestions for additional functionality and new products (13).

Figure 3 shows that the sales team applies both a formal and informal approach to uncovering new customers - this is achieved through face-to-face meetings (13), attending trade shows, pursuing tip-offs from existing customers, researching the current market (14) and scanning potential customer websites (15). Competitors also act (unwittingly) as external knowledge resources, as the company conducts regular competitor product workshops where software is reverse engineered to uncover the knowledge embedded in the product (8).

In addition, Figure 3 identifies the customer focus groups (4) which include customers (typically educators) and resellers. During these sessions participants are encouraged to contribute ideas to the new product development process. The Technical Director (TD) outlined the rationale for organised customer oriented group sessions.

We are very focused on the end user and what technology they need to make their lives better and easier and what we need to do to improve our software. (TD)

From the reseller perspective, the TD commented that the nature of HelpRead products is such that if changes are made to the software, it impacts the reseller's business model. As a result, during the planning stage of any new HelpRead products the participation of resellers is vital to the continued success of their relationship with the company. The SD also identified the reseller as a key knowledge source for the organisation.

I had one guy the other week actually who phoned me up, now he doesn't buy off us directly, he buys our product through a reseller. Yet he phoned me up to say 'I just wanted to let you know that your competition has been in to see me'. (SD)

He attributed this willingness to act as a source of knowledge to the trust relationship developed between HelpRead and the established reseller network.

• Knowledge Acquisition through Employee Skills

Across all functions, there is agreement that the company only hires experienced people (12). This criterion was explained on the basis that HelpRead software required significant programming competencies which were difficult to attract in Northern Ireland. On the sales side, while a technical background is not a prerequisite for employment, extensive sales experience is essential. Once employed, training needs analysis (11) is carried out to assess how each new employee can enhance their competencies. This is done with a view to sending every employee on five days of training per annum (9). The TD outlined that, due to the complex nature of the software, this training is primarily technical. However, to ensure HelpRead employees are *'not just nerds'*, a personal training scheme (17) is also provided to encourage the development of well-rounded individuals. In addition to this, an assistive technology expert trains new staff in the nature of learning disability (16) and how the software supports this need - this is coupled with the TD providing training in HelpRead software. All employees receive training, which is justified by the CEO and the TD based on the importance of understanding the firm's specialist software and the requirement it fulfils, in terms of supporting those with learning disabilities.

That's the key, it's not learning the software it's learning why that is useful to somebody with dyslexia. And that again is done through training; it's done through talking to people who have dyslexia and just building up that knowledge through experience. (TD)

Figure 4. Knowledge Codification at HelpRead

Types of Knowledge	Knowledge Activity	Instances of Knowledge Activity
Software development/Project	1. Codify minutes of weekly meeting	Codify minutes to facilitate knowledge sharing amongst technical staff
	2. Codify risk assessment discussion	Codify matrix on whiteboard during the course of risk assessment discussion
	3. Document Post Implementation Review (PIR) outcome	Codify matrix on whiteboard during the course of PIR discussion
Product	4. Codify minutes of focus group	Codify minutes to facilitate knowledge sharing amongst meeting participants e.g. TD, Sales, Customers/ Resellers – act as initial functional specification document for new project
	5. Codify minutes from brainstorming sessions	Codify requirements and functional specification for new product features and new products
Software development	6. Codify existing programming code	Refine all code from all software development projects into a format that can be stored
	7. Using methodologies during software development at an individual level to codify functional requirements	Codify requirements and functional specification requirements using variations on software development methodologies e.g. UML, IML
	8. Codify content for Technical Frequently Asked Questions (FAQ)	Codify software development knowledge which is posted to Technical FAQ
Project	9. Software developers create personal timetables for projects	Based on previous projects individuals typically codify personalised timetables for their own information
	10. Codify project timetable at weekly meeting	Codify Microsoft Project timetable based on previous project experience
Company	11. Codify minutes of monthly meeting	Codify minutes to facilitate knowledge sharing amongst all staff

- Knowledge Acquisition through Other Sources

Figure 3 illustrates that HelpRead's focus on external sources of knowledge acquisition extends to receiving feedback from Lionbridge Technologies, Paris, who conduct software compliance testing for MS VeriTest certification (5). The QA Manager is responsible for maintaining communication with this group.

Figure 3 highlights that no formal software development methodology is in place. During the analysis stage of each project developers are encouraged to leverage explorative programming techniques (10), as a means of informing the difficulty levels required to complete particular functionality. This knowledge acquisition activity has been tried and tested through several projects and has resulted in time saving during the development phase of many projects.

Codifying Knowledge

Knowledge codification activities at HelpRead are largely focused on the knowledge required to produce software with the exception of company knowledge. Figure 4 presents *11 codification activities*, these activities deal with *4 different types of knowledge* which include software development, project, product and company. Codification is well defined due to compliance guidelines. Knowledge must be auditable and transparent, particularly in terms of versioning documentation when maintenance activity occurs. At HelpRead, the focus of knowledge codification is on the knowledge required to support software production.

Codification is primarily achieved through organised meetings i.e. weekly meetings (1), monthly meetings (11), focus groups (4), post implementation reviews (PIR) (3), risk assessments (2) and brainstorming sessions (5). After much discussion and eventual consensus, these meetings result in the generation of project related documentation. The QA Manager refines the output from these sessions into Microsoft Word documents for project specifications. These include Microsoft Project timetables for individual projects (10), images from photographs of whiteboards from PIR (3) and risk assessment (2) groups and Microsoft documents for minutes of meetings. As part of his role, the QA Manager makes each of these documents available in the relevant document libraries on the company Intranet.

The software development team are responsible for distilling and refining the material they post to the Intranet. This involves documenting and organising code (6) into accessible chunks and assigning them to the relevant project folder. They are required to develop the Intranet based Technical FAQ (8) by posting relevant technical material and experiences gathered on the use of software methodologies (7) during the development of project components.

Codifying this project and software development material into a refined and comprehensive format provides the organisation with valuable knowledge resource that may be leveraged to inform better decisions around development projects in the future. Figure 4 shows that individual developers typically codify their own personal project timetable (9) based on their role in the project, incorporating any module integration that needs to occur. They use this as a personal time management tool.

Storing Knowledge

The focus on IS9001:2000 compliance means that documentation previously stored as paper-based files has moved to the Intranet where it is accessible to all staff. As a result storing knowledge at HelpRead culminates in *24 incidences of knowledge activities* which are listed in Figure 5. Knowledge storage deals with *7 knowledge types* which include sales, software development, product, company, employee and customer knowledge. Seven out of the ten knowledge types identified at HelpRead are leveraged during knowledge storage activities. In particular, the important and valuable knowledge required to support the sales and software development processes is stored. In addition, the TD requires the storage of company

performance knowledge to support his strategic requirements.

In order to further organise and present codification activities, the subsequent discussion of Figure 5 is broken down into five emergent sections. Project, programming and feedback focus on software related knowledge storage activity supporting the work of the development team, while the focus on storing company knowledge fulfils knowledge needs a senior management level. The storage of sales knowledge is pursued in order to support the needs of the organisation's sales function.

- Storing Project Related Knowledge

The QA Manager has driven knowledge storage activities at HelpRead and he moderates the storage and maintenance of all documentation, with the exception of the activities of the development team who make some of their own changes to documentation.

I'm pretty happy with them knowing what's right and they're not typically by nature they are not a long-winded crowd. I wouldn't exactly call them nerds but ah they are sort of leaning towards that persuasion. (QA Manager)

The Intranet stores all project related documentation in document libraries. In Figure 5, this documentation ranges from minutes from all formal meetings including weekly (13) and monthly meetings (11), focus groups (23) and brainstorming (24) sessions for new products, requirements specification and design documentation (14), project costing (16), risk assessment (12), MS Project timetable (18) for the project and documentation generated from PIR (17). The storage of this knowledge provides transparency to those working on development projects, in terms of weekly progress made by each developer, as well as suggested solutions to complex features. Photographs are taken of all whiteboards gener-

Figure 5. Knowledge Storage at HelpRead

Types of Knowledge	Knowledge Activity	Instances of Knowledge Activities
Sales	1. Store sales invoices	Store sales information from Goldmine and documents generated by sales team
	2. Store internal sales for NI and UK	Store to Sale Director's personal computer by individual sales people
	3. Store internal sales for US	Store to Sale Director's personal computer by individual sales people
Software Development/Product	4. Store Technical support issues	Store technical issues via customer phone calls and emails
Software development	5. Store code	Store old code to inform new developers
	6. Store Technical know-how	Store Helpful programming hints, available through the Intranet Technical FAQ
	7. Store legacy code	Store Older code on the server, available to all developers for reuse
Company	8. Store Non Conformance issues	Store irregularities raised in the organisation
	9. Track days to process an information request	Store transactional data from all departments
	10. Track Days to deliver product	Store time taken to deliver each order
	11. Store minutes from monthly meetings	Store Minutes taken at each meeting as means of sharing what is happening in the company available on Intranet
Software development/Project	12. Record of whiteboard and minutes during risk assessment of project	Whiteboard based on risk assessment discussion is photographed and stored on related document library on Intranet with associated documentation
	13. Store minutes from weekly meetings	Store Minutes taken at each meeting as means of sharing skills discussed at that meeting available on Intranet
	14. Store functional, requirements and design specification	Store functional requirements in relevant project folder
	15. Senior Developers record own personal timetables	Developers use MS Project or word to Store individual timetables to manage time at their allocated component
	16. Store all project costing information	Store in related document library of company intranet
	17. Record whiteboard and minutes taken during PIR	Whiteboard based on PIR discussion is photographed and stored on related document library on Intranet with associated documentation
	18. Store project timetables	Store MS project timetable in related document library of company Intranet
	19. Store self documentation of code	Store relevant documentation with code, as self documentation of code is encouraged
Product	20. Log Software feature requests	senior management, developers and sales team on site visits store software feature requests
Software development/Sales/Employee	21. Store employee skills matrix	Details of all employee skills are stored on Intranet
Product/Customer	22. Record customer information and conversation	Store customer knowledge in Goldmine after customer interaction takes place
Software development/Project/Product	23. Store ideas generated from focus groups	Store customer ideas from focus group in related document library of company intranet
	24. Store ideas generated from internal brainstorming sessions	Store ideas from brainstorming sessions in related document library of company Intranet

ated during PIR and risk assessment processes and these are stored in the relevant project library on the company Intranet (12, 17). Individual developers store mini-timetables relating to their own components on their local machines (15). During the course of a project, developers are responsible for updating specification documents and timetables if changes are made.

- Storing Programming Code

Figure 5 shows that all code is stored (5), archived and accessible through the Intranet. Legacy code is stored (7) on another server and this may be accessed by the development team. Storing code in

an organised and readily accessible format means that HelpRead do not 'reinvent the wheel' when it comes to duplicating code modules. Figure 5 includes the Technical FAQ implemented (6) by the development team on the Intranet using Wiki technology. The TD and the most senior developers have instigated this endeavour as a means of storing helpful technical hints. The Development Manager (DM) emphasised the need to store the TD's technical knowledge.

Because the company started small a lot of the knowledge is in here in people's heads. If TD went under a bus we'd be doomed. (DM)

Complete self documentation of code (19) by all of the developers for each project is required as shown in Figure 5. This knowledge store acts as an efficient knowledge transfer mechanism in future projects or in the case of a developer leaving the company. As noted by the DM:

Learning is facilitated by speaking inside documents. (DM)

From the perspective of a long serving software developer at HelpRead, storing meaningful documentation or comments as part of the individual software modules during the development process is the most effective way to speed up a new developer's learning curve during future projects.

• Storing Feedback

HelpRead's focus on product feedback is evident in Figure 5, in terms of storing both employee and customer feedback. The *Fly Spray*^TM^ system, accessible through the Intranet, allows all employees and customers to log software bugs and feature requests (20). This is a quick and transparent mechanism for managing open issues and for collating suggestions for new products or components.

• Storing Company Performance Knowledge

The focus on monitoring company performance is highlighted in Figure 5 - a digital dashboard available on the Intranet tracks company performance in real time. This includes the percentage of general e-mail inquiries responded to within 8 working hours (9), the number of non-conformance reports outstanding (8), time to deliver shipped product (10), the average number of open technical support issues (4) and the employee skills matrix (21). The TD emphasised the importance of collecting and monitoring this performance information.

We record it as a collective memory for the company so we can avoid making that mistake again. So you know the way little kids walk along, and they fall and they get up and they walk and they remember it and they say 'oh, must remember to put my feet a little bit forward next time'. It's like that for the company. (TD)

• Storing Sales Knowledge

From a sales perspective, Figure 5 shows that *Goldmine*^TM^ is used to store all customer related activity including sales invoices (1), personal customer and conversation details. The Sales Director for NI and UK encourages the sales team to store all interactions with the customer in the system (22).

You're talking to a customer and he may mention I don't know that their kids are doing something; its good salesman's craft to have a note of it so next time you can say 'how did your son do in his exam?' (SM)

He explained that this strategy is '*good salesman craft*', keeping an up to date set of customer records and contact dates allows the sales teams to exhaust every customer opportunity. In order to promote transparency in the organisation, all employees have access to *Goldmine*^TM^. All regional sales teams (NI/UK and US) keep a local copy of all sales transactions and customer prospects at the regional Sales Director's personal computer (2) (3). This is used by each sales team to track sales at a local level.

Maintaining Knowledge

The heightened focus on obtaining quality certification, coupled with the growth of the organisation, increased the need for more rigorous documentation control at HelpRead. Figure 6 presents *8 knowledge maintenance activities* focused around

Figure 6. Knowledge Maintenance at HelpRead

Types of Knowledge	Knowledge Activity	Instances of Knowledge Activities
Project	1. Maintain project timetable	Update documents for individual projects
	2. Maintain functional and requirements specification	Update documents for individual projects
Software Development	3. Maintain Technical FAQ	Update Technical FAQ with relevant technical content
	4. Maintain code documentation	Update changes in code with relevant documentation/comments
Customer	5. Maintain individual customer contact	All details on customer and conversations are kept and updated through regular contact with customer
	6. Update reseller contact on regular basis	All reseller details are kept and maintained on a regular basis
Software development/sales	7. Update Employee skills matrix	Matrix maintained as a means of identifying the right people for projects
Environment	8. Maintain knowledge of external environment	Maintain environment knowledge by attending trade shows and related events

5 knowledge types. HelpRead maintains software development, customer, project, sales and environment knowledge.

Knowledge maintenance activity supports both the software development and sales functions at HelpRead. In order to further present the activities in Figure 6, maintenance activity is considered in terms of the knowledge leveraged to support these business processes.

• Maintaining Software Development/ Project Related Knowledge

HelpRead employees are required to actively maintain project related documentation. Figure 6 shows that this involves updating specification documentation (2) and project timetables (1). The maintenance of documentation is closely monitored by the QA Manager. The Technical FAQ is a newer incentive and this is updated less frequently (3). This is due to the fact that the development team are under constant pressure to get software fixes for existing products, new features and completed new products to completion which means they have little time for 'housekeeping'. As the Technical FAQ is new, it is yet to become an integral part of a developer's

daily workload. Its value, therefore, has yet to be proven. The employee skills matrix is maintained on a regular basis (8) as it informs the selection of developers for specific projects, depending on their skill set. Figure 6 also identifies the focus on maintaining complete documentation in all code generated (4). This is partly due to the departure of a developer who left a gap in the project team and, as result, a lot of time was spent understanding his components, due to poor comments and associated documentation. As a result of increased testing and analysis of code by testers, the quality team require improved documentation standards.

• Maintaining Sales Related Knowledge

Reminders are updated regarding customer status and opportunities for re-establishing contact (6) are provided by the Goldmine system (Figure 6). While the Sales Director admitted that this has never been formally outlined as part of a sales person's role, his team are good at maintaining their resources.

The sales staff here are very very motivated to be looking after their own areas and are highly driven. I suppose we've been fortunate in a way that the professionalism of the staff we've employed we've never had a problem like that. (SD)

Current and updated customer files are effectively maintained as standard at HelpRead and, according to the Sales Director, it would be obvious if this was not happening regularly. The sales team actively maintain relationships with their reseller network through face-to-face meetings and over the telephone (7). Industry related knowledge is maintained through attending open days and relevant trade shows such as the Learning and Skills Council UK (5).

Transferring Knowledge

Knowledge transfer activity occurs on both an organised and ad-hoc basis at HelpRead. There are *17 knowledge transfer activities* identified in Figure 7, these activities use *9 types of knowledge.* From Figure 7, environment knowledge is the only type of knowledge not leveraged during knowledge transfer activity as it is not important to senior software developers at an operational level - it is primarily sales and senior management who are concerned with scanning the external market. Nine of the ten knowledge types identified at HelpRead are leveraged during transfer activity; knowledge type is not a discriminating characteristic of knowledge transfer. From Figure 7, it is evident that knowledge transfer activity spans across the organisation involving many types of employees with different knowledge requirements. While the other knowledge activities are discussed in terms of their process driven knowledge focus, knowledge transfer activity is considered based on the formal or informal nature of the transfer activity.

•   Formal Knowledge Transfer Activity

Figure 7 shows that weekly (2) and monthly meetings (10) are held to facilitate formal knowledge transfer sessions. At the weekly meetings,

senior developers are required to account for themselves and progress made, particularly in terms of meeting project timetable deadlines (17) and any other issues they have encountered during the previous week. At the monthly meetings there is a more general discussion at an organisational level, as explained by the SD:

If the TD's going to the States for a fortnight, he stands up and says right I'm going to the States for a fortnight, this is who I'm going to be seeing, this is what I'm going to be doing and just so that everybody knows......if you're sat programming at the cold face or whatever and you're watching these [managers] disappearing here and there and what have you it's nice to know what they're up to. (SD)

The main purpose of these meetings is to transfer knowledge across all levels of the organisation establishing a sense of loyalty and trust between senior management and staff. The TD also organises brainstorming sessions (14) for this group (QA, Sales, TD and technical team) to encourage creativity during new product development (Figure 7). The TD leverages novel techniques, such as De Bono techniques in creative thinking, as a means of generating new and innovative ideas for software products.

As highlighted in Figure 7, post implementation reviews (PIR) (3) and risk assessments (1) are formally organised and conducted as part of each project. The PIRs, in particular, operate as an effective knowledge transfer mechanism. It gives the QA Manager, Project Manager and development team the opportunity to consider the time taken, the cost, the success areas, the technical issues experienced and the lessons learned during the course of the project. The TD explained:

PIR is the time when people learn most. (TD)

A PIR is carried out immediately after project completion as it gives all staff involved an op-

Figure 7. Knowledge Transfer at HelpRead

Types of Knowledge	Knowledge Activity	Instance of Knowledge Activity
Software development/ Project	1.Discuss Risk Assessment	Discuss risk assessment review with team involved in project
	2.Discuss project related issues at weekly meetings	By conducting formal technical meeting held on weekly basis where staff take responsibility for completing tasks committed to and documented in previous meetings
	3.Discuss issues arising at PIR	Discuss Post implementation review issues
Software Development	4.Exchange technical knowledge amongst development team	Informal exchange of technical knowledge among the development team
	5.Participate in Ad hoc meetings	General business knowledge exchanged through face to face meetings
	6.Technical Director (TD) shares technical skills	Employees ,particularly software developers, elicit undocumented technical knowledge from TD
Software development/ Project/ Product	7.Senior developers share ideas with line manager	Developers share their ideas with line managers on a regular basis during general conversation
Software development/ sales/ learning disability	8.Induct new hires	Train new hires - training focus is on the software produced by the company
Software Development/ Sales/ Product	9.Informal employee induction process	Employee induction also occurs informally, employees are brought up to speed in their relevant areas by other team members
Company	10. Discuss issues arising at organisation wide monthly meetings	Formal face -to-face meeting of entire organisation
Technical/ Employee	11. Cross train testers	Cross-skilling employees to improve their expertise in current roles
Customer	12. Transfer sales knowledge	When sales team exchange customer lead knowledge on an ad hoc basis
Product	13. Train new employees in company software features	Each new employee has formal training with TD or other technical staff in software product
	14. Discuss ideas at Internal Brainstorming session	QA, TD, Sales and technical team participate in brainstorming exercise
	15. Sales manager transfers product knowledge	sales manger exchanges product knowledge with senior management team
Project	16. Discuss issues arising from informal PIR for QA	Discuss issues such as loss of time, mistakes made and room for improvement
	17. Transfer project timetable knowledge at weekly meeting	Regularly discuss project timetables to exchange project relate knowledge i.e. progress or problems arising

portunity to deal with the outstanding issues from the project while it is recent. As pinpointed by Figure 7, the serious focus on maintaining quality standards means that the QA team has their own informal PIR for each project (16). Their objective is to reduce bugs per 1000 lines of code to negligible percentage for a new project.

Figure 7 illustrates that another occurrence of organised knowledge transfer is new employee induction. A full time trainer is employed to train new hires in areas such as the software produced by the organisation and the markets served (8).

Informal induction then takes place in each key functional area (9) i.e. sales and software development. All employees are inducted in terms of the features provided by HelpRead software (13). A new developer is provided access to existing code and given small components to work on as an introduction to the group. From the QA perspective, their focus on efficiency in testing code and compliance means that software testers are cross skilled (11) on the job through trial and error approach to a new task assigned to them. The QA manager commented:

He'll have to liaise with our install engineer... who also has a lot of Active Directory experience and he'll be learning from him. So at the end of writing this test script he should have a fair idea. (QA Manager)

This approach has resulted in the development of a highly skilled team of testers.

- Ad-hoc Knowledge Transfer Activity

Due to the size of the organisation and the positive attitude toward knowledge transfer ad-hoc meetings (5), informal discussions enabled through close physical proximity facilitates effective knowledge transfer across the organisation. Although in terms of new features or product ideas, the path of communication is informal, it is also well defined. Figure 7 details this informal process. A senior developer approaches his line manager to discuss his idea (7) and this is then conveyed by the line manager to the TD, QA Manager and SD. Knowledge transfer inside the technical team from an informal perspective is quite efficient and it seems that the atmosphere within the team means that knowledge hoarding is not an issue (Figure 7). The longest serving senior software development, newly appointed DM, describes a recent incident where on completing the development of speech output functionality, he passed this knowledge on to the developer of one product, who then passed to it to another developer. This instance of knowledge transfer in the development team exemplifies how knowledge transfer can facilitates faster development time across software projects (4).

However, the DM added that, while this is an exemplary knowledge transfer activity, most of this knowledge - particularly that of the TD (6) - has yet to be captured and stored in the Technical FAQ. As a result of this lack of formal codification, the company has experienced knowledge leakage with the resignation of one developer. In a team of ten developers, where much knowledge transfer

is ad-hoc and informal in nature, the loss of one head can have a significant impact on project progress. The DM explained:

He was the first person to [leave] in a long time and it was the first time we ever had a handover of a project and his last week was just spent documenting what he had there. Now you can imagine someone who's leaving, their heart isn't in it anymore and the documentation wasn't great. (DM)

As staff turnover at HelpRead was traditionally very low, this was the first developer to leave in five years - this turn of events highlighted the need for increased mechanisms for knowledge transfer in the organisation, however the DM outlined a problem with this:

The problem is knowing what to write down because we don't know the questions until we're asked them. (DM)

Up to the recent growth phase, the informal approach, particularly in terms of the knowledge transfer amongst the software development team, was sufficient but the unexpected loss of a team member affected the collective knowledge of the team. The SD also commented that informal sales knowledge transfer occurred amongst the sales team (12) and from sales to other senior managers (15).

Creating New Knowledge

New software product ideas are created on the back of a number of knowledge acquisition activities involving employees, learning experts, customers, resellers and competitors. Figure 8 illustrates *5 knowledge creation activities* dealing with *4 types of knowledge,* including software development, product, project and customer. HelpRead's focus on innovative software development in the niche market of learning disability is reflected in its knowledge creation activity. The company's focus

Figure 8. Knowledge Creation at HelpRead

Types of Knowledge	Knowledge Activity	Instances of Knowledge Activities
Product	1. Generate ideas for new products through brainstorming	Ideas for new products from brainstorming and from these the initial requirements specification is derived
	2. Generate ideas for new products through focus groups	Ideas for new products from focus groups and from these the initial requirements specification is derived
Software Development/ Project/ Product	3. Generate ideas through ad hoc discussion	Ideas about development projects are derived from ad-hoc discussion amongst the development team
Customer/ Project/ Product	4. Derive ideas from lessons learned at post implementation review	Discussion about how things could be improved resulting from PIR generates new ideas
Customer	5. Generate ideas through environment scanning	Environment scanning can lead to ideas about new customers/markets that could be targeted

on developing products that cater for the specific needs of its customers is a strategic priority for the organisation, resulting in a close connection particularly between the product, project and customer knowledge necessary to fulfil this objective.

The software/product development and sales processes are supported by knowledge creation activity at HelpRead. From Figure 8, these activities can be presented based around these core business processes.

• Product-oriented Knowledge Creation

While only five knowledge creation activities were identified, the nature of these activities is valuable in nature. Figure 8 presents brainstorming sessions (1) and focus groups (2) as idea factories where ideas are incubated and grown until an initial software specification is documented by a member of the team. In addition, PIRs (4) provide a forum for all involved to examine all aspects of each completed project. The TD described what happened in the PIRs:

We examine the spec, examine the product, did it do, was it a success or not? It's very simple. Did it go out the door on time on budget delivering the functionality we wanted? It's a yes or no. (TD)

The project review process facilitates the discussion, codification and storage of lessons learned from past project experiences. There is a particular emphasis on how teams can improve time management techniques to ensure timely product completion. Ad-hoc discussion, particularly amongst the development team, can also lead to new product ideas (3). Evidently, it is through a number of knowledge transfer activities such as brainstorming sessions and focus groups that knowledge creation occurs. It is the discussion that takes place at these organised groups that supports a focus on knowledge creation activity. This is otherwise difficult to achieve in a software SME where employees suffer from resource limitations, such as the time pressures associated with software development activity.

• Sales-oriented Knowledge Creation

From a sales perspective, new ideas are supported by focusing on the company's external environment. Figure 8 shows that new sales prospects may be generated by scanning the customer environment through the web, at trade shows and through interaction with existing customers (5).

Distribution of Knowledge Activity at HelpRead Ltd.

At 82 instances, HelpRead generates significant numbers of knowledge activities. Figure 9 identifies that the majority of activities present them-

Figure 9. Distribution of Knowledge Activities at HelpRead Ltd.

	KA /Company	HelpRead Ltd.	Percentage	Knowledge Focus by Activity
73%	Acquire	17	21%	53% Product Knowledge (9 of n=17 activities)
	Codify	11	13%	90% SW Dev, Project and Product Knowledge (10 of n=11 activities)
	Store	24	29%	71% SW Dev, Product, Project Knowledge (17 of n=24 activities)
	Maintain	8	10%	63% Project and SW Dev Knowledge (5 of n=8 activities)
27%	Transfer	17	21%	83% Product, Project and SW Dev Knowledge (14 of n=17 activities)
	Create	5	6%	80% Product Knowledge (4 of n=5 activities)
	Total	82	100%	

selves through knowledge acquisition, storage and transfer at HelpRead. It is also important to note that, at this time HelpRead Ltd. were not in a new product development phase, it would be anticipated that the volume of activity would increase if KA were identified during a new product development process.

Figure 9 displays the distribution of knowledge activities and the type of knowledge focus for each of these activities - these statistics are derived from the individual tables of knowledge activities in the previous sections. The difference in intensity between these types of activities is indicative of HelpRead's current position as a growing organisation. Knowledge acquisition intensity at 21 percent (n=82) shows that HelpRead are focused on building a collective organisational memory that facilitates continued growth through the introduction of new hires and new products. This is particularly important to them in terms of acquiring external knowledge to inform new product development. From Figure 9, it is evident that 53 percent of all knowledge acquisition activity is focused on gathering product knowledge. This supports Groen's (2006, p124) view that in high-technology SMEs *"intensive interaction is needed to enhance the product creation process with knowledge from external sources"*.

At 13 percent (n=82) codification activity is relatively low intensity - this is reflective of the uncertainty around what the company needs to know in the future. This is predominantly evident with the Technical FAQ, which lacks buy-in from the entire development team. The Software Development Manager admitted that as a team *"they didn't know what they should know"*. Most codification activity is directly related to refining the discussions at group meetings into documents which are made available over the Intranet. Otherwise, codification takes place amongst the development team where code components and lessons learned from exploring software methodologies are broken down and refined for storage purposes. Over 90 percent (n=11) of all codification activity identified in Figure 9 is related to product development knowledge. Thus, codification is largely not a sales related activity. The well defined scope of the Goldmine sales system means no knowledge activity is required to support the refinement and distillation of sales related knowledge. In addition, the experience of the sales team means they know what important customer and sales related knowledge should be stored for future use.

The high occurrence of storage activities (29 percent in Figure 9) is indicative of the importance placed on storing knowledge in the new Intranet-based quality system - approximately

74 percent (based on Figure 5, 17 out of n=24 storage activities) of storage activity involves the Intranet. These activities primarily include storing software project documents and employee skills documents, in line with the compliance requirements outlined by IS9001:2000. The codification intensity also includes the level of customer information captured and stored by the sales team. This 29 percent reflects the move to store the knowledge gathered from acquisition, codification and transfer activities.

As many of the acquisition, storage and transfer processes are newly in place, the focus on maintenance is not as strong as the emphasis on other activities. Maintenance activities are at 10 percent. Figure 9 shows the focus on software and product development knowledge. The TD, the QA Manager and the senior developers highlighted issues around maintaining the Technical FAQ. This appears to be two pronged. Firstly, the development team work to strict deadlines that are monitored on a weekly basis which does not allow for a lot of free working time and, secondly, one senior developer identified the problems associated with knowing what knowledge was valuable to store. As Intranet usage becomes embedded into employee's daily routines, these should increase.

As a smaller organisation with a software development team of 5 employees and 2 software product offerings, the company did not need to consider a formalised approach to leveraging KA. Their recent growth phase has highlighted a greater need to achieve this. Surprisingly, transfer activity is high intensity at 19 percent in Figure 9 - with closer inspection of the analytic memos; the role of the TD is integral to this. This reflects his role as a strategy maker - he is a pivotal player in pushing knowledge transfer to facilitate a smooth expansion period amongst the development team. At 6 percent, knowledge creation is very low. While Figure 9 shows that 80 percent of knowledge creation activity is focused on product knowledge, in line with company strategy, the lack of other types of knowledge creation may be at-

tributed to the pressures associated with the rapid growth in employee headcount and the increased product portfolio.

An investigation of the knowledge activities at HelpRead illustrates in Figure 9 that approximately 73 percent of activity lies in knowledge acquisition, codification, storage and maintenance. From this, the company's ability to acquire knowledge and build knowledge stores is confirmed. However, knowledge transfer and creation activity at 27 percent intensity is low by comparison, particularly in view of the TD's heavy involvement in a large proportion of transfer activity. This indicates that HelpRead has more work to do in terms of developing their knowledge transfer and creation activities in the longer term. While these activities are more difficult to grow, they are the most valuable knowledge generators for the organisation.

FUTURE RESEARCH DIRECTIONS

This chapter has presented the analysis of findings from one case study in which the researcher sought to investigate the company's approach to KM. This study may be leveraged in future research to inform both research and practice. From a research perspective, the next step is to abstract the knowledge activities identified in this company to a higher level of understanding as a means of further characterising a software SMEs approach to KM. This would support Tan *et al.* (2009) who contend that while testing existing theories in a small firm context has advanced the nature of research in the area, greater attention needs to be attributed to theory building in technology, innovation and corporate social responsibility in small business research.

In addition, there is a need to leverage this classification of knowledge activities in order to confirm and/or extend it, in both the software and other high-technology sectors. Doing this should both confirm the validity of the classification, as well as extend its applicability in alternative knowledge domains. While it has been established that SMEs and MNEs differ, larger organisations could leverage the classification across functional areas as a KM diagnostic tool. This could provide large organisations with the capability of tangibly measuring their knowledge activities. From the point of view of practitioners, this classification of KA provides a tangible and actionable starting point for firms to practically assess their KM approach, providing them with the ability to diagnose their KM strengths and weaknesses in order to better prepare for changing circumstances both within and outside the organisation.

CONCLUSION

At HelpRead knowledge creation was quite low with a significant amount of this activity occurring at a senior level. This may be characterised as a weakness of how this organisation manages their knowledge activity. In support, Chan and Chao (2008) advocate that SMEs should be more open to employee ideas, creativity and innovations.

Undoubtedly, organisations large and small need to leverage the wealth of knowledge available to them. The company is over reliant on the Technical Director to champion knowledge initiatives. To overcome this, it is imperative that the value of these activities is understood across the organisation. Notwithstanding the weaknesses in HelpRead's current approach to knowledge activities, leveraging and growing their existing capabilities means that they can aim to do things better e.g. make better decisions around project timetabling, assigning new developers to specific projects and gathering ideas from customers. Taking this one step further, HelpRead could aspire to improve their focus on developing transfer activities and generating new knowledge in a formalised approach to prepare for and even anticipate environmental changes in the future.

REFERENCES

Ägerfalk, P., & Fitzgerald, B. (2008). Outsourcing to an Unknown Workforce: Exploring Opensourcing as a Global Sourcing Strategy. *Management Information Systems Quarterly, 32*(2), 385–409.

Alavi, M. (1997). KPMG Peat Marwick U.S.: One Giant Brain. *Harvard Business School Case*, 9-397-108, Rev. July 11.

Alavi, M., & Leidner, D. E. (2001). Knowledge Management and Knowledge Management Systems: Conceptual Foundations and Research Issues. *Management Information Systems Quarterly, 25*(1), 107–136. doi:10.2307/3250961

Barthelme, F., Erime, J. L., & Rosenthal-Sabroux, C. (1998). An architecture for knowledge evolution in organisations. *European Journal of Operational Research, 109*(2), 414–427. doi:10.1016/S0377-2217(98)00067-8

Brown, S.J. & Duguid, P. (2000). Balancing Act: How To Capture Knowledge Without Killing It. *Harvard Business Review*, May-June, 78(3), pp. 73-80.

Cecez-Kecmanovic, D. (2000). *Understanding Knowledge Sharing in Organizational Decision Making Supported by CMC*. IFIP TC8/WG8.3 International Conference on Decision Support through Knowledge Management, 9-11 July 2000, Stockholm, Sweden, pp. 77-90.

Chan, I., & Chao, C. K. (2008). Knowledge Management in Small and Medium Sized Enterprises. *Communications of the ACM, 51*(4), 83–88. doi:10.1145/1330311.1330328

Choo, C. (1996). An Integrated Information Model of the Organization: The Knowing Organization. URL=http://www.fis.utoronto.ca/people/faculty/choo/FIS/KO/KO.html1contents. (Last accessed March 18TH 2008).

Davenport, T. H., & Prusak, L. (1998). *Working Knowledge. How Organizations Manage What They Know*. Boston: Harvard Business School Press.

Earl, M. J., & Hopwood, A. G. (1980). From Management Information to Information Management. In Lucas, L., & Lincoln, S. (Eds.), *The Information Systems Environment*. Amsterdam: North Holland Publishing Company.

Fahey, L., & Prusak, L. (1998). The Eleven Deadliest Sins of Knowledge Management. *California Management Review, 9*, 449–459.

Hansen, M., Nohria, N & Tierney, T. (1999). What's Your Strategy for Managing Knowledge? *Harvard Business Review*, March-April, 77(2), pp. 106-116.

Holsapple, C., & Joshi, K. (2004). A Knowledge Management Ontology. In Holsapple, C. W. (Ed.), *Handbook on Knowledge Management* (*Vol. 1*, pp. 89–128). Berlin: Verlanger.

Holsapple, C., & Singh, M. (2004). The Knowledge Chain Model: Activities for Competitiveness. In Holsapple, C. W. (Ed.), *Handbook on Knowledge Management* (*Vol. 2*, pp. 657–678). Berlin: Verlanger.

Holsapple, C. W., & Whinston, T. (1987). Knowledge-based organizations. *The Information Society, 2*, 77–90. doi:10.1080/01972243.1 987.9960049

Huber, G. P. (1990). A theory of the effects of advanced information technologies on organizational design, intelligence, and decision making. *Academy of Management Review, 15*(1), 47–71. doi:10.2307/258105

Huber, G. P. (1991). Organisational Learning: The contributing Processes and the Literatures. *Organization Science, 2*(1), 88–115. doi:10.1287/orsc.2.1.88

Joe, C., & Yoong, P. (2004). Harnessing the Knowledge Assets of Older Workers: A Work in Progress Report.in *Proceedings of the 2004 DSS Conference*, Prato, Italy.

Kayworth, T., & Leidner, D. (2004). Organizational Culture as a Knowledge Resource. In Holsapple, C. W. (Ed.), *Handbook of Knowledge Management* (*Vol. 1*, pp. 235–252). Berlin: Verlanger.

Kraaijenbrink, J., Faran, D., & Hauptman, A. (2006). Knowledge Integration by SMEs – Framework. In Jetter, A., Kraaijenbrink, J. Schroder, H., Wijnhoven, F., (eds). *Knowledge Integration: The Practice of Knowledge Management in Small to Medium Sized Enterprises,* pp. 17-28 New York: Springer

Lee, G. L., & Oakes, I. (1995). The 'pros' and 'cons' of total quality management for smaller firms in manufacturing: some experiences down the supply chain. *Total Quality Management, 6*(4), 413–426. doi:10.1080/09544129550035341

Leonard-Barton, D. (1995). *Wellsprings of knowledge: building and sustaining the sources of innovation*. Boston: Harvard Business School Press.

Miles, M. B., & Huberman, A. M. (1994). *Qualitative data analysis: An expandedSourcebook*. Thousand Oaks, CA: Sage.

Nevo, S., Wade, M. R., & Cook, W. D. (2007). An examination of the trade off between internal and external IT capabilities. *The Journal of Strategic Information Systems, 16*, 5–23. doi:10.1016/j.jsis.2006.10.002

Nonaka, I. (1991). The Knowledge Creating Company. *Harvard Business Review*, November-December, 69, pp. 96-104.

O'Dell, C., & Grayson, C. J. J. (1998). *If Only We Knew What We Know: The Transfer of Internal Knowledge and Best Practice*. New York: The Free Press.

Patton, M. (1990). *Qualitative Evaluation and Research Methods*. Newbury Park, CA: Sage Publications.

Pentland, B. (1995). Information systems and organizational learning: the social epistemology of organizational knowledge systems. *Accounting. Management and Information Technologies, 5*(1), 1–21. doi:10.1016/0959-8022(95)90011-X

Sparrow, J. (2000). Knowledge Features in Small Firms. *Operations Research Society KMAC Conference,* University of Aston, 17-18 July.

Szulanksi, G. (1996). Exploring Internal Stickiness: Impediments to the Transfer of Best Practice within the Firm. *Strategic Management Journal, 17,* 27–43.

Tan, J., Fischer, E., Mitcherll, R., & Phan, P. (2009). At the Center of the Action: Innovation and Technology Strategy Research in the Small Business Setting. *Journal of Small Business Management, 47*(3), 233–262. doi:10.1111/j.1540-627X.2009.00270.x

Welsh, J., & White, J. (1981). A small business is not a little big business. *Harvard Business Review,* (July-August): 18–32.

Wiig, K. M. (1993). *Knowledge Management Foundations – Thinking About Thinking – How People and Organizations Create, Represent, and Use Knowledge.* Arlington, TX: Schema Press.

KEY TERMS AND DEFINITIONS

Knowledge: Information that is important for an employee to complete a task.

Knowledge Activity: A transaction or manipulation of knowledge, constituent parts of an organisation's approach to Knowledge Management.

Small to Medium Enterprise (SME): An organisation with between 50 and 250 employees.

Knowledge Acquisition: Identify and capture knowledge from a source.

Knowledge Codification: Assess, distil refine knowledge into a useful format.

Knowledge Storage: Store knowledge in some artefact i.e. system.

Knowledge Maintenance: Update knowledge store on continual basis.

Knowledge Transfer: Send or exchange knowledge to/with appropriate receiver.

Knowledge Creation: Create new knowledge important to the organisation.

Chapter 5
Business Agility and Process Agility:
How Do They Relate to Each Other?

Giorgio Bruno
Politecnico di Torino, Italy

ABSTRACT

Agility is an essential feature for SMEs and this chapter intends to examine if and how business processes, as currently understood, are able to promote it. Over the last years a number of viewpoints have emerged which exerted great influence on the design of notations and languages for business processes: the majority of them can be referred to as the centralized viewpoint, the role viewpoint, the conversational viewpoint, the case viewpoint and the cooperative one. These viewpoints provide different levels of agility and then beneficial results can be expected from their integration, which is the purpose of the proof-of-concept notation, AgileBPN, presented in this chapter. In AgileBPN, business processes are organized around conversations and role processes (encompassing the tasks pertaining to a given role); shared artifacts are represented as cooperative objects. The notation is illustrated with the help of an example referring to a business process meant to handle applications in a certain organization.

INTRODUCTION

Agility is an essential feature for SMEs, since "these do not apply standardised processes to such a degree as large companies" (Riss, Rickayzen, Maus & van der Aalst, 2005).

In general, agility is the ability to react to external stimuli, quickly and effectively. In a business context, agility is associated with the business practices at different levels (corporate, individual and group).

At the corporate level, agility means the adaptation of the current business practices or the introduction of new ones, in response to new market needs, to initiatives of competitors or to changes in regulations.

Since business practices are carried out through business processes (Davenport, 1993), an impor-

DOI: 10.4018/978-1-60960-463-9.ch005

tant driver of corporate agility is an expressive notation able to capture the essential features of the business problem being considered. As notations are made up of building blocks addressing specific classes of sub-problems, the issue is to identify the building blocks as well as the most appropriate composition mechanisms. Agility is achieved because the building blocks provide partial solutions already available, which can be arranged in the order needed, by means of the composition mechanisms.

Over the last years, a number of viewpoints have emerged which exerted great influence on the design of notations and languages for business processes.

These viewpoints propose different ways of organizing the basic constituents of cooperative environments, which are the operational activities, the coordination activities and the common field of work (Schmidt & Simone, 1996). Operational activities are units of work meant to produce some changes in the underlying common field of work, which is a repository of artifacts (business data and documents). Coordination activities are responsible for organizing the operational activities in the proper sequence.

When an activity is to be carried out by a person, it is referred to as manual activity or task; the term "task" will be used in this chapter to denote a manual activity. On the contrary, automated activities are performed by external services. The people taking part in a process are referred to as the participants in the process.

At the beginning of CSCW (Computer Supported Cooperative Work), coordination was left to the users who tried to achieve it by means of various means, including shared databases and e-mails (Holt, 1985). Then, explicit coordination techniques were introduced in order to come up with repeatable processes.

However, there are marked differences among the above mentioned viewpoints in the extent to which the participants in the business processes are involved in the coordination activities.

In the centralized viewpoint, where efficiency is the major goal, coordination is carried out by the business processes through control-flow elements, which are responsible for organizing the operational activities in sequential, alternative, repetitive and concurrent paths, as needed.

A business process is then like a master who distributes the work among the participants.

This is a rigid approach in that, when an activity has been completed, the selection of the next one to be carried out is automatically made through the control-flow elements.

Well-known notations and languages, such as BPMN (OMG, 2008) and BPEL (OASIS, 2007), support the centralized viewpoint.

While it is generally accepted that rigid processes made a significant contribution to repetitive, standardized work (i.e. routines), they do not seem to be adequate to situations requiring knowledge intensive work (Riss, Rickayzen, Maus & van der Aalst, 2005).

Knowledge intensive work is usually associated with individual agility, which is the ability for the participants to take part in the coordination of the work to be done; they do so, by autonomously selecting the tasks to carry out, when needed, on the basis of their judgment and experience.

The conversational viewpoint and the case viewpoint promote individual agility through conversations and through the handling of individual artifacts, respectively.

The conversational viewpoint emphasizes conversations, which are patterns of interaction between pairs of participants. A well-known such pattern is the conversation for action (Winograd, 1987-1988), in which two parties, i.e. a requester and a provider, reach mutual agreement through a number of negotiations. A business process can then be described in terms of roles and conversations between roles, roles and conversations being building blocks (Dietz, 2006). In particular, a role building block is a compound entity encompassing the "space of action" of the participants playing that role in the business process being considered.

This space of action shows the conversations the participants may be involved in as well as the tasks that are needed to support them. Agility is achieved not only because conversations proceed through negotiations but also because the space of action may include optional tasks in addition to mandatory ones; for example, an optional task may enable a participant to start a certain conversation if needed.

While conversations focus on the interactions and on the related actions, it is not infrequent that a business process is meant to handle the life cycle of a particular class of artifacts, such as purchase orders or insurance claims.

The case viewpoint (where case denotes the artifact to be handled by the business process) considers the state of the case, rather than the completion of the process activities, as the primary driver of the process evolution (van der Aalst, Weske & Grünbauer, 2005). The control flow turns out to be much simpler and agility is achieved because the participants select the tasks to perform on the basis of the state of the case.

Traditionally, the cooperative development of shared artifacts, such as documents and software, is considered to be part of the groupware domain, because there is no explicit control flow to handle. Recent work includes the collaborative development of process descriptions based on wiki systems (Neumann & Erol, 2009).

However, integrating the cooperative viewpoint in the business processes promotes agility at the group level in that a number of participants can be quickly involved in a collective action without the need to explicitly define conversations or tasks.

An example could be the preparation of a complex quote in response to a request for quote: the account manager that received the request for quote could organize a wiki document to collect the suggestions of a number of advisors before proceeding with the finalization of the quote.

An agile notation should be able to support all the above-mentioned viewpoints. This is not an easy goal for several reasons: conversations and case handling seem to be orthogonal notions and representing shared artifacts in business processes is still an open issue.

This chapter presents a proof-of-concept notation, called AgileBPN (Agile Business Process Notation), in which all the above-mentioned viewpoints are addressed; it does so with the help of an example of which several versions are discussed. In AgileBPN, business processes are organized around conversations and role processes (encompassing the tasks pertaining to a given role); shared artifacts are represented as cooperative objects.

This chapter is organized as follows. Section 2 illustrates the viewpoints on business processes in more detail. Section 3 introduces conversation patterns, while section 4 presents the architecture of business processes as well as the standard role processes implied by the conversations. Section 5 explains how a role process can combine two or more conversations. Section 6 shows a case of individual agility in a role process, while section 7 illustrates how shared artifacts can be included in the business processes. Section 8 presents the conclusion and the future work.

VIEWPOINTS ON BUSINESS PROCESSES

This section discusses five major viewpoints on business processes, i.e. the centralized viewpoint, the role viewpoint, the conversational viewpoint, the case viewpoint and the cooperative one.

Probably, the most popular viewpoint is the centralized one, which considers business processes essentially as orchestrators of operational activities. Efficiency is the major goal, which is achieved by means of a rigid control flow: in this context, a business process is like a master distributing the work among the participants.

An example is a business process handling a purchase requisition (PR) as follows. First, the PR is entered by a requester, e.g. through a suitable form; then the process hands it to the appropriate approver (e.g. the requester's supervisor) so as to get it evaluated. If the evaluation is positive, the process hands the PR to a member of the purchasing department (i.e. a buyer) so as to get it turned into a purchase order; otherwise it notifies the rejection to the requester.

In the centralized perspective, participants are meant to interact with the processes and not with each other. They are presented with to-do lists showing the tasks that have been assigned to them by the processes; by clicking on the items of their todo lists, they can perform the corresponding tasks.

When an activity has been completed, the decision on the next one to be carried out is taken by the process through a control-flow building block.

A business process involves a number of participants denoted by their roles; in the example above, three roles are mentioned, i.e. requester (the role of the participants entitled to enter purchase requisitions), approver and buyer. Swimlanes are usually associated with roles so as to group the corresponding tasks.

Activities and control-flow elements are the major building blocks, while swimlanes are the major structuring mechanisms. Well-known notations and languages, such as BPMN (OMG, 2008) and BPEL (OASIS, 2007), support the centralized viewpoint.

It is not easy for participants to understand their real involvement when they look at the model of a business process based on the centralized perspective. They can find their tasks in the swimlane associated with their role, but the task flow for a given participant is hard to identify because the task flows of all the participants are mixed, in the process model.

The participation of users in processes is made more evident, if the process is decomposed into several "role" components: this is the essence of the role viewpoint. In the RAD (Role Activity Diagramming) approach (Ould, 2005), each role component is structured as a process including the tasks pertaining to the role; components interact with each other by means of send/receive operations.

The conversational viewpoint starts from the consideration that it is usually possible to identify a number of portions in a business process, each portion encompassing a flow of tasks involving the same pair of participants. While the actual tasks depend on the business problem being addressed, their flow, instead, usually falls into a number of standard patterns.

A well-known pattern is the conversation for action (Winograd, 1987-1988), which can be expressed as follows. R (i.e. the participant who initiates the conversation, also referred to as the conversation initiator) makes a request to F (i.e. the other party, also referred to as the conversation follower): F can accept, decline or even make a counter-offer. In the last case, R can accept the counter-offer, can cancel the request or can make another request. In case of acceptance, F will assert the task is completed, and R can accept or can reject the result. Such patterns are called conversations, because they are aimed at producing an effect on the real world through the interactions of two parties, and the interactions are very similar to speech acts (Austin, 1976).

As a matter of fact, the purpose of an interaction is to communicate an intention of the originator (of the interaction) to the recipient. Examples of intentions are making a request, accepting a request, and providing a reply.

A similar pattern is the conversation for approval whose purpose is to get the initiator's request evaluated by the follower.

For example, the above-mentioned purchase requisition process might be extended so as to enable the approver to ask for some modifications to the purchase requisition. Then the requester may update the purchase requisition or may withdraw it. In the first case, the approver will subsequently evaluate the updated purchase requisition and the result may be its approval or rejection or even a new request for change.

If the business logic relies on a number of conversations, the overall business process might be very complicated at the task level; however, if building blocks centered on conversations are provided, the resulting business process turns out to be much simpler.

Agility in design is achieved by means of such building blocks, because the architecture of the business process can be quickly obtained by identifying the roles involved and then introducing the conversations required, which can be obtained by customizing standard patterns, as shown in the next section.

Empirical findings (Thom, Reichert & Iochpe, 2009) show that common business processes are mainly made up of standard conversation patterns.

Several modeling approaches based on conversations have been proposed; they characterize the language/action perspective, or LAP (Weigand, 2006).

In the Action Workflow approach (Medina-Mora, Winograd, Flores & Flores, 1992), a typical conversation takes place between a requester and a performer and is made up of four major phases (request, commitment, performance and evaluation) forming the so-called workflow loop.

In the DEMO approach (Dietz, 2006), workflow loops are subdivided in three phases (order, execution and result) and are encapsulated in transactions. Business processes are compositions of roles and transactions, where transactions connect two roles and roles include tasks and control-flow logic. In the hierarchical structure provided by DEMO, tasks are compared to atoms, transactions to molecules, and business processes to fibers (Dietz, 2003).

The viewpoints examined so far emphasize the activities and the control-flow issues, while leaving aside the business entities that the activities are meant to handle.

However, there are situations requiring a different viewpoint, in which the handling of the life cycle of a particular business entity is the major purpose of a business process. The business entity to be handled is referred to as the case (van der Aalst, Weske & Grünbauer, 2005) of the process, which is denoted as a case-handling process; this viewpoint can be called case viewpoint, consequently.

Case-handling processes require a stronger integration between control-flow issues and data-flow ones, because the process evolution is driven by the state of the case rather than by the completion of its activities (Künzle & Reichert, 2009). As a matter of fact, a task may be enabled as soon as the needed attributes of the case have been set by another task (even if this task is not yet completed).

Agility is achieved because the participants can look at the case as a whole: when performing a task, they are not constrained to provide only the mandatory information items, but, to a certain extent, they can enter additional information items as well. If it happens that the information items introduced with a certain task, say, T1, include the mandatory information items for a subsequent task, say, T2, then T2 becomes unnecessary and can be skipped.

Winograd states that conversations "form the central fabric of cooperative work" (Winograd, 1987-1988). The term conversation is to be taken in a broad sense including not only conversations for action, but also other kinds of conversation, such as those for clarification, for possibilities or for orientation. From this point of view, cooperation is achieved through interactions between individuals.

However, while it is important to understand the constituents of cooperative work, i.e. interactions and conversations as goal-oriented grouping of interactions, it must also be recognized that in most cases the purpose of cooperative work is the production of shared artifacts, such as documents and software. In this viewpoint referred to as cooperative viewpoint, the participants share a space of actions "such that the actions of one group member can affect the space of actions of the others" (Kaplan & Carroll, 1992). This common space is referred to as social space and is made up of a number of entities, referred to as social entities, which are visible to all the participants: by acting on the social entities, they can influence each other.

There is a growing interest in wiki systems, for their potential in terms of availability, customizability and agility in use (Leuf & Cunningham, 2001).

A wiki document is a social entity in that it enables a number of users with different roles to work out a shared document by taking advantage of the internal mechanisms provided by wiki systems (e.g. access control and version management). The customization of a wiki document may imply the introduction of a hierarchy of pages and consequently the definition of the participants entitled to work on them (Bruno, 2009).

Business processes can benefit from the introduction of social entities, such as wiki documents.

An example could be the preparation of a complex quote in response to a request for quote: the account manager that received the request for quote could organize a wiki document to collect the suggestions of a number of advisors before proceeding with the finalization of the quote.

The integration between business processes and social entities is a new field of research; in section 7, a proposal based on the notion of cooperative object is presented.

CONVERSATIONS

This section illustrates how conversations are represented in AgileBPN.

Basically, conversations are patterns of interaction between two parties referred to as initiator (the one who starts the conversation) and follower. The purpose of an interaction is to communicate an intention of its originator to its recipient. Examples of intentions are making a request, accepting a request, and providing a reply.

Conversations are represented in terms of interaction flows and various types of models have been proposed. State models are the most used for sequential conversations, i.e. when parallel interactions cannot occur; a well-known example is the model of conversations for action (Winograd, 1987-1988).

In the domain of choreographies (which address conversations taking place between two or more participants), there are a number of solutions: BPSS (Hofreiter, Huemer & Winiwarter, 2005) is based on UML activity diagrams (OMG, 2007), interaction Petri nets (Decker & Weske, 2007) draw on Petri nets, and Let's Dance (Zaha, Dumas, ter Hofstede, Barros & Decker, 2008) introduces specific precedence and inhibition constructs.

Research on PAISs (Process-Aware Information Systems) (Dumas, van der Aalst & ter Hofstede, 2005) and on case handling (van der Aalst, Weske & Grünbauer, 2005) advocates a stronger connection between the activities and the business entities to be acted on; for this reason, in AgileBPN, the intention communicated by an interaction is supported by a business entity providing all the details needed. For example, the interaction named "submit purchase requisition" points to a business entity, which is the purchase requisition being submitted by the originator.

Given an interaction, the associated business entity is referred to as its support entity.

From a complementary viewpoint, a conversation is a coordination mechanism enabling the participants to act on the same business entities at different times and with different purposes.

In analogy with case-handling processes (van der Aalst, Weske & Grünbauer, 2005), there are conversations aimed at handling the life cycle of a particular business entity, which can be referred to as the conversation case.

In a conversation for approval, which will be shown later on in this section, there is one business entity (i.e. the item to be evaluated) flowing along the various interactions: this item is the case of the conversation.

In general, the support entity of the first interaction of the conversation will be considered to be the conversation case.

All the conversations with the same purpose have the same structure and differ in the types of the support entities of their interactions. Such structures, called conversation patterns, can be defined independently of the types of the business entities exchanged by the parties; generic types are used instead of the actual ones. In process models, conversation patterns are customized by replacing generic types with actual types.

The models shown in Figure 1 represent a simple conversation for action (SimpleCfA); two representations are shown, i.e. a state model and a UML sequence diagram (OMG, 2007).

As a general rule, the initiator is meant to be located on the left side of the model and the follower on the right side. Data-driven constraints are not considered so as to keep the examples reasonably simple: in order for them to be handled, an information model including the relevant attributes of the generic types should be added.

The conversation is started with interaction r, meant to convey a request; R denotes the type of its support entity. The type of an interaction support entity is referred to as the interaction support type.

The follower may reply with one of two alternative interactions, r- and s, thus ending the conversation. Interaction r- means that the request has been rejected, while interaction s conveys the response (i.e. the outcome of the action performed by the follower). Interaction r- returns the request, and, for this reason, it has the same support type as interaction r. The support type of interaction s is different as it represents the outcome of the action performed.

This pattern becomes more complicated, if counter-offers are included (Winograd 1987-1988).

The sequence diagram organizes the interaction flow in fragments: the "alt" fragment includes a number of alternative sections.

In addition to being patterns of interactions, conversations are also patterns of work because an interaction is produced by an originator's task and is handled by a recipient's task.

Although the actual tasks will be determined in the process models, it is useful to analyze a conversation in isolation in order to find out which tasks are needed: such tasks are referred to as the implicit tasks of the conversation.

The representation of tasks is easier with state models than with sequence diagrams; this is the reason why state models have been chosen in AgileBPN. Basically, tasks are associated with transitions, while interactions are shown in the states.

The first interaction, r, in pattern SimpleCfA is produced by a proactive task, represented by the transition entering state r. A proactive task has no input state; as a matter of fact, it is up to

Figure 1. Models of SimpleCfA: state model (a), sequence diagram (b)

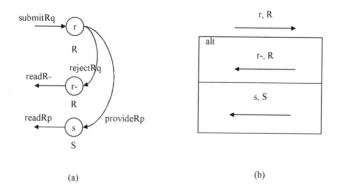

(a)

(b)

the initiator to start a new conversation whenever they want to. The standard name of this task is submitRq (submit request).

The follower reacts to a request with one of two alternative tasks, rejectRq (reject request) or provideRp (provide response). They are optional tasks in that it is up to the follower to select one of them. They are also reactive tasks because they are caused by an incoming interaction and produce an outgoing one.

Interactions r- and s end the conversation; the initiator can take notice of them by means of tasks readR- (take notice of rejection) and readRp (take notice of response), which have no output states because these interactions are final ones.

The support types, R and S, are shown near the corresponding states.

Two more patterns, used in the following sections, are shown in Figure 2.

Pattern SimpleCfApproval handles simplified conversations for approval. The conversation is started with a request (r) and the follower may accept (r+) or reject it (r-). The same support entity is meant to go backward and forward between the parties, and hence there is only one generic type involved, R.

Pattern Notification consists of one interaction (n), interpreted as a notification (i.e. a simple communication requiring no reply). The generic interaction support type is N.

PROCESS MODELS

In AgileBPN, business processes are made up of two major kinds of building blocks, i.e. conversation types and role processes, as illustrated in the simple example that follows.

This example is concerned with a business process meant to handle applications in a given organization. Its requirements, kept to a minimum, are as follows. An applicant is assumed to apply for one of the available positions by filling out an online application form; then the application is handled by one of the recruiters associated with the position indicated in the application. The recruiter can accept or reject the application and the outcome is communicated to the applicant.

Two roles, Applicant and Recruiter, are involved and their interactions follow the SimpleCfApproval pattern; therefore a conversation type, called ApplyForJob, based on this template, is introduced. The model of this business process, called ApplicationHandler v.1 is shown in Figure 3. An extended version of this business process will be discussed in the next section.

Several notations have been proposed in order to integrate conversations in business processes; among them stand out Action Workflow (Medina-Mora, Winograd, Flores & Flores, 1992) and DEMO (Dietz, 2003).

The processes in DEMO and in AgileBPN have a similar structure based on conversations (called

Figure 2. Models of SimpleCfApproval (a) and Notification (b)

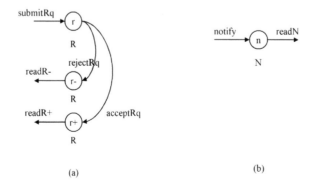

(a)

(b)

Figure 3. Business process ApplicationHandler v.1 (a) and its conversation table (b)

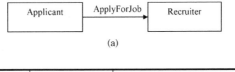

(a)

Conversation type	Pattern	Follower
ApplyForJob	SimpleCfApproval (R = Application)	The process selects one recruiter from among those associated with the position indicated in the application.

(b)

transactions in DEMO) and role processes. However, in AgileBPN, conversations are not restricted to conversations for action (as in DEMO) and they integrate case-handling as well; in addition, role processes can accommodate cooperative objects as illustrated in a subsequent section.

In AgileBPN, roles are shown as boxes and conversations as directed links originating from the box associated with the initiator role and ending in the box of the follower role. In general, conversation types can be completely defined in separate models; alternatively, they may be obtained as customizations of standard conversation patterns. This is the case of conversation type ApplyForJob, which derives from pattern SimpleCfApproval, as shown in the conversation table. This table (in the Pattern column) indicates which actual types are meant to replace the generic types: in ApplyFor-Job, the generic type R is to be substituted with the actual type Application. In order to describe the actual types along with their attributes and relationships, an information model is needed: it is omitted for the sake of simplicity.

The model basically shows that conversations of type ApplyForJob can take place between applicants and recruiters; it is an architectural description leaving out two important aspects, i.e. how the followers of conversations are to be determined and how the participants are expected to behave on the basis of the conversations they are involved in.

As to the first issue, i.e. the determination of the follower of a given conversation, there are two major alternatives: the follower is selected by the initiator or the choice is made by the process on the basis of a business rule. The first situation is illustrated in the next section, when recruiters are entitled to ask reviewers to provide their evaluations of the applications. On the other hand, when an applicant submits an application, they cannot select the recruiter who will follow the conversation, because such a choice is based on a company policy. The selection mechanism is explained in the follower column of the conversation table; the description given is informal, but if an information model were provided, it could be made more precise, e.g. by means of a navigational language such as OCL (OMG, 2005).

The behavior of the participants is defined in the role boxes, which, when expanded, show the role processes. A role process encompasses the tasks the participants playing that role are expected to carry out. Since a role is involved in a number of conversations, a role process may take advantage of the implicit tasks associated with these conversations, as shown in Figure 4.

The conversations in which a role is involved are shown as conversation processes in the corresponding role process. A conversation process is labeled with the conversation type it refers to and is represented as a rectangle with rounded corners including the interactions of the conversa-

Figure 4. Role processes in business process ApplicationHandler v.1

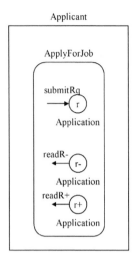 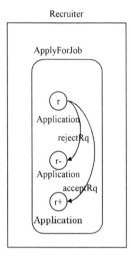

tion type as well as the implicit tasks needed. The tasks are those pertaining to the function (initiator or follower) carried out by the role with respect to the conversation type and the generic support types are replaced with the actual support types (on the basis of the pattern column in the conversation table).

Complications arise when a role is involved in two or more conversation types: this situation, analyzed in the next section, requires the introduction of new tasks (in addition or in alternative to the implicit ones), whose purpose is to combine interactions belonging to different conversation types.

ROLE PROCESSES

This section discusses two major factors of complexity, one at the role level and the other at the process level.

Complexity increases at the role level when there are two or more conversation types to handle; an additional control flow is then needed to integrate the separate conversation processes.

A relevant part of the overall control flow is defined in the conversation types; however, there may be situations in which an ordering of conversations has to be established as a consequence of company policies. In such cases, a process-level control flow is needed, which is then external to the conversations.

The discussion of these issues is based on an extended version of business process ApplicationHandler (introduced in the previous section). In the new situation, four roles are involved, i.e. applicants, recruiters, reviewers and members of the personnel department.

Applicants submit applications as before. However, recruiters cannot decide on an application without getting three external reviews before. Therefore they send the applications to three reviewers and when the reviews are available, they will take the final decision (whether to accept or to reject the application). In case a reviewer refuses to evaluate an application, they will appoint another one. The selection of the reviewers is made by the recruiters.

In case an application is accepted, (a member of) the personnel department will complete the hiring procedure through a series of interactions with the applicant: for the sake of simplicity, only one interaction (from the personnel department to the applicant) is to be considered. This interaction is supposed to bring the application back to the applicant with some hiring details.

The analysis of the requirements above reveals that the conversations taking place between recruiters and reviewers are simple conversations for action; hence they derive from the SimpleCfA pattern. Their type is called GetReview: the generic support types R and S are replaced with the actual support types Application and Review. The conversations between the personnel department and the applicants amount to notifications; their type is called FinalizeHiring and the generic support type N is replaced with Application.

The model of business process Application-Handler v.2 is shown in Figure 5 along with its conversation table.

In process ApplicationHandler v.2, when an application is accepted, further work is to be done by the personnel department; however, its members are not involved in the evaluation of applications and hence an external control flow is needed to bring them the accepted applications.

In other terms, when an ApplyForJob conversation ends successfully, a conversation FinalizeHiring is meant to follow. The connection between these two conversations is obtained by means of notification N, which has the purpose of relaying interaction ApplyForJob.r+ from a recruiter (the source of the link) to a member of the personnel department, selected by the process. As to the notation, notification links are labeled by the interaction to be relayed written between parentheses.

The requirements do not impose on recruiters the burden to carry out an explicit conversation with the personnel department, and therefore an automatic notification is needed. Recruiters are not aware of such automatic notifications, because they are part of a higher structuring level.

The role process of recruiters, shown in Figure 6, turns out to be more complex than the one in the first version of the business process, as recruiters are involved in several conversations (of type ApplyForJob and GetReview) which need to be combined on the basis of the requirements above.

A conversation type is a model describing how the actual conversations based on that type are expected to proceed over time. This model is state-based as an actual conversation moves from state to state depending on the decisions taken by the participant involved. When several conversations need to be integrated, the standard conversation processes (derived from the corresponding conversation types) are extended with the addition of new states and with the introduction of new tasks whose actions span two or more actual conversations.

When a recruiter receives an application to evaluate, they have to get three reviews from suitable reviewers; therefore a new task askForReviews is needed. The implicit tasks, rejectRq and approveRq, are no longer needed. The effect of task askForReviews is to place the application in a new state, i.e. state p (the decision is pending), and to start three GetReview conversations, each with a distinct reviewer.

Figure 5. The model of process ApplicationHandler v.2

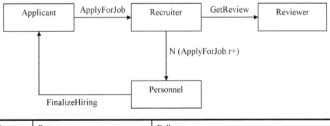

Conversation type	Pattern	Follower
ApplyForJob	SimpleCfApproval (R = Application)	The process selects one recruiter from among those associated with the position indicated in the application.
GetReview	SimpleCfA (R = Application, S = Review)	The reviewer is selected by the recruiter.
N	Notification (N = Application)	The process selects one member of the Personnel Department.
FinalizeHiring	Notification (N = Application)	The follower is the applicant related to the application.

Figure 6. The recruiter role process in business process ApplicationHandler v.2

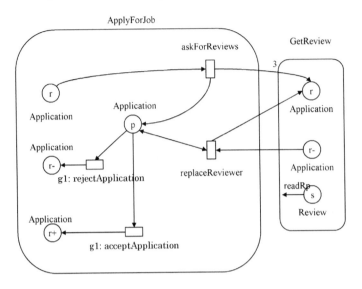

g1: 3 correlated reviews available

If a task, such as askForReviews, has two or more output states, it is not represented as a link but as a small rectangle; in general, this representation (resembling that of Petri nets) is needed when there are two or more inputs and/or two or more outputs.

If a task is connected to the initial state of a conversation process, then the execution of this task will result in the activation of a new conversation of that type; if a multiplicity (e.g. 3) is shown near the connection, then several new conversations will be started by the task.

Since the input state ApplyForJob.r and the output state GetReview.r have the same support type, the same application received with interaction ApplyForJob.r is transmitted to the outgoing interactions GetReview.r.

As a matter of fact, task askForReviews spans four conversations: the ApplyForJob conversation that triggered the execution of the task and the three GetReview conversations started by the task. Parent-child relationships are established between conversations by tasks like askForReviews: the ApplyForJob conversation can be considered as the parent of the three GetReview conversations.

This interpretation is based on the fact that task askForReviews appears inside the ApplyForJob conversation process.

Reviewers can reply with a declination or a review. In the first case, the recruiter has to involve another reviewer, as indicated by task replaceReviewer. This task, triggered by a negative conclusion of a GetReview conversation, is meant to start a new conversation GetReview with another reviewer. Task replaceReviewer spans one ApplyForJob conversation and two GetReview conversations: the newly started GetReview conversation is a child of the ApplyForJob conversation because the task belongs to the ApplyForJob conversation process.

When three reviews are available, the recruiter can either accept or reject the pending application. The corresponding tasks are called acceptApplication and rejectApplication: their effect is to move a pending application from state p to state r+ or state r-, respectively.

Such tasks are guarded because their activation is subjected to the availability of three correlated reviews (where correlation is based on parent-child relationships between conversations). A guard (e.g. g1) is a condition that has to be satisfied in order for the task to be carried out; it is given an informal description in the absence of an information model.

AGILE ROLE PROCESSES

Conversations are meant to introduce some agility in the interactions between two parties, because negotiations can take place at any stage (Winograd, 1987-1988).

In the conversation pattern SimpleCfApproval, this agility is achieved by giving the follower the opportunity of deciding which interaction to perform after receiving a request, i.e. whether to accept or reject it. Since interactions are produced by tasks, such decisions are embodied in the selection of the appropriate task to carry out. This kind of agility is referred to as conversational agility.

Another kind of agility, referred to as role agility, can be achieved at the role level, if the participants can select the tasks to perform on

the basis of their personal judgment grounded on their skills and experience.

In the recruiter process shown in Figure 6, there are two "rigid" situations, in correspondence with tasks askForReviews and replaceReviewer. These tasks are mandatory, because they have no alternatives. Too much rigidity prevents the participants from taking smart reactions in response to exceptional situations.

For example, if the application requires careful handling, the recruiter might want to involve more than three reviewers, so as to select the most appropriate reviews, or they may want to involve another reviewer as soon as they suspect that a reviewer is not going to deliver their review; or, in extreme situations, they might want to provide a review themselves.

In addition, the number of the needed reviews can be changed on the basis of urgency requirements.

A revised model of the recruiter process is shown in Figure 7. When the application is in state r, tasks askForReviews and writeReview may be

Figure 7. The agile recruiter process

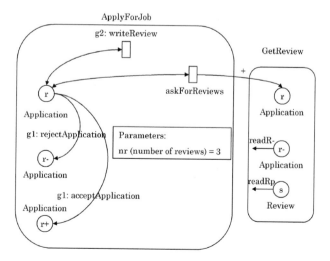

g1: the needed number of reviews (specified by parameter nr) are available

g2: the task has not yet been carried out in the current conversation

carried out in any order; for this reason, there are bidirectional links between state r and these tasks.

Task askForReviews enables the recruiter to involve one or more reviewers (and not exactly three as in the previous model, shown in Figure 6) and may be performed several times. The multiplicity "+", which is shown near the connection from this task to the initial state of conversation process GetReview, means that one or more conversations can be started by the task.

Task writeReview may be carried out once because of guard g2.

The number of the reviews required is specified by parameter nr, which may be changed occasionally, when needed.

Agile processes can be compared to maps in that they are used for orientation purposes, and not as a prescribed sequence of actions (Suchman, 1987). The emphasis is placed on the tasks to be carried out and on the artifacts to be acted on, rather than on the explicit ordering relationships between the tasks.

The role process shown in Figure 7 is a case of "constrained flexibility" (de Man, 2009), as the states of the conversations establish the flexibility regions in which the participants can take their decisions.

COOPERATIVE OBJECTS

This section discusses how the cooperative development of shared artifacts is represented in AgileBPN by means of cooperative objects. In particular the use of wiki systems is addressed, owing to their potential in terms of availability, customizability and agility in use (Neumann & Erol, 2009).

In AgileBPN, a cooperative object is an encapsulated cooperative environment, consisting of operational activities, coordination activities and the common field of work.

The common field of work of a wiki cooperative object is a collection of web pages on which

operational actions (e.g. editing) can be performed by taking advantage of the internal mechanisms of wiki systems, which include access control and version management (Bruno, 2009).

The coordination actions are mainly concerned with the handling of the working group and this takes place through conversations.

As an example, this section presents a new version of the business process ApplicationHandler in which applications are evaluated cooperatively by recruiters and reviewers. In particular, upon receiving an application, a recruiter generates a wiki document (in its initial form) and invites a number of reviewers to cooperatively write the evaluation of the application in the wiki document.

In AgileBPN, a wiki cooperative object implies two major roles, moderator and contributor. The moderator is responsible for generating the wiki document and for inviting the contributors, who act essentially as writers. The moderator is a writer as well, and, in addition, they can freeze the wiki document thus stopping further changes.

The moderator manages the working group with the simple conversations shown in Figure 8; their type is named WikiConversation.

The moderator is the initiator of the conversation, while its follower is a contributor.

The initial interaction (i) enables the moderator to invite a contributor to take part in the cooperative effort; the support entity is the wiki document to be acted on. Either party can end

Figure 8. Model of WikiConversation

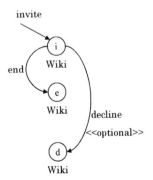

the conversation: the moderator when the editing period has elapsed, a contributor any time. Task decline is optional as indicated by the stereotype associated with the transition.

The actions and the interactions carried out through a wiki cooperative object by the moderator and the contributors can be represented by means of the behavioral model shown in Figure 9, where the left side addresses the moderator's behavior and the right side the contributor's one. The behavioral model of a cooperative object shows the tasks and the conversations pertaining to the participant roles as well as the ordering constraints. The ordering constraints depend both on the internal mechanisms (which, for example, prevent two participants from editing the same piece of document) and on coordination interactions. The behavioral model of wiki documents is named WikiDocument and draws on conversation type WikiConversation.

After generating the wiki document, the moderator is entitled to invite contributors (by starting WikiConversations with them), to contribute to the document as well as to coordinate the working group (with task moderate). State g is the initial state of the wiki document, while state e is the final state. When the time allotted to the writing

of the wiki document has elapsed, the moderator can freeze it, thus bringing it to the final state. When the wiki document is frozen, all the ongoing WikiConversations are ended.

When WikiConversations are in state g, contributors may work on the related wiki documents; they can do so until they decline or the conversations are ended by the moderator.

Tasks contribute and moderate are mapped to the internal mechanisms of wiki systems.

When a role is meant to operate on a cooperative object, there is no need to explicitly introduce the related behavioral tasks in the role process, because they are automatically implied by the cooperative object itself.

The new version of process ApplicationHandler (version 3) is shown in Figure 10. Type EvaluationWiki draws on pattern WikiDocument which is a cooperative object.

In a role process, a cooperative object appears as a building block, shown as a square, which is connected to the task meant to activate it.

The new version of the recruiter process is shown in Figure 11.

Upon receiving an application to evaluate, a recruiter performs task genWikiDocument thus producing an instance of EvaluationWiki (i.e. a

Figure 9. Behavioral model of WikiDocument

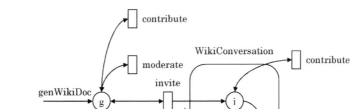

Figure 10. The model of process ApplicationHandler v.3

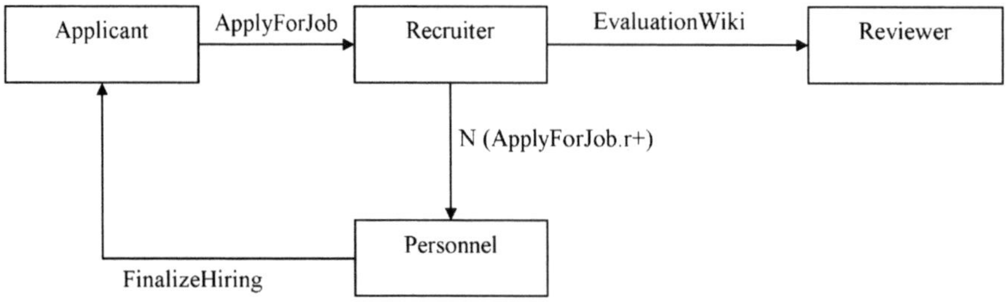

Conversation type	Pattern	Follower
ApplyForJob	SimpleCfApproval (R = Application)	The process selects one recruiter from among those associated with the position indicated in the application.
EvaluationWiki	WikiDocument	
N	Notification (N = Application)	The process selects one member of the Personnel Department.
FinalizeHiring	Notification (N = Application)	The follower is the applicant related to the application.

wiki document). Then, they can invite reviewers as contributors on the basis of the behavioral model shown in Figure 9.

Task genWikiDocument brings the application to state p; the application remains in this state until the recruiter takes the final decision, which has to be preceded by the freezing of the wiki document as prescribed by guard g1.

Figure 11. The recruiter process including a cooperative object

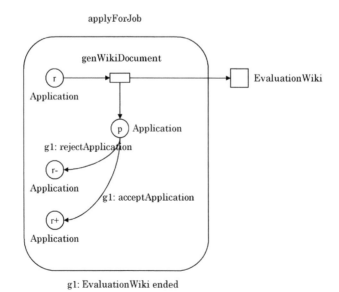

CONCLUSION

Agility is an essential feature for SMEs, since "these do not apply standardised processes to such a degree as large companies" (Riss, Rickayzen, Maus & van der Aalst, 2005).

The notations and languages for business processes differ in the viewpoints they are based on; this chapter has considered five major viewpoints (i.e. the centralized viewpoint, the role viewpoint, the conversational viewpoint, the case viewpoint and the cooperative one) and has discussed how they address agility issues. In particular, three forms of agility have been emphasized: conversational agility, role agility and group agility.

The first form is related to conversations between two parties because negotiations can take place at any stage. Role agility is the ability of the participants (playing a given role) to select the tasks to perform on the basis of their personal judgment grounded on their skills and experience.

Role agility is promoted by the case viewpoint because a participant can look at a case (i.e. the business object to be acted on) as a whole and the process evolution is driven by the state of the case rather than by the completion of its activities (Künzle & Reichert, 2009).

In this chapter, group agility is mainly related to the cooperative development of shared artifacts: in particular the use of wiki systems is addressed, owing to their potential in terms of availability, customizability and agility in use (Neumann & Erol, 2009).

A proof-of-concept notation, AgileBPN, has been presented which aims at integrating all the above-mentioned viewpoints. In AgileBPN, business processes are organized around conversations and role processes (encompassing the tasks pertaining to a given role); shared artifacts are represented as cooperative objects. The definition of a wiki cooperative object has been presented: it is a novel approach in which the operational actions related to the underlying technology are integrated with coordination activities based on conversations.

Increasing attention is expected to be directed to holistic approaches like AgileBPN, as it is now recognized that the "the most important processes for organizations today involve knowledge work" (Davenport, 2005).

There are two major directions of future development for the research presented in this chapter. One is the integration of process models and information models with the purpose of making the annotations in models more formal. The other direction is concerned with the definition of a suitable personal workspace in which participants can perform their actions and can observe the results of the actions of the other participants.

REFERENCES

Austin, J. L. (1976). *How to do things with words*. Oxford, UK: Oxford University Press.

Bruno, G. (2009). Requirements elicitation as a case of social process: an approach to its description. In *7th Int. Conference on Business Process Management: BPMS2'09 Workshop*. Springer (in press).

Davenport, T. H. (1993). *Process innovation*. Boston: Harvard Business School Press.

Davenport, T. H. (2005). *Thinking for a living*. Boston: Harvard Business School Press.

de Man, H. (2009). Case management: Cordys approach. *BPTrends*. Retrieved September 18, 2009, from http://www.bptrends.com.

Decker, G., & Weske, M. (2007). Local enforceability in Interaction Petri Nets. [New York: Springer.]. *Lecture Notes in Computer Science, 4714*, 305–319. doi:10.1007/978-3-540-75183-0_22

Dietz, J. L. G. (2003). The atoms, molecules and fibers of organizations. *Data & Knowledge Engineering, 47*(3), 301–325. doi:10.1016/S0169-023X(03)00062-4

Dietz, J. L. G. (2006). The Deep Structure of Business Processes. *Communications of the ACM, 49*(5), 59–64. doi:10.1145/1125944.1125976

Dumas, M., van der Aalst, W. M. P., & ter Hofstede, A. H. M. (2005). *Process-Aware Information Systems: bridging people and software through process technology*. New York: Wiley. doi:10.1002/0471741442

Hofreiter, B., Huemer, C., & Winiwarter, W. (2005). Business collaboration models and their business context-dependent web choreography in BPSS. *International Journal of Web Information Systems, 1*(1), 33–42. doi:10.1108/17440080580000081

Holt, A. W. (1985). Coordination technology and Petri nets. [New York: Springer.]. *Lecture Notes in Computer Science, 222*, 278–296. doi:10.1007/BFb0016217

Kaplan, S. M., & Carroll, A. M. (1992). Supporting Collaborative Processes with ConversationBuilder. *Computer Communications, 15*(8), 489–501. doi:10.1016/0140-3664(92)90028-D

Künzle, V., & Reichert, M. (2009). Towards object-aware process management systems: issues, challenges, benefits. In *Lecture Notes in Business Information Processing, 29* (pp. 197–210). New York: Springer.

Leuf, B., & Cunningham, W. (2001). *The Wiki way: quick collaboration on the web*. Reading, MA: Addison-Wesley.

Medina-Mora, R., Winograd, T., Flores, R., & Flores, F. (1992). The Action Workflow approach to workflow management technology. In J. Turner & R. Kraut (Eds.), *4th Conference on Computer Supported Cooperative Work*. New York: ACM.

Neumann, G., & Erol, S. (2009). From a social wiki to a social workflow system. In *Lecture Notes in Business Information Processing, 17* (pp. 698–708). New York: Springer.

OASIS. (2007). *Web Services Business Process Execution Language, V.2.0*. Retrieved September 18, 2009, from http://docs.oasis-open.org/wsbpel/2.0/wsbpel-v2.0.pdf.

OMG. (2005). *UML 2.0 OCL Specification*. Retrieved September 18, 2009, from http://www.omg.org/docs/ptc/ 05-06-06.pdf.

OMG. (2007). *Unified Modeling Language: Superstructure, V.2.1.1*. Retrieved September 18, 2009, from http://www.omg.org/docs/formal/07-02-03.pdf.

OMG. (2008). *Business Process Modeling Notation, V.1.1*. Retrieved September 18, 2009, from http://www.bpmn.org.

Ould, M. (2005). *Business Process Management: a rigorous approach*. The British Computer Society.

Riss, U. V., Rickayzen, A., Maus, H., & van der Aalst, W. M. P. (2005). Challenges for business process and task management. *Journal of Universal Knowledge Management, 0*(2), 77–100.

Schmidt, K., & Simone, C. (1996). Coordination mechanisms: towards conceptual foundation of CSCW systems design. *Computer Supported Cooperative Work, 5*, 155–200. doi:10.1007/BF00133655

Suchman, L. A. (1987). *Plans and situated actions: the problem of human-machine communication*. Cambridge, UK: Cambridge University Press.

Thom, L. H., Reichert, M., & Iochpe, C. (2009). Activity patterns in Process-Aware Information Systems: basic concepts and empirical evidence. *International Journal of Business Process Integration and Management, 4*(2), 93–110. doi:10.1504/IJBPIM.2009.027778

van der Aalst, W. M. P., Weske, M., & Grünbauer, D. (2005). Case handling: a new paradigm for business process support. *Data & Knowledge Engineering, 53*(2), 129–162. doi:10.1016/j.datak.2004.07.003

Weigand, H. (2006). Two decades of the Language-Action Perspective: introduction. *Communications of the ACM, 49*(5), 44–46. doi:10.1145/1125944.1125973

Winograd, T. (1987-1988). A Language/Action Perspective on the design of cooperative work. *Human-Computer Interaction, 3,* 3–30. doi:10.1207/s15327051hci0301_2

Zaha, J. M., Dumas, M., ter Hofstede, A. H. M., Barros, A., & Decker, G. (2008). Bridging global and local models of service-oriented systems. *IEEE Transactions on Systems, Man and Cybernetics. Part C, Applications and Reviews, 38*(3), 302–318. doi:10.1109/TSMCC.2008.919193

Chapter 6

E-Procurement Process:
Negotiation and Auction Approaches for SMEs

Paolo Renna
University of Basilicata, Italy

Pierluigi Argoneto
University of Basilicata, Italy

ABSTRACT

E-procurement transactions in Business to Business (B2B) environment showed a constant and positive trend in the last years. The most popular methodologies to support these tools are all related to dedicated protocols able to facilitate the agreements among customers and suppliers. This chapter proposes a Multi Agent Architecture integrated with several multi-attribute auction mechanisms specifically designed to support the e-procurement processes. Moreover, differently from other cases proposed in literature, the suppliers' proposal formulation is strongly influenced by their production plans. A simulative environment has been developed in order to evaluate different performances: the customer and suppliers' utilities, the profit distribution among the involved agents and the time necessary to reach an agreement. The mentioned approaches are compared with a negotiation process. The simulation results highlight the weakness and strength points of each auction protocol and why they can be considered as a relevant tool in B2B environments.

INTRODUCTION

The growth of Information and Communication Technologies (hereafter ICT) changed the way the enterprises do their business. Among the newest procurement mechanisms, auction and negotiation are the most used in B2B transactions. The procurement process in B2B involves buyers that require good or services and suppliers that can provide them. Generally, this is a multi-attribute process and it includes variable as price, volume, due date, quality, etc. Electronic procurement

DOI: 10.4018/978-1-60960-463-9.ch006

(hereafter e-procurement) is the procurement process performed through ICT and network systems. The benefits of e-procurement compared to traditional procurement process can be summarized as follows (Favier et al., 2000; Ordanini et al.,2004):

- an higher number of suppliers can be involved in the process;
- a strong reduction of transaction costs could be reached (both considering purchasing and processing costs);
- more rapid information flow on inventory is possible because of the reduction of stock levels and, therefore, of the inventory costs;
- an increasing level of service to the customers as a consequence of all the previous point.

To reach these results, Multi Agent Systems (hereafter MAS) are the most common technology utilized to sustain the e-procurement processes. An agent is defined as an autonomous problem solving unit that may collaborate with other agents and that tries to achieve optimized results in its problem area (Bradshaw, 1997; Turowski, 2002). In e-procurement applications that technology is the most appropriate tool to be implemented in order to make transactions able to take into accounts both buyers and sellers' identities and goals, providing a better global satisfaction (Favir et al., 2000). Generally speaking, the dispute among buyers and suppliers has been mainly solved by using two approaches: negotiation and auction. Negotiation can be defined as a form of decision making process where two or more parties jointly search a space of possible solution with the goal reaching a deal (Rosenschein and Zlotkin, 1994). An electronic negotiation protocol is a model of the negotiation process in which at least some activities are supported or performed by information systems and the remainder is conducted with an electronic medium. The protocol may be complex and with many rules governing the parties as they move through different stages and phases of the process. Typically, designers try to achieve certain goals for the outcome of a negotiation and for the negotiation process itself, such as, Pareto optimality of the result, maximization of the bid taker's revenue/utility, stability, and speed of convergence (Raiffa, 1996). These objectives are achieved through:

- specification of the structure of the negotiation problem and process,
- specification of rules of feasible activities, and their sequencing and timing; and
- imposition of limitations on the form and content of information exchange.

Every electronic negotiation protocol restricts the negotiators' freedom in order to meet one or more of the above objectives. Generally, the following parameters are used to evaluate the results of the negotiation:

- *time*: negotiations that end without delay are preferable to negotiations that are time-consuming. It will be assumed that a delay in reaching an agreement causes an increase in the cost of communication and computation time spent on the negotiation. We want to prevent the agents from spending too much time on negotiation resulting in not keeping to their timetables for satisfying their goals;
- *efficiency*: it is preferred that the outcome of the negotiations will be efficient. It increases the number of agents that will be satisfied by the negotiation results and the agents' satisfaction levels from the negotiation results. Thus it is preferable that the agents reach Pareto optimal agreements;
- *simplicity*: negotiation processes that are simple and efficient are preferable to complex processes. Being a "simple strategy" means that it is feasible to build it into an

automated agent. A "simple strategy" is also one that an agent will be able to compute in a reasonable amount of time;

- *stability*: a set of negotiation strategies for a given set of agents is stable if, given that all the other agents included in the set are following their strategies, it is beneficial to an agent to follow its strategy too. Negotiation protocols that have stable strategies are more useful in multi-agent environments than protocols that are unstable.

Differently, auction theory is an applied branch of game theory and is not commonly applied as a protocol for B2B interactions. Also in this case, there are many possible designs, or sets of rules that can be used: typical issues studied by auction theorists include the efficiency of a given auction design, optimal and equilibrium bidding strategies and revenue comparison. Carter et al. (2004) defined an electronic auction (e-auction) as a real-time auction between a buyer (including an organization) and multiple invited suppliers, where suppliers can submit several bids during the specified time period of the auction. Within the first ten years of its usage, from 1995 until 2004, e-auctions were involved in transactions totaling over $70 billion worth of goods and services (Zaccone, 2004). Five different types of e-auctions could be found (Buxton, 2008):

1. *Reverse English*; this kind of auction is the most common type of procurement sale. Bidders offer decreasing prices to be able to sell their product to the buyer;
2. *Reverse Japanese*; in a Reverse Japanese Auction, the price of an item is continually decreased, according to a specified decrement, and at pre-set intervals. Bidders must place a bid at each interval to continue participating in the market. The auction closes when a single supplier, the lowest bidder, remains in the market.

3. *Sealed first-price auction*; in this kind of auction all bidders simultaneously submit sealed bids so that no bidder knows the bid of any other participant. The highest bidder pays the price they submitted [McAfee and McMillan,1987]. This type of auction is distinct from the English auction, in that bidders can only submit one bid each. Furthermore, as bidders cannot see the bids of other participants they cannot adjust their own bids accordingly.
4. *Vickrey auction*; this mechanism is identical to the sealed first-price auction except that the winning bidder pays the second highest bid rather than their own [Krishna, 2002].
5. *Weighted/Multi-Attribute*; in this case a score function is defined as a factor that represents the value of bid.

There are many contradictory opinions on the value of e-auctions in the marketplace and who, if anyone, benefit most. There is increasing evidence from the private sector and wider public sector that e-auctions can deliver incremental benefits (Kumar and Chang, 2007) as:

- incremental savings in the cost of goods and services;
- savings in process time and costs associated with the Best and Final Offer (BAFO) stage of a procurement;
- valuable intangible benefits such as:
  - suppliers' standardized processes and communication throughout the BAFO stage;
  - encouraging unambiguous and accurate specification which helps to crystallize the buyer's requirement and provides the necessary clarity between buyer and supplier;
  - producing a history of the BAFO process that would highlight the impartiality of the buyer's sourcing decisions. Internal audit departments

see this as being advantageous, particularly if they wish to review the audit trail for the award of a particular contract.

Summarizing, the mechanism promotes costs savings while increasing access to potential suppliers and enhancing buyer supplier relationships (Losch and Lambert, 2007). Opponents to the system suggest the costs savings are smaller than most expect or often nonexistent when the total procurement costs are considered (Emiliani, 2006). Starting from this analysis, the focus of the chapter concerns the development and evaluation of different auction mechanisms in a neutral e-marketplace for B2B applications. The methodology to support the e-marketplace is based on MAS and the computation of the performances is obtained by a discrete event simulation tool. A negotiation approach is used as a benchmark.

The remainder is structured as follow: Section 2 presents an overview of the literature concerning auction protocols in e-procurement; Section 3 discusses the difference between negotiation and auction while the Multi Agent Architecture is illustrated in Section 4. The proposed negotiation protocol is described in Section 5. The best supplier auction, the modified Vickrey auction and the one shot auctions are respectively presented in Section 6, Section 7 and Section 8. The developed simulation environment and the simulation results are respectively presented in Sections 9 and Section 10. Finally, conclusions and further research paths are withdrawn in Section 11.

LITERATURE REVIEW

Many authors proposed researches concerning electronic procurement applications in B2B environment. Beil and Wein (2003) considered a manufacturer who uses a reverse, or procurement, auction to determine which supplier will be awarded a contract. Each bid consists of a price and a set of non price attributes (e.g., quality, lead time, etc.). The manufacturer is assumed to know the parametric form of the suppliers' cost functions (in terms of the non price attributes), but has no prior information on the parameter values. The proposed mechanism, indeed, maximizes the manufacturer's utility within the open-ascending format. Chen Ritzo et al. (2005) compare the multi-attribute auctions with the price-only auctions. They presented an ascending auction mechanism for a buyer whose utility function is known and dependent on three attributes; in particular, they considered quality and lead time for the two attributes in addition to price. Compared with the price-only auction, they find that the mechanism designed was effective in increasing both buyer utility and bidder (supplier) profits. Parkes and Kalagnanam (2005) provided an iterative auction design for an important special case of the multi-attribute allocation problem with special (preferential independent) additive structure on the buyer value and seller costs. Auction *Additive & Discrete* provides a refined design for a price-based auction in which the price feedback decomposes to an additive part with a price for each attribute and an aggregate part that appears as a price discount for each supplier. In addition, this design also has excellent information revelation properties that are validated through computational experiments. The auction terminates with an outcome of a modified Vickrey-Clarke-Groves (hereafter VCG) mechanism. Jin et al. (2006) discussed multiple unit auctions for industrial procurement where the cost structures of suppliers capture economies and diseconomies of scale caused by the nature of the production cost and the opportunity value of suppliers' capacities. They proposed a Binary Tree algorithm with Bounds (hereafter BTB) which efficiently exploits the model as optimality properties. BTB outperforms general integer optimization software in computational time, especially with existence of substantial economies and diseconomies of scale. Zhang et al. (2007) studied iterative multi-attribute auctions for multi-unit procurement. A mechanism called Iterative Multi-attribute Multi-unit Reverse Auction (hereafter IMMRA) was proposed based on the assumption of the modified myopic best-response strategies. Results from numerical experiments show that the IMMRA achieves market efficiency in most instances. The inefficiency occurs occasionally in special cases when cost structures are significantly different among suppliers. Numerical results also show that the IMMRA results in lower buyer payments than the traditional Vickrey- Clarke-Grove payments in most cases without significantly hurting market efficiency. Goeree et al. (2006) compare the performances of first price simultaneous, first price sequential, simultaneous descending and simultaneous ascending auctions in various bidding environments with single-unit demands. They find that simultaneous ascending auctions are the most efficient, but at the same time they yield lower and more variable revenues than other auction formats. Renna (2009) discussed the evaluation of real added-value services in e-business applications. In particular, an innovative approach has been proposed through a link between production plan and negotiation in a neutral e-marketplace. The methodology is based on a multi-agent architecture and on an open source simulation tool. The research underlines how, through the simulation, real added value can be evaluated and who, among customers and suppliers, have more opportunity to improve their business. In particular, three approaches have been tested: negotiation, auction and cooperation. From the analysis of the literature in here analyzed, the following limits can be highlighted:

- the most part of researches, concerning auction mechanism, do not have any link with suppliers' production plan information;
- the proposed protocols are evaluated by using some test case, but never in a dynamic environment;

- the most part of researches deeply investigate the agreement in a negotiation (very often involving just two agents), but anyone evaluate the real value added by this approach and how the generated utility is distributed among suppliers and buyers participating to an e-marketplace.

This chapter aims at understanding what kind of advantages can get both suppliers and buyers by the implementation of a particular auction mechanism and under which conditions it could be particularly advantageous apply one of them instead of another. The research presented in this chapter differs form the ones reported in literature on the following innovative aspects:

- the auction mechanisms are implemented using information coming from the agent's production plan and, therefore, is more realistic;
- several auction mechanisms are fully implemented and compared among them with a complete statistical test case;
- a discrete simulation environment has been developed in order to test all the approaches in a dynamic environment. The objective is to develop a decision support system able to select the more appropriate auction mechanism to use, depending on the environment conditions.

Before deeply explain our model, the following section describes some theoretical concerns regarding negotiation and auction.

AUCTIONS VS. NEGOTIATIONS

This section lays out some insights based on the theoretical literature related to the choice of award mechanisms. In an important paper, Goldberg (1977) recognized that "competitive bidding is one of several devices for transmitting information between organizations. As such it is both a substitute and complement for alternative devices such as negotiated contracts". Furthermore, as Goldberg explains, the information transmitted by an auction is primarily restricted to price, and when projects are complex the relative significance of price may be dwarfed by other considerations, such as how to deal with adaptation due to unforeseen events and problems. Indeed, it is widely believed that when competitive bidding is used to award what is typically a fixed-price or unit-price contract, the contractors strategically read the plans and specifications to determine where they will fail. To see this consider a contractor who sees a flaw in the plans can use this information to submit a low bid, and recover significant profits when necessary changes are implemented. Thus, competitive bidding may lead to adverse selection, which is more problematic when projects are complex. This disadvantage of auctions has been recognized by Goldberg (1977) who writes that "in competitive bidding for complex contracts, conveyance of information at the pre-contract stage is likely to be a substantial problem". The industry literature suggests that one merit of negotiations is that buyers and contractors spend more time discussing the project and ironing out possible pitfalls before work begins and that complementing this with cost-plus contracts will allow for the needed flexibility of adapting work for complex projects. This argument leads to the consideration that more complex projects are more likely to be negotiated, and as such, a positive correlation between project complexity and the choice of negotiations exists. A more recent paper by Bajari and Tadelis (2001) explores the effects of complexity on contractual choice, not award mechanisms. They show that fixed price contracts provide good ex ante cost incentives but impose high frictions when ex post adaptations are needed. Cost plus contracts, on the other hand, better accommodate ex post adaptation but suffer from the lack of ex ante cost incentives. They conclude that fixed-price contracts perform well for simple projects with

few anticipated changes, while cost-plus contracts are better suited for more complex projects, for which many changes are anticipated. As most practitioners agree, "a cost-plus contract does not lend itself well to competitive bidding." (Heinze, 1993). Indeed, most negotiated contracts are of the cost-plus-fee type. On the other hand, once a set of blueprints is in place for a fixed-price contract, it is rather straightforward to request fixed-price bids and adopt an auction. The second consideration is regarding a rather straightforward implication of auction theory. It is well known that increasing the number of bidders in an auction will reduce the expected winning bid. Therefore, in a situation in which there are few bidders available to participate in an auction, the gains from holding the auction will be relatively low and in turn, negotiations will more likely be seen as the chosen mechanism. Thus, in environments where there are more available bidders, the likelihood of choosing auctions will increase. The arguments above imply a causal relationship between project characteristics (complexity) and award mechanisms and environmental characteristics (degree of competition) and award mechanisms. A third consideration is implied from the first one, though the causal relationship may be less clear. When negotiation is considered it is common practice for a private owner to forgo the competitive bidding process entirely and to hand-pick a contractor on the basis of reputation and overall qualifications to do the job. This is consistent with an argument that more expertise is needed to complete complex projects, and such expertise is part of a contractor's reputation. Thus, we would expect more reputable contractors to be selected when negotiations are used. This argument assumes that the choice of award mechanism is independent of the set of available contractors and that therefore the choice is sequential: first an award mechanism is chosen and then the buyer searches for a reputable and competent contractor. One might argue that the mere existence of reputable contractors may make negotiations with such a contractor more attractive, causing the buyer to forgo competition. This is less likely to be beneficial if the project is simple, since reputation for competency may no and should not imply that the contractor will offer attractive cost bids. Hence, if competence concerns are not an issue, even the availability of a reputable contractor should not induce a buyer to forego competition. Nevertheless, this reverse causality cannot be refuted, but the empirical hypothesis is the same: more reputable and experience contractors should be selected when negotiations are used. As the simulation output seems to suggest us, for the issue and the typology of exchanged goods considered in this chapter, both negotiation and auction approaches can be fruitfully applied as a reward mechanism for SME's involved in an e-markeplace

MULTI AGENT ARCHITECTURE

In this paragraph is reported a brief description of the Multi Agent Architecture proposed in [Renna, 2009]. Figure 1 shows the class diagram: as therein showed, seven classes can be detected:

- *planner*; this class, operating in the simulation environment, has in charge the data setting and the initialization of all the considered parameters;
- *model*; this class controls the events occurring among customers and suppliers. In particular, it supervises the orders data requested by the customers, the identification of the registered participants and the events timetable. Initially it operates by monitoring the negotiation, then collecting the final reports;
- *customer*; it is in charge of manage data regarding orders and to define the optimal strategy to adopt during the negotiation/auction stage. It operates by using the negotiation/auction algorithm to manage the knowledge during the interaction phases;
- *customers' database*; this class manages the customers' knowledge stored in a spe-

Figure 1. Class diagram

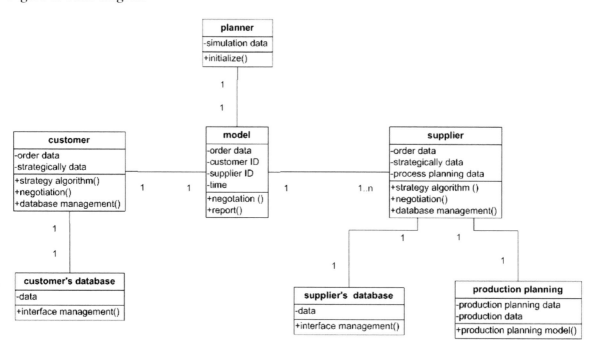

cific database by using an opportune interface linked to the previous described class;

- *supplier*; this class receives the orders data and knows the strategies regarding the suppliers as well as the process plan data. It operates by using the negotiation/auction algorithm and communicate with the production plan class in order to obtain the process plan alternatives;
- *production planning*; it manages both production planning data and orders features requested by the customers. It operates by using the production planning algorithm in order to provide the production planning alternatives to the suppliers' class;
- *suppliers' database*; this class manages the knowledge regarding the suppliers: it is stored in a specific database by an appropriate interface linked to the suppliers' class.

NEGOTIATION PROCESS

Figure 2 shows, through an UML activity diagram, the detail of the negotiation process involving Customer Negotiation Agent (CNA), Supplier Negotiation Agent (SNA) and Supplier Planning Agent (SPA).

The activities of the agents are the following:

- The CNA puts the order on the network of suppliers and negotiates it with the SNA;
- The SNA, who is in charge with order processing and counter-proposal formulation;
- The SPA receives information on the order characteristics (volume, price and due date) and provides the production planning alternatives to the SNA.

The process is characterized by the following characteristics (Negotiation constraints):

- the negotiation is a multi-lateral one and it involves one customer and many suppliers (one to many approach);
- the negotiation is an iterative process with a maximum number of rounds, r_{max}; after that an agreement is reached or the negotiation fails;
- during each round the supplier can submit a new counter-proposal (N) to the customer while, at $r=r_{max}$, it can only accept (A) or reject (R) the proposal;
- the agreement is reached only if, at round $r<r_{max}$, the customer accepts the supplier's counter proposal; in this case customer and supplier sign an electronic contract;
- supplier and customer's behavior is assumed to be rationale according to their utility functions;
- the customer does not know suppliers' utility functions and vice versa; however supplier and customer can only argue, by applying a proper learning algorithms, the oncoming behavior of their counterparts.

The negotiation process starts with the customer's order submission. The order is processed through the *Customer Order Inputting Menu* and it is delivered to the CNA. The order is represented by the array (i, V_i, dd_i, p_i), being $i \in \{1,...,n\}$ the selected product from the supplier's catalogue, V_i the required quantity, dd_i the suitable delivery date and p_i the asked price.

The activity diagram of Figure 2 carries out the following actions:

- *Transmits order*; the CNA transmits the order array (i, V_i, dd_i, p_i) to the SNA;

Figure 2. UML Activity diagram

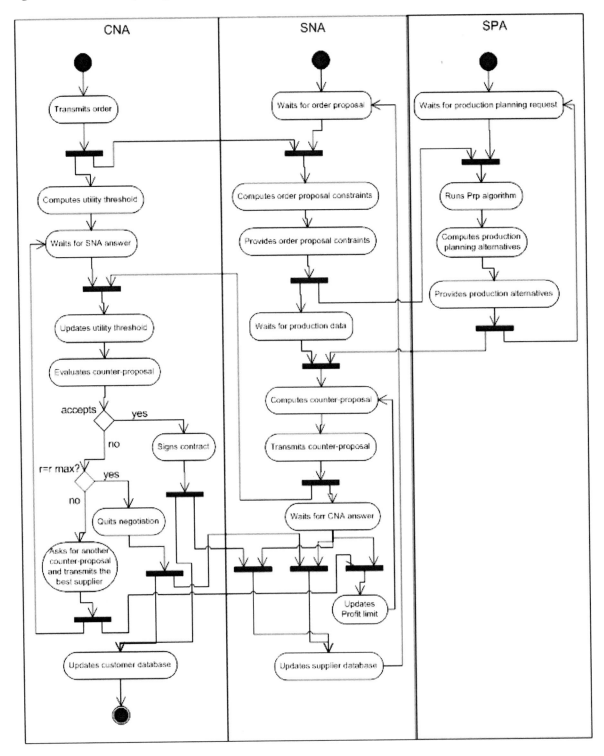

Computes utility threshold; The CNA computes its utility function and the lower threshold level according to the following expression (1):

$$Thu(r) = Thu_{max} \cdot \left(1 - \frac{r-1}{r_{max}-1}\right)^2 + F \cdot \left(\frac{r-1}{r_{max}-1}\right)$$

$$\left(1 - \frac{r-1}{r_{max}-1}\right) + Thu_{min} \cdot \left(\frac{r-1}{r_{max}-1}\right)^2$$

(1)

where:

- Thu_{max} is given by the sum of the maximum values reached by the considered utility functions (obtained when all the requested parameters are fully satisfied);
- F is the utility function slope.
  - *Computes Order Proposal Constraints;* the SNA computes a feasible range of variation of both the required price (Δp_i) and due date (Δdd_i) by using the values reported in Table 2;
  - *Provides Order Proposal Constraints;* the values Δp_i and Δdd_i are transmitted to the SPA and they will be considered as bounds by the agents;
  - *Runs PrP;* the SPA runs the production planning (PrP) algorithm (for details see Perrone et al., 2005);
  - *Computes Production Alternatives;* as output of the PrP algorithm, the SPA computes an array of production planning alternatives PA_j $(j=1...m)$ that associate a supplier profit (Pr_j) and an offered volume (V_j) to each combination of offered due date (dd_j) and price (p_j), that is $PA_j = (Pr_j, V_j, dd_j, p_j) \; \forall j$, where $V_j \leq V_i$;

- Provides production alternatives; the set of values PA_j is transmitted to the SNA;
- Computes counter-proposal; if $r=1$, the SNA builds the set of alternatives $K_0 = \{1,2,..k,...,n^*\}$ such as:

$$Pr_k = Pr_{max} = \max_{j=1,...,n} \{Pr_j\} \; \forall k \in K_0 \qquad (2)$$

and it searches within K_0 for the alternative j^* such as:

$$j^* | \min_{j \in K_0} \left(\frac{|dd_j - dd_i| + |p_j - p_i| + |V_j - V_i|}{3} \right) \qquad (3)$$

On the other hand, if $r>1$, the SNA applies a profit reduction strategy according to the negotiation round: it computes the new acceptable profit at the round r as reported in (4):

$$Pr_r = Pr_{max} - \frac{PR_{max} - PR_{min}}{r_{max}} \cdot r \text{, being the}$$

value PR_{min} reported in Table 2. (4)

Afterwards SNA builds the set of production alternatives $Kr = \{1,2,..k,...,m^*\}$ such that:

$$Pr_k \geq Pr_r \; \forall k \in K_r \qquad (5)$$

and it finds the alternative j^* that minimizes the relation (3) with $j \in Kr$. The array (V_j^*, dd_j^*, p_j^*), both in cases $r = 1$ and $r > 1$, represents the supplier counter-proposal;

- *Transmits counter proposal;* the array (V_j^*, dd_j^*, p_j^*) is transmitted to the CNA. The SNA remains waiting for a CNA request;

- *Updates utility thresholds*; the CNA updates the utility function thresholds at the round *r* according to the expression (1).

Evaluates counter-proposal; the CNA evaluates the utility related to the counter-proposal:

$$U_r^{c\cdot p} = U_v + U_{dd} + U_p \qquad (6)$$

where U_v, U_{dd}, U_p are respectively the utilities of the volume, the due date and the price, computed as reported in (7), (8) and (9):

$$U_v = \max\left(\left(\frac{V_{j*} - V_{min}}{V_i - V_{min}}\right); 0\right), \text{ being } V_{min} = 0.3 * V_i; \qquad (7)$$

$$U_{dd} = Max\left(Min\left(\frac{dd_{j*} - dd_{min}}{dd_i - dd_{min}}; \frac{dd_{max} - dd_{j*}}{dd_{max} - dd_i}\right); 0\right)$$
, being $dd_{max} = dd_i + 5$ and $dd_{min} = dd_i - 5$, (8)

$$U_p = \begin{cases} Min\left(\left(\frac{p_i}{p_{j*}}\right); 1\right), & if\ p_{j*} < p_{max} \\ 0 & otherwise \end{cases}, \text{ being}$$
$p_{max} = 1.6 * p_i$. (9)

In case $U_r^{c\cdot p} \geq Thu(r)$, the CNA accepts (A) the counter-proposal and it signs the agreement with SNA; afterwards they update their database with the agreement data. Conversely, if $U_r^{c\cdot p} < Thu(r)$ and $r < r_{max}$, CNA asks for a new counter-proposal (N) otherwise, if $r = r_{max}$, CNA rejects the proposal and quits the negotiation.

The constants reported in equations (7, 8, and 9 means that the customer sets the limit for an acceptable counter-proposal; for each of them the satisfaction is null if the counter-proposal goes over these limits. These values contribute to the customer's strategy development.

BEST SUPPLIER AUCTION (BSA)

The auction mechanism in here proposed is dissimilar from the explained negotiation process: consequently, in order to compare this two approaches, the auction timeline has been fixed equal to the maximum round r_{max} and the first proposal, submitted by the SNA, is computed as in the negotiation protocol. Subsequently, at the end of each step, the CNA transmits to all the involved agents the information regarding the identity of the supplier who made the best proposal. This knowledge allows, at the subsequent rounds, to the improvement of all the proposals except for the best one. This rule is utilized to protect the suppliers' profit: in fact it could be strong reduced because of an indiscriminate modification of all the bids. At the last round, in case the utility related to one of them (computed as reported in equation 6) is bigger than the threshold value, the CNA signs the agreement with the supplier who made the best proposal. To obtain an homogeneous comparison between the models, the considered utility threshold is represented in Figure 3: in case $r < r_{max}$ the values are constant and equal to Thu_{max}, differently, when $r = r_{max}$ the value is the same obtainable at the last round of negotiation (putting the value $r = r_{max}$ in equation (1)).

Figure 3. Customer Threshold function

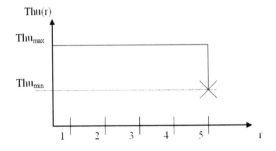

The main characteristics of the BSA are the following:

- at each step, all the suppliers are forced to improve their bids in order to satisfy the customer's request, except for the one who made the best proposal;
- information regarding the identity of the best supplier allows to improve the global utility only if a real competition is present. In fact, it is obvious that the best supplier will not improve its proposal until when other suppliers do not demonstrate to be competitive (i.e. they will be able to submit a new better proposal). In this way, the advantage obtained by the customer is balanced by this shared information;
- the approach could be compared with the negotiation because of the possibility to follow the same timeline until its maximum value ($r=r_{max}$).

MODIFIED VICKREY AUCTION (MVA)

The traditional Vickrey protocol regards auction with one attribute, generally the price. It is a type of sealed-bid auction: all bidders simultaneously submit sealed bids so that no bidder knows the bid of any other participant. In this research is proposed a *modified Vickrey auction*: it is a multi-attribute auction (volume, due date and price are considered) in which the proposals are elaborated taking into account information coming from the agents' production plan. The basic agents' behaviors are described in Figure 2. The approach in here proposed follows the classical formulation proposed by Vickrey in his original paper: the highest bidder wins, but the price paid is the second-highest bid. The difference lies in the fact that the "price" concept has been substituted by the "utility" one (see equation 6). Specifically: the seller's bid, elaborated by the SNA, is computed as explained for the negotiation: in case

two bids fully satisfy the customer's request the process ends, otherwise it keeps on. At each subsequent round, until $r=r_{max}$, the suppliers improve their proposals. At the end of the auction the CNA evaluate the best two bids, named $(V_{b1}, dd_{b1}, p_{b1})$ and $(V_{b2}, dd_{b2}, p_{b2})$ -both satisfying the minimum threshold value $U_{r}^{c-p} \geq Thu(r)$ - and signs the agreement with the agent who submitted the proposal with the maximum related utility. Supposing to be the supplier *1* the winner, and to keep maintain the parallel with the original Vickrey auction, the attributes it has to satisfy are relaxed taking into account the second best proposal. Particularly, the CNA transmits to the winner these parameters:

- $V^*=Min(V_{b1}, V_{b2})$: that choice gives to the winning supplier the chance to provide a minor quantity of volume in confront to the value expressed in the best proposal: at the same time, having considered the global utility related to the bids and not the single elements in it, the second best proposal could be characterized by an attribute $V_2 > V_1$. In this case the winning supplier could not be forced to supply the volume V_2, because of its production planning constraints, and maintain its original proposal V_1;
- $dd^*=Max(dd_{b1}, dd_{b2})$; the customer allows the best supplier to extend the due date to the value proposed in the second best proposal;
- $p^*=Max(p_{b1}, p_{b2})$; the price can be incremented considering the price expressed in the second best proposal.

At this point, the SNA runs its production planning algorithm maximizing its profit with the constraints (V^*, dd^*, p^*) and transmits the definitive parameters to the CNA. Finally, the CNA computes its new utility value and updates its database.

The characteristics of the MVA could be summarized as follows:

- the suppliers are forced to improve the proposal in order to satisfy the order's attribute until the last step, except for the case in which at least two proposals fully satisfies the customer's request;
- the tradeoff between customer and supplier, with this approach, is obtained by the attributes relaxation considering the second best proposal;
- also this case could be compared with the negotiation, because of the possibility to follow the same timeline until its maximum value ($r=r_{max}$).

ONE SHOT AUCTIONS

In the following explained cases, the customer try to reach an agreement in a single step. Each supplier submit a bid to the customer: if the best among the proposals has an utility greater than threshold value, computed as in equation (6), the agreement is signed. Each supplier has to perform some strategy to select, among all the alternatives, the definitive bid. In this chapter two different policies have been adopted: the *maximum customer's benefit* and the *expected profit*.

Policy 1: Maximum Customer's Benefit (MCB)

In this policy, firstly the supplier computes a minimum acceptable value (threshold) regarding its profit. This value is computed by using the expression (4), putting $r=r_{max}$. Potentially, each proposal with a profit greater than the threshold could be utilised as a bid for the customer. The selected one will be the proposal obtained by using the equation (3).

Theoretically, this strategy should lead to the maximum benefit for the customer, but at the same time leads to the reduction of the supplier's profit. This policy is used as a benchmark for all other approaches, but particularly for the one proposed in the next paragraph. The characteristics of the MCB can be summarized as follows:

- the willing time in which is possible to find an agreement is really short, because the protocol is performed in just one shot;
- the agents with this policy have a very low "intelligence";
- the suppliers' point of view is taken into account at all.

Policy 2: Expected Profit (ExP)

In this case, each supplier decides which proposal submits to the customer computing its expected profit. The way they do this is explained by the following algorithm:

the probability to win the auction is computed, among all the production alternatives PA_j, as:

$$Prob_j = \frac{1}{3}\left(Prob_V + Prob_{dd} + Prob_p\right) \qquad (10)$$

being:

$$Prob_V = \frac{V_j}{V_i}, \qquad (10.a)$$

$$Prob_{dd} = \left[1 - \left(\frac{|dd_j - dd_i|}{dd_{max} - dd_i}\right)\right], \qquad (10.b)$$

$$Prob_p = \frac{1}{p_{max} - p_i}\left[Min\left(\frac{p_i}{p_j}, 1\right) - \frac{p_i}{p_{max}}\right], \qquad (10.c)$$

Figure 4. Volume probability

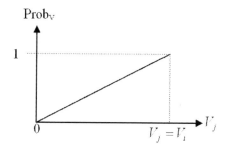

with *ith* and *jth* indexes already defined.

The expression (10) represent a normalized average: the more the output is higher the more the *jth* counter-proposal is closer to the customer's request and, therefore, the more increases the probability to obtain an agreement. In particular, expression (10) is composed by three different components $\left(Prob_V, Prob_{dd}, Prob_p\right)$: their trends are respectively reported in Figure 4, Figure 5 and Figure 6.

The probability regarding the volume ($Prob_V$) assumes is higher value when the supplier exactly offers the volume required by the customer. It decreases proportionally to the difference existing between these two values.

The probability regarding the due date ($Prob_{dd}$) assumes is higher value when the supplier exactly offer the value of due date required by the customer. It decreases proportionally to the increment of the delay: the minimum (null) value is reached when the due date assumes its maximum value (dd_{max}).

The probability regarding the price ($Prob_p$) assumes is higher value when the supplier exactly offers the price required by the customer. It decreases proportionally to the increment of the price: the minimum (null) value is reached when the price assumes its maximum value (p_{max}).

the second step is the evaluation of the expected profit (*ExP*) for each production alternatives, computed by the following expression (11):

Figure 5. Due date probability

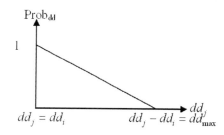

$$Ex\,P_j = Pr_j \cdot Prob_j\,, j=1...m \qquad (11)$$

It estimates the profit that the supplier can gain with the generic production alternative PA_j, for each *j* value;

finally, the supplier choose the bid to submit to the customer by using the expression (12):

$$PA_{j*}\,|\,j = \max_j\left(Ex\,P_j\right) \qquad (12)$$

Expression (12) evaluates the best compromise between the supplier's profit and the probability to reach an agreement with the customer.

At this point, the customer evaluates the counter proposal and, if $U^{c-p} > Thu_{min}$ is verified, the agreement is signed. Otherwise both customer and supplier quit the process. The main characteristics of the *ExP* mechanism are the following:

- the approach try to maximize the suppliers' profit finding a compromise between

Figure 6. Price probability

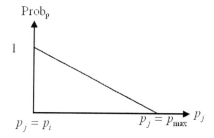

Table 1. Resources cost and production capacities

	Suppliers			
	1	*2*	*3*	*4*
FC_{il} ∀ *i,l* (€/hour)	300	150	300	150
CRG_j ∀ *j* (€/hour)	15	30	15	30
COV_j ∀ *j* (€/hour)	30	60	30	60
$CAPR_{jt}$ ∀ *j,t* (hours)	8	8	16	16
$CAPO_{jt}$ ∀ *j,t* (hours)	8	8	8	8

, the process plan *l* fixed cost when selected for job *l*;
, *j* time unit cost when used during ordinary time;
, *j* time unit cost when used during over time;
, resource *j* ordinary time capacity at time *t*;
, resource *j* overtime capacity at time *t* .

the customer's request and the probability to obtain a certain gain;

- the time the mechanism needs to try to reach an agreements is short, because the protocol is performed in just one shot;
- the customer point of view is strongly taken into account in the dibs elaboration.

SIMULATION ENVIRONMENT

To evaluate the proposed mechanisms, it has been specifically developed a distributed simulation environment based on the proposed Multi Agent Architecture, by using Java development kit package. The modeling formalism in here adopted is a collection of independent objects interacting via messages. This formalism is quite suitable for MAS development. In particular, each object represents an agent and the system evolves through a message sending engine managed by a discrete event scheduler. Specifically, the following agents have been developed: the CNA, the SNA, the SPA, the *Scheduler Agent* and the *Model Agent*. The former three agents have been deeply described in the previous sections. The *Scheduler Agent* is in charge with the system evolving by managing the discrete events of the simulation engine. Differently, *Model Agent* is in charge of the suppliers' and customers' interaction. Moreover, the customer and supplier agents have been provided with a local database to manage their own data. Finally, the SPA has been linked with the production planning algorithm (proposed in Perrone et al. (2005)) by a proper interface.

The simulator can be customized by the parameters reported in the class diagram of Figure 1. It automatically generates a report of the simulations and, in particular, the number of the reached agreements as well as the profit obtained by each supplier. Table 1 reports the simulative data for each supplier.

Data reported in Table 1 describes the competitive arena composed by different suppliers in terms of capacity and costs. The production alternatives have been computed, for each supplier, using the following bounds.

Table 2. Production alternatives bounds

	min	*max*
Δp	p_i	$p_i + 0.4 \cdot p_i$
Δdd	$dd_i - 5$	$dd_i + 5$
Pr	$\mathrm{Pr}_{\min} = 0,4 \cdot \mathrm{Pr}_{\max}$	$\mathrm{Pr}_{\max}$ [see equation (2)]

The parameters reported in Table 2 are part of the suppliers' strategy.

The simulations have been conducted for 48 orders; for each experimental class have been defined:

- *order*: the ordinal number referred to the orders;
- t_a : time in which customer's request is done. For each time bucket (T=30 periods) four orders are generated;
- dd_i : requested due date. t_a and dd_i are fixed and distributed uniformly over the time bucket T.
- V_i : requested volume. It leads to the workload of the network of suppliers.
- p_i : requested price.

Orders input has done during a time horizon of 360 periods (days), subdivided in 30 buckets: in each of them has been possible to make a re-planning. Each part type is considered to be manufactured only by one types of manufacturing resources and, according with one of the process plan in order to evaluate only the auction policies,

it is considered just one type of product with a production time of one hour.

The simulations have been conducted considering three parameters:

- *overlap*; it is the overlap among the considered orders, in term of days;
- *workload*; it is the volume that the customer requires;
- *mark-up*; it determines the price of the orders.

Combining three different level of variability, defined in Table 3, for all three parameters, 27 different experimental classes are obtained (see Table 4). The *workload* for each supplier could be interpreted as the volume required at each period. The *mark-up* is the parameter used to obtain price by using the following expression (13):

$$price = (\lambda \cdot workload) \cdot mark - up, \qquad (13)$$

being λ=225 the average, among the suppliers, of production costs.

Table 3. Parameters values

	Low	Medium	High
Overlap	0	3	6
Workload	60	100	140
Mark-up	1.1	1.4	1.7

Table 4. Experimental classes

Exp. No.	Overlap	Workload	Mark-up
1	Low	Low	Low
2	Medium	Low	Low
3	High	Low	Low
4	Low	Low	Medium
5	Medium	Low	Medium
6	High	Low	Medium
7	Low	Low	High
8	Medium	Low	High
9	High	Low	High
10	Low	Medium	Low
11	Medium	Medium	Low
12	High	Medium	Low
13	Low	Medium	Medium
14	Medium	Medium	Medium
15	High	Medium	Medium
16	Low	Medium	High
17	Medium	Medium	High
18	High	Medium	High
19	Low	High	Low
20	Medium	High	Low
21	High	High	Low
22	Low	High	Medium
23	Medium	High	Medium
24	High	High	Medium
25	Low	High	High
26	Medium	High	High
27	High	High	High

The considered performance measures are the following:

- *customer utility (CU)*; it is the sum of the utilities of all the orders ended with an agreement (see equation 6);
- *total suppliers utility (TSP)*; it is the sum of the profits of all the suppliers over all the 48 orders;

distribution index (DI); it is an index taking into account how the *TSP* is distributed, considering each single supplier's profit *SP*. It is computed as:

$$DI = \sum_{i=1}^{n} \left| \frac{TSP}{n} - SP_i \right| \qquad (14)$$

being N the number of suppliers;

The *DI* index is then normalized by the following expression:

$$DI^* = \frac{DI}{TSP} \tag{15}$$

The *DI** index allows to evaluate the profit distribution in an a-dimensional manner, to obtain a more intuitive comprehension.

- *rounds (R)*; it is given by the global amount of round each model needs to reach an agreements, for all the 48 considered orders.

SIMULATION RESULTS

Table 5 reports the average value of the performance measures over all the experimental classes.

The above results allow to highlights the differences existing among the different proposed approaches. In particular, the following considerations can be drawn:

- the customer's utility performance keeps an high level for the all the auction mechanism: *BSA*, *MVA* and *MCB* have a very low difference among them (about 2%). Moreover, all of these methods outperform the negotiation. As the reader can notice, the *MVA*, with a value R=801, leads to an utility value for the customer very close to the one obtained with *MCB*, with a strong reduction of R (R=192);

- the negotiation leads to the best performance for the suppliers (*TSP*=209,912); therefore, this approach seems to be the most promising for them. Among auction approaches, the *ExP* leads to the higher level of suppliers' performance (*TSP*=176,678), the closest to the negotiation;

- the *DI** is comparable for all the approaches, except for the ExP: in this case the obtained value is the worst.

- *BSA* and *MVA* lead to the maximum value of R. The better ones are *MCB* and *ExP*, with a value of R=192. The negotiation could be considered, form this point of view, as a compromise among the other approaches.

To obtain a deeper analysis of the obtained results, a discussion for each parameter (overlap, workload and mark-up) has been conducted.

Overlap

Table 6 reports the customer's utility considering as only variable parameter the overlap among the orders. The value of the standard deviation (*st. dev*) highlights that *MVA* and *MCB* mechanism are very robust among the overlap variability. While this result could be considered obvious for the *MCB* approach, because of the fact that the suppliers always choose the best proposal for the customer, it is excellent for the *MVA*. Differently

Table 5. Simulation results

	CU	*TSP*	*DI*	*DI**	*R*
Negotiation	128.06	209,912	243,816	1.16	475
BSA	137.73	176,096	195,418	1.11	800
MVA	139.30	166,996	189,761	1.14	801
MCB	140.47	150,999	157,812	1.05	192
ExP	113.51	176,678	241,777	1.37	192

Table 6. Customer's utility

	Negotiation	*BSA*	*ExP*	*MCB*	*MVA*
Low	130.96	136.78	128.15	137.70	138.58
Medium	130.68	141.26	117.00	142.99	142.15
High	122.55	135.15	95.38	140.72	137.17
st.dev	4.78	3.17	16.66	2.65	2.57

the customer's utility possesses an high fluctuation for the *ExP* model. More generally, except for the Negotiation and the *ExP*, all the approaches increase the utility when the overlap assumes the medium value: in fact the re-planning activity allows to adapt the bids to the customer's requests.

In the same condition, Table 7 reports the suppliers' utility. The *st.dev* value highlights that the negotiation is the best approach for them. *ExP*, *MCB* and *MVA* have a very high fluctuation: this is because the considered approaches are substantially different from negotiation. In the *BSA*, for example, the increment of the overlap leads to the reduction of the suppliers' profit because of the increasing pressure on the production planning. This situation, to keep an high level of customer's utility leads to a strong reduction of the profit. The *MCB* and *ExP* have the same macro-behavior: moreover *ExP* has the highest fluctuation

because the overlap increment reduces the number of production alternatives with an high profit that could be considered.

Workload

Table 8 reports the customer's utility considering as only variable parameter the workload. In this case, the reader can notice that the *st.dev* has bigger values if compared to the ones reported in Table 6: this because the workload is a parameter that leads to a bigger fluctuation of the customer's utility. The evolution of the workload from Low to High level leads to reduce the performance value for all the considered mechanism, except for the *ExP*. In this case the customer's utility increases (starting from 107.60 to 116.38) when the workload passes from Low to High. This is

Table 7. Suppliers' utility

	Negotiation	*BSA*	*ExP*	*MCB*	*MVA*
Low	211,348	186,228	196,621	165,690	178,340
Medium	205,747	173,064	179,082	158,118	141,258
High	212,642	168,996	154,333	129,191	154,346
st.dev	3,665	9,007	21,246	19,262	18,806

Table 8. Customer's utility

	Negotiation	*BSA*	*ExP*	*MCB*	*MVA*
Low	132.35	142.47	107.60	143.33	143.06
Medium	130.58	140.04	111.97	141.47	141.44
High	121.26	130.69	116.38	136.61	133.40
st.dev	5.96	6.22	4.39	3.47	5.17

Table 9. Suppliers' utility

	Negotiation	BSA	ExP	MCB	MVA
Low	135,262	110,023	114,932	98,253	108,986
Medium	218,008	182,015	119,510	156,316	175,266
High	276,467	236,249	125,118	198,431	216,738
st.dev	70,950	63,321	5,102	50,300	54,350

because of the bigger number of generated profitable production planning alternatives.

Table 9 reports the suppliers' utility. All the approaches have a high fluctuation of the considered performances except for the *ExP*.

Mark-Up

The mark-up level is the parameters with the smaller impact on the customer utility: the fluctuations are very limited. This means that the proposed approaches are really robust in respect of the market price fluctuations.

As the reader can (obviously) notice, the increment of the mark-up parameter leads to an increment of the suppliers' profit. The mark-up parameter has a weak effect if compared to the workload.

Summarizing, these simulation results demonstrate how the proposed agent architecture and the integration among the agents and their production plan to elaborate bids are effectively able to support Small and Medium Enterprises in e-procurement process. Moreover, the numerical results could give to all the potential participants in an e-marketplace a quantitative support to consider how improve their satisfaction as well as whether take part in such a context or not.

CONCLUSION AND FURTHER RESEARCHES

This chapter deals with the investigation of different kind of auction based protocols, compared with the more common negotiation. In particular,

Table 10. Customer's utility

	Negotiation	BSA	ExP	MCB	MVA
Low	126.19	135.92	105.96	139.89	137.89
Medium	128.91	138.38	108.24	140.42	139.88
High	129.10	138.89	108.57	141.10	140.14
st.dev	1.63	1.59	1.42	0.60	1.23

Table 11. Suppliers' utility

	Negotiation	BSA	ExP	MCB	MVA
Low	148,572	119,098	114,761	99,927	108,641
Medium	208,285	176,023	133,517	154,260	166,780
High	272,880	233,167	153,811	198,812	225,744
st.dev	62,170	57,034	19,530	49,523	58,552

two innovative auction protocols have been proposed: the *BVA* and the *MVA*. Moreover, other innovations have been introduced in the *MCB* and *ExP* protocols, while negotiation has been used as a benchmark. All the proposed approaches have been implemented by a Multi Agent Architecture and a simulation environment has been developed by the JAVA package. The evaluated performance indexes concern: the customer and suppliers' utilities, the profit distribution among the involved agents and the time necessary to reach an agreement. To consider a simulative environment as close as possible to realty, three parameters have been considered as input data: the suppliers' workloads, the mark-up and the overlap degree among orders.

The obtained results can be placed at three different levels. Regarding the proposed auction protocols, the main innovation of this chapter are concerning:

- the link among the suppliers' proposal formulation and their production plans: the last ones provide the information and bounds to the agents to formulate their proposals, leading to a more realistic process;
- the implementation of multi-attribute auctions for all the proposed mechanisms, particularly for the Vickrey's one. In the eyes of the authors this result it is a very innovative tool to support e-business applications for SMEs'.

Regarding the comparison of the models among themselves, all the considered auction protocols result to be competitive with the negotiation. Specifically:

- the *BSA* is the approach that leads to the best compromise between suppliers and customer;
- *ExP* leads to a positive level of performance, especially among the ones performed in a single shot;

- the MVA obtains performances values very close to the BSA: ;
- the *BSA* leads to the best global customer's satisfaction.

Lastly, at strategic level the research shows that:

- discrete event simulation is a powerful tool to design and test distributed environment based on agent technology;
- the simulations provide complete information in several environmental conditions: major effects of the parameters variation on performances have been deeply investigated.

Further researches will deeply follow the subsequent paths:

- the simulations will be extended to a competitive environment increasing the number of suppliers. The objective is the investigation of the performances with a different number of suppliers and different competitive characteristics for each of them. More precisely, it will be investigated the case when the suppliers have a different risk attitude. Specifically, for each of them will be considered different production planning costs (resources, fixed costs, etc.) because of their influence on the agent's behavior;
- the results of the simulations can be used as a knowledge based management system both for suppliers and customers. A proper learning algorithm will be developed in order to select the most appropriate strategy for the proposal formulation. The methodologies that can support this approach could be the Q-learning method or the fuzzy logic;
- the possibility to make a coalition when the auction protocol is performed. It will be investigated the effect of suppliers co-

alition on the performance. The issues to face with are: how the suppliers decide to form a coalition; how the coalition computes the proposal combining the information of each production planning algorithm and how the profit is distributed among the suppliers of the coalition when an agreement is reached. The most promising approach in this field seems to be the game theory methodology.

REFERENCES

Antonnette, G., Giunipero, L.C., Sawchuk, C., (2002). *E-Purchasing Plus: Transforming Supply Management through Technology*. New York: JGC Enterprises.

Bajari, P., & Tadelis, S. (2001). Incentives Versus Transaction Costs: A Theory of Procurement Contracts. *32. The Rand Journal of Economics*, 387–407. doi:10.2307/2696361

Beil, D. R., & Wein, L. M. (2003). An inverse-optimization-based auction mechanism to support a multi-attribute RFQ process. *Management Science*, *49*(11), 1529–1545. doi:10.1287/mnsc.49.11.1529.20588

Bradshaw, J. M. (1997). An introduction to software agents. In Bradshaw, J. M. (Ed.), *Software Agents*. Menlo Park, CA: AAAI Press.

Buxton, A. (2008). *Does Procurement eAuction Design Matter? Trading Partners,* http://www.tradingpartners.com/usa/download.php?Id=85&Field=File&Force=Y&Stream=N, 26 Mach 2008, (Accessed on August 4, 2009).

Carter, C. R., Kaufmann, L., Beall, S., Carter, P. L., Hendrick, T. E., & Petersen, K. J. (2004). Reverse auctions – grounded theory from the buyer and supplier perspective. *Transportation Research Part E, Logistics and Transportation Review*, *40*(3), 183–270. doi:10.1016/j.tre.2003.08.004

Chen Ritzo, C., Harrizon, T., Kwasnica, A., & Thomas, D. (2005). Better, faster, cheaper: An experimental analysis of a multi-attribute reverse auction mechanism with restricted information feedback. *Management Science*, *51*(12), 1753–1762. doi:10.1287/mnsc.1050.0433

Emiliani, M. L. (2006). Executive Decision Making Traps and B2B online reverse auctions. *Supply Chain Management: An International Journal*, *11*(1), 6–9. doi:10.1108/13598540610642411

Favier J., Condon C., Aghina W., Rehkopf F., (2000). Euro eMarketplaces top hype. *Forrester Research*, Inc., May 2000.

Goeree, J. K., Offerman, T., & Schram, A. (2006). Using first-price auctions to sell heterogeneous licenses. *International Journal of Industrial Organization*, *24*(3), 555–581. doi:10.1016/j.ijindorg.2005.07.011

Goldberg, V. P. (1977). Competitive Bidding and the Production of Precontract Information. *8. The Bell Journal of Economics*, 250–261. doi:10.2307/3003497

Hinze, J. (1993). *Construction Contracts. McGraw-Hill Series in Construction Engineering and Project Management*. New York: Irwin/McGraw-Hill.

Jin, M., Wu, S. D., & Erkoc, M. (2006). Multiple unit auctions with economy/diseconomy of scale. *European Journal of Operational Research*, *174*(2), 816–834. doi:10.1016/j.ejor.2005.02.075

Krishna, V. (2002). *Auction Theory*. San Diego, CA: Academic Press.

Kumar, S., & Chang, C. W. (2007). Reverse Auctions: How much total supply chain cost savings are there? – A conceptual overview. *Journal of Revenue and Pricing Management*, *6*(3), 229–240. doi:10.1057/palgrave.rpm.5160088

McAfee, R. P., & McMillan, J. (1987). Auctions and Bidding. *Journal of Economic Literature (American Economic Association), 25* (2), 699–738, June 1987. Retrieved from http://www.jstor.org/stable/2726107, on 2009-11-16.

Ordanini, A., Micelli, S., & Di Maria, E. (2004). Failure and success of B-to-B Exchange Business Models: A Contingent analysis of their performance. *European Management Journal, 22*(3), 281–289. doi:10.1016/j.emj.2004.04.013

Parkes, D. C., & Kalagnanam, J. (2005). Models for iterative multiattribute Vickrey auctions. *Management Science, 51*(3), 435–451. doi:10.1287/mnsc.1040.0340

Perrone, G., Bruccoleri, M., & Renna, P. (2005). *Designing and Evaluating value added services in Manufacturing e-marketplaces. Netherlands.* Netherlands: Springer. doi:10.1007/1-4020-3152-1

Raiffa, H. (1996). *Lectures on negotiation analysis.* Cambridge, MA: PON.

Renna, P. (2009). A multi-agent system architecture for business-to-business applications. *International Journal of Services and Operations Management, 5*(3), 375–401. doi:10.1504/IJSOM.2009.024152

Turowski, K. (2002). Agent-based e-commerce in case of mass customization. *International Journal of Production Economics, 75,* 69–81. doi:10.1016/S0925-5273(01)00182-7

Vickery Auction. (n.d.). http://en.wikipedia.org/wiki/Vickrey_auction, Wikipedia Website, Accessed on November 16, 2009.

Zaccone, S. (2004). The Yin and Yang of Reverse Auctions and Trust. *Converting Magazine, 22*(5), 34–36.

Zhang, Z., & Jin, M. (2007). Iterative Multi-AttRibute Multi-Unit Reverse Auctions. *The Engineering Economist, 52*(4), 333–354. doi:10.1080/00137910701675239

Chapter 7
Well–Being and E–Business as an Influential Innovation

Simona Šarotar Žižek
University of Maribor, Slovenia

Matjaž Mulej
University of Maribor, Slovenia

Sonja Treven
University of Maribor, Slovenia

ABSTRACT

The contemporary world is full of innovations, causing both good and bad consequences, including the essential problem of well-being of co-workers. Most troubles of this kind cannot be resolved with measures of the usual management and/or economic theory that have caused these troubles. Therefore, the question is raised: what could be done about the well-being of co-workers, if principles and measures of innovative business, social responsibility, and requisite holism were used in synergy.

The electronic business plays a central role in the economy, facilitating the exchange of information, goods, services, and payments, being an innovation causing changes influencing well-being. On one hand the e-business raises productivity and competitiveness, on the other hand it negatively effects well-being of co-workers in all organizations, including SMEs. Most humans tend to prefer their established routine, not change, including innovation.

In this chapter the authors will introduce well-being and its benefits, first. Then, they will discuss connection between well-being and e-business and both positive and negative effects of this connection.

DOI: 10.4018/978-1-60960-463-9.ch007

INTRODUCTION

E-business has a crucial impact on the contemporary enterprises, including small and medium-size enterprises (SMEs). SMEs use e-business mainly because of its numerous advantages. However, the positive and negative influences of e-business on employees' (subjective) well-being are rarely considered. To strengthen its positive and weaken its negative influences on co-workers' well-being, which is important also in economic terms, we suggest the concept of social responsibility, paying regard to humans as multilayered beings, increasing their holism through the personal development.

After the introduction we shall discuss SMEs followed by e-business and its meaning for SMEs. On this basis we shall concentrate on the positive psychology and well-being with a special emphasis on the subjective well-being. This will lead us to social responsibility (SR) and discussing SR concept for SME's against disadvantages of e-business. Our contribution ends with some conclusions.

SMALL AND MEDIUM-SIZE ENTERPRISES (SME)

Issues of well-being differ in SME from the ones in bigger organizations and public sector, because the situation at work and organization and management of it differ for natural reasons:

- Every person makes a bigger percentage, which is crucial, if anybody is missing.
- It is difficult to be narrowly specialized and still cover all needs.
- It is difficult to have time to adapt to novelties.
- It is difficult to hide in the mass rather than to be in overt interaction.
- Etc.

Thus it makes sense to spend some time in defining SME first.

Definitions of SME

Scientific, political, and business literature provides many different definitions of SME (Meyer, 2000, p. 1; summarized after Schneider, 2004, p. 7). Storey (1994, p. 8) sees no single, uniformly acceptable, definition of SME. Unfortunately, definitions related to »objective« measures of size such as number of employees, sales turnover, profitability, net value, etc., when examined at a sector level, mean that in some sectors all firms may be found small, while in other sectors there are possibly no small firms (Storey 1994, pp 8-9).

The Bolton Committee (1971; summarized after Storey, 1994, p. 9) attempted to overcome this problem by formulating an »economic« definition and a »statistical« definition. In the economic definition small firms must satisfy three criteria (Bolton Committee, 1971; summarized after Storey, 1994, p. 9):

- They have a relatively small share of their market.
- They are managed by owners or part-owners in a personalized way, rather than through a formalized management structure.
- They are independent, rather than parts of a large enterprise.

Given this »Economic« definition, Bolton devised a »Statistical« definition that was designed to address the three main issues (Bolton Committee 1971; summarized after Storey, 1994, p. 9):

1. To qualify the current size of the SME sector and its contribution to economic aggregates such as gross domestic product, employment, exports, innovation, etc.

Table 1. Bolton Committee definitions of SME

SECTOR	DEFINITION
Manufacturing	200 employees or less
Construction	25 employees or less
Mining and quarrying	
Retailing	Turnover of £50,000 or less
Miscellaneous	
Services	
Motor trades	Turnover of £100,000 or less
Wholesale trades	Turnover of £200,000 or less
Road transport	Five vehicles or less
Catering	All excluding multiples and brewery-managed houses

Source: Bolton Committee, 1971; summarized after Storey, 1994, p. 9

2. To compare the extent to which the small firm sector has changed its economic contribution over time.

3. The statistical definition, in principle, must enable comparison between the contributions of small firms in various countries.

For definitions used by the Bolton Committee see Table 1, which illustrates (ibid., p. 9):

- The use of different definitions of SME in different sectors,
- Criteria upon which the judgment of »smallness« was made per sectors.

Storey (1994, 10) mentions criticism of Bolton's both »economic« and »statistical« definitions: the following aspects are questionable:

- Criteria that a small business is »managed by its owners or part owners in a personalized way, and not through a formal management structure« is almost certainly incompatible with its »statistical« definition of small manufacturing firms which could have up to 200 employees.

- Emphasis upon the inability of the small firm to affect its environment – most notably its inability to influence, by changing the quality which it produces, the price at which a product or service is sold in the marketplace.

Storey (1994, p. 13) considered that the term SME has been coined to overcome some of these problems. This process led the European Commission, which disaggregated the SME sector into three components (Storey 1994, p. 13):

- Micro-enterprises: with 0 - 9 employees;
- Small enterprises: with 10 - 99 employees;
- Medium enterprises: with 100 - 499 employees.

This definition says that the SMEs – except agriculture, hunting, forestry and fishing – employ less than 500 workers. Storey (1994, p. 13) mentions that the major advantage of the EC definition is that it uses as criteria only employment, and it does not vary its definition per industries. Therefore in almost all aspects the EC definition is currently more appropriate than those of the Bolton Committee (Storey 1994, p. 13):

- The EC definition is exclusively based upon employment, rather than several criteria.
- The use of 100 employees as a small firm limit is more appropriate, given the rises in productivity over the last two decades.

Significance of SME

Schneider (2004, 9) mentions that SMEs have a high economic relevance in Germany and in many other countries; in Germany the interest in the SME is increasing after »decades of the large-scale enterprises« due to the increased meaning of this class of society. Schneider (2004, p. 9) regrets that big companies like Siemens, Daimler Chrysler, or Nestlé create the headlines, whereas the medium-size enterprises are the power of the German economy regarding flexibility, innovation, and tax quantity. Many academic surveys and publications study medium-size enterprises. Now it is time of growing interest for »medium-size renaissance« due to plentiful new foundations in Eastern Germany, after decades in an economic climate favoring big industries. Schneider (2004, p. 9) is convinced that in Germany, the importance of research concerning SMEs is reflected in the rising number of university institutes committed only to the research and education of medium-size management. German universities founded more than 16 such institutes during the last decade. Figures from the USA also indicate the importance of SMEs for the American economy. Meyer (2001, 1 ff; summarized after Schneider, 2004, p. 9) displays this significance with the list of the 500 best SMEs: SMEs have the highest growth and profit rates. Therefore many big corporations are getting more interested in management tools of SMEs.

In the past, the social parties and trade unions favored the big corporations; but today all groups of society focus on medium-size enterprises, and their economic potential and influence in different market segments. The Bonn Institute for Medium-size Enterprise Research proved this relevance of SMEs: SMEs (Schneider, 2004, p. 9):

- Carry 45,9% of the German tax load,
- Employ 64% of the German workforce,
- Provide 80% of professional apprenticeship,
- Create 52.1% of the Gross National Products,
- Have a rate of 44,1% of all German investments,
- Represent 99.6% of all taxpaying enterprises in Germany.

Success Factors and Main Problems of SMEs

Schneider (2004) mentions success factor and the main problems of SMEs: success factors include high flexibility, innovation, reliability, motivation of employees, and customer loyalty, as well as customer-specific goods and services, which are, last but not least, determined by the strong influence of the entrepreneur. SMEs have also many problems, including: too high costs for duties and bureaucracy, low capital capacities, too little management potential; this makes good inventions and innovations from the markets or from the enterprise difficult to implement consequently and profitably in products, methods, and new market offers (Schneider, 2004).

Perhaps, E-business can offer alternative chances.

E-BUSINESS

E-business is a novelty aimed to become innovation. Thus, it requires a change in the way of working and established habits, which influences well-being of employees both positively and negatively. The negative impacts might be smaller, if e-business is clearer to the tackled persons. Hence, let us spend some time on e-business.

Definitions of E-Business

Harris (2002; summarized after Jackson et al., 2003, p. 5) sees are numerous definitions of e-Commerce and e-Business; many people treat them somewhat synonymously. Jackson et al. (2003, p. 5) present the following definition:

- E-Commerce has a more restrictive meaning limited to buying and selling of goods online. This may also extend to »back-end« processes where supply-chains are managed through electronic stock-ordering systems (which, as Harris points out, pre-date the Internet in the form of EDI).
- E-Business is a broader concept describing arrangements where organizations have redesigned their business structures, processes and services to take advantage of Internet capabilities. The essential features of an e-Business include:
  - Making greater use of electronic devices in the processing and communicating of data.
  - Allowing for increased interaction of databases and hardware devices (thanks largely to the »open protocols« that govern the transfer of data between systems).
  - Enabling users to engage »interactively« with systems and services – for instance, to purchase goods, check on orders, or collaborate in virtual teams or communities.

Bocij et al. (2006, p. 17) argue: »Electronic business (e-business) is all electronically mediated information exchange, both within an organization and with external stakeholders supporting the range of business processes. E-business involves increasing the efficiency of information flows and business processes within an organization and with other partners such as customers, suppliers, distributors and other intermediaries« (Bocij et al., 2006, p. 17).

Singh and Waddell (2003, vi) see e-business as a revolution bringing new ways of dealing with customers and business partners, new revenue streams, new methods of processing information, new organizational structures, skill sets, electronic supply chains and new standards and policies, forcing the need for adaptable business strategies. Singh (2003, p. 1) defines e-business as innovation, which is based on technology, evolves with technological developments, digitizes and automates business process, is global, and leads to improved competitiveness and efficiencies, increased market share, and business expansion. After Singh (2003, p. 1) e-business models include business-to-business, business-to-customer, government-to-government, government-to-business, government-to-customer, and numerous others results of new developments.

Justification of E-Business

Reasons for e-business in companies include reaching out to customers at greater geographic distances, having a shop front 24 hours a day, seven days a week, acquiring a new channel of business, and integrated business process (Singh, 2000; summarized after Singh, 2003, p. 4). Whinston et al. (1998; summarized after Singh, 2003, p. 4) mention, that e-business improves company image, requires less floor space, leads to increased data accuracy, and offers opportunities for more challenging responsibilities and training. Zhuang and Lederer (2003; summarized after Singh, 2003, p. 4) alert that these benefits are referred to as non-financial benefits and are not easy to quantify.

Advantages of e-business include:

- It can help increase profits (increasing sales and reducing costs).
- Promotional message reaches out to potential customers in every country in the world.

- It can reach narrow market segments that are widely scattered geographically.
- It is useful in creating virtual communities, which become ideal targets markets.
- It uses low cost medium for disseminating information and processing transactions.
- It enables error reduction.
- It increases efficiency through automation of business processes.
- It reduces cost of handling sales inquiries and determining product availability.
- It increases sales opportunity for the seller.
- It increases purchasing opportunity for the buyer.
- Businessmen can identify new suppliers and business partners.
- Efficient providing of competitive bid information is possible.
- It provides buyers a wider range of choices than traditional commerce.
- It replaces the traditional roadblocks of business such as waiting for the mail to bring a catalogue or product specification sheet, waiting for a fax transmission.
- Buyers can have instant access to the information on the web.
- It helps us change the methods of governance.
- It protects against fraud and theft losses because electronic payment can be easier to monitor than payments made by cheques.
- It enables people to work from home with an added benefit in reduction in traffic and pollution caused by employees commuting to the office.
- Products and services can be made available in remote areas through e-commerce, etc. (Altekar, 2005, pp. 382-383).

Altekar (2005) and Singh (2003, pp. 4-5 defined advantages of e-business):

- Tangible benefits may include increased revenue from new customers acquired on-line, acquisition of new business partners for discounted or cheaper raw materials and saving resulting from reduced errors. Intangible benefits are non-quantifiable, such as improved customer satisfaction and improved morale of employees.
- Intangible benefits should be taken into account for evaluation converted to quantifiable benefits wherever possible, too.

»Many of benefits are realized in the long term; therefore justification of innovations suggested by Singh (1997) needs an evaluation method considering that such investments require a longer period for returns, and strategic advantages such as improved quality, improved flexibility, image and business efficiencies of automated business process and data management are taken into account« (Singh, 2003, p. 5).

Milutinović and Patricelli (2002) argue that the highest e-business achievers are companies combining above-average IT spending with a deep commitment to e-business best practices. Companies with Internet get e.g.: competitive advantage, improved customer satisfaction, reduced operating costs, or generate new sources of revenue, create new markets for products, and increase profits.

Disadvantage of E-Business

Disadvantages of e-business include (Altekar, 2005, pp. 382-383):

- Some business processes like foods and high cost items such as jewelry and antiques may never lend themselves to e-business.
- Low critical mass of potential customer.
- Investment in e-business's worth cannot be determined easily.
- Costs, depending on technology, can change dramatically during short-lived electronic commerce implementation proj-

ects, because the underlying technologies change so rapidly.

- Trouble in recruiting and retaining employees with technological, design, and business process skills needed to create an effective electronic commerce presence.
- Fraud has not been completely eliminated in e-business transaction.

We add disadvantages with large expenditure (cost of technology, software, networking requirements, fees paid to consultants and experts, training expenses) and involvement of the whole organization in e-business integration and changing organization structure, managerial leadership, and well-being of employees.

Issues Concerning E-Business

Singh (2003, 1) presents that technological development applied to e-business results in new issues in the organization, in dealing with business partners and customers, requires new laws and regulations, and automated business process. Conducting business electronically is for enterprises a change from traditional ways of working, leading to large scale transformation of existing business. Singh (2003, p. 1) suggested that for attaining business efficiencies from e-business, organizations must effectively manage e-business environment and all changes associated to digitizing and maintaining the environment.

Jackson et al. (2003, p. 5) mention that realizing the full benefits of the Internet, as well as the e-Commerce and e-business functions it supports, is not easily done using traditional systems of work and organization. Therefore it is an e-Business orthodoxy that organizations need to »reinvent« their business processes or entire business models in order to fully benefit from their Internet investments.

Hence the basic principles of human resources management (HRM) are particularly important for management and marketing of established organizations moving into e-Business for the first time. Although they are often regarded as quite separate business disciplines, there are a number of synergies, which are generated by effectively integrating HRM and the management of customers (marketing) and other key stakeholders such as business partners. Jackson et al. (2003, p. 68) demonstrate: synergies generated by integrating internal and external stakeholder relationships make an organization's only source of sustainable competitive advantage and well-being of employees.

Jackson et al. (2003, p. 68) suggest that e-Business is just about technological change. Firms set up specifically to operate through the Internet are ideally placed to recruit staff and deal with customers in the most effective way, although many are struggling with current economic conditions. Established firms, however, may have a whole history of embedded working practices and customer relationships that require significant change, if e-Business should be implemented successfully. Becoming an e-Business requires a diverse range of skills. In the e-Business world companies must anticipate the need for transformation and be ready to re-examine their organizations to the core. E-Business tools encourage the dissemination of information contribute to moving away from centralized, hierarchical approaches by reducing or even eliminating the need for privileged points of contacts in organizations and transforming traditional relationships within and between organizations.

In the traditional economy, partnership forms are managed in traditional styles. The traditional economy is successively being transferred into an IT-based economy: the classical globalization is shifting towards e-Globalization (Abouzeedan and Busler, 2007, p. 303). Globalization and e-globalization are highly significant for smaller firm's mechanisms of survival and growth; because of this studying the way firms are using bridging tactics, including strategic alliances, to increase their chance of survival and growth is an important issue (Abouzeedan and Busler 2006, 243). Abouzeedan and Busler (2006, p. 243) reviewed important existing knowledge about Information Technology's (IT) impact on the management and other functional aspects of SMEs and suggest 'Firm Impact Sphere' as a new approach to understand the interaction between the firm's activity and its environment.

These facts and factors are not engineering issues only, but tackle humans too, making the positive psychology an important topic.

POSITIVE PSYCHOLOGY

Maslow (1954) was the first to use the term positive psychology. Positive psychology has flourished in the last 10 years. »Maslow and Seligman's call for more serious attention to the positive side of life has been echoed by many, including visionaries in psychiatry such as Karl Menninger, and business gurus, notably Peter Drucker.« (Lopez & Gallagher, 2009). Seligman at al. (2005, p. 410) mention that positive psychology is an umbrella term for the study of positive emotions, positive character traits, and enabling institutions. Positive psychology is the study of how human beings prosper in the face of adversity (Linley in Joseph 2004, 32). Linley in Joseph (2004, p. 32) mention positive psychology's focus on identifying and enhancing the human strengths and virtues that make life worth living, i.e., "the good life" (Selingman 2002a, b; Selingman & Csikszentmihalyi, 2000), and allow individuals and communities to thrive (Sheldon, et al., 2000). Sheldon and King (2001, p. 216) mention that positive psychology is an attempt to urge psychologists to adopt a more open and appreciative perspective regarding human potentials, motives, and capacities. It is becoming increasingly clear that the normal functioning of human beings cannot be accounted for within purely negative (or problem-focused) frames of reference (ibid., p. 216).

One of research models of positive psychology is well-being because of the practical importance of well-being.

After Seligman (2002b, p. 3) the field of positive psychology at the subjective level is about positive subjective experience: well-being and satisfaction (past); flow, joy, the sensual pleasures, and happiness (present); and constructive cognitions about the future - optimism, hope, and faith. At the individual level positive personal traits are important: the capacity for love and vocation, courage, interpersonal skill, aesthetic sensibility, perseverance, forgiveness, originality, future-mindedness, high talent, and wisdom. At the group level (after Seligman and Csikszentmihalyi, 2000; summarized after Seligman, 2002b, p. 3) it is about the civic virtues and the institutions that move individuals toward better citizenship: responsibility, nurturance, altruism, civility, moderation, tolerance, and work ethic.

Applied positive psychology, which is concerned with facilitating good lives and enabling people to be at their best, has applications that span almost every area of applied psychology (clinical psychology, counseling and psychotherapy, humanistic psychology etc.) and beyond (education, development of specific happiness-increase interventions, management) etc. (Liney et al. 2009, p, 35). According to Liney et al. (2009, p, 35) applications of positive psychology in society are also important as they are also in the field of Industrial Organizational Psychology. Applications are presented throughout the work on transformational behavior, appreciative inquiry, and strengths-based organization.

This brings us to the issue of well-being. It should also be defined to be better understood and more acceptable in organizational management and governance.

WELL-BEING

Definition of well-being after SNDR (2005, p. 5):

- »…comprises objective descriptors and subjective evaluations of physical, material, social and emotional well-being, together with the extent of personal development and purposeful activity, all weighed by a set of values" (Felce and Perry 1995);
- »Paradigms for empirical enquiry into well-being …revolve around two distinct philosophies. The first of these can be broadly labelled hedonism…and reflects the view that well-being consists of pleasure or happiness. The second view…is that well-being consists of more than just happiness. It lies instead in the actualization of human potentials. This view has been called eudaimonism… The two traditions – hedonism and eudaimonism – are founded on distinct views of human nature and what constitutes a good society" (Ryan and Deci 2001).
- »There is no accepted definition of well-being" (Hird 2003).

"Well-being is more than the absence of illness or pathology; it has subjective (self-assessed) and objective (ascribed) dimensions; it can be measured at the level of individuals or society; it accounts for elements of life satisfaction that cannot be defined, explained or primarily influenced by economic growth." (SDRN, 2005, p. 2). Well-being is a complex construct whose meaning remains contested and key distinctions are between: (i) hedonic and eudaemonic well-being; and (ii) objective and subjective measures (SDRN, 2005, p. 4).

Ryan and Deci (2001) present hedonic tradition, in which psychologists have concentrated on the assessment of "subjective well-being". This has three elements: (i) life satisfaction; (ii) the presence of positive mood; and (iii) the absence of negative mood. All this together is summarized as happiness (ibid: 144). Ryan and Deci (2001, p. 146/7; summarized after SDRN, 2005, p. 5) mention that the eudaimonic theorists argue that well-being and happiness are distinct: not all sources of pleasure foster well-being. They presented self-determination theory positing that there are three basic psychological needs – autonomy, competence and relatedness – and theorize that fulfillment of these needs is essential for psychological growth and well-being (Ryan and Deci, 2001, p. 146/7; summarized after SDRN, 2005, p. 5)

Felce and Perry (1995) presented objective domains of well-being and subjective evaluations of well-being, the two main approaches to measuring well-being in research. »Objective measures of well-being consist of survey data related to material and social circumstances, which may foster – or detract - from well-being. These include income, housing, educational attainment, access to, and use of, public services. Objective measures have not provided a coherent explanation for trends in well-being. Notably, rising economic growth and GDP per capita in developed countries have not been accompanied by commensurate increases in reported life satisfaction.« (SDRN 2005, p. 2). The objective well-being includes material and social circumstances, which influence an individual's personal objective well-being; it consists of the following dimensions (McAllister 2005, p. 9; summarized after: Prosenak and Mulej 2007a, p. 3): material, physical, social, and emotional well-being, development and activity.

»Subjective measures are usually based on survey questions asking respondents to rate their own happiness or satisfaction with life as a whole. These measures have been shown to be statistically robust and have largely superseded more specific measures of subjective well-being and emotional state«. (SDRN 2005, p. 2). McAllister (2005) and Arthaud-Day et al. (2005; summarized after Prosenak and Mulej 2007a, p. 3) mention, that subjective well-being stems from individual's perception of objective well-being. Because the perception depends on individual's subjective starting points (knowledge, emotions, mentality and values), a high objective well-being does not necessary simultaneously mean a high subjective well-being (Prosenak and Mulej 2007a, 3). We know also of relative well-being, which depends on one's comparison with people playing important roles in one's life (Revkin, 2005). Diener and Seligman show the following partial formula for high well-being (2004, p. 25; summarized after Prosenak and Mulej 2007a, p. 3): living in a democratic and stable society that provides material sources to meet needs, having supportive friends and family, rewarding and engaging work and an adequate income, being reasonably healthy and having treatment available in case of mental problems, having important goals related to one's values, philosophy or religion that provide guidance, purpose and meaning to one's life. In our contribution we will use subjective well-being.

Defining well-being is a complex matter. This is a reason for us to apply points following of common ground suggested by SDRN:

- »Well-being is more than the absence of illness or pathology.
- Well-being has both subjective and objective dimensions. It can be assessed in subjective terms (seeking individuals' views in surveys) or objectives terms (by measuring access to physical, environmental, social and other resources). There are pros and cons to each approach. Both types of information are useful and together they provide a fuller picture of well-being.
- The terms »life satisfaction«, »happiness«, »quality of life« and »well-being« are often used interchangeably. The significance of seeing the terms as interchangeable is that they express a global assessment of satisfaction, rather than capturing a momentary mood. Such measures of well-being potentially give policymakers an indication of overall levels of satisfaction in the population and suggest the impact of living in the current regime.
- The burgeoning literature on happiness (e.g. Layard 2005, Nettle 2005, Martin 2005) is concerned with subjective well-being, and draws on the same pool of survey evidence regarding »quality of life« and »life satisfaction«.
- Most researchers agree about the domains that make up well-being: physical well-being; material well-being; social well-being; development and activity; emotional well-being. The elements can be paraphrased as physical health, income and wealth, relationships, meaningful work and leisure, personal stability and (lack of) depression. Mental health is increasingly seen as fundamental to overall health and well-being. These elements are sometimes viewed as »drivers« of well-being.
- Both individual and societal well-being is important and measurable. Veenhoven (1997) describes quality of life as »the presence of conditions deemed necessary for the good life, and the practice of good living as such«. The interaction between the two is where much of the link with policy comes: what enhances personal well-being may be negative for society, or possibly vice versa, and the balance of well-being now and well-being in future must be taken into account.
- Well-being is an important area for future policy as it accounts for elements in life experience that cannot be defined, explained, or primarily influenced by economic growth« (SDRN 2005, 6).

Obviously, there is a practical difference between the organizational and individual well-being as well as between the objective and subjective one. Let us now turn to the latter. This might help influential persons in organizations attain more of well-being of their co-workers, be them subordinates, bosses, or peers, and on this basis more of good business results of the organization and of its members.

SUBJECTIVE WELL-BEING

Definition and Measuring of Subjective Well-Being

Subjective well-being is the main subject in the context of positive psychology (Musek and Avsec, 2006, 51). After Diener et al. (2002, p. 63) the subjective well-being is defined as a person's cognitive and affective evaluations of his or her life, which include emotional reactions to events as well as cognitive judgment of satisfaction and fulfillment. Diener and Seligman (2004) define the subjective well-being or welfare as the evaluation of an individual's life taking into account his or her positive emotions, work, life satisfaction, and meaning. For Musek and Avsec (2002, p. 10) the subjective well-being is the main notion, which combines a series of evaluations, which refer to the individual's life, cognitive and emotional, general and more specific.

Diener (1984, p 543-544) mentions the following three hallmarks of subjective well-being:

- It is subjective – it resided within the experience of the individual.
- It includes positive measures – it is not just the absence of negative factors, as is true of most measures of mental health.
- Subjective well-being measures typically include a global assessment of all aspects of a person's life.

Lucas, Diener in Suh (1996, summarized after Diener et al., 2002, p. 64) demonstrated that multi-item life satisfaction, pleasant affect, and unpleasant affect scales formed factors that were separable from each other, as well as from

other constructs such as self-esteem. This means that concept of the subjective well-being covers three components: (i) the positive emotions and humors, (ii) the absence of negative emotions and humors, and (iii) the evaluation of life satisfaction (Musek, 2005, p. 178). A second factor of the subjective well-being tackles the emotional aspect of well-being, which is composed of two independent components – positive and negative affections. A measuring device had to be built for measuring the above three components. Watson, Clark & Tellegen (1988: summarized after Musek, 2005, p. 178) mention that positive and negative affection (PA and NA) is measured by numerous instruments and most often the PANAS questionnaire (Positive Affect Negative Affect Scale) is used.

Implications of Subjective Well-Being

According to Diener and Seligman (2004, p. 1) the individual's income, when increasing, is becoming less relevant for the growth of well-being; on the other hand interpersonal relations and satisfaction at work are becoming more and more relevant. Non-economic indicators of social well-being are found important by these authors, such as social capital, democratic management and human rights, having effect on the satisfaction and profitability at the workplace. Diener and Seligman (2004, p. 1) claim that the expected (economic) results are most often the effect of well-being and not vice versa. They also discovered that people who are at the top of the well-being scale have more income and are more successful at work as those in the lower region of such a scale. Satisfied employees are better co-workers and therefore help their colleagues in various ways. Furthermore, people with a higher level of well-being have better social relations. Such people are more likely to get married, stay married and have a successful marriage. And finally, well-being is also connected with health and longer living, but the connections between them are far from being completely understood. Therefore a high level of well-being is not precious only in the context of well-being, but it can also be economically useful. These facts show that monitoring of well-being at the organization and state levels is necessary for well-being to become a central topic for the creation of the policy of management, and that accurate measuring of well-being forms a basis of such a policy (Diener and Seligman, 2004, p. 1). Authors suggest that positive and negative emotions, commitment, purpose and meaning, optimism and trust as well as a wide concept of a full life be used as variables for measuring of well-being. At the same time they point out that for the measuring of well-being researches are important, which cover social conditions, income, physical health, mental disorders and social conditions. James (2007) warns about the border between well-being and the end of motivation because of the affluence combined with complacency: the border is not objective but subjective.

People with high well-being indicated significant life benefits, such as (Pavot and Diener, 2004, p. 116):

- Individuals reporting high subjective well-being had stronger social relationships than less happy individuals (Diener & Seligman, 2002).
- People with higher levels of subjective well-being were more likely to be married at a later measurement (Marks & Flemming, 1999; Lucas, Clark, Geogellis & Diener, 2003).
- High individual subjective well-being is a strong predictor of marital satisfaction (Glenn & Waver, 1981).
- In the workplace employees higher in dispositional positive affect receive higher supervisor rating and better pay (Diener, Nickerson, Lucas & Sandvik, 2001).
- In stressful circumstances, positive affect is associated with more effective coping

and better overall outcomes (Frederickson & Joiner, 2002).

- High subjective well-being is associated with lower levels of suicidal ideation and behavior (Diener & Seligman 2002).
- Subjective well-being is related to successful outcomes in a variety of life domains, because people with higher subjective well-being are more successful in relationships, more successful on the job, and better equipped to successfully cope with stress.

In summary we can say, that subjective well-being is associated with improved social connectedness, positive health outcomes, and increased resistance to the negative effects of stress, and success in the workforce and society (Pavot and Diener, 2004, p. 129). What links e-business with it?

The Influence of E-Business on Well-Being of Employees

The integration of e-business into the operations of enterprises is an innovative attempt and brings big changes, which also the employees must face. The individuals basically do not like changes and oppose them, because changes require adaptations in different fields (knowledge, manner of work, habits, skills, ...). All this usually causes their stress, weakens their concentration and increases possibility of mistakes and related punishment and failure, rather than benefit. E-business in SME-s also causes employees to not be treated as creative[1] and equal, although this would reduce their need for resistance or even revolt, strikes, and similar disturbances in creativeness within working process. That means that e-business could establish a model of managing the employees, which does not contain enough holism, expressed in the form of social responsibility and fair treatment; thus it would not offer a solution to the issue of well-being and its positive economic consequences. The use of e-business might lead to absentism, other serious illnesses or medical disorders, dislike of work instead of enjoying creative opportunities at work, searching for all possible ways of veiled strike, demonstrating the managers that their instructions are not factual enough to be achievable, etc., just like any other restructuring of other technological or non-technological novelty (Hrast et al., editors, 2009, especially Kieselbach, Dodič Fikfak).

When the employees do not stand the challenge of e-business as a novelty that is supposed to become innovation, they face a low self-esteem etc.; from this many negative consequences arise, also from the economic point of view. They also have less and less contacts to other people. We should be aware that the human is a social entity exercising a part of her integration into the social environment at her working place as well. The modern technology can destroy their ambitions to work and moves them away from their inner essence. So they experience more and more often the negative emotions (fear, sorrow, anger, …) and become apathetic and depressive. They can be thrilled by their feeling of being unable to manage their lives and that their living conditions are not good. Equally they might be dissatisfied with the results in their key areas of life – work, spare time, relations, and health. They think that their lives are incomplete and unfulfilled.

A negative influence can also be felt at the posture of employees working with computers, their eyesight, and blood circulation in their lower extremities.

However, the changes bring chances for learning and personal and personality development, if they present a challenge and new opportunity for innovativeness/creativeness. In this case the individual is filled with positive emotions, which has a positive effect on well-being. That means also a positive impact on life satisfaction.

All this shows that the perception of employees is crucial and that for establishing e-business in SME-s one must provide qualification, training, and communication. They can improve the employees' will and capacity to accept the novelty such as e-business because they feel more social responsibility expressed by their employers.

SOCIAL RESPONSIBILITY

Social responsibility (SR) is becoming more and more a hot topic. Writing about SR can be found (also) with following authors: Božičnik et al. (2008), Daft and Marcis (2001), Daft (1994), Steiner and Steiner (2003), Lahovnik (2008), Martin (2001), Harrison (1995), Prosenak and Mulej (2007 and 2008), Prosenak, Mulej, and Snoj (2008), Schwartz and Carroll (2003), Hrast et al. (2006, 2007, 2008, 2009, 2010), Rozman and Kovač (2006), Hrast and Zavašnik, ed. (2007), Knez-Riedl (2002, 2003a, b, c, 2004, 2006a, b, c, 2007a, b, c), Waddock and Bodwell (2007), Crowther and Caliyurt, ed. (2004), Crowther et al., ed. (2004), EU (2001) etc. 1.5 million hits on an official EU website about SR proves it to be an important topic (Google gives you 25 million hits on SR) [2] (Mulej et al., 2009, p. 4). We have no room to cite ideas of all these and other related authors. A generalized summary only can follow.

After surveying the relevant literature, Prosenak and Mulej (2008, p. 10) defined SR as a concept in which care for social and environmental problems should be included in activities to achieve our own goals. They say SR scoops three dimensions: (i) social, (ii) environmental and (iii) economic. EU definition (2001, 347 final, p. 5; sum. after: Mulej and Hrast, 2008, p. 43) is also important for our topic: "…SR of companies is a concept, with which companies voluntarily implement social and environmental care into their business activities and into their interactions with stakeholders". But companies are people's tools; that's why SR should be considered as ethical guide for individuals when active and making decisions.

Concerning the definition of SR, which is mostly used on EU level – concept of voluntary participation that takes care of stakeholders and of quality of their relations, the following SR stakeholders are defined (Štoka Debevec, 2007):

- Employees, which need the following attributes guaranteed: safe and healthy working place, decent conditions and pay for their work, workers' rights, duties and needs respected, and also the understanding for reconciliation of their working and private needs;
- Suppliers, from which companies demand a transparent and fair attitude and also respect the same rules themselves;
- Nature, which alarms us more and more about its exploitation and our inappropriate handling its resources; and
- Environment as social community in which companies function and exploit conditions that are available and in the same way companies are expected to return these benefits to society in terms of its future development.

Fields of Activity and Benefits from SR

Nickels and Wood (1997, p. 92-93) say that the SR concept covers all areas of organization; it is based on conviction that companies shouldn't only take care of their profits, but should also contribute to prosperity in society. Socially responsible behavior covers not only acting according to law and avoiding unethical deeds, but also an active involvement in society and a help with solving problems of society. Johnson and Scholes (1997, p. 211-212) show that SR of companies includes their actions on internal (care for employees, working conditions and working place and working orders adequacy) and external basis (care for environment, safety of products and services, market and suppliers choice, employment and local society activities). Frideric, Davis and Post (1988, p. 33) consider the following areas as central in SR: (i) quality and safety of products, (ii) consumers

relations, (iii) employees relations, (iv) charity and care for people, (v) society relations, (vi) care for environment and (vii) economic influences.

Need of many to emphasize SR as a necessary feature of companies, shows how distant have companies become from their natural role: the company has become self-sufficient. Goerner et al. (2008) emphasize that American capitalism has changed into something against what it has arisen centuries ago. Toth (2008) similarly thinks that the current model of capitalism is obsolete and in need of renovation. Naomi Klein (2009) talks, similarly like Božičnik et al. (2008) about capitalism of disaster. SR leads the way out of this blind alley.

Mulej and Hrast (2008, p. 47) also summarize the common denominator of definitions of SR and its benefits. SR can cover an upgrading of the informal system thinking methods, too. But SR can also mean a lot more – a new way from the blind alley of humanity of today. After the phases of competitiveness based on natural resources, on investing, and on innovating, in the fourth phase humankind is coming closer and closer to affluence. The latter is found a climax in human wishes and a blind alley, too, because more and more people, having everything they consider necessary, no longer have motivation to work and shop[3] SR, combined with acting according to requisite holism, and with creativity, oriented towards Fromm's transition of humans from owners to creators, could save the current human civilization, so it wouldn't deteriorate like all the others have done in their times of affluence. It is a process of social innovation and it is a rightfully wanted goal (Mulej and Hrast 2008, p. 41). This process is of vital importance to crisis prevention and solving because the essence of SR is prevention of misuse/abuse of legal, economic and natural laws. Its intention is to replace short-term and narrow-minded standards with broader and more long-term criteria of what is right and what is wrong, and later to establish what is useful, and what is not so (Mulej and Hrast 2008, p. 46).

New Perspectives on SR

There is a long line of new perspectives concerning the SR development. We will sum up some of the propositions that will serve us as a foundation to develop our own perspective concerning SR aimed at solving the potential e-business crisis by reaching requisite holism standards of behavior.

SR is supposed to constructively contribute to solving of complex issues, such as: (i) climate change, (ii) limitation of natural resources, (iii) increase of differences and stress, and (iv) global competition (Prosenak and Mulej 2008, pp. 10-11). Prosenak and Mulej (2008, pp. 10-12) see deficiency in the present concept of SR: (i) problems-solving in un-holistic manner, (ii) morally questionable activities, and (iii) one-sidedness, instead of a (requisitely) holistic pressure of share-holders and other owners on companies' leaderships. Therefore they find the present concept of SR too un-holistic to be the solution and that is why we need the Dialectical Systemic approach to the problem, which will include and connect all necessary aspects for achieving the requisite holism.

Considering that all subjects are inter-connected because they are interdependent, we should take care of a requisitely holistic quality of life (objective and subjective welfare/well-being) including human solidarity (that is based on acknowledging the meaning and strengthening of ethics of interdependence). This includes e.g. respect towards ecological sensibility and natural limitations, which demands reconciliation of narrower, broader, short-term and long-term perspectives with ecological and other nature-respecting perspectives as a necessary element of values of people, expressed with SR (Prosenak and Mulej, 2008, p. 13).

That shows that SR could be an efficient concept also against the current disadvantages of e-business of SME's, but it needs to be supplemented with requisite holism, which helps individuals to come closer to requisite holism in standards of behavior, which leads to socially responsible actions.

APPLICATION OF SR CONCEPT IN SME's AGAINST DISADVANTAGES OF E-BUSINESS IN TERMS OF WELL-BEING

Social responsibility tends to increased well-being of employees and result in better work. But this potential benefit is hard to attain, if coworkers are viewed as employees only rather than as complex multilayered individual human beings. E-business is no exception, experience says, which we have no room to tackle in any detail here.

Individual as a Multi-Layered Being

Individual is the foundation of SR that is based on individual's personal responsibility. Hence the organizations should look at humans as multilayered, not only as professional entities. In synergy, not only separately, we define humans as: (i) physical, (ii) mental, (iii) social, (iv) spiritual, (v) professional, and (vi) economic entities. Humans are marked by requisitely, though not absolutely, holistic pattern of relatively permanent characteristics, due to which individuals differ from each other. All these and other attributes form synergies.

In today's unstructured world, populated with competent individuals, where everything is spinning around intelligence and non-material things, that means flows of knowledge. But emotions and imagination are not parts of some section in organization but rather a philosophy, a viewpoint (Nordström and Ridderstråle 2001, p. 109 and p. 213). Such a world fills people with doubt and hesitation: they neither have a clear mission nor strive to find it. Neuman (2001, p. 19) also discusses that. A modern human is numb and bored (Lesar, 2002, p. 11). Solution lies in a spiritual motivation which carries a will to meaning in its centre – an inner wish of individual to accept her life as worthy and meaningful (Musek, 1998). That is why we evaluate that it is necessary to develop (subjective and objective) wellbeing as well as the spiritual side of individual in order to get her nearer to requisite holism.

Requisite Holism of Individual

Study of holism/wholeness, conducted by Bertalanffy (1968, edition 1979), is crucial to our research, but as a requisite one it was authored by Mulej (2000 – on basis of publications in 1974, 1975, 1979, etc). Works such as Treven and Mulej (2005a, b), Mulej and Kajzer (1998a, b), Sruk (1995), Mautner (1995),… can be added to the list. Mulej's and Kajzer's law of requisite holism also managed to enter encyclopedia (François 2004). Chopra (2006, p. 120) means holism when he talks about entireness, which is defined as including of everything without anything being left behind. He also connects wholeness to a personality; it's a state of personality, which shows at times, when »I am« as individual is the same as »I am« everywhere. Sadly, entireness/holism/wholeness isn't executable for natural reasons, when it comes to human acting: there are too many attributes, that is why there are so many specializations. Only requisite holism of behaviour is executable. That is why systems theory is important to our research, but not in all versions, such as the descriptive and matemathical ones etc., but as knowledge about achieving the requisite holism of behaviour, that includes observing, comprehending, thinking, emotional and spiritual life, decision-making, communication, and practical action (Mulej, 2009, p. 4).

If holism is applied to an individual personality as an employee, beside philosophy, management, spiritualism, sociology, psychology is crucial, too. It defines personality, its basic attributes, structure of personality, and personality development. So, existential analysis and Frankl's[4] understanding of human development and her actions in the world are very important; his concept emphasizes, that

the spiritual motivation has a priority with no doubt, where a will to a meaning is a priority – an inner wish of an individual to experience her life as valuable and meaningful. Frankl, the founder of logo-therapy, defines lack of meaning of life as a basic »neurosis« of the modern human, which manifests itself as sense of meaninglessness, emptiness of life – as emptiness of being. Musek (1999, p. 7) emphasizes, that questions of self-awareness and of borders of personality exceed the framework of scientific research and pass into the area of philosophical, even transcendental aspects of personality. So, here we pass to the area of spiritualism that is important for the development of welfare and/or well-being of an individual, which also provides for some positive consequences.

Therefore requisite holism of an individual, being employed on a basis of welfare/well-being, is defined as both practice and self-awareness. All this presents a good basis for SR, realization of which would contribute to well-being of employees in SME's, too, with good economic outcomes included.

CONCLUSION

E-business is a novelty that provides for changes in the given habits of employees. Even if it is an technological innovation rather than a failure, if makes pressure over humans who tend to prefer routine over novelty; it requires innovation of habits and related values, culture, ethics, and norms – more social responsibility and holism. This impacts employees' well-being and, through it, employees' own as well as company's effectiveness of work. Therefore, well-being may not be left aside when owners and managers intend to introduce e-business style in their organizations. Consequences of one-sidedness might be crucial in this case like in all other cases. Principles and measures of innovative business, social responsibility and requisite holism should be used and be so in synergy rather than in separation.

REFERENCES

Abouzeedan, A., & Busler, M. (2006). Information Technology (IT) and Small and Medium-sized Enterprises (SMEs) Management. *Global Business Review, 7*(2), 243–257. doi:10.1177/097215090600700204

Abouzeedan, A., & Busler, M. (2007). Internetization Management. *Global Business Review, 8*(2), 303–321. doi:10.1177/097215090700800208

Altekar, R. V. (2005). *Supply Chain Mangement. Concepts and Cases.* Upper Saddle River, NJ: Prentice Hall of India.

Arthaud-Day, M. L., Rode, J. C., Mooney, C. H., & Near, J. (2005). The Subjective Well-being Construct: A test of Its Convergent, Discriminant, and Factorial Validity. *Social Indicators Research, 74*, 445–476. doi:10.1007/s11205-004-8209-6

Bertalanffy, L. v. (1950). An outline of General System Theory. *The British Journal for the Philosophy of Science, 1*(2), 134–165. doi:10.1093/bjps/I.2.134

Bertalanffy, L. v. (1968, edition 1979). *General Systems Theory. Foundations, Development, Applications. Revised Edition. Sixth Printing.* New York: Braziller.

Bocij, C. D., Hickie, S., & Greasley, A. (2006). *Business information systems; Technology, Development and Management for the e-business, 3th edition.* Upper Saddle River, NJ: Prentice Hall.

Božičnik, S., Ećimović, T., & Mulej, M. (Eds.). (2008). *Sustainable future, requisite holism, and social responsibility. Maribor: ANSTED University, Penang in co-operation with SEM Institute for climate change.* Korte, and IRDO Institute for Development of Social Responsibility. CD.

Chopra, D. (2006). *Knjiga skrivnosti.* Maribor: Litera.

Crowther, D., Barry, D. M., Sankar, A., Goh, K. G., & Ortiz Martinez, E. (2004b). *S.R.W. Social Responsibility World of RecordPedia 2004. Penang: Ansted Service Center.* Ansted University Asia Regional Service Center.

Crowther, D., & Caliyut, K. T. (Eds.). (2004): *Stakeholders and Social Responsibility.* Penang: ANSTED University.

Daft, R., & Marcis, D. (2001). *Understanding Management.* London: Thomson Learning.

Daft, R. L. (1994). *Management* (3rd ed.). United States of America: The Dryden Press.

Diener, E. (1984). Subjective Well-being. *Psychological Bulletin, 95*(3), 542–575. doi:10.1037/0033-2909.95.3.542

Diener, E., Lucas, R. E., & Oishi, S. (2002). Subjective Well-Being. In Snyder, C. R., & Lopez, S. J. (Eds.), *Handbook of positive psychology.* New York: Oxford University Press.

Diener, E., Nickerson, C., Lucas, R. E., & Sandvik, E. (2001). *Dispositional affect and job outcomes.* Manuscript submitted for pulication.

Diener, E., & Seligman, E. M. (2004). Beyond Money; Toward an Economy of Well-being. *Psychological Science in the Public Interest, 5*(1), 1–31. doi:10.1111/j.0963-7214.2004.00501001.x

Diener, E., & Seligman, M. E. (2002). Very happy people. *Psychological Science, 13*, 81–84. doi:10.1111/1467-9280.00415

Dodič Fikfak, M. (2009). Prestrukturiranje gospodarstva in kazalniki zdravja. V: *Delo – most za sodelovanje/4. mednarodna konferenca Družbena odgovornost in izzivi časa 2009.* Hrast, A. in M. Matjaž (urednika). Maribor: IRDO – Inštitut za razvoj družbene odgovornosti, 63.

EU. (2001). [Commission of the European Communities, 2001]: Green Paper on Promoting a European Framework for Corporate Social Responsibility, COM (2001) 366 final, Brussels. Retrieved July 1, 2009, from http://eur-lex.europa.eu/LexUriServ/site/en/com/2001/com2001_0366en01.pdf

Felce, D., & Parry, J. (1995). Quality of life: its definition and measurement. *Research in Developmental Disabilities, 16*(1), 51–74. doi:10.1016/0891-4222(94)00028-8

François, Ch. (Ed.). (2004). *International Encyclopedia of Systems and Cybernetics* (2nd ed.). Munich: Saur.

Frankl, V. E. (1962). *Man's search for meaning: An introduction to logotherapy.* Boston: Beacon Press.

Frankl, V. E. (1994). *Zdravnik in duša: osnove logoterapije in bivanjske analize.* Celje: Mohorjeva družba.

Frankl, V. E. (2005). *Človek pred vprašanjem o smislu: izbor iz zbranega dela.* Ljubljana: Pasadena.

Fredericson, B. L., & Joiner, T. (2002). Positive emotions trigger upward spirals toward emotional well-being. *Psychological Science, 13,* 172–175. doi:10.1111/1467-9280.00431

Friderick, W. C., Davis, K., & Post, E. J. (1988). *Business and Society: Corporate Strategy, Public Policy, Ethics* (6th ed.). New York: McGraw-Hill Publishing Company.

Glenn, N. D., & Weaver, C. N. (1981). The contributions of marital happiness to global happiness. *Journal of Marriage and the Family, 43,* 161–168. doi:10.2307/351426

Goerner, S., Dyck, R. G., & Lagerroos, D. (2008). *The New Science of Sustainability. Building a Foundation for Great Change.* Chapel Hill, N.C: Triangle Center for Complex Systems.

Harris, L. (2002). History, Definition and Frameworks. In Harris, L., & Dennis, C. (Eds.), *Marketing and e-Business.* London: Routledge. doi:10.4324/9780203166963.ch1

Harrison, S. (1995). *Public Relations: an introduction.* New York: Routledge.

Hird, S. (2003). What is Well-being? A brief review of current literature and concepts. *NHS Scotland,* March 2003. Retriven June 28, 2009, from http://phis.org.uk/doc.pl?file=pdf/What%20is%20wellbeing%202.doc.

Hrast, A., & Matjaž, M. (2009). *Delo – most za sodelovanje/4. mednarodna konferenca Družbena odgovornost in izzivi časa 2009.* (Ed.). Maribor: IRDO – Inštitut za razvoj družbene odgovornosti.

Hrast, A., & Mulej, M. (Eds.). (2008). *Družbena odgovornost 2008. Zbornik 3. IRDO Konference o družbeni odgovornosti.* Maribor: IRDO Inštitut za razvoj družbene odgovornosti. CD.

Hrast, A., Mulej, M., & Knez-Riedl, J. (Eds.). (2006). *Družbena odgovornost in izzivi časa 2006. Maribor: IRDO Inštitut za razvoj družbene odgovornosti.* Na CD.

Hrast, A., Mulej, M., & Knez-Riedl, J. (Eds.). (2007). *Družbena odgovornost 2007.* Maribor: IRDO Inštitut za razvoj družbene odgovornosti. CD.

Hrast, A., & Zavašnik, A. (Eds.). (2007). *Uvajanje družbene odgovornosti v poslovno prakso malih in srednje velikih podjetij v Sloveniji: Priročnik s primeri dobre prakse.* Maribor: GZS – Območna zbornica Maribor.

Jackson, J., Harris, L. & Eckersley, Peter M. (2003). *E-business fundamentals.* London and New York: Routledge Taylor & Francis Crou

James, O. (2007). *Affluenza – a contagious middle class virus causing depression, anxiety, addiction and ennui.* London: Vermillion, an imprint of Ebury Publishing, Random House UK Ltd etc.

Johnson, G. & Scholes, K. (1997). *Exploring Corporate Strategy*. Hertfordshire: Prentice Hall Europe.

Kieselbach, T. (2009). Health in restructuring: Empirical evidence and policy recommendations. In Hrast, A., & Mulej, M. (Eds.), *Delo – most za sodelovanje/4. mednarodna konferenca Družbena odgovornost in izzivi časa 2009. Maribor: IRDO – Inštitut za razvoj družbene odgovornosti, 58.*

Klein, N. (2009). *Doktrina šoka: razmah uničevalnega kapitalizma*. Ljubljana: Mladinska knjiga.

Knez-Riedl, J. (2002). Družbena odgovornost malih in srednje velikih podjetij. In M. Rebernik (Ed.) *Slovenski podjetniški observatorij 2002*, (pp 91 – 112), 2nd part.

Knez-Riedl, J. (2003a). Corporate social responsibility and communication with external community = Korporacijska društvena odgovornost i komuniciranje sa vanjskim okruženjem. *Informatologia, 36*(3), 166–172.

Knez-Riedl, J. (2003b). Social responsibility of a family business. *MER, Rev. manag. razvoj, 5*(2), 90-99.

Knez-Riedl, J. (2003c). Corporate social responsibility and holistic analysis. In G. Chroust in Ch. Hofer (Ed.), *IDIMT-2003: Proceedings, (Schriftenreihe Informatik, Bd 9),* Linz: Universitätsverlag R. Trauner, 187-198.

Knez-Riedl, J. (2004). Slovenian SMEs: from the environmental responsibility to corporate social responsibility. In Sharma, S. K. (Ed.), *An enterprise odyssey: building competitive advantage* (pp. 127–139). Zagreb: Zagreb International Review of Economics & Business.

Knez-Riedl, J. (2006c). *Družbena odgovornost in univerza*. In A., Hrast et al. (2006), referenced here.

Knez Riedl, J. (2007a). Kako DOP povečuje konkurenčnost. In *Projekt CSR – Code to Smart Reality*, Maribor: GZS-OZ.

Knez-Riedl, J. (2007b). Družbena odgovornost podjetja in evropski strateški dokumenti, *Projekt CSR – Code to Smart Reality*. Maribor: GZS OZ Maribor.

Knez-Riedl, J. (2007c). Obvladovanje celovite (družbene) odgovornosti. *Razgledi MBA*, 12 [i.e. 13],(1/2), 37-43.

Knez-Riedl, J., & Hrast, A. (2006a). Managing corporate social responsibility (CSR): a case of multiple benefits of socially responsible behaviour of a firm. In R. Trappl (Ed.), *Cybernetics and systems 2006: proceedings of the Eighteenth European Meeting on Cybernetics and Systems Research.* (pp 405-409). Vienna: Austrian Society for Cybernetic Studies.

Knez-Riedl, J., Mulej, M., & Dyck, R. G. (2006b). Corporate Social Responsibility from the Viewpoint of Systems Thinking. *Kybernetes, 35*(3/4), 441–460. doi:10.1108/03684920610653737

Lahovnik, M. (2008). Družbena odgovornost ko dejavnik korporacijskega upravljanja podjetij v Sloveniji. *Naše gospodarstvo,* 54 (5/6): 10-21.

Layard, R. (2005). *Happiness: lessons from a new science*. London: Allen Lane, Penguin Grou.

Lesar, I. (2002). *Med iskanjem smisla in izbiro smisla*. Ljubljana: Inštitut za psihologijo osebnosti.

Lewin, K. (2005). *A Dynamic Theory of Personality – Selected Papers*. Read Books.

Linley, A., & Joseph, S. (Eds.). (2004). *Positive Psychology in Practice*. Newspaper of the National Association of School Psychologists, Retrieved May 25, 2009, from http://people.hofstra.edu/Jeffrey_J_Froh/Froh_Review.pdfSeligman, M.E. [2.2.2009].

Linley, A., Joseph, S., Maltby, J., Harrington, S., & Wood, A. M. (2009). Positive Psychology Applications. In C. R. Snyder & S. J. Lopez (Ed.) 2002. *Oxford Handbook of Positive Psychology.* New York: Oxford University Press.

Lopez, S. J., & Gallagher, M. W. (2009). A Case for Positive Psychology. In C. R. Snyder & S. J. Lopez (Ed.) 2002. *Oxford Handbook of Positive Psychology.* New York: Oxford University Press.

Lucas, R. E., Clark, A. E., Georgellis, Y., & Diener, E. (2003). Re-examining adaptation and the set point model of happiness: Reactions to changes in marital status. *Journal of Personality and Social Psychology, 84,* 527–539. doi:10.1037/0022-3514.84.3.527

Lucas, R. E., Diener, E., & Suh, E. (1996). Discriminant validity of well-being measures. *Journal of Personality and Social Psychology, 71,* 616–618. doi:10.1037/0022-3514.71.3.616

Marks, G. N., & Flemming, N. (1999). Influences and consequences of well-being among Australian young people: 1980-1995. *Social Indicators Research, 46,* 301–323. doi:10.1023/A:1006928507272

Martin, J. (2001). *Organizational Behaviour.* London: Thompson Learning.

Martin, (2005). *Making Happy People: the nature of happiness and its origins in childhood.* Fourth Estate pubs.

Maslow, A. H. (1954). *Motivation and Personality.* New York: Harper&Row.

Mautner, T. (1995). *A dictionary of philosophy.* Oxford: Blackwell Publishers Ltd.

McAllister, F. (2005). *Wellbeing Concepts and Challenges. Discussion Paper Prepared by Fiona McAllister for the Sustainable Development Research Network (SDRN).* Retrieved May 1, 2009, from http://www.sd-research.org.uk/wellbeing/documents/SDRNwellbeingpaper-Final_000.pdf.

Meyer, J. (Ed.). (2000). *Jahrbuch der KMU-Forschung.* München. 1f Meyer, J. (Ed.). (2001). *Flensburger Forschungsbeiträge zur kleinen und mittleren Unternehmen.* Koln. 1ff

Milutinovič, Ž., & Patricelli, F. (2002). *E-business and e-challenges.* Amsterdam: IOS Press.

Mulej, M. (1974). Dialektična teorija sistemov in ljudski reki. *Naše gospodarstvo,* 21 (3-4): 207-212.

Mulej, M. (1979). *Ustvarjalno delo in dialektična teorija sistemov. Razvojni center.* Celje.

Mulej, M. (2009). Lack of requisitely holistic thinking and action – a reason for products to not become winners. In Rebernik, (Eds.), *PODIM 2009. University of Maribor.* Faculty of Economics and Business, Institute for Entrepreneurship and Small Business Management.

Mulej, M. et al. (2000). *Dialektična in druge mehkosistemske teorije: (podlage za celovitost in uspeh managementa).* Maribor: Ekonomsko-poslovna fakulteta.

Mulej, M., Božičnik, S., Ženko, Z., & Potočan, V. (2009). Nujnost in zapletenost ustvarjalnega sodelovanja za inoviranje in pot iz krize 2008. In Hrast, A. & Mulej, M. (Ed.). *Delo – most za sodelovanje/4. mednarodna konferenca Družbena odgovornost in izzivi časa 2009.* Maribor: IRDO – Inštitut za razvoj družbene odgovornosti, Musek, J. & Avsec, A. (2002). Pozitivna psihologija: subjektivni (emocionalni) blagor in zadovoljstvo z življenjem. *Anthropos,* 34, (1/3), 41-68.

Mulej, M., & Hrast, A. (2008). Družbena odgovornost podjetij. V: *Skupaj smo močnejši, Zbornik 2. konference nevladnih organizacij Podravja* (pp 41-52). Regionalno stičišče Podravja.

Mulej, M., & Kajzer, S. (1998a). Tehnološki razvoj in etika soodvisnosti. *Raziskovalec, 28,* 1.

Mulej, M., & Kajzer, S. (1998b). Ethic of interdependence and the law of requisite holism. In M. Rebernik & M. Mulej (Ed.) *STIQE '98* (pp 56-67). Maribor: ISRUM.

Mulej, M. (1975). *Osnove dialektične teorije sistemov*. Lecture notes. Univerza v Ljubljani, Fak. za telesno kulturo, Ljubljana.

Musek, J. (1998). *Človek celostno bitje*. Educy: Ljubljana: Inštitut za psihologijo osebnosti.

Musek, J. (2005). *Psihološke in kognitivne študije osebnosti*. Ljubljana: Znanstveni inštitut Filozofske fakultete.

Musek, J., & Avsec, A. (2002). Pozitivna psihologija: subjektivni (emocionalni) blagor in zadovoljstvo z življenjem. *Anthropos*, [online]. *34*(1/3), 41-68. Dostopno na: http://www.educy.com/jmusek/Teksti/Pozitivna%20psihologija.pdf. [16.2.2009].

Musek, J., & Avsec, A. (2006). Osebnost, samopodoba in psihično zdravje. *Anthropos*, *38*(1/2), 51–75.

Musek, J., Tušak, M., & Zalokar Divjak, Z. (1999). *Osebnost in zdravje*. Ljubljana: EDUCY.

Nette, D. (2005). *Happiness: the Science behind you smile*. Oxford, UK: OU

Neumann, E. (2001). *Ustvarjalni človek*. Ljubljana: Študentska založba.

Nickels, W. G., & Burk Wood, M. (1997). *Marketing: Relationships, Quality, Value*. New York: Worth Publishers Inc.

Nordström. Kjell A. & Ridderstråle, J. (2001). *Ta nori posel – Funky business, ko zaigra talent, kapital pleše*. Ljubljana: GV založba.

Pavot, W. in E. Diener. (2004). The subjective evaluation of well-being in adulthood: Findings and implications. *Ageing International, 29*(2), 113–135. doi:10.1007/s12126-004-1013-4

Prosenak, D., & Mulej, M. (2007). How can marketing contribute to increase of well-being in transitional (and other) societies? In B. Snoj & B. Milfelner (Ed.), *1st International Scientific Marketing Theory Challenges in Transitional Societies Conference* (pp 127-133). Maribor: University of Maribor, Faculty of Economics and Business.

Prosenak, D. & Mulej, M. (2008). O celovitosti in uporabnosti obstoječega koncepta družbene odgovornosti poslovanja = About holism and applicability of the existing concept of corporate social responsibility (CSR). *Naše gospodarstvo*, 54 (3/4), 10-21.

Prosenak, D., Mulej, M., & Snoj, B. (2008). A requisitely holistic approach to marketing in terms of social well-being. *Kybernetes, 37*(9/10), 1508–1529. doi:10.1108/03684920810907832

Revkin, A. C. (2005). A New Measure of Well-Being from a Happy Little Kingdom. *The New York Times*, 4. 10. Retriven May 25, 2009, from http://www.nytimes.com/2005/10/04/science/04haphtml?ex=1171947600&en=5a41a93522961d05&ei=5070.

Rozman, R., & Kovač, J. (Eds.). (2006). *Družbena odgovornost in etika v organizacijah. Proceedings of the 7th scientific conference on organisation. (In Slovenian).*, Kranj: Univerza v Mariboru, Fakulteta za organizacijske vede in Zveza organizatorjev Slovenije; Ljubljana: Univerza v Ljubljani, Ekonomska fakulteta.

Ryan, R. M., & Deci, E. L. (2001). On Happiness and Human Potentials: A Review of Research on Hedonic and Eudaimonic Well-Being. In s Fiske (Ed) *Annual Review of Psychology* (Annual Reviews Inc, Paolo Alto California).

Schneider, B. (2004). *The Successful Management of Small and Middle-sized Enterprises in a Specific Sector – with a Practical Analysis*. München in Mering. Reiner Hampp Verlag.

Schwartz, S. M., & Caroll, A. B. (2003). *Corporate social responsibility: A three domain approach*. New York: Business Ethics Quarterly.

Seligman, M. E. (2002). *Authentic happiness: Using the new positive psychology to realize your potential for lasting fullfillment*. New York: Free Press.

Seligman, M. E. (2002). Positive Psychology, Positive Prevention, and Positive Therapy. In C. R. Snyder & S. J. Lopez (Ed.) (2002). *Handbook of positive psychology.* New York: Oxford University Press, page: 3-13.

Seligman, M. E., & Csikszentmihalyi, M. (2000). Positive psychology: An Introduction. *The American Psychologist, 55*(1), 5–14. doi:10.1037/0003-066X.55.1.5

Seligman, M. E., Steen, T. A., Park, N., & Peterson, C. (2005). Positive Psychology Progress, Empirical Validation of Interventions. *American Psychologist* 60(5), 410-421. Retriven March 13, 2009. http://pq.2004.tripod.com/apa_positive_psychology_progress_july_august_2005.pdf., [12.6.2009].

Sheldon, K., Frederickson, B., Rathunde, K., & Csikszentmihalyi, M. in J. Haidt. (2000). *Positive psychology manifesto (Rev. ed.),* [online]. Dostopno na: Retriven June 22, 2000, fromhttp://www.positivepsychology.org/akumalmanifesto.html [22.6.2000].

Sheldon, K. M., & King, L. (2001). Why positive psychology is necessary. *The American Psychologist, 56*(3), 216–217. doi:10.1037/0003-066X.56.3.216

Singh, M. (1997). *Effective implementation of new technologies in the Australian manufacturing industries.* PhD Thesis, Monash University, Melbourne, Australia.

Singh, M. (2000). Electronic Commerce in Australia: Opportunities and factors critical for success. *Proceedings of the 1ˢᵗ World Congress on the Management of Electronic Commerce (CD-ROM),* Hamilton, Ontario, January, 19-21.

Singh, M. (2003). Innovation and Change Management. In *M. Singh M. & D. Waddell. (2003). E-business innovation and change management.* Hershey, PA: Idea Group Publishing.

Singh, M., & Waddell, D. (2003). *E-business innovation and change management.* Hershey, PA: Idea Group Publishing.

Snyder, C. R., & Lopez, S. J. (Eds.). (2002). *Handbook of positive psychology.* New York: Oxford University Press.

Sruk, V. (1995). *Filozofija.* Ljubljana: Cankarjeva založba.

Steiner, G. A., & Steiner, J. F. (2003). *Business, Government and Society: A Managerial Perspective, Text and Cases* (10th ed.). New York: McGraw-Hill.

Štoka Debevec, M. (2008). Pregled dogajanj na področju družbene odgovornosti v Evropski uniji. In Hrast, A. (Eds.), *Prispevki družbene odgovornosti k dolgoročni uspešnosti vseh udeležencev na trgu.* Maribor. Referenced here.

Storey David John. (1994). *Understanding the Small Business Sector.* Thompson.

Sustainable Development Research Network. (2006). *Wellbeing Concepts and Challenges.* Online Available: Retrieved June 26, 2009, from http://www.sd-research.org.uk/wellbeing/documents/FinalWellbeingPolicyBriefing.pdf.

Toth, G. (2008). *Resnično odgovorno podjetje.* Ljubljana: GV Založba.

Treven, S. (2005, sept.). in & Mulej, M. (2005a). Sistemski pristop k obvladovanju raznolikosti zaposlenih v globalnem okolju. *Organizacija, 38*(7), 321–329.

Treven, S. in & Mulej, M. (2005b). Teorija sistemov, inovativna družba in management stresa v delovnem okolju. *Naše gospodarstvo,*51(3/4), 56-63.

Veenhoven, R. (1997). Advances in the Understanding of Happiness, publishing in French in. *Revue Québécoise de Psychologie, 18,* 29–74.

Waddock, S., & Bodwell, C. C. (2007). *Total Responsibility Management*. Sheffield: Greenleaf Publishing Limited.

Watson, D., Clark, L. A., & Tellegen, A., A. (1988). Develpoment and validation of a brief measure of positive and negative affect: The PANAS scales. *Journal of Personality and Social Psychology, 54*, 1063–1070. doi:10.1037/0022-3514.54.6.1063

Whinston, A., Stahl, D., & Choi, S. (1998). *The economics of electronic commerce*. Indianapolis, Indiana: Macmillan Technical Publishing.

Zhuang, Y & Lederer, A. (2003). An instrument for measuring the business benefits of e-commerce retailing. *International Journal of Electronic Commerce, 7*(3).New York: Spring.

ENDNOTES

[1] A small empirical anecdote illustrates the point: during the decades of supporting the organizations in their development of innovative business we have also encountered managers, who told us they could not expect any innovative suggestions from their employees since none of them had suggested anything for many years; this means they are supposed to not be creative. To such statements we responded with a double question: 1. If they are not innovative, how do they manage to survive with the modest pay they get? 2. How many of those making no suggestions in the company, successfully deal with grey economy at home? The answer was that the great majority show creativity, where the leadership conditions and styles allow or even promote it. At home they are autonomous, not subordinated. Therefore they feel better and can accomplish more, even innovations. – They are not the problem, but their managers are.

[2] On 5th March 2009 e-browser Google offered more than 55 million hits on keyword Social Responsibility. In June 2009 they were beyond 200 million.

[3] The danger of affluence is visible in the increasing role of marketing and aggressive advertisement and the growing number of people trying to forget about reality by abusing drugs, etc.

[4] Viktor Frankl (1962, 1994, 2005)

Chapter 8

Copying with Dynamic Change:
Collaborative Business Interfacing for SMEs under Integrated eOperations

Jayantha P. Liyanage
University of Stavanger, Norway

ABSTRACT

The business environment around the world is in a continuous evolution process due to changes in global dynamics. Even though the energy sector has relied much on the known sources, the production process has gone through some notable changes due to inherent challenges and developments in knowledge management and technology use. The Offshore oil & gas production industry today, at least in the North Sea, is at a cross-road where the traditional operational concepts are seriously challenged due to various risk factors and commercial uncertainties. Subsequently, 'Intergrated eOperations' (IO) was adapted as the business solution for a sustainable future seeking major benefits by major players in the sector. This has begun to re-engineer the traditional practices and commercial operations, and the industry continuously seeks novel solutions for 24/7 online real-time operations. In this unique 'eBusiness' environment, SMEs encounter various technical and operational challenges to cope with the mass scale dynamic change process. In order to utilize IO for commercial advantage, SMEs are in the process of exploring various interface solutions today. With respect to the ongoing developments and the scopes of IO, 'Collaborative business interfacing' that is discussed in this chapter is to enable the SMEs to be 'smarter together' to capitalize on the potentials of IO through a strategic capability acquisition process. In the IO setting, and the eBusiness environment that it is expected to create, strategic business change is not an option for SMEs but an inevitable issue for survival and growth.

INTRODUCTION

The environment for Engineering asset management has been subjected to significant changes over the last few years. Various attempts have been made in industrial sectors towards technological and service innovation, knowledge management, information, collaboration, etc. to realize operational excellence in hard times (Child & Faulkner,

DOI: 10.4018/978-1-60960-463-9.ch008

1998, Dyer, 2000, Tidd, 2001, Gunasekaran, Khalil, 2003, During, Oakey, et.al., 2004, Timo, Markku, et.al. 2005, Wang, Heng, et.al. 2006, Liyanage, 2008a). Different industrial sectors seem to have different orientations, in this context, seeking feasible implementation solutions.

In the North Sea Offshore petroleum industry, *Integrated eOperations* is seen as the new business solution for complex engineering assets to cope with challenging commercial conditions (OLF, 2003). North Sea oil & gas production industry in particular has already begun to invest billions of USDs on various application solutions targeting productivity improvements in offshore production assets. At the beginning, a major portion of these investments were made seeking technological innovation to enable a 24/7 real-time online operating mode. This has resulted in a completely different e-business solution around offshore assets, where the industry as a whole today undergoes a complete re-engineering process involving producers, authorities, trade unions, external service providers, third party contractors, etc. This process began in early 2000s and will continue at least for another decade targeting the full scale *Integrated eOperations* status towards 2015 or so (Liyanage, Herbert, et.al. 2006, Liyanage & Langeland, 2007, McCann, Omdal, et.al. 2004).

The major oil & gas producers are the principal drivers of this dynamic change process. The external organizations are expected to device suitable strategies and measures, and implement advanced technologies to cope with the mass scale change process to remain competitive. While major business partners, such as engineering contractors, drilling service providers, etc., have taken early measures to implement adaptive strategies to capitalize on *Integrated eOperations*, there are various other organizations who are lagging behind the development process. This particularly is the case for SMEs who encounter various technical and operational challenges to cope with the mass scale dynamic change process. As an active and a critical component of the industry structure and

corporate value chains, SME integration is a commercially vital issue in many different contexts (Wang, Heng, et.al., 2007, Tai, Wang, et.al. 2007). However, as Lin and Patterson (2007) discuss, there are notable barriers for SMEs in coping with industry transformation strategies, where risk distribution plays a major role.

In order to utilize *Integrated eOperations* for commercial advantage, SMEs are in the process of exploring various interface solutions today. Commercially advantageous business interface solutions do not solely rests on innovative technologies and advanced ICT infrastructures, but also on other soft organizational, managerial, and work-processes related issues that are critical to have a seamless interface with the Offshore assets. (Liyanage & Bjerkebæk, 2007, Liyanage, 2008b, Liyanage & Herbert, 2008). For instance, business-to-business trust has become a major issue of attention lately (Lin & Pettrson, 2007) due to inherent risks associated with organizational exposures. The required transition is not a choice for SMEs but an unavoidable business requirement to survive and grow in the emerging highly collaborative 24/7 online real-time operational environment.

With reference to recent development in more global scale, Sabbaghi & Vidyanathan (2007) highlights that in integration context the cultivation of anticipatory stance for SMEs to cope with emerging business challenges is vital for competitive performance rather than resorting to reactive strategies. Such anticipation can largely be generated through a realistic comparison of opportunities presented by strategic changes in industrial sectors against the capabilities that an organization possesses. However, given the limitations in access to resources coupled with other practical bottlenecks encountered by SMEs, novel interface solutions seem to be necessary in the implementation of adaptive measures. The objective of this chapter is to discuss these complex set of business interface solutions for SMEs to survive in this dynamic mass scale change process within the petroleum sector. This is based on current developments in the Norwegian Offshore industry towards dynamic *Integrated eOperations*.

'INTEGRATED E-OPERATIONS' [IO]

Over the last decade the Petroleum industry has been undergoing a number of major challenges globally. The increasing demand for energy together with the favorable oil price generated a wave of rapid responses all over the world. This included; major mergers and acquisitions, liberalization of new markets for exploration and production, etc. Subsequently, in global scale the competition became tough, while the opportunities for commercial growth got expanded. At the same time, the industry was exposed to unprecedented challenges in the new business environments, in political, technical, and operational terms, demanding novel solutions to oil & gas operations. Some of the new fields that were found in fact introduced major engineering challenges having specific technical characteristics, for instance in terms of depth, geographical formations of reserves, pressure and temperature, geological conditions, etc. On the other hand some of the new exploration regions were known to be quite sensitive in business scale due to elevated risk factors, particularly in Alaskan, South American, Eastern European, and Asian sectors. The industry

was required to resort to technological innovation and capitalization of advanced technologies to overcome engineering challenges, while seeking new operational concepts to reduce commercial exposure and business risks.

Apart from the events in the global scale, the assets on the Norwegian continental shelf have also been undergoing obvious changes in terns of production capacity. A good number of producing fields have reached their stage of maturity while a number of others have shown the signs of declining production. Incidentally, a good portion of the newly found fields were assessed to be marginal in capacity, raising concerns about the economical feasibility as well as underlying risks of investments for field development and operation. Subsequently, the industry, together with representative organizations such as *Norwegian Oil Industry Association (OLF)*, began to review the emerging status of the Continental shelf and made some early attempts to develop business road maps to ensure that the future of oil & gas production is sustainable and life extension of producing fields, as well as exploitation of marginal fields, are commercially feasible. This provided the basis for the systematic development of *Integrated eOperations* across producing fields on the Norwegian shelf (Figure 1).

IO, since its inception in early 2000s, in fact systematically introduced a new *eBusiness* solution for the offshore petroleum industry, targeting

Figure 1. Embracing Intergated eOperations (IO) as the eBusiness solutions for sustainability of Commercial operations in the Offshore petroleum industry, involves a number of critical issues

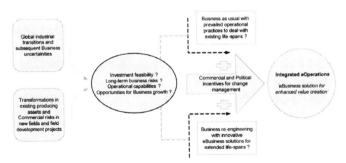

capitalization of innovative solutions for enhanced value creation. The value creation potential is targeted in terms of;

- Enhanced production and reserve exploitation
- Effectiveness in Operations and maintenance cost control, and
- Enhanced health, safety, and environmental performance

The new report issued by OLF claims that the updated value potential of IO implementation process will be approx. NOK 300 billion (OLF, 2007).

Development and implementation of IO solutions is in fact a long-term process involving several distinctive stages due to the inherent complexities and challenges (Liyanage & Bjerkebæk, 2007). The initial stage of the transition took place at a very slow pace and only involved some internal applications and pilot tests within the premises of some major oil producers and drilling service providers. The success achieved was so encouraging that some of the major developments are in progress at the moment involving various other actors across the industry. Interestingly, the success achieved has helped much in eliminating initial skepticisms towards major resource commitments and financial investments, and at the

moment it appears that IO related developments are going through a major transformation across the petroleum sectors world-wide aiming at the realization of '*smart fields*', '*i-fields*', '*smart assets*', etc. While these terms may sound different, it implies that the development and operational practices of offshore assets is subjected to a re-engineering process and that more technically advanced operational concepts will be implemented to enhance the value created by producing assets. The scale of re-engineering involved is seen quite large and the breadth of the scope of IO and '*i-field*' concept is acknowledged to be quite wide. With respect to the current pace of development, this holistic eBusiness solution can at least be expected to go through 3 stages of development (as shown in Figure 2), as it will gradually be adapted as the global solution for efficient and sustainable oil & gas reserve exploitation.

IO solutions are not certainly '*off-the-shelf*', and every organization and region involved take steps to device specific solutions for distinctive producing assets depending on the operational conditions and business plans. However, the solutions will be based on learning across different sectors, utilization of common application solutions and operational principles. In this context, there appears to some form of harmony that will probably enable faster interfacing solutions for collaborative global operations.

Figure 2. IO is progressing gradually as an adaptive global business solution for the petroleum industry

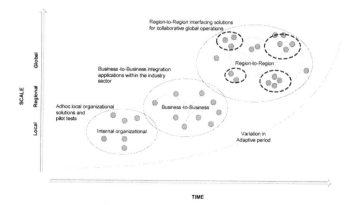

The development and implementation of IO as the solution for future commercial activities, actively promote the mutual benefits of '*being smarter together*'. This sets the focus on integrating the traditionally fragmented industry so that active business-to-business collaboration can be established, primarily based on technological capabilities and advanced ICT infrastructures. The business sectors that are affected by the ongoing developments are quite broad, and includes for instance; *oil & gas producers, drilling companies, engineering companies, support service providers, external discipline experts, equipment manufacturers, instrumentation and surveillance solution providers, technology developers, ICT solutions providers, spare part vendors, logistic companies, R&D organizations*, etc. It implies that apart from multinational organizations and large scale regional companies, a considerable number of SMEs are also involved in various capacities, and subsequently are affected directly by the ongoing development. However, the adaptive capabilities of the SMEs to this large scale dynamic change process are not very visible and clear, but obviously the business challenges are quite many requiring smart business interface solutions to capitalize on the opportunities presented by IO.

THE CASE OF '*SME*' UNDER '*INTEGRATED E-OPERATIONS*'

IO, seemingly, provides a unique set of business opportunities for SMEs, but the ability of these organizations to capitalize on the full potential obviously comes through a relatively different approach to device suitable business solutions. Over the last few years, the engagement of SMEs were very evident in various capacities, but their product and service provisions remained largely fragmented across the industrial sector and inter-competitive.

Barriers and Impediments

The question in terms of commercial future is in fact, whether this conventional approach to SMEs' business transactions can provide favorable conditions to establish strategic measures and interface solutions to reap the commercial benefits of IO.

First and foremost, coupling with IO process in principal demands considerable investments for various change adaptive measures. This primarily requires acquisition of strategic technological capabilities to equalize with the basic industry standards to penetrate into eBusiness environment. Inability to do so, has significant commercial disadvantages, particularly when ICT-based collaborative applications invade the offshore industry as a cost saving and knowledge management measure for enhanced asset productivity. However, this require major investments where the risks are relatively high for SMEs, given various business influence factors as, limited business transaction volume in the provision of own products or services, fluctuations in activity level in response to oil price, limitations in contractual periods and work packages given, etc.

On the other hand there is a greater need for various organizational development processes and human capability enhancement measures in preparation for the innovative product or the service provision demanded by IO. This particularly aims at better organization and management of internal organizational resources and capabilities so that the organization remains flexible and adaptive to the needs and demands of various major clients who are active in IO setting. However, there is a limit to what SMEs can actually do in this context due to major bottlenecks in the access to and deployability of core resources in the provision of solutions to the multiple clients with varying scopes. These clients primarily include, major oil producers, drilling contractors, and large scale engineering companies, who create relatively specific business packages with limited scope seeking limited-term cost-effective engagements. Often, the investments required by such organizational and human issues are relatively less in comparison to technology and ICT implementation. However, it brings a much greater proportion of business challenges due to the inherent sensitivity and the fluidity of the change processes involving critical decisions on soft organizational issues.

In general, there is an inherent un-proportionality between the commitment of capital investments and actual transitional efforts in acquiring technological and organizational capabilities to cope with the IO-based dynamic change, as diagrammatically illustrated in Figure 3.

In general, there is a number of critical issues encountered by SMEs that hinders the successful exploitation of opportunities presented by IO. This for instance includes;

- Limited availability of investment capital and large commercial risks due to fluctuating work volumes in business contracts
- Limitation with respect to access to core resources and the constraints for deploying in-house resources during high activity periods

Figure 3. Capital commitment and Transitional efforts required are un-proportional in the acquisition of Technological and Organizational-Human capabilities to cope with IO process

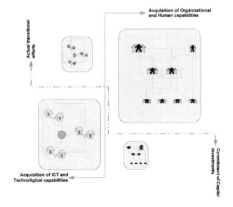

- Large scale transitional efforts for implementing organizational development processes
- Contractual conditions that are limited in temporal and content terms, and even short of proper incentives
- Recruiting the talents and developing training modules with the risk of high employee turnover due to out-competing employment conditions offered my major players
- Specific product and/or service provision niche where the company has acquired know-how through years of commercial engagement and resource commitment, that induces an exit barrier to capitalize on other emerging business areas
- Relatively lesser motivation / inclination / ability to test novel competitive technologies and application solutions, and launch specific industry oriented R&D work
- Short of bargaining power in business transactions with majors due to intense sectoral competition for similar of alternative solutions

The present barriers and impediments have affected the SMEs considerably over the last few years in their constant effort to penetrate into the IO based eBusiness environment. In most cases, SMEs appear to struggle with conventional business strategies that provide less room for diversification of business solutions across the Offshore industry, and subsequently with limited space for growth. However, the ongoing developments today and emerging conditions in the Petroleum industry provide ample of opportunities to capitalize on innovative business interface solutions.

Collaborative Business Interfacing

As the conventional competitive strategies and the IO entry barriers constantly challenge the SMEs, specific solutions are being explored by some of the forward-looking organizations for long-term engagement and subsequent business growth. The very fragmented product and service provision interface that has always provided extreme competition across similar or auxiliary solutions among SMEs does not appear to be the choice for innovative SMEs to survive under the current dynamic conditions. Under the present very dynamic transformation processes, the potential eBusiness solutions under testing and review by major players in industry, as well as consequently emerging trends, are quite complex and send mixed signals to the external environment. The change dynamics have been quite chaotic, and the future business positions of those organizations that are forceful in defining and shaping the future of the IO scenario are relatively ill-defined. In this setting, efforts to gather the fullest business intelligence to interpret the industry cues with greater degree of certainty is not possible to know specific roles and roadmaps of different leading players, which in turn introduces a relatively vulnerable business setting for the SMEs. The difficulties to comprehend how different business solution providers intend to position themselves to capitalize on the novel opportunities of IO, compel the SMEs to change their stance and the competitive dynamics to acquire their business position in a highly sensitive and interactive IO business setting.

The fragmented product and service provision strategies is less likely to provide a strategic platform for business positioning for SMEs where long-term growth can be assured. The coping strategies to face the future need to be deeply embedded into the very principles of IO, and mutually reinforcing. These principles have a clear focus and define what the future of the industry will be, and thus provide SMEs a specific set of '*strategic business interfacing scopes*' to develop competitive business interfacing solutions. Such *scopes* for instance include;

- Being smarter together through effective knowledge management

- 24/7 operational capability following the sun
- Development of 24/7 online support systems accessible from anywhere anytime
- Real-time decision making support through shared plant data
- Business-to-business integration solutions
- etc.

These scopes play a pivotal role for SMEs' in defining the scale and nature of their future commercial transactions. They open up greater opportunities for the SMEs to re-engineer business interface solutions and to device IO capitalization process targeting successful IO entry. Specific commercial solutions need to have an explicit contribution to one or more of the scopes allowing the operators and other leading players to gain commercial strengths necessary to execute their functions in a dynamic operational setting. Some of the commercially important business areas (or '*business interfacing nodes*') where SMEs are expected to make a significant contribution includes;

- ICT solutions and application software for complex data management
- Asset operations, maintenance, and work processes optimization related tasks
- Organizational development and competency management support
- Expert services and consultancy for trouble shooting
- On-call expert availability and knowledge management services
- Cooperative resource pooling and extra capacity bank for ready deployment on urgent demands
- Etc.

Over the last few years there has been so much of a focus on the data management and decision support solutions, and subsequently the industry has inundated with various application solutions provided by programmers and database specialists. Given the industry's dependence on a stream of technical and operational data from offshore assets in the IO setting to manage high-risks and complex production conditions under 24/7 online real-time environment, the market potential for such companies have been extremely good and subsequently a good number of SMEs have begun to provide data management solutions to the major players.

Equally, the industry in general has a greater difficulty in access to talent and experience due to the ageing factor and recruitment difficulties. On one hand a good portion of the experienced crew is about to retire in a few years time, and on the other the number of new breed engineers are inadequate to fill up the available positions both in technical and operational capacities. For few years, before the financial crisis hit the sector, the recruitment process was elevated to the extreme highs to get hold and develop necessary organizational competencies for IO related operations. In this setting, SMEs seems to have stepped-in to take over some of the challenges for instance in terms of in-sourcing services, training programs, etc. Due to the lack of internal competencies and other resources some of the major producers, drilling contractors, and engineering companies have begun to resort to outsource specific work packages relating to operations and engineering projects, and has begun to rely much on the external expertise that SMEs have begun to capitalize today. With the ongoing pace and nature of development in IO, these '*business interfacing nodes*' will be excellent entry points to the SMEs for a number of years to the future, and they provide unique commercial opportunities that can be exploited in many ways.

The IO process has given specific challenges to the SMEs in terms of development of specific capabilities to cope with the new eBusiness environment. While some companies do possess certain core capabilities that are matured today

to a very competitive scale owing to continuous business engagements, not all of them have acquired the capabilities in its fullest scale, nor can practically do so. This by far is a matter of available resources and organizational capacity for developing a broad set of core capabilities required that ramifies into various technological and organizational aspects. Some of distinctive business capabilities favorable for successful commercial operations include, for instance;

- Ability to deploy and/or adapt to mass scale ICT infrastructure solutions, e.g. fiber-optic net, wireless applications, web-based solutions, etc., for sharing of technical and operational data and information management
- Ability to configure into advanced data integration solutions and platforms, for instance based on ontologies, semantics, and standards (e.g. ISO and W3C), for real-time data sharing to enhance collaborative decision making capabilities
- Ability to build and operate *Onshore remote support centers* (OSC) fully equipped with advanced communication and real-time surveillance technologies to enhance collaboration among disciplines (e.g drilling and well, maintenance, engineering projects, reservoir, production, etc.) and to provide online support to offshore operations
- Ability to acquire/develop and utilize advanced information management and decision making tools, for example visualization, 3D/4D simulation, dynamic process simulation, failure diagnostic and prognostic, data interpretation, etc.
- Ability to establish / utilize and configure into business-to-business collaborative platforms, for instance between operators, drilling service providers, engineering service companies, subject experts, logistic

companies, etc., for dynamic work planning, coordination, and work process optimization in an integrated environment

- Ability to utilize novel competency management solutions, for instance based on virtual training and other advanced tools.

The capability acquisition and development process is quite slow among the SMEs due to internal constraints. This has obviously contributed to a notable lag in the IO-entry process. However, as aforementioned, the SMEs' lack of individual capacity is not a panacea to under-perform in the IO environment. SMEs have no option but to organize their commercial transactions strategically, in such a way that it provides innovative and holistic solutions satisfying the operational principles for reaching the scopes of the IO.

Obviously, the product and service profile of the SMEs that compete in the offshore sector are quite varied. It ranges from pure technology and/or software providers to maintenance and inspection program developers, operational risk analysts, safety and environmental advisors, etc. Each and every player can be included in one or two specific business interface niches based on their business expertise and core capabilities, while some have bit more complicated overlapping commercial transactions through special business arrangements. However, in general SME sector posses a large body of knowledge and expertise across a range of disciplines that is of great importance under the present industrial conditions and challenges for further development of IO. Perhaps

the greatest challenge by far to the SMEs is the nature and the dynamics of the inter-.competition and the provision of duplicating products and services to the same market. It seems to have contributed much to the redundancy of resources and capabilities as well as to the loss of bargaining power in commercial engagements. Despite that this has been the situation for quite sometimes now, the majority has not yet comprehended that *'being smarter together'* has the greatest potential to contribute to the business future of SMEs in the IO environment.

The concept of *'being smarter together'* encompasses a notion of cooperative and coordinated deployment of knowledge, resources, and capabilities in an effective manner to reach a set of specific goals. It in fact, rests much on the cooperative strategies and collaborative business solutions rather than individual engagements in standalone scales. For SMEs in this context, mutually reinforcing business partnerships among the sector seems to have the potential to pay larger dividends, for instance through specific measures such as business ventures (Figure 4).

This is a matter of developing distinctive IO-entry capabilities through strategic collaborative measures in such a way that the partnerships help meeting a given success criteria, for instance, flexible business conditions to respond to industry needs, adaptive commercial actions to cope with change, agile business responses, holistic commercial solutions, compilation of strategic resources, pooling of core competencies, etc. It allows required level of diversification of product

Figure 4. 'Being smarter together' to acquire distinctive IO-entry capabilities

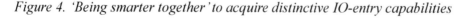

& service provision process embedded into integrated solutions, catering different client groups varying from major producers to small-scale producers in the region. With respect to developments of IO in a more global scale, in later stages, this even has the considerable business potential to grow into other geographical regions establishing collaborative product and service provision networks serving the industrial sector.

BRIDGING THE GAPS AND FUTURE RESEARCH

The good intentions and innovative solutions, obviously, do not themselves justify the success of solution implementation process. Given the very dynamic nature of current developments within IO and the scale of transition moving away from traditional practices, there are some specific gaps that need to be resolved for successful business interfacing. Major issues needing solutions are known to be 'soft', while some 'technical' issues also remain to be seen. These include;

- Mutual trust between change agents and solution providers
- Robust IT systems interfaces for mutual data exchange
- Performance-based incentive schemes
- Developing 'open' business solutions based on distinctive business interests
- Security assurance measures of data flow across organizations
- Internal organizational willingness for change implementation
- Organizational alignment for change adaptation
- Concerns on possible loss of talents into other organizations
- Contractual conditions set by the majors
- Business relationships in a virtual operational environment

- Inter-organizational communication patterns and social dimensions for collaboration
- Etc.

Obviously, these gaps require some novel thinking and innovative solutions that breaks the boundaries of conventional practices and that can drive the industry to realize success in the new business environment. It provides a fruitful environment for serious R&D work exploring the critical dimensions of collaborative business interfacing in virtual settings.

CONCLUSION

Many industrial sectors today are in the verge of a transition process. While some transitionary processes have been caused by technological push and economical risk, there has also been a greater impact of other complex global and industry specific issues. Equally, the petroleum industry in certain regions is subjected to elevated risks demanding novel solutions to ensure a sustainable future. In North Sea over the last few years, the concept of *Integrated eOperations* has been able to provide the future vision to the offshore oil & gas production industry to overcome the unprecedented challenges. Despite it is an inevitable transition to safeguard the future of the industry, not all the organizations across the sector have acquired the same level of maturity in the transitions process. This particularly includes SMEs who obviously require novel solutions to ensure successful IO-entry. Under the current industrial conditions, SMEs have to rely on collaborative business interfacing solutions to cope with the dynamic change, rather than been resorting to conventional fragmented product and service provision solutions. It is the '*being smarter together*' principle that can make a difference in SMEs future business transactions and sustainable commercial success. It provides them the necessary basis for capability development, and to capitalize on the business potentials of IO. However, with reference to the current pace of development, the SMEs seem to have a long way forward before such strategic business interfacing solutions can become fully operational.

REFERENCES

Child, J., & Faulkner, D. (1998). *Strategic for co-operation: Managing alliances, networks, and joint ventures.* Oxford, UK: Oxford University Press.

During, W., Oakey, R., & Kauser, S. (2004). *New technology-based firms in the new millennium.* New York: Elsevier.

Dyer, J. H. (2000). *Collaborative advantage: Winning through extended enterprise supplier networks.* Oxford, UK: Oxford University Press.

Gunasekaran, A., & Khalil, O. (Eds.). (2003). *Knowledge and information technology management: Human and social perspectives.* Hershey, PA: Idea group Publishing.

Lin, A., & Patterson, D. (2007). An investigation into the barriers to introducing virtual enterprise networks. In Wang, Y.C., Heng, M.S.H., Chau, P.Y.K. (ed.) (2006). *Supply chain management: Issues in the new era of collaboration and competition*, pp.23-44. Hershey, PA: Idea Group.

Liyanage, J. P. (2008a) Rapid virtual enterprising to manage complex and high-risk assets. InZemliansky, P., St. Amant, K., (ed.), *Handbook of Research on Virtual Workplaces and the New Nature of Business Practice*, pp 702-709. Hershey, PA: IGI Global.

Liyanage, J. P. (2008b). Integrated eOperations-eMaintenance: Applications in North Sea Off-shore assets. In Kobbacy, K. A. H., & Murthy, D. N. P. (Eds.), *Complex systems maintenance handbook* (pp. 585–610). New York: Springer. doi:10.1007/978-1-84800-011-7_24

Liyanage, J.P., & Bjerkebæk, E., (2007). Key note paper: Use of advanced technologies and information solutions for North sea offshore assets: Ambitious changes and socio-technical dimensions. *Journal of International Technology and Information Management (JITIM)*, 1-10. International Information Management Association (IIMA).

Liyanage, J. P., & Herbert, M. (2008). Collaborative dynamic networks (CDNs) and Virtual support enterprises (VSEs). In Putnik, G. D., & Cunha, M. M. (Eds.), *Encyclopaedia of Networked and Virtual Organizations* (pp. 237–243). Hershey, PA: IGI-Global.

Liyanage, J. P., Herbert, M., & Harestad, J. (2006). Smart integrated e-operations for high-risk and technologically complex assets: Operational networks and collaborative partnerships in the digital environment. In Wang, Y. C. (Eds.), *Supply chain management: Issues in the new era of collaboration and competition* (pp. 387–414). Hershey, PA: Idea Group.

Liyanage, J. P., & Langeland, T. (2007). Smart assets through digital capabilities. In Khosrow-Pour, M. (Ed.), *Encyclopaedia of Information Science and Technology.* Hershey, PA: Idea Group.

MCcann. A. Omdal, S. Nyberg, R. K. & Mydland, Ø, (2004), *Statoil's First Onshore Support Center: The Result of New Work Processes and Technology Developed to Exploit Real-Time Data*, Society of Petroleum Engineers (SPE), 90367.

OLF (Oljeindustriens landsforening / Norwegian Oil Industry Association), (2003), *eDrift for norsk sokkel: det tredje effektiviseringsspranget* (eOperations in the Norwegian continental shelf: The third efficiency leap), OLF (www.olf.no). (*in Norwegian*)

OLF (Oljeindustriens landsforening / Norwegian Oil Industry Association), (2007), *Oppdatert verdipotensiale for Integrerte operasjoner på norsk sokkel* (Updated value potential for Integrated operations on Norwegian shelf), OLF (www.olf. no). (*in Norwegian*)

Sabbaghi, A., & Vaidyanathan, G. (2007). Integration of global supply chain management with small and medium suppliers. In Wang, Y.C., Heng, M.S.H., Chau, P.Y.K. (ed.) (2006). *Supply chain management: Issues in the new era of collaboration and competition*, pp 127-164. Hershey, PA: Idea Group.

Tai, J. C. F., Wang, E. T. G., et al. (2007), Virtual integration: Antecedents and role in governing supply chain integration. In Wang, Y.C., Heng, M.S.H., Chau, P.Y.K. (ed.) (2006). *Supply chain management: Issues in the new era of collaboration and competition*, pp 63-104. Hershey, PA: Idea Group.

Tidd, J. (Ed.). (2001). *From knowledge management to strategic competence: measuring technological, market and organizational innovation*. New York: Imperial College Press.

Timo, S., Markku, T., & Anne, T. (2005). *Managing business in multi-channel world: Success factors for E-business*. Hershey, PA: Idea Group Pub.

Wang, W. Y. C., Heng, M. S. H., et al. (2007), Implementing supply chain management in the new era: A replenishment framework for the supply chain operations reference model. In Wang, Y.C., Heng, M.S.H., Chau, P.Y.K. (ed.) (2006). *Supply chain management: Issues in the new era of collaboration and competition*, pp 1-22. Hershey, PA: Idea Group.

Wang, Y. C., Heng, M. S. H., & Chau, P. Y. K. (Eds.). (2006). *Supply chain management: Issues in the new era of collaboration and competition*. Hershey, PA: Idea Group.

Section 2
Applications, Surveys and Case Studies

Chapter 9

SME Adoption and Use of ICT for Networked Trading Purposes:
The Influence of Sector, Size and Age of Firm

Fintan Clear
Brunel University, UK

Adrian Woods
Brunel University, UK

Keith Dickson
Brunel University, UK

ABSTRACT

Based on empirical evidence gained by a telephone survey of 375 SMEs (Small and Medium-sized Enterprises), this chapter uses logistical regressions as a means of identifying the potential for relationships between three variables - industry sector, firm size (as measured by employment), and age of firm - as they influence ICT ownership, ICT use and ICT benefits. Such inter-relationships can then be used to identify networked trading practice and proclivity. Data was gathered for firms on the basis of four industrial sectors ('Media', 'Logistics', 'Internet Services' and 'Food Processing') in a region encompassing West London and adjacent counties. Logistical regressions on the sample data suggest that possession, application and the benefits derived from ICT can be explained on the basis of single and multiple variables or as the result of none, and are individuated as either 'just sector', 'just size', 'sector and size', 'sector and age', 'sector, size and age' or 'no variable'.

DOI: 10.4018/978-1-60960-463-9.ch009

INTRODUCTION

There are over 4.7 million enterprises in the UK (BERR, 2007). The majority of these - nearly 3.5 million – are 'one-man-bands' (i.e they have no employees) leaving around 1.2 million which have employees. Further breakdown shows that just over one million (1,019,295) have between one and nine employees (constituting 'micro firms'), 160,820 have between 10 and 49 employees ('small firms'), 26,690 have between 50 and 249 employees ('medium-sized firms') and nearly 6,000 have over 250 employees and above ('large firms'). Thus 'Small and Medium-sized Enterprises' (SMEs) – that is, firms with between 0 and 249 employees - account for over 99 percent of all businesses in the UK, and thus have a significant role to play in the UK economy (Beaver, 2002). The European Commission (2002) observes that SMEs "generate a substantial share of European GDP and. .. are a key source of new jobs as well as a fertile breeding ground for entrepreneurship and new business ideas." (European Commission, 2002, p.1). Additionally Tse and Soufani (2003) speculate that:

"Small firms might carry even more importance in the new economy...While the traditional economic structure favours size and physical matters, the new economy is earmarked by relationships, network and information. It is in this light that it can be seen that small firms would become an ever more important engine in the new economy" (Tse and Soufani, 2003, p. 306 as cited in Fillis et al, 2004).

Whatever 'outrageous fortunes' some ICT (Information and Communications Technology) and e-business initiatives may suffer, if we accept the role that electronic mediation or 'networked trading' already plays, and will continue to play, in economic activity (see e.g. Turban, 2004; Laudon & Laudon, 2005), then it is clear that its study in an SME and small firm context is of critical interest. However, even though SMEs constitute 99% of all UK firms, the balance of research in the field does not reflect this primacy. With notable exceptions, research dwells mainly on large firm perspectives.

Arguably, examinations of large information systems in the literature tend to downplay financial resource issues, for example, due to the fact that they are the province of large firms and their significant resource bases and for whom necessary financial provision will be made – even in difficult economic circumstances. Many researchers examining ICT adoption in small firms however attest to financial constraints having critical influence. Martin and Matlay (2001), Dixon *et al.* (2002) and Taylor and Murphy (2004) are critical of literature that ignores the heterogeneity of SMEs. Any literature that broadly ignores critical considerations may appear somewhat irrelevant to SMEs. In a fast-paced and highly dynamic world, for policy makers, technology providers, and 'small firms' to work with the world as it really is, clear evidence of how small and medium-sized enterprises exploit ICTs and the Internet is continuously required. Perhaps this might help avoid incidents in which "firms continue to choose technologies which may not be very effective for their environment" (Gupta and Hammond, 2005, p. 307).

Empirical evidence of how SMEs exploit ICTs, gathered on the basis of industry sector, firm size and age should help provide richer pictures of business reality, and thus contribute to more effective ICT investment. Thus to complement existing evidence, this chapter addresses the question as to the extent of influence that industry sector, firm size and age might have on SME adoption and exploitation of ICTs. For the purposes of this study however, firms with no employees (i.e., single operators or 'one-man-bands') have been excluded. Exploration of sector, size and age differences is undertaken therefore on the basis of firms with employees only.

The chapter is structured such that the next section reviews the literature, and this is followed by the methodology section. The project findings follow this, and the chapter ends with some concluding remarks.

LITERATURE REVIEW

While much of the academic literature focuses on large firms, much less is evident on the experiences of SMEs in terms of ICT usage (Martin and Matlay, 2001; Dixon *et al.,* 2002) or on the emergence of networked trading which proponents such as Straub (2002) argue is becoming the dominant commercial paradigm. IT adoption practice in SMEs cannot be based on the same theoretical frameworks applied to large organisations (Ordanini, 2006), as afterall, small businesses are not simply scaled-down versions of large businesses (Westhead and Storey, 1996; Curran and Blackburn, 2001; Quayle, 2002). For any theory on SMEs to be relevant, consideration of their "motivations, constraints and uncertainties" (Westhead and Storey, 1996, p. 18) must be made which are different in comparison to their larger cousins.

The small but growing SME literature evinces a number of themes, including 'promoters of' and 'inhibitors to' ICT and e-business adoption. Writers addressing these include Purao and Campbell (1998), Hadjimanolis (1999), Poon and Swatman (1999), Van Akkeren and Cavaye (1999), Reimensheder and McKinney (2001), Martin and Matlay (2001), Dixon *et al.* (2002), Quayle (2002), Riquelme (2002) and MacGregor and Vrazalic (2004). Thus Dixon *et al.* (2002) list a set of inhibitors to ICT use that they view as typical for the literature: a generalised lack of awareness of the potential of ICT; a lack of an IT skills base; concerns about security and privacy issues; apparent high initial set-up costs; and a lack of staff to implement ICT.

Adoption is often explored by use of models that include so-called 'stage models'. These show potential adopters ascending through stages of

relatively more-complex ICT use with, for example, a first stage or rung typically citing email use, and a last stage exhibiting pervasive use of electronic mediation on an intra- and inter-firm basis. However stage models have been the subject of much criticism when seen as the policy engine for public-sector support to firms. Martin and Matlay (2001) and Simpson and Docherty (2004) imply that the Cisco-sponsored stage model as originally adopted by UK Government and styled the 'DTI Adoption Ladder' was too simplistic. For example, it assumed that ICT ownership and ICT use were one and the same. No account was made of the motivations of owner-managers which are noted as the key aspect in adoption narratives. In sum, the model offered "both a limited and a limiting vision of government-inspired support for the ICT implementation and development needs of firms operating in the small business sector of the UK economy" (Martin and Matlay, 2001).

Simpson and Docherty (2004) are particularly critical of some business support mechanisms as delivered on the ground and based on the stage model paradigm; Levy and Powell (2003) argue for a 'contingent' approach in which adoption behavior is seen to be based more on apparent business need than on a linear and apparently seamless progression towards some vaguely-defined 'digital nirvana' where pervasive and integrated operations are transacted between and amongst firms. Ill-fitting policy can help contribute to distrust of government support agencies by small firms as Simpson and Docherty (2004) note with the potential effect of inhibiting small firms from seeking what should be 'disinterested' advice on critical issues such as data security. However MacGregor and Vrazalic (2005) find some taxonomies 'manufactured' and reflections of research design rather than reality on the ground. Vega *et al.* (2008) criticise a failure to study contextual factors affecting e-Business adoption by SMEs such as 'supply-push', 'demand-pull', 'complementary innovations', 'cultural aspects' and 'government intervention' with Meckel *et al.* (2004) pointing to studies by Kalkota and Robinson (1999) and Mehrtens *et al.* (2001) who underline the influence of larger enterprises with adoption behaviour by small firms related to their role as customers or suppliers to their larger brethren. Nevertheless Parker and Castleman (2009) conclude in an examination of the e-business adoption literature that decision-making by small firms is idiosyncratic with owner-managers as likely to pursue social imperatives in regard to family, friends and other businesses as economically-rational goals. When citing Watson *et al.* (2000), Fillis *et al.* (2004) echo Parker and Castleman (2009) to an extent and are highly critical of the academic literature by warning of "the continued belief by many researchers in the sole value of formalised, structured, prescriptive ways of conceptualising business behaviour despite the realities of non-linear, sometimes chaotic behavior" (p.350).

Though Bodorick *et al.* (2002) did not focus on SMEs specifically, Simpson and Docherty (2004) note their argument that e-commerce readiness and adoption are likely to vary by industry sector. Martin and Matlay (2001) concur, finding that micro-businesses that focus on providing business services were more likely to adopt ICT than similar-sized manufacturing firms. Dixon *et al.* (2003) find that wholesaling and retailing may be more likely to use ICT as other sectors. In relation to e-business, Drew (2003) finds that high technology and knowledge intensive firms are more proactive in electronically-mediated trading than others. However, other researchers such as Levy and Powell (2001) argue that there is little evidence for such differential patterns of ICT adoption on the basis of sector.

Researchers who find evidence for size as a significant factor in eCommerce adoption include Van Beveren and Thompson (2002), Daniel and Myers (2000), Kai-Uwe Brock (2000) and Windrum and De Berranger (2003). The general thesis is that the larger the number of employees, the greater the ability of the firm to adopt new technologies. Dixon *et al.* (2003), citing the work of Kai-Uwe

Brock (2000), suggest that ICT use in SMEs can vary according to a number of factors including firm size. However Levy and Powell (2003) argue that size is not such a differentiating factor in ICT adoption, finding instead that the owners' knowledge and attitude to growth dominates.

In terms of age of firm, Kai-Uwe Brock (2000) argues that younger firms may be more likely to use ICT (cited in Dixon *et al.*, 2003). Daniel and Myers (2000) found that the older the SME, the less likely they were to use e-commerce (cited in Simpson and Docherty, 2004).

With the literature lacking consistency on sector, size and age effects, we chose to focus on these three aspects as independent variables in the study (with firm size measured by number of employees). We sought to analyse a sample of data related to what ICT a firm possessed, what use it made of ICT, and what benefits it derived from ICT use. Then logistical regression modelling was applied as a means to identify possible relationships between the three variables. Such vistas might contribute to an understanding of the complexity of forces at play. In the next section, the methodology is explored.

METHODOLOGY

Using a structured questionnaire of 30 questions, quantitative empirical evidence was obtained for 375 firms located in a region that encompassed West London boroughs and adjacent counties. Using a listing of around 2000 firms sourced from a commercial database provider and based on a telephone survey approach, responses gained from owner-managers were input directly into an SPSS database. There are firms in near-equal measure across four industrial sectors which are a) 'Media', b) 'Logistics', c) 'Internet Services', and d) 'Food Processing'. Selection of sectors was based on primacy of economic activity in the study region. Out of a possible seven sectors, the final selection of four were thought to test whether there is evidence to support a thesis dichotomising 'informational' sector ICT use versus 'physical' sector ICT use. 'Informational' here implies sectors in which there is a primacy of service activity, while the 'physical' implies sectors which have a primacy of economic activity in which production or some tangible work effort is an attribute. The underlying hypothesis therefore is that 'Internet Services' and 'Media' ('Informational') should make greater use of ICT than 'Food Processing' or 'Logistics' ('Physical').

Analysis of relevant data was undertaken using binary logistic regression tests. Logistic regression is similar in some senses to multiple linear regression, but whereas the latter can only accommodate continuous data, logistic regression can accommodate dependent variables that are categorical. With the binary logistic test, multiple regressions are undertaken "but with an outcome variable that is a categorical dichotomy and predictor variables that are continuous or categorical" (Field, 2005, p. 218). Whereas a chi square test would look at the three independent variables in isolation from each other, logistic regression combines statistical examination of the three 'predictor' variables of sector, size and

age of firm to produce dichotomous results that highlight which of these variables has primacy in terms of influence on the dependent variables (such as 'company website' or 'customer satisfaction'). In these logistic regression tests, reference categories are used as a basis for comparison. Thus where the significance of the logistic regression test is less that 0.05, the odds generated predict the likelihood of an individual sector, size, or age of firm having a particular technology, for example, in comparison with the reference category. For sector the reference category is 'Food Processing'; for size the reference category is 'medium' (ie 50-249 employees); and for age of firm, '10 years plus' is used as the reference category.

SAMPLE

Tables 1 to 3 describe the sample. Of the 375 firms in the sample (see Table 1 for sector by firm size data) approximately one quarter were in each of the following sectors (figures in parentheses are rounded): 'Media' (24%), 'Logistics' (27%), 'Internet Services' (23%) and 'Food Processing' (27%). In terms of size 'micro' firms (1 to 9

Table 1. Sector by firm size

Sector	Firm Size (by numbers of employees)			Total
	1 - 9	**10 - 49**	**50 - 249**	
Media	59	27	3	90
	66.3%	30.3%	3.4%	100%
Logistics	49	37	13	99
	49.5%	37.4%	13.1%	100%
Internet Services	49	34	5	88
	55.7%	38.6%	5.7%	100%
Food Processing	46	41	12	99
	46.5%	41.1%	12.1%	100%
Total	203	139	33	375
	54.1%	37.1%	8.8%	100%

Chi square significance: 0.45

Table 2. Age of firm by sector

Sector	Age of Firm			Total
	1-5 years	6 – 10 years	10+ years	
Media	21	14	54	89
	23.6%	15.7%	60.7%	100%
Logistics	24	13	62	99
	24.2%	13.1%	62.6%	100%
Internet Services	27	47	14	88
	30.7%	53.4%	15.9%	100%
Food Processing	20	25	54	99
	20.2%	25.3%	54.5%	100%
Total	92	99	184	375
	24.5%	26.4%	49.1%	100%

Chi square significance: 0.00

employees) represent 54% of the sample, 'small' firms (10 to 49 employees) represent 37% and 'medium'-sized (50-249 employees) represent around 9%. The average size of the sample as measured by employment was 18.6 but there were significant differences in size between sectors: 'Logistics' and 'Food Processing' both had around 23 employees against 'Internet Services' and 'Media' averages with around 13 employees.

Table 2 has data on age of firm by sector which shows that nearly one half of the sample (49%) were more than ten years old with just over a quarter (26.4%) being between five and ten years and just a bit less than a quarter (24.5%) being between one and five years in age. Firms younger than one year – which accounted for one firm only – have been removed from the sample for analysis purposes. With the proportion of firms aged between '1 - 5 years' being more-or-less the same for all sectors, differences really start to show in the '6-10 years' category where the proportion of 'Internet Services' firms (around 53%) is markedly greater than those for 'Logistics' (13%) and 'Media' (nearly 16%) with 'Food Processing' (25%) lying between the two. At '10+ years' the contrast between 'Internet Services' (16%) and the rest (between 55% and 63%) is

even more marked. Thus 'Internet Services' firms stand out as the youngest overall, with 84% of them less than ten years old.

Table 3 completes the array of cross-tabular data defining the sample. There appears to be a limited relationship between the two variables shown in that the largest firms tend to be amongst the oldest of the firms. At the 'small' firm level, 19% are amongst the youngest (i.e. '1 - 5 years') in the sample while 52% are amongst the oldest (i.e. '10+ years'); for 'medium'-sized firms, this effect is more marked with 6% being amongst the youngest and 70% being amongst the oldest.

FINDINGS

As noted above, the empirical data is being analysed to identify a) the information technology possessed by firms, b) how the information technology is applied, and c) the benefits obtained from that information technology use. The results for the sample for these three areas are shown in Tables 4, 5 & 6 respectively. Table 4 makes clear how ubiquitous possession of the Internet and email are for the firms, and these are followed closely by 'own computer network (LAN/WAN)' and

Table 3. Age of firm by size

Firm Size (by numbers of employees)	Age of Firm			Total
	1- 5 years	6 – 10 years	10+ years	
1 - 9	64	50	89	203
	31.5%	24.6%	43.8%	100%
10 - 49	26	41	72	139
	18.7%	29.5%	51.8%	100%
50 - 249	2	8	23	33
	6.1%	24.2%	69.7%	100%
Total	92	99	184	375
	24.5%	26.4%	49.1%	100%

Chi square significance: 0.04

'company website'. 'Wireless access' comes some way behind these though still more than 50% of firms in the sample exploit this technology. The other technologies are used by fewer than 50% of the sample, with the laggard being 'groupware' (eg 'Lotus Notes') at about 23%.

Table 5 shows the applications that the information technology is used for. The clear leader is 'document management' at nearly 87%, with 'sales or marketing' the nearest to this at nearly 75%. With a number of applications coming at around 50%, three applications lag behind the rest with ERP (enterprise resource planning) being some way behind the rest at 27%.

Benefits obtained for the firms by information technology use are noted in Table 6. Two 'benefits' are out in front at around 83% ('enable us to keep up with competitors' and 'faster response to customers'), followed closely by three further benefits ('improved product/service quality', 'improved productivity' and 'improved customer satisfaction') which are between 77% and 73%. With two further benefits at around 60% ('increased sales' and 'improved staff satisfaction'), 'improved working on joint projects with other firms' trails at about 53% with 'reduced staff numbers' lagging at just over 24%.

It is possible to speculate that in many instances it would be (the firm's) sector that was the most

Table 4. Information technology

What information technology does your firm possess?	(%)
Internet	99.2
Email	98.7
Own computer network (LAN/WAN)	85.7
Company website	82.0
Wireless access	53.2
Intranet	39.4
Extranet/Electronic data exchange	31.0
Video/Audio conferencing	28.6
Groupware	22.8

Table 5. Application of information technology

How does your firm make use of its information technology ?	(%)
Document management	88.6
Sales or marketing	74.6
Design	54.0
Production planning & control	54.0
Human resource management	52.3
Market research	42.3
Stock control	41.8
Enterprise resource planning (ERP)	27.2

Table 6. Benefits from information technology

What benefits does your firm derive from its use of information technology ?	(%)
Enable us to keep up with competitors	82.8
Faster response to customers	82.5
Improved product/service quality	77.0
Improved productivity	74.6
Improved customer satisfaction	73.0
Increased sales	61.4
Improved staff satisfaction	59.9
Improved working on joint projects with other firms	52.8
Reduced staff numbers	24.3

important independent variable of the three, but in some cases it might be size of firm, and then in others, age of firm. As there are significant relationships between sector, employment size and age of firm, care had to be exercised in establishing whether any significant relationship between these three variables existed. Thus a series of logistical regressions were undertaken that allowed the authors to control for the effects that the independent variables have on a specified dependent variable. The easiest way to approach logistical regression is to see it as a parallel to conventional linear regression but instead of predicting the value of the independent variable, it predicts the probability that the independent variable *exists*. The closer the probability is to one, the more likely the independent variable will

occur, and conversely the closer the probability is to zero, the less likely the event will occur. Thus situations are identified in which the independent variable may either be present or not present, thus offering a useful statistical tool by which to begin to divine the possible inter-relationships and causal factors amongst variables.

As an illustration, a significant age effect may be identified that is generated by sector of firm. So while for example 'Internet Services' firms might tend to be younger than firms in the other three sectors, logistical regression modelling suggests that this could be explained by sector. Further, 'Media' and 'Internet Services' firms might tend to be smaller in employment size than the other two sectors, but again the modelling shows that this may be explained by sector. A last illustration

Table 7. No Independent variables

No independent variables	Email
	Internet
	Reduced staff numbers
	Improved staff satisfaction

would be that the older the firm, the larger it is measured by employment.

Tables A1, A2 and A3 (see appendices) give details of how the three independent variables are singularly associated with what ICT the firm has, how this is used and what benefits the firm derives from its ICT use. Then, taking into account that they are significantly associated themselves, we identify which variable, or variables, are statisti-

cally significant as tested by a logistical regression model. The results from these three tables are summarised below in Table A4 such that columns identifying 'no variable', 'just sector', 'just size', 'sector and size', 'sector and age' and 'sector, size and age' are shown.

Table 7 shows that in terms of the logistic regression statistical tests for email and the Internet, none of the three independent variables of sector,

Table 8. Just sector

Dependent Variable	Sector Data
Company website	IS (9.3) Media (3.0)
Video/Audio conferencing	IS (6.5) Media (2.5)
Sales or Marketing	IS (3.4)
Design	IS (10.3) Media (5.1) Logs (0.31)
Market Research	IS (2.6)
Document management	Media (0.19)
Improved productivity	IS (3.2) Media (2.7) Logs (0.52)
Improved product / service	IS (6.0) Media (3.3) Logs (2.2)
Improved customer satisfaction	IS (3.0)
Improved working on joint projects with other firms	IS (3.6)
Increased sales	IS (2.2) Logs (0.4)
Enable us to keep up with competitors	Sector significant*

Table notes:

IS = 'Internet Services'; Logs = 'Logistics'; Food Pro. = 'Food Processing'

Figures in brackets show increases or decreases in the odds ratio for sector categories as against the reference category. Categories not displayed have odds equivalent to the reference category.

* At the whole sector level the data shows significance; at the individual sub-sector level no significance was shown.

size or age showed significance. Both technologies are almost universal in adoption at around 99% (see Table 4) and therefore offer ubiquity above and beyond sector, age and size considerations. The benefits from ICT 'Reduced staff numbers' and 'Improved staff satisfaction' also show no identifiable sector, size or age primacy, though as the apparent benefits of ICT, they were not recognised as such by all the firms polled. Table 7 shows that well over half of the sample (about 60%) felt that 'Improved staff satisfaction' was a benefit of ICT while less than one quarter (just over 24%) felt that 'Reduced staff numbers' was a benefit. Given how ICT has been lauded by technology providers and others as a means of reducing headcount, it is noteworthy that a majority of SMEs do not share this perspective.

Table 8 shows the results of logistic regression statistical tests pointing to sector being the primary influence. As an explanation of the data, take 'Design': the right-hand column shows that 'Internet Services' firms in the sample are 10.3 times as likely and 'Media' firms 5.1 times as likely to use their ICT for 'Design' as the reference sector 'Food Processing'. 'Logistics' firms on the other hand are 0.31 times (i.e. less than one third) as likely as 'Food Processing' firms to use ICT for design purposes; to put it another way, 'Media' and 'Food Processing' firms are 3.2 times as likely to use I it for design purposes as 'Logistics' firms. That 'Internet Services' is by far the most likely sector of firms to adopt, use and benefit from ICT for this sample may be unsurprising given the nature of their work, though the magnitude of this primacy ranges from over 10 times

in the case of 'Design' to just over twice in the case of 'Increased sales'. 'Media' comes in second place (eg 'Company website') or 'second equal' (eg 'Sales or Marketing') for the most part. The other two sectors generally vie for third and fourth place, though there are cases where either one or both may be 'second equal'. This general pattern is broken with 'Document management' with 'Internet Services', 'Logistics' and 'Food Processing' all equally as likely to use ICT for this purpose, with 'Media' trailing in this regard. Here the underlying hypothesis that 'Informational' industries should make greater use of ICT than 'Physical' industries falls down. In these terms 'Logistics' is a sector that depends heavily upon documentation to further business ends, and the large array of different document types includes e.g. despatch notes, bills of lading, delivery notes, VAT declarations (etc). The need for quick and flexible responses to business demands and the close relationships with trading partners appears to be a driver for the use of electronic documentation. In the same vein, 'Food Processing' is a sector that in recent years has been obliged to exploit electronic forms of documentation along food supply chains in order a) to maximise the life of foodstuffs on retailers' shelves in a highly competitive but concentrated UK market, and b) in order to assure food safety as much as possible (Clear, forthcoming).

Two dependent variables show 'just size' primacy in the logistic regression tests (see Table 9). 'Groupware' is relatively complex software that allows individuals working remotely to collaborate synchronously using the same data

Table 9. Just size

Dependent Variable	Size Data
Groupware	Micro (0.35)
Human resource management	Micro (0.11)

Table notes:

Figures in brackets show increases or decreases in the odds ratio for size categories as against the reference category. Categories not displayed have odds equivalent to the reference category.

sources, and as such this exemplifies the notion of 'networked working' if not 'networked trading' as such. An ability to work with such software implies that a firm has a sophisticated level of knowledge and skills in ICT use. 'Human resources management' is a function that will be undertaken by an owner-manager in small firms, and will only become a discrete function at a certain size of firm. The likelihood is that 'micro' firms are less likely to have this discrete function than the larger firms, and the findings bear this out. In fact the pattern for both dependent variables is identical with 'micro' firms least likely to have either 'groupware' or 'Human resource management' as against 'small' and 'medium'-sized firms. Put another way, 'small' and 'medium'-sized firms are three times more likely to have groupware and 10 times more likely to have a human resource management function than 'micro' firms.

Table 10 shows dependent variables that show the influence of both sector and size in terms of their adoption or apparent benefit. In sector terms 'Internet Services' have primacy of influence, with 'Media' coming second or 'second equal', thus echoing for the most part the pattern noted

above for 'Just Sector' in Table 9. Size shows the primacy of the 'medium'-sized firm for the most part in adoption or benefit terms. Thus 'Intranet', 'Extranet/EDI', 'Own computer network (LAN/WAN)', 'Wireless' and 'Enterprise Resource Planning (ERP)' are all dependent variables that fit a general pattern identifying the primacy of both 'Internet Services' and 'Medium'-sized firms in these terms. The one exception is 'Stock control' with 'Food Processing' having the greatest primacy according to the logistic regression tests. Given that 'Food Processing' is the only sector involved in manufacturing, such a finding is to be expected.

Table 11 shows the one dependent variable in this data – 'Faster response to customers' – that is influenced primarily by sector and age according to the logistic regression tests. The pattern for sector echoes findings noted above in terms of the odds ratios: 'Internet Services' has primacy with 'Media' being 'second equal' with 'Logistics' and 'Food Processing'. Age is an independent variable that appears only twice in these findings. It is notable that the 'youngest' firms (ie 1-5 years) and the 'oldest' firms (ie more than 10 years) are

Table 10. Sector and size

Dependent Variable	Sector Data	Size Data
Intranet	IS (7.4)	Small (0.15) Micro (0.09)
Extranet/Electronic data exchange	IS (2.2) Logs (0.48)	Micro (0.29)
Own computer network (LAN/WAN)	IS (5.2)	Micro (0.11)
Wireless	IS (5.0) Logs (0.5)	Small (0.37) Micro (0.33)
Stock control	Media (0.2) Logs (0.1) IS (0.07)	Small (0.24) Micro (0.18)
Enterprise Resource Planning (ERP)	IS (3.3) Media (2.5)	Micro (0.27)

Table notes:
IS = 'Internet Services'; Logs = 'Logistics'; Food Pro. = 'Food Processing'
Figures in brackets show increases or decreases in the odds ratio
for sector and size categories as against the reference category for data showing significance. Categories not displayed have odds equivalent to the reference category.

Table 11. Sector and age

Dependent Variable	Sector Data	Age Data
Faster response to customers	IS (3.3)	6-10 (0.37)

Table notes:

IS = 'Internet Services'

Figures in brackets show increases or decreases in the odds ratio

for sector and age categories as against the reference category for data showing significance. Categories not displayed have odds equivalent to the reference category.

around 2.7 times as likely to cite this as a benefit of ICT as the 'middle-aged' firms (ie 6-10 years).

Table 12 shows the one dependent variable – 'Production Planning and Control' – that the findings of the logistic regression tests show all three independent variables having significance. In line with findings above, size data shows that 'small' and 'medium'-sized firms are 3.7 times as likely to use their ICT for 'Production Planning and Control' purposes as 'micro' firms. As opposed to the pattern for age data shown in Table 11, the 'middle-aged' firms (6-10 years) are more likely (over twice as much) to have 'Production Planning and Control' as their younger or older counterparts.

To summarise the findings, for 'Email', 'Internet', 'Reduced staff numbers' and 'Improved staff satisfaction', none of the three independent variables influence their use or perception of benefit. Out of the 26 logistical regressions applied, 'just sector' was evident for 12 of them, with 'sector & size' scoring six, 'just size' scoring two, 'sector & age' and 'sector, size & age' scoring one each, with four dependent variables showing the influence of no independent variables

at all. Clearly, in trying to understand a picture on information technology owned by a firm, how it is used, and what benefits the firm derives from its use, the sector in which the firm is located can be seen as the most important independent variable overall. The fact that 20 of the 26 models point to sector (either uniquely or in combination) underlines this primacy, thus bearing out the views of Simpson and Docherty (2004) and Bodorick *et al.* (2002) that industry sector has the greatest influence on ICT and e-business adoption. Size by itself scores only two while size in combination with sector scores six. The age of the firm comes across as having little critical influence, appearing only in combination for two findings.

Looking through the results for sector either by itself or in combination with size, the industry sector that stands out, understandably, is 'Internet Services'. Only in the cases of 'stock control' and 'documentation management' is this industry sector *not* uniquely the highest. For 'stock control' 'Food Processing' firms have primacy while for 'documentation management' 'Internet Services' usage is on a par with 'Food Processing' and 'Logistics' firms. Notwithstanding these cases, the

Table 12. Sector, size & age

Dependent Variable	Sector Data	Size Data	Age Data
Prod Plan & Control	Sector significant*	Micro (0.27)	6-10 (2.2)

Table notes:

Figures in brackets show increases or decreases in the odds ratio

for sector, size and age categories as against the reference category for data showing significance. Categories not displayed have odds equivalent to the reference category.

* At the whole sector level the data shows significance; at the individual sub-sector level no significance was shown.

primacy of 'Internet Services' suggests that such firms have staff with competencies in information technology that allow them to install and use ICT relatively easily compared to the other sectors and thus to gain benefits from its use. There is also evidence to show that as firm size increases firms become much more likely to use ICT in areas such as production planning and control systems and human resource management as their scale makes the investment worthwhile and firms feel that they need ICT to enable them to keep up with their competitors. Further, as can be seen in the 'size and sector' findings, large firms irrespective of sector use ICT in certain ways. So there appears to be a size effect which means that once a firm reaches a certain size irrespective of sector it starts to invest in ICT and then gain the benefits from it in specific ways. In regard to what appears to be a fairly limited 'age of firm' effect, it was implied earlier that only 16% of 'Internet Services' firms were more than 10 years of age as against proportions for other sectors of 55% for 'Food Processing', 61% for 'Media' and 63% for 'Logistics' firms. The two cases where age of firm shows primacy point to '6-10' years as the most influential age category with regard to 'production planning & control' and the least influential age category with regard to 'faster response to customers'. However the question arises as to whether 'Internet Services' firms and their relative youth is affecting the results –is t what appears to be an age effect in fact a disguised sector effect? Such speculation begs further research on the subject.

The findings in this study have implications for the manner in which technology providers and training providers approach their markets. While the logistic regression tests show no particular influence for technologies such as email and Internet, adoption behaviour for other technologies and the manner in which they are used by firms in this study implies that technology vendors and training providers should package their products and services with sectoral considerations in mind. In terms of training, these findings echo

the Leitch Report (2006) in giving support to the principle of 'Sector Skills Councils' (originally established from 2002) through which employers from different industrial sectors can voice their skills needs in order to influence training provision through public-private collaboration. Through these mechanisms the UK government intends that small firms maintain and improve their competitive advantage and allow "the production of innovative, high quality, high value-added products and services" (HM Treasury 2005: 5).

CONCLUSION

Based on empirical evidence gained by a telephone survey of 375 SMEs (Small and Medium-sized Enterprises), this chapter uses logistical regressions as a means of identifying the potential for relationships between three variables - industry sector, firm size (as measured by employment), and age of firm - as they influence ICT ownership, ICT use and ICT benefits. Data was gathered for firms on the basis of four industrial sectors ('Media', 'Logistics', 'Internet Services' and 'Food Processing') in a region encompassing West London and adjacent counties. The majority of the tests (20 out of 26) point to sector either uniquely or in combination as having prime influence on the adoption and use of ICT and perceived benefits. In terms of networked trading, perhaps unsurprisingly, 'Internet Services' is the one sector of the four studied that is consistently shown to be the most likely adopter and user of different technologies to exploit e-business and to derive the benefits thereof. 'Media' follows in second place or at least 'second equal' for the most part, with 'Food Processing' and 'Logistics' the trailing independent variables in the logistic regression tests.

However the findings point to areas of use in which other sectors 'challenge' this primacy such as in the case of 'documentation management' where the two 'physical' sectors studied ('Food

Processing' or 'Logistics') are just as likely to exploit ICT. Size was the critical independent variable for two of the dependent variables concerned, that is possession of groupware and application of ICT for human resources management, but otherwise size was evident only in combination with sector. Age was the one independent variable that appeared to have little overall influence in terms of the aspects explored. Nevertheless a question is begged about how the relative youth of 'Internet Services' firms may be unduly influencing the age data such that what might appear to be an age effect (however limited in scope) may be a disguised sector effect. Contra-indicators notwithstanding, the thesis that 'Informational' sectors ('Internet Services' and 'Media') are more likely than the 'Physical' sectors (Food Processing' or 'Logistics') to adopt, use and gain benefits from ICT was borne out.

The findings in this study have implications for the manner in which technology providers and training providers approach their markets. While the logistic regression tests show no particular influence for technologies such as email and Internet, adoption behaviour for other technologies and the manner in which they are used by firms in this study implies that technology vendors and training providers should package their products and services with sectoral considerations in mind.

ACKNOWLEDGMENT

The authors would like to acknowledge the financial support provided by WestFocus* under the Higher Education Innovation Fund (HEIF 2) and the contributions of the other project team members: David Barnes, Romano Dyerson, G. Harindranath and Wendy Gerrish (all Royal Holloway, University of London), Lisa Harris (Southampton University), Paul Wallin (Kingston University) and Alan Rae (Ai Consultants). (*WestFocus is a partnership between universities, SMEs and community groups in South and West London and the Thames Valley, UK.)

REFERENCES

Beaver, G. (2002). *Small Business and Enterprise Developmen*. Upper Saddle River, NJ: Prentice Hall.

BERR. (Department of Business, Enterprise and Regulatory Reform), (2007).*Table 1 UK Private Sector, Number of enterprises, employment and turnover in the private sector by number of employees, UK, start 2007*, BERR Enterprise Directorate Analytical Unit.

Bodorick, P., Dhaliwal, J., & Jutla, D. (2002). Supporting the e-business readiness of small and medium-sized enterprises: approaches and metrics. *Internet Research: Electronic Networking Applications and Policy, 12*(2), 139–164. doi:10.1108/10662240210422512

Clear, F. (forthcoming), Food and Drink Manufacturing and the Role of ICT, in Bourlakis, M. *et al., Intelligent Agrifood Chains and Networks: Current Status, Future Trends & Real-life Cases*. New York: Routledge.

Curran, J., & Blackburn, R. (2001). *Researching the small enterprise*. New York: Sage.

Daniel, E., & Myers, A. (2000), *Levelling the playing field: electronic commerce in SMEs*. Retrieved from http://mn-isweb-1.som.cranfield.ac.uk/publications/ISRC_2001_SME-Report.pdf (accessed 15/12/09)

Dixon, T., Thompson, B., & McAllister, P. (2002). *The Value of ICT for SMEs in the UK: A Critical Review of Literature*. Reading: Report for the Small Business Service Research Programme, The College of Estate Management.

Drew, S. (2003). Strategic uses of e-commerce by SMEs in the East of England. *European Management Journal, 21*(1), 79–88. doi:10.1016/S0263-2373(02)00148-2

DTI. *(2003). Small Business Service,* Excel Tables - SME Statistics UK 2003, Table 1: UK Whole Economy.*Retrieved from*http://www.sbs.gov.uk/default.php?page=/analytical/statistics/smestats.php*(accessed 10-07-09)*

European Commission (2002). *Benchmarking National and Regional E-business Policies for SMEs.*final report of the Ebusiness Policy Group of the European Union, Brussels, 28 June.

Field, A. (2005). *Discovering Statistics Using SPSS* (2nd ed.). London: Sage.

Fillis, I., Wagner, B., & Johansson, U. (2004). Factors Impacting on E-Business Adoption and Development in the Smaller Scottish Firm. *International Journal of Entrepreneurial Behaviour and Research, 10*(3), 178–191. doi:10.1108/13552550410536762

Gupta, A., & Hammond, R. (2005). Information systems security issues and decisions for small businesses. An empirical examination. *Information Management & Computer Security, 13*(4), 297–310. doi:10.1108/09685220510614425

Hadjimolis, A. (1999). Barriers to Innovation for SMEs in a Small less developed Country (Cyprus). *Technovation, 19*(9), 561–570. doi:10.1016/S0166-4972(99)00034-6

Kai-Uwe Brock, J. (2000). Information and communication technology in the small firm. In Carter, S., & Dylan-Jones, D. (Eds.), *Enterprise and the Small Business* (pp. 384–408). Upper Saddle River, NJ: Financial Times/Prentice Hall.

Kalakota, R., & Robinson, M. (1999), *e-Business: Roadmap for Success*. Reading, MA:Addison-Wesley.

Laudon, K., & Laudon, J. (2004). *Management Information Systems: Managing the Digital Firm.* Upper Saddle River, NJ: Prentice-Hall.

Levy, M., & Powell, P. (2003). Exploring SME Internet Adoption: Towards a Contingent Model. *Electronic Markets, 13*(2), 173–181. doi:10.1080/1019678032000067163

MacGregor, R., & Vrazalic, L. (2005). A basic model of electronic commerce adoption barriers. A study of regional small businesses in Sweden and Australia. *Journal of Small Business and Enterprise Development, 12*(4), 510–527. doi:10.1108/14626000510628199

Martin, L., & Matlay, H. (2001). "Blanket" Approaches to Promoting ICT in Small Firms: Some Lessons from the DTI Adoption Model in the UK. *Internet Research: Electronic Networking Applications and Policy, 11*(5), 399–410. doi:10.1108/EUM0000000006118

Meckel, M., Walters, D., Greenwood, A., & Baugh, P. (2004). A taxonomy of e-business adoption and strategies in small and medium sized enterprises. *Strategic Change, 13*(5), 259–269. doi:10.1002/jsc.682

Mehrtens, J., Cragg, P., & Mills, A. (2001). A model of Internet adoption by SMEs. *Information & Management, 39*(3), 165–176. doi:10.1016/S0378-7206(01)00086-6

Ordanini, A. (2006). *Information Technology and Small Businesses: Antecedents and Consequences of Technology Adoption.* Northampton, MA: Edward Elgar.

Parker, C., & Castleman, T. (2009). Small firm eBusiness adoption: a critical analysis of theory. *Journal of Enterprise Information Management, 22*(1/2), 167–182. doi:10.1108/17410390910932812

Poon, S., & Swatman, P. (1999). An Exploratory Study of Small Business Internet Commerce Issues. *Information & Management, 35*(1), 9–18. doi:10.1016/S0378-7206(98)00079-2

Purao, S., & Campbell, B. (1998). Critical Concerns for Small Business Electronic Commerce: Some Reflections Based on Interviews of Small Business Owners. In *Proceedings of the Association of Information Systems Americas Conference*, Baltimore. *MD Medical Newsmagazine, 14-16*(August), 325–327.

Quayle, M. (2004). E-commerce the challenge for UK SMEs in the Twenty-First Century. *Journal of Operations and Production Management, 22*(10), 1148–1161. doi:10.1108/01443570210446351

Reimenscheider, C., & McKinney, V. (2001). Assessing Beliefs in Small Business Adopters and Non-Adopters of Web-Based E-Commerce. *Journal of Computer Information Systems, 42*(2), 101–107.

Riquelme, H. (2002). Commercial Internet Adoption in China: Comparing the Experience of Small, Medium and Large Business. *Internet research. Electronic Networking Applications and Policy, 12*(3), 276–286. doi:10.1108/10662240210430946

Simpson, M., & Docherty, A. (2004). E-commerce adoption support and advice for UK SMEs. *Journal of Small Business and Enterprise Development, 11*(3), 315–328. doi:10.1108/14626000410551573

Straub, D. (2002). *Foundations of Net-Enhanced Organizations*. New York: Wiley.

Taylor, M., & Murphy, A. (2004). SMEs and e-business. *Journal of Small Business and Enterprise Development, 11*(3), 280–289. doi:10.1108/14626000410551546

Treasury, H. M. (2005). *Cox Review of Creativity in Business: building on the UK's strengths* Retrieved from http://www.hm-treasury.gov.uk./independent_reviews/cox_review/coxreview_index.cfm (accessed 10/12/09).

Treasury, H. M. (2006). *Prosperity for All in the Global Economy-World Class Skills: Final Report* ('The Leitch Report'), Retrieved from http://www.dcsf.gov.uk/furthereducation/uploads/documents/2006-12%20leitchreview1.pdf (accessed 10/12/09).

Tse, T., & Soufani, K. (2003). Business Strategies for Small Firms in the New Economy. *Journal of Small Business and Enterprise Development, 10*(3), 306–320. doi:10.1108/14626000310489781

Turban, E., King, D., Lee, J., & Viehland, D. (2004). *Electronic Commerce - A Managerial Perspective*. Upper Saddle River, NJ: Prentice Hall.

Van Akkeren, J., & Cavaye, A. (1999), Factors affecting entry-level Internet adoption by SMEs: an empirical study In *Proceedings of the Australasian Conference in Information Systems, 2*, Brisbane, 1999, pp. 1716-1728.

Van Beveren, J., & Thompson, H. (2002). The use of electronic commerce by SMEs in Victoria, Australia. *Journal of Small Business Management, 40*(3), 250–253. doi:10.1111/1540-627X.00054

Vega, A., Chiasson, M., & Brown, D. (2008). Extending the research agenda on diffusion: the case of public program interventions for the adoption of e-business systems in SMEs. *Journal of Information Technology, 23*(2), 109–117. doi:10.1057/palgrave.jit.2000135

Watson, R., Berthon, P., Pitt, L., & Kinkhan, G. (2000). *Electronic Commerce: The Strategic Perspective*. Orlando, FL: Dryden Press.

Westhead, P., & Storey, D. (1996). Management Training and Small Firm Performance: Why is the Link so Weak? *International Small Business Journal*, *14*(4), 13–24. doi:10.1177/0266242696144001

Windrum, P., & de Berranger, P. (2003). The adoption of e-business technology by SMEs. In Jones, O., & Tilley, F. (Eds.), *Competitive Advantage in SMEs: Organising for Innovation and Entrepreneurship*. New York: Wiley.

APPENDIX

Table A1. Logistic regression tests for ICT

IT	Logistic Regression Result		
	Sector	Size	Age
Email	NS	NS	NS
Internet	NS	NS	NS
Company Website	IS (9.3) Media (3.0)	NS	NS
Intranet	IS (7.4)	Small (0.15) Micro (0.09)	NS
Extranet/EDI	IS (2.2) Logs (0.48)	Micro (0.29)	NS
Own computer network (LAN/WAN)	IS (5.2)	Micro (0.11)	NS
Wireless	IS (5.0) Logs (0.5)	Small (0.37) Micro (0.33)	NS
Groupware	NS	Micro (0.35)	NS
Vid/Aud. Conf.	IS (6.5) Media (2.5)	NS	NS

Table notes:

IS = 'Internet Services'; Logs = 'Logistics'; Food Pro. = 'Food Processing'

NS = Not statistically significant; otherwise data is statistically significant at 5% or better.

Figures in brackets show increases or decreases in the odds ratio for sub-sector and age categories as against the reference category for data showing significance. Categories not displayed have odds equivalent to the reference category.

Table A2. Logistic regression tests for applications

Applications	Logistic Regression Result		
	Sector	Size	Age
Stock control	Media (0.2) Logs (0.1) IS (0.07)	Small (0.24) Micro (0.18)	NS
Sales/Mktg.	IS (3.4)	NS	NS
Design	IS (10.3) Media (5.1) Logs (0.31)	NS	NS
Mkt Research	IS (2.6)	NS	NS
Doc Mgmt	Media (0.19)	NS	NS
Prod Plan & Control	S	Micro (0.27)	6-10 (2.2)
Human Resources Mgmt	NS	Micro (0.11)	NS
Enterprise Resource Planning (ERP)	IS (3.3) Media (2.5)	Micro (0.27)	NS

Table notes:

IS = 'Internet Services'; Logs = 'Logistics'; Food Pro. = 'Food Processing'

NS = Not statistically significant; otherwise data is statistically significant at 5% or better.

Figures in brackets show increases or decreases in the odds ratio for sub-sector, size and age categories as against the reference category for data showing significance. Categories not displayed have odds equivalent to the reference category.

S= Statistically significant at overall sector level but not significant at sub-sector level

Table A3. Logistic regression tests for the benefits from ICT

Benefits from ICT	Logistic Regression Result		
	Sector	Size	Age
Improved productivity	IS (3.2) Media (2.7) Logs (0.52)	NS	NS
Improved product / service	IS (6.0) Media (3.3) Logs (2.2)	NS	NS
Faster response to customers	IS (3.3)	NS	6-10 (0.37)
Improved customer satisfaction	IS (3.0)	NS	NS
Improved working on joint projects with other firms	IS (3.6)	NS	NS
Increased sales	IS (2.2) Logs (0.4)	NS	NS
Reduced staff numbers	NS	NS	NS
Improved staff satisfaction	NS	NS	NS
Enable us to keep up with competitors	S		

Table notes:

IS = 'Internet Services'; Logs = 'Logistics'; Food Pro. = 'Food Processing'

Data is statistically significant at 5% or better

NS = Not statistically significant

Figures in brackets show increases or decreases in the odds ratio for sub-sector and age categories as against the reference category for data showing significance. Categories not displayed have odds equivalent to the reference category.

S= Statistically significant at overall sector level but not significant at sub-sector level.

Table A4. Summary of findings for logistic regression tests

No independent variables	Just Sector	Just Size	Sector and Size	Sector and Age	Sector, Size and Age
Email	**Company Website** IS (9.3) Media (3.0)	**Groupware** Micro (0.35)	**Intranet** [IS (7.4)] [Small (0.15) Micro (0.09)]	**Faster response to customers** [IS (3.3)] [6-10 (0.37)]	**Prod Plan & Control** [Sector Signif]* [Micro 0.27] [6-10 (2.2]
Internet	**Vid/Aud. Conf.** IS (6.5) Media (2.5)	**Human Resources Mgmt** Micro (0.11)	**Extranet/EDI** [IS (2.2) Logs. (0.48)] [Micro (0.29)]		
Reduced staff numbers	**Sales/Mktg.** IS (3.4)		**Own computer network (LAN/WAN)** [IS (5.2)] [Micro (0.11)]		
Improved staff satisfaction	**Design** IS (10.3) Media (5.1) Logs (0.31)		**Wireless** [IS (5.0) Logs (0.5)] [Small (0.37) Micro (0.33)]		

continued on following page

Table A4. continued

No independent variables	Just Sector	Just Size	Sector and Size	Sector and Age	Sector, Size and Age
	Improved productivity IS (3.2) Media (2.7) Logs (0.52)		**Stock control** [Media (0.2) Logs (0.1) IS (0.07)] [Small (0.24) Micro (0.18)]		
	Improved product / service IS (6.0) Media (3.3) Logs (2.2)		**Enterprise Res. Planning (ERP)** [IS (3.3) Media (2.5)] [Micro (0.27)]		
	Mkt Research IS (2.6)				
	Doc Mgmt Media (0.19)				
	Improved cust. satisfaction IS (3.0)				
	Improved working on joint projects with other firms IS (3.6)				
	Increased sales IS (2.2) Logs (0.4)				
	Enable us to keep up with competitors [Sector Signif]*				
4	12	6	2	1	1

Table notes:
IS = 'Internet Services'; Logs = 'Logistics'; Food Pro. = 'Food Processing'.
Results shown are statistically significant at 5% or better.
Figures in brackets show increases or decreases in the odds ratio for sub-sector and age categories as against the reference category for data showing significance. Categories not displayed have odds equivalent to the reference category.
* Overall sector data shows significance but no individual sub-sector shows significance

Chapter 10
Collaborative Networks:
Challenges for SMEs

Kathryn Cormican
National University of Ireland, Ireland

ABSTRACT

The business landscape has changed dramatically in recent years. Innovative organisations are re-structuring their business models. They are moving away from discrete linear value chains towards open innovation models such as networks. Small to Medium Sized Enterprises (SMEs) recognise that in order to survive they must be equipped with the relevant competencies required to design, develop and deploy innovative solutions that meet the needs of the end user. More and more small firms are collaborating with each other in order to create value added products and access new markets. However, the task of working in a collaborative network is not easy. SMEs find it particularly difficult to engage in these activities and experience many challenges in this regard. Moreover, there are very few support structures and systems available to guide successful knowledge sharing and collaboration. This chapter explores the fundamental concepts of collaborative networks and knowledge sharing, synthesises and presents some of the challenges faced by SMEs and identifies some critical success factors that should be considered to help overcome the barriers identified.

INTRODUCTION

Open innovation is a new paradigm that has emerged for managing innovation (Chesbrough, 2003; Gassmann, 2006). It proposes that organizations should exploit external competencies such as knowledge, infrastructure and relationships

to help accelerate the generation, development and commercialization of technologies and innovations. Chesbrough (2006) defines open innovation as '*the use of purposive inflows and outflows of knowledge to accelerate internal innovation, and to expand the markets for external use of innovation, respectively.* (p. 1)' Literature suggests that there are two components that are central to the open innovation model. These are

DOI: 10.4018/978-1-60960-463-9.ch010

'exploration' and 'exploitation' (van de Vrandea (2009); Lichtenthaler, 2008; Chesbrough & Crowther, 2006; Geiger & Makri, 2006). Exploration can be defined as the search for new knowledge, technology, competences, markets or relations and exploitation can be defined as is the further development of existing knowledge, technology, competences, markets or relations (Li et al., 2008). In light of this, open innovation models comprise a variety of internal and external technology sources and a variety of internal and external technology commercialisation methods (Chesbrough, 2003). Effective knowledge sharing and collaboration is central to the success of open innovation. Collaboration is a process of shared discovery or creation in order to create value (Hardin & Shrage, 1998). It involves two or more individuals with complementary skills interacting with each other to create a shared understanding that neither had previously possessed, nor could have possessed on their own.

Small to medium sized enterprises (SME) are beginning to adopt open innovation models in order to create value added products and services. To do this they must reorganise their operational structures. Consequently, they are forming enterprise networks. Enterprise networks are a coalition of independent organisations with complementary competencies and skills. They enable organisations to share competencies, combine resources and innovate outside of their individual capabilities. However, collaborating in an enterprise network is not easy. It demands that individuals re-orientate their mindset and that leaders create new organizational structures and work processes. SMEs find it particularly difficult to collaborate in

networks (Cormican & Dooley, 2007). They fail to understand how they can actively participate and benefit from these endeavours. They also lack the essential resources such as time and skills needed to participate (Bougrain & Haudeville, 2002). Furthermore, much of the discussions on open innovation models and enterprise networks to date have focused on larger organisations. There has been little debate about or analysis of SME involvement in such initiatives. There is also a lack of support structures and systems available to guide successful knowledge sharing and collaboration in a networked environment.

This chapter aims to provide a better understanding of knowledge sharing in collaborative networks. The networked enterprise is defined; the rationale for establishing a network is presented and the benefits and business case are also explored and discussed. A comparative analysis of traditional organisational structures and the new networked enterprise structure is provided. The characteristics and traits of enterprise networks are identified and discussed. The chapter then discusses the importance of knowledge sharing and what motivates people to share knowledge. The key challenges that SMEs encounter are synthesised and documented. The remainder of the chapter focuses on highlighting critical success factors that should be considered to help overcome these barriers.

THE NETWORKED ENTERPRISE

Traditionally organisations competed across linear supply chains (see Figure 1). These sup-

Figure 1. Linear supply chain model (Source: Author)

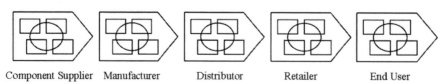

| Component Supplier | Manufacturer | Distributor | Retailer | End User |

Figure 2. Networked enterprise (Source: Author)

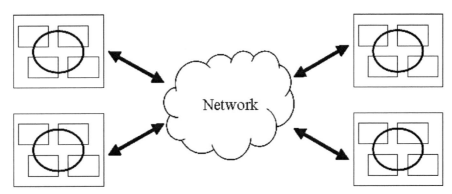

ply chains focused on improving the efficiency and effectiveness of existing product/market combinations. However the business landscape has changed dramatically in recent years. Innovation is radical, product life cycles are shortening, customers are more discerning and prices and margins are falling. Organisations must seek not fractional but exponential levels of improvement to survive. Consequently, progressive organisations are restructuring and reconfiguring their business models. They are moving away from discrete linear supply chains towards value networks. These emerging structures (see Figure 2) seek to support open innovation models by sharing competencies and resources and optimising linkages and relationships.

According to Achrol & Kotler, (1999) a networked enterprise is *"an interdependent coalition of business entities"* (either independent companies or autonomous organizational units) that operate *"without hierarchical control but have strong lateral connections* (p. 148)". Camarinha-Matos et al., (2008) state that these entities are *"largely autonomous, geographically distributed, and heterogeneous in terms of their operating environment, culture, social capital and goals* (p. 57)". A networked enterprise has shared objectives; participants collaborate to achieve common or compatible goals. They are organized around customer needs and come together to exploit new opportunities and create value for the customer.

A networked enterprise comprises a distinct system of designers, suppliers, manufacturers and infrastructure providers that focus on their individual core competencies and compete on capabilities. They maximize productivity by creating partnerships among independent specialized firms, many of which are small to medium sized enterprises (SME's). One of the greatest advantage of the collaborative network is its ability to take on larger projects in a more efficient and flexible manner than would be possible for an individual organisation. As these value networks are created industries polarise between knowledge companies and physical companies. Knowledge companies create the value proposition (i.e. the promise of a product or service) and they control the customer relationship and while the physical companies realize this promise by manufacturing or distributing the product, service or solution. Table 1 compares the characteristics of traditional organisational structures and the new networked enterprise.

Collaborative networks are organised to optimise core competencies, they have flatter structures and they promote interaction among organisational units and people. They are characterised by flexibility, specialisation and emphasis on relationship management instead of market transactions. They promote knowledge sharing, learning and change faster as well as more effective decision making (Mendelson, &

Table 1. Comparative analysis between traditional organizational structures and the networked enterprise (Adapted from Cormican & O'Sullivan, 2004)

Dimension	Traditional Structure	Networked Enterprise
Environment	Stable	Dynamic
Core Competence	Discipline specific	Specialised skills
Added Value	Transform materials	Synthesise information
Size	Large	Small
Capability	Supervision	Collaboration
Development	Sequential	Concurrent
Organisation	Functional, hierarchical, centralised	Autonomous cross functional teams
Management	Hierarchy	Relationship
Focus	Discipline	Market
Communication	Formal information system	Continuous, flexible and multi-directional
Decision making	Vertical	Vertical and lateral
Location	Co-located	Work across time and space
Contact	Face to face	Digital networks

Pillai, 1999). Collaborative networks also help firms to minimise the costs associated with finding, organising, and using knowledge. They can also help employees to do their jobs more effectively. Collaborative networks are credited with the following benefits:

- **Increased creativity and innovation:** Networks are an effective mechanism for generating, sharing, and applying organisational knowledge. Information and knowledge are critical components for creativity and innovation which fuels growth and profitability. Networks also promote divergent thinking and the cross fertilisation of ideas.
- **Faster knowledge transfer:** Networks are an effective mechanism for generating, sharing, and applying organisational knowledge. They can help SMEs leverage knowledge assets more effectively and enable participants to locate and communicate with experts more quickly.
- **Enhanced agility and productivity:** Workers with easier access to relevant

skills and resources perform more productively. They spend less time looking for information and more time on leveraging and using it. They also make more effective decisions faster.

- **Optimised resources:** Networks come together to pool resources. This means that the limitations and deficiencies of an organisation can be supplemented by the expertise of another.
- **Higher profits:** Key performance indicators such as shorter lead times, lower costs, increased flexibility, better ideas and more satisfied customers have a significant impact on the bottom line and ultimately lead to higher profit margins.

CHARACTERISTICS OF A NETWORK

Networks also have special characteristics that can help to define them. These characteristics can be grouped into the following categories (a) membership; (b) lifecycle; (c) goals; (d) culture;

(e) added value; (f) digital technologies. Each of these features is discussed in more detail.

Membership

The network must have a critical mass of suitable partners. According to Thompson (2009), they must include the right individual from the right company, from the right industry. The networked enterprise may consist of representatives from large organisations as well as SMEs. Members should have complimentary skills, they should be willing to work together and demonstrate commitment by assigning senior people to the initiative. While membership in a network is fluid and will change regularly each partner must play an active role, contribute to the end product and form a link in the network, regardless of location.

Life Cycle

All networks are temporary and have predefined lifecycles. The lifecycle of the network will vary according to the goals and mission of the initiative. However research suggests that there are at least four significant life-cycle phases are which are similar to those found in the theory of group dynamics (e.g. forming, norming, storming and performing). These are:

- **Preparation of a network** (identifying, sourcing and selecting partners)
- **Establishment of a network** (idea generation, setting goals and objectives, resolving legal issues, developing contracts, etc.)
- **Operation of a network** (day-to-day management of the network)
- **Decomposition of a network** (dissolvent or break up of the network)

Goals

For networks to be effective they must have a shared vision or purpose and obtainable goals.

For networks to be effective, participants' efforts must clearly link back to the strategic goals and value proposition of the organization. The strategic planning process should define goals that reflect the needs of the participating organisations. These goals should then be communicated to and agreed by all participants. Performance measures that align with the goals should be developed in order to help keep everybody focussed in the same direction.

Culture

Collaboration is a voluntary process; it cannot be hierarchically imposed or closely controlled (Miles et al., 2000). A culture based on the desire to share skills and information must replace the traditional control-based culture. The desire and ability to take risks is an absolute prerequisite to membership in such an organisation. Trust in the collaborative network is based primarily on trust between people.

Added Value

A balanced distribution of risks as well as profits within the enterprise network is a necessary for successful co-operation. In order for the network to survive, some added value must be achieved and perceived. In general, partners who cannot perceive any added value by co-operating with others will concentrate on their individual activities and will not put sufficient effort into the network. Mutual benefits in terms of shared added value become a stabilising factor for a co-operative behaviour in a network.

Digital Technologies

Members in a network work in a virtual space. Networks are composed of co-workers geographically and organisationally linked through digital technologies. Communication and transactions are supported by ebusiness technologies. Work is organised around value adding projects that are carried out by small multi-skilled self managed teams. The interactions among these teams are supported by digital technologies.

KNOWLEDGE SHARING CHALLENGES FOR SMEs

Effective knowledge sharing is central to the success of collaborative networks. The strategic importance of knowledge sharing has been well documented in the literature (Mooradian et al., 2006, Bock et al, 2005; Kreiner, 2002; Tidd, 2001). Research suggests that individuals share knowledge for self motivating or personal reasons such as to gain personal advantage or reward (Wasko & Faraj, 2000). Some people may expect that their contributions will earn them a good reputation and improve their status within their social group (Cabrera & Cabrera, 2002). Others may choose to share knowledge for altruistic or social reasons such as to do the right thing or to help develop relationships with others (Ardichvili et al., 2003; Wasko & Faraj, 2000). For example, such individuals may be committed to the organisation or network and they may want to see the organisation benefit from their knowledge.

However, research indicates that knowledge sharing is a complex activity (Cormican & Dooley, 2007) and a significant barrier to collaboration (Hendriks, 1999). Hansen (1999) found that the key problems with transferring knowledge in organisations centre around two key factors. These are (a) people are not willing to share and (b) people are not able to share.

- People are not willing to share knowledge because they may operate in an environment of secrecy and competition and do not trust their colleagues with their knowledge (Mooradian et al., 2006; Dirks & Ferrin, 2001; Hansen, 1999). Cabrera & Cabrera (2002) found that many people

did not have sufficient time to participate in knowledge sharing activities. They also found that many people did not understand the value in sharing their knowledge with others and so were not motivated to share their knowledge with others.

- People are not able to share knowledge with others because it is not easy to take individual's personal knowledge and transform it into an asset that can be absorbed and used by an organisation (Bock et al., 2005; Warkentin et al., 2001; Hildreth, 2000). It is also difficult to transfer knowledge that was created in one organization to another organization. This is because knowledge is socially constructed and developed in a context specific environment. As each organisation's learning experience is unique it is difficult to capture knowledge from one setting and use it in another (Cabrera & Cabrera, 2002). Furthermore organizational knowledge is often tacit in nature and embedded in a unique and often unspoken culture or system of norms and beliefs (Hansen, 1999). This makes organizations knowledge difficult to copy or reproduce in another setting.

In order to identify where the barriers currently exist with respect to knowledge sharing in a collaborative environment, a qualitative study using focused workshop techniques was undertaken across 8 regions in Europe namely Spain, Italy, Netherlands, Denmark, Czech Republic, Poland, Ireland and UK. The workshops were targeted at owner managers of SMEs employing less that 50 people in the knowledge sector who had some experience of collaborating in a network. On average 20 people participated in each workshop. The aim of the workshop was not to focus on the specifics of the individual projects but instead to identify and prioritise the current problems and future challenges associated with sharing knowledge across a collaborative networked environment.

Table 2. Challenges for SMEs

Dimension	Description
Motivation	• Members are unclear about the rationale and associated benefits of working in the network. • Participants are uncertain about the drivers, goals, advantages, rewards and returns for sharing information and knowledge with others. • Feelings of isolation and decreased interpersonal contact experienced by virtual team members can lead to motivational challenges. • It is more difficult to implement and maintain common goals when team members are divided by time zones and geographical locations. • Lack of face-to-face interaction can lead to feelings of anonymity and low social control, which in turn can cause social loafing • It is more difficult to receive positive feedback in a virtual setting
Size	• Large groups increase the levels of complexity in the network. Work tasks and communication channels are then divided which causes problems with co-ordination. • As size increases there are more problems with cultural diversity, trust, and information security. • Security becomes particularly problematic as size increases.
Cognitive distance	• Different mindsets of individuals and organisations can result in misunderstanding and disagreement since their behaviour is grounded on different values and beliefs. • Members from separate organizations have different motivations and incentives. • Members prioritise the work they must deliver for their "home organisation" over what they must deliverable for the network.
Trust	• It is difficult to establish trust when members come from different educational and cultural backgrounds and have different professional loyalties. • Members are afraid to share propriety information with other organisations. They often fear that competitors may gain access to proprietary data if they share information such as sales forecasts, proprietary intellectual property or promotional plans with collaborating partners.
Skills	• Members do not know how to share information and knowledge. • They do not know what information and knowledge to share and the format in which it should be transferred.
Time	• Members cite the lack of sufficient time to capture and transfer critical knowledge. • They do not have sufficient time to rethink and redesign their knowledge processes.
Communication	• There is too much unimportant information transferred between members. • It is more difficult for information to flow in a virtual environment. • People often do not know what information to share, where critical information can be found and how to transfer it to others. • Information is often incorrectly formatted in documents and files and people are unable to communicate effectively. • There is a lack of a common language between representatives from different organisations and consequently information is often misinterpreted between its creation and its application. • There is a loss of non-verbal cues, such as facial expressions, which can impede understanding. • Difficult to communicate and retain contextual information about other team members

Nominal group techniques were used to organise and correlate the workshop results. This method provides a reliable structure for a group discussion (see Langford et al., 2002, McDaniel & Gates, 2001, Oakland, 2000). It is used when the issues are complex and the information required is in unorganised thoughts. The findings from this study are synthesized and presented in Table 2.

Knowledge sharing and collaboration is not easy. Many organizations find the implementation of good knowledge practices difficult. SMEs experience even more problems with this as they lack the sophisticated systems enjoyed by larger organizations. It seems that the key problems that SMEs face with knowledge sharing and collaboration lie with managing the individual in an organizational setting. In light of this, attention must be paid to redesigning and restructuring internal processes and management systems to support the new collaborative business environment. This is not an easy task for small firms. However, changes in the work environment can make substantial improvements in knowledge sharing and collaboration. SMEs that wish to promote knowledge sharing must develop and foster appropriate work environments. The following section discusses some of the critical success factors that should be considered and adopted.

SOLUTIONS AND RECOMMENDATIONS

There are many factors that affect successful knowledge sharing and collaboration in SMEs. However, processes and systems can have a significant impact on collaboration. Owner/managers of SMEs must purposefully construct strategies and structures so as to enhance knowledge generation, transfer and reuse for innovation. These should include people, process as well as technology related issues. Some of the most appropriate and relevant critical success factors are introduced. These include (a) goals; (b) leadership; (c) size; (d) composition; (e) ownership; (f) accountability; (g) trust; (h) empowerment; (i) resources and finally (j) communication. Key decision makers may use this discussion as a guide to help overcome some of the challenges highlighted on our study.

Goals

Collaborative networks comprise experts from a wide variety of functions and disciplines and this diversity can create serious barriers for shared understanding. Inadequate definition of the goal, work content, cost, schedule or technical requirements will quickly bring the project into trouble. The establishment of clear goals provides the form and focus which can help maintain motivation.

Long term goal clarity is achieved when all employees know where the organisation is attempting to go in the future and why knowledge transfer is important to get there. Short-term goal clarity is achieved when managers set tangible and measurable goals for employees' work, which are in alignment with the overall goals of the organisation. Goals must be clearly defined and communicated to all so that everyone can work towards a similar end. All team members must understand their role in the process. Detailed procedures should be developed by the team members to minimize resistance within the organization.

Leadership

Strong leadership is imperative in order to clearly define the vision for the network and guide the members. Bell & Kozlowski (2002) state that the key functions of team leaders are to develop a cohesive unit, to shape processes, and to continuously monitor and manage team performance. Chinowsky & Rojas (2003) believe that team leaders must constantly re-emphasize the ultimate goal of the team to ensure focus is maintained on the big picture. Continuous performance feedback should also be provided to members. They should exhibit a number of essential attributes, including: *'leadership, results catalyst, facilitator, barrier burster, business analyser, coach, and living example'* (Fisher & Fisher, 2001) (p. 110).

Furthermore, employees who are actively encouraged to share ideas, take risks, and initiate change are more inclined to be successful at inter firm collaboration (Cormican & O'Sullivan, 2003a). Thus, it is the leadership of the network nodes that must communicate to the participants a mindset of shared partnership as well as the value-adding joint benefit and long-term future of the network in order to facilitate participants to engage with each other and collaborate within the network. Hertel et al., (2004) believe that issues with low motivation can be handled by leaders by creating high task interdependence from the outset and using team-based rewards to maintain high perceived outcome interdependence with the teams. Lurey & Raisinghani (2001) also believe that the creation of team-based reward systems is important. However, Hertel et al., (2005) stresses that team leaders should ensure that assigned team roles are not in conflict with team members' commitments to other work units

Size

In general, the smaller the number members in the network, the higher the probability of success. Some initiatives require a greater diversity of skills but, all other things being equal, a larger size tends to lead to a lower per capita performance. If a network is too large it becomes difficult to maintain close cohesion and they can more readily break up into factions. Conversely, it can also be argued that it is more difficult to bring together the range of skills and approaches that lead to the problem solving and idea generation when the team has less than four members. Therefore, it seems that the ideal team size should consist of four to seven members where they can convene easily and frequently, communicate with all members without formal systems and understand everyone else's roles and skills.

Composition

Composition has been shown to be central to the success of the network. Finding good performers will contribute to productivity but, unless they collectively possess the functional background, skills, and experience necessary to implement the project deliverables, the network is not likely to succeed. A well balanced skill mix is also essential for success. Each team must have adequate functional or technical expertise, problem solving and decision making skills, and interpersonal skills.

Ownership

Unless mutual benefits to collaboration are established and communicated to all parties from the outset, people will remain unwilling to participate and reluctant to learn new procedures for information exchange. Member companies must also take ownership of the network and be willing to contribute financially to its development. They must have a stake both in the process and the outcome. The issue of intellectual property contribution and ownership is something that should be decided on as part of the strategic partnership agreement and should be communicated to all network participants prior to beginning any collaborative initiative.

Accountability

Johnson et al., (2001) note that self-discipline and accountability is also essential. The concept of mutual accountability requires moving from a parochial view of the world in which the individuals own function, values and goals are paramount. In order for members to become mutually accountable, members must be clear on the contributions for which they are individually responsible and also, for which the group is jointly responsible. These may include; the purpose, goals, approach, and deliverables. Commitment and trust are two critical dimensions to mutual accountability. When people work together toward a common objective, trust and commitment follow. Consequently, networks enjoying a strong common purpose and approach inevitably hold themselves, both as individuals and as a group, responsible for the output and performance.

Trust

Establishing trust is potentially the greatest barrier to overcome in collaboration, and it must be established from the outset to allow knowledge sharing. Trust can be defined as the '*willingness to be vulnerable to the actions of another party based on the expectation that the other will perform a particular action important to the trustor, irrespective of the ability to monitor or control that other party'* (Mayer et al., 1995, p. 712). Jarvenpaa et al. (2004) state that, *'where members rely on IT-mediated interactions, successful collaboration depends on trust'* (p. 250). Trust is important in collaborative networks as many tasks are carried out independently and team members must rely on each others' expertise to carry out these tasks successfully. Rosen et al. (2007) stress that a psychologically safe team culture needs to be created by team leaders, so that team members can freely share ideas and offer constructive criticisms.

Trust is something that cannot be imposed on a network but instead must be 'normed and formed' over time, as with any group dynamic. However, an organisations culture (i.e. values, norms and beliefs) and climate (i.e. policies, practices and procedures) have a significant impact on nurturing trust (Cormican & O'Sullivan, 2003a). For example, workers should be afforded a certain degree of autonomy (Gupta and Govindarajan, 2000) and failure should not be punished (Leonard & Sensiper, 1998). Rezgui (2007) believes that *'open communication channels, and participation and involvement in decision-making, enhance sharing of information and facilitate virtual team cohesion, which in turn promotes trust'* (p. 102). Many other authors mention the importance of free-flowing information (Hinds & Pfeffer 2003; Gibbert & Krause 2002; Jarvenpaa & Staples 2000) and open communication (Ardichvili et al, 2003; Hinds & Pfeffer 2003; Wasko & Faraj 2000).

Empowerment

Kirkman et al., (2004) highlight empowerment as an important factor in the performance of virtual teams. Chinowsky & Rojas (2003) believe that these teams should be given the power to make independent decisions; *'Teams receiving the greatest independence and opportunity to make*

overall project decisions will function as better teams and reduce the likelihood that geographic separation will affect the project outcome' (p. 105). Employee empowerment involves the delegation of decision making to employees while holding them accountable for outcomes (Kirkman & Rosen, (2000). Empowerment means giving employees much more scope to make decisions and allowing organizations to become less bureaucratic. This ownership is lauded to be imperative for the success of teams. More specifically, it is believed to have a positive impact on the team's decision making ability. It also increases employee motivation and productivity.

Virtual workers must show high levels of initiative and pro-activity. Accordingly, it is important that team members feel empowered to improve processes and respond to changing customer demands as required. However, if organizations really want to empower employees, they have to do more than just cede authority and control, they have to help their employees manage their autonomy. Members must have access to relevant skills and information to perform their jobs well. In other words, employees must be enabled to do the work. Enabling people involves helping them develop the competencies they need to manage additional power and autonomy efficiently. When enablement is not part of the effort, it is likely to fail.

Resources

Effective knowledge sharing and transfer demands time, energy and resources. However these resources are often in short supply and most SMEs do not have sufficient time and support to rethink and redesign their work processes. Organisational resources may be categorised as tangible such as money and equipment, or intangible which would include, time and support. SME owner/ managers should demonstrate tangible support for effective collaboration through by allocating specific budgets to it. For example, management can demonstrate their support by providing funding for supporting mechanisms such as face-to-face meetings that allow the network members to 'norm and form'.

Methods and tools are essential to equip members with the appropriate skills for effective collaboration. Rosen et al., (2007) and Griffith et al., (2003) stress the need to provide adequate tools to support highly-interdependent work. Collaborative networks are emerging organisational structures and there is insufficient research and support systems to guide their development and implementation. However an effective and structured approach to knowledge sharing and collaboration should be designed and deployed. The use of methods and tools can enable knowledge transfer to happen quickly and predictably. Cormican and O'Sullivan, (2003b) note that methods and tools should:

- Be context specific
- Meet the needs of the user
- Be simple and user friendly
- Be available to all members
- Make appropriate use of proven and available management techniques and tools
- Take into consideration the organisations' culture and value systems. Furthermore, implementing tools that align with existing processes and workflow is imperative. In other words, methods and tools must be appropriate to the job at hand; they should act as a means to an end (i.e. an enabler to an existing process) rather than an end in itself (i.e. an additional or separate activity in the organisation).

Time is often cited as a critical success factors for effective collaboration. It is important to remember that networks take time to develop. Trust and independence is built over time and results in increasing flows of information throughout the network. There must be extra willingness and flexibility during the early stages of establishing a structure. Furthermore time must be allowed for

redesigning and restructuring internal processes to support effective knowledge transfer. Communication Effective project implementation involves synthesising and reusing existing knowledge and information (Cormican & O'Sullivan, 2004). Many small firms face difficulties in transferring knowledge and information from one organisational unit to another and consequently project team members are not equipped with all the necessary information to perform tasks and make informed decisions. In order to avoid repeating mistakes, reinventing solutions and expending resources into solving problems that might have already been solved, it is important that the right information is available to the right people, in the right format, at the right time. Furthermore, it is essential that this information is reliable, accurate, complete and up to date. Johnson et al., (2001) emphasize the importance of effective communications in virtual environments and the need for additional training for team members to ensure they understand the constraints of using a virtual environment. Team members required more linguistic precision in their communication, since they ware unable to modify their speech with descriptive gestures or facial movements (Townsend et al., 1998). Kayworth & Leidner (2000) also stress the importance of continuous communication. Rezgui (2007) recommends the inclusion of face-to-face interactions where possible and in particular during its inception stage of the lifecycle, where the vision, mission, and goals can be communicated and shared. According to (Lurey & Raisinghani, 2001, p. 533). '*These dispersed work groups, then, must take ample time during the initial design phases to consider their future goals and develop healthy and supportive environments if they are to reach their complete potential*' Zigurs (2003) also stresses the importance of interspersing face-to-face communication with virtual meetings to help to build relationships and commitment that can enhance team performance.

Technology is an essential element to collaboration in a network as much work is not co-located and conducted over digital networks. Olson & Olson (2000) highlight the need for the organisation to have some experience in collaboration technology before implementing virtual structures. Avolio & Kahai (2003) believe that leaders in virtual environments need to use the collaborative technology tools to build and sustain relationships and to deal with greater workforce diversity as '*electronic media may help take group*

members' attention away from individual differences, enabling greater unity' (p. 333).

This section presented ten critical success factors that were found to enhance knowledge sharing in collaborative networks. These success factors are a synthesis of best practice in the area and useful to support the management of collaborative networks. Table 3 demonstrates how these success factors can address the challenges that were identified earlier.

Table 3. Key solutions aligned to challenges

Challenge	Critical Success Factor
Motivation	• Member must take ownership of the network and be willing to contribute to its development. • Members must have a stake both in the process and outcome. • A strong leader who is able to clearly define the vision and set with obtainable goals is needed. • Goals must reflect the needs of the participating organisations. • Goals must be communicated to all so that everyone can work towards a similar end. • Clear performance measures should be developed to keep the vision and strategy focussed. • Clear roles and policy guidelines should be developed to minimize resistance.
Size and Composition	• The network should comprise four to seven members. • Members must have the functional background, skills, and experience necessary to implement the project deliverables. • Members must also possess problem solving, decision making and interpersonal skills.
Cognitive distance	• Mutual benefits must be defined and communicated. • Intellectual property issues should be agreed in advance. • Mutual accountability is necessary. • Members must know what they are responsible for. • Initiative, commitment, self discipline and pro-activity are essential. • Members should be encouraged to share ideas, take risks, and initiate change.
Trust	• Flexibility should be afforded to members at the early stages of development. • Members must be empowered to improve processes and respond to changing customer demands. • Workers should be given a certain degree of autonomy. • Failure should not be punished. • Members should be involved in the decision making process. • Communication channels should be open.
Skills	• Members must have access to relevant skills, methods and tools to perform their jobs well. • Tools must align with actual work processes. • Members must be equipped with the appropriate skills for sharing knowledge. • Specific budgets must be allocated to the network.
Time	• Time must be allocated at the early stages of the lifecycle to define goals and develop supportive environments. • Time must be afforded to redesign work processes.
Communication	• The right information must be available to the right people, in the right format, at the right time. • Information is reliable, accurate, complete and up to date. • Training should be provided to ensure that members understand the constraints of working in a virtual environment. • Face-to-face meetings should be scheduled where possible. • Members must be equipped with skills in collaboration technologies before implementing virtual structures.

CONCLUSION

We are experiencing a major distortion in the market place. Competition is becoming increasingly intense. It is more and more difficult for companies in general and small to medium enterprises (SMEs) in particular to gain and maintain competitive advantage. Consequently, we are experiencing a major change in the way companies operate. Open innovation models are emerging. SMEs are changing their business models in order to compete and survive. Organisations with specific and complementary competencies are organising themselves around collaborative networks in order to design, develop and deploy innovative products and services for mutual gain. To do this they must share knowledge, competencies and resources. However, SMEs are finding this to be a major challenge. They recognise that it is not easy to build relationship with other organisations

It seems that many of the problems highlighted focus on the 'softer' side of knowledge sharing and integration rather than the technical infrastructure. The key problems with collaboration lie with work practices and organizational structures. In light of this attention must be paid to redesigning and restructuring internal processes and management systems to support the new collaborative business environment. While effective knowledge sharing cannot be forced or mandated, changes in the work environment can make substantial improvements in knowledge sharing and collaboration. Managers SMEs can reduce the risk of failure by exploring the factors that facilitate the process. Factors such as developing ownership and building a trust are important but they are not sufficient. Factors such as creating a shared vision and strategic compatibility as well as design appropriate systems support structures have to be considered. Successful initiatives require support and backing from key leaders in order to overcome the natural resistance of organisations to change. Inter firm collaboration may demand even greater leadership and support than previous internally focused initiatives. Therefore leaders must focus on the specific, tangible business benefits of these efforts, and participants across collaborating organisations must understand and support those benefits. Such foundation building will be critical in overcoming the barriers to inter firm collaboration.

REFERENCES

Achrol, R. S., & Kotler, P. (1999). Marketing in the network economy. *Journal of Marketing*, *63*, 146–163. doi:10.2307/1252108

Ardichvili, A., Page, V., & Wentling, T. (2003). Motivation and barriers to participation in virtual knowledge-sharing communities of practice. *Journal of Knowledge Management*, *7*(1), 64–77. doi:10.1108/13673270310463626

Avolio, B., & Kahai, S. (2003). Adding the "E" to E-leadership: How it may impact your leadership. *Organizational Dynamics*, *31*(4), 325–338. doi:10.1016/S0090-2616(02)00133-X

Bell, B. S., & Kozlowski, S. W. J. (2002). A typology of virtual teams: Implications for effective leadership. *Group & Organization Management*, *27*(1), 14–49. doi:10.1177/1059601102027001003

Bock, G.-W., Zmud, R. W., Kim, Y.-G., & Lee, J.-N. (2005). Behavioral intention formation in knowledge sharing: Examining the roles of extrinsic motivators, social-psychological forces and organizational climate. *Management Information Systems Quarterly*, *29*(1), 87–112.

Bougrain, F., & Haudeville, B. (2002). Innovation, collaboration and SMEs internal research capacities. *Research Policy*, *31*(5), 735–747. doi:10.1016/S0048-7333(01)00144-5

Cabrera, A., & Cabrera, E. F. (2002). Knowledge sharing dilemmas. *Organization Studies*, *23*(5), 687–710. doi:10.1177/0170840602235001

Camarinha-Matos, L. M., Afsarmanesh, H., & Ollus, M. (2008). *Methods and tools for collaborative networked organizations*. New York: Springer. doi:10.1007/978-0-387-79424-2

Chesbrough, H. W. (2003). *Open Innovation: The new imperative for creating and profiting from technology*. Boston: Harvard Business School Press.

Chesbrough, H. W. (2006). Open Innovation: A New Paradigm for understanding industrial innovation. In H. Chesbrough, W. Vanhaverbeke & J. West (Eds), *Open innovation researching a new paradigm*. Oxford, UK: Oxford University Press.

Chesbrough, H. W., & Crowther, A. K. (2006). Beyond high tech: early adopters of open innovation in other industries. *R & D Management, 36*(3), 229–236. doi:10.1111/j.1467-9310.2006.00428.x

Chinowsky, P. S., & Rojas, E. M. (2003). Virtual teams: Guide to Successful Implementation. *Journal of Management Engineering, 19*(3), 98–106. doi:10.1061/(ASCE)0742-597X(2003)19:3(98)

Cormican, K., & Dooley, L. (2007). Knowledge sharing in a collaborative networked environment. *Journal of Information and Knowledge Management, 16*(2), 105–115. doi:10.1142/S0219649207001706

Cormican, K., & O'Sullivan, D. (2003a). A scorecard for supporting enterprise knowledge management. *Journal of Information and Knowledge Management, 2*(3), 191–201. doi:10.1142/S0219649203000395

Cormican, K., & O'Sullivan, D. (2003b). A collaborative knowledge management tool for product innovation management. *International Journal of Technology Management, 26*(1), 53–67. doi:10.1504/IJTM.2003.003144

Cormican, K., & O'Sullivan, D. (2004). Auditing best practice for effective for product innovation management. *Technovation, 24*(10), 819–829. doi:10.1016/S0166-4972(03)00013-0

Dirks, K. T., & Ferrin, D. L. (2001). The role of trust in organizational settings. *Organization Science, 12*(4), 450–467. doi:10.1287/orsc.12.4.450.10640

Fisher, K., & Fisher, M. D. (2001). *The Distance Manager: A Hands-On Guide to Managing Off-Site Employees and Virtual Teams*. New York: McGraw-Hill.

Gassmann, O. (2006). Opening up the innovation process: towards an agenda. *R & D Management, 36*(3), 223–228. doi:10.1111/j.1467-9310.2006.00437.x

Geiger, S., & Makri, M. (2006). Exploration and exploitation innovation processes: The role of organisational slack in R&D intensive firms. *The Journal of High Technology Management Research, 17*, 97–108. doi:10.1016/j.hitech.2006.05.007

Gibbert, M., & Krause, H. (2002). Practice exchange in a best practice marketplace. In Davenport, I. T. H., & Probst, G. J. B. (Eds.), *Knowledge Management Case Book: Siemens Best Practices* (pp. 89–105). Erlangen, Germany: Publicis Corporate Publishing.

Griffith, T. L., Sawyer, J., & Neale, M. (2003). Virtualness and knowledge in teams: managing the love triangle of organizations, individuals, and information technology. *Management Information Systems Quarterly, 27*(2), 265–287.

Hansen, M. T. (1999). The search-transfer problem: the role of weak ties in sharing knowledge across organization subunits, *Administrative Science Quarterly, 44*(1), 82, 112.

Hardin, S. R., & Schrage, M. (1998). Delivering Information Services through Collaboration. *Bulletin of the American Society for Information Science, 24*(6). http://www.asis.org/Bulletin/Aug-98/hardin.html.

Hendriks, P. (1999). Why share knowledge? The influence of ICT on the motivation for knowledge sharing. *Knowledge and Process Management, 6*(2), 91–100. doi:10.1002/(SICI)1099-1441(199906)6:2<91::AID-KPM54>3.0.CO;2-M

Hertel, G., Konradt, U., & Orlikowski, B. (2004). Managing distance by interdependence: Goal setting, task interdependence, and team-based rewards in virtual teams. *European Journal of Work and Organizational Psychology, 13*(1), 1–28. doi:10.1080/13594320344000228

Hildreth, P., Kimble, C., & Wright, P. (2000). Communities of practice in the distributed international environment. *Journal of Knowledge Management, 4*(1), 27–38. doi:10.1108/13673270010315920

Hinds, P., & Pfeffer, J. (2003). Why organizations don't 'know what they know: cognitive and motivational factors affecting the transfer of expertise. In Ackerman, M., Pipek, V., & Wulf, V. (Eds.), *Beyond Knowledge Management: Sharing Expertise*. Cambridge, MA: MIT Press.

Jarvenpaa, S. L., Shaw, T. R., & Staples, D. S. (2004). Toward contextualized theories of trust: The role of trust in global virtual teams. *Information Systems Research, 15*(3), 250–267. doi:10.1287/isre.1040.0028

Jarvenpaa, S. L., & Staples, D. S. (2000). The Use of Collaborative Electronic Media for Information Sharing: An Exploratory Study of Determinants. *The Journal of Strategic Information Systems, 9*, 129–154. doi:10.1016/S0963-8687(00)00042-1

Johnson, P., Heimann, V., & O'Neill, K. (2001). The "wonderland" of virtual teams. *Journal of Workplace Learning, 13*(1), 24–29. doi:10.1108/13665620110364745

Kayworth, T. R., & Leidner, D. E. (2000). The global virtual manager: A prescription for success. *European Management Journal, 18*(2), 183–194. doi:10.1016/S0263-2373(99)00090-0

Kirkman, B. L., & Rosen, B. (2000). Powering up teams. *Organizational Dynamics, 28*(3), 48–66. doi:10.1016/S0090-2616(00)88449-1

Kirkman, B. L., Rosen, B., Tesluk, P. E., & Gibson, C. B. (2004). The impact of team empowerment on virtual team performance: The moderating role of face-to-face interaction. *Academy of Management Journal, 47*(2), 175–192. doi:10.2307/20159571

Kreiner, K. (2002). Tacit knowledge management: the role of artefacts. *Journal of Knowledge Management, 6*(2), 112–123. doi:10.1108/13673270210424648

Langford, B. E., Schoenfeld, G., & Izzo, G. (2002). Nominal grouping sessions vs focus groups. *Qualitative Market Research: An International Journal, 5*(1), 58–70. doi:10.1108/13522750210414517

Leonard, D., & Senipser, S. (1998). The role of tacit knowledge in group innovation. *California Management Review, 40*(3), 112–132.

Li, Y., Vanhaverbeke, W., & Schoenmakers, W. (2008). Exploration and exploitation in innovation: Reframing the interpretation. *Creativity and Innovation Management, 17*(2), 107–126. doi:10.1111/j.1467-8691.2008.00477.x

Lichtenthaler, U. (2008). Open innovation in practice: an analysis of strategic approaches to technology transactions. *IEEE Transactions on Engineering Management, 55*(1), 148–157. doi:10.1109/TEM.2007.912932

Lurey, J., & Raisinghani, M. (2001). An empirical study of best practices in virtual teams. *Information & Management, 38*, 523–544. doi:10.1016/S0378-7206(01)00074-X

Mayer, R. C., Davis, J. H., & Schoorman, F. D. (1995). An integrative model of organizational trust. *Academy of Management Review, 20*(3), 709–734. doi:10.2307/258792

McDaniel, C. D., & Gates, R. H. (2000). *Contemporary Marketing Research* (4th ed.). Cincinnati, OH: Southwestern College Publishing.

Mendelson, H., & Pillai, R. R. (1999). Information age organizations, dynamics and performance. *Journal of Economic Behavior & Organization, 38*(3), 253–281. doi:10.1016/S0167-2681(99)00010-4

Miles, R. E., Snow, C. C., & Miles, G. (2000). The Future.org. *Long Range Planning, 33,* 300–321. doi:10.1016/S0024-6301(00)00032-7

Mooradian, T., Renzl, B., & Matzler, K. (2006). Who Trusts? Personality, trust and knowledge sharing. *Management Learning, 37*(4), 523–540. doi:10.1177/1350507606073424

Oakland, J. S. (2000). *Total Quality Management: Text with Cases.* Boston: Butterworth Heinemann.

Olson, G. M., & Olson, J. S. (2000). Distance Matters. *Human-Computer Interaction, 15,* 139–178. doi:10.1207/S15327051HCI1523_4

Rezgui, Y. (2007). Exploring virtual team-working effectiveness in the construction sector. *Interacting with Computers, 19,* 96–112. doi:10.1016/j.intcom.2006.07.002

Rosen, B., Furst, S. A., & Blackburn, R. S. (2007). Overcoming Barriers to Knowledge Sharing in Virtual Teams. *Organizational Dynamics, 36*(3), 259–273. doi:10.1016/j.orgdyn.2007.04.007

Thompson, K. (2009). *The Networked Enterprise: Competing for the future through virtual enterprise networks.* Tampa, FL: Meghan-Kiffer Press.

Tidd, J. (2001). Innovation management in context: environment, organization and performance. *International Journal of Management Reviews, 3*(3), 169–183. doi:10.1111/1468-2370.00062

Townsend, A., DeMarie, S., & Hendrickson, A. (1998). Virtual Teams: Technology and the workplace of the future. *The Academy of Management Executive, 12*(3), 17–29.

Van de Vrandea, V., de Jongb, J. P. J., Wim Vanhaverbekec, W., & de Rochemontd, M. (2009). Open innovation in SMEs: Trends, motives and management challenges. *Technovation, 29*(6-7), 423–437. doi:10.1016/j.technovation.2008.10.001

Warkentin, M., Bapna, R., & Sugumaran, V. (2001). E-knowledge networks for inter-organizational collaborative e-business. *Logistics Information Management, 14*(1), 148–163. doi:10.1108/09576050110363040

Wasko, M., & Faraj, S. (2000). It is what one does: Why people participate and help others in electronic communities of practice. *The Journal of Strategic Information Systems, 9*(2-3), 155–173. doi:10.1016/S0963-8687(00)00045-7

Zigurs, I. (2003). Leadership in Virtual Teams: Oxymoron or Opportunity? *Organizational Dynamics, 31*(4), 339–351. doi:10.1016/S0090-2616(02)00132-8

Chapter 11
E–Sourcing Electronic Platforms in Real Business

Luís Sampaio
Technological University of Lisbon, Portugal

José Figueiredo
Technological University of Lisbon, Portugal

ABSTRACT

The authors carried out this research in a specific context within the electronic markets - business-to-business (B2B). The purpose is to assert the major blocks needed to be covered by an e-purchasing tool in order to be successful. Another goal is to identify how this e-purchasing tool allows buyers (firms) to practice Strategic Sourcing. After an enlarged literature review on E-Sourcing Electronic Platforms (ESEP) and e-purchasing markets they defined a methodological framework and construct a case study. Their strategy was to use one case study only. The use of a single case study is addressed and justified. Within their case study the authors took advantage of the data collected in a survey recently conducted by Vortal (Portuguese firm that owns several B2B platforms in different electronic markets). Finally some conclusions are tentatively constructed.

INTRODUCTION

The first electronic markets (EM) originated with the emergence of the Internet and the World Wide Web boom in the beginning of the 90s. EMs can be divided in two main groups: Business-to-Consumer (B2C) and Business-to-Business (B2B). In this research we focus in B2B.

We begin contextualizing B2B EM (E-Economy, E-Business, E-Commerce, Physical and EM, E-Sourcing versus E-Procurement, Strategic Sourcing) and identify some of the main characteristics of ESEP (core building blocks, main buyers and suppliers benefits, E-Government and evolution). We reflected on the physical and virtual value chain model in order to take advantage of the integration of both chains. Then we put forward a methodological framework. In

DOI: 10.4018/978-1-60960-463-9.ch011

a reflective process, we tried to understand two questions: What characteristics should a successful e-purchasing tool have, and how can a successful e-purchasing tool allow firms to practice Strategic Sourcing policies?

After we build up one Case Study based on the Civil Construction Sector platform (ECON-STROI – www.econstroi.com), a platform owned and managed by Vortal S.A. We used and reflected on the data of a survey conducted by Vortal S.A in October 2008 addressing more than fifty buyer firms.

Finally we draw some conclusions and outline some recommendations.

BACKGROUND

Etymologies and Markets

E-Economy

Beginning in 1993 the Internet evolved into a service integrated global network with a diversity of multimedia uses. Negroponte in his early texts on Wired, some of them later compiled in a book (Negroponte, 1995), explored the E-economy metaphor as being a shifting from processing atoms to processing bits. This text and others of the same time stressed the fact that the main attribute of this E-Economy is immateriality. However this New Economy is characterized by three distinctive but important factors beyond immateriality: it is global; it favors' intangible things - ideas, information, knowledge, relationships; and It is deeply inter-linked (Kelly, 1998).

E-Business

E-business refers to a broader view of E-Commerce, not just the buying and selling of goods and services, but also servicing customers, cooperation with business partners, and conducting electronic transactions within the organization (Turban, et al.,

2002). The key concept in E-Economy is system dynamics, while in E-Business is the activity and in E-Commerce is the transaction.

An interesting example of the differences between E-Commerce and E-Business is addressed by Gottschalk (2006). The example is on handling customer complaints. As long as customers do not complain E-Commerce may be sufficient for electronic transactions with customers. The front end of the business is electronic and this front end is the only contact customers have with the business. However, if a customer complains, then other parts of the business need to get involved.

E-Commerce

According to Timmers (1999) E-Commerce reasons of growing are:

- Low entry cost compared to other solutions such as EDI. With low entry cost, a fast return on investment is possible;
- A promise of protecting the investment. Whereas EDI-based systems have a tendency to be specific to the trading or supply-chain relationship, Web-based systems interoperate among suppliers;
- Connectivity and communication meeting information needs;
- If a critical mass is already built and increasing this attracts even more users and providers of the technology and of business solutions (social network effect);
- Technology-driven 'virtuous innovation cycle' with constant opportunity creation as a consequence of the very rapid progress of electronic commerce technologies.

E-Commerce is usually divided in several categories. The classification of these categories is based on the nature of the transactions (who is selling to whom). The two more widely used categories of E-commerce are:

- **Business-to-Business (B2B):** involves transactions between businesses. Example: www.commerceone.com;
- **Business-to-Consumer (B2C):** businesses sell directly to consumers. Example: www.amazon.com.

Beyond these two categories the most important businesses in E-Commerce are: Consumer-to-Consumer (C2C), Consumer-to-Business (C2B), Business-to-Administration (B2A), among others. From these categories B2A is the most important because of the growing significance of E-Government all over.

E-Markets

An EM is an inter-organizational information system that allows buyers, sellers, independent third parties, and multi-firm consortiums to exchange information on prices and product offerings (Mahadevan, 2000). With the beginning of the EMs, two types of markets can be assessed: Physical and Electronic. Both these markets have the same three main functions (Bakos, 1998):

- Matching buyers and sellers;
- Facilitating the exchange of information, goods, services, and payments associated with a market transaction;
- Providing an institutional infrastructure, such as a legal and regulatory framework which enables the efficient functioning of the market.

EMs executes much more efficiently these functions because they extend the matches possibility among buyers and sellers, simplify the process of buying and of presenting proposals and perform worldwide without boundaries. Regardless all these advantages, EMs cannot fully threaten physical markets because of the need of physical communication channels.

Beyond the similarities at a market function level, from an economics perspective, EMs have fundamental differences from physical markets, namely transparency, size, and cost, (Bichler, 2001).

EMs are more transparent than physical markets because the several market participants can observe all the trading process from end-to-end. From a size perspective, EMs are not circumscribed by the normal boundaries that physical markets face, allowing a wider potential of trading. Finally from a cost point of view, EMs are able to reduce the transaction costs and to eliminate intermediates.

Electronic Markets Benefits

Following what we just said, Baker (2000) and Hartman et.al (2001) identified the major benefits of EMs in three groups of drivers: Process improvements; Cost reductions; New business generation.

A different approach (buyer/supplier) to the EMs benefits is addressed by Siegelmann, et al. (1996) and Feldman (2000):

- **Buyer advantages:**
  - Access to more information structured and stored in one place, so that it supporst consumers decision making processes;
  - Easier market research and comparison;
  - Consumers can conduct their researches anytime and anywhere: Some EMs include online product sampling (i.e. book excerpts, CD recording samples and so on);
  - Lower costs (because of information system usage), lower prices and higher quality (higher competition among suppliers), and wider selection of goods (aggregating significant number of vendors).

- **Supplier advantages:**
  - Improved economic efficiencies reducing margins and speeding up complicated business deals;
  - Better distribution, with no middlemen and shrinking distribution channels;
  - Possibility to gather more customer information;
  - Marketing communications allowing competing on other dimensions than only price;
  - Operational benefits which include reduced errors, time and overhead costs in information processing, easier entry into new markets (especially geographically remote) and faster time to market.

The adoption of EMs allows an important number of win-win situations both to buyers and suppliers. Buyers and suppliers benefit from process improvement and new business models can be created at virtually no extra cost. Buyers have cost reductions benefits. However, with EMs, suppliers can face a shrinking on their margins due to a more competitive and open market.

EMs also have some disadvantages as significant technological investment in infra-structures is required, issues related to security/privacy of data and finally legal problems related with EMs that perform worldwide, Kowalkiewicz (2004).

Business Dimensions of Electronic Markets

According to Thorelli (1986), Elofson et.al (1998), Lief (1999), Kaplan, et al. (1999), Sculley, et al. (1999), and Hartman et al. (2001) EMs can be segmented along six dimensions:

- Business model;
- Order processing mechanism;
- Revenue model;
- Market characteristics;
- Product specifics;
- EMs services.

Business Model

The business model of the EM depends on its ownership model. In this dimension we can have three types of EMs: focusing on sellers, focusing on buyers and neutral marketplaces, which do not favor either sellers or buyers but attract both (Kaplan, et al. (1999)) and Rosson (2000).

Order Processing Mechanism

The literature refers to five main order process mechanisms: Catalogs, Auction, Reverse Auction, Exchange and Community. Another order process mechanism can be added – ESEP

Revenue Model

It is possible to identify five major sources of revenue (Reilly, 2000; Trepp, 2000): Transaction fees, membership/subscription fees, advertising, professional service fees and value added service fees.

Market Characteristics

B2B EMs can be divided in two different types: horizontal and vertical (Blodget, et al. 2000):

- **Vertical:** Aimed at a specific industry and completely oriented toward the distinct need of a particular group (Rosson, 2000). This type of market focus on the efficiency of the supply chain of a given Industry;
- **Horizontal:** Are not customized to a specific industry. Aim to improve inefficiencies among multiple supply chains.

Other important characteristic of EMs is their Public or Private Dimension. The Public EM is an open trading environment that allows relationships from many-to-many. The Private EM is controlled by the buyer that manages the relationship with the business partners through the EM. There is also the Consortia EMs where a group of buyers manages the EM.

Product Characteristics

Some products are more suitable to be placed at EM than others. The characteristics of the products more suitable to marketplaces can be divided in 4 groups:

- Highly standardized merchandises/commodity type products that can be easily compared across suppliers are more suitable for EMs than highly customized products with individual specifics and infrequent purchase patterns (Lee et al., 2000). Although Ebay (www.ebay.com) history proves that high differentiated products can be commercialized through EMs;
- Product with a short life-cycle can create large quantities of obsolete products. EM provides new points of sale to these products;
- Low-value goods with relatively high traditional transaction costs are perfectly suitable to be traded on various B2B Markets (Kafka,2000);
- Products with high volatile prices.

E-Market Services

The services delivered by EMs need to be contextualized regarding the phase of the transaction when they occur. According to Schmid (1993) the exchange between demanders and suppliers is carried out through business transactions that can be divided in three phases: Information, negotiation and execution.

E-Sourcing

Sourcing

The purchasing/sourcing/negotiation processes started to have more visibility in the Firms with the creation of the first Purchasing Department Business Units (PDBU). Although the gathering of all buyers in a single unit introduced economies of scale at the first PDBU is was possible to observe that big savings (at different levels) were yet to be done. There are two main bottle-necks in the process (Simchi-Levi et al., 2003) within the first PDBU:

- Skills of the Buyers were low;
- Information available to them in order they could take decisions was very limited.

Behind these, PDBU started to have a wider range of tasks (Lamoreaux, et al. 2008):

- Determine what a company needs to buy, from whom and where;
- Location of current and potential supply sources;
- Who the suppliers are?
- Understanding the market dynamics affecting the related supply chain.

The Sourcing phase has more potential savings than the Procurement phase. The Total Cost of Ownership (TCO) is the most common KPI to address Sourcing. However a new indicator is achieving more relevance: Total Value Management (Lamoreaux, et al. 2008).

According to Lamoreaux, et al. (2008) Total Value Management (TVM) is an extension of the TCO and beyond the price and the logistics cost takes also in consideration the value of the products/services bought to the specific Strategic Supply Chain objectives.

E-Sourcing and E-Procurement

In a survey conducted by Aberdeen (2006) it is mentioned that the E-Sourcing / E-Procurement revolution began in the mid- to late-90's and accelerated through the early years of the new millennium. So with the Internet boom many firms shifted from paper based transactions to on-line based transactions. Aberdeen (2002) defined E-Sourcing as the use of Web-based applications, decision support tools, and associated services to streamline and enhance Strategic Sourcing processes and knowledge management.

E-Procurement is concerned with the operational aspects of the purchasing: requisition order, authorization of the requisition order, place the requisition order, receipting and invoice reconciliation. E-Sourcing and E-Procurement are not the same, so they will deliver different kinds of value to the firm. According to Giga Research (2004) there is an eight-step cycle firms must follow to achieve optimal results from online buying initiatives, see Figure 1.

We resume the differences between E-Sourcing and E-Procurement below:

- **E- Sourcing:** Strategic Phase focused in the Cost of Goods Savings;
- **E-Procurement:** Transactional/Operational Phase focuses in Process efficiency savings.

After a clear distinction between E-Sourcing and E-Procurement it is important to understand the reasons why firms started to adopt E-Sourcing solutions. According to Aberdeen (2007), the main pressures that lead to the adoption of E-Sourcing solutions are:

- Streamline the sourcing process (68%);
- Reduce supply costs (45%);
- Increase of spend under management (30%);
- Improve visibility into sourcing initiatives (28%);
- Improve supplier management and collaboration (27%);
- Centralize processes (27%).

The needs for E-Sourcing are related with pressure of the competitors, customers pressures to

Figure 1. E-Sourcing and E-Procurement different steps deliver different kinds of value- Adapted from Giga Research (2004)

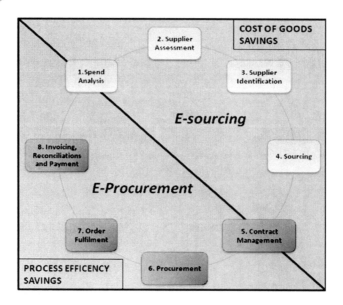

reduce prices and the need to give more visibility to the sourcing process. Firms are pressured and many of them face a global competition. Firms need to be more efficient in their purchasing processes, in order to maintain their competiveness.

E-Sourcing offers benefits in a wide range of areas, however two factors stand up:

- **High Material Costs:** if a firm has 1 million Euros of expenses in material cost per year without an E-Sourcing tool, with an E-Sourcing tool it would save an average of 143.000 Euros per year!
- **Sourcing Administration Cost:** if a firm has 1 million Euros of expenses in material supply without an E-Sourcing tool, with an E-Sourcing tool it would save more than 600.000 Euros per year!

Strategic Sourcing

Inadequate sourcing competencies are costing mid-size firms in the U.S. more than $134 billion in missed supply savings opportunities annually (Aberdeen, 2005). Such huge amount in missed saving opportunities annually is not negligible. In many mid-size companies this miss of savings represents the difference between success and bankruptcy. Strategic Sourcing is considered the best approach to address this problem. But what is Strategic Sourcing?

Strategic Sourcing to Lamoreaux, et al. (2008) is mainly a source of value. It is concerned with finding the right price, not the lowest price. Sometimes value is gained by selecting a lower cost provider, and sometimes value is gained by selecting a higher cost provider with greater quality, reliability or status.

Aberdeen (2005) identified four major problems to middle-size companies that interfere with Strategic Sourcing practices:

- Lack of formal sourcing procedures;
- Lack of sourcing and commodity skills;

- Insufficient system infra-structures;
- Problems for not having a powerful negotiation position with the suppliers.

The first three problems are reachable and the best in class firms need to create formal procedures to cut expenses. They need to adopt specialized brokers that know from /what to buy/ from whom to buy/ when to buy and invest on minimal information structure that helps the firms collaborators to execute more efficiently their purchasing processes.

The Strategic Sourcing KPIs that best-in-class purchasing business units must have, according to Aberdeen (2005) are: Year-over-Year Cost Reduction, Cost of Goods sold, Purchase Price Variant, Percent of Spend Strategically Sourced and Total Spend as a percent of Revenue.

What did E-Sourcing Change and How to Implement an E-Sourcing Tool

The main sub-Processes at the Sourcing and E-Sourcing are the same: Create RFX, Approve RFX, Select Suppliers, Send RFX to the Market, Source and Analysis, Contract Management. But in E-Sourcing these sub-processes are executed much more efficiently.

These advantages are bottom line in the Aberdeen (2005) report: an E-Sourcing tool allows reducing sourcing administration cost in 60% and Cut sourcing cycles in half. The implementation of new software is always a delicate process with entrance barriers and key factors of success. People usually have some resistance to change so the requirements need to comply with people's expectations. Rocha, et al. (2008) defined four guidelines to an effective implementation of an E-Sourcing tool (mainly focused on ESEPs):

- **Strategy:** Definition of the goals and the direction to achieve those same goals;
- **Processes:** Improving the processes that

will produce better tangible results;

- **People:** Managing the old issue "Resistant to change by the end users";
- **Technology:** Access to Internet. Performance and Security of the E-Sourcing tool.

Core Building Blocks of an ESEP

Before presenting the core blocks of an ESEP it is important to give an overview through the online process of purchasing (E-Sourcing and E-Procurement).

Returning to Figure 1, there are 8 steps to fulfill the online purchasing process: Spend analysis, Supplier performance assessment, Supplier identification, Sourcing, Contract management, Procurement, Order fulfillment and Invoicing, payment and reconciliation, where:

1. **Spend analysis:** Allows answering the question "Who buys what, from whom?" (www.emporion.com). The Spend Analysis mechanism works through Data Mining algorithms and allows the improvement of many aspects: Better understanding of spend patterns, identification of key suppliers, spend visibility until the points of order, accurate categorization and which outcomes are important savings for the firms;

2. **Supplier assessment:** The performance of the suppliers is evaluated at this step;

3. **Supplier identification:** At this step the best suppliers to respond to a given e-RFXs or bid are identified;

4. **Sourcing:** This step includes development of RFXs, bid and negotiation processes;

5. **Contract management:** Once a supplier (or suppliers) is chosen, the contract that documents terms and conditions of the sourcing agreement must be generated, reviewed, accepted and maintained in a repository where those terms are accessible in the E-Procurement system;

6. **Procurement:** Step where operational activities are executed. Examples: the approval process for the requisition, the submission of the order to the supplier and the response from the supplier;

7. **Order fulfillment:** This step is the follow up of the purchased goods, knowing if they were received as expected so that the payment is due;

8. **Invoicing, payment and reconciliation:** The billing and invoices process are followed up at this phase. Lamoreaux et al. (2008) believes that on average up to 70% of identified savings from E-Sourcing enabled awards are never realized because the associated supply chain activities are not successfully tracked and performance is not carefully monitored.

According to Aberdeen (2002) the following components are the core building blocks of an effective E-Sourcing platform: Negotiation; Collaboration; Project Management; Knowledge Management; Document Management; and Analytics.

Aggregating the 8 steps of the online purchasing process and the core building blocks of an ESEP it is possible to build the diagram in Figure 2.

Regardless of the core blocks already mentioned to integrate a new E-Sourcing software tool it is very expensive to build all the core blocks. So it is normal that some features of the tool are not implemented.

Therefore we separate two different kinds of core blocks of the ESEP:

- **Critical path content:** Negotiation, Collaboration (Requirements specification and collaboration with the supplier is a requisite), Document Management (The attachment of documents is necessary). These are absolutely necessary processes to the performance of the ESEP;
- **Value Add Services content:** Project Management, Knowledge Management

Figure 2. *Online Purchasing Process and Core building blocks of an ESEP*

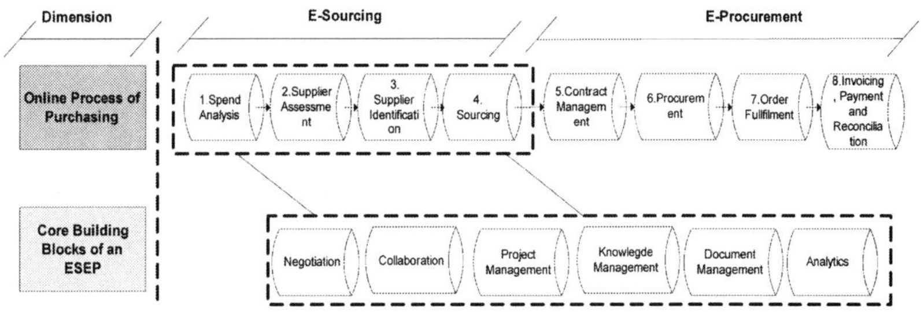

and Spend Analysis. They are very important but an ESEP can perform without them.

For example, the developments required for a start-up software provider that wants to deliver a product focused at the sourcing step must allow the E-RFX and Award sub-process. These two sub-processes can be defined as the critical path of the sourcing step.

Thinking in the Value Chain terms critical pass features are support activities and value add services are primary activities. In fact critical path content is critical to a successful operation but tens to be not strategic, while Value Added Services is always strategic and anticipating trends.

Main Benefits at ESEP

ESEP solutions are transversal. However buyers and suppliers have different perspectives on benefits and, in order to take advantage of the e-purchasing tool we will analyze and explore these different perspectives.

We mentioned that, in EM systems, both buyers and suppliers take advantage of process improvement and new business generation, but only the buyers achieve cost reduction benefits.

Bellow we identify some concrete transversal benefits to the different purchasing order mechanisms, using Tascomi Services (2000-2004) approach: Printing cost per page; Postage cost per gram; Phone cost per minute; Faxing costs per

minute; Archived documents secure storage per box; Staff time; and Advertising space (linage) costs.

The Buyer Benefits

Each purchasing order mechanism (although related with the others) maximizes a certain type of benefit and has its own core application area. ESEP is the purchasing order mechanism closer to Strategic Sourcing (without the cost centric approach of the others purchase order mechanisms). Therefore their benefits are similar to the E-Sourcing benefits already described. However ESEP buyer benefits depend of the core building blocks included in the software. Each block fulfils a certain type of benefit. ESEP systems that include all the core building blocks identified allow a broader approach to all the online purchasing process and maximize the Strategic Sourcing benefits.

The Supplier Benefits

On a general perspective supplier selling products in EMs achieve a more transparent purchasing process. They can increase their business opportunities, reduce customer acquisition costs and practice competitive pricing information. Naturally a fierce competition obliges suppliers to push their efficiency forward.

However, suppliers have different kinds of benefits regarding the purchase order mechanism of the EM. According to the Blodget, et al. (2000) there is space for a lot of supplier benefits.

E-Government

After the Internet boom E-Commerce started to have important developments and some pioneer countries began to reformulate their legislation regarding Public Tendering.

On March 2004 the European Union published two decisive directives 2004/18/CE and 2004/17/CE regarding the coordination of the contract award process in the EU. These directives obliged the EU members to adapt their Public Tendering Processes to an online process until 31/01/2006.

On December 2004 the Commission to the European Communities submitted an Electronic Public Tendering Action Plan to the European Parliament. The action plan was divided in three different branches:

- Several intermediate stages in order to help and support the EU Members to implement ESEP;
- Encourage each EU member to build its own Action Plan;
- Settle the 31st of January 2006 as the limit to the EU members to provide the new legislation.

Regarding implementation, each EU members had two main issues in hands in order to adopt the 2004/18/CE and 2004/17/CE directives:

- Choose and implement the model of electronically public tendering. According to the Science and Technology Minister (2001) there are three types of models: Public Model, Private Model and the Mix Model;
- Adapt the new legislation and the procedures defined in 2004/18/CE and 2004/17/CE directives.

The choice of the implementation model is highly related with the specificities of each country and at this moment (where electronic public tendering still is a recent issue) no conclusion can be made on which is the best model.

This aspect is highlighted by the different choices of models made by the EU members – some examples:France: Mix Model: www.marches-publics.gouv.fr; United Kingdom: Public Model www.ogcbuyingsolutions.gov.uk; Denmark: Mix Model: www.doip.dk; Portugal: Private Model: vortalGOV, Construlink www.compraspublicas. pt, Bizdirect- www.biz.gov.pt (in the Private Model management can be accomplished by more than one private firm).

Evolution

The e-purchasing solutions had their "boom" in 1999, 2000 and early 2001 when they had a 400% growth during these two and half years (Giga Research, 2004). However, the first e-purchasing solutions were focused at the E-Procurement step of the online purchasing process. According to Giga Research (2004), as companies learned that E-Procurement (cost centric approach) was the tail, and not the head of the business value, the vendor's revenues started declining until 2003. According to Forrester (2009) the vendors revenues recovered quite modestly during 2004 (9%) and 2005 (5%). From 2006 to 2009 (2008 and 2009 values are forecasts) the e-purchasing tools revenues grew approximately 20% each year. This was not obtained through a came back of the E-Procurement solutions (11% growth), but from the growth and appearance of other segments (Supplier performance management – 115%, Services Procurement – 35%, Supplier Network – 24%, Spend Analysis – 25%, between others) that allowed a broader and more valuable coverage of the e-purchasing process.

The Physical and the Virtual Value Chain on ESEPs

Porter (1985) proposed a value chain analysis based on five primary activities (Inbound Logistics, Operations, Outbound Logistics, Marketing/Sales and Services) and four main support activities (Procurement, Technology Development, Human Resource Management and Firm Infrastructure). We will refer this value chain as "Physical Value Chain" (PVC).

Sviokla et, al. (1995) created the concept of Virtual Value Chain (VVC) basing the value generation in information, and not in physical assets. According to Sviokla creating value through information is achieved in five steps: Gathering Information, Organizing Information, Selecting Information, Synthesizing Information and Distributing information.

The Internet allowed the creation of VVC where value is generated through information. But, what were the impacts of VVC in the PVC and what can we do to integrate both? Weiber, et, al. (1998) purposed a three level division we present

in Figure 3. In a first level VVC changed the way business is made in marketplaces. At a second level the VVC allows the creation of new markets (online auctions and EMs). Finally through the combination of VVC and PVC a Virtual-Actual Value Chain rises up where "marketspace" and marketplace are integrated.

After this quick overview, ESEP platforms aggregate the main operations of the VVC and in order to create value they must integrate the primary activities as well as assemble the practices of collaboration and aggregation of information. To illustrate the connections in ESEP platforms and VVC we analyze the main steps of an e-RFx in Figure 4 where several levels of value through information are segmented.

The e-RFx process is sustained in a B2B EM, a market where VVC applies and where all the players (buyers and sellers) are emulated. The visibility and availability of transactions allows more degrees of action and the exploitation of value. So, we can guarantee that ESEP aggregates value through specific features designed to explore the primary activities of the Virtual Value Chain.

Figure 3. Virtual Value Chain, Physical Value Chain and Virtual-Actual Value Chain- Adapted from Weiber, et, al. (1998)

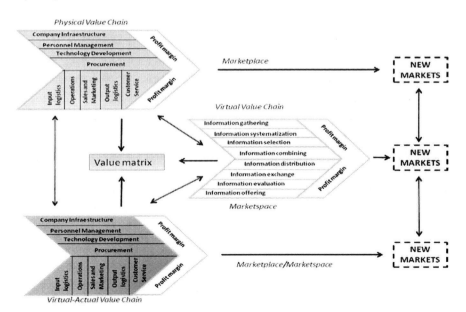

Figure 4. Standard E-RFx process at an ESEP and VVC information flow

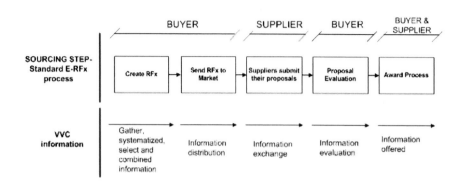

RESEARCH METHODOLOGY

Research Approach

The research approach was carried out using qualitative and quantitative research methods. We used both methods in order to take advantages of their complementary. We used a Case Study strategy which has an important quantitative research component – data from a survey conducted by Vortal on November/December 2008. We used only one case because we think that in this situation it would provide a better reasoning. As Robert Yin once said "The single case showed how investigations of such topics could be done, thus stimulating much further research and eventually the development of policy actions" (Yin,1984, pp 43). Others say the analysis of the near-histories and hypothetical histories often introduce fewer biases than those of real histories (March et al., 1999).

The Major Blocks of a Successful E-Purchasing Tool

We concluded that the successful e-purchasing tool should have to cover the 8 steps of the online purchasing process (Spend Analysis, Supplier Assessment, Supplier Identification, Sourcing, Contract Management, Procurement, Order Fulfillment and Invoicing, Reconciliation/Payment). But will the successful e-purchasing tool

be circumscribed to these 8 steps? We think not. Lamoreaux, et al. (2008) argues that E-Sourcing delivers significant savings by streamlining the bid process for either long term conditions or spot buy opportunities of indirect/direct material and/or services. We absolutely agree. Although the Reverse Auction mechanism has a very cost centric approach it is important to the e-purchasing tool to have a Reverse Auction module that allows the buyers to achieve significant savings when buying undifferentiated products/services. So far the e-purchasing referential tool covers the 8 steps of the e-purchasing process and has a Reverse Auction module. Would it be interesting to cover more parts? We think yes.

Analyzing the Criteria for Sourcing Solution Selection, we observe that 55% of the responses assume integration to back office and ERP systems as critical criteria for selecting an ESEP. We understand and agree with the result registered in this survey. We think it is essential for the e-purchasing tool to be connected to other systems of the firm (ERP or not). So, so far the successful e-purchasing tool covers the 8 steps of the e-purchasing process, has a Reverse Auction module and has integration services with the main ERP firms. Would it be interesting to cover more parts? Again we think yes. Raisch, W. (2001) argues that EMs will evolve from simple matchmaking services focused on transactions to E-Commerce. The next phase of evolution will be centered on providing value-added services that support the transaction. This will span the transformation of the EMs from a central matchmaker into a value-added service provider. Value Added Services (inside the transactions) allow many times a better performance of the transaction both for buyers and suppliers, and increases their competiveness. We believe this is in fact and a future trend.

The proposed baseline suite is now completed and is constituted by:

- Integration with ERP;
- E-purchasing 8 steps process;
- Reverse Auctions block;
- Value Added Services to the buyer related with the main transactions;
- Value Added Services to the supplier related with the main transactions;
- Value Added Services outside the main transactions.

Case Selection

Our Case Study is based on a Vortal survey on EMs, with more emphasis to the ECONSTROI platform. In this Case Study the results of the Vortal survey "Buyers feedback to the ECON-STROI platform" were interpreted. The goal of this survey was to understand and formalize in a structured way the buyer's opinion about ECONSTROI current blocks/features and also to understand future needs expected by the buyers. Even not completely aligned this Case Study is suitable to our research because it is in line with our initial questions:

- **An ESEP "inside-out" perspective** that allows understanding in an empirical approach several aspects of the e-B2B leader service provider in Portugal;
- **The buyers survey allows an important sample** on the end-users feedback relative the blocks/features and general performance of the ECONSTROI platform.

Data Collection

The data collection of this research comes from the Vortal survey to ECONSTROI buyers between November and December 2008. The goal of the Vortal survey was to understand the opinion of the users and to identify future needs of the ECONSTROI users.

The Vortal survey to ECONSTROI buyers had the following characteristics:

- 50 buyers firms that use ECONSTROI for more than a year;
- 198 end users were selected (the end users were randomly selected, independently of their role in the Buyer firms);
- From the 198 end users selected, 36 didn't answer to the survey. Survey response percentage above 80%;
- The answers scale of the survey was between 1 and 5. Where 1: Very Unsatisfied, 2: Unsatisfied, 3: Satisfied 4: Good Satisfaction and 5: Totally Satisfied.

The data collected from the survey allowed us to reflect on:

- Satisfaction and importance degree of 13 different functionalities offered by ECONSTROI;
- Satisfaction degree to the market value allowed by ECONSTROI;
- Understand if buyers are satisfied with ECONSTROI and would recommend it to other firms;
- End user suggestions to improve ECONSTROI.

Strengths and Weakness of this Research

The major strengths of this research methodology approach are:

- The use of qualitative and quantitative data allowing complementarities;
- The use of a wide number of different sources of information;
- The use of real data from a professional community in an "inside-out" perspective.

The main weaknesses of the research methodology are: The survey was directed to the buyers, not allowing conclusions on the suppliers side; The Vortal survey is a short sample (50 firms).

Vortal

Vortal was founded in December 2000 by a group of twenty four firms who composed the initial stakeholders. Vortal mission is to electronically integrate company and government processes, making transactions more secure, confidential, quick, easy and efficient through innovative ser-

vices. The Civil Construction Market was the first EM created by Vortal with the ECONSTROI B2B platform. After 2003 Vortal began its expansion, geographically and to different sectors.

In 2006 Vortal, decided to amplify the scope of their B2B markets launching three new B2B platforms directed to specific markets: Vortal INDUSTRY Vortal ENERGY&UTILITIES Vortal OFFICE&SUPPLIES. In 2008 Vortal created one more market: Vortal HEALTH, addressing the healthcare area.

Characteristics, Main Process and Major Functionalities of the Vortal EMs

Vortal has six different EMs that have approximately the same *modus operandi* in the online purchasing process, which major functionalities are presented in Table 1.

Table 1. Vortal buyer side major functionalities

Buyer side major functionalities			
Functionality	**Brief Description**	**Step of the e-purchasing process**	**Target market**
Request for Proposals	Buyer creates the requirements of the request and launches to the suppliers.	Sourcing	All six markets
Request for Information	Buyer creates a request for information in the platform.	Sourcing	ECONSTROI
Vortal Orders	Allows the buyers to publish their orders online.	Order Fulfillment and Contract Management	ECONSTROI
Reverse Auctions	Buyers can make perform several types of auctions.	Value Added Service	All six markets
ECONSTROI-connect	Target to clients with specific needs of integration with other systems.	Value Added Service	ECONSTROI
Directories of Firms	The Vortal "virtual community".	Supplier Identification, Supplier Assessment and Categorization	All six markets
Guaranting	An exclusive payment method for purchases negotiated on ECONSTROI.	Value Added Service	ECONSTROI
Electronic Invoice	Send electronically invoice to the suppliers awarded.	Invoice, Reconciliation and Payment	All six markets
Purchasing Monitor	Business intelligence in the purchasing of Vortal platforms.	Spend Analysis	All six markets
Security mechanisms	Encryption, Decryption, Digital Signature, Time-stamping and Electronic Receipt.	Not applied	Vortal GOV and Vortal HEALTH
Comparative map of proposals	Allow buyers to compare the suppliers proposals in the ESEP.	Sourcing	All six markets

ECONSTROI operates since 2001 and is the Vortal EM with a larger variety of functionalities. It is also possible to understand in Table 1 that the Vortal platforms cover seven of the eight steps of the referential purchasing online process. The E-Procurement step is not available (there isn`t a strong e-catalogues block).

From the supplier side Vortal has the major functionalities described in Table 2. The "submit proposals" functionality allows completing the E-rfx process (together with the "Request for Proposal"). The other functionalities represent value added services.

ECONSTROI CASE STUDY

We begin by interpreting the value of service allowed by 13 different functionalities of ECON-STROI. ECONSTROI has many more function-alities, but the survey was centered on the items in Table 3.

Analyzing Table 3 it is possible to make the following conclusions:

- The "Call Center" and the "Consultant Presence" are the services to which clients attribute more importance. Probably this is connected with the end user information

technology (IT) knowledge and literacy. People between 20-40 years old usually have a higher IT know-how than the others situated in the range of the 40-60 years old;

- The importance of the service accomplished by "Suppliers" had a significant grade of 4, 17, together with a not quite satisfactory grade of 2, 7. This service item shows the importance buyers give to have competitive suppliers;

"Budgets and *Rides"* (4, 15) and *"Guaranting"* (3, 98) functionalities were given significant importance by the buyers. These functionalities are Value Added Services outside the main transaction. This aspect gives strengths that a successful e-purchasing suite must have a block with value added services outside the main transactions

Market Value

Another important aspect of the survey is the market value given from using ECONSTROI platform, resumed in Table 4.

Analyzing Table 4 it is possible to make the following analysis:

- "Process simplification and higher control of the purchasing process" is the aspect

Table 2. Vortal supplier side major functionalities

Supplier side major functionalities		
Functionality	**Brief Description**	**Target market**
Submit Proposals	Allows the suppliers to submit their proposals to a certain Request for Proposal.	All six markets
iobra	It is a powerful tool to discover the civil construction ongoing works in Portugal and Spain.	ECONSTROI
Offers and Promotions	Allows the supplier to endorse offers and promotions to their potential buyers. If the buyer is interested he can create automatically an electronic order to a specific offer/promotion.	ECONSTROI
Directories of Firms	The Vortal "virtual community". Important repository of information of the sector and with detailed information on each company.	All six markets
Business Cockpit	Performs some business intelligence. Examples: supplier market share at a certain segment, number of awards won, competitive ranking and buyers feedback.	All six markets
"Boleias"-rides	Allows a supplier to invite other suppliers to a certain request.	ECONSTROI
Forward Auctions	Allows sellers to perform seller driven auctions.	All six markets

Table 3. Service value of ECONSTROI

VALUE OFSERVICE	Importance of the Service (1 to 5)	Degree of satisfaction with the service (1 to 5)
Usability of ECONSTROI platform	3.72	3.45
Spend Cost Centres process	3.48	3.2
Creation of Request for Proposals process	4.08	3.32
Selecting /adding suppliers process	4.18	3.21
Online follow up of the Request for Proposals and communications sent to the suppliers.	4.02	3.17
Suppliers	4.17	2.7
Comparative map of proposals	3.96	3.11
Approbation workflow and award process	3.85	3.11
Go live process after the Request for proposal is awarded	3.79	3.08
Budgets and Rides service,	4.15	3.27
Guaranting	3.98	3.13
Call Center	4.27	3.63
Consultant Presence	4.27	3.84

Table 4. Market value of using ECONSTROI platform

MARKET VALUE	Degree of satisfaction (1 to 5)
Process – Simplified Process and higher control of the Purchasing process.	3,42
Suppliers – Identification of better suppliers.	3,16
Proposals – Quality of received proposals.	2,97
Costs – Cost Reduction	3,28
Change – Better Management of the change.	3,34
Relationship – Better relationship with the suppliers.	3,18

with best grade (3, 42). This corroborates that the purchasing process though an EM is much simpler and allows a better control of the items purchased;

- The "Quality of received proposals" (2, 97) and the "Suppliers" (3, 16) are the aspects with which the buyers are not so highly satisfied;
- Buyers are quite satisfied with the cost reduction allowed by ECONSTROI (3, 28).

To complement the market value given by the buyers to ECONSTROI we analyze the answers of the buyers to the questions below and display the results in Figure 5.

- Are you satisfied with ECONSTROI?
- Would you recommend the use of ECONSTROI to other firms?

These are very significant values that justify the 800% growth of ECONSTROI between 2002 and 2007.

Figure 5. User satisfaction opinions

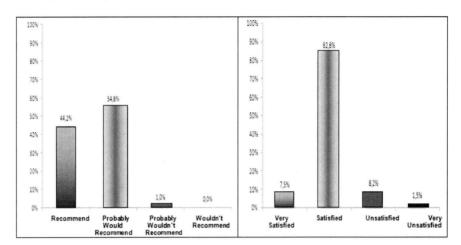

SWOT Analysis

Once again, buyers give a very important value to access a broader number of suppliers. Buyers also highlighted that the purchasing process in the EM is much simpler than at a physical market. Buyers give an important market value to ECONSTROI (all answers above 2,9) and the capability of the EM to allow different source of benefits.

Finally some of the end user improvement suggestions are aligned with what we stated an e-purchasing tool should really have, namely addressing:

- **Value Added Services at the main transactions:** Performing other types of actions at the award phase;
- **Connecting of e-purchasing suites with ERP:** ECONSTROI already has a connecting system with any type of ERPs, but many buyers firms have the ECONSTROI-connect functionality, although they need it;
- **Value Added Services outside at the main transactions:** Access to a larger number of technical contents and chat communication systems.

According to what was perceived from the survey we display in Table 5 our SWOT analysis.

ECONSTROI vs. Referential Suite

It is important to compare the blocks covered by ECONSTROI with the proposed baseline suite. There are relevant similarities between ECONSTROI and the e-purchasing tool (wide coverage of the e-purchasing process, value added services related with the transactions and outside the main transactions), Reverse auctions block and Integration ERP.

However there are two main differences between ECONSTROI and the previously purposed baseline suite e In fact ECONSTROI: Only covers seven of the eight steps of the e-purchasing process; Vortal has a Forward Auction block.

We realize the covering of the e-purchasing step isn't critical. The e-procurement step doesn't return a relevant value to the buyers and probably is a strategically option by Vortal.

The Forward Auction will be added to the successful (baseline) e-purchasing tool. A forward auction block may stimulate the supplier's participation and improve their performance.

The final version of the successful e-purchasing suite is displayed in Figure 6.

Table 5. ECONSTROI SWOT analysis

STRENGTHS	OPPORTUNITIES
- Very good market image: 90,3% of the firms interviewed are very satisfied or satisfied with ECONSTROI; - 99% of the firms would recommend ECONSTROI; - Several Added Value Services available (Budgets and *Rides, Guaranting*, among others); - ECONSTROI is available in 3 languages (Portuguese, Spanish and English); - Relevant external certifications: Certified by the ISO 27001 and Microsoft Gold Partner; - Vortal was the 2007 winner of the Innovation Prize for SME`s awarded by COTEC.	- Presence outside Portugal, first steps were already taken in Spain; - The E-Procurement block; - Platform availability in more languages; - Growing pattern of electronic public tendering.
WEAKNESSES	THREATS
- Buyers expect an increased in the number of proposal by e-Rfx; - Doesn`t cover all the blocks of the procurement step of the e-purchasing referential process;	- New competitors are certainly around the corner; - Technologies change. ECONSTROI needs to be alert to new techniques, software, and technologies.

Independently of these differences it is possible to argue that ECONSTROI is generally aligned with the proposed e-purchasing suite in Figure 6.

CONCLUSION

We conclude that the successful e-purchasing tool must have the positioning of a combined suite, because these mechanisms will have sustainable demand in the near future, are simpler to manage, cover all the e-purchasing process, allow data model benefits and allow for price competitive advantages comparing to the buying of several standalone mechanism.

Regarding the business dimensions of the successful e-purchasing tool we believe it should be neutrally managed (attracting both buyers and suppliers), and adopt the structure of an ESEP

Figure 6. Main blocks of the successful e-purchasing tool, upon case study reflexion

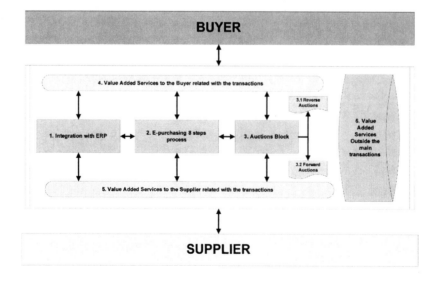

(only purchasing order mechanism that engages with Strategic Sourcing goals).

We conclude that the successful e-purchasing tool should have a wide spectrum, although the high investment required (gradual investment is suggested). The combined suite would be divided in six main blocks: Integration with ERP, cover of the E-purchasing 8 steps process, Auctions Block (Reverse and Forward), Value Added Services to the buyer /supplier connected with the transactions and Value Added Services outside the main transactions.

We believe that the combined suite must have an important concern with value added services because clients tend to valorize these differentiations. We also conclude that the e-purchasing suite should have a forward auction block because suppliers (and their proposals) are a key element to the EM.

We believe the combined suite is an important mechanism to the managers of the PDBU (as to the entire firm) to perform best in class Strategic Sourcing practices because:

- Allows the managers of the buyers firms to have a clear view of all the steps of the e-purchasing process;
- Enable mechanism oriented to maximize the Strategic Sourcing KPI.

Regarding Vortal, we conclude that ECONSTROI structure is generally aligned with the proposed e-purchasing suite .The improvements suggested by users elucidated the value they give to Value Added Services at the main transactions, connecting of e-purchasing suites with ERP, and Value Added Services outside at the main transactions.

ECONSTROI buyers are quite satisfied and give an important value to the operations allowed in ECONSTROI. One of the key factors of success of this EM was the ability to build an important "Virtual Community". A very significant number of buyers and suppliers make transactions in

ECONSTROI and both are able to retrieve value from the EM (WIN-WIN). Buyers achieve better business, important savings (administrative, processes and in the cost of the materials) and discover new suppliers, while suppliers achieve new business opportunities.

Finally, we recommend a more profound Study over the entrance barriers; initial investments required and return of investment that e-purchasing tools face (both standalone as combined suite mechanisms).

REFERENCES

Aberdeen (2002). Making E-Sourcing Strategic -From tactical Technology to core business strategy.

Aberdeen (2005). Strategic Sourcing in the Mid-Market Benchmark-The Echo Boom in Supply Management.

Aberdeen (2006). *E-Sourcing: The Art & Science of the Deal*.

Aberdeen (2007). The Advanced Sourcing & Negotiation Benchmark Report –"The Art and Science of the Deal.

Baker, H. (2000). *E-Sourcing 21st Century Purchasing*. New York: Scheer.

Bakos, Y. (1998).The emerging role of electronic markets on the Internet. Communications of the ACM.

Bichler, M. (2001). *The Future of E-Markets, Multidimensional Market Mechanisms*. University Press. doi:10.1017/CBO9780511492532

Blodget, H., & McCabe, F. (2000). *The B2B Market Maker Book*. New York: Merrill Lynch.

Elofson, G., & Robinson, W. (1998). Creating a Custom Mass-Production Channel on the Internet. *Communications of the ACM*, 41.

Feldman, S. (2000). Electronic Marketplaces IEEE Internet Computing.

Forrester (2009). *The Forrester Wave: E-Sourcing – Q1 2009.*

Giga Research(2004). Market Overview 2004: E-Procurement and E-Sourcing – What will take to break the Glass Floor in Demand?.

Gottschalk, P. (2006). *E-business strategy – Sourcing and Governance Electronic Commerce.* Hershey, PA: Idea Group Publishing.

Hartman, E., Gemuenden, H., & Ritter, T. (2001) Determining the Purchase Situation: Conerstone of Supplier Relationship Management. 17th IMP Conference, Oslo, Norway.

Kafka, S. (2000).e-Marketplaces Boost B2B Trade, Forrester Report.

Kaplan, S, Sawhney, M. (1999). *The Emerging Landscape of Business to Business E-Commerce.* Business 2.0 Magazine.

Kelly, K. (1998). *The new rules of the New Economy.* New York: Penguin Books Ltd.

Kowalkiewicz, M. (2004). *From traditional markets to electronic markets for learning – opportunities an threats.* Poznan University of Economics.

Lamoreaux, M., Bush, D., Strovink, E., Beuc, M., Degasperi, A. (2008), *The E-Sourcing Handbook – A Modern Guide to Supply and Spend Management Success.* Carmel, IN: Iasta Publishing.

Lee, E., White, M., & Austrian, B. (2000). *B2B e-Markets & Trading Hub Primer.* San Francisco: Bank of America Securities.

Lief, V. (1999). *Net Marketplaces Grow Up.* Cambridge, UK: Forrester Research.

Mahadevan, B. (2000). Business Models for Internet based E-Commerce: An Anatomy. *California Management Review,* 42.

March, J.G., Sproull, L.S. e Tamuz, Michal, (1999), Learning from samples of one or fewer, The Pursuit of Organizational Intelligence. Thousand Oaks, CA: Sage Publications.

Negroponte, N. (1995). *Being Digital.* New York: Knopf Doubleday Publishing G.

Porter, M. (1985). *Competitive advantage, creating and sustaining superior performance.* Washington, DC: First Free Press Edition.

Raisch, W. (2001). *The E-Marketplace- Strategies for Success in B2B Ecommerce.* New York: McGraw Hill.

Reilly, G. (2000). *E-Commerce Revenue Models: Don`t be Just One Horse.* Gartner Group Strategic Analysis Report.

Rocha, M. P., Macara, J. C., & Sousa, F. V. (2008). *A Contratação Pública Electrónica e o Guia dos Contractos Públicos. Edition.* Semanário Económico, Diário Económico & Academia Vortal.

Rosson, P. (2000). Electronic Trading Hubs: Review and Research Questions. 16[th,] Schmid, B. (1993). *Electronic Markets. Electronic Markets,* 3.

Science and Technology Minister (2001). *Electronic Acquisition of things, materials and services by the Public administration.*

Sculley, A. (1999). *B2B Exchanges. The Killer Applications in the Business-to-Business Internet Revolution. New York: ISI Publications.* W.: Woods.

Siegelmann, H., Avital, O, (1996).Electronic Commerce.

Simchi-Levi, D., Kaminsky, P., & Simchi-Levi, E. (2003). *Designing & Managing the Supply Chain* (2nd ed.). New York: McGraw Hill.

Sviokla, J., & Rayport, J. (1995). *Exploiting the Virtual Value Chain.* Boston: Harvard Business School Review, Nov-Dec.

Tascomi Services (2000-2004). *E-Sourcing cost benefits factors –Issues and Opportunities within local government.*

Thorelli, H. (1986). Networks: Between Markets and Hierarchies. *Strategic Management Journal,* 7.

Timmers, P. (1999). *Electronic Commerce, Strategies and Models for Business-to-Business Trading.* London: John Wiley & Sons, Ltd.

Trepp, L. (2000). *Valuing the new industrial model: B2B Internet Exchanges.* Electronic Market Center, Inc, Philadelphia; Turban, E., King, D., Lee, J., Warkentin, M. & Chung, H. (2002). *Electronic Commerce 2002 – A Managerial Perspective.* International Edition; Weiber, R., Kollmann, T., (1998). *Competitive advantages in virtual markets - perspectives of "information-based marketing" in cyberspace.* Germany: University of Trier.

Yin, R. (1984). *Case study research: Design and methods.* Thousand Oaks, CA: Sage Publications.

Chapter 12
Search Engine Marketing in Small and Medium Companies:
Status Quo and Perspectives

Tom Alby
uniquedigital GmbH, Germany

Burkhardt Funk
Leuphana University Lüneburg, Germany

ABSTRACT

Search Engine Marketing (SEM) is one of the most effective online advertising channels which let companies efficiently acquire new and reactivate existing customers at low acquisition costs. In this chapter the authors briefly review the scientific literature on SEM with respect to managerial decision problems along the levers of SEM, mainly bid optimization, keyword selection, and adCopy creation. Based on a case study they discuss challenges of SEM campaigns operated by small and medium enterprises (SME). After briefly describing the technical requirements for effectively controlling SEM campaigns the authors focus on keyword selection and how to address the long tail issue in SEM. A/B-Tests are shown to be an appropriate measure for optimizing the combination of ad copies and landing pages. Finally they discuss bid optimization at a keyword level taking into account spill-over effects between keywords.

INTRODUCTION

It has always been a huge challenge for companies of all sizes to optimize the allocation of their marketing spendings. As search engine marketing is becoming an important part in the media mix of SMEs they face some serious questions: Does it make sense for SMEs to use sophisticated SEM tools or to engage a dedicated agency? Is there an efficiency gap in which human campaign management and optimization is too time consuming and automated software tools do not work due to a lack of data? How can firms handle this lack of

DOI: 10.4018/978-1-60960-463-9.ch012

analyzable data that comes with restricted budgets? In this paper we will discuss these questions.

The Pay per Click (PPC) model has been very attractive for advertisers since its invention for a variety of reasons. The first reason is search itself: Like all search engines, Google does not disclose the details of its organic search ranking algorithms, the part of search that cannot be paid for. As a result, advertisers can never be sure that their site will be listed on a specific position, even if their offer is the most relevant. Moreover, there is a time lag between creating a page with a product offer and its inclusion in a search engine's index, let alone until a page ranks at the desired position, and this time lag can be between a few hours and months. Removing a result can be equally difficult, letting most marketers not feel comfortable with the technical complexity of optimizing a site for ranking in organic search results. This approach is called search engine optimization or SEO.

In contrast to this, the PPC model has been attracting marketers since the system is much more transparent, even although more sophisticated technical factors have been introduced. Nevertheless, basically, everyone can bid for a keyword, and ads will appear immediately on a position that the advertiser is more or less able to influence. Finally, marketers are enabled to determine the return on investment (ROI) for each campaign, given that effectiveness can be tracked precisely and instantly. This does not mean that search engine marketing is the only choice for marketers: Since organic results attract most of the clicks and these clicks are not charged, SEO still is of interest. However, search engine optimization is based on completely different approaches, and the ROI of SEO efforts can not be covered here.

More than ten years after its birth, the PPC industry is still growing. Although growth has slowed down, there are still new users coming online that search for products, enabling Google and other search engines to monetize the additional searches coming in. The number of advertisers per keyword determines how much Google will earn per click, given that each advertiser bids per each keyword separately, and each advertiser has to determine what bid is profitable; the more competition, the higher will be the bid to get a higher position on the SERP that usually translates to more traffic.

With ten or hundred thousands of keywords, optimization can be a full-time job for one or more employees, and even with tools, keyword and ad copy generation as well as analysis and reporting still require human work. While this is not rocket science, many companies decide not to build the necessary expertise internally, but outsource this part of their marketing to specialized agencies, or they use tools that allow them to optimize bidding more or less automatically.

The first crucial question for most SMEs is whether PPC advertising makes sense at all. In some niche markets, search volumes for relevant keywords are so low that setting up and managing a campaign may be more expensive than the expectable outcome. This can happen to SMEs as well as to the big brands. If the answer is "yes", though, the second question is how to determine whether an agency or the use of a commercial tool will provide a better ROI that would justify the expense. We review these challenges and give possible answers in this paper.

The answer to the first question depends on the goals of online marketing activities. For online shops, the cost per order will most probably be the most important key performance indicator (KPI): How much money has to be spent in order to generate a specific sale? This approach relies on a transaction base where customers are not very loyal and will most probably select a different shop the next time they search for a product the shop has to offer. In contrast to this, other online shops measure the customer lifetime value, since they expect a customer to return, and they are willing to pay more for a new customer ("cost per lead"). In other cases, especially when there is nothing to sell, users are expected to perform a specific action such as signing up for a newsletter ("cost per action"). The latter is of particular interest for advertisers that pursue a branding approach in their PPC auctions: As opposed to other forms of marketing where contact with a brand is difficult to assess, one of the advantages of the PPC model is the measurability of its effectiveness[1]; after a few days if not hours, advertisers are able to differentiate between keywords that result in the desired action and those that do not.

Unfortunately, the existence of data alone does not necessarily mean that conclusions can be drawn out of it, and this is one of the biggest challenges that PPC campaigns for SMEs face: If a keyword results in a sale, does this automatically mean that this keyword is a good keyword? If a keyword led to 10 sales in 1.000 searches, some significance is assumed, but how about 1 sale per 1.000 searches? What about hundreds or thousands of keywords that only lead to a sale once in a while with no pattern becoming obvious? What is the (automated) optimization strategy if data does not give any hint into which direction to go? We could describe this as the SME's dilemma: They are usually too big to neglect this form of online marketing or to bid only on a few keywords but, at the same time, they are too small to have enough data for automated bidding. In this case, SMEs are in the most expensive area of PPC: Manual optimization of a large number of keywords without a tool-driven support. In a similar fashion, these companies are by far not the most attractive clients for agencies since they require much more manual work due to the lack of data; at the same time, these clients will have a closer eye on what the agency costs with respect to the benefits. However, this problem does not affect SMEs only as mentioned before. The more a business operates in a niche, the less likely people will search for products in that niche, and the less likely an algorithmic approach is possible. At the same time, even if SMEs operate in a non-niche market, the cost of bidding tools may make them unattractive.

SCIENTIFIC BACKGROUND

While finding optimal algorithms for retrieving relevant search results has a long standing tradition in computer science (information retrieval), SEM has been established as an active field of research only recently, probably due to the fact that information retrieval has been a popular field already long before the web and search engines for them had been introduced. Research in the field of search has focused on 3 areas:

- User search behavior
- Advertiser strategies and benefits
- Search engine auction mechanisms and strategies

These categories have recently been used in a literature review (Yao & Mela, 2009) in order to dissect the needs and strategies of each party separately. However, it is debatable whether each party should be isolated for a detailed analysis since they all depend on each other, and a full understanding of the mechanisms of the search engine marketing systems can only be obtained by reviewing each perspective in the context of the other stakeholders. As an example, an advertiser's bidding strategy depends on the user's search behavior that, again, is influenced by the product that is offered. As Rutz & Bucklin have pointed out in their research about click histories and branding effects (2009), users may learn more about a subject after performing an initial search and will then rephrase their search in order to dig deeper into the topic. This mechanism must be understood by advertisers in order to make sure that users stay aware of a product offer during their exploration of a topic.

Furthermore, search engines have introduced features such as search suggestions that are displayed while the initial search is entered by the user. After this initial search, further suggestions are shown if the first result set is not satisfactory. Finally, users queries have been the subject of research in order to understand the intent of a query automatically (Jansen, Booth and Spink 2007) or at least categorize them (Nelson & Bayrak 2009). Understanding the intent of a query would not only allow search engines to improve the quality of the organic search results, but also to provide more relevant ads that, as a consequence, may attract more users to click on them and thus result in a higher revenue for the search engine.

Since most search engines do not disclose search logs, most research exploits the few nuggets that researchers could get hold of, in particular the 2006 America Online (AOL) data that resulted in serious privacy concerns (Strohmaier & Kröll 2009). A first analysis of the AOL data is presented by Pass, Chowdhury and Torgeson (2006), including search patterns over different time frames. In the absence of data of the most popular search engine, Google, such user search data must be interpreted carefully since the demographics of such search engines' users is not unlikely to be different from the average Google user. Moreover, user behavior changes over time since more and more users have become used to searching with a search engine. A snapshot from one search engine from one year and from another search engine from another year will skew the results; understanding user search behavior and its development requires a more solid data source. Together with Stanford researchers, Microsoft has developed a mechanism to disclose search logs and, at the same time, keep the privacy of the search users (Korolova, Kenthapadi, Mishra & Ntoulas 2009). However, apart from Microsoft, no other search engine has used this mechanism to the best of our knowledge.

Furthermore, since most keyword auctions take place on Google but researchers cannot review Google's query logs, some important pieces are missing. Using more advanced tracking systems, advertisers are able to track if a user clicks on an ad for a specific term and returns to the site with a different term so that spillover from one type of keyword to another is measurable (Rutz

& Bucklin 2008). However, advertisers cannot see what users have searched for if they have not clicked on their ads. On the contrary, Google cannot see what happens after the click, provided that Google's tracking product such as Google Analytics or Google conversion tracking are not deployed.

Whilst search engines do not disclose query logs, almost all offer keyword suggestions to advertisers; in addition, reports are offered for download so that broad keyword matches can be added to the keyword portfolio. Nevertheless, building and maintaining a keyword portfolio still is a laborious task so that some research has focused on how a keyword portfolio can be created algorithmically. The most simple approaches are based on keyword co-occurrence, more sophisticated approaches are based on concept hierarchies (Chen, Xue and Yu 2008) or semantic similarity (Abishek & Hosanagar 2007). Also, some research has gone into the more or less automated generation of ad copies or at least preparing the keywords for inclusion in ad copy (Bartz, Barr & Aijaz 2008).

Most work, though, has gone into the analysis of bidding behavior in keyword auctions resulting in simple heuristics but also advanced computational models. Kitts & Leblanc (2004) were the first to present a trading agent that offers an automated bidding approach. Many other have followed (Borgs et al., 2007; Cary et al., 2007; Hosanagar and Cherepanov, 2008).

Search engine marketing is only one part of the digital marketing portfolio, and advertisers that run SEM campaigns may also book display banner campaigns or engage in affiliate marketing campaigns. While users come to a search engine with an information need in mind, display advertising creates more interest for a product and, thus, implies more searches for a product. With isolated tracking for each channel, it is impossible to understand the interaction between the channels. As a consequence, sales that were made via search engine marketing but that were initiated by display advertising would be added to the search engine marketing although they would not have taken place without display advertising. Using a tracking for all channels, it is possible to trace the journey of a user and identify the impact of a specific channel. Unfortunately, not too much research has been done in this area, although the optimal allocation of budgets within the channels with respect to their interaction has great business potential. Some work has been done by Manchanda et al (2006), proving that display advertising has a positive impact on online shop sales. With more tracking features available, we expect more research in this area soon.

CASE STUDY

The case study demonstrates the complexity that companies face when employing SEM. Data on the campaign as well as individual keyword level are used to explain how SMEs can successfully exploit the market potentials in general and what decisions have to be made in detail.

The research site of the field study described in this chapter is a medium-size German retailer who operates physical outlets as well as an online shop (in the remainder of this chapter the retailer is referred to as "the company"). The company offers around 5,000 different products with prices between 1.00 EUR and 1,000.00 EUR. The product portfolio ranges from apparel to technical equipment.

The online advertising of the company encompasses paid search, search engine optimization (on- and offsite) and Affiliate Marketing. Only a small fraction of the budget has gone into online display advertising. The Online Marketing was started by the company 5 years ago and has been run by a large online marketing agency (in the remainder of the chapter it is referred to as "the agency") also based in Germany for the last 3 years. The online marketing campaign of the company is strictly performance oriented. So, the focus is put on generating sales and acquiring new

customers instead of enhancing brand awareness and recognition. Two key performance indicators (KPIs) are used to monitor success and to control spendings and budget allocation: cost per acquisition (CPA) and cost income ratio (CIR). Both KPIs are determined on the lowest level of granularity possible enabling decision making on keyword level[2].

Technical Setting and Data Structure

To be able to evaluate the Online Marketing performance it is necessary to track campaign costs as well as sales, revenues and the product mix sold. Beside Google Analytics there is a wide range of independent tracking solutions. They differ in price[3], functionality, and quality, e.g.:

- Reporting facilities (user frontend, different reporting formats, reporting scheduling, APIs)
- Data collection and aggregation (how much data is collected? On what level is the data aggregated and archived?)
- Technical tracking approach (e.g. log file analysis, invisible pixel)
- Extended functionality (e.g. bidding agent, display ad serving, cross-channel tracking)
- Non-functional requirements (e.g. usability, service levels, scalability)

For the company a scalable tracking solution, named etracker.com, is employed. Each click coming from the search engine is redirected through etracker using a URL which encodes keyword, match type, ad copy text, and landing page. Etracker checks whether the user is already known to the tracking system or otherwise sets a cookie containing a unique user-ID and saves the data under the user-ID. Before starting the campaign website goals (e.g. generating sales or leads) are defined and associated with specific web pages. On these web pages an image tag from etracker, invisible to the user, is included and signals the fact that a user reached a website goal to the tracking system. Now sales can be associated with the initial clicks from the search engine.

In Figure 1 a simplified data model of the company is shown. *Campaign* and *AdGroup* encompass all entities which have ever been active in the company's SEM campaign. The table *Keyword* aggregates daily data on keyword and match type level and yields information on clicks, impressions, average position, and costs (the data directly stems from the search engines). The list of individual *Sales* are associated with *Keywords* (if a *Sale* occurs, it is associated with the last *Keyword* search for before the *Sale*), *Baskets,* and *Users*. For those *Users* who have generated at least one *Sale* the *History* of clicks is available. This information gives insight into the ways users take from visitors to customers and helps to understand the contribution to the sales outcome of individual keywords.

Account Structure

Search engines enable advertisers to hierarchically structure SEM accounts. Google and Yahoo! offer three levels: (i) account, (ii) campaigns,

and (iii) ad groups. An SEM account (one per advertiser) encompasses several campaigns and each campaign again contains several ad groups. On the level of individual campaigns advertisers can choose language and geographical settings as well as daily budgets. In addition advertisers can roughly determine bidding behavior and ad scheduling. Last but not least advertisers using Google have to decide whether the ads should be served only on Google itself or also on search partners or in the so called content network. On ad group level a maximum cost per click and a landing page URL can be set, which serve as default values and can be overwritten on keyword level. Ad groups are also associated with one or more ad copies (see Figure 1 and section on ad copy) and contain the keywords.

The Google account of the company includes 14 campaigns and around 250 active ad groups. The 14 campaigns focus different aspects: 6 of them concentrate on generic product categories, another 5 on foreign brand terms, and 1 summarizes all keywords related the corporate brand. The last 2 campaigns were set up to separate ads which are shown in the content network (only a small fraction of the overall budget goes into ads

Figure 1. Simplified data model (only selected entity types and attributes are shown)

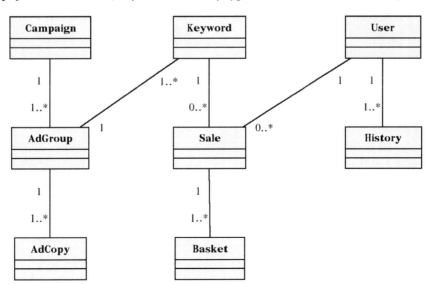

on the content network). Most ad groups (around 100) are centered on foreign brands.

Finding the right structure and granularity on the ad group level largely depends on the variety of products and services offered by the advertiser. Each product category should receive one ad group, since ad copies and keywords will be specific to the given product category. Sometimes it can be useful to add further ad groups for certain target groups (e.g. men's wear).

Keywording and Match Types

As discussed in section above the company has to choose a set of keywords from millions of possible keywords and keyword combinations. To determine a basic set of keywords when starting with SEM, there are two major criteria: first, relevance of a keyword to the intended website goal, e.g. lead generation, second, search volume (impressions) of the keyword per time interval. The attractiveness with respect to cost and market share is further determined by the competition for the keyword[4].

In addition search engines enable the advertisers to define so called stop words (or negative matches). Whenever such a stop word is part of the user query the ad is not displayed. E.g., an online bank might want to advertise for its premium checking account by bidding for the keyword "checking account" and avoiding the ad to be displayed when a user searches for "free checking account". The company has not only to decide on the set of keywords but also on the match type of each selected keyword. The matching option determines how closely related the user query should be to a keyword defined by the advertiser. Yahoo! and Google offer three different match types:

- **Exact:** the ad only appears when the user query is exactly the same as the keyword or keyword combination
- **Phrase:** the keyword or keyword combi-

nation has to be part of the user query or can be identical with the user query
- **Broad:** the ad is displayed when the user query contains similar keywords

To generate a set of keywords for the company's SEM campaign product names[5] (or types) and some typographical variations of it are used as a starting point. These keywords are combined with a range of generic expressions like "buy", "online", and "discount". In addition, generic product categories are a good source for additional keywords. For this purpose the agency uses a proprietary tool which has access to internal as well as external databases and services and applies standard linguistic methodology. To get a rough estimate on the potential number of clicks per keyword and time interval services provided by the search engines are used. Over the last three years about 18,500 keywords and keyword combinations (more than 75% are keyword combinations) were used. Some of them have been promoted temporarily (e.g. repeating seasonal offerings or short-term product specials). Others were tested for performance (see section on results) and were not able to meet the minimum requirements with respect to KPIs. In the last month (August 2009) around 12,500 keywords were used in the campaign (generating around 15 Mio. impressions). It was decided to concentrate on supposedly relevant keywords. This will become important when it comes to decision making and performance evaluation on the individual keyword level (see section on bid management).

As shown in Figure 2 around 80% of the impressions are generated by only 2.5% of all keywords. Studying clicks generated by individual keywords only slightly changes the outcome (80% come from 4.5% of the keywords). This situation is typical for SEM campaigns where only a small fraction of keywords generates the largest part of the traffic.

When it comes to successful keyword selection a major task is to cancel low performing keywords

Figure 2. Keywords are decreasingly sorted by the number of impressions as represented by the full line (whenever the ad from the company appears it is counted as an impression). The dashed line indicates the aggregated fraction of impressions up to a given keyword number.

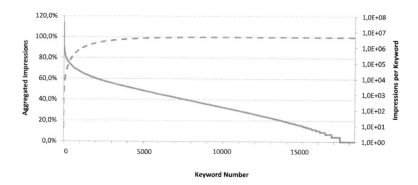

and to iteratively test new (and paused) keywords within budget constraints and KPI limits. Low performing keywords are obviously those that do not meet KPI targets (see section on Results). Depending on budget constraints low performing keywords can also be those that are not able to acquire enough impressions and clicks within a given time frame and that are thus not decidable with respect to performance. To give an example: the average keyword in the portfolio of the company shows a click through rate of 0.9% and a conversion rate (CVR) of about 1% (search engine marketing only). So, on average 10,000 search requests and about 100 clicks are required to generate one sale. Following simple Poisson statistics and assuming that no sale is observed for a keyword after a while the company needs to spend about 25,00 EUR to exclude the conversion rate to be higher than 1% at a confidence level 75%. This calculation uses the company's average cost per click of 0.15 EUR. So starting with a keyword portfolio of 100.000 keywords makes it necessary to spend about 2.5 Mio. EUR to select well performing keywords discard the rest. Due to this fact, limiting the long tail (Elberse, 2008) has after its initial advent (Anderson, 2004) been the preferred strategy in recent times when

generating the initial keyword portfolio. Thus it is important to at least have some strong hypotheses on what search terms user might look for when they intend to buy from the company. The initial keyword portfolio of the company encompassed all brand related terms, exact product names, and also those keywords that were known from the generic search to perform well. Currently, researchers work on estimating conversion rates of fresh keywords based on experiences with similar keywords (Rutz and Bucklin, 2009). This might in future help to have a more efficient keyword portfolio at the start-up of a SEM campaign.

Ad Copy and Landing Page

Since ad copies are gate keepers between search engines and the landing pages of the advertisers, they should on the one hand encourage users to click on it and on the other hand make sure that only users with a specific interest in the products and services of the advertiser click on the ad to avoid unnecessary costs. Following a recent study from Google (2008) the ad copy may also positively influence brand awareness from users who did not click on ads. Thus, ad copies play an important role in SEM. In case of Google, the ad copies consist of a 25-character title, 2 lines of text with 35characters each and the so called display URL which can be different from the underlying link which refers to the landing page. In the internet there are many blogs on how to write good ad copies. Some of them are straightforward and generic to all kinds of ad copies (e.g. tell customers your USP, be specific, include a call to action), others relate to the search channel (e.g. use keyword in title and display URL, care for proper formatting).

Search engines support A/B-tests of ad copies by splitting the search traffic for an ad group and directing it to different ad copies. Based on the resulting click through rates (CTR) the search engine can automatically decide on which ad copy to prefer in future ad delivery. For the company not only CTR data is used but the agency also takes into account differences in CPA data. Over a period of 3 years the company has tested more than 1,680 ad copies which at least differed in title, text, or display URL from each other. To reach statistically significant conclusions it is necessary to restrict the number of ad copies to be tested. During such an A/B-test typically 3 ad copies per ad group are running at the same time. To roughly estimate the test duration we employ the following formula (Funk, 2009):

$$T_{Test} \approx \frac{N_{copy} \left(\dfrac{CL}{e} \right)^2 CVR \left(1 - CVR \right)}{CTR * I}$$

where N_{copy} is the number of ad copies to be tested, e is the accepted error, CL is the confidence level, and $CTR*I$ is the number of clicks expected from the search engines per time unit. Requiring an error of 0.2% (corresponding to a 20% uncertainty on the conversion rate of 1%), a confidence level of 1σ, $CTR*I$ to be 500 clicks per day and assuming the numbers from above, it takes about 15 days to reach a conclusion. In smaller companies (and search engine accounts) this duration might even be longer. Thus, it is important to start a search account with a small set of ad groups and ad copies in order to enable early decision-making on poor performing elements. Figure 3 shows that it is not possible to infer the conversion rate from the click through rate, there is no positive

Figure 3. Click through (CTR) and conversion rates (CVR) of selected ad copies (the error bars of the conversion rate indicate the statistical 2σ error interval, the error of the CTR is too small to be shown)

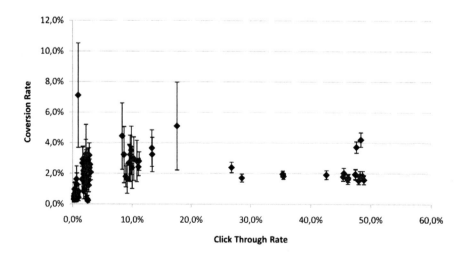

correlation ($R^2 < 0.1$). Instead, due to the fact that an over-selling ad copy will generate high CTRs while falling short in conversions, the opposite can be the case in practice.

The company uses around 17,500 different landing pages. This high number compared to the number of keywords in the account results from linking directly to individual product pages which are identical in structure but display different products. Performance testing of such a large number of landing pages cannot be done on individual level; instead the underlying template of the product pages can be varied and tested. Again, due to statistical limitations of small and medium search accounts, SMEs should refrain from trying to evaluate the overall conversion of ad copies and landing pages in combination but separately determining ad copy and landing page conversion. To do so the best performing ad copy is selected and different landing pages are tested against each other (and vice versa). Obviously, this procedure is not able to systematically analyze potential cross-dependencies between ad copies and landing pages but serves as a starting point for exploring most likely successful combinations.

Bid Optimization

The auction mechanisms in SEM have been described above. As a result of its application, setting maximum bids (b_{max}) for individual keywords and match types is an important and recurring task for the advertiser. Search engines offer the possibility to determine default values for b_{max} on ad group level. Whenever b_{max} is not defined on keyword level this default value is used. To understand how the bids can systematically be set we briefly look at the simplified cause-effect-chain on individual keyword level: the maximum bid placed on a given keyword (and to a certain extend other factors which Google summarizes under the so called quality factor) influences the position at which the ad is displayed on the SERP. The position itself governs the *CTR*. And finally, b_{max} but also the *CTR* determine the cost per click and thus the budget spend per time interval.

The functional dependency between budget per keyword (and day) and the number of clicks is shown in Figure 4a. Two aspects should be noted: first, the fitting functions are non-linear at higher daily budgets. That means, as we would expect, that the marginal CPCs increases with daily budget. Second, for different time intervals the steepness of the function (corresponding to the CPC) var-

Figure 4. In the left panel (a) the dependency between clicks per day and the daily budget spent on a given keyword is displayed for three non-overlapping time intervals. The right panel (b) shows the conversion rate as a function of position (2σ error intervals)

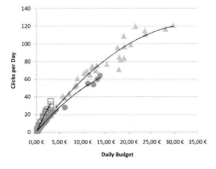
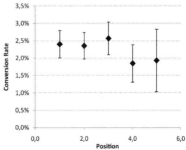

ies. That can be attributed either to changes in customer demand, the competition on the search engines, or changes in the relevant products. As a result the fitting functions have to be gauged using most recent data. For the company seasonal effects can be observed leading to differences in level and curvature of the function.

In the next step the conversion rate is needed to determine the number of sales as a function of budget. Even though for some heavy-traffic keywords one can observe a weak correlation between position and CVR, often the conversion rate can be assumed to be roughly independent of the position (Figure 4b). Since there are no other relevant dependencies of the *CVR*, this translates Figure 4a directly into the number of sales as a function of budget. Deriving this function yields the marginal CPA which can be compared with a maximum target value of the company, thus leading to the optimal daily budget for the keyword under consideration. For heavy-traffic keywords this method can easily be used. But for the great majority of keywords, first, it is necessary to aggregate them into groups and then apply the method to the group.

Very often, not the marginal maximum CPA is given, but advertisers want to spend a fixed budget on SEM or want to achieve an average overall CPA. From a computer science perspective the corresponding optimization problem[6] (e.g. on 12.500 keywords as in the case of the company) shows an exponential complexity. That means that in worst case the time needed to solve the problem increases exponentially. Theoretically correct, in practice this problem can be simplified using the method from above due to the fact that the cost and benefit of individual keywords are always much smaller than the total budget spent. Given that, a simple heuristic can be applied: Sort all keywords in decreasing order with respect to marginal CPAs and then determine what the best alternative will be to spend the next EUR (this procedure is often referred to as bang-per-buck); repeat this until the budget is spent or the overall average CPA is reached.

Figure 5 represents the number of sales which can be generated through keyword advertising assuming a cut-off at a given CPA. The steep rise in of the full line at around 1.00€ is due to a very well performing corporate brand term – a behavior

Figure 5. The full line indicates the number of sales (per arbitrary time interval) which can be reached by allowing only keywords with CPA less than a given limit. The dashed line represents the number of sales as a function of average cost per acquisition.

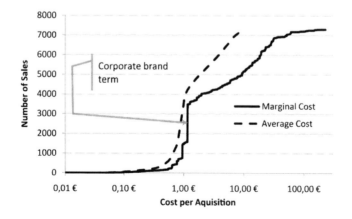

which is typical in SEM campaigns. So far we have only discussed single keyword statistics.

The company's data show that many users click more than once on search engine ads before buying a product. About 31% of all sales include more than one click in the interaction history. But, the method described above only takes into account single keywords by simply assuming that only the last click on a keyword is responsible for a sale that happened afterwards ("last cookie counts"). In a more advanced model we take the interaction (click) history of a user and calculate a so called assisted cost per acquisition

$$CPA_{assist} = \frac{Cost_{keyword}}{\displaystyle\sum_{i \in CLICKSTREAMS} O_{keyword,i} \frac{S_i}{N_i}}$$

Where $O_{keyword,i}$ is the number of occurrences of *keyword* in clickstream i, S_i is the number of sales in i, and N_i is the number of clicks in i. Table 1 shows that the CPAs of selected keywords from the company's portfolio can change significantly. From the table one can see that branded keywords get slightly more expensive while generic keywords get cheaper.

While this supports the observation of a "generic-to-brand spill over" from Rutz and Bucklin (2008), the effect is lower than some researchers have expected[7]. This is – as mentioned above – the first step towards taking into account the user journey when it comes to the evaluation of the performance of individual placement units (here: keyword and match type) in Online Advertising.

CONCLUSION

SMEs are more likely to face an efficiency gap in search engine marketing since they may not be able to afford sophisticated bidding tools, or, in a similar fashion, these tools may not be applicable with respect to niche markets that will not offer enough data for algorithm-based optimization. Further research is necessary in order to provide a solution for this group that takes a different approach than the current heuristic-based approaches. However, even if data is available, many problems are related to the fact that the large number of decision problems overweight data availability. Therefore, we need appropriate and robust models and specifical fitting functions.

The results of this research are relevant for the current status of search engine marketing, but search evolves, and the upcoming changes will offer new opportunities to SMEs apart from the abovementioned challenges. SERPs have looked the same for years: 10 organic results and a number of paid results above, below and next to the organic results. A few search engines had experimented with completely different approaches of presenting results, but none of them was considerably successful. Users have been conditioned what a SERP looks like since the first days of the web. However, at the same time, a significant number of search queries indicates that other media than text would be a more relevant result, especially for local searches or searches for visual ("asian restaurant in holborn london" or "picture of london bridge"). As a consequence, search engines have been experimenting how to

Table 1. Difference in CPA for selected keywords when taking into account assisting clicks

Keyword	CPA [EUR]	CPA$_{assist}$ [EUR]	ΔCPA %
Keyword 1	69.99	63.62	-8
Keyword 2	68.39	62.75	-9
Keyword 3	72.69	58.62	-19

add other media into the text-dominated SERPs, and the term "Universal Search" has been coined for the result of these experiments. We will call a Universal search results page as USERP in order to be able to distinguish such result pages from the text-only SERPs.

While it may sound trivial to add images and videos to a SERP, this has a significant impact on user behavior and, consequently, on the performance of Search Engine Marketing and Search Engine Optimization campaigns. Users are more likely to click on an image or a video than on text, and click rates on standard formats are more likely to drop compared to SERPs without other formats. This, however, would cannibalize search engines' revenues if clicks on ads decrease, and Google has started to test other formats in ads, too. Pictures and Videos of products could attract more clicks on USERPs. This will result in new challenges but also opportunities for SMEs, since a photo or the preview picture of a video will most probably determine the click through rate instead of the offer described in the ad copy. Some first studies have already been done by the authors, and Figure 6a illustrates how much more users are attracted to images in comparison to Figure 6b, a text-only SERP, although the single ad at the top still gets some attention.

SERPs with no other media than text attract most of the attention at the top, and ads in this space are much more likely to be clicked on than ads on the right, as shown in Figure 6a. Interestingly enough, the last result gets more attention than the ones before, a phenomenon that can be explained by the need to find an "edge" when scrolling through a list of links.

With Google's increasing dominance in the search engine world, new challengers are able to receive extraordinary attention, given that it seems impossible to gain significant market share without a feature that clearly shows a benefit for the user to change the default search engine. Worse, since the data that Google is able to collect from users makes its product continuously better, it is unclear what such a feature could be that could challenge Google. As a consequence, the launch of Wolfram Alpha was anticipated with high interest, given that this search engine was announced as the next giant step in the world of search engines. But while Wolfram Alpha's features and capabilities are impressive, these features do not target the mainstream market. Bing is another challenger, and in combination with Yahoo's search background, Bing is in the process of gaining market share. Nevertheless, Bing is still lacking features that would make it

Figure 6. Images on a SERP lead to different attention patterns

unique in comparison to Google. Currently, Bing is still trying to catch up in our opinion.

This quasi-monopoly has several consequences for SMEs. Without significant pressure from competitors, Google is able to dictate the rules. If you don't like these rules, you have no alternative, taking into account that the majority of all users uses Google and ads on other search engines are only seen by a fraction of web users. Optimization requires data, and if data is scarce, then optimization is difficult and more labor-intensive or even impossible. Optimizing bidding strategies with data from one of Google's competitors alone seems to be difficult if not impossible. In some countries, spendings for Yahoo!'s search ads have already dropped since the extra time to manage a campaign on a second platform could not be justified by the outcome with respect to the low search user base of Yahoo! in these countries. A new competitor will be required to provide a Google-compatible interface for campaigns in order to decrease the entrance cost for existing Google customers, unless additional traffic in a significant area would justify the expense.

Finally, competition is good for the customer. Apple's operating System MacOS X has seriously challenged Microsoft's Windows, and Microsoft's new version of Windows has not only included MacOS alike features but also several new features that MacOS X lacks. Competition in the search engine market would be beneficial for users as well as for advertisers – the latter need a choice where to spend their money, even though it is currently easier and cheaper for them since they are able to focus on one platform. Unfortunately, we don't expect such a choice to come up in the next few years.

REFERENCES

Anderson, C. (2004). The Long Tail. *Wired Magazine, 12*(10), 170–177.

Bartz, K., Barr, C., & Aijaz, A. (2008). Natural language generation for sponsored-search advertisements. In *Proceedings of the 9th ACM Conference on Electronic Commerce* (p. 1–9). New York: ACM New York.

Battelle, J. (2006). *The search. How Google and its rivals rewrote the rules of business and transformed our culture.* New York: Portfolio.

Borgs, C., Chayes, J., & Etesami, O. (2007). Dynamics of bid optimization in online advertisement auctions. *Proceedings of the WWW, 2007,* 531–540. doi:10.1145/1242572.1242644

Cary, M., Das, A., & Edelman, B. (2007). Greedy Bidding Strategies for Keyword Auctions. *Electronic Commerce, 2007,* 262–271.

Chen, Y., Xue, G.-R., & Yu, Y. (2008). *Advertising Keyword Suggestion Based on Concept Hierarchy* (p. 251). Web Search & Data Mining.

Elberse, A. (2008). Should You Invest in the Long Tail? *Harvard Business Review, 86*(7), 88–96.

Feldman, J., Muthukrishnan, S., Pál, M., & Stein, C. (2007). *Budget Optimization in Search-Based Advertising* (pp. 40–49). Electronic Commerce.

Funk, B. (2009) Optimizing Price Levels in E-Commerce Applications with Respect to Customer Lifetime Values. *Proceedings of the International Conference on E-Commerce,* pp. 169-175.

Hosanagar, K., & Cherepanov, V. (2008). Optimal Bidding in Stochastic Budget Constraint Slot Auctions. *Electronic Commerce, 2008,* 20–29.

Jansen, B. (2007). Click Fraud. *Computer, 40*(7), 85–86. doi:10.1109/MC.2007.232

Jansen, B. (2007). The Comparative Effectiveness of Sponsored. *ACM Transactions on the Web, 1*(1), 1–25.

Jansen, B., Booth, D., & Spink, A. (2007). Determining the user intent of web search engine queries. In *Proceedings of the 16th international conference on World Wide Web* (p. 1149–1150). New York: ACM.

Kitts, B., & Leblanc, B. (2004). Optimal Bidding on Keyword Auctions. *Electronic Markets, 14*(3), 186–201. doi:10.1080/1019678042000245119

Korolova, A., Kenthapadi, K., Mishra, N., & Ntoulas, A. (2009). Releasing Search Queries and Clicks Privately. *Proceedings of the WWW, 2009*, 171–180. doi:10.1145/1526709.1526733

Manchanda, P., Dubé, J.-P., Goh, K. Y., & Chintagunta, P. K. (2006, February). The effect of banner advertising on internet purchasing. *JMR, Journal of Marketing Research, 43*(1), 98–108. doi:10.1509/jmkr.43.1.98

Nelson, S., & Bayrak C. (2009). Categorizing Web Queries. *SIGSOFT Software Engineering Notes. March 2009 34(2)*.

Rutz, O., & Bucklin, R. (2008). *From Generic to Branded: A Model of Spillover in Paid Search Advertising*. Retrieved from http://ssrn.com/abstract=1024766.

Rutz, O., & Bucklin, R. (2009). *A Shrinkage-based Approach to Measuring Keyword Conversion Rates in Paid Search*. Under first round review at Quantitative Marketing and Economics.

Sen, R., Bandyopadhyay, S., Hess, J. D., & Jaisingh, J. (2008). Pricing Paid Placements on Search Engines. *Journal of Electronic Commerce Research, 9*(1), 33–50.

Strohmaier, M., & Kröll, M. (2009). Studying databases of intentions: do search query logs capture knowledge about common. *fifth international conference on Knowledge capture*, 89-96.

Yao, S., & Mela, C. F. (2009). Sponsored Search Auctions: Research Opportunities in Marketing. *Foundations and Trends in Marketing, 3*(2), 75–126. doi:10.1561/1700000013

Aggarwal, G., Feldman, J., Muthukrishnan, S., & Pal, M. (2008). *Sponsored search auctions with markovian users*. WINE'08, 621–628. New York: Springer.

Aggarwal, G., Muthukrishnan, S., Pál, D., & Pál, M. (2009). *General auction mechanism for search advertising*. Proceedings of the 18th international conference on World wide web - WWW '09, 241. New York: ACM Press.

Croft, B., Metzler, D., & Strohman, T. (2009). *Search Engines: Information Retrieval in Practice*. Reading, MA: Addison-Wesley.

Edelman, B., & Ostrovsky, M. (2007). Strategic bidder behavior in sponsored search auctions. [New York: Elsevier.]. *Decision Support Systems, 43*(1), 192–198. doi:10.1016/j.dss.2006.08.008

Edelman, B., Ostrovsky, M., & Schwarz, M. (2007). Internet Advertising and the Generalized Second-Price Auction: Selling Billions of Dollars Worth of Keywords. [American Economic Association Publications.]. *The American Economic Review, 97*(1), 242–259. doi:10.1257/aer.97.1.242

Feldman, J., Muthukrishnan, S., Pal, M., & Stein, C. (2007). Budget optimization in search-based advertising auctions. portal.acm.org, 40-49.

Ghose, A., & Yang, S. (2008). An empirical analysis of sponsored search performance in search engine advertising. In *Proceedings of the international conference on Web search and web data mining* (p. 241–250). New York: ACM.

Goel, G., & Mehta, A. (2008). Online budgeted matching in random input models with applications to adwords. In *Proceedings of the nineteenth annual ACM-SIAM symposium on Discrete algorithms* (p. 982–991). Society for Industrial and Applied Mathematics Philadelphia, PA, USA.

Jones, K. B. (2008). *Search Engine Optimization: Your Visual Blueprint for Effective Internet Marketing*. New York: Wiley.

Manning, C. D., Raghavan, P., & Schütze, H. (2008). *Introduction to Information Retrieval.* Cambridge, MA: Cambridge University Press.

Meghabghab, G., & Kandel, A. (2008). *Search Engines, Link Analysis, and User's Web Behavior: A Unifying Web Mining Approach.* New York: Springer.

Mehta, A., Saberi, A., Vazirani, U., & Vazirani, V. (2007). Adwords and generalized online matching. *46th Annual IEEE Symposium on Foundations of Computer Science (FOCS'05)*, 264-273. New York: ACM.

Moran, M., & Hunt, B. (2009). *Search Engine Marketing – Driving Traffic to your Company's Web Site.* New York: IBM Publishing.

Papadimitriou, C., & Zhang, S. (2008). Internet and network economics. *4th international workshop, WINE 2008, Shanghai, China, December 17 - 20, 2008; proceedings.* Berlin: Springer (Lecture notes in computer science, 5385).

Rutz, O., & Bucklin, R. (2007). A model of individual keyword performance in paid search advertising. papers.ssrn.com, (November).

Varian, H. (2007). Position auctions. [New York: Elsevier.]. *International Journal of Industrial Organization, 25*(6), 1163–1178. doi:10.1016/j.ijindorg.2006.10.002

ENDNOTES

[1] Not every factor is measurable; as an example, while a user does not click on an ad, she might still perceive an ad.

[2] In order to guarantee privacy the data of the company (especially prices, budget, and sales figures) has been sanitized.

[3] It involves a fix component and variable component which depends on the number of clicks served.

[4] See for example the external keyword tool from Google: https://adwords.google.com/select/KeywordToolExternal

[5] Sometimes it can be useful to also use product numbers as keywords (e.g. from an offline catalogue). Since there are no are only a few competitors bidding on these kind of keywords, the cost per click is low.

[6] In the literature these problems are known as integer programming problems.

[7] It should be noted that the effect varies from advertiser to advertiser depending on, e.g. brand awareness, spending, and product type

Chapter 13

Information and Technology Management (ITM):
Competitive Advantage through Customer Relationship: The Case of an Automobile Dealership

Marjorie Luísa Biehl
Unisinos University, Brazil

Brandon Link
Unisinos University, Brazil

Adolfo Alberto Vanti
Unisinos University, Brazil

Gustavo Schneider
Unisinos University, Brazil

ABSTRACT

A competitive market gives the organizations a constant update on the management process of their businesses and allows the creation of new ways to take competitive advantage. Retail businesses need to identify the value perceived by customers as a strategic source of value generation. This chapter presented a competitive value generation methodology by identifying the most important values perceived by customers of a Volkswagen Car Dealer. There was application and analysis of two strategic instruments of research, a qualitative and another qualitative/quantitative one. As a result, the study obtained a proposal for value generation by setting the following strategic variables referent credibility/reliability.

INTRODUCTION

Strategic management is constantly passing through changes in order to attend to new demands related to the uncertainties the market has been imposing. This way, the present treatise approaches such uncertainties – both quantitatively and qualitatively – which encase the strategy of a company within customer relationship and competitive value generation, through a model based

DOI: 10.4018/978-1-60960-463-9.ch013

on Compensatory Fuzzy Logic (CFL) that frames up mathematically the classical SWOT analysis, added of Objectives and Actions (SWOT-OA). This framework based on CFL is translated in Strengths, Weaknesses, Opportunities, Threats, Objectives and Actions, which turns the linguistically-expressed knowledge of specialists into a widening-associative quantification of the Boolean logic, allowing the researchers and readers of this study to analyze the importance of each of its strategic variables.

According to Mintzberg and Quinn (2001) the strategy is characterized as a corporate transformation process, subjected to usual fixing. Due to this diagnosis, it is important to establish connections between strategic integration links and advance into a predictability of their behaviour, for according to Bonabeau (2002), predicting the unpredictable depends a lot on emerging phenomena formed amid the interaction of different organizational levels. This kind of situation instigated the writing of the present treatise, i.e. taking in account situations that are not standards represented in the strategic planning, and for this reason the following question was defined: How is it possible to generate competitive value through costumer relationship in a car part-seller company?

THEORICAL REFERENCE

Value Generation and Costumer Relationship

According to Dominguez (2000), as times has passed by, successful companies have transferred their focuses from improving internal processes to market approach developing, having as objective to supply costumers' needs and desires as well to generate superior value to them. It is a regard that the costumer is the one who determines how much goods and services are worth, and for that reason participation, feeling of together and connectivity have become key-words when creating

and maintaining a long-term relationship between costumers and companies.

Porter (1990) states that competitive advantage sprouts from the value a company can generate to its shoppers and goes beyond its operating expenses. This relation between competition and value generation characterizes the efficacy of a company to compete by creating sustainable value through time. This can still be cContaR palaVraSwiden according to Gibson et al. (1988) who states that such process is the level by which organizations reach their missions, aims and objectives.

Value generation, for the client, is not only about adding characteristics and benefits to products, neither reducing prices. These market strategies only happen if clients notice an improvement on the value, and they consequently feel pleased (BARNES, 2002). Value pops out when the human being establishes utilities or purposes to the objects.

The management of perceived value allows the company to get to know their costumers better and the market to fit its marketing approaches to the clients, centering the arguments on value proposing, instead of just pricing (KOTLER, 1998). Proposing value varies between desired and received value, i.e. before or after the usage, or even as for the objective intended. In the context of perceived value, quality and price, the "mean-end" model proposed by Zeithaml (1988) associates price, quality and value. For Chang and Wildt (1994), perceived value is formed of a judiciousness of the information obtained about the product, the real product price and the price that the costumer has in mind for the goods he or she is looking for.

Peppers and Rogers (2001) state it is essential to treat customers in a non-ordinary way. This is the idea for changing companies' behavior towards each client, based on the information the companies have about them, and also on the information the customers expose. Loyalty is, then, framed out on the level of satisfaction, credibility and trust between clients and company. For Moutella (2002), loyalty is conquered in a long-term relationship through attitudes which show trust, respect, care and attention one to another. Offering customers a pleasant and reliable relationship means to invest on the conquest of their loyalty, building on them a feeling of thinking deep and seriously before trying another brand.

Loyalty is a continuous process for obtaining faithfulness and has a differential competitive which will assure its survival. This way, the effort on client retention is, above all, an investment which will assure a raise in the sales and a decrease in the expenses. Barney (2001) clarifies that the expense when losing a customer multiplies in new different expenses, either with him or also with other possible clients who were negatively influenced.

METHODOLOGICAL PROCEDURES

The present research joins theory and practice, because it's motivated by the necessity of solving real problems from the business world. The tools for collecting data were divided in the following categories:

A: Interview with clients, chosen for their knowledge about the studied company. These interviews were composed by ten questions, listed below, followed by the corresponding authors and key-words:

1. Which satisfactory criteria do you consider to have more importance when shopping? (Kaplan and Norton, 1997) Satisfactory criteria.
2. What are the unsatisfactory reasons that would lead you not to buy goods or services? (Kaplan and Norton, 1997) Unsatisfactory criteria.
3. In which ways do you consider convenient carrying out post-market activities? (Greenberg, 2001) Post-market activities.
4. Within the next twelve months, which reasons will bring you back to our company? (Chalmeta, 2005) Post-market activities.
5. What is important for you during the contact with the staff? (Kotler, 1998) Service.
6. What do you appreciate the most in our company? (Karsaklian, 2000, apud CAMPOS, 2004) Value.
7. Which criteria do you have in mind when shopping? (Zeithaml and Bitner apud Barnes, 2002) Value generation.
8. What can you observe in the chosen product? (Barnes, 2002) Key-elements for value generation.
9. What characterizes good business for you? (Dominguez, 2001) Proportional benefits.
10. What is really worth for your satisfaction? (Barnes, 2002) Customer Satisfaction.

B: Logical model of quali-quantitative type, based on compensatory fuzzy logic (CFL) in which it is first defined strategic variables related to SWOT analysis, added of Strategic Objectives and Actions (SWOT-OA). This model is defined with the structures of matrices, and the relation among the variables is based on CFL, validated by the manager of the company.

Compensatory fuzzy logic, according to Espin and Vanti (2005) aims to compensate Boolean logic – which uses only extremes of decision, as 0 or 1 –, and also to work with the principle of gradual levels within the interval [0,1] in order to measure the truthfulness of its predicates, considering 0 or 1 as extreme truth or untruth. From this analysis, it is possible to identify 0,5 as full uncertainty or maximum vagueness. A complete representation of the scale of truthfulness is shown in Table 1.

The values of truthfulness above are obtained to be included as data input into the matrices and also to calculate the results of these predicates, which must be sensitive to the changes of basic predicate truth values or to the verbal meaning of the truth values, calculated as shown below:

Table 1. Scale of truthfulness (Source: the authors)

Truth Value	Category
0	False
0.1	Almost false
0.2	Slightly false
0.3	Somewhat false
0.4	Falser than true
0.5	As true as false
0.6	Truer than false
0.7	Somewhat true
0.8	Slightly true
0.9	Almost true
1	True

$$v(p_1 \wedge p_2 \wedge ... \wedge p_n) = (v(p_1).v(p_2)...v(p_n))^{1/n}$$
$$v(p_1 \vee p_2 \vee ... \vee p_n) = 1 - ((1 - v(p_1)).(1 - v(p_2))...(1 - v(p_n)))^{1/n}$$

This formula transfers the classical linguistic knowledge from SWOT, reaching to compensate the lack of associative properties from conjunction and disjunction operators. Plus, it widens its framework to fit strategic objectives and actions, in order to turn SWOT analysis into an alignment, ranging from threatens and opportunities to objectives and actions which the company should perform.

This way, the formula tests the matrices continuously, applying geometric means which operate with conjunctions to carry out disjunctions, until they reach the limit multiplication of the matrix objective x objective and final calculus of the importance of the variables. Such model was programmed in Delphi language and it is used on academic exercises in Administration and Accountancy courses.

For data input, the manager of the company followed some questions to define the quantification of each cross among the variables. These questions are:

- How true is it for each characteristic of the company to be recommended to purpose each objective?
- How true is it for each characteristic of the environment to be recommended to purpose each objective?
- How true is it for each characteristic of the company along with each one of the environment to be taken into account to choose the strategies that lead to the company's vision?
- How true is it for each characteristic to be a characteristic of the company? Represent the evaluation of the presence of characteristics.
- How true is it for each characteristic to be a characteristic of the environment? Represent the evaluation of the presence of characteristics of the environment.
- How true is it for the accomplishment of each objective to influence (or to have great importance) accomplishment in other objectives?
- How true is it for the performance of each action to influence (or to have great importance) accomplishment of each objective?

After the fulfilling of the matrices, it was possible to analyze them along with the equations framed out through computer systems. This way, the relative importance of each variable was generated.

The result of the practical work is shown through giving priority to the strategic variables concerned with the knowledge of a specialist, and subsequently the analysis of these variables was realized along with the interviews (ten questions). That process led to the final analysis of value generation and customer loyalty relationship. Following the final analysis described above, the results were presented – element by element – through the consolidation board.

Such study was performed in a Volkswagen car dealer, active in the market since 1958, in

Montenegro, a city in southern Brazil. In the beginning it was built a quantitative ground of data input which was validated afterwards. This will be numerically explained in the next steps with a sequence of matrices.

Studied Case

The company in which the research was made authorized the release of this treatise. The company's name is Comercial Auto Montenegrina Ltda – COMAUTO, a Volkswagen car dealer, being more than 50 years old, as well the leader of the market in Caí River Valley. Its mission is to include clients' expectations in the focus of its acting, keeping their loyalty and trust. Approaching twenty-one cities around its headquarters, COMAUTO has as great characteristic to set and keep contact with costumers from the rural and hinterland inhabitants.

Qualitative Tool: Interviews

When analyzing the answers from the interviews, it was noticeable that customers from COMAUTO have a large range of different responses, mainly when asked about the satisfactory and unsatisfactory criteria in the moment of the purchase of goods or services. The average number of elicited items per client as satisfactory criteria was seven, being *price* and *technology* named unanimously. Other elicited items by most of the clients were *service, brand, model* and *maintenance cost.* Only one client elicited *promotion* as a priority when shopping.

The second question of the interview was about the reasons which would led him or her not to buy a product in a place. In this case two answers were elicited by all the clients: *price* and *market's opinion.* The clients confessed they get to know other people's and specialist's opinions of a product before the purchase.

Other criteria were remembered and got significant importance by the interviewed customers, such as the *car resale value*, being elicited as of greatest importance. *Service (contact with staff)* was not mentioned as decisive factor for a purchase, but it was pointed out as an essential factor for quitting; *technology* and *characteristics of the product* were also mentioned by the customers. The least remembered criterion was *means of payment.*

Another question aimed to identify by which ways the costumer thinks it is more appropriated to realize post-market activities. The result showed that four out of five customers believe that feedbacking about the purchase and the service performed is *unpleasant.* When asked about the reasons that would bring the costumers back to the dealership, *good and qualified service* were the most elicited answers – costumers also mentioned the preventive maintenance. Customers also pointed out that *accurate and attentive salespeople* is the most important element when purchasing. They believe the salesperson must know the products really well and be able to explain every single detail about them. The value attributed to COMAUTO, by the costumers, is Volkswagen brand, followed by its staff.

Important information analyzed during the purchase, concerning the choice of the product by the clients, was classified as personal reasons which are directly connected to each costumer's lifestyle. Methods as comparing different brands and products, researching about the quality of the product, trusting in the brand, supplying necessities and expecting to find everything the costumer wishes in the product are some of the criteria elicited on the interviews.

After choosing the product, clients confessed to observe some specifications. The most remarkable ones were related to the quality of the product, differentials and its characteristics. It is important to point out that clients really want to possess the product at the moment of the purchase, thus, *availability* assumes great importance when choosing a product. Other concerns elicited by just one customer are about *call center services* and *the reading of the user manual.*

Sale success is not only about completing it. It is necessary for the client to notice he or she has done great business. This was perceived by most clients as cost-benefit ratio: the amount paid versus the quality and reliability of the product. This fact was also considered important because it is allied with a large range of means of payment – which makes the purchase easier – and the supply of costumer's expectations.

One of the interviewed clients highlighted other clients' opinions about the purchase as advantageous business. In the search for client loyalty, it becomes really important to recognize which things are important to assure customer's satisfaction. It is possible to state that two items were pointed out as great priority: respect and courtesy from staff to client and the expectation to have all the necessities supplied by the product – the pleasure of owning desired goods. Afterwards, responsibility values were elicited, which means the fact of the dealership be as good as its word, and also the social value related to the good relationship among staff members, clients and the company.

Qualitative and Quantitative Tool: Strategic Variables Definition and Matrices Filling

After the analysis of external and organizational environments, the following variables were elicited:

- **Strengths:** No Volkswagen competitor (S1), stability (S2), loyalty (S3), infrastructure (S4), sales potential (S5), service (S6), brand (S7), price (S8), technology (S9), maintenance cost (S10), credibility in the dealership (S11), product/service quality (S12), promotion (S13), means of payment (S14), resale value (S15), market opinion (S16), post-market activities (S17), cost-benefit ratio (S18), what one gets compared to what one gives (S19), satisfaction

(S20), warranty (S21), customer service (S22), product availability (S23).

- **Weaknesses:** improving sales department (W1), overstocking (W2), post-market activities (W3), lack of performance indicators (W4), lack of strategic planning (W5), strengthening credit rating (W6), necessity to update IT (W7), strategies focused on the client (W8), competitive strategy (W9), meet deadlines (W10), unpredictability of risks (W11).

- **Opportunities:** new design (OP1), improve automotive technology (OP2), sales expansion (OP3), easier means of payment (OP4), sustainable activities (OP5), implementation of business risks analyses (OP6), added value in processes/relationship (OP7), customization of services (OP8), loyalty (OP9).

- **Threatens:** economic crisis (T1), sustainable crisis (T2), falling reputation of Volkswagen's (T3), competition (T4), dependence from the car factory – delivery deadline (T5), unsatisfied client (T6).

To widen the analysis of the importance the company should focus on its strategic planning, it was also elicited Strategic Objectives and Actions, in order to make the quantification of the matrix crosses possible. Afterwards, data will be processed on the software developed for it. The "additional" variables are:

- **Strategic Objectives:** market expansion (OB1), client satisfaction (OB2), client loyalty (OB3), increasing/managing customers' perceived value (OB4), increasing competitive differential (OB5), manage value/relationship chain (OB6), cash and client union – long term (OB7) increasing profits per dealings (OB8).

- **Actions:** increasing car accessories sales (A1), skilled salespeople (A2), training/rewarding (A3), strengthening post-market activities (A4), staff commitment (A5), searching solutions for clients (A6), marketing investments (A7).

From the verbalization of the executive department, matrices were built. They quantify strategic relationship from SWOT plus strategic

Table 2. Quantification of Swot matrix (Source: the authors)

SWOT	OP1	OP2	OP3	OP4	OP5	OP6	OP7	OP8	OP9	T1	T2	T3	T4	T5	T6	Presence
S1	0,7	0,9	0,7	0,7	0,6	0,8	0,6	0,7	0,8	0,6	0,7	0,5	0,9	0,7	0,5	0,9
S2	0,8	0,9	0,8	0,9	0,5	0,6	0,7	0,7	0,9	0,4	0,7	0,4	0,7	0,7	0,4	0,9
S3	0,8	1,0	0,7	0,6	0,7	0,8	0,7	0,8	1,0	0,7	0,6	0,6	0,6	0,7	0,4	0,8
S4	0,3	0,4	0,7	0,4	0,5	0,4	0,6	0,6	0,6	0,5	0,6	0,5	0,6	0,5	0,6	0,7
S5	0,7	0,7	0,7	0,9	0,6	1,0	1,0	1,0	0,9	0,4	0,7	0,3	0,8	0,6	0,6	0,9
S6	0,0	0,2	0,9	0,4	0,5	0,7	0,8	1,0	0,8	0,5	0,6	0,6	0,7	0,7	0,4	0,8
S7	0,9	0,9	1,0	0,5	1,0	0,9	0,9	0,7	1,0	0,7	0,7	1,0	0,9	1,0	0,3	1,0
S8	0,5	0,7	0,7	1,0	0,5	0,9	0,9	0,7	0,8	0,6	0,9	0,7	0,7	0,5	0,6	0,7
S9	0,8	1,0	0,9	0,4	0,7	0,7	0,8	0,9	0,9	0,6	1,0	0,2	0,6	0,5	0,2	0,9
S10	0,5	0,5	0,8	0,9	0,6	0,3	0,7	0,5	0,9	0,9	0,9	0,4	0,4	0,5	0,4	0,7
S11	0,4	0,6	0,9	1,0	0,8	0,8	0,9	0,9	1,0	0,8	0,6	0,6	0,8	0,8	0,3	0,9
S12	0,8	0,7	1,0	0,5	0,7	0,7	1,0	0,8	1,0	0,5	0,6	1,0	0,9	0,5	0,1	0,9
S13	0,6	0,5	0,8	1,0	0,5	0,8	0,6	0,6	0,4	0,7	0,5	0,4	0,8	0,6	0,2	0,7
S14	0,5	0,5	0,8	1,0	0,5	0,9	0,6	0,8	0,5	0,9	0,8	0,5	0,6	0,5	0,1	0,6
S15	0,4	0,8	0,8	0,6	0,5	0,6	0,6	0,4	0,6	0,8	0,8	0,1	0,9	0,5	0,3	0,9
S16	0,7	0,9	0,9	0,9	0,4	0,7	0,7	0,9	0,8	0,7	0,8	0,3	0,9	0,8	0,4	1,0
S17	0,7	0,6	0,8	0,2	0,6	0,7	0,9	0,9	1,0	0,5	0,5	0,4	0,8	0,7	0,4	0,9
S18	0,5	0,5	1,0	0,6	0,5	0,8	0,4	0,6	1,0	0,4	0,8	0,4	1,0	0,4	0,0	1,0
S19	0,5	0,7	0,9	0,7	0,5	0,2	0,9	0,9	1,0	0,7	0,7	0,3	0,9	0,4	0,4	1,0
S20	0,6	0,9	1,0	1,0	0,8	0,2	1,0	1,0	1,0	0,7	0,8	1,0	0,9	1,0	1,0	1,0
S21	0,9	0,9	0,7	0,3	0,5	0,3	0,8	0,8	0,8	0,5	0,9	0,6	0,7	0,5	0,6	0,9
S22	0,7	0,5	0,7	0,5	0,5	0,5	0,8	1,0	0,9	0,6	0,7	0,7	0,8	0,7	0,4	0,7
S23	0,7	0,8	0,9	1,0	0,5	0,6	0,6	0,7	0,6	0,4	0,8	0,4	0,6	1,0	0,5	0,7
W1	0,7	0,7	0,8	0,3	0,5	0,7	0,8	0,8	0,7	0,7	0,8	0,9	0,8	0,3	0,9	0,7
W2	0,6	0,4	0,7	0,6	0,5	0,7	0,5	0,6	0,3	0,3	0,7	0,3	0,6	0,6	0,6	0,6
W3	0,5	0,6	0,7	0,4	0,6	0,8	1,0	0,6	0,8	0,7	0,7	0,8	0,8	0,7	0,8	0,7
W4	0,4	0,5	0,8	0,7	0,5	0,8	0,8	0,6	0,4	0,8	0,8	0,6	0,8	0,4	0,7	1
W5	0,3	0,4	0,9	0,8	0,5	1,0	0,9	0,4	0,6	0,8	1,0	0,6	0,9	0,6	0,8	1,0
W6	0,4	0,2	0,6	1,0	0,5	0,9	0,4	0,4	0,5	1,0	0,9	0,5	0,7	0,3	0,5	0,8
W7	0,6	0,7	0,8	0,7	0,5	0,8	0,8	0,9	0,7	0,8	0,8	0,6	0,7	0,6	0,8	1,0
W8	0,6	0,7	0,9	0,6	0,7	0,7	1,0	0,7	0,8	0,9	1,0	0,8	0,8	0,5	1,0	1,0
W9	0,7	0,8	0,9	0,7	0,7	1,0	1,0	0,6	0,7	0,9	1,0	0,8	0,7	0,6	0,9	1,0
W10	0,5	0,6	0,8	0,5	0,5	0,8	0,8	0,7	0,8	0,8	0,8	0,8	0,9	1,0	1,0	0,8
W11	0,6	0,7	0,8	0,7	0,6	1,0	0,9	0,7	0,7	1,0	0,9	0,9	0,9	1,0	1,0	1,0
Presence	0,7	0,9	1,0	0,7	0,8	1,0	1,0	1,0	1,0	1,0	1,0	0,6	0,9	0,9	1,0	

objectives and actions (SWOT-OA). From this relation, everything is processed in a conjunctive way, containing:

- Swot matrix between itself and relative Presences;
- Swot matrix before each objective;
- Actions before each objective;
- Objective before each objective.

Data Input (Tables 2, 3, 4, 5 and 6)

ANALYSIS AND CONCLUSION

When pointing the main values present in the interviews and the results from the matrices SWOT-OA, it is established the relation of values elicited by the clients and the priorities evidenced

Table 3. Quantification: strategic objectives x weaknesses and strengths (Source: the authors)

Strategic OBectives								
Company's charac-ter-istics	OB1	OB2	OB3	OB4	OB5	OB6	OB7	OB8
Strengths and Weak-nesses								
S1	0,6	0,5	0,7	0,4	0,6	0,6	0,5	0,6
S2	0,7	0,7	0,6	0,7	0,8	0,8	0,7	0,8
S3	0,6	0,8	1,0	0,9	1,0	0,9	0,7	0,9
S4	0,3	0,6	0,5	0,6	0,6	0,6	0,3	0,5
S5	0,7	0,9	0,9	0,8	0,8	1,0	0,8	0,7
S6	0,7	0,9	1,0	0,9	1,0	1,0	0,7	0,7
S7	0,9	0,9	0,9	0,8	0,4	0,7	0,7	0,8
S8	0,6	0,7	0,5	0,4	0,5	0,7	0,6	0,8
S9	0,9	0,7	0,8	0,9	1,0	0,9	0,7	0,9
S10	0,4	0,6	0,4	0,9	0,8	0,6	0,7	0,7
S11	0,8	1,0	1,0	0,8	0,8	0,9	0,7	0,8
S12	0,9	1,0	0,8	1,0	1,0	0,8	0,7	1,0
S13	0,7	0,8	0,4	0,3	0,7	0,6	0,6	0,0
S14	0,6	0,6	0,3	0,4	0,6	0,7	0,6	0,6
S15	0,6	0,7	0,4	0,6	0,6	0,5	0,1	0,6
S16	0,9	1,0	0,7	0,9	0,7	0,7	0,5	0,7
S17	0,8	1,0	1,0	0,8	0,8	1,0	0,8	0,9
S18	0,9	0,9	0,9	0,9	0,8	0,7	0,7	0,8
S19	0,6	0,9	0,8	0,9	0,7	0,6	0,6	0,7
S20	0,8	1,0	1,0	1,0	1,0	0,9	0,9	1,0
S21	0,6	0,7	0,3	0,6	0,4	0,4	0,0	0,0
S22	0,6	0,7	0,7	0,8	0,8	1,0	0,4	0,6
S23	0,4	0,7	0,5	0,5	0,6	0,3	0,6	0,6
W1	0,9	0,9	0,7	0,8	0,7	0,7	0,6	0,8
W2	0,6	0,4	0,3	0,3	0,6	0,1	0,6	0,6

continued on following page

Table 3. continued

W3	0,7		0,8	1,0	0,9	0,9	1,0	0,7	1,0
W4	0,6		0,3	0,4	0,6	0,7	0,6	0,6	0,7
W5	0,7		0,6	0,6	0,4	0,4	0,8	0,7	0,7
W6	0,7		0,5	0,3	0,5	0,6	0,7	1,0	0,9
W7	0,8		0,7	0,8	0,9	0,8	0,9	0,8	0,9
W8	0,8		0,9	0,9	1,0	0,9	1,0	0,7	0,7
W9	0,9		0,8	0,8	0,7	1,0	0,9	0,8	0,8
W10	0,7		0,9	0,9	0,8	1,0	0,6	0,6	0,6
W11	0,8		0,8	0,4	0,5	0,7	0,9	0,8	0,6

Table 4. Quantification: strategic objectives x opportunities and threatens (Source: the authors)

Environmental characteristics															
Strategic OBectives	OP1	OP2	OP3	OP4	OP5	OP6	OP7	OP8	OP9	T1	T2	T3	T4	T5	T6
OB1	0,9	0,8	1,0	0,9	0,9	0,9	0,8	0,9	0,6	0,4	0,4	0,2	1,0	0,4	0,2
OB2	0,8	0,9	0,5	0,7	0,7	0,0	1,0	1,0	0,9	0,5	0,6	0,4	0,7	0,6	0,5
OB3	0,6	0,7	0,6	0,3	0,6	0,0	0,9	0,9	1,0	0,4	0,5	0,3	0,7	0,6	0,0
OB4	0,7	1,0	0,6	0,6	0,7	0,0	1,0	1,0	1,0	0,7	0,6	0,4	0,8	0,3	0,1
OB5	0,8	0,9	0,5	0,7	0,8	0,7	1,0	1,0	0,0	0,6	0,9	0,6	0,7	0,3	0,4
OB6	0,2	0,5	0,8	0,6	0,4	1,0	0,8	0,7	1,0	0,9	0,7	0,7	0,8	0,5	0,4
OB7	0,4	0,6	0,7	0,9	0,5	0,8	0,8	0,8	0,9	0,6	0,5	0,4	0,6	0,5	0,5
OB8	0,6	0,6	0,6	1,0	0,6	0,9	0,9	0,9	1,0	0,4	0,6	0,4	0,6	0,3	0,5

Table 5. Quantification: strategic objectives x strategic objectives (Source: the authors)

Strategic Objectives								
Strategic Objectives	OB1	OB2	OB3	OB4	OB5	OB6	OB7	OB8
OB1	1,0	0,6	0,6	0,8	0,8	0,7	0,6	0,5
OB2	0,6	1,0	1,0	0,7	0,9	0,4	0,3	0,4
OB3	0,5	1,0	1,0	0,9	0,7	0,9	0,7	0,6
OB4	0,4	0,9	1,0	1,0	0,9	0,8	0,6	0,7
OB5	0,8	0,9	0,8	0,9	1,0	0,7	0,6	0,6
OB6	0,9	0,6	0,8	0,9	0,6	1,0	0,6	0,7
OB7	0,7	0,5	0,4	0,5	0,8	0,6	1,0	0,7
OB8	0,5	0,5	0,7	0,7	0,6	0,7	0,8	1,0

Table 6. Quantification: strategic objectives x actions (Source: the authors)

Strategic Objectives								
Actions	OB1	OB2	OB3	OB4	OB5	OB6	OB7	OB8
A1	0,3	0,4	0,7	0,7	0,9	0,7	0,6	1,0
A2	0,9	0,8	0,8	0,9	0,8	1,0	0,7	0,9
A3	0,8	0,7	0,6	0,7	0,8	0,8	0,8	0,9
A4	0,6	0,8	0,9	0,9	0,8	0,7	0,7	0,7
A5	0,7	0,9	0,9	0,9	0,7	0,9	0,9	0,9
A6	0,8	1,0	1,0	1,0	1,0	1,0	0,8	1,0
A7	0,9	0,3	0,4	0,6	0,8	0,8	0,8	0,8

in the environmental and organizational information cross, as well as the company's strategies.

Eleven items about organizational and environmental characteristics were classified for the analysis. Such analyses pointed out during

Table 7. Results generated by the system for the importance of strategic themes to venture (Source: The authors)

Strengths		Weaknesses		Threatens	
S1	0,8043604	W1	0,8158772	T1	1
S2	0,7981586	W2	0,7383458	T2	1
S3	1	W3	1	T3	1
S4	0,6956393	W4	0,772778	T4	1
S5	1	W5	1	T5	1
S6	1	W6	0,7511479	T6	1
S7	1	W7	1	**Objectives**	
S8	0,8246542	W8	1	OB1	1
S9	0,838707	W9	1	OB2	1
S10	0,7811538	W10	1	OB3	1
S11	1	W11	1	OB4	1
S12	1	**Opportunities**		OB5	1
S13	0,7544819	OP1	0,7294334	OB6	1
S14	0,7797789	OP2	0,7934641	OB7	0,8030922
S15	0,753872	OP3	1	OB8	1
S16	0,8365966	OP4	1	**Actions**	
S17	1	OP5	1	A1	1
S18	1	OP6	1	A2	1
S19	1	OP7	1	A3	0,8719984
S20	1	OP8	1	A4	0,8795971
S21	0,7849978	OP9	1	A5	0,9216325
S22	1			A6	1
S23	0,7972017			A7	0,839109

the interviews are wide, which is a classical characteristic of this kind of tool. In SWOT-OA analyses, such studies are more specific, detailed and longer, due to the logic of relating variables among themselves, and not analyzing them individually. Only the ones which got an importance level of 1 (one) were listed. Different analyses done in detail can be found in Biehl (2009). From now on, the results of the application of both tools are presented as well as the comparisons between them (Table 7).

Consolidation Board

This board's objective is to show the relation between obtained results from the interviews and the enlargement of the analysis of SWOT matrices which relates each of the variables among themselves. The most important information obtained from the interviews is elicited in Table 8 along with the results from the matrices – pointed out as

the most important ones, i.e. graded 1 (one). The rest of the variables are not mentioned in Table 8.

The variables *W5: Lack of strategic planning; W8: strategies focused on the client; W9: Competitive strategy* and *W11: unpredictability of risks,* shown to be graded 1 in SWOT analysis, are related to the company's planning, which wasn't elicited in the interviews. However it is important to state this has great importance in the analysis and in the strategic planning of the company.

The proposals of value shown to the clients in Table 9 are the attributes that suppliers offer through their products and services, in order to generate loyalty and satisfaction in target segments. Proposal of value is the fundamental concept for understanding the vectors of the essential measures of market satisfaction, attracting, keeping and participation.

Competitive advantage sprouts from the value a company can generate for its shoppers and it

Table 8. Relation with environmental and organizational characteristics (Source: the authors)

Interviews	SWOT
Service	T6: Unsatisfied Client; S6: Service
Market Opinion;	OP3: Sales Expansion; T3: Falling reputation of VW's; T4: Competition; S5: Sales Potential; S7: Brand
Price;	OB4: Increasing/managing customers' perceived value OB8: Increasing profits per dealings; S18: Cost-benefit ratio
Cost-benefit ratio;	S5: Sales potential; S18: Cost-benefit ratio; S19: What one gets compared to what one gives; S20: Satisfaction
Technology/Quality of the product;	S5: Sales potential; S12: Quality; W7: necessity to update IT
Post-market activities: diversity of opinions;	S17: Post-market activities; W3: Post-market activities; S22: Customer service; T6: Unsatisfied client
Clients expect courtesy and supplied necessities – Satisfaction;	W8: strategies focused on the client; OP7: added value in processes/relationship; OP8: customization of services (in order to get) OP9: Loyalty; S6: Service; S20: Satisfaction
Means of payment;	T1: Economic crisis; OP4: Easier means of payment; OP6: Implementation of business risks analyses; W11: Unpredictability of risks
Credibility in the dealership	T1: Economic crisis; OP4: Easier means of payment; OP6: Implementation of business risks analyses; S3: Loyalty; S5: Sales potential; S11: Credibility in the dealership; W10: Meet deadlines
Brand;	OP5: Sustainable activities; T2: Sustainable crisis; T3: Falling reputation of Volkswagen's; T4: Competition; T5: Dependence from the car factory – delivery deadline; S7: Brand
Car Resale Value	T1: Economic crisis; S5: Sales potential; S7: Brand

Table 9. Relation to strategic planning: strategic objectives and actions (Source: the authors)

Interviews	SWOT
Service	OB2: Client satisfaction; OB3: Loyalty; OB4: increasing/managing customers' perceived value; OB5: manage value/relationship chain; OB6: manage value/relationship chain; A2: skilled salespeople;
Market Opinion;	OB2: client satisfaction; OB4: increasing/managing customers' perceived value; OB5: increasing competitive differential; A5: staff commitment; A6: searching solutions for clients; A7: marketing investments;
Price;	OB4: increasing/managing customers' perceived value; OB8: increasing profits per dealings; A1: increasing car accessories sales;
Cost-benefit ration;	OB4: increasing/managing customers' perceived value; A3: training/rewarding; A5: staff commitment; A7: marketing investments;
Technology/ quality of the product;	OB2: client satisfaction; OB8: increasing profits per dealings; A3: training/rewarding; A4: staff commitment; A6: searching solutions for clients;
Post-market activities: diversity of opinions;	OB2: client satisfaction; OB3: Loyalty; OB4: increasing/managing customers' perceived value; OB5: increasing competitive differential; OB6: manage value/relationship chain; A3: training; A4: strengthening post-market activities; A5: staff commitment; A6: searching solutions for clients;
Clients expect courtesy and supplied necessities – Satisfaction;	OB2: client satisfaction; OB3: Loyalty; OB4: increasing/managing customers' perceived value; OB5: increasing competitive differential; OB6: manage value/relationship chain; A5: staff commitment; A6: searching solutions for clients;
Means of payment;	OB2: client satisfaction; OB5: increasing competitive differential; OB8: increasing profits per dealings; AC6: searching solutions for clients;
Credibility in the dealership	OB2: client satisfaction; OB3: Loyalty; OB4: increasing/managing customers' perceived value; A5: staff commitment; AC6: searching solutions for clients;
Brand;	OB5: increasing competitive differential; A1: increasing car accessories sales; A2: skilled salespeople; A7: marketing investments;
Car Resale Value	OB4: increasing/managing customers' perceived value; A1: increasing car accessories sales;

goes beyond operating costs, being based on value generation from its positioning framed on strategic planning, i.e. the capacity of companies to manage the perceived values from clients. When these factors are identified, as shown in the case study, it is important to focus the strategies to supply what costumers need, and make them become satisfied in order to build loyalty on them. It is necessary to manage relationship with clients as seriously as the processes of manufacturing.

Gale (1996) apud Campos (2004) defends that quality is the general opinion of costumers about your products or services when compared to other companies. He also adds that the value of the client is the quality perceived by the market adjusted to the relative price of goods.

This study was realized with the application of two tools: interviews (qualitative tool) and SWOT-OA analysis (quantitative/qualitative tool). To become the market leader, besides pricing, it is necessary to have the best strategy, actions and objectives to defeat competitors. Thus, the necessity of updating IT identified a priority of acting in this area, plus a marketing and sales services channel improvement in order to build costumers' loyalty. The focus on the relationship with the costumer was related mainly to a strategic positioning of trust and credibility, which was highlighted as relevant aspect in the research.

About the generalization of the research, even being an applied study, it was possible to establish a methodological proposal which widens the exclusive usage of interviews (qualitative tools). With this kind of application, the verbalized knowledge from specialists was structured and quantified in order to generate value and build loyalty in the organizational environment.

REFERENCES

Barnes, J. G. (2002). *Segredos da gestão pelo relacionamento com clientes - CRM: é tudo uma questão de como você faz com que eles se sintam.* Rio de Janeiro, Brazil: Qualitymark.

Barney, J. (2001). Is the resource-based view a useful perspective for strategic management research? Yes. *Academy of Management Review, 26,* 41–56. doi:10.2307/259393

Biehl, M. L. (2009). *Geração de valor competitivo através da relação com o cliente: caso de uma empresa do setor de autopeças.* Trabalho de Conclusão de Curso, Unisinos.

Bonabeau, E. (2002). Predicting the unpredictable. *HBR80* (3), pp. 109. March.

Campos. Daniel M. e. (2004). *A análise do valor percebido pelo cliente como ferramenta para a formulação de estratégias competitivas uma aplicação de conjoint analysis.* Dissertação de mestrado. Universidade Municipal de São Caetano do Sul. São Paulo.

Chalmeta. R. (2005). Methodology for customer relationship management. *The Journal of Systems and Software.* Espanha.

Chang, T. Z; Wildt, R. (1994). Price, product information and purchase intention: an empirical study. *Journal of the Academy of Marketing Science, 22*(1), winter.

Dominguez, S. V. (2000). O Valor Percebido como elemento estratégico para obter a lealdade dos clientes. Caderno *de pesquisas em Administração, São Paulo, 07*(4), outubro/dezembro.

Espín, R.; Vanti, A.A. (2005). Administración Lógica: Un estudio de caso en empresa de comercio exterior. Revista BASE. *São Leopoldo, RS - Brasil, ago, 1*(3), pp.4-22.

Gibson, J. L., Ivancevich, J. M., & Donnelly, J. H. (1988). *Organizações: comportamento, estrutura e processos.* São Paulo: Atlas.

Greenberg. P.(2001). *CRM na velocidade da luz: conquista e lealdade de clientes em tempo real na internet.* Rio de Janeiro: Campus.

Kaplan, R. S., & Norton, D. P. (1997). *A Estratégia em Ação – Balanced Scorecard.* 9 ed. Rio de Janeiro: Campus.

Kotler. P.(1998). *Princípios de Marketing.* Rio de Janeiro: Pretince-Hall.

Lopes, J., Filho, J. F. R., & Pederneiras, M. (2008). *Educação Contábil.* Análise das metodologias e técnicas de pesquisa adotadas nos estudos brasileiros sobre *Balanced Scorecard:* um estudo dos artigos publicados do período de 1999 a 2006. Ed. São Paulo: Atlas.

Mintzberg, H. & Q., J. (2001). *O processo da estratégia.* 3. ed. Porto Alegre: Bookmam.

Moutella. C.(2002). *Fidelização de clientes como Diferencial Competitivo.* Fonte www.portaldomarketing.com.br, acesso em 20/11/2008.

Peppers, D., & Rogers, M. (1997). [*– Instrumentos para Competir na Era da Interatividade.* Rio de Janiro: Campus.]. *EMPRESA, 1,* 1.

Peppers, D., Rogers, M., & Dorf, B. (2001). *Marketing One to One – Ferramentas para implementação de Programas de Marketing Direto One to One.* São Paulo: Makron Books.

Porter, M. E. (1990). *Vantagem competitiva. Trad. Elizabeth M. P. Braga. RJ.* Campus.

Zeithaml, V. (1988). Consumer Perceptions of Price, Quality, and Value: A Means-End Model and Synthesis of Evidence. [July.]. *Journal of Marketing, 52*(3), 2–22. doi:10.2307/1251446

Chapter 14
E–Commerce Penetration in the SADC Region:
Consolidating and Moving Forward

Bwalya Kelvin Joseph
University of Botswana, Botswana

ABSTRACT

E-Commerce, and recently mobile commerce (m-Commerce: ePayment, eTickets, eBanking etc.), has shown a lot of potential for development in the Southern African Development Community (SADC) bloc given the growth in e-adoption of the region. Partly, this has been attributed to sound policies and initiatives thereby creating an enabling environment for e-Commerce to thrive. However, despite this positive note, there are also challenges that are being faced on an everyday basis concerning e-Commerce business and how this impacts the SME (Small Medium Enterprise) sector. This chapter aims to present these challenges and recommend on what should be done in order to consolidate and move forward the adoption of e-Commerce applications in the SADC region. It looks at exploratory studies of e-Commerce penetration specifically from four SADC member countries: South Africa (arguably currently considered the most economically sound and leader of e-Commerce utilization in Africa), Mozambique, Zimbabwe and Botswana. Arguably, a look at these four countries is believed to be adequately representative of the SADC bloc. In Africa, other than e-Commerce, there has been a transition (change of business models) where businesses are now done using m-Commerce (distributed dynamic computing where the host and agent keep on changing their locations). This chapter also reviews the growth of this new business model, and further looks at Africa's infrastructure preparedness to adopt this new business model. It also looks at mobile phone subscription rates in the SADC region, level of trust in these business models, and the general value that this kind of business undertaking brings.

DOI: 10.4018/978-1-60960-463-9.ch014

INTRODUCTION

The world markets have kept transforming the way businesses and any form of transactions is done. There has been a paradigm shift where the traditional approach of static (fixed) mode of doing business is transcending into mobile, anytime, anywhere type of business models. Traditional market places have been turned into mobile marketplaces – thanks to the rapidly changing technology innovations. In this kind of business models, the cost of doing business is greatly reduced and more people with internet or any appropriate telecommunications-based tools such as mobile phone can be easily reached. In every context, e-Commerce has evolved from the much narrower set of structured computer-based business activities known as Electronic Data Interchange (EDI), which preceded the emergence of the Internet and the World Wide Web (WWW) to anywhere, anytime type of business. E-Commerce continues to broaden in scope as different technologies and context keeps changing to include other aspects of e-services such as e-government, e-health, etc. As is the case the world over, many countries even in Africa have realized the benefits that come with appropriate use and adoption of e-Commerce applications. In general terms, if properly applied, e-Commerce will have a major impact on the way businesses, especially the SMEs, are conducted. It has a great potential to revolutionize both national and international trade, touching virtually all aspects of economic and social life paradigms within countries. Nevertheless, for the case of Africa, basic commercial processes, infrastructure and systems are underdeveloped thereby limiting the growth and adoption of e-Commerce applications. With the desire to encourage the growth of e-Commerce applications, some African countries and regional groupings such as SADC are putting in place sound institutional, legal and ethical regulatory frameworks to make sure e-Commerce applications are being adopted in all socio-economic setups. Further, deliberate policies and initiatives are being put in place to create a level and enabling environment for the growth of e-Commerce usage in some of the African countries. This is important because if the end goal of e-Commerce applications – effective interaction between the consumer and the producer- is achieved, then African businesses can adequately participate in global business value chains.

In all respects, it is a rather difficult task to provide a precise definition of e-Commerce. However, let's consider several definitions of e-Commerce taken from different sources. E-Commerce can be broadly defined as "The conduct of commerce in goods and services, with the assistance of telecommunications and telecommunications-based tools" (IDRC, 2007). It includes various types of business transactions between Consumers (C), Government (G), and Business entities (B). E-Commerce overlaps with the understanding given to e-business and e-government. The three terms (e-Commerce, e-government and e-business) are used interchangeably. The Department of Communications (DoC) of South Africa incorporates e-government in its definition of e-Commerce: "The use of electronic networks to exchange information, products, services and payments for commercial and communication purposes between individuals (consumers) and businesses, between businesses themselves, within government or between the public and government, and last, between business and government" (IDRC). With this definition, the major concept of e-government (which is desire for constructive interaction between the government, citizens and businesses for cheap and efficient service delivery) is emphasized. One of the notable definitions of e-Commerce has been that given by the Pan African Initiative: "Electronic commerce is about doing business electronically. It is based on the processing and transmission of data, including text, sound and video. It encompasses many diverse activities including electronic trading of goods and services, online delivery of digital content, electronic fund transfers, electronic share trading, electronic bills of lading, commercial auctions, online sourcing, public procurement, direct consumer marketing, and after-sales service" (IDRC). The European Union has adopted a definition which directly links to the common definition of e-government: "E-Commerce is sometimes also categorized under four main areas of activity: business-to-business (B2B), business-to-government (B2G), business-to-consumer (B2C) and consumer-to-consumer (C2C)". Thus, with all these definitions, the common characteristics of e-Commerce are that it involves the selling and buying of services, with interaction of the buyer and the seller being brought about by means of a telecommunications medium (e.g. internet).

Implementation of e-Commerce applications usually comes with main challenges and these challenges have to be overcome if the value of e-Commerce is to be fully exploited. For the case of Africa, this is emphasized because of the limitation in the telecommunications infrastructure, lack of proper regulatory frameworks and policies, and lack of effective awareness campaigns on the benefits of e-Commerce applications. The ECA/IDRC Pan-African Initiative on e-Commerce of 2001 recognized the existence of many principles of commercial law which have been rendered obsolete, and in many instances pose a threat to the survival of e-Commerce. Another important concern of e-Commerce applications has been that of security and trust. Convincing the consumer of e-Commerce services, especially in an African context, is a mammoth, multi-dimensional problem which calls for concerted efforts from multiple fronts – the government, the private sector, businesses and the community at large. In this regard, regional consortia, blocs and forums such as SADC, COMESA, NEPAD have formed groupings with a view of coming up with amalgamated efforts in the formation of policies and setting of an enabling environment for e-Commerce to thrive. These international efforts have attempted to identify the most important policy issues relating to e-Commerce. The new generation of African leaders has shown a commitment towards the need for greater consistency in these national and regional e-Commerce approaches. This is in conformance with the United Nations Commission on International Trade Law (UNCITRAL) which drafted the Model Law on Electronic Commerce in 1996 (IDRC, 2007). The Model Law's aim was to provide the basis for countries to develop their national polices with the aim of creating a more secure legal environment for electronic commerce.

Many countries, enterprises and parastatals have now started employing mobile commerce (m-Commerce) as a new form of e-Commerce in a bit to reach more market players and consumers. The idea of the mobile market place is for services to be offered anywhere and anytime. With the rate at which the African mobile industries and networks (wireless local area networks (WLANs), wireless local loops (WLL), satellite based networks, mobile Internet protocol (IP), and wireless asynchronous transfer mode (ATM) networks, GSM and CDMA technology) are growing, m-commerce is likely to have significant impact in Africa. This chapter defines m-Commerce as the buying and selling of goods and services using information and communication technology (ICT) gadgets such as mobile telephones, the internet or personal digital assistants (PDAs). As e-Commerce, it also involves the interaction of businesses, government and the consumer: B2B, B2C, B2G and C2C. M-Commerce applications are a form of e-Commerce with high prospects to being encapsulated into the African socio-economic frameworks. As Mensah et al. (2005) puts it, approximately 0.03 per cent of Africans own bank accounts, compared to 6 per cent of Africans who have a mobile telephone. Jukic et al. (2009) defines m-Commerce as an extension of conventional, Internet-based e-Commerce, which adds a different mode of network and accommodates different end users' characteristics. It can also be defined as a platform for conducting commercial transactions via a "mobile" telecommunications network using a communication, information, and payment (CIP) device such as a mobile phone or a palmtop unit (Muller-Veerse, 1999). As aforementioned, one major plus in implementing m-Commerce applications is that they have an influence on the market dynamics thereby directly impacting on the level of interaction between the seller and the buyer. The major characteristic of m-Commerce is that it has to have a mobile network. Jukic et al. (2009) state that a mobile network has basically two characteristics: The first is the ability to maintain communication between non-static locations and the second critical feature is the capability to keep track of the location. Although m-Commerce comes with many advantages compared to e-Commerce when implemented in the African setup, it is still imperative to address the issues of e-Commerce before we transcend to m-Commerce applications as these issues can still spill-over to m-Commerce when it is applied at advanced stages. The m-Commerce business model can thrive in South Africa. South Africa has an advanced e-readiness index and is a country considered to be where information resource utilization has thrived (Ifinedo, 2005). Since third-generation mobile technology can provide broadband access, mobile communications are expected to play an increasing role in making high-speed Internet available in developing countries (UN MDGs Report, 2009).

Given this background, it is clear that the way forward in Africa's e-Commerce applications is to encourage the adoption of m-Commerce applications through massive awareness campaigns. This is because Africa is adopting mobile technologies (e.g. wireless networks) at a faster rate than static technologies such as broadband internet access due to higher costs and lack of established networks.

This chapter aims to outline some of the policy mechanisms and implementation strategies that have been adopted in the SADC bloc and provides some perspectives on the various initiatives that have been embedded in various programming mechanisms at various national levels of the

countries in the SADC bloc. The different policies are being looked at as efforts towards creating an enabling environment to allow countries to stimulate and develop niche markets in the global economy. The chapter looks at status of adoption of e-Commerce in South Africa, Mozambique, Zimbabwe and Botswana (representative of the SADC bloc). Further, it looks at the mobile phone subscription and internet penetration rates in the SADC region, level of trust in these business models, awareness of these business models and the different challenges that come with the implementation of e-Commerce business models. The chapter also investigates how the success of e-Commerce can spill-over to SMEs in the SADC region which are at the helm of this technology and business model. At the end of the chapter, a look at the way forward of these new business models is investigated and recommendations of what SADC countries should do if such models were to be a success is given.

Next, the background section where characteristics of e-Commerce, the general adoption trends of e-Commerce in the SADC region, and the factors affecting the adoption of e-Commerce are discussed is presented. Then, the exploratory studies covering the aforementioned countries are presented. Thereafter, e-Commerce penetration in the SADC bloc covering the SADC institution, legal and regulatory framework of e-Commerce is discussed. After that, the chapter discusses the way forward for e-Commerce encapsulation into SADC regional and national socio-economic cultures. At the end of the chapter, further research directions and the conclusion are given.

BACKGROUND

a) Characteristics of e-Commerce

The implementation of e-Commerce applications has always been looked at as a value-adding preposition to SMEs and other business entities. The major characteristics of e-Commerce implementation have been a global marketplace with better profit margins and easy access to market players e.g. service or product consumers. This is coupled with a reduction in various expenses related to product or service marketing (advertising product or service awareness campaigns), order processing requests, customer relations and inventory management, information storage and telecommunications, etc. There are main benefits attributed to e-Commerce applications as evidenced by the increased interaction between the consumer and the producer of services. Schwab Entrepreneur (2003) ascertains that in any e-Commerce establishment, creating effective payment channels is a necessary condition for e-Commerce development and for bringing down overall transaction costs. Chege et al. (2002) further ascertains that e-Commerce accords people the opportunity to participate in a global marketplace unrestricted by geographical barriers or boundaries; accessibility to information improving the competitiveness of firms, leveling the playing field leading to improved customer service and satisfaction. The Green Paper on e-Commerce for South Africa (2000) identifies the following as the main benefits to e-Commerce adoption: Improved response time, reduced competitive prices, improved competitive positioning, increased consumer convenience and choice, ease of concluding deals and financial transactions, extended global market reach, increased revenue potential and improved and convenient customer service (Lehlokoe & Malema, 2000).

M-Commerce has been defined as a new version of e-Commerce which has shown a lot of success propensity in African environments. This can be evidenced by the extent of basic cellular phone usage in Africa which is a good enough indicator of the magnitude of wireless potential (Jukic et al., 2009). Apart from the many different versions of e-Commerce definitions given in the previous section, kuo and Yu (2005) quoting from Mylonopoulos and Doukidis (2003) describes m-Commerce as an interactive ecology system of individuals and corporations, and this ecology system is built upon the social economic background and various succeeding technologies. Through the applications of wireless and mobile technologies, it is a learning process that the two parties jointly create brand new experiences within social interactions. Thus, m-Commerce is being succinctly defined as follows: through any highly mobile device and wireless communication network, activities related to commerce transaction, data access, network service, and so on, processed without any boundaries of time and space; or intended to promote business operations and the efficiency of commercial procedures are within the coverage of m-Commerce.

There are several advantages and disadvantages associated with e-Commerce applications. The e-Commerce debate forum for South Africa has identified the following as some of the major advantages of e-Commerce:

- E-Commerce offers a considerable degree of economic growth to any kind of business, especially the SMEs. By opting to employ e-Commerce, you can expand your market margins to global horizons or squeeze them to highly focused market segments, as per subjective business acumen and discretion.

- Enables the application of innovative business models or process re-engineering and implementation of higher degree of specialization or enhancing productivity and customer care.

- Enables the sharpening of a business's marketing and promotion strategies to be remarkably on target by observing customer's ordering patterns.

- As regards business partners, e-Commerce aids in minimizing supply chain inefficiencies, bringing about reduced inventory requirement and lessened delivery delays, thereby rendering you more confident about your business collaborations with your suppliers and service companies.

Some of the disadvantages of e-Commerce applications are the following:

- E-Commerce overdependence on the internet makes it unsuitable to a large chunk of people who have not embraced internet as an integral part of their lifestyles. Its motivation of universal market reach is not achieved in places where internet penetration rates leave much to be desired.
- Many people, especially in Africa, are yet to invest full trust on e-Commerce applications because of privacy and security issues as they face a dilemma each time they need to divulge highly personal information online.
- Lack of so many people with the keen interest of investing their time in fully exploiting the advantages that online transactions have to offer.

As has been outlined, there are many advantages that are associated with e-Commerce applications and these can be enjoyed when all the barriers for e-Commerce applications have been dealt with. Looking at the disadvantages of e-Commerce applications outlined above, it is worth noting their overdependence on internet as a communications medium. For the case of Africa where mobile (wireless) communications are being encapsulated into the socio-economic cultures at a faster rate, it is important to move to m-Commerce. Whether it is e-Commerce or m-Commerce, there are challenges that need to be overcome to harness their full potential. The next section looks at the different factors that affect the adoption of e-Commerce by ordinary citizens.

b) General Adoption Trends of e-Commerce in the SADC Region

Generally, there has been low volume of e-Commerce activity and adoption in the SADC region probably due to the major market players' reluctance to carry out awareness campaigns for e-Commerce, among other reasons. South Africa, however, has shown a higher propensity to e-business transactions in such a way e-Commerce characteristics in South Africa straddle the line between developed and developing countries. The Google country directory currently records about 6 942 South African websites and there is a growing incidence of on-line consumer purchasing e.g. the most successful www.computicket. com. Other countries such as Zambia, Botswana and Zimbabwe show a potential for growth in e-Commerce applications but lack volatile fiscal policies for creating an enabling environment for their growth. This can be evidenced by the large number of people accessing the internet as shown in the Table 1.

Table 1 has shown that a sizable number of people in the SADC region have access to the internet. However, it is wrong to assume that these people go online for e-Commerce's sake. This data provided suggests there is a sizable number of people accessing the internet and if all the constraints that hinder fruitful e-Commerce applications are taken care of, and proper awareness campaigns are instituted, then there are chances that e-Commerce can thrive in the SADC bloc.

The level of adoption of e-Commerce in the SADC region encompasses two groups: a) countries that have a more developed ICT infrastructure than the rest and to an appreciable extent participate in the e-world. These are South Africa, Seychelles, Mauritius, Tanzania and Uganda. These countries also face serious challenges such as shortage of skilled manpower, bad socio-economic conditions, exorbitant subscription fees, no regulatory frameworks, and relatively low level of PC penetration. b) Countries with a potential to

Table 1. Internet penetration in the SADC region (2009)

AFRICA	Population (2009Est.)	Internet Users Dec/2000	Internet Users Latest Data	Penetration (% Population)	User Growth (2000-2009)	% Users in Africa
Angola	12,799,293	30,000	**550,000**	4.3%	1,733.3%	0.8%
Botswana	1,990,876	15,000	**100,000**	5.0%	566.7%	0.2%
Lesotho	2,130,819	4,000	**73,300**	3.4%	1,732.5%	0.1%
Madagascar	20,653,556	30,000	**316,100**	1.5%	953.7%	0.5%
Malawi	15,028,757	15,000	**139,500**	0.9%	830.0%	0.2%
Mauritius	1,284,264	87,000	**380,000**	29.6%	336.8%	0.6%
Mozambique	21,669,278	30,000	**350,000**	1.6%	1,066.7%	0.5%
Namibia	2,108,665	30,000	**113,500**	5.4%	278.3%	0.2%
Rwanda	10,746,311	5,000	**300,000**	2.8%	5,900.0%	0.5%
Seychelles	87,476	6,000	**32,000**	36.6%	433.3%	0.0%
South Africa	49,052,489	2,400,000	**4,590,000**	9.4%	91.3%	7.0%
Swaziland	1,337,186	10,000	**48,200**	3.6%	382.0%	0.1%
Tanzania	41,048,532	115,000	**520,000**	1.3%	352.2%	0.8%
Uganda	32,369,558	40,000	**2,500,000**	7.7%	6,150.0%	3.8%
Zambia	11,862,740	20,000	**700,000**	5.9%	3,400.0%	1.1%
Zimbabwe	11,392,629	50,000	**1,421,000**	12.5%	2,742.0%	2.2%

Source: Internet World Stats (August, 2009) - http://www.internetworldstats.com/stats1.htm

further develop e-Commerce transactions. These are Namibia, Botswana, Swaziland, Lesotho, DRC, Zimbabwe, Angola, Malawi, Zambia, and Mozambique (SADC report, 2002). Namibia and Botswana shows significant growth and potential to participate in the e-world having put in place acceptable regulatory and policy frameworks, awareness campaigns to support e-Commerce penetration. It is anticipated that continued growth in these countries might see them moving into Group 1 in the near future.

c) Factors Affecting Citizen Adoption of e-Commerce

Apart from a few countries such as South Africa, Egypt and Kenya, there are very few countries that have adopted online transactions to any appreciable extent due to a couple of reasons. There are many factors that have contributed to the low adoption rates of e-Commerce by ordinary Africans. Mensah et al. (2005) relates this to Africans not being aware of the major opportunities that are offered by e-Commerce. This can be attributed to lack of awareness campaigns to the masses on the benefits of e-Commerce applications. Another major reason for the slow adoption of e-Commerce applications can be the paucity in internet penetration rates coupled with undeveloped ICT infrastructures. Also, the institutional, legal and regulatory frameworks to curb the different issues that come with online transactions have not been put in place in Africa. The other larger factor limiting the growth of e-Commerce in Africa has been lack of consumer protection. If a person's information or money has been stolen, in most cases, there are no legal frameworks and instruments to bring the culprit to book. Most countries in Africa are cash-based, limiting the adoption of online payments using credit cards. Local culture is also one factor that has an impact on the adoption rates of e/m-Commerce.

There are also other factors that have an impact on the adoption and implementation of e/m-Commerce. Chege et al. (2002) has outlined the implications that come with cross-border e-Commerce applications. Different countries have different legal systems and this could present a problem when trying to enforce contracts in different countries. Other challenges are the lack of technologically advanced telecommunications infrastructure, lack of legal and regulatory frameworks supportive of ICT developments and the high rate of illiteracy (ECA-CORDIST, 2009). Rahmati (2008), also quoting Markus and Soh (2002), suggested that in addition to examining the impact of national culture on the adoption of m-Commerce one should not lose sight of physical, social and economic arrangements that shape e-Commerce business models and influence individual use of these technologies. In addition to the e-Commerce adoption factors mentioned here, it is only possible to implement and operate e-Commerce initiatives if there are modern banking and insurance firms operating, and these do not exist in most African countries. It is also important to raise awareness and to offer training programs that target the business community in particular and the public in general (Mensah et al., 2005).

During an ECA/IDRC study in 2000/01, it was found that businesses and others in the North African countries of Egypt, Morocco and Tunisia were adopting ecommerce and recognized the important role of government in setting up the appropriate conditions within which e-Commerce can be developed (Mensah et al., 2005). The same survey covered three countries in Southern Africa (Mozambique, Namibia and South Africa) and found that e-Commerce had a "high profile in only one of the three countries surveyed at this time, although processes are under way in the other two which could lead to more attention to the issues involved"(Mensah et al., 2005). The reason behind this could be that South Africa has put in appropriate regulatory and institutional frameworks and incentives such as the Green Pa-

per on e-Commerce, outlining thorough analyses of what needs to be done, coupled with proper awareness campaigns.

To get a feeling of the actual level of e-Commerce adoption and encapsulation into socio-economic frameworks of the SADC block, let's look at the different exploratory studies from different countries of SADC. Four (4) countries are surveyed: Botswana, Zimbabwe, Mozambique and South Africa. These represent the two groups of levels of e-Commerce adoption outlined above and I feel this is representative enough of the bloc. By looking at the 4 countries, it will be known how e-Commerce has been used in different economic fronts, what benefits have been experienced and what challenges have been met.

EXPLORATORY STUDIES

a) Botswana

Botswana has been referred to as an emerging economic powerhouse due to its fast growing economy and rich diamonds reserves and cattle industry. It is situated in Southern Africa just north of South Africa. It is completely landlocked and has a semi-arid climate. Botswana has a population of about 1.6 million and is a parliamentary republic. The GDP in 2008 was 526.04 billion dollars. Through fiscal discipline and sound management, Botswana has transformed itself from one of the poorest countries in the world to a middle-income country with a per capita GDP of nearly $15,800 in 2008. The economy is structured with agriculture still providing a livelihood for more than 80% of the population but supplies only about 50% of food needs and accounts for only 3% of GDP. Substantial mineral deposits were found in the 1970s and the mining sector grew from 25% of GDP in 1980 to 38% in 1998 (COMNET-IT 2002).

Mobile penetration has passed the 80% mark, almost three times the continent's average. A nationwide fibre backbone network supports a wide range of services, and this landlocked country's access to international bandwidth is being improved. Broadband services are available in the form of ADSL and various wireless technologies, including a city-wide WiMAX network in the capital Gaborone, launched in mid-2008.

While much hesitation is evident on e-Commerce technology in Botswana, there is hope that it will be fully adopted in business environments in the near future as this is evidenced by the escalating number of companies now attempting to employ e-Commerce. The many players in the e-Commerce market of Botswana have done some awareness campaigns on the potential of e-Commerce. Most organizations including hotels are offering online payment options. Financial organizations such as First National Bank Botswana, Barclays Bank of Botswana are now offering Mobile Banking having realized the potential that this kind of business model has on their returns. Another business offering e-Commerce applications is the Botswana Craft (http://www.botswanacraft.bw) which has shopping cart facilities and accepts Visa and MasterCard.

Botswana has an appropriate legal and institutional framework and has granted appropriate powers to the regulatory authority to enable it to function fully. However, it is required that power be extended to include regulatory ICT. Botswana has inadequate policies for development of ICT infrastructure and it does not have appropriate policies for maximizing benefit. There is also no existence of any policies relating to creating trust in the digital economy (which has a direct impact on the growth of e-Commerce), reforming the legal system to enable it to cope with a paperless economy or recognizing and protecting Intellectual Property Rights in electronic data (SADC Report, 2002). Botswana proposed a Cybercrime Bill in 2007 which may contribute a great deal to the development of e-Commerce in Botswana.

b) Zimbabwe

Despite having been disturbed by a decade-old deep political and economic crisis, the e-Commerce landscape in Zimbabwe has not been hard hit. After the signing off of the unity government, things like dwindling local currency, hyperinflation is slowly being done away with. Growth of the country's three mobile networks has been slowed down, but an immense pent-up demand is now being addressed with major infrastructure upgrades, including the introduction of 3G mobile and other wireless broadband services. It is worth noting that Zimbabwe's backbone network is being upgraded, including fibre optic links which also improve Internet connectivity. A power-sharing agreement reached on the political level following violent elections in March 2008 is seen as a first step towards Zimbabwe's efforts to reclaiming its foregone economic place in Africa.

The ICT infrastructure backbone is relatively developed in comparison to other SADC countries. Out of a total of 19 commercial banks that are operational in the country, 12 offer online services. There are a large number of ATMs installed (compared to other SADC countries). There are also a large number of credit card, debit card and smart card users in Zimbabwe. The ICT skill levels within Zimbabwean society are not the lowest, but are far from exemplary. Strong development in education is necessary to ensure Zimbabwe's e-readiness standing. Further, the Institutional framework of Zimbabwe is appropriate although it can be improved through extending the power of the regulator and ministry regarding ICTs. Zimbabwe does not seem to have appropriate policies aimed at developing infrastructure for ICT. However, Zimbabwe has extensive policies and programs for taking advantage of opportunities created by ICT top maximize benefits (SADC Report, 2002).

The penetration of e-Commerce in Zimbabwe is thwarted by a number of factors including the high cost in ICT procurement and roll-out strategies to the door steps of the people. Ndlovu (2009) mentions that despite Zimbabweans being of an average IT literacy standing, they do not engage in ICT activities because the ICT infrastructure is not very much developed. Computer and internet penetration, and correspondingly e-Commerce adoption, is very low in Zimbabwe due to the cost of owning a PC or MAC and the cost of having an internet connection. Another problem that has contributed to low adoption rates of e-Commerce has been unreliable supply of electricity as inadequate power generation and unreliable transmission and distribution capacity has a direct impact on ICT development strategies (Ndlovu, 2009).

Another ICT usage component that is directly used to measure e-Commerce is the use of ICT gadgets and the internet technology in electronic banking. Dube et al. (2009) investigated the current status of adoption and use of internet banking (IB) in Zimbabwe. In their study, they found out that while the Zimbabwean banking sector is significantly well developed technologically in comparison with other African banking systems, internet banking is not being fully utilized by banks and consumers alike as seventy five percent (75%) of the banks on average use fifty percent (50%) and below of the internet banking capacity. The study recommended that banks in Zimbabwe should vigorously promote the usage of IB among customers while policy makers such as the Government and the Reserve Bank of Zimbabwe should increase investments targeted at infrastructure development so as to encourage banks and individuals alike to adopt the innovation (Dube et al., 2009).

On the policy front, Zimbabwe is committed to putting in place a society with an acceptable level of e-readiness. Zimbabwe is now pursuing more rigorous wireless last mile connection technologies like Wi-Max, Wi-Fi, 3G, CDMA etc. Already, Powertel and Telone are involved in CDMA rollouts in and around Harare (Ndlovu, 2009). The regulatory framework is also well-established. With these interventions, it is anticipated that e-

Commerce will at long last be adequately adopted in the socio-economic frameworks of Zimbabwe.

c) Mozambique

Mozambique has been referred to as one of the fastest-growing economies on the African continent following its long stench of civil wars. The mobile sub-sector in Mozambique has experienced excellent growth rates following the introduction of competition in 2003, but market penetration is still well below the African average. Internet usage has increased in recent years following the introduction of various kinds of broadband services, and the mobile operators have entered this market segment with the launch of mobile data services. Further improvements can be expected from the ongoing rollout of 3G mobile services and a national fibre backbone network as well as the arrival of the first international submarine fibre optic cable to the country's shores in 2009.

The adoption of e-Commerce in Mozambique has been thwarted by limitation in the development of the ICT infrastructure. This is expected as Mozambique cannot afford novel ICT infrastructure developments as it is one of the least developed and poorest countries in the world. In 1997, Mozambique initiated the e-Commerce policies which were officiated in 2000. The current situation is that Mozambique is rolling out sacrifice policies, deliberate initiatives to develop efficient e-Commerce supporting infrastructure such as reliable electivity supply to supply the functionality of different ICT gadgets. These policies have also included the funding, with support of UNDP, of workshops for user training, and development of e-content. Also, within this framework, Mozambique has subscribed to the Pan African e-Commerce initiative with AISI's conduction of different e-Commerce workshops nationwide. Despite these initiatives, Mozambique's commercial banks do not have central communication links between them. This may have an impact, albeit a negative one, on e-Commerce penetration.

Mozambique's ICT industry continues to be in a bad state. There are 0.9 PCs per 1000 people and a small proportion of the population uses the Internet. The dial-up fees for Internet connection are not very high compared to regional averages. Only 7% of households in Mozambique have access to electricity. This effectively limits any kind of electronic transaction (SADC Report, 2002). The skill levels of the population to participate in the electronic world from a general educational viewpoint are mediocre. There are a few schools that have access to the Internet which do not impact on the future e-readiness of Mozambique. Mozambique has a rudimentary ICT policy and regulatory framework. It does not appear to have sufficient policies for infrastructure development as aforementioned. There are extensive projects aimed at maximizing benefits but they are not aimed at delivering services through ICT applications (SADC Report, 2002).

The last two years has seen Mozambique undertaking legal and regulatory reform and has integrated the idea of ICT as an integral enabler of socio-economic development as a national strategic imperative. Yet, despite these positive developments on a policy level, Mozambique is still plagued by low levels of infrastructure development and low HDI value as a result of the effect of damaging civil wars. Not much has been done in as far as ICT infrastructure development is concerned.

d) South Africa

South Africa is the leader of e-Commerce, not only in the SADC region, but in Africa at large although further economic growth and ICT development should take place before it can be compared to developed and other developing countries such as South Korea, Brazil and Singapore. The South African telecommunications infrastructure is quite developed, the ICT literacy levels are above Africa's average, there are sound regulatory, institutional and legal frameworks, and appro-

priate ICT usage awareness campaigns. The ICT landscape in South Africa presents an enabling environment for the growth of e-Commerce. The important contribution to South Africa's e-Commerce adoption strength is e-Commerce legislation in 2001 and the Green Paper of e-Commerce (2000) which outlined the different strategies for the growth of e-Commerce in South Africa. Another important development was the creation of the State Information Technology Agency, SITA, in April, 1999. These initiatives are further complimented by the department of Communications (DoC) which has launched a series of initiatives under the collective label of the "Info.Com 2025" program, which seeks to achieve broad-based growth and equitable development through communications and information technologies (COMNET-IT, 2002). South Africa has an appropriate institutional framework and has granted appropriate powers to the regulatory authority to enable it to function properly. South Africa has appropriate policies aimed at creating trust in the digital economy, reforming the legal systems to cope with paperless economy and recognizing and protecting intellectual property in electronic data (SADC Report, 2002).

The ITU Report (2009) mentions that South Africa is the largest African economy; ranked 87th in the world (10 places down from 2002) and is the top among Sub-Saharan economies. Despite this rhetoric, the country needs to do more in enabling its citizens have access to and use ICTs. International Internet bandwidth is only 852 bits/s/user (which is similar to Ethiopia, compared to, for example, Tunisia with 1800 bits/s/user) and only 4.8 per cent of households had access to the Internet in 2007 (ITU Report, 2009).

Unlike Mozambique, South Africa has dedicated initiatives to further develop its ICT infrastructure both from the policy and implementation fronts. It is currently the leader in the convergence of telecommunication and information technologies thus positioning itself as potential e-Commerce leader. Some of the initiatives done in this regard have been the legalization of VoIP Internet telephony in 2005, investing of billions of dollars by various stakeholders into IP-based Next Generation Networks capable of delivering converged services more efficiently, encouraging telecom carriers and ISPs into delivering audio and video content over their networks, arrival of new international submarine fibre optic cables to the country's shores in 2009, implementation of their own fibre and broadband networks by many municipalities and major metro areas, the issuance of mobile TV licenses (as expected in 2009), and the putting in place of an enabling environment for the digital media to reach a level of development to foster an associated advertising and marketing industry, etc. These interventions, which are done both from the private and public sectors, have made sure that e-Commerce is made to develop as online advertising and payments in South Africa grew at the fastest rate among all countries in the English-speaking world in 2008 and is likely to repeat this performance in years to come.

South Africa closely follows the UNCITRAL Model Law on Electronic Commerce and it is being looked at as a basis to introduce primary legislation on commercial transacting (in particular to deal with legal recognition of data messages, contracting by electronic means, jurisdiction and evidence). In addition to the aforementioned interventions, concrete initiatives done to develop e-Commerce in South Africa have been the following: Discussion paper launched in July 1999; Stakeholder working group submissions collated November 1999; Green Paper: issued November 2000; E-Law Conference: Stakeholders invited to discuss proposed framework/outline of the Bill and make recommendations; E-Bill (2nd quarter 2001) dealing with legislative issues; E-Legislation: to be passed (3rd quarter 2001) and promulgated before the end of the year; and policy Directions (beyond e-legislation) including policy positions, regulations and guidelines and self-regulatory measures - contracts, industry norms and practices, codes.

For the banking sector, South Africa has put in place the WIZZIT initiative, a startup mobile banking provider that offers a transaction banking account accessible via mobile phone and debit card. The company operates as a division of the South African Bank of Athens, targeting 16 million people (48 per cent of adults) who are unbanked or who have difficulties in having access to formal financial services. Since its launch in December 2004, WIZZIT has more than 50,000 customers (ECA report, 2009).

The different efforts towards institutionalization of e-Commerce / m-Commerce business models in South Africa are slowly paying off. The South Africa's case can be an example to the other African countries that want to engulf e-business models into their socio-economic setups. In summary, the ICT densities, which may be partially related to the adoption levels of e-Commerce for the countries surveyed in this chapter, but Zimbabwe, are shown in the table below.

Africans have realized that for them to benefit from what e-Commerce or m-Commerce has to offer, there is need to put in place acceptable ICT infrastructures. The Internet Society (ISOC) and AfriNIC (African Network Information Center) infrastructure project have rolled out a collabora-

Table 2. ICT Densities in 2007 (Source: ITU Database 2008)

	Internet Users per 100 inhabitants	Main (fixed) telephone lines per 100 inhabitants	Mobile cellular telephone subscribers per 100 inhabitants
Botswana	4.25	7.68	75.84
Mozambique	0.93	0.33	15.42
South Africa	8.16	9.56	87.08

tive project aiming to establish national Internet eXchange Points (IXPs) where service providers can peer, hence allowing faster access to Web sites and paper (Chabossou et Al., 2009). The Economic Comission of Africa (ECA) has delved to continue working with its member States to support e-Commerce and especially m- Commerce activities from a policy perspective, including incorporating privacy and data protection, security, wireless regulatory (Mensah et al., 2005). These initiatives are paving way for further adoption of m-Commerce in the African business culture.

E-COMMERCE PENETRATION IN THE SADC REGION

a) General Perspective

As partially shown in the exploratory studies above, the SADC region shows a lot of disparities in the adoption levels of e-Commerce. The status of e-Commerce in SADC countries appears to be largely divided into three categories (IDRC 2006):

• Countries such as South Africa and Mauritius, clearly spelled out e-Commerce vision and achieved an appropriate legal structure supporting e-Commerce penetration;

• Countries such as Botswana and Seychelles that have recognized the potential of e-Commerce but are still developing the facilities and environment it; and

• Countries such as the Democratic Republic of Congo and Angola, where establishing an effective Internet infrastructure still poses a major national challenge.

The different levels in e-Commerce adoption can be attributed to a wide range of reasons and factors: Technical factors such as limitation in telecommunications infrastructure (high costs in telecommunications-related services and availability of computers); human factors (availability of trained people and lack of policy research capacity in e-Commerce); and, policy and structural factors (legal and policy environment established by the government; and integrative mechanisms).

Limitation in telecommunications infrastructure is evident even throughout the whole of Africa thus having an impact on the level of adoption of e-Commerce. Generally, Africa has the lowest telephone densities (main lines per 100 inhabitants) in the world. The continent has only 2% of world telephone lines. Africa has 35 of the world's 49 countries with least developed telecommunication infrastructures in the world, and until quite recently, the continent has had the lowest annual growth in teledensity (Ajayi, 2002). For the case of South Africa, as afore-hinted, the ICT landscape is adequately regulated. South Africa is in transition from being a monopoly (TELKOM) to being a duopoly of TELKOM and SNO (Pehrson and Ngwira, 2006)

b) SADC Institution, Legal and Regulatory Frameworks of E-Commerce

SADC, with a view of promoting e-Commerce growth in the region, has put in place appropriate institutional, legal and regulatory instruments. The first initiative towards the development of the ICT infrastructure was the putting in place of the SADC Protocol on transport, communications and Meteorology in 1996. This protocol had the following milestones: Development of a regional policy and regulatory framework; provision of universal service; deployment of the relevant infrastructure; and capacity building. In 2002, SADC published a paper: Policy guidelines on making ICT a priority in turning SADC into an Information Based Economy and created the following specialized associations to undertake specific tasks:

- **TRASA (1997) now CRASA:** established to coordinate and harmonize regulatory issues in the sub-region as a result of accelerated transformation in the sector.
- **SATA:** formed with the objective of harmonizing interconnectivity in terms of setting up of radio, fiber and microwave backbone links in the Region (SRII)

Another initiative was the SADC's declaration on ICT which aimed at achieving efficient communication and information exchange; with special consideration to, Rural and remote areas; under-privileged urban areas; education; health; gender and media grouping. This declaration identified 5 priority implementation areas which are: Regulatory environment for ICT; infrastructure for ICT development; community participation and governance in ICT development; ICT in business development (such as e-Commerce and m-Commerce); and human resource capacity for ICT development.

The most recent initiative, and directly related to the development of e-Commerce, has been the E-SADC (regional ICT strategy). This strategy aims at addressing all the major aspects of e-applications including e-Commerce, e-education, e-health, e-agriculture, e-government, and e-parliament. This initiative/ framework aims to achieve harmonization and coordination of national efforts as an integration strategy. The implementation of E-SADC will seek to achieve the harmonization of national policy and regulatory frameworks, creation of a framework for the development of ICT infrastructure, strengthening capacity at the sub-regional level in ICT for development and building a critical mass to facilitate regional integration through ICTs.

A look at the different initiatives and strategies employed by SADC, it is evident to note that the regional grouping has realized that universal and affordable access to information infrastructures is the single, biggest growth factor for e-Commerce. Appropriate regulation and liberalization of the

markets entails that prices charged by telecommunications operators for access to crucial services can be lowered to be an affordable level for ordinary citizens. This is because the pricing trend is a major factor in determining the effectiveness and affordability of e-Commerce / m-Commerce opportunities on the whole. As the ECA report (2009) puts it, Africa is well placed in exploring the new opportunities presented by m-Banking (m-Commerce) as it has core demand for such services. It is worth mentioning that these fiscal policies for encouraging the development of e/m-Commerce should be adapted to the country level to adapt to the local conditions as the context may be unique for any different country.

Having looked at the current status of e/m-Commerce adoption in the SADC region and what interventions are being authored at regional level, let's now look at what should be done to consolidate e/m-Commerce applications and move forward.

E-Commerce Consolidating and Moving Forward

The many challenges that come with the implementation of e-Commerce should be known from context to context if adoption of e-Commerce can be realized. The cases explored in the SADC region have shown that while there are disparities in the uptake of e-Commerce in different African countries, there is reason to believe that the situation is likely to change in the near future. This is because there is commitment from multiple fronts on encouraging the encapsulation of e/m-Commerce in different socio-economic setups. On the policy front, a lot has been highlighted what has, and is being done. One question that immediately pops up is: Are these policy interventions maturing into implementations? What is the major line of interventions that should be done in order to make sure that a level ground is set for e/m-Commerce development in the SADC region? Are the ordinary citizens in the SADC seeing and realizing the benefits of e/m-Commerce implementations and what are the awareness campaigns being put in place to encourage adoption of e/m-Commerce? Answers to these and other questions in this line need to be found in order to push the adoption and encapsulation of e/m-Commerce in the SADC block further. The following outlines some of the interventions that are desirable to improve e/m-Commerce implementation landscape in the SADC regions:

- Since mobile and wireless communications are being adopted at a very faster rate in the African context, it is logically coherent to ascertain that the variant version of e-Commerce which is m-Commerce be encouraged. It is assumed that when m-Commerce business model is adopted, more people in the market will be reached.

- Before any deliberate policies are drawn for encouraging e/m-Commerce, there is need for African countries to make sure that appropriate ICT backbone infrastructures are put in place. This can be done by erecting reliable and costless fibre infrastructures for faster data transmission rates. Hotspots, base stations and adequate GSM coverage need to be installed so that all mobile agents are captured to promote anytime, anywhere business models (m-Commerce).

- There should be proper market regulation in the ICT sector. This can be achieved by putting in place sound ICT policies that favor growth of e-applications such as e-Commerce, e-Governance, e-Health, etc. whilst it is important that local regulatory instruments be authored, there is need to start with a regional policy framework and then adapt it to the local conditions. Existing "model laws" and codes should be adopted where applicable. SADC countries should join a uniform legislative initiative to avoid divergent legal approaches, establish basic rules of cross-border e-trade and

to facilitate legal and technical interoperability. In this regard, African governments need to act on their responsibility for creating an economic, legal and regulatory environment that will enable and foster the growth of e-Commerce within their national economies. Each government should develop and publicize a specific agenda, accompanied by a proposed timetable, for the actions that it will undertake to create an enabling environment for e-Commerce within its national economy.

- Encourage in-depth discussions on legal, social, economic and technological aspects and implications of policies for the facilitation of e-Commerce.

- Promote and raise awareness at door-steps and community levels (general public/consumers), policy makers, and producers; these awareness campaigns should be pursued through the most common ways through which the community can be reached. This can be through public platforms such as the television, radio programs, or even drama. A concerted educational campaign is necessary to educate the public about the benefits and pitfalls of e-Commerce services, and to strengthen their consumer rights and consumer voice.

- There is need to create a stakeholders forum where both the private and the public players are given a platform to interact and exchange ideas. This will make sure that the concerns of even smaller market players are taken into consideration in the development of the e/m-Commerce strategy.

- There should be targeted support for SMEs and special target groups. This support can come in form of putting in place an intermediation service capable of connecting African e-business start-ups with prospective players in the developed world for sole purpose of exchange of ideas and technology. This may help create e/m-Commerce incubators and help identify research and help locate market niches for African e-entrepreneurs.

- Because it has been identified that skilled manpower on e/m-Commerce fundamental principles in the SADC region may be lacking, it is important a region labor pool on e/m-Commerce be established. This can be achieved by putting in place strategic training programs and mechanisms using ICTs thereby developing effective e-business mentoring, twinning and intermediation mechanisms.
- It is important to put in place vibrant legal frameworks so that both the consumer and the producer of a service in the e/m-Commerce platform are protected.
- It is important to make sure that there is a guided policy on e/m-Commerce. This will guide e/m-Commerce policy development which requires very specialized expertise in areas such as taxation, online contracting and intellectual property. This policy development should be done through a consultative process through awareness-raising workshops and launches, with a wide spectrum of participation from government, industry, NGOs, academia.

FUTURE RESEARCH DIRECTIONS

The changing of a paradigm to an m-Commerce centric is much more feasible in the SADC bloc given the rate at which mobile technology adoption is growing and the paucity in static ICT infrastructure. Traditional Internet access through stationery computers is limited in the SADC bloc. This is because of exorbitant rates charged to access it, and its compromising network throughput and data latency. However, mobile phones are a must-have for a majority of citizens in this part of Africa. Telecommunications companies have opted to provide access to the internet through

mobile phones (using Wireless Access Protocol) or any related mobile technologies such as Personal Digital Assistants (PDAs). Also, in many cases do you find public places such as restaurants or airports installed with vibrant hotspots for Wi-Fi internet access on mobile devises e.g. a laptop. This presents an opportunity where m-Commerce can reach many potential consumers as more people can now have internet access through conventional means. M-Commerce implementation in the SADC bloc presents a huge opportunity which should be tapped.

Future research directions should focus on how mobile commerce should actually be pursued with an emphasis on how trust should be encouraged when using these platforms and what is the level of legal security. Also, future work should investigate what is the best way to encourage adoption of m-Commerce by ordinary individuals especially those in remotest parts of the SADC bloc.

CONCLUSION

This chapter has described what e-Commerce is, and what the adoption factors pertaining the same are and what the different challenges that are faced in its implementation are. Following the rapid growth in adoption of basic ICTs especially mobile technologies, this chapter has looked at how a new business model of a mobile marketplace is being engulfed in the SADCs socio-economic hierarchy. It has been shown that m-Commerce has a lot of potential in Africa because over two thirds of the potential target consumers by the SMEs and other business establishments are known to possess a mobile phone with internet access. To investigate the issues surrounding the successful implementation of e/m-Commerce models in the SADC bloc, four countries: Botswana, Zimbabwe, Mozambique and South Africa, have been investigated. This is because it is considered that the four countries present all the bands of the socio-economic spectrum of the SADC bloc and therefore are representative enough.

The exploratory studies have reviewed different adoption statuses, e-readiness of individual countries towards encapsulation of e/m-Commerce models, and perception of ordinary citizens on the e-business models. Issues of lack of adequate ICT infrastructure, lack of policy implementation follow-ups, lack of awareness campaigns to the ordinary citizens on the opportunities that come with e/m-Commerce implementation, the paucity of internet penetration rates, lack of consumer protection, and lack of trust in online applications have emerged as major issues. It is suffice to emphasize that at the region level, SADC has put in place appropriate institutional, legal and regulatory frameworks to encourage the development of e-business models. The onus is on the individual countries to adopt the policies and tune them to be relevant to their local conditions by developing locally authored implementation guidelines.

Given the above gaps in laying an enabling environment for e/m-Commerce to thrive, it has been observed that certain measures and incentives have to be implemented for e/m-Commerce applications to move forward. Specifically, in a broader context, the following interventions, among others, have to be put in place: there should be authored strategies to improve basic national ICT infrastructure (such as erecting a reliable ICT network backbone) and to reduce the costs of using this infrastructure sustainably; building the professional capacity of people, putting in place deliberate human resource development programs to be able to address the different issues that come with e/m-Commerce implementation; putting in place proper awareness campaigns for the benefits of using e-Commerce applications; putting in place appropriate legal, institutional and regulatory frameworks at the national level, and putting in place vibrant e/m-Commerce strategy implementation programs.

Although these different interventions for developing e-business models in the SADC bloc

have been identified, it is important to do more investigations on the local context so that traditional e-Commerce models can be adapted to the local conditions.

REFERENCES

Ajayi, O. (2002). *Information Communications Technology in Africa*. Retrieved July 26, 2009, from www.wireless.ictp.it/school_2002/.../ajayi/Trieste_-2_-_ICT_in_Africa.doc

Chabossou, A., Stork, C., Stork, M., & Zahonogo, Z. (2009). Mobile Telephony Access and Usage in Africa. *Southern African Journal of Information and Communication, Issue No. 9*. Retrieved August 14, 2009, from www.whiteafrican.com/wp-content/.../04/researchictafrica-ictd2009.pdf

Chege, L., Gustav, C., & Mahachi, J. (2001). *E-Commerce and value chain management – the prospects and challenges for the South African construction industries. Construction Informatics Digital Library*. Retrieved August 15, 2009, from http://itc.scix.net/cgi-bin/works/Show?_id=w78%2d2001%2d62&sort=DEFAULT&search=E%2d COMMERCE%20AND%20VALUE%20CHAIN%20MANAGEMENT%20%96%20THE&hits=1261

COMNET-IT. (2002*). Country profiles of e-Governance, UNESCO*. Retrieved August 3, 2009, from www.portal.unesco.org/...governance...doc/E%2Bgovernance%2Bstudy%2Bfull%2Btext.doc

Dube, T., Chitura, T., & Runyowa, L. (2009). Adoption and Use of Internet Banking in Zimbabwe: An exploratory study. *Journal of Internet Banking and Commerce*. Retrieved August 3, 2009, from www.arraydev.com/commerce/JIBC/2009-04/Dube%20etal.pdf

ECA CORDIST. (2009). *Workshop on Legal and Regulatory Framework for the Knowledge Economy Report.* Presented at the first Meeting of the Committee on Development Information, Science & Technology (CODIST), Addis Ababa, Ethiopia ECA report. (2009). Mobile Commerce in Africa: An overview with specific reference to South Africa, Kenya and Senegal. *First Session of the Committee on Development Information, Science and Technology (CODIST-I). Addis Ababa, Ethiopia.* Retrieved July 30, 2009, from www. uneca.org/codist/codist1/.../E-ECA-CODIST-1-23-EN.pdf

Ifinedo p. (2005). Measuring Africa's e-readiness in the global networked economy: A nine-country data analysis. *International Journal of Education and Development using Information and Communication Technology (IJEDICT)*, 1(1), 53-71.

Jukic, N., Sharma, A., Jukic, B., & Parameswaran, M. (2009). M-Commerce: Analysis of Impact on Marketing Orientation. *Loyola University Chicago research series.* Retrieved August 10, 2009, from sba.luc.edu/research/wpapers/011020.pdf.

Kuo, Y.-F., & Yu, C.-W. (2005). 3G telecommunication operators' challenges and roles: A perspective of mobile commerce value chain. *Science Direct.* Retrieved August 3, 2009, from http://www.sciencedirect.com/science?_ob=ArticleURL&_udi=B6V8B-4H99JC0-2&_user=778200&_rdoc=1&_fmt=&_orig=search&_sort=d&_docanchor=&view=c&_searchStrId=979257359&_rerunOrigin=google&_acct=C000043160&_version=1&_urlVersion=0&_userid=778200&md5=a04f3e5c0e758f5c3aa042dc7459d6fb

Lehlokoe, D., & Malema, F. (2000). *A Green Paper on Electronic Commerce for South Africa – for public discussion 2001.* Retrieved August 17, 2009, from www.polity.org.za/polity/.../green_papers/greenpaper/execsum.PDF

Mensah, A. O., Bahta, A., & Mhlang, S. (2002). *E-Commerce challenges in Africa: issues, constraints, opportunities.* ECA briefing paper. World Summit on the Information Society, Geneva 2003, Tunis 2005

Ndlovu, R. (2009). *ICT guide – Zimbabwe.* Retrieved August 5, 2009, from www.kubatana.net/docs/inftec/ndlovu_ict_guide_zimbabwe.doc

Pehrson, B., & Ngwira, M. (2006). *Optical Fibre for Education and Research Networks in Eastern and Southern Africa.* Retrieved August 8, 2009, from www.ubuntunet.ssvl.kth.se/.../Sarua-fibre-final-report-draft-2006-03-04.pdf

Rahmati, N. (2008). National Culture and Adoption of Mobile Commerce: An Overview. *European and Mediterranean Conference on Information Systems 2008* (EMCIS2008). May 25-26 2008, Dubai

Report, I. T. U. (2009). *Measuring the Information Society – The ICT Development Index.* Retrieved July 15, 2009, from www.itu.int/ITU-D/ict/publications/idi/2009/.../IDI2009_w5.pdf

Report, U. N. (2009). The Millennium Development Goals. Retrieved August 2, 2009, from www.un.org/millenniumgoals/.../MDG%20Report%20 2009%20ENG.pdf

SADC. (2002). *SADC e-Readiness Review and Strategy.* Recommendations of the SADC e-Readiness Task Force. Retrieved July 17, 2009 from www.schoolnetafrica.org/fileadmin/resources/SADC_report.pdf

Schwab Entrepreneur. (2003). *ASAFE: Strategic Challenges for E-Commerce Promotion in Central Africa.* Retrieved August 4, 2009, from www.weforum.org/pdf/.../CaseStudy_ASAFE_Yitamben.pdf

KEY TERMS AND DEFINITIONS

E-Commerce: in this business model, business transactions (including payments uusing credit cards) are done with the help of ICTs.

SADC: A regional socio-economic grouping for countries in Southern Africa

Adoption: acceptance and encapsulation of a technology, in this case e-Commerce.

Electronic government (e-Government): Is a platform through which the government interacts with its citizens and business entities for the sake of exchange of information, public services and participatory democracy through the use of ICT platforms.

SME (Small Medium Enterprise): is a small scale business establishment whose headcount or turnover falls below certain limits.

ICTs: This acronym stands for information and communications technologies.

ICT Infrastructure: It encompasses all the devices, networks, protocols and procedures that are employed in the telecoms or information technology fields to foster interaction amongst different stakeholders.

Regulatory Framework: A set of guidelines that coordinates the following of set principles, e.g. market competition and liberalization, ethic, etc.

Chapter 15
Conservation of Information and e-Business Success and Challenges:
A Case Study

Huilien Tung
Auburn University, USA

Hsiang-Jui Kung
Georgia Southern University, USA

Désirée S. Lawless
Woodward, USA

Donald A. Sofge
Naval Research Laboratory, USA

William F. Lawless
Paine College, USA

ABSTRACT

Guided by the authors' theory of the (COI), which holds that the transformation pairs of information uncertainty between time and frequency remain constant (or alternately uncertainty for geospatial position and spatial frequency), they describe a case study on an international corporation based in Taiwan to demonstrate COI factors associated with the challenges and successes in the adoptions of e-business by the firm and by small and medium size enterprises in general.

BACKGROUND

e-Business is business exchanges on the Internet which utilize information and communication technologies to support business activities and processes. Beside regular selling and buying transactions, web-based customer service and collaboration with business partners are central components of e-Business.

Web applications are the glue joining Information Technology (IT) infrastructure with the business processes that e-Business services deliver to constituents. Reviewing web applications over the past ten years, scholars agree that more features are offered every year, producing more complexity as web design methods and technologies advance

DOI: 10.4018/978-1-60960-463-9.ch015

(Kung, Tung & Case, 2007). However, a Standish Group (2002) survey on web applications development shows that 84 percent of development projects do not meet business needs, 56 percent do not have the required functionality, 79 percent are behind schedule, and 63 percent are over budget. These challenges are especially hard on small to medium sized businesses.

We will use theory and a case study to discuss the challenges and successes that e-Business organizations face from ever evolving technologies, different e-business process requirements, different e-platforms, and different e-infrastructures.

THEORY

We review the state of interdependence theory and the evidence in support of it. This section engages in mathematical modeling. Whenever possible, we will summarize the results to minimize the need by readers for mathematics to better understand the material. In fact, the conclusion to draw is that understanding is a byproduct of a strongly independent worldview; an interdependent worldview, should one exist, precludes the existence of a "single understanding" or "situational analysis". Instead, the conclusion is that in an interdependent world, single perspectives or worldviews reflect human and cultural tradeoffs coupled to a residual, irreducible level of uncertainty. A single perspective in isolation is static, but two together, existing in a state of interdependence (i), can produce a potent dynamic. What follows is our approach to a theory of i.

In sum, dynamics are the result of competitive behaviors represented by the existence of two mutually incommensurable view points (Republicans and Democrats; conservatives and liberals; market economists and socialists; etc.). These polar opposite views serve many key but seldomly appreciated functions in society: Under conflict, we learn better (Dietz et al., 2003); we make better political decisions (e.g., Coleman,

2003); and we make better economic decisions (Hayek, 1944). But how can this conflict be modeled? And what relationship can be established to winning and losing across social, political or market landscapes?

A Hilbert Space (HS) is an abstract space defined so that vector positions and angles permit the calculations of distance, reflection, rotation and geospatial measurements, or subspaces with local convergences where these measurements can occur. That would allow real-time determinations of the situated, shared situational awareness in localizing the center of a target organization, $\sigma_{x\text{-}COG}$, to represent the shared uncertainty in social-psychological-geospatial terms, and σ_k to similarly represent the spatial frequencies of an organization's patterns displayed across physical space (e.g., the mapping of social-psychological or organizational spaces to physical networks). It would establish an "oscillation" between two socio-psycho-geospatial operators A and B such that

$$[A,B] = AB - BA = iC \neq [B,A]. \qquad (1)$$

This type of an oscillation defines a social-psychological decision space within an organization. It is called an "oscillator" because decision-making occurs during rapid-fire turn-taking sessions driven by big self-interests that "rotate" attention for the topic under discussion in the minds of listeners or deciders first in one valence direction (e.g., "endorsing" a proposition) followed by the opposite (e.g., "rejecting" a proposition) to produce a "rocking" or back and forth process, like an organizational or social-psychological harmonic oscillator (SPHO) within an organization, or like the merger and acquisition (M&A) negotiations between a hostile predator organization and its prey target. But these oscillations may not occur in the minds of the agents who are driving the discussion (e.g., oscillation occurs in the minds of neutral jury members as first a prosecutor's case is presented to them followed by a defense attorney's case, but specifically not in the partisan minds of the prosecutor or defense attorney, unless they are seeking a compromise; or not in the minds of a predator organization competing for its prey M&A target organization but more likely in the observers more neutral to the M&A process yet who are not neutral to making a profit; in Lawless et al., 2009).

A democratic space could be defined as a space where decisions characterized by SPHOs are made by majority rule (e.g., jury, political, or faculty decisions); the lack of an SPHO identifies decisions made by minority (consensus) or authoritarian rules (e.g., decisions where countervailing views are suppressed, as in common to military, authoritarian government or CEO business decisions; Lawless et al., 2007).

The key to building the abstract representations necessary to construct an SPHO may be to locate opposing clusters of the shared interpretations of concepts geospatially across physical space or via a socio-psychological network anchored or mapped to physical network space. SPHOs should generalize to entertainment or stories. Similar to a decision process involving drivers and neutrals, we propose that a story or stage production, as found by Hasson and his colleagues (2004) in their study of inter-subjectivity among viewers of a Clint Eastwood movie, engages and holds an audience's attention with this rocking process. SPHO rocking produces fluctuations that produce information characteristic of an organization's stability response. This insight suggests that the reverse engineering of terrorist organizations may be possible (Lawless et al., 2007).

The operators A and B are community interaction matrices that locate social objects interdependently, ι, in social space (shared conceptual space) that are in turn separately anchored (embedded or situated) in geospatial or physical space. ι states are non-separable and non-classical; disturbances collapse ι states into classical information states. Two agents, one as an web-based firm's President and the second as

the Chief Technology Officer (CTO), meet in the President's office, the choice of seating location reflecting the relative social power of the President over the subordinate CTO, but the CTO holding a skill set required by the organization that permits the two to negotiate while both are aware of their different functions and relative social ranks in the organization (Ambrose, 2001), generating bistable social perspectives that reflect the separate social constituencies that drive compromises (Wood et al., 2009); e.g., in contrast to the gridlock in the Department of Energy's (DOE) Hanford cleanup driven by its consensus-ruled Citizens Advisory Board (CAB) where compromises can be easily blocked, compromises made by the majority-ruled DOE Savannah River Site (SRS) CAB have accelerated environmental remediation at SRS (Lawless et al., 2008).

Per Bohr (1955), complementarity actors and observers and incommensurable cultures generate conjugate or bistable information couples that he and Heisenberg (1958) suggested paralleled the uncertainty principle at the atomic level. We have built a model to test their speculation and to extend it to role conflicts (Lawless et al., 2009). But even for mundane social interactions, Carley (2002) concluded that humans became social to reduce uncertainty. Thus, the information available to any human is incomplete, producing uncertainty. More importantly, this uncertainty has a minimum irreducibility that promotes the existence of tradeoffs between any two factors in an interaction (uncertainty in worldviews, stories or business models, ΔWV, and their execution, Δv; uncertainty in centers of gravity Δx_{COG} and spatial frequencies, Δk; and uncertainty in energy, ΔE, and time, Δt).

The uncertainty in these oscillations can be reformulated[1] to establish that Fourier pairs, consisting of standard deviations, are equal to:

$$\sigma_A \sigma_B \geq \tfrac{1}{2} \qquad (2)$$

Equation (2) indicates that as variance in factor *A* broadens, variance in factor *B* narrows.

To summarize, a model of interdependence in the interaction or organizations must be able to:

1. Reflect orthogonal perspectives (i.e., Nash equilibriums; cf. Luce & Raiffa, 1967); e.g., between prosecutors and defense attorneys (Busemeyer & Trueblood, 2009); between actions and observations or between multiple cultures (Bohr, 1955); between USAF combat fighter jet pilots and book-knowledge of air combat maneuvering (Lawless et al., 2000); between game-theory preferences and actual choices made during games (Kelley, 1992); and to capture the discrepancy between the views of managers and the decisions made by their organizations (Bloom et al., 2007).

2. Allow rotation vectors as a function of the direction of rotation. Permit measurements between vectors and rotations.

3. Enable a mathematics of interdependent (*ı*) bistability where measurements disturb or collapse the *ı* states that occur during social-psychological interactions in physical space.

4. Test the proposition that information in organizational interactions can be modeled by the conservation of information.

What we have accomplished above is to model social rotations as part of an SPHO. What we have not done to this point is to link SPHO with winners and losers in society, politics, or the market place. However, the existence of an SPHO should it be established would alone signify the value of stability to organizations and social systems. An SPHO allows us to study organizations as they search for stability (mergers; in Lawless et al., 2009). We will do this next with a case study.

CASE STUDY

MiTAC Inc. was founded in 1974 as the original member of MiTAC-SYNNEX Group. The group now consists of more than 40 companies from different fields such as electronic gases & chemicals, design and manufacturing of IT and mobile communication devices, system integration and Internet technology, as well as distribution and fulfillment. MiTAC-SYNNEX Group has been trying to form a unique group, called the "N-Dimensional Network Organization"[2], a tight network (i.e., reduced uncertainty) of different specialized units interlinked to achieve common goals. They define the N-Dimensional Network Organization as one organization that combines a problem-solving group domain of knowledge, group synergy, e-Centric skills and growth.

The original core business of MiTAC Inc. was the personal computer (PC) market. In 1974, MITAC introduced the INTEL microprocessor system to Taiwan and the first super-minicomputer (Perkin-Elmer, 32-bit) and then moved on to model system integration. Later, it developed the first commercial Chinese terminal, a computerized taxation system and the first auction system in Taiwan. In the 1980s, MiTAC launched the first Chinese terminal named Ha-Tun, developed the first multi-processor system in Taiwan, established the Traffic Surveillance system for the National Chungshan freeway and got involved in different systems such as population, land, military and police administration. In the 1990s, it entered the communication, network and education fields, produced industrial computers, built the island-wide united Credit Card Center networking system, and expanded into mainland China. Aiming at becoming a trend leader, MiTAC has been moving toward the field of Internet service by providing e-commerce web services in the 2000s. From 2000 to the present, it also developed a Self-service Counter System (SCS) for financial markets, constructed a Taipei Easy Card system using Smart Card technology, teamed up with Thales and Fubon Back to play a major part with the Taiwan High-Speed Consortium, and become the first company in Taiwan to attain a CMMI Maturity Level 3 appraisal for Systems Engineering and Software Engineering.[3]

MiTAC expanded from commercial computer production and system integration to IT distribution. It is now the largest IT system integration provider in Taiwan. As stated on its website, its goal is "to incorporate advanced technology and management knowledge, providing customers with comprehensive, dynamic solutions to improve productivity and working efficiency to better compete in the marketplace."[4]

MiTAC Inc. has accomplished a number of system integration projects. Their clients include governmental organizations, militaries, financial institutes, and private enterprises. In response to the "Digital Taiwan Plan" authorized by the Taiwan government, the wide-range of its clients demonstrates MiTAC's managing concept of "e-Government, e-Industry, and e-Society". We list major projects from all three of these areas.

E-GOVERNMENT

MiTAC has developed various information systems for different Taiwan government branches that illustrate its versatility.

- **Integrated Tax System (ITS):** ITS is a full-scale operation service for the outsourcing program of Taiwan's Internal Revenue Service. It is a dual-phased, cross platform system that provides data exchange through Internet and Gateways using different platforms.

- **Integrated Taxation Administration Information System (M-ITAIS):** The M-ITAIS includes taxpayer registration, tax return filing and processing, auditing, compliance, billing collection management, enforcement audit selection, and

other related services. MiTAC is responsible to operate, maintain and continuously upgrade the Taxation Administration Information System. We discuss this project in more detail below as a "success" eBusiness project that MiTAC has implemented.

- **Integrated Land Administration Information system:** Taiwan land administration computerization project and its maintenance.

- **Healthcare field:** Mainframe system upgrade and database integration, and computerization for 369 villages and towns for the Bureau of National Health Insurance.

- **Government field:** The Office Automation computerization systems for the Taiwanese Presidential Palace, the National Security Office, the Executive Yuan, the Legislative Yuan, and the Judicial Yuan.

- **Military field:** Tactical Communication System and Logistics Information Management System for the Taiwanese Air Force; military real estate control system; Coast Guard Administration Information System and Vessel Satellite Monitoring System; Military Police Integrated Information System; Advanced Air Defense System (AADS) for the Taiwanese Air Force; Multiple Integrated Laser Engagement System (MILES) for the Taiwanese Army; and Command Control Communication Computer Intelligence Surveillance and Reconnaissance for Taiwanese tri-services.

E-BUSINESS

- **Silo and Mill Automatic control System:**[5] These Automatic control system are to increase operation performance for warehouse businesses. A complete silo automation management and control system changes the traditional storage and delivery of agriculture products process and lowers operational cost (reduce personnel and time) while increasing production. It manages the intake, shipping and delivery process under a precise product flow monitor model. Consisting of a front end control system and management system, it is mainly a chain-reaction control system run from a computer programmed controller and other equipment, including field conveying equipment control and management system controls.

MiTAC has built Silo automatic control systems for Taichung and Kaohsiung harbor (Far-Eastern Silo) and a mill automatic control system for Lien-Hua Fu-Kung flour factory, Great Wall enterprise Co., and Great Wall Chuang-hua.

- **Credit Card Operation Management System**.
- **Banking Everybody Information System:** The purpose for establishing this system is to assist not only the decision-making for the executive and operation mangers, but also expand the system to permit all clients to be able to get their own internal or external banking information.
- **Logistics, Finance and Stocks Management System**.
- **Bank Foreign Exchange System:** MiTAC Bank Foreign Exchange System has 4 major functions: Outward Remittance, Inward Remittance, Inter-bank Transfer and Foreign Deposits on a common platform. This platform serves to form a foundation for all foreign exchange transactions.

E-SOCIETY

- **Integrated Highway Surveillance control System:** A highway surveillance system was assigned to provide the public with a more convenient and safer driving environment by monitoring traffic and car accidents. The system should also generate revenue for the government. There are three sub-systems in the MiTAC Integrated Highway Surveillance System (MIHSS): Traffic Control System (MIHSS-100), Toll Collection System (MIHSS-200) and Operation Management System (MIHSS-300). MiTAC has developed and installed the Taiwan Chungshan Highway's first stage traffic control system, toll counting system, and central computer system for the second Northern Highway northern section control center and tunnel control center. The Traffic Control System uses surveillance equipment to collect instant traffic information and send it back to the control center. The central computer then makes the best assessment and decision based on operational models and policies. The Operation Management System mainly provides strategic and management support.
- **Cab Driving Simulation System**.
- **Hog Auction Management System**.
- **Automatic Fare Collection System (AFC):** With the experience of designing and installing automatic control systems, MiTAC moved to serve the rapid-transportation field. It has completed numerous projects involving system design and implementation of Highway, Railway, Mass Rapid Transit, and High Speed Rail automation. Its specialties are manifested by the Automatic Fare Collection systems. The AFC that MiTAC assigned and implemented is successful due to its ability to handle operations on a grand project scale, to provide real time traffic information and control, and to generate sufficient revenue to operate the system. MiTAC has com-

pleted Taipei's EasyCard System AFC, Taiwan High Speed Rail System AFC, and the Electronic Toll Collection System in recent years for Taiwan as it constructed a rapid transit network to serve its public. Taipei EasyCard System is a multi-operator and multimodal system. Since its operation, it has issued over 7 million cards with transactions recorded at around 3 million per day. Taiwan's High Speed Rail System serves over 300,000 passengers per day and is designed for future interoperability with Taipei's EasyCard system.

Challenge: E-Government Project

E-government may be described as the general use of information and communication technology and the specific use of e-commerce to carry out government operations. It includes providing citizens and organizations with more convenient access to government information and services, and with delivering government agency services to citizens, business partners and suppliers or other government agencies (UN & ASPA, 2002). Taiwan government authorities have been promoting a "Digital Taiwan" plan. MiTAC has finished some major projects under this umbrella.

MiTAC has developed significant e-Government projects which include a full-scale integrated Tax system, Integrated Taxation Administration Information System, Integrated Land Administration Information system, Healthcare field system,

and other government and military systems. We discuss the project MiTAC did for Taiwan's Patent Office, the TiPOnet, to describe the challenges for government as it moves into the eBusiness world to better serve its people; there are also challenges that a medium-size IT company faces as it develops an e-system for government authorities in this territory unfamiliar to both the government and the company.

TIPOnet

The challenges that digital technologies pose for national and international regulation of intellectual property rights are receiving considerable attention these days from many governments such as the United States, Taiwan and China. In September 1995 the United States issued its White Paper on Intellectual Property and the National Information Infrastructure (Samuelson, 1996). To promote e-filing and international harmonization with other countries, the TIPOnet project was proposed in early 2002 by MiTAC to Taiwan's Patent Office to integrate information technology under business processes re-engineering (BPR) to create an IT-activated, paperless and online infrastructure. The TIPOnet project was designed to enhance administrative efficiency and service quality as well as to increase the competitiveness of domestic industries. On January 6, 2003, the Executive Yuan agreed to incorporate the TIPOnet project into the "Digital Taiwan Plan" for "Challenge

Table 1. TIPOnet total cost breakdown (in NT$ million) [7]

	2003	2004	2005	2006	2007	Total
Hardware	*	59.7	52.3	47.6	47.5	207.1
Operation	*	3.8	4.8	8.3	12.6	29.5
Maintenance	*	*	7.1	13.4	19.1	39.7
Application Development	53.0	168.8	187.7	183.3	25.0	617.8
Grand Total	53.0	232.2	251.9	252.7	104.2	894.1

*There were no costs associated with Hardware, Operation and Maintenance in the first stage of system design.

2008—National Development Plans",[6] Taiwan's plan to develop a Knowledge-based economy in Taiwan formulated by the Council for Economic Planning and Development.

TIPO awarded the TIPOnet development project, valued at over $26 million (NT$ 894 million), to MiTAC in January 2003. TIPOnet is a five-year development project. Table 1 shows the total cost breakdown of the TIPOnet project. The total hardware cost is about $6 million (NT$207 million), operation $0.88 million, maintenance $1.2 million, and application development $18 million. Table 2 shows the software cost breakdown in employee-months. The total application development required over twenty-nine hundred employee-months, over four hundred employee-months for project management, over eight hundred employee-months for operations, and over one hundred employee-months for training.

MiTAC Inc. has since developed other large-scale e-government development projects in Taiwan. But intellectual property systems are a brand new area for MiTAC. In order to reduce the risk to MiTAC with the TIPOnet development project, MiTAC teamed up with IBM and Reed Technology and Information Service Inc. (RTIS). IBM has been involved in the development of patent and trademark application system for the United States Patent and Trademark Office (USPTO). RTIS has been working with USPTO for over thirty years in publishing the USPTO Gazette and in converting paper-based patents to electronic documents.

In February 2001, the Chief Information Office (CIO) consortium provided guidance for FEA (federal enterprise architecture) to the United States federal government (CIO Council, 2001). The FEA is a collection of reference models that defines a common taxonomy and ontology for describing IT resources. It includes the Performance Reference Model (PRM), the Business Reference Model (BRM), the Service Component Reference Model (SRM), the Data Reference Model (DRM) and the Technical Reference Model (TRM). The purpose of the FEA framework is to identify opportunities to simplify processes and unify work across agencies and within the lines of business for the federal government. The TIPOnet enterprise architecture (EA) framework adopted a simplified view of the relationships among FEA reference models.

The TIPOnet enterprise architecture (EA) framework represents the TIPOnet EA in three fundamental tiers or layers (i.e., business, services, and technical), all of which are intersected by three critical architectural dimensions (i.e., information and data, operational, and security and privacy). This means that the three basic perspectives of the TIPOnet EA (the business view, the services view, and the technical view) must always be considered in the context of three pervasive sets of considerations: information and data flows; operational objectives and measures; and security and privacy controls. Since it is a service-oriented system, TIPOnet utilized SRM to plan and map services that the system offers. The SRM defines seven major services: portal,

Table 2. Software cost breakdown (in employee-months)

	2004	2005	2006	2007	Total
Application Development	879	919	902	239	2,939
Project Management	128	119	167	15	429
Operation	102	204	240	312	858
Training	20	40	40	5	105
Grand Total	1,129	1,282	1,349	571	4,331

e-filing, e-examining, e-search, e-publishing, knowledge management (KM), and management information system (MIS). TIPOnet set out to launch an e-filing system on 26 August 2008 for patents and trade marks.[8] To encourage applicants to use online instead of paper filings, from the time when it was first launched, the application fee was reduced by approximately EUR 13 per document (about 16%) for patents and EUR 6.5 (about 10%) for trademarks. Now some of the applications for patents are free. Since the launching of this new electronic filing service, the response from all types of users has been positive. The e-filing service has been utilized by individuals, agents and companies alike, with many of the first-time applicants becoming long-term users.

CHALLENGES

Although TIPOnet was finished on time, it did not follow the original project time-line allotted for each component/phase of its project life cycle. This project is not listed as one of MiTAC's "most successful" cases because it suffered project creep, delay of certain phases, and the project life-cycle was not completed in a timely and cost-effective way. Due to the nature of the project and the customer, there was no room for negotiation in the budget or for time increases. MiTAC had to come up with alternative solutions for these problems. MiTAC faced two major challenges: step in a new and unfamiliar field to design a system, and try to follow a yet-to-mature model. First, and as the first intellectual property project MiTAC had taken on, TIPOnet's startup had not been easy. It took MiTAC two years to do the requirements analysis to meet business (TIPO) needs and to design the system to have all the required functionalities. This caused a major delay in the beginning (requirement analysis and design phase) of the project. And the learning curve for this project was steep. Unlike the financial market that MiTAC was familiar with and also has had

many models to follow, the procedure of applying and processing patents and trademarks had to be uniquely defined, mapped and implemented. Then the second major challenge revealed itself.

MiTAC was asked to adopt the FEA framework. Adopting this framework meant that MiTAC inherited both its advantages and disadvantages. One of the weaknesses in the FEA framework is that it does not contain a detailed description sufficient to generate specification documents for each cell of an FEA-F Matrix (Leist & Zellner, 2006). There is no standard artifact description for some cells. Each organization has to define the meta model for each cell such as data, function, network, people, time and motivation. Such cells represent different areas of interest for each perspective. Therefore, the resulting framework is not a definite solution. Many studies compare the similarities and differences between different enterprise architecture frameworks, but few studies report the empirical implementation of FEA frameworks (Kim et al, 2005; Meneklis et al., 2005). These deficiencies made MiTAC's work more difficult and farther steepened its learning curve. But by taking advantage of its strong background in software development, MiTAC gained time back by adding extra software developers to its team to help with the coding process during the development phase and to finish the project in time.

SUCCESS: INTEGRATED TAXATION ADMINISTRATION INFORMATION SYSTEM (M-ITAIS)

A good taxation system is the foundation of a government's economic growth plan. Taiwan's previously paper-based taxation system created many obstacles. From the public's perspective, members of the public had to fill out different forms for different level units (federal, city, or local) and they had to go to each location, to get in line and either fill out a tax return or deal with several different tax issues. The process was time-consuming, error-prone and sometimes the paperwork got lost, causing many to repeat the process. From the official side, the lack of a standardized data format increased costs and time; officials were also overloaded with many different cases. To make matter worse, there was no central database for different tax units to share tax data. Taiwan's government wanted a good taxation system to serve its people better and to stimulate economic growth. This could be better done by utilizing Information technology and the Web to reduce bottom-line costs, and thus to generate revenue that could be used for public development.

During the past three decades, MiTAC won several projects to design and deploy the Integrated Taxation Administration Information System (M-ITAIS) in Taiwan for many government agencies. To "overhaul" the manual system, there were two major challenges/requirements for a TAIS: a common platform (to reduce uncertainty) and a "one stop" portal for both tax officials and citizens. With its strong background in information technology, web service and financial market experience, MiTAC designed ITAIS as a web-service system with a Service Oriented Architecture (SOA) to ensure interoperability across different government units.[9] It consisted of three major parts of e-Business: G2C (Government to Consumer), G2B (Government to Business) and G2G (Government to Government). It was a prime model for e-Government to serve the public (consumers), to perform eBusiness functions (G2B), and to interoperate government units (G2G). M-ITAIS includes taxpayer registration, tax return filing and processing, auditing, compliance, billing collection management, enforcement audit selection, and other related functions. It has significant features such as the All-in-one Functional Center, transparency and accountability for all tax officials. It also simplifies service and the automation of administrative assessments. Mi-TAIS provides the government of Taiwan with an effective and cheaper way to collect taxes and at the same time to offer a better and faster service to its citizens.

M-ITAIS has become both a benchmark model of a desired taxation system and MiTAC's most famous successful project based on customer satisfaction, increased productivity, reduced operational costs, an efficient but complex system, and the revenue that it generates. The annual tax revenue collected is over 50 billion USD which has drawn international attention. Delegations from countries of Asia, Latin America and the USA have visited the Financial Data Center in Taiwan to observe its "best practices" model.

Success Factors of M-ITAIS

1. Understand the customer's needs and goals for a project. This is critical for any system design. MiTAC has a strong background in the financial sector and it has been designing systems for different levels of organizations for about 30 years. Although it was a familiar field, MiTAC must still make sure it understands the needs for each office. However, the rotations that we described in the earlier section under theory tell us that beliefs and actions can be orthogonal; thus, we cannot rely on the average responses from customers but instead must consider the widest range of them and, more importantly, their actions.

2. Provide professional and specialized team and management. With extensive backgrounds in all aspects of hardware, software, communication, networking, integrated testing, training, maintenance and consulting services, MiTAC was able to implement an e-Tax net which connects all levels of government units for data sharing and processing.

3. Provide the logistics necessary for operations. MiTAC has strong Supply Chain management and since it could draw knowledge, man-power from other companies in their Group on the supply chain, it was able to

obtain adequate resources to finish its target project.

4. All-in-One service is the key success feature of M-ITAIA. The main purpose of setting up a ITAIS was to provide the government tax officials and citizens a central portal for their taxation needs. All-in-One services offer real-time data, standardized forms, accountability, and best of all, convenience. It saves time and cost.

5. Cross-platform design. Since the e-Tax net connects different levels of government tax units, it has to be able to perform on different platforms.

MITAC BETAS

Many formulas exist for stock market beta, including with statistical regressions. Beta represents market volatility. We estimated beta with the covariance of a target organization *A* against a standard, such as the S&P 500, divided by variance of the standard (see www.answers.com/topic/beta-coefficient). In order for the data to be synchronized, we matched the dates of the available data for MITAC, the S&P 500 Index, the Goldman Sachs Taiwan Select 50 Index (TS 50), and the USA Today E-Business 25 Index. The time period chosen was from March 1, 2007 to May 21, 2009.

MiTAC's betas indicate that MiTAC is a very stable organization. Whether compared to the

S&P 500 Index, the TS 50 Index, or the eBusiness 25 Index, MiTAC's responses to market perturbations have been uniformly stable.

DISCUSSION

From MiTAC's various projects and our COI theory, we try to find the common competiveness/success factors as listed below.

Innovation

Since its founding in 1974, MiTAC has always tried to use the most current technology in order to position itself as a trend leader. It evolved from a PC and Software Development Company to a system integration enterprise that can provide a total solution for its customers. To be a trend leader, MiTAC has to be innovative in technology products, in management, and in services to its customers. Their (MiTAC-SYNNEX Group) 3V business model (Velocity, Visibility and Value), and their N-Dimension Network concept have helped MiTAC create a synergy that seamlessly unites its partners, customers, employees, and companies. MiTAC's products and services have won awards from government, technology shows, and its customers almost every year, providing proof that it is an innovative firm. With so many successfully designed and implemented projects,

Table 3. SD of MiTAC = 8.507

COVAR		
MiTAC	S&P 500	1942.277
	Goldman Sachs Taiwan Select 50 (USD) Index	136.0038
	USA TODAY E-BUSINESS 25 INDEX	155.3663
Beta 1 (S&P 500 and MiTAC)		.03
Beta 2 (TS 50 and MiTAC)		.30
Beta 3 (eBusiness 25 and MiTAC)		.39

such as the M-ITAIS we discussed above, MITAC has set a benchmark for financial markets.

Sophisticated Supply Chain Management and Integrated Design-and-Manufacturing System

Supply chains are the life-blood of all kinds of organizations. They are often the unseen forces without which an organization cannot function. A good supply chain will ensure that materials are available to begin production and that finished products are ready for delivery to the customer. A supply chain is best satisfied when the interrelated components expressed in a business plan, business objectives and profitability, and productivity extend through a planning horizon sufficient to schedule the labor, equipment, facilities, material, and finances required to accomplish the production plan. In that this plan affects many interdependent company functions, it integrates information from across the supply chain (e.g., marketing, manufacturing, engineering, finance, materials). There must be interaction across management and the other units (i.e., oscillation) of an organization. There must be units to provide real-time information on customer needs, even before customers or suppliers can articulate these needs. MiTAC's approach, PLM (Product Lifecycle Management), is its way to address this particular part of its supply chain to reduce time and cost with precise production management. Combining the MiTAC-Synex group's horizontal development strategy, MiTAC's supply chain is completed with products Design & Manufacturing (manufacturing and Research & Development), Internet Technology & Mobile Solutions, and Distribution & Fulfillment. MiTAC's different but interdependent functional units and other companies of the group in its supply chain communicate (oscillate back and forth) through the whole chain which enables it to identify and solve problems to provide the best and most effective service to its customers and follow its "all service

in one" model. Since systems are developed by distinct groups with different points of view, only by reducing uncertainty and increasing the rate of information exchange is it possible to reach the "best" design.

Vertical and Horizontal Development Strategy

MiTAC's horizontal (i.e., supply chain) is completed from products to e-Commerce to take full advantages of its network. Its vertical chain consists of units from material (production) to system (integration and delivery).

Precise Management

Unique business model and management concepts enable administrators to control all of the information relevant to an organization's or government's businesses. Management teams must continually strive for focus, alignment and synchronization among the interdependent functions of an organization to reduce its time and cost factors.

Great Customer Service/ Management

MiTAC's complete system life-cycle, integration, development, consultation and maintenance processes not only provide real-time information exchanges for its customers, but also help to keep its customers involved in system design and development. This has increased customer satisfaction and has served to ensure that the systems it designs meet its customer's needs. MiTAC is also involved in many government IT projects to build good relationships with government authorities that not only provide framework and regulations to follow but also a great resource for future projects.

e-Centric and Digitalization of its Operations are "Must-Haves" in the Information Age

Partnerships

MiTAC partners with other companies for specialized functions when MiTAC cannot fulfill a customer's needs or make its products sufficiently competitive. It has partnered with different companies, some very famous, with different specialties to build solutions for its customers. For example, MiTAC teamed up with HITACHI, MITSUBISHI and others for a transportation solution; with HP, IBM, Microsoft, Oracle and others for computer integration; with CORNING, CISCO, MOTOROLA and others for communication integration; and CISCO, SYMANTEC, and WATCHGUARD for security integration. MiTAC has also invested with Anjes, Sinfotek, and Onsys to build up a professional Internet service team and to team up with banks on various other projects.

LESSON LEARNED AND FUTURE TRENDS

For an eBusiness to be successful, future systems must be functional across different platforms, able to provide real-time responses, and able to reduce computational time. For better management, evaluation and decision making, it is ideal to implement Web-based performance metrics to provide feedback, pinpoint the components that need improvement and reduce uncertainty. But like most decisions made, states of interdependence can positively or adversely impact the resulting decision (Lawless et al., 2007). An organization has to involve the entire supply chain and its customers as early in the process as possible to avoid unnecessary costs. New product development should not be kept separate from the supply chain focus because not only the products (system) created but routing can adversely impact the finances of new products. Utilizing the most current information technology and Internet technology are also critical for eBusiness success.

What we have done is to create a model of social rotations (i.e., SPHOs, Nash Equilibria; etc.). What we have not done is to link rotations with population effects from the fluctuations or perturbations caused by rotations (Nash equilibria). Once we do so, our model will become dynamic and predictive. We predict that these fluctuations will generate limit cycles, our next area of research.

CONCLUSION

We have devised a theory of social rotations to model social, political and market conflict and competition. We used our ideas about rotation to study stability and to apply them to MiTAC, which we found to be one of the more successful international companies. We suspect that our theory of rotations and findings about MiTAC may well contradict the prevailing view of Nash Equilibria. In this prevailing view, set out by Luce and Raiffa (1969), where it was believed that cooperation can avoid the traps of Nash Equilibria, it was taken to its logical extreme by Axlerod (1984) who believed that Nash Equilibria led to the worst social welfare outcomes: "the pursuit of self-interest by each [participant] leads to a poor outcome for all" (Axlerod, 1984, p. 7; also p. 8) that can be avoided when sufficient punishment exists to discourage competition. Instead, we suspect when all is said and done, that competition is the mechanism by which a company like MiTAC or a society can best learn, govern, defend, and feed itself.

ACKNOWLEDGMENT

For the fifth author, this material is based upon work supported by, or in part by, the U. S. Army Research Laboratory and the U. S. Army

Research Office under contract/grant number W911NF-10-1-0252.

REFERENCES

Ambrose, S. H. (2001). Paleolithic technology and human evolution. *Science, 291*, 1748–1753. doi:10.1126/science.1059487

Axelrod, R. (1984). *The evolution of cooperation.* New York: Basic.

Bloom, N., Dorgan, S., Dowdy, J., & Van Reenen, J. (2007). Management practice and productivity. *The Quarterly Journal of Economics, 122*(4), 1351–1408. doi:10.1162/qjec.2007.122.4.1351

Bohr, N. (1955). Science and the unity of knowledge. In Leary, L. (Ed.), *The unity of knowledge* (pp. 44–62). New York: Doubleday.

Busemeyer, J., & Trueblood, J. (2009). Comparison of quantum and Bayesian inference models. In P. Bruza, Sofge, D.A., Lawless, W.F., Van Rijsbergen, K., & Klusch, M. (eds). *Quantum Interaction. Third International Symposium, QI-2009.* Berlin:Springer-Verlag.

Carley, K. M. (2002). *Simulating society: The tension between transparency and veridicality. Social Agents: ecology, exchange, and evolution.* University of Chicago, Argonne National Laboratory.

CIO (Chief Information Officer) Council. (2001). *A Practical Guide to Federal Enterprise Architecture.* Version 1.0. Retrieved June 30, 2006, http://www.gao.gov/special.pubs/eaguide.pdf

Cohen, L. (1995). *Time-frequency analysis: theory and applications.* Upper Saddle River, NJ: Prentice Hall Signal Processing Series.

Coleman, J. J. (2003). The benefits of campaign financing. *CATO Institute Briefing Papers.* www.cato.org/pubs/briefs/bp-084es.html. Washington.

Dietz, T., Ostrom, E., & Stern, P. C. (2003). The struggle to govern the commons. *Science, 302,* 1907. doi:10.1126/science.1091015

Gershenfeld, N. (2000). *The physics of information technology.* Cambridge, MA: Cambridge University Press.

Hasson, U., Nir, Y., Levy, I., Fuhrmann, G., & Malach, R. (2004). Intersubject Synchronization of Cortical Activity During Natural Vision. *Science, 303,* 1634–1640. doi:10.1126/science.1089506

Hayek, F. A. (1944/1994). *The road to serfdom.* Chicago, UK: Routledge Press/University of Chicago Press.

Heisenberg, W. (1958/1999). *Language and reality in modern physics. Physics and philosophy. The revolution in modern science* (pp. 167–186). New York: Prometheus Books.

Kelley, H. H. (1992). Lewin, situations, and interdependence. *The Journal of Social Issues, 47,* 211–233. doi:10.1111/j.1540-4560.1991.tb00297.x

Kim, J., Kim, Y., Kwon, J., Hong, S., Song, C., & Baik, D. (2005). An enter-p rise architecture framework based on a common information technology domain (EAFIT) for improving interoperability among heterogeneous information systems. *Proceedings of the 2005 Third ACIS Int'l Conference on Software Engineering Research.*

Kung, H., Tung, H., & Case, T. (2007). Managing E-Government Application Evolution: A State Government Case. *International Journal of Cases on Electronic Commerce, 3*(2), 36–53.

Lawless, W. F., Bergman, M., Louçã, J., Kriegel, N. N., & Feltovich, N. (2007). A quantum metric of organizational performance: Terrorism and counterterrorism. *Computational & Mathematical Organization Theory, 13,* 241–281. doi:10.1007/s10588-006-9005-4

Lawless, W. F., Castelao, T., & Ballas, J. A. (2000). Virtual knowledge: Bistable reality and the solution of ill-defined problems. *IEEE Systems Man, and Cybernetics, 30*(1), 119–126. doi:10.1109/5326.827482

Lawless, W. F., Sofge, D. A., & Goranson, H. T. (2009). Conservation of Information: A New Approach To Organizing Human-Machine-Robotic Agents Under Uncertainty. In P. Bruza, Sofge, D.A., Lawless, W.F., Van Rijsbergen, K., & Klusch, M.(eds). *Quantum Interaction. Third International Symposium, QI-2009*. Berlin:Springer-Verlag.

Lawless, W. F., Whitton, J., & Poppeliers, C. (2008). Case studies from the UK and US of stakeholder decision-making on radioactive waste management. *Practice Periodical of Hazardous, Toxic, and Radioactive Waste Management, 12*(2), 70–78. doi:10.1061/(ASCE)1090-025X(2008)12:2(70)

Leist, S., & Zellner, G. (2006). Evaluation of Current Architecture Frameworks. *ACM Symposium on Applied Computing* (pp. 1547-1553). Dijon, France: ACM.

Luce, R. D., & Raiffa, H. (1967). *Games and decision*. New York: Wiley.

Meneklis, B., Kaliontzoglou, A., Douligeris, C., & Polemi, D. (2005). *Engineering and Technology Aspects of an e-Government Architecture Based on Web Services, Proceedings of the Third European Conference on Web Services.*

OMB (Office of Management and Budget). (2006). *FEA Practice Guidance*. Retrieved June 30, 2006, http://www.whitehouse.gov/omb/egov/documents/FEA_Practice_Guidance.pdf

Rieffel, E. G. (2007). Certainty and uncertainty in quantum information processing. *Quantum Interaction: AAAI Spring Symposium*, Stanford University:AAAI Press.

Samuelson, P. (1996). Intellectual Property Rights and the Global Information Economy. *Communications of the ACM, 39*(1), 23–28. doi:10.1145/234173.234176

Standish Group. (2001). *Extreme chaos*. Retrieved May 30, 2006, http://www.standishgroup.com/sample_research/PDFpages/extreme_chaos.pdf

UN & ASPA. (2002). *Bench-marking e-government: A global perspective*. Retrieved May 30, 2006, http://unpan1.un.org/intradoc/groups/public/ documents/UN/UNPAN021547.pdf

Wood, J., Tung, H.-L., Marshall-Bradley, T., Sofge, D. A., Grayson, J., & Lawless, W. F. (2009). Applying an Organizational Uncertainty Principle: Semantic Web-Based Metrics. In M. M. Cunha, Eva Oliveira, Antonio Tavares & Luis Ferreira (Eds.). *Handbook of Research on Social Dimensions of Semantic Technologies and Web Services*. Hershey, PA: IGI Global.

ENDNOTES

[1] Given $[A,B] = iC$, and $\delta A = A - <A>$, then $[\delta A, \delta B] = iC$; further, $<\delta A^2><\delta B^2> \geq \frac{1}{4} <C^2>$, giving the Heisenberg uncertainty principle $\Delta A \Delta B \geq 1/2 <C>$ (for details, see Gershenfeld, 2000, p. 256). The uncertainty equation models the expected variance around the expectation value of the operators while the right hand side gives the expectation value of the commutator. In signal detection theory, the uncertainty principle becomes the Fourier pair $\sigma_A \sigma_B \geq \frac{1}{2}$ (see Cohen, 1995; Rieffel, 2007).

[2] http://www.msgroup.com.tw/index.htm N-dimension Organization = Domain knowledge + Synergy +e-Centric + Growth

[3] CMMI is a numeric scale used to "rate" the maturity of a software development process or team. There are five levels of maturity in CMMI: 1. performed, 2. managed, 3.

defined, 4. Quantitatively Managed and 5. Optimizing. To achieve CMMI level three, a process that qualifies for CMMI level two is instituted as a corporate standard. Then it is tailored and applied to standard process to individual projects. http://tynerblain.com/blog/2006/03/10/foundation-series-cmmi-levels-explained/

[4] http://www.mitac.com.tw/english/about.htm

[5] http://www.mitac.com.tw/english/project05.htm

[6] Developed by the Council for Economic Planning and Development, Challenge 2008 –National Development Plan is combination of new policies and strategy to guide Taiwan's IT development to meet the global IT challenge and move toward to eBusiness era. http://www.cepd.gov.tw/encontent/m1.aspx?sNo=0001451&ex=1&ic=0000069

[7] 1.00 TWD = 0.0308623 USD rate on September 27, 2009 http://www.xe.com/ucc/convert.cgi?Amount=1&From=TWD&To=USD&image.x=55&image.y=11

[8] http://tiponet.tipo.gov.tw/home/

[9] In computing, **service-oriented architecture (SOA)** provides a set of principles of governing concepts used during phases of systems development and integration. Such an architecture will package functionality as *interoperable services*: software modules provided as a service can be integrated or used by several organizations, even if their respective client systems are substantially different. http://en.wikipedia.org/wiki/Service-oriented_architecture

Chapter 16
The Diffusion of Internet Technology in Rural Minnesota:
An Empirical Study

Susan M. Jones
Southwest Minnesota State University, USA

Ronald G. Stover
South Dakota State University, USA

ABSTRACT

The research problem for this study was to determine to what extent organizational size, organizational complexity, and organizational social ties impacted the creation of an organizational Web page and its relative time of adoption among the organizational members of the chamber of commerce in a small city in Minnesota. The research utilized a cross-sectional design, with data being gathered via a self-administered mail survey. A total of 173 surveys were completed and returned for a response rate of 48.60%.

Two independent variables were statistically significant in predicting whether an organization would have a Web page: 1) organizational size measured by the number of paid employees; and 2) organizational complexity indexed by the number of unique job descriptions, physical locations in Minnesota, and physical locations in other states. The results of this research provide practical information to formal organizations considering the adoption of an organizational Web page.

INTRODUCTION

Three theories provided the foundation for this study: network theory, Everett M. Rogers' ([1962] 2003) diffusion of innovations theory, and Peter Blau's (1970) structural differentiation theory of formal organizations. Each of these theories contributed to a theory of diffusion developed by these authors. The goal of this research study was to determine whether the propositions developed in this theory of diffusion provided a reasonable

DOI: 10.4018/978-1-60960-463-9.ch016

basis for describing the diffusion of Web page technology.

BACKGROUND

The adoption of a specific technology – a Web page – by organizations in a rural setting is the focus of this research study. In this section of the chapter, two tasks are accomplished. First, concepts critical to this study are defined. Second, key independent and dependent variables that have been identified in the literature in prior diffusion studies are described.

Critical Concepts

There are three concepts critical to this study: 1) innovation; 2) diffusion; and 3) ideal types. These concepts are defined in the following sections of this chapter.

Innovation. A review of the literature indicates varying perceptions among researchers about the concept of innovation itself. "It seems to us that we have, at the moment, only a slender thread of agreement or commonality among the writers on innovation. That thread of agreement is one to which we have already referred: the agreement on the nature of the process" (Becker and Whisler, 1967, pp.467). Indeed, innovation is described as a "process" by a number of researchers (Evan and Black, 1967; Feldman, 2002; Knight, 1967; Landry et al., 2002; Mirvis et al., 1991; Shepard, 1967). These researchers also believe that innovation occurs over a period of time.

Despite many researchers viewing innovation as a process, there is variation in their actual definitions of this phenomenon. A number of researchers make the distinction between "invention" and "innovation." Becker and Whisler (1967) felt that innovation was a process that followed invention. Innovation and invention were viewed as separate and unique processes, in terms of their timing and location, by these researchers. Knight (1967)

pointed out that innovation could relate to any change which was new to a particular organization, not necessarily new to society. Mohr (1969) summed up the difference between invention and innovation by noting, "Invention implies bringing something new into being; innovation implies bringing something new into use" (p. 112). Smits (2002) pointed out that excellence in producing an invention and excellence in producing a given innovation are two very different things. Shepard (1967) makes an interesting point that innovation can also be not doing something. " ... [I]t is an innovation if an organization learns not to do something it formerly did and proceeds to not do it in a sustained way" (p. 470).

Many researchers also equate innovation with economic benefit. Archibugi and Iammarino (2002) point out that innovations are becoming increasingly costly and rapidly obsolete. This obsolescence provided incentive, they theorized, for innovators to commercialize or sell their innovations in increasingly larger and larger markets. Dispersion of an innovation via commercialization perhaps alludes to the increasing globalization of the marketplace. A positive economic outcome can serve as an incentive to innovate Feldman (2002) believed. She noted, "Innovation is the ability to blend and weave different types of knowledge into something new, different, and unprecedented that has economic value" (p. 49). Evan and Black (1967) argued that the innovation process within organizations is necessary for long-term survival due to pressures placed upon the organization by its surrounding environment.

Some researchers have distinguished between "radical" and "incremental" innovations. Dewar and Dutton (1986) viewed "radical" innovation as those that involve fundamental changes and that are a clear deviation or alteration from current practices in the organization. Shepard (1967) pointed out that it is typically in times of organizational crisis that radical innovations are adopted; " ... [T]he uncertainty and anxiety generated by the crisis make organization members eager to adopt new structures that promise to relieve the anxiety" (p. 473).

One of the leading researchers and theorists in the area of innovation, Everett Rogers ([1962] 2003), focused on the perception of the adopter in his definition of innovation. Rogers viewed any idea, practice, or object that is perceived as new by a given actor as being an innovation. "It matters little … whether or not the idea is 'objectively' new as measured by the lapse of time since its first use or discovery. … if the idea seems new to the individual, it is an innovation" (p. 12). This view is particularly relevant for this study. The innovation being studied – use of an organizational Web page – while in existence in society for more than a decade can still be perceived as "new." The newness of this innovation is perhaps particularly true for potential adopters of this technology that are located in rural areas, as are the respondents in this study.

This study focuses on innovation, not invention. The definition of innovation used in this study follows that developed by Knight (1967) who stated that, "An innovation is the adoption of a change which is new to an organization and to the relevant environment" (p. 478).

Diffusion. A corollary concept to innovation is diffusion. A key question to be investigated, once a new concept or idea has been considered or identified as potentially useful within a given setting, is how does use of the innovation spread or diffuse to others? Researchers offer a variety of perspectives on this topic, viewing diffusion as a key way in which change occurs in society. Katz et al. (1963) viewed diffusion as one of the major mechanisms of social and technological change. Wejnert (2002) believed that the diffusion process could apply to the spread of ideas and concepts, technical information, and practices within a given social system. " … [T]he spread denotes flow of movement from a source to an adopter typically via communication and influence. Such communication and influence alter an adopter's … probability of adopting an innovation" (p. 297).

Researchers also note that technological innovations, in particular, may alter as they move through the diffusion process. "Technologies develop as they diffuse, and as they progress, they become more attractive to potential adopters, affecting the base to which the initial innovation is modified; thus, rate, direction, diffusion, and adoption are intertwined" (Podolny and Stuart, 1995). Mirvis et al. (1991) theorized that collected experience and improvements diffused, along with the technology itself.

Katz et al. (1963) emphasized the link between the social structure and the diffusion process. Specifically, they highlighted the importance of channels of communication within a social structure and the impact which the existing values or cultures could have on adoption or non-adoption of the innovation. Similarly, Rogers ([1962] 2003) stressed the importance of communication links and the influence of peers in the diffusion process. "This dependence on the experience of near peers suggests that the heart of the diffusion process consists of the modeling and imitation by potential adopters of their network partners who have previously adopted. Diffusion is a very social process that involves interpersonal communication relationships" (Rogers, [1962] 2003, p. 19).

In this research study the following definition of diffusion employed by Rogers ([1962] 2003) will be used: "*Diffusion* is the process by which (1) an *innovation* (2) is *communicated* through certain *channels* (3) over *time* (4) among members of a *social* system" (p. 11).

Ideal Types. An ideal type is a concept that is constructed by a researcher to generalize and simplify data. Major similarities and characteristics within the data are emphasized in a given ideal type category; minor differences are ignored. When each data point in a population is assigned to an ideal type category, a taxonomy is formed (Hughes et al., 2002).

Researchers have used a wide variety of adopter taxonomies in innovation studies. Of particular importance to this study is the taxonomy developed by Rogers ([1962] 2003), a leading researcher in the area of innovation. His taxonomy consists of five adopter categories: 1) innovators, 2) early adopters, 3) early majority, 4) late majority, and 5) laggards. Rogers' taxonomy is used in this study to categorize one dependent variable – the relative timing of the adoption of Web page technology.

Rogers provided a description for each of the adopter categories in his taxonomy. He described adopters in the "innovators" category as venturesome. Innovators have a great interest in new ideas, causing them to venture outside their local network of peers. Often innovators control substantial financial resources to help them to absorb setbacks if a new innovation is not successful. Innovators serve as gatekeepers as they bring innovations into their social circles. "Early adopters," according to Rogers, tend to be more integrated into the local social system. Early adopters often serve as opinion leaders within their social circles, providing information and advice about innovations to others. Early adopters are role models for others in their social circles because they are respected by their peers. Those in the "early majority" adopter category adopt innovations just before the average member of the social system. The early majority interacts frequently with their peers; however, they seldom hold positions of opinion leadership. The "late majority" adopters adopt innovations just after the average member of a social system. Those in the late majority category tend to be cautious and skeptical about new innovations. Generally, peer pressure is necessary to cause a member of the late majority to adopt an innovation. Members of this adopter group have fewer financial resources so they must be reasonably certain about the success of an innovation before adopting it. "Laggards" are the last in a social system to adopt an innovation. Members of this group are the most localized and isolated of all of the groups. Laggards tend to have traditional values and are suspicious of innovations and change. Based on his empirical research, Rogers determined that the distribution

of adopters of a given new innovation over time mirrored a normal Bell curve ([1962] 2003).

Critical Dependent Variables

Two aspects of the adoption of an innovation have been emphasized in the literature as dependent variables: 1) the adoption or non-adoption of the innovation; and 2) the relative timing of the adoption.

Adoption or Non-Adoption of an Innovation. The great majority of the innovation researchers consider the adoption or non-adoption of the innovation to be the dependent variable in the adoption process (Corwin, 1975; Dewar and Dutton, 1986; Evan and Black, 1967; Guthrie, 1999; Landry et al., 2002; Majumdar, 1995). Katz et al. (1963) set forth a caution regarding the distinction between first use of a new innovation at a particular point in time and continued use over time. " … [F]irst-use may or may not be followed by continued use …. Thus a measure of 'sustained use' might be appropriate for some purposes, but for other purposes it may be of interest to consider only 'ever use'" (p. 240).

Date / Time of Adoption. The date / time of adoption has also been viewed as a key dependent variable by a number of innovation researchers. Becker (1970), in his study of the adoption of innovations by local health officers in the states of Michigan, Illinois, and New York in 1967, viewed the time of adoption as the dependent variable. "The major dependent variable is *time of adoption*, the determination of which enables the researcher to test the hypothesis that the diffusion of a particular innovation was indeed associated with informal communication patterns among adopters and to discover characteristics associated with individuals who are pioneer, early, or late adopters" (p. 270).

Katz (1961) also pointed out the importance of the variable of time. " … [I]t is the element of time, perhaps more than any other, which makes the study of diffusion possible" (p. 72). Katz was referring to his comparison of two key diffusion studies: the hybrid seed corn studies of Ryan and Gross (1943) and the research by Katz et al. (1963) describing the response of doctors to the availability of the new drug tetracycline. Katz (1961) felt time was a key dependent variable as he found that later adopters could depend to some degree on the accumulated experience of the earlier innovators.

Critical Independent Variables

A very important question facing sociologists studying the diffusion of innovation pertains to the factors impacting an organization's decision to adopt a new innovation such as the use of an organizational Web page. Specifically, an investigation of factors or independent variables impacting use of this new technology is critically important. " … [T]here are few other topics as important as the issue of the determinants and effects of technological change" (Powell, 1987, p. 197).

Each of the key independent variables that has been identified by prior research as critical for understanding technological innovation is described in the following paragraphs, along with their applicability to this study.

Organizational Size. Many researchers have studied the impact of organizational size on the propensity of organizations to adopt new innovations. Some have found a positive association between organizational size and willingness of the organization to adopt new innovations. Rogers ([1962] 2003), for example, found that the size of an organization was consistently positively related to its degree of innovativeness. He noted, "Large size was highly related to innovativeness" (p. 409). With regard to size, Corwin (1975) also found positive effects. He identified many of the attributes of larger firms that contributed to their willingness to innovate. " … [R]ecent research … suggests that this variable [size] should not be discounted. Larger organizations tend to be char-

acterized by more conflict and uncertainty which can lead to change, and to permit more flexibility and autonomy; larger organizations, perhaps, are more secure than smaller ones, and are in a better position to take risks associated with innovation; and greater manpower and other resources are more likely to be available in larger than in smaller organizations" (p. 5). Other researchers have found similar results. In a survey of the adoption of Internet-based technology, Guthrie (1999) found a positive relationship between organizational size and the degree of innovativeness. Larger organizations tend to use the World Wide Web (WWW) to a greater degree, his research showed, because they had more fiscal and personnel resources to devote to implement this new technology, as well as more effective marketing strategies than did smaller organizations.

Dewar and Dutton (1986) in their study of footwear manufacturers in the mid-1970's found that organizational size appeared to have a particularly significant impact on the adoption of more radical innovations. Their findings showed that the larger footwear manufacturers had more engineers, more research equipment, larger labs, and more slack time at their disposal, all of which facilitated the adoption of new innovations.

On the other hand, not all researchers have found a positive relationship between large organizational size and a high degree of organizational innovation. " … [T]here is no agreement on the relative importance of size vis-à-vis other aspects of organizational structure. Empirical studies using size as a major variable have come to rather contradictory conclusions" (Hall et al., 1967, p. 904). Other researchers note that size is no guarantee that more resources will be devoted to the adoption of new innovations. Mohr (1969) attempted to identify the determinants of innovation in public agencies by studying full-time local health departments in Illinois, Michigan, New York, Ohio, and Ontario in the 1960's. He concluded that large size was not a guarantee that increased resources would be allocated to the adoption of new innovations. Majumdar (1995) conducted a study of firms in the U.S. telecommunications industry in 1987. His findings indicated that organizational size had an insignificant impact on the innovative activity of the firms.

Organizational Complexity. Rogers ([1962] 2003) defined complexity as, " ... the degree to which an organization's members possess a relatively higher level of knowledge and expertise, usually measured by the members' range of occupational specialties and their degree of professional training (expressed by formal training)" (p. 412). Therefore, Rogers associated the number of unique occupations within an organization and the level of educational credentials required for these positions to be an indicator of the complexity of the organization.

Hall et al. (1967) expanded on this definition of complexity. They included not only the division of labor, but also the spatial dispersion of the organization. In other words, Hall et al. viewed organizations that had sub-divisions in multiple geographical locations as being more complex than those organizations that had just one location.

There is nearly unanimous agreement among researchers about the positive association between a higher degree of organizational complexity and increased adoption of innovations in organizations (Corwin, 1975; Dewar and Dutton, 1986; Evan and Black, 1967; Guthrie, 1999; Hage and Aiken, 1967; Majumdar, 1995; Sapolsky, 1967). Perhaps the focus on organizational complexity extends back to Durkheim's ([1933] 1997) *The Division of Labor in Society*. "By determining the main cause of the progress of the division of labour, we have at the same time determined the essential factor in what is called civilisation. It is itself a necessary consequence of the changes occurring in the volume and density of societies" (p. 276). Hage and Aiken (1967) also support the significance of Durkheim's work. "Since the publication of the English translation of Durkheim's *The Division of Labor*, the degree of complexity or specializa-

tion has been a key concept in the organizational literature" (p. 507).

Blau and Scott (1962) also focused on the significance of organizational complexity. They theorized that complexity in the form of specialization of job positions appeared to be essential for organizations to make rewards proportional to contributions.

Researchers have built upon the earlier work of Durkheim and Blau, relating the presence of occupational specialties within an organization to the level of innovation adoption. Dewar and Dutton (1986) found that " ... [T]he more different types of knowledge that are present, i.e., the more complex or specialized the organization, the higher the rate of radical innovation adoption" (p. 1424). Guthrie (1999) found a similar relationship between complexity / specialization and innovation in his study of the adoption of Internet technology by medium and large organizations in the U.S. in 1996. Guthrie (1999) noted, " ... [T]here is a strong association between complex organizational structures and the adoption of new information technologies" (p. 585).

Rogers ([1962] 2003) also focused on the importance of organizational complexity relative to the adoption of innovations. "Complexity encourages organizational members to grasp the value of innovations" (p. 412).

Thus, the research on this topic indicates that organizational complexity can take a number of forms. These include: 1) the level of professional training possessed by members of the organization; 2) the range of occupational specialties found within the organization; and 3) the degree of spatial dispersion of the components of the organization. Each of these indicators of organizational complexity will be considered in this diffusion study.

Organizational Social Ties. One focus in innovation research has been the concept of organizational social ties. Researchers in this area believe that the pattern of ties linking the members or actors within a society may impact the adoption of an innovation. For example, Landry et al.

(2002) focused on organizational social ties and their impact on innovation adoption. They studied manufacturing firms in diverse industries in the Montreal area in 2000. They found that trust is a key aspect of organizational social ties. Their findings indicated that firms that were characterized by a high level of trust among organizational members were more likely to innovate. " … [N]etworks develop as actors develop reliable and effective communication channels across organizational boundaries" (p. 687). The social ties or networks that develop between a given organization and the outside may serve as a conduit across which information about new innovations may travel.

Granovetter (1983) has been a key theorist and researcher in the area of social ties. He made a distinction between a "weak" social tie, which he considered to be an acquaintance, and a "strong" social tie, which he considered to be a relative or a friend with whom a close relationship is maintained. Regarding the diffusion of innovation, Granovetter believed that weak ties may play the most significant role initially, when information about the innovation is being dispersed. He noted, "Weak ties provide people with access to information and resources beyond those available in their own social circle …" (p. 209). He argued bridging social circles via the connections or links provided by these weak ties then facilitates the spread of new ideas and innovations.

While weak social ties are important in sharing initial information about a new innovation, Granovetter asserts strong social ties play the greatest role in determining whether a new innovation will be adopted. "Weak ties provide the bridges over which innovations cross the boundaries of social groups; the decision-making, however, is influenced mainly by the strong ties network in each group" (p. 219). Granovetter indicates that it is via the weak social ties that information about a new innovation travels from one social group or organization to another. However, when the adoption decision is made, it is the parties with whom the decision maker maintains strong social

ties that may have the most impact on the innovation decision.

Further, Granovetter viewed the ties linking business and professional individuals and organizations to be weak social ties because they tend to be limited to interaction in the work setting. As Wellman and Wortley (1990) note, "Few weak ties extend outside the job" (p. 583). These weak ties have a fairly high probability of serving as information conduits for the sharing of data on a new innovation between social groups (Granovetter, 1983). Much of the transmission of new information about innovations appears to occur within the work setting via weak social ties, which dominate formal organizations (Granovetter, 1983; Wellman and Wortley, 1990).

In their study of the diffusion of hybrid seed corn in the 1930's and 1940's, Ryan and Gross (1943) alluded to the difference between weak and strong network ties in their study findings. They stated, "Commercial channels, especially salesmen, were most important as original sources of knowledge, while neighbors were most important as influences leading to acceptance" (p. 15). In this situation, the salesmen appear to have a weak tie to the potential adopters of the seed corn, while the neighbors appear to have a far stronger tie with the potential adopters. This parallels the work of Granovetter (1983) and Wellman and Wortley (1990) with respect to the diffusion of innovation within organizations.

MAIN FOCUS OF THE CHAPTER

This section of the chapter includes several parts. First, the problem statement of this research study is identified. Second, the research design is described. Third, the theories that provide a basis for this study are described, along with the theory of diffusion developed by the authors. Fourth, a summary of the research findings is provided. Fifth, theoretical implications are presented. Sixth, practical implications of this study are described. Finally, suggestions for future research are offered.

Problem Statement

The research question which this study seeks to answer is as follows:

To what extent do organizational size, organizational complexity, and organizational social ties impact the creation of an organizational Web page and its relative time of adoption?

The Research Design

The study population consisted of the 356 organizational members of the chamber of commerce in a small midwestern city. Through the use of a mailed self-administered survey to respondents representing these organizations, the authors sought to determine the extent to which organizational size, organizational complexity, and organizational social ties impacted the adoption of a Web page by business organizations.

No sampling method was needed since the survey was sent to all of the organizational members of the chamber of commerce rather than to only a select group. Since no sampling technique of the population was used in this survey research, the survey results should provide an unbiased representation of Web page adoption by the entire population of organizational members of the chamber of commerce. Members of the chamber of commerce span a broad spectrum of industries and range in size from very small to very large.

A list of the organizational members was obtained from the chamber of commerce's Web site. This listing provided the following information for each member: 1) organization name, 2) current address, 3) phone number, and 4) a brief description of the organization's purpose or products / services. This information was used to create a mailing list for the survey conducted by the authors.

Study Population and Unit of Analysis. The study population was selected for two key reasons. First, membership in the chamber of commerce serves as a network or link among key organizational leaders in the community. The importance of such professional contacts and networking has been highlighted as an important aspect of innovation. As Wejnert (2002) noted, " … [A]doption of an innovation by a network's more prominent members induces adoption across community members …" (p. 313). Second, membership in the chamber of commerce potentially provides a good cross section of the business organizations located in this community.

Data Collection. The data were collected for this study during the October—December 2004 time period. A survey packet consisting of three components was developed. The first component was a cover letter for the survey signed by one of the study authors and by the president and chief executive officer (CEO) of the chamber of commerce. The letter explained to the members of the chamber the rationale for the study. The second component of the packet was the survey instrument. It was printed on one sheet of tan ledger-sized paper (11" X 17"). When folded in half, all four pages of the survey could be included on this one sheet of paper. The final component of the survey packet mailed to potential respondents was a self-addressed, stamped, return mail envelope. The survey packets were addressed to the "Owner / General Manager" of each organization, as per the suggestion of Dillman (2000).

To encourage and remind potential respondents to complete the survey, a second complete survey package (including the survey instrument, a second copy of the original signed cover letter, and a self-addressed, stamped, return mail envelope), along with a half-page "reminder message" was mailed to those potential respondents who had not returned a completed survey in early December 2004. This second mailing of the complete survey package generated additional completed surveys. The final overall response rate was 173 surveys completed out of a possible 356, for a total response rate of 48.60%.

This response rate appears to be quite favorable, considering that 'organizations' are the unit of analysis. Dillman points out that organizations may be a difficult group to survey when he notes, "Surveys of business and other organizations face challenges different from those for any other type of survey. These potential difficulties may help explain why a review of 183 business surveys (in selected journals published since 1990) revealed an average response rate of 21%" (2000, p. 323). The overall response rate for this survey was substantially higher than the one referenced by Dillman. The Statistical Package for the Social Sciences (SPSS) software package was used to conduct the analysis on the data received from the survey respondents.

The dependent variables were each operationalized with a separate question on the survey. Respondents were asked to identify if they had or had not adopted an organizational Web page. If a Web page were in use, respondents were asked to identify its date of adoption.

Theoretical Basis

Three differing theories may contribute to the explanation for diffusion of Web page technology: network theory; the diffusion of innovations theory developed by Rogers ([1962] 2003); and a structural differentiation theory of formal organizations developed by Blau (1970). In this section of this chapter, each theory is described and discussed. They then serve as the basis for a "theory of diffusion" developed by the authors. Propositions developed from this theory of diffusion are tested to determine if the theory provides a reasonable basis for describing the adoption of Web page technology.

Network Theory. The preponderance of theoretical analysis conducted by sociologists with regard to innovation and diffusion is based on network theory. Specifically, network theorists try to understand the objective pattern of ties linking the members or actors within a society.

A common goal of network theorists is to explain patterns among these ties that operate beneath the surface of the social system. For these theorists, a "social system" is a set of elements or components that are related to one another in a fairly stable manner over a period of time. It is important to note, however, that change and adaptation are also continuous processes within a social system (Hughes et al., 2002, pp. 18-19).

A key element in network analysis is the concept "node," by which network researchers mean any unit of analysis in network theory (i.e., individuals, groups, organizations, clusters of ties, or nation-states) (Wellman, 1983). "Ties" or communication channels link nodes in a network. Various types of ties can link the nodes in a social network, including oral, written, personal and impersonal modes of communication. Wellman believes that an actor's position in the social structure plays a key role in his or hers network relationships. He notes, "The most direct way to study a social structure is to analyze the pattern of ties linking its members. ... Try to describe these patterns and use the descriptions to learn how network structures constrain social behavior and social change" (p. 157).

Rogers' Diffusion of Innovations Theory. Rogers is perhaps the key theorist regarding the diffusion of innovations. The first edition of Rogers' landmark text *Diffusion of Innovations* was published in 1962. Since that time, it has been updated a number of times, with the fifth edition being published in 2003. During this time, Rogers has completed an extensive amount of research he based on his theory. His work has ranged from the study of agricultural innovations to the diffusion of health and family planning innovations to educational innovations.

For Rogers ([1962] 2003), the diffusion process consists of four main elements: 1) the innovation, 2) communication channels, 3) time, and 4) the social system. "These elements are identifiable in every diffusion research study and in every diffusion campaign or program" (p. 11).

An innovation refers to an idea, a practice, or an object that is perceived as new by the potential adopter. An organizational Web page, which is the focus of this study, would be an example.

Communication channels form a link between an information source and the potential adopter of the innovation, may be personal or impersonal, and are used to share information about an innovation. An example of a personal communication channel would be sharing information with a neighbor about the latest gardening techniques. An example of an impersonal communication channel would be learning about these same new gardening techniques via a television program.

Time refers to the point at which a potential adopter actually decides whether or not to adopt the new innovation. Characteristics of the innovation can impact the point in time at which an innovation is adopted; characteristics of the adopter can also have significant impact.

The **social system** is the set of social elements or social components that are related to one another in a fairly stable manner over time. The social system impacts the adoption of an innovation. For example, if the members of a social system have very little education or few financial resources, they may be unlikely to adopt a technological innovation such as the Internet. Change and adaptation occur continually in a social system. The resulting decision by the potential adopter to implement the innovation or not to do so impacts the social system in which the potential adopter functions. Katz et al. (1963) observe, " ... [T]he diffusion of innovation is one of the major mechanisms of social and technical change" (p. 237).

According to Rogers, the innovation-decision process involves both the seeking of information by the potential adopter and the subsequent processing of this information. When a potential adopter is faced with an innovation, he or she will seek out information about the costs and benefits

of the innovation. A common source from which information is sought is others within the social system of the potential adopter, particularly those who have previously adopted the innovation.

Blau's Structural Differentiation Theory. Although Blau's (1970) theory of structural differentiation does not explicitly address the adoption of innovations, it is important for this study because Blau attempts to predict patterns of structure and functioning in formal organizations. It is important to understand such patterns as they relate to formal organizations and innovation. These patterns of structure and functioning are theorized by Blau to result from a variety of independent variables that act upon the organization. Two of the independent variables he identified and studied – organizational size and organizational complexity -- may have a significant impact on the adoption of an innovation by a formal organization.

Blau was quite specific about his definition of size as it relates to this proposition and the theory itself. "The operational definition of size is number of employees" (Blau, 1970, p. 204). Blau refers to two opposite effects that an increase in organization size may have. On the one hand, a larger organizational size will generally require additional managers and supervisors in the organization (Blau refers to this as the indirect effect). On the other hand, structural differentiation will occur as the organization becomes larger, leading to more workers per manager (Blau refers to this as the direct effect). Blau's research indicated that the direct effect of structural differentiation more than offsets the increase in management employees that occurred as organizations became larger.

Summary of Existing Theories

Based on the three theories described above and an extensive review of the existing research, three organizational characteristics appear to have special significance in the diffusion and adoption of an innovation -- organizational size, complexity within the organization, and social ties. These three characteristics are the three independent variables that will serve as a cornerstone of the theory of diffusion to be described in the next section of this chapter. That theory will be a key component of this research study.

A Theory of Diffusion

The theory of diffusion developed by the authors is based on aspects of each of the three theories discussed in the previous sections of this chapter – network theory, Rogers' diffusion theory, and Blau's structural differentiation theory of formal organizations. The goal of the creation of this theory was to develop a reasonable, comprehensive theory to explain the diffusion and adoption of a technological innovation by a formal organization. This theory of diffusion will be diagrammed, its major propositions will be outlined, and its key variables will be identified in the following sections of this chapter.

Theory Overview. Certainly, aspects of network theory can be applied to this study of the adoption of Web page technology. "Computer networks are inherently social networks, linking people, organizations, and knowledge" (Wellman, 2001, p. 2031). Web pages link organizations to the Internet, the largest and most fully connected social network of all (Wellman, 2001). The contribution of network theory to this research study is particularly evident in the independent variable, organizational social ties, which is included in this study. The diffusion theory developed by Rogers ([1962] 2003) provides the basis for the dependent variables used in this present research study: 1) adoption or non-adoption of the innovation, and 2) relative date / time of adoption. Blau's (1970) theory of structural differentiation in formal organizations contributes greatly to this theory of diffusion because it provides the basis for two of the independent variables used in this current research study: 1) organizational size, and 2) organizational complexity.

A model of the theory of diffusion appears in Figure 1. The indicators of each of the independent

Figure 1. Diagram of the theory of diffusion

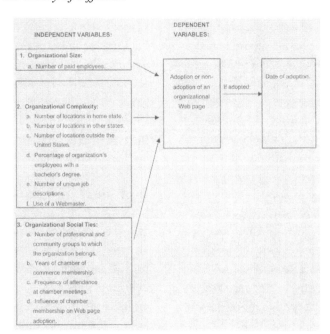

variables that are tested in this research study are also listed in this model diagram.

Propositions and Tests of Hypotheses

The findings of this study are summarized around the propositions of, and hypotheses developed from, the theory of diffusion model. Six propositions were developed based on the three theories described above. Hypotheses derived from each proposition were developed and tested in a two-stage process. The first three hypotheses (H_1, H_2, and H_3) were tested to determine the significance of the relationship between the independent variables of 1) organizational size, 2) organizational complexity, and 3) organizational social ties and the adoption or non-adoption of an organizational Web page. For any of the first three hypotheses that were supported with a statistically significant relationship, the second step was to test three subsequent hypotheses (H_4, H_5, and H_6) pertaining to the relative date of Web page adoption. The findings from this study are summarized below.

Proposition #1: Organizational size is associated with adoption of new innovation.

Hypothesis 1 (H1): *There is an association between the size of an organization and the creation of a Web page by that organization.*

Chi square was used to test the statistical significance of the relationship between the two variables included in this proposition: organizational size and the existence of an organizational Web page. The chi square value testing this relationship has an asymptotic significance level of .001, assuming a two-sided test of significance. This value is statistically significant at the .05 level. The fact that chi square is statistically significant and the phi correlation coefficient is moderately positive at .364 indicates there is a statistically significant, positive relationship between the number of em-

ployees and the existence of an organizational Web page. Therefore, the null hypothesis is rejected and the research hypothesis (H_1) is accepted. Based on the survey responses received in this study, there does indeed appear to be a positive association between the size of an organization as measured by its number of employees and the creation of a Web page by that organization.

Proposition #2: Organizational complexity is associated with adoption of new technology.

Hypothesis 2 (H2): *There is an association between organizational complexity and the creation of a Web page by that organization.*

Four indicators were used to measure the independent variable in this hypothesis. They were: 1) the number of additional locations, if any, at which the business operates in Minnesota, 2) whether the organization has locations in states other than Minnesota, 3) the proportion of organizational employees who have at least a bachelor's degree, and 4) the number of unique job descriptions which the organization has.

Three of the indicators of organizational complexity provide statistically significant support for research hypothesis two (H_2): 1) number of additional locations in Minnesota, 2) additional locations in other states, and 3) number of unique job descriptions that the organization has. Only the indicator for the proportion of the organization's employees who have a bachelor's degree or higher was not statistically significant in indicating whether the organization would have a Web page. The three indicators of the independent variable that were statistically significant had a phi correlation coefficient of moderate strength (i.e., at least .2501) or higher. On the basis of these results, the conclusion can be drawn that there is an association between organizational complexity and the existence of an organizational Web page.

Proposition #3: Organizational social ties are associated with adoption of new innovations.

Hypothesis 3 (H3): *There is an association between the presence of an organization's number of social ties and the creation of a Web page by that organization.*

Three indicators were used to measure the independent variable to test this research hypothesis. The indicators were: 1) the number of professional and community organizations to which the organization belongs, 2) the number of years of membership in the Chamber of Commerce, and 3) the frequency of attendance at Chamber of Commerce meetings.

None of the indicators of organizational social ties provided statistically significant support for research hypothesis three. Therefore, the null hypothesis #3 is accepted. Thus, none of these three indicators of organizational social ties were further analyzed in research hypothesis #6 to determine if this independent variable has a statistically significant impact on the relative time of Web page adoption by the organization.

Proposition #4: Organizational size is associated with the relative date on which a new innovation is adopted.

The survey respondents who had adopted an organization Web page were sub-divided into two groups: "early adopters" and "late adopters." A frequency distribution for the date of Web page adoption reported by the survey respondents was developed. The respondents that fell into the "early adopters" group had adopted an organizational Web page in the 1993—2000 time frame; respondents that fell into the "late adopters" group had adopted an organizational Web page in the 2001—2004 time frame. A natural break in the data occurred between 2000 and 2001.

Hypothesis 4 (H4): *There is an association between the size of an organization and the relative date on which an organization adopts an organizational Web page.*

Since Hypothesis #1 indicated a significant relationship between organizational size and the existence of an organizational Web page, Hypothesis #4 was tested for significance to determine if there is an association between organizational size and the timing of Web page adoption. However, since the chi square value was not statistically significant at the .05 level, the null hypothesis #4 is accepted and research hypothesis #4 is rejected. Based on the survey responses received in this study, there does not appear to be statistical significance between the size of an organization and the relative date on which the organization adopted a Web page.

Proposition #5: Organizational complexity is associated with the relative date on which a new innovation is adopted.

Hypothesis 5 (H5): *There is an association between organizational complexity and the relative date on which an organization adopts an organizational Web page.*

Only the three indicators that were statistically significant in Hypothesis #2 were carried forward for testing Hypothesis #5 to determine if there is a statistically significant association between organizational complexity and the relative time when an organizational Web page is adopted. The three indicators that were tested in Hypothesis #5 include: 1) number of additional locations in Minnesota, 2) whether the organization has additional locations in other states, and 3) number of unique job descriptions that the organization has.

Two of the indicators of organizational complexity provided statistically significant support for research hypothesis five (H$_5$). These statistically significant variables were: 1) the presence of additional locations in other states, and 2) the number of unique job descriptions of the organization. These same two indicators of the independent variable also had a correlation coefficient of moderate strength (i.e., .2501 to .4999). On the basis of these results, the conclusion can be drawn that there is an association between organizational complexity and the relative date on which the organization adopted a Web page.

Proposition #6: An organization's social ties are associated with the relative date on which a new **innovation** is adopted.

Hypothesis 6 (H6): *There is an association between an organization's number of social ties and the relative date on which an organization adopts an organizational Web page.*

None of the three indicators of organizational social ties was statistically significant in the testing of Hypothesis #3. Therefore, none of these indicators for this variable was carried forward for the testing of Hypothesis #6 to determine if there is a statistically significant association between an organization's number of social ties and the relative date when an organizational Web page is adopted.

Findings in Relation to the Research Question

On the basis of the results described above, there does appear to be statistically significant support for a number of components within the theory of diffusion as summarized in Table 1:

Issues, Controversies, Problems

Theoretical Interpretation of the Results

Based upon the findings of this study, it is believed that the original theory of diffusion proposed and diagrammed above should be modified. Organizational social ties has been removed from the theory of diffusion as an independent variable. The revised model of this theory is diagrammed in Figure 2.

The results of this research do provide support for two of the independent variables identified as indicators of Web page technology: 1) organizational size, and 2) organizational complexity. The selective combination of key aspects of three well-researched and well-publicized theories does provide a fairly good theoretical explanation for the adoption of a new technological innovation such as an organizational Web page. It is encouraging that a number of the operationalizations of

Figure 2. Diagram of the modified theory of diffusion

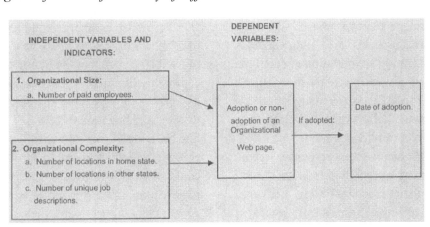

Table 1. Statistically Significant Results

Hypothesis	Independent Variable	Dependent Variable	Statistically Significant Indicators
# 1	Organizational Size	Existence of an organizational Web page.	1) Number of paid employees.
# 2	Organizational Complexity	Existence of an organizational Web page.	1) Number of unique job descriptions.
			2) Number of physical locations in Minnesota.
			3) Whether the organization has physical locations in other states.
# 5	Organizational Complexity	Relative date of Web page adoption.	1) Whether the organization has physical locations in other states.
			2) Number of unique job descriptions.

the independent variables in this research study proved to be statistically significant.

Also as a result of this study, the authors believe that two mediating or intervening variables may impact the respondent organization's decision to adopt an innovation such as Web page technology. Responses by respondents to several of the open-ended survey questions lend support to the need to consider mediating variables that may intervene between the independent variables of 1) organizational size, and 2) organizational complexity and the dependent variable of Web page adoption. The two proposed mediating variables are 1) the organization's motivation to adopt the innovation due to perceptions of the innovation's potential benefit; and 2) sources of assistance and / or information available to the organization as a potential adopter of an innovation.

Respondents' handwritten responses to the open-ended survey questions provide a starting point for operationalization of these mediating variables. For example, respondents indicated that a company sponsor, communication, and the desire to get their organization's name out to the public are among the reasons they were motivated to adopt an organizational Web page. These responses could relate to the first mediating variable – the organization's motivation for adoption of the innovation. Since nearly 86% of the 173 respondents to this survey are "for-profit organizations", the desire to minimize costs and maximize profits may serve as a motivation for the adoption of a new innovation.

For firms in competitive industries, the desire to capture market share may be a strong motivator. With the advent of the Internet and electronic commerce, competitors may now exist anywhere globally if they provide customers with access to their organizational Web site and offer online ordering of their merchandise. The desire to compete with these remotely located competitors could serve as an impetus for the adoption of Web page technology by for-profit organizations also. Any or all of these possibilities could serve as operationalizations of this "motivation or perceived potential" mediating variable.

A multitude of resources provided information to adopters of Web page technology in this survey according to the responses received. On-line research, a company sponsor, education, experience in the industry, a trained professional, and software are but a few of the many sources of information on Web page technology used by survey respondents. These responses could represent possible operationalizations of the second mediating variable – sources of assistance or information available.

Inclusion of these two mediating variables would modify the theory as diagrammed in Figure 3.

Practical Implications

The results of this research provide some relevant information to organizations in a rural setting that are considering the adoption of Web page technology. First, this study does indicate a statistically significant, positive relationship between organizational size operationalized as the number of employees and the existence of an organizational Web page. For organizations that currently do not have an organizational Web page but that are growing in terms of number of employees, it may be beneficial to consider adopting a Web page. A Web page may even be a necessity to compete effectively, once the host organization reaches a certain size.

Second, organizations with multiple locations within the United States appear to be more likely to adopt Web page technology. The presence or addition of multiple organizational locations may also provide organizational owners and managers with an indicator of the appropriate time to adopt such technology.

In sum, organizations that are larger and have multiple locations within the United States appear to have characteristics that lead to the adoption of an organizational Web page. However, the ideal timing of this adoption is more difficult to pinpoint from the variables included in this research study. Only the presence of multiple organizational locations in states outside the home state of the organization and a larger number of job descriptions within the organization appear to affect the timing of the adoption of Web page technology.

Figure 3. A potential theory of diffusion

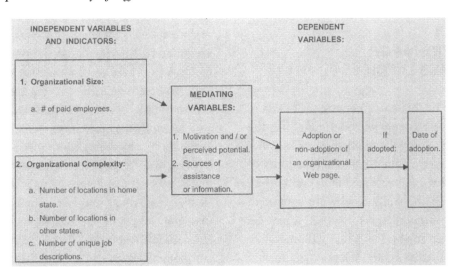

Limitations of the Study

This research study has several limitations. First, this research study investigated the adoption of Web page technology in only one small midwestern city. This focus can be very useful for the city under study to identify characteristics of organizations that have and have not adopted Web page technology. However, applying the results of this study to other cities should be done with caution. The results of this one case cannot be assumed to be universally applicable.

Second, this study provides a snapshot of the extent to which Web page technology was being utilized at one point in time: the fourth quarter of 2004. The relative proportion of organizations utilizing Web page technology can shift and is likely to be somewhat different from the results presented here if measured at a different point in time.

Third, the operationalization of the independent variables used in this research study may be the reason for the failure to accept some of the research hypotheses. It is possible that other operationalizations of these independent variables may have produced statistically significant results. Additional indicators of the independent variables are suggested in the section "Suggestions for Future Research" below.

SUGGESTIONS FOR FUTURE RESEARCH

The findings of this study suggest areas where additional research may be beneficial. First, the present study could be replicated on another organizational population, preferably in a city of similar size that is also located in a rural setting, to determine if the study results are consistent across different populations. Second, it may be helpful to re-do the present study with the same study population at a later date(s). This further research would transform the present study from its present cross-sectional state to one that is longitudinal. Third, further research should be done to identify additional theoretically relevant variables that may improve the overall explanatory power of the theory of diffusion model. A number of possible variables found in the literature include: 1) formalization, 2) centralization, and 3) innovation cost. Fourth, rather than eliminating the indicators of organizational social ties from the theory of diffusion, these indicators could instead be tested to determine if they apply to types of social organizations other than the chamber of commerce. Fifth, a study similar to this one could be done utilizing the two mediating variables proposed in the revised version of this theory: 1) the organization's motivation to adopt the innovation due to perceptions of the innovation's potential benefit, and 2) sources of assistance and/or information available to the organization as a potential adopter of an innovation. A study based on this more elaborate version of the model has the potential to provide an even richer, more valuable explanation of the adoption of an innovation by a formal organization.

CONCLUSION

This research adds to the growing body of theoretical knowledge on the adoption of innovations by organizations. This study, however, is somewhat unique as it focused on the adoption of new Internet technology. There are few detailed studies in this area, especially related to Web page and Internet utilization by formal organizations.

This study may also serve as a model for other researchers considering combining aspects of pre-existing theories into a single theoretical model that may better explain the focus of their research. In many cases there may be no pre-existing theory that aptly explains the research topic at hand. In cases such as in this study, the integration of components of several pre-existing theories may provide the best theoretical explanation.

Replication and expansion of this study will serve to validate or invalidate the worth of the theory of diffusion presented here. As Blau (1968) noted, "The only connection between different empirical investigations ... is the generalizations derived from each that go beyond its limited evidence" (p. 455). It is hoped that the present study has made a contribution toward these generalizations described by Blau.

REFERENCES

Archibugi, D., & Iammarino, S. (2002). The Globalization of Technological Innovation: Definition and Evidence. *Review of International Political Economy, 9*, 98–122. doi:10.1080/09692290110101126

Becker, M. H. (1970). Sociometric Location and Innovativeness: Reformulation and Extension of the Diffusion Model. *American Sociological Review, 35*, 267–282. doi:10.2307/2093205

Becker, S., & Whisler, T. L. (1967). The Innovative Organization: A Selective View of Current Theory and Research. *The Journal of Business, 40*, 462–469. doi:10.1086/295011

Blau, P. (1968). The Hierarchy of Authority in Organizations. *American Journal of Sociology, 73*, 453–467. doi:10.1086/224506

Blau, P. (1970). A Formal Theory of Differentiation in Organizations. *American Sociological Review, 35*, 201–218. doi:10.2307/2093199

Blau, P. M., & Scott, W. R. (1962). *Formal Organizations*. San Francisco: Chandler Publishing Company.

Corwin, R. G. (1975). Innovation in Organizations: The Case of Schools. *Sociology of Education, 48*, 1–37. doi:10.2307/2112048

Dewar, R. D., & Dutton, J. E. (1986). The Adoption of Radical and Incremental Innovation: An Empirical Analysis. *Management Science, 32*, 1422–1433. doi:10.1287/mnsc.32.11.1422

Dillman, D. A. (2000). *Mail and Internet Surveys*. New York: John Wiley & Sons, Inc.

Durkheim, E. (1997). *The Division of Labor. Translated by W. D. Halls*. New York: Free Press. (Original work published 1933)

Evan, W. M., & Black, G. (1967). Innovation in Business Organizations: Some Factors Associated With Success or Failure of Staff Proposals. *The Journal of Business, 40*, 519–530. doi:10.1086/295016

Feldman, M. P. (2002). The Internet Revolution and the Geography of Innovation. *International Social Science Journal, 54*, 47–56. doi:10.1111/1468-2451.00358

Granovetter, M. S. (1983). The Strength of Weak Ties: A Network Theory Revisited. In Collins, R. (Ed.), *Sociological Theory* (pp. 201–233). San Francisco: Jossey-Bass, Inc.

Guthrie, D. (1999). A Sociological Perspective on the Use of Technology: The Adoption of Internet Technology in U.S. Organizations. *Sociological Perspectives, 42*, 583–603.

Hage, J., & Aiken, M. (1967). Program Change and Organizational Properties: A comparative Analysis. *American Journal of Sociology, 72*, 503–519. doi:10.1086/224380

Hall, R. H., Haas, J. E., & Johnson, N. J. (1967). Organizational Size, Complexity, and Formalization. *American Sociological Review, 32*, 903–911. doi:10.2307/2092844

Hughes, M., & Kroehler, C. J. Vander Zanden & James W. (2002). *Sociology: The Core*. 6th Ed. New York: The McGraw-Hill Companies, Inc.

Katz, E. (1961). The Social Itinerary of Technical Change: Two Studies in the Diffusion of Innovation. *Human Organization, 20,* 70–82.

Katz, E., Levin, M. L., & Hamilton, H. (1963). Traditions of Research on the Diffusion of Innovation. *American Sociological Review, 28,* 237–252. doi:10.2307/2090611

Knight, K. E. (1967). A Descriptive Model of the Intra-Firm Innovation Process. *The Journal of Business, 40,* 478–496. doi:10.1086/295013

Landry, R., Amara, N., & Lamari, M. (2002). Does Social Capital Determine Innovation? To What Extent? *Technological Forecasting and Social Change, 69,* 681–701. doi:10.1016/S0040-1625(01)00170-6

Majumdar, S. K. (1995). The Determinants of Investment in New Technology: An Examination of Alternative Hypothesis. *Technological Forecasting and Social Change, 50,* 235–247. doi:10.1016/0040-1625(95)90095-0

Mirvis, P. H., Sales, A. L., & Hackett, E. J. (1991). The Implementation and Adoption of New Technology in Organizations: The Impact on Work, People and Culture. *Human Resource Management, 30,* 113–139. doi:10.1002/hrm.3930300107

Mohr, L. B. (1969). Determinants of Innovation in Organizations. *The American Political Science Review, 63,* 111–126. doi:10.2307/1954288

Podolny, J. M., & Stuart, T. E. (1995). A Role-Based Ecology of Technological Change. *American Journal of Sociology, 100,* 1224–1260. doi:10.1086/230637

Powell, W. W. (1987). Review Essay: Explaining Technological Change. *American Journal of Sociology, 93,* 185–197. doi:10.1086/228714

Rogers, E. M. (2003). *Diffusion of Innovations* (5th ed.). New York: The Free Press of Glencoe. (Original work published 1962)

Ryan, B., & Gross, N. C. (1943). The Diffusion of Hybrid Seed Corn in Two Iowa Communities. *Rural Sociology, 8,* 15–24.

Sapolsky, H. M. (1967). Organizational Structure and Innovation. *The Journal of Business, 40,* 497–510. doi:10.1086/295014

Shepard, H. A. (1967). Innovation-Resisting and Innovation-Producing Organizations. *The Journal of Business, 40,* 470–477. doi:10.1086/295012

Smits, R. (2002). Innovation Studies in the 21st Century: Questions from a User's Perspective. *Technological Forecasting and Social Change, 69,* 861–883. doi:10.1016/S0040-1625(01)00181-0

Wejnert, B. (2002). Integrating Models of Diffusion of Innovations: A Conceptual Framework. *Annual Review of Sociology, 28,* 297–326. doi:10.1146/annurev.soc.28.110601.141051

Wellman, B. (1983). Network Analysis: Some Basic Principles. In Randall, C. (Ed.), *Sociological Theory* (pp. 155–200). San Francisco: Jossey-Bass, Inc.

Wellman, B. (2001). Computer Networks as Social Networks. *Science, 293,* 2031–2034. doi:10.1126/science.1065547

Wellman, B., & Wortley, S. (1990). Different Strokes for Different Folks: Community Ties and Social Support. *American Journal of Sociology, 95,* 558–588. doi:10.1086/229572

Compilation of References

Aberdeen (2002). Making E-Sourcing Strategic -From tactical Technology to core business strategy.

Aberdeen (2005). Strategic Sourcing in the Mid-Market Benchmark-The Echo Boom in Supply Management.

Aberdeen (2007). The Advanced Sourcing & Negotiation Benchmark Report –"The Art and Science of the Deal.

Aberdeen (2006). *E-Sourcing: The Art & Science of the Deal.*

Abouzeedan, A., & Busler, M. (2006). Information Technology (IT) and Small and Medium-sized Enterprises (SMEs) Management. *Global Business Review, 7*(2), 243–257. doi:10.1177/097215090600700204

Abouzeedan, A., & Busler, M. (2007). Internetization Management. *Global Business Review, 8*(2), 303–321. doi:10.1177/097215090700800208

Achrol, R. S., & Kotler, P. (1999). Marketing in the network economy. *Journal of Marketing, 63,* 146–163. doi:10.2307/1252108

Adshead, A. (2001). The E-Supply Chain is Only as Strong as Its Weakest Link. *Computer Weekly, 2,* 42–46.

Afuah, A. (2001). Dynamic Boundaries of the Firm: Are Firms Better Off Being Vertically Integrated in the Face of a Technological Change? *Academy of Management Journal, 44*(6), 1211–1228. doi:10.2307/3069397

Afuah, A., & Tucci, C. L. (2003). *Internet business models and strategies* (2 Ed.). New York: McGraw Hill.

Ägerfalk, P., & Fitzgerald, B. (2008). Outsourcing to an Unknown Workforce: Exploring Opensourcing as a Global Sourcing Strategy. *Management Information Systems Quarterly, 32*(2), 385–409.

Ajayi, O. (2002). *Information Communications Technology in Africa.* Retrieved July 26, 2009, from www.wireless.ictp.it/school_2002/.../ajayi/Trieste_-2_-_ICT_in_Africa.doc

Alavi, M., & Leidner, D. E. (2001). Knowledge Management and Knowledge Management Systems: Conceptual Foundations and Research Issues. *Management Information Systems Quarterly, 25*(1), 107–136. doi:10.2307/3250961

Alavi, M. (1997). KPMG Peat Marwick U.S.: One Giant Brain. *Harvard Business School Case,* 9-397-108, Rev. July 11.

Al-Hakim, L., & Memmola, M. (Eds.). (2009). *Business web strategy: Design, alignment, and application.* Hershey, PA: IGI Global.

Altekar, R. V. (2005). *Supply Chain Mangement. Concepts and Cases.* Upper Saddle River, NJ: Prentice Hall of India.

Ambrose, S. H. (2001). Paleolithic technology and human evolution. *Science, 291,* 1748–1753. doi:10.1126/science.1059487

Anderson, V., & Boocock, G. (2002). Small Firms and Internationalisation: Learning to Manage and Managing to Learn. *Human Resource Management Journal, 12*(3), 5–24. doi:10.1111/j.1748-8583.2002.tb00068.x

Anderson, C. (2004). The Long Tail. *Wired Magazine, 12*(10), 170–177.

Antonnette, G., Giunipero, L.C., Sawchuk, C., (2002). *E-Purchasing Plus: Transforming Supply Management through Technology.* New York: JGC Enterprises.

Anwer, S., & Ikram, N. (2006, December 6). *Goal oriented requirement engineering: A critical study of techniques.* Paper presented at the XIII Asia Pacific Software Engineering Conference (APSEC'06), Bangalore, India.

Arbore, A., & Ordanini, A. (2009). Environmental drivers of e-business strategies among SMEs. In Lee, I. (Ed.), *Electronic Business: Concepts, methodologies, tools, and applications* (*Vol. 1*, pp. 185–196). Hershey, PA: IGI Global.

Archibugi, D., & Iammarino, S. (2002). The Globalization of Technological Innovation: Definition and Evidence. *Review of International Political Economy, 9*, 98–122. doi:10.1080/09692290110101126

Ardichvili, A., Page, V., & Wentling, T. (2003). Motivation and barriers to participation in virtual knowledge-sharing communities of practice. *Journal of Knowledge Management, 7*(1), 64–77. doi:10.1108/13673270310463626

Arthaud-Day, M. L., Rode, J. C., Mooney, C. H., & Near, J. (2005). The Subjective Well-being Construct: A test of Its Convergent, Discriminant, and Factorial Validity. *Social Indicators Research, 74*, 445–476. doi:10.1007/s11205-004-8209-6

Audretsch, D., van der Horst, R., Kwaak, T., & Thurik, R. (2009). *First Section of the Annual Report on EU Small and Medium-sized Enterprises: European Commission.* Directorate General Enterprise and Industry, EIM.

Austin, J. L. (1976). *How to do things with words.* Oxford, UK: Oxford University Press.

Avolio, B., & Kahai, S. (2003). Adding the "E" to E-leadership: How it may impact your leadership. *Organizational Dynamics, 31*(4), 325–338. doi:10.1016/S0090-2616(02)00133-X

Axelrod, R. (1984). *The evolution of cooperation.* New York: Basic.

Baina, S., Ansias, P.-Y., Petit, M., & Castiaux, A. (2008, June 16). *Strategic business/ IT alignment using goal models.* Paper presented at the Third International Workshop on Business/ IT Alignment and Interoperability, BUSITAL'08, Montpellier, France.

Bajari, P., & Tadelis, S. (2001). Incentives Versus Transaction Costs: A Theory of Procurement Contracts. *32. The Rand Journal of Economics*, 387–407. doi:10.2307/2696361

Baker, H. (2000). *E-Sourcing 21st Century Purchasing.* New York: Scheer.

Bakos, Y. (1998). The emerging role of electronic markets on the Internet. Communications of the ACM.

Baldwin, J., Sabourin, D., & Smith, D. (2004). Firm Performance in the Canadian Food Processing Sector: The Interaction Between ICT, Advanced Technology Use and Human Resource Competencies. In OECD (Ed.), *The Economic Impact of ICT, Measurement, Evidence and Implications* (pp. 153-181), OECD, Paris.

Barnes, J. G. (2002). *Segredos da gestão pelo relacionamento com clientes - CRM: é tudo uma questão de como você faz com que eles se sintam.* Rio de Janeiro, Brazil: Qualitymark.

Barney, J. (2001). Is the resource-based view a useful perspective for strategic management research? Yes. *Academy of Management Review, 26*, 41–56. doi:10.2307/259393

Barthelme, F., Erime, J. L., & Rosenthal-Sabroux, C. (1998). An architecture for knowledge evolution in organisations. *European Journal of Operational Research, 109*(2), 414–427. doi:10.1016/S0377-2217(98)00067-8

Bartz, K., Barr, C., & Aijaz, A. (2008). Natural language generation for sponsored-search advertisements. In *Proceedings of the 9th ACM Conference on Electronic Commerce* (p. 1–9). New York: ACM New York.

Battelle, J. (2006). *The search. How Google and its rivals rewrote the rules of business and transformed our culture.* New York: Portfolio.

BCC. (2008). *Annual Report on the SME sector in Romania.* Bucharest: Bucharest Chamber of Commerce Publications.

Beaver, G. (2002). *Small Business and Enterprise Developmen.* Upper Saddle River, NJ: Prentice Hall.

Becker, M. H. (1970). Sociometric Location and Innovativeness: Reformulation and Extension of the Diffusion Model. *American Sociological Review, 35*, 267–282. doi:10.2307/2093205

Becker, S., & Whisler, T. L. (1967). The Innovative Organization: A Selective View of Current Theory and Research. *The Journal of Business*, *40*, 462–469. doi:10.1086/295011

Becker, A. L., Prikladnicki, R., & Audy, J. L. N. (2008, May 13). *Strategic alignment of software process improvement programs using QFD.* Paper presented at the BIPI'08, Leipzig, Germany.

Beckinsale, M., Levy, M., & Powell, P. (2006). Exploring Internet Adoption Drivers in SMEs. *Electronic Markets*, *16*(4), 361–370. doi:10.1080/10196780600999841

Beil, D. R., & Wein, L. M. (2003). An inverse-optimization-based auction mechanism to support a multi-attribute RFQ process. *Management Science*, *49*(11), 1529–1545. doi:10.1287/mnsc.49.11.1529.20588

Bell, B. S., & Kozlowski, S. W. J. (2002). A typology of virtual teams: Implications for effective leadership. *Group & Organization Management*, *27*(1), 14–49. doi:10.1177/1059601102027001003

BERR. (Department of Business, Enterprise and Regulatory Reform), (2007). *Table 1 UK Private Sector, Number of enterprises, employment and turnover in the private sector by number of employees, UK, start 2007*, BERR Enterprise Directorate Analytical Unit.

Bertalanffy, L. v. (1950). An outline of General System Theory. *The British Journal for the Philosophy of Science*, *1*(2), 134–165. doi:10.1093/bjps/I.2.134

Bertalanffy, L. v. (1968, edition 1979). *General Systems Theory. Foundations, Development, Applications. Revised Edition. Sixth Printing.* New York: Braziller.

Bichler, M. (2001). *The Future of E-Markets, Multidimensional Market Mechanisms.* University Press. doi:10.1017/CBO9780511492532

Biehl, M. L. (2009). *Geração de valor competitivo através da relação com o cliente: caso de uma empresa do setor de autopeças.* Trabalho de Conclusão de Curso, Unisinos.

Blau, P. (1968). The Hierarchy of Authority in Organizations. *American Journal of Sociology*, *73*, 453–467. doi:10.1086/224506

Blau, P. (1970). A Formal Theory of Differentiation in Organizations. *American Sociological Review*, *35*, 201–218. doi:10.2307/2093199

Blau, P. M., & Scott, W. R. (1962). *Formal Organizations.* San Francisco: Chandler Publishing Company.

Bleistein, S. J., Aurum, A., Cox, K., & Ray, P. K. (2004). Strategy-oriented alignment in requirements engineering: Linking business strategy to requirements of e-business systems using the SOARE approach. *Journal of Research and Practice in Information Technology*, *36*(4), 259–276.

Blodget, H., & McCabe, F. (2000). *The B2B Market Maker Book.* New York: Merrill Lynch.

Bloom, N., Dorgan, S., Dowdy, J., & Van Reenen, J. (2007). Management practice and productivity. *The Quarterly Journal of Economics*, *122*(4), 1351–1408. doi:10.1162/qjec.2007.122.4.1351

Bocij, C. D., Hickie, S, & Greasley, A. (2006). *Business information systems; Technology, Development and Management for the e-business, 3th edition.* Upper Saddle River, NJ: Prentice Hall.

Bock, G.-W., Zmud, R. W., Kim, Y.-G., & Lee, J.-N. (2005). Behavioral intention formation in knowledge sharing: Examining the roles of extrinsic motivators, social-psychological forces and organizational climate. *Management Information Systems Quarterly*, *29*(1), 87–112.

Bodorick, P., Dhaliwal, J., & Jutla, D. (2002). Supporting the e-business readiness of small and medium-sized enterprises: approaches and metrics. *Internet Research: Electronic Networking Applications and Policy*, *12*(2), 139–164. doi:10.1108/10662240210422512

Bohr, N. (1955). Science and the unity of knowledge. In Leary, L. (Ed.), *The unity of knowledge* (pp. 44–62). New York: Doubleday.

Bonabeau, E. (2002). Predicting the unpredictable. *HBR80* (3), pp. 109. March.

Borgs, C., Chayes, J., & Etesami, O. (2007). Dynamics of bid optimization in online advertisement auctions. *Proceedings of the WWW, 2007*, 531–540. doi:10.1145/1242572.1242644

Bougrain, F., & Haudeville, B. (2002). Innovation, collaboration and SMEs internal research capacities. *Research Policy*, *31*(5), 735–747. doi:10.1016/S0048-7333(01)00144-5

Božičnik, S., Ećimović, T., & Mulej, M. (Eds.). (2008). *Sustainable future, requisite holism, and social responsibility. Maribor: ANSTED University, Penang in co-operation with SEM Institute for climate change.* Korte, and IRDO Institute for Development of Social Responsibility. CD.

Bradshaw, J. M. (1997). An introduction to software agents. In Bradshaw, J. M. (Ed.), *Software Agents*. Menlo Park, CA: AAAI Press.

Brown, S.J. & Duguid, P. (2000). Balancing Act: How To Capture Knowledge Without Killing It.*Harvard Business Review*, May-June, 78(3), pp. 73-80.

Bruno, G. (2009). Requirements elicitation as a case of social process: an approach to its description. In *7th Int. Conference on Business Process Management: BPMS2'09 Workshop*. Springer (in press).

Busemeyer, J., & Trueblood, J. (2009). Comparison of quantum and Bayesian inference models. In P. Bruza, Sofge, D.A., Lawless, W.F., Van Rijsbergen, K., & Klusch, M. (eds). *Quantum Interaction. Third International Symposium, QI-2009*. Berlin:Springer-Verlag.

Buxton, A. (2008). *Does Procurement eAuction Design Matter? Trading Partners,* http://www.tradingpartners.com/usa/download.php?Id=85&Field=File&Force=Y&Stream=N, 26 Mach 2008, (Accessed on August 4, 2009).

Cabrera, A., & Cabrera, E. F. (2002). Knowledge sharing dilemmas. *Organization Studies, 23*(5), 687–710. doi:10.1177/0170840602235001

Camarinha-Matos, L. M., Afsarmanesh, H., & Ollus, M. (2008). *Methods and tools for collaborative networked organizations*. New York: Springer. doi:10.1007/978-0-387-79424-2

Campos. Daniel M. e. (2004). *A análise do valor percebido pelo cliente como ferramenta para a formulação de estratégias competitivas uma aplicação de conjoint analysis.* Dissertação de mestrado. Universidade Municipal de São Caetano do Sul. São Paulo.

Carley, K. M. (2002). *Simulating society: The tension between transparency and veridicality. Social Agents: ecology, exchange, and evolution*. University of Chicago, Argonne National Laboratory.

Carrizo, D., Dieste, O., & Juristo, N. (2008, September 12). *Study of elicitation techniques adequacy.* Paper presented at the 11th Workshop on Requirement Engineering, Barcelona, Spain.

Carter, C. R., Kaufmann, L., Beall, S., Carter, P. L., Hendrick, T. E., & Petersen, K. J. (2004). Reverse auctions – grounded theory from the buyer and supplier perspective. *Transportation Research Part E, Logistics and Transportation Review, 40*(3), 183–270. doi:10.1016/j.tre.2003.08.004

Cary, M., Das, A., & Edelman, B. (2007). Greedy Bidding Strategies for Keyword Auctions. *Electronic Commerce, 2007*, 262–271.

Cassivi, L., Lefebvre, E., Lefebvre, L. A., & Léger, P.-M. (2004). The impact of e-collaboration tools on firms' performance. *International Journal of Logistics Management, 15*(1), 91–110. doi:10.1108/09574090410700257

Cecez-Kecmanovic, D. (2000). *Understanding Knowledge Sharing in Organizational Decision Making Supported by CMC.* IFIP TC8/WG8.*3 International Conference on Decision Support through Knowledge Management*, 9-11 July 2000, Stockholm, Sweden, pp. 77-90.

Chabossou, A., Stork, C., Stork, M., & Zahonogo, Z. (2009). Mobile Telephony Access and Usage in Africa. *Southern African Journal of Information and Communication, Issue No. 9*. Retrieved August 14, 2009, from www.whiteafrican.com/wp-content/.../04/researchictafrica-ictd2009.pdf

Chaffey, D. (2004). *E-Business and E-Commerce Management* (2nd ed.). Upper Saddle River, NJ: Prentice-Hall.

Chalmeta. R. (2005). Methodology for customer relationship management. *The Journal of Systems and Software*. Espanha.

Chan, I., & Chao, C. K. (2008). Knowledge Management in Small and Medium Sized Enterprises. *Communications of the ACM, 51*(4), 83–88. doi:10.1145/1330311.1330328

Chan, Y. E., & Reich, B. H. (2007). IT alignment: what have we learned? *Journal of Information Technology* (22), 297–315. doi: 10.1057/palgrave.jit.2000109

Chang, T. Z; Wildt, R. (1994). Price, product information and purchase intention: an empirical study. *Journal of the Academy of Marketing Science, 22*(1), winter.

Chege, L., Gustav, C., & Mahachi, J. (2001). *E-Commerce and value chain management – the prospects and challenges for the South African construction industries. Construction Informatics Digital Library.* Retrieved August 15, 2009, from http://itc.scix.net/cgi-bin/works/Show?_id =w78%2d2001%2d62&sort=DEFAULT&search=E%2d COMMERCE%20AND%20VALUE%20CHAIN%20 MANAGEMENT%20%96%20THE&hits=1261

Chen, Y., Xue, G.-R., & Yu, Y. (2008). *Advertising Keyword Suggestion Based on Concept Hierarchy* (p. 251). Web Search & Data Mining.

Chen Ritzo, C., Harrizon, T., Kwasnica, A., & Thomas, D. (2005). Better, faster, cheaper: An experimental analysis of a multi-attribute reverse auction mechanism with restricted information feedback. *Management Science, 51*(12), 1753–1762. doi:10.1287/mnsc.1050.0433

Chesbrough, H. W. (2003). *Open Innovation: The new imperative for creating and profiting from technology.* Boston: Harvard Business School Press.

Chesbrough, H. W., & Crowther, A. K. (2006). Beyond high tech: early adopters of open innovation in other industries. *R & D Management, 36*(3), 229–236. doi:10.1111/j.1467-9310.2006.00428.x

Chesbrough, H. W. (2006). Open Innovation: A New Paradigm for understanding industrial innovation. In H. Chesbrough, W. Vanhaverbeke & J. West (Eds), *Open innovation researching a new paradigm.* Oxford, UK: Oxford University Press.

Child, J., & Faulkner, D. (1998). *Strategic for cooperation: Managing alliances, networks, and joint ventures.* Oxford, UK: Oxford University Press.

Chinowsky, P. S., & Rojas, E. M. (2003). Virtual teams: Guide to Successful Implementation. *Journal of Management Engineering, 19*(3), 98–106. doi:10.1061/(ASCE)0742-597X(2003)19:3(98)

Choo, C. (1996). An Integrated Information Model of the Organization: The Knowing Organization. URL=http://www.fis.utoronto.ca/people/faculty/choo/FIS/KO/KO.html1contents. (Last accessed March 18TH 2008).

Chopra, D. (2006). *Knjiga skrivnosti.* Maribor: Litera.

Chung, L., Nixon, B. A., Yu, E., & Mylopulos, J. (2000). *Non-functional requirements in software engineering.* Norwell, MA: Kluwer Academic Publishers.

CIO (Chief Information Officer) Council. (2001). *A Practical Guide to Federal Enterprise Architecture.* Version 1.0. Retrieved June 30, 2006, http://www.gao.gov/special.pubs/eaguide.pdf

Clear, F. (forthcoming), Food and Drink Manufacturing and the Role of ICT, in Bourlakis, M. *et al., Intelligent Agrifood Chains and Networks: Current Status, Future Trends & Real-life Cases.* New York: Routledge.

Cohen, L. (1995). *Time-frequency analysis: theory and applications.* Upper Saddle River, NJ: Prentice Hall Signal Processing Series.

Coleman, J. J. (2003). The benefits of campaign financing. *CATO Institute Briefing Papers.*www.cato.org/pubs/briefs/bp-084es.html. Washington.

COMNET-IT. (2002*). Country profiles of e-Governance, UNESCO.* Retrieved August 3, 2009, from www.portal.unesco.org/...governance...doc/E%2Bgovernance%2Bstudy%2Bfull%2Btext.doc

Corbett, O., & Molloy, O. (2000). *Alignment of business and IT strategies* (p. 13). Galway, Ireland: National University of Ireland, Galway.

Cormican, K., & Dooley, L. (2007). Knowledge sharing in a collaborative networked environment. *Journal of Information and Knowledge Management, 16*(2), 105–115. doi:10.1142/S0219649207001706

Cormican, K., & O'Sullivan, D. (2003a). A scorecard for supporting enterprise knowledge management. *Journal of Information and Knowledge Management, 2*(3), 191–201. doi:10.1142/S0219649203000395

Cormican, K., & O'Sullivan, D. (2003b). A collaborative knowledge management tool for product innovation management. *International Journal of Technology Management, 26*(1), 53–67. doi:10.1504/IJTM.2003.003144

Cormican, K., & O'Sullivan, D. (2004). Auditing best practice for effective for product innovation management. *Technovation, 24*(10), 819–829. doi:10.1016/S0166-4972(03)00013-0

Corwin, R. G. (1975). Innovation in Organizations: The Case of Schools. *Sociology of Education, 48*, 1–37. doi:10.2307/2112048

Cross, G. (2000). How E-Business is Transforming Supply Chain Management. *The Journal of Business Strategy, 21*(2), 36–43. doi:10.1108/eb040073

Crowther, D., Barry, D. M., Sankar, A., Goh, K. G., & Ortiz Martinez, E. (2004b). *S.R.W. Social Responsibility World of RecordPedia 2004. Penang: Ansted Service Center.* Ansted University Asia Regional Service Center.

Crowther, D., & Caliyut, K. T. (Eds.). (2004): *Stakeholders and Social Responsibility.* Penang: ANSTED University.

Curran, J., & Blackburn, R. (2001). *Researching the small enterprise.* New York: Sage.

Daft, R., & Marcis, D. (2001). *Understanding Management.* London: Thomson Learning.

Daft, R. L. (1994). *Management* (3rd ed.). United States of America: The Dryden Press.

Daniel, E., & Myers, A. (2000), *Levelling the playing field: electronic commerce in SMEs.* Retrieved from http://mn-isweb-1.som.cranfield.ac.uk/publications/ISRC_2001_SME-Report.pdf (accessed 15/12/09)

Davenport, T. H., & Prusak, L. (1998). *Working Knowledge. How Organizations Manage What They Know.* Boston: Harvard Business School Press.

Davenport, T. H. (1993). *Process innovation.* Boston: Harvard Business School Press.

Davenport, T. H. (2005). *Thinking for a living.* Boston: Harvard Business School Press.

de Man, H. (2009). Case management: Cordys approach. *BPTrends.* Retrieved September 18, 2009, from http://www.bptrends.com.

Decker, G., & Weske, M. (2007). Local enforceability in Interaction Petri Nets. [New York: Springer.]. *Lecture Notes in Computer Science, 4714*, 305–319. doi:10.1007/978-3-540-75183-0_22

DeLone, W. (1988). Determinants of Success for Computer Usage in Small Business. *Management Information Systems Quarterly, 12*(1), 51–61. doi:10.2307/248803

Denney, R. (2005). *Succeeding with use cases working smart to deliver quality.* Upper Saddle River, NJ: Addison Wesley Professional.

Dewar, R. D., & Dutton, J. E. (1986). The Adoption of Radical and Incremental Innovation: An Empirical Analysis. *Management Science, 32*, 1422–1433. doi:10.1287/mnsc.32.11.1422

Dholakia, R., & Kshetri, N. (2004). Factors Impacting the Adoption of Internet Among SMEs. *Small Business Economics, 23*(3), 311–322. doi:10.1023/B:SBEJ.0000032036.90353.1f

DIDA. (2009). *Description of the Italian enterpreneurs.* Rome: DIDA Publications.

Diener, E. (1984). Subjective Well-being. *Psychological Bulletin, 95*(3), 542–575. doi:10.1037/0033-2909.95.3.542

Diener, E., & Seligman, E. M. (2004). Beyond Money; Toward an Economy of Well-being. *Psychological Science in the Public Interest, 5*(1), 1–31. doi:10.1111/j.0963-7214.2004.00501001.x

Diener, E., & Seligman, M. E. (2002). Very happy people. *Psychological Science, 13*, 81–84. doi:10.1111/1467-9280.00415

Diener, E., Lucas, R. E., & Oishi, S. (2002). Subjective Well-Being. In Snyder, C. R., & Lopez, S. J. (Eds.), *Handbook of positive psychology.* New York: Oxford University Press.

Diener, E., Nickerson, C., Lucas, R. E., & Sandvik, E. (2001). *Dispositional affect and job outcomes.* Manuscript submitted for pulication.

Dietz, J. L. G. (2003). The atoms, molecules and fibers of organizations. *Data & Knowledge Engineering, 47*(3), 301–325. doi:10.1016/S0169-023X(03)00062-4

Dietz, J. L. G. (2006). The Deep Structure of Business Processes. *Communications of the ACM, 49*(5), 59–64. doi:10.1145/1125944.1125976

Dietz, T., Ostrom, E., & Stern, P. C. (2003). The struggle to govern the commons. *Science, 302*, 1907. doi:10.1126/science.1091015

Dillman, D. A. (2000). *Mail and Internet Surveys*. New York: John Wiley & Sons, Inc.

Dirks, K. T., & Ferrin, D. L. (2001). The role of trust in organizational settings. *Organization Science*, *12*(4), 450–467. doi:10.1287/orsc.12.4.450.10640

Dixon, T., Thompson, B., & McAllister, P. (2002). *The Value of ICT for SMEs in the UK: A Critical Review of Literature*. Reading: Report for the Small Business Service Research Programme, The College of Estate Management.

Dodič Fikfak, M. (2009). Prestrukturiranje gospodarstva in kazalniki zdravja. V: *Delo – most za sodelovanje/4. mednarodna konferenca Družbena odgovornost in izzivi časa 2009*. Hrast, A. in M. Matjaž (urednika). Maribor: IRDO – Inštitut za razvoj družbene odgovornosti, 63.

Dominguez, S. V. (2000). O Valor Percebido como elemento estratégico para obter a lealdade dos clientes. Caderno *de pesquisas em Administração, São Paulo, 07*(4), outubro/dezembro.

Drew, S. (2003). Strategic uses of e-commerce by SMEs in the East of England. *European Management Journal*, *21*(1), 79–88. doi:10.1016/S0263-2373(02)00148-2

DTI. *(2003). Small Business Service,* Excel Tables - SME Statistics UK 2003, Table 1: UK Whole Economy. *Retrieved from* http://www.sbs.gov.uk/default.php?page=/analytical/statistics/smestats.php *(accessed 10-07-09)*

Dube, T., Chitura, T., & Runyowa, L. (2009). Adoption and Use of Internet Banking in Zimbabwe: An exploratory study. *Journal of Internet Banking and Commerce*. Retrieved August 3, 2009, from www.arraydev.com/commerce/JIBC/2009-04/Dube%20etal.pdf

Dumas, M., van der Aalst, W. M. P., & ter Hofstede, A. H. M. (2005). *Process-Aware Information Systems: bridging people and software through process technology*. New York: Wiley. doi:10.1002/0471741442

During, W., Oakey, R., & Kauser, S. (2004). *New technology-based firms in the new millennium*. New York: Elsevier.

Durkheim, E. (1997). *The Division of Labor. Translated by W. D. Halls*. New York: Free Press. (Original work published 1933)

Dyer, J. H. (2000). *Collaborative advantage: Winning through extended enterprise supplier networks*. Oxford, UK: Oxford University Press.

Earl, M. J., & Hopwood, A. G. (1980). From Management Information to Information Management. In Lucas, L., & Lincoln, S. (Eds.), *The Information Systems Environment*. Amsterdam: North Holland Publishing Company.

EC. (2008). *Communication from the Commission to the Council, the European Parliament, the European Economic and Social Committee and the Committee of the Region*s - "Think Small First" - A "Small Business Act" for Europe (Vol. {SEC(2008)2101} {SEC(2008)2102}): European Commission Directorate-General for Enterprise.

ECA CORDIST. (2009). *Workshop on Legal and Regulatory Framework for the Knowledge Economy Report*. Presented at the first Meeting of the Committee on Development Information, Science & Technology (CODIST), Addis Ababa, Ethiopia ECA report. (2009). Mobile Commerce in Africa: An overview with specific reference to South Africa, Kenya and Senegal. *First Session of the Committee on Development Information, Science and Technology (CODIST-I). Addis Ababa, Ethiopia*. Retrieved July 30, 2009, from www.uneca.org/codist/codist1/.../E-ECA-CODIST-1-23-EN.pdf

Elberse, A. (2008). Should You Invest in the Long Tail? *Harvard Business Review*, *86*(7), 88–96.

Eleftheriadou, D. (2008). *Small and Medium-Sized Enterprises Hold the Key to European Competitiveness: How to Help Them Innovate Through ICT and E-Business*. The Global Information Technology Report, World Economic Forum.

Elofson, G., & Robinson, W. (1998). Creating a Custom Mass-Production Channel on the Internet. *Communications of the ACM*, 41.

Emiliani, M. L. (2006). Executive Decision Making Traps and B2B online reverse auctions. *Supply Chain Management: An International Journal*, *11*(1), 6–9. doi:10.1108/13598540610642411

Escofet, E., Rodríguez, M. J., Garrido, J. L., & Chung, L. (2009). Strategic alignment as a way of addressing the barriers to e-business adoption. In S. Krishnamurthy (Ed.), *Proceedings of the 6th IADIS International Conference E-Commerce* (pp. 27-34). Algarve, Portugal: IADIS Press.

Espín, R.; Vanti, A. A. (2005). Administración Lógica: Un estudio de caso en empresa de comercio exterior. Revista BASE. *São Leopoldo, RS - Brasil, ago, 1*(3), pp.4-22.

Esposito, J. L. (2002, November 14). *A framework relating questionnaire design and evaluation processes to sources of measurement error.* Paper presented at the International Conference on Questionnaire Development, Evaluation, and Testing Methods, Charleston, SC.

Esteves, J. (2006, July 6). *Establishing the relationship between enterprise systems benefits, business complexity, and business alignment in SMEs.* Paper presented at the European and Mediterranean Conference on Information Systems (EMCIS´2006), Costa Blanca, Alicante, Spain.

EU. (2001). [Commission of the European Communities, 2001]: Green Paper on Promoting a European Framework for Corporate Social Responsibility, COM (2001) 366 final, Brussels. Retrieved July 1, 2009, from http://eur-lex.europa.eu/LexUriServ/site/en/com/2001/com2001_0366en01.pdf

European Commission (2002). *Benchmarking National and Regional E-business Policies for SMEs.*final report of the Ebusiness Policy Group of the European Union, Brussels, 28 June.

European Commission. (2008). *The European E-Business Report 2008: The Impact of ICT and E-Business on Firms, Sectors and the Economy.* 6th Synthesis Report of the Sectoral E-Business Watch. Retrieved September 2, 2009 from http://www.ebusiness-watch.org.

European Commission. (2009). *Europe's Digital Competitiveness Report.* Annual Information Society Report – Volume 1, European Union. Retrieved September 9, 2009 from http://eur-lex.europa.eu.

Evan, W. M., & Black, G. (1967). Innovation in Business Organizations: Some Factors Associated With Success or Failure of Staff Proposals. *The Journal of Business, 40,* 519–530. doi:10.1086/295016

Fahey, L., & Prusak, L. (1998). The Eleven Deadliest Sins of Knowledge Management. *California Management Review, 9,* 449–459.

Favier J., Condon C., Aghina W., Rehkopf F., (2000). Euro eMarketplaces top hype. *Forrester Research,* Inc., May 2000.

Feindt, S., Jeffcoate, J., & Chappel, C. (2001). Identifying Success Factors for Rapid Growth in SME E-Commerce. *Small Business Economics, 19,* 51–62. doi:10.1023/A:1016165825476

Felce, D., & Parry, J. (1995). Quality of life: its definition and measurement. *Research in Developmental Disabilities, 16*(1), 51–74. doi:10.1016/0891-4222(94)00028-8

Feldman, J., Muthukrishnan, S., Pál, M., & Stein, C. (2007). *Budget Optimization in Search-Based Advertising* (pp. 40–49). Electronic Commerce.

Feldman, M. P. (2002). The Internet Revolution and the Geography of Innovation. *International Social Science Journal, 54,* 47–56. doi:10.1111/1468-2451.00358

Feldman, S. (2000). Electronic Marketplaces IEEE Internet Computing.

Field, A. (2005). *Discovering Statistics Using SPSS* (2nd ed.). London: Sage.

Fillis, I., Wagner, B., & Johansson, U. (2004). Factors Impacting on E-Business Adoption and Development in the Smaller Scottish Firm. *International Journal of Entrepreneurial Behaviour and Research, 10*(3), 178–191. doi:10.1108/13552550410536762

Fisher, K., & Fisher, M. D. (2001). *The Distance Manager: A Hands-On Guide to Managing Off-Site Employees and Virtual Teams.* New York: McGraw-Hill.

Forrester (2009).*The Forrester Wave: E-Sourcing – Q1 2009.*

François, Ch. (Ed.). (2004). *International Encyclopedia of Systems and Cybernetics* (2nd ed.). Munich: Saur.

Frankl, V. E. (1962). *Man's search for meaning: An introduction to logotherapy.* Boston: Beacon Press.

Frankl, V. E. (1994). *Zdravnik in duša: osnove logoterapije in bivanjske analize.* Celje: Mohorjeva družba.

Frankl, V. E. (2005). *Človek pred vprašanjem o smislu: izbor iz zbranega dela.* Ljubljana: Pasadena.

Frary, R. B. (1996). *A brief guide to questionnaire development.* Washington, DC: ERICAE Clearinghouse on Assessment and Evaluation.

Fredericson, B. L., & Joiner, T. (2002). Positive emotions trigger upward spirals toward emotional well-being. *Psychological Science, 13,* 172–175. doi:10.1111/1467-9280.00431

Friderick, W. C., Davis, K., & Post, E. J. (1988). *Business and Society: Corporate Strategy, Public Policy, Ethics* (6th ed.). New York: McGraw-Hill Publishing Company.

Funk, B. (2009) Optimizing Price Levels in E-Commerce Applications with Respect to Customer Lifetime Values. *Proceedings of the International Conference on E-Commerce,* pp. 169-175.

Gassmann, O. (2006). Opening up the innovation process: towards an agenda. *R & D Management, 36*(3), 223–228. doi:10.1111/j.1467-9310.2006.00437.x

Geiger, S., & Makri, M. (2006). Exploration and exploitation innovation processes: The role of organisational slack in R&D intensive firms. *The Journal of High Technology Management Research, 17,* 97–108. doi:10.1016/j.hitech.2006.05.007

Gershenfeld, N. (2000). *The physics of information technology.* Cambridge, MA: Cambridge University Press.

Gibbert, M., & Krause, H. (2002). Practice exchange in a best practice marketplace. In Davenport, I. T. H., & Probst, G. J. B. (Eds.), *Knowledge Management Case Book: Siemens Best Practices* (pp. 89–105). Erlangen, Germany: Publicis Corporate Publishing.

Gibson, J. L., Ivancevich, J. M., & Donnelly, J. H. (1988). *Organizações: comportamento, estrutura e processos.* São Paulo: Atlas.

Giga Research (2004). Market Overview 2004: E-Procurement and E-Sourcing – What will take to break the Glass Floor in Demand?.

Glenn, N. D., & Weaver, C. N. (1981). The contributions of marital happiness to global happiness. *Journal of Marriage and the Family, 43,* 161–168. doi:10.2307/351426

Goeree, J. K., Offerman, T., & Schram, A. (2006). Using first-price auctions to sell heterogeneous licenses. *International Journal of Industrial Organization, 24*(3), 555–581. doi:10.1016/j.ijindorg.2005.07.011

Goerner, S., Dyck, R. G., & Lagerroos, D. (2008). *The New Science of Sustainability. Building a Foundation for Great Change.* Chapel Hill, N.C: Triangle Center for Complex Systems.

Goldberg, V. P. (1977). Competitive Bidding and the Production of Precontract Information. 8. *The Bell Journal of Economics,* 250–261. doi:10.2307/3003497

Gottschalk, P. (2006). *E-business strategy –Sourcing and Governance Electronic Commerce.* Hershey, PA: Idea Group Publishing.

Granovetter, M. S. (1983). The Strength of Weak Ties: A Network Theory Revisited. In Collins, R. (Ed.), *Sociological Theory* (pp. 201–233). San Francisco: Jossey-Bass, Inc.

Greenberg. P. (2001). *CRM na velocidade da luz: conquista e lealdade de clientes em tempo real na internet.* Rio de Janeiro: Campus.

Griffith, T. L., Sawyer, J., & Neale, M. (2003). Virtualness and knowledge in teams: managing the love triangle of organizations, individuals, and information technology. *Management Information Systems Quarterly, 27*(2), 265–287.

Gunasekaran, A., & Khalil, O. (Eds.). (2003). *Knowledge and information technology management: Human and social perspectives.* Hershey, PA: Idea group Publishing.

Gupta, A., & Hammond, R. (2005). Information systems security issues and decisions for small businesses. An empirical examination. *Information Management & Computer Security, 13*(4), 297–310. doi:10.1108/09685220510614425

Guthrie, D. (1999). A Sociological Perspective on the Use of Technology: The Adoption of Internet Technology in U.S. Organizations. *Sociological Perspectives, 42,* 583–603.

Haag, S., Raja, M. K., & Schkade, L. L. (1996). Quality function deployment usage in software development. *Communications of the ACM, 39*(1), 41–49. doi:10.1145/234173.234178

Hadjimolis, A. (1999). Barriers to Innovation for SMEs in a Small less developed Country (Cyprus). *Technovation, 19*(9), 561–570. doi:10.1016/S0166-4972(99)00034-6

Hage, J., & Aiken, M. (1967). Program Change and Organizational Properties: A comparative Analysis. *American Journal of Sociology*, 72, 503–519. doi:10.1086/224380

Hall, R. H., Haas, J. E., & Johnson, N. J. (1967). Organizational Size, Complexity, and Formalization. *American Sociological Review*, 32, 903–911. doi:10.2307/2092844

Halleux, P., Ludovic, M., & Andersson, B. (2008, June 16). *A method to support the alignment of business models and goal models.* Paper presented at the Third International Workshop on Business/IT Alignment and Interoperability, BUSITAL'08, Montpellier, France.

Hansen, M., Nohria, N & Tierney, T. (1999). What's Your Strategy for Managing Knowledge? *Harvard Business Review*, March-April, 77(2), pp. 106-116.

Hansen, M.T. (1999). The search-transfer problem: the role of weak ties in sharing knowledge across organization subunits, *Administrative Science Quarterly, 44*(1), 82, 112.

Hardin, S. R., & Schrage, M. (1998). Delivering Information Services through Collaboration. *Bulletin of the American Society for Information Science*, 24(6). http://www.asis.org/Bulletin/Aug-98/hardin.html.

Harindranath, G., Dyerson, R., & Barnes, D. (2008). ICT Adoption and Use in UK SMEs: A Failure of Initiatives? *Electronic Journal Information Systems Evaluation*, 11(2), 91–96.

Harris, L. (2002). History, Definition and Frameworks. In Harris, L., & Dennis, C. (Eds.), *Marketing and e-Business*. London: Routledge. doi:10.4324/9780203166963.ch1

Harrison, S. (1995). *Public Relations: an introduction.* New York: Routledge.

Hartman, E., Gemuenden, H., & Ritter, T. (2001) Determining the Purchase Situation: Conerstone of Supplier Relationship Management. 17th IMP Conference, Oslo, Norway.

Hasson, U., Nir, Y., Levy, I., Fuhrmann, G., & Malach, R. (2004). Intersubject Synchronization of Cortical Activity During Natural Vision. *Science*, *303*, 1634–1640. doi:10.1126/science.1089506

Hayek, F. A. (1944/1994). *The road to serfdom.* Chicago, UK: Routledge Press/University of Chicago Press.

Heisenberg, W. (1958/1999). *Language and reality in modern physics. Physics and philosophy. The revolution in modern science* (pp. 167–186). New York: Prometheus Books.

Henderson, J. C., & Venkatraman, N. (1999). Strategic alignment: Leveraging information technology for transforming organizations. *IBM Systems Journal*, *38*(2), 472–484. doi:10.1147/SJ.1999.5387096

Hendriks, P. (1999). Why share knowledge? The influence of ICT on the motivation for knowledge sharing. *Knowledge and Process Management*, *6*(2), 91–100. doi:10.1002/(SICI)1099-1441(199906)6:2<91::AID-KPM54>3.0.CO;2-M

Hertel, G., Konradt, U., & Orlikowski, B. (2004). Managing distance by interdependence: Goal setting, task interdependence, and team-based rewards in virtual teams. *European Journal of Work and Organizational Psychology*, *13*(1), 1–28. doi:10.1080/13594320344000228

Hildreth, P., Kimble, C., & Wright, P. (2000). Communities of practice in the distributed international environment. *Journal of Knowledge Management*, *4*(1), 27–38. doi:10.1108/13673270010315920

Hill, J., & Scott, T. (2004). A consideration of the roles of business intelligence and e-business in management and marketing decision making in knowledge-based and high-tech start-ups. *Qualitative Market Research: An International Journal*, *7*(1), 48–57. doi:10.1108/13522750410512877

Hinds, P., & Pfeffer, J. (2003). Why organizations don't 'know what they know: cognitive and motivational factors affecting the transfer of expertise. In Ackerman, M., Pipek, V., & Wulf, V. (Eds.), *Beyond Knowledge Management: Sharing Expertise*. Cambridge, MA: MIT Press.

Hinze, J. (1993). *Construction Contracts. McGraw-Hill Series in Construction Engineering and Project Management.* New York: Irwin/McGraw-Hill.

Hird, S. (2003). What is Well-being? A brief review of current literature and concepts. *NHS Scotland*, March 2003. Retriven June 28, 2009, from http://phis.org.uk/doc.pl?file=pdf/What%20is%20wellbeing%202.doc.

Hofreiter, B., Huemer, C., & Winiwarter, W. (2005). Business collaboration models and their business context-dependent web choreography in BPSS. *International Journal of Web Information Systems, 1*(1), 33–42. doi:10.1108/17440080580000081

Holsapple, C. W., & Whinston, T. (1987). Knowledge-based organizations. *The Information Society, 2,* 77–90. doi:10.1080/01972243.1987.9960049

Holsapple, C., & Joshi, K. (2004). A Knowledge Management Ontology. In Holsapple, C. W. (Ed.), *Handbook on Knowledge Management* (*Vol. 1,* pp. 89–128). Berlin: Verlanger.

Holsapple, C., & Singh, M. (2004). The Knowledge Chain Model: Activities for Competitiveness. In Holsapple, C. W. (Ed.), *Handbook on Knowledge Management* (*Vol. 2,* pp. 657–678). Berlin: Verlanger.

Holt, A. W. (1985). Coordination technology and Petri nets. [New York: Springer.]. *Lecture Notes in Computer Science, 222,* 278–296. doi:10.1007/BFb0016217

Hosanagar, K., & Cherepanov, V. (2008). Optimal Bidding in Stochastic Budget Constraint Slot Auctions. *Electronic Commerce, 2008,* 20–29.

HRAKK. (2009). *Description of the main contents of the Finnish entrepreneurs.* Hyvinkaa: HRAKK Publications.

Hrast, A., Mulej, M., & Knez-Riedl, J. (Eds.). (2006). *Družbena odgovornost in izzivi časa 2006. Maribor: IRDO Inštitut za razvoj družbene odgovornosti. Na CD.*

Hrast, A., & Matjaž, M. (2009). *Delo – most za sodelovanje/4. mednarodna konferenca Družbena odgovornost in izzivi časa 2009.* (Ed.). Maribor: IRDO – Inštitut za razvoj družbene odgovornosti.

Hrast, A., & Mulej, M. (Eds.). (2008). *Družbena odgovornost 2008. Zbornik 3. IRDO Konference o družbeni odgovornosti.* Maribor: IRDO Inštitut za razvoj družbene odgovornosti. CD.

Hrast, A., & Zavašnik, A. (Eds.). (2007). *Uvajanje družbene odgovornosti v poslovno prakso malih in srednje velikih podjetij v Sloveniji: Priročnik s primeri dobre prakse.* Maribor: GZS – Območna zbornica Maribor.

Hrast, A., Mulej, M., & Knez-Riedl, J. (Eds.). (2007). *Družbena odgovornost 2007.* Maribor: IRDO Inštitut za razvoj družbene odgovornosti. CD.

Hsu, C.-C., & Sandford, B. A. (2007). The Delphi technique: Making sense of consensus. *Practical Assessment. Research Evaluation, 12*(10), 1–8.

Hua, S., Rajesh, M., & Theng, L. (2008). *Barriers to the Adoption of E-Commerce Among Small and Medium-Sized Entreprises: A Study on the Non-Adopters in Malaysia.* Working paper presented at the 3rd International Colloquium on Business & Management (ICBM) held in Bangkok. Retrieved November, 9, 2009, from http://icbm.bangkok.googlepages.com/ICBM.2008.Sim.Chia.Hua.RP.pdf.

Huber, G. P. (1990). A theory of the effects of advanced information technologies on organizational design, intelligence, and decision making. *Academy of Management Review, 15*(1), 47–71. doi:10.2307/258105

Huber, G. P. (1991). Organisational Learning: The contributing Processes and the Literatures. *Organization Science, 2*(1), 88–115. doi:10.1287/orsc.2.1.88

Hughes, M., & Kroehler, C. J. Vander Zanden & James W. (2002). *Sociology: The Core.* 6th Ed. New York: The McGraw-Hill Companies, Inc.

Hwang, H., Ku, C., Yen, D., & Cheng, C. (2004). Critical Factors Influencing the Adoption of Data Warehouse Technology: A Study of the Banking Industry in Taiwan. *Decision Support Systems, 37*(1), 1–21. doi:10.1016/S0167-9236(02)00191-4

Ifinedo p. (2005). Measuring Africa's e-readiness in the global networked economy: A nine-country data analysis. *International Journal of Education and Development using Information and Communication Technology (IJEDICT), 1*(1), 53-71.

Ivis, M. (2001). *Analysis of barriers impeding e-business adoption among Canadian SMEs* (pp. 1–9). Ottawa, Canada: Canadian Chamber of Commerce.

Jackson, J., Harris, L. & Eckersley, Peter M. (2003). *E-business fundamentals.* London and New York: Routledge Taylor & Francis Crou

James, O. (2007). *Affluenza – a contagious middle class virus causing depression, anxiety, addiction and ennui.* London: Vermillion, an imprint of Ebury Publishing, Random House UK Ltd etc.

Jansen, B. (2007). Click Fraud. *Computer, 40*(7), 85–86. doi:10.1109/MC.2007.232

Jansen, B. (2007). The Comparative Effectiveness of Sponsored. *ACM Transactions on the Web, 1*(1), 1–25.

Jansen, B., Booth, D., & Spink, A. (2007). Determining the user intent of web search engine queries. In *Proceedings of the 16th international conference on World Wide Web* (p. 1149–1150). New York: ACM.

Jap, S. (2000). The Relationship-Technology Interface: A Path to Competitive Advantage. In Boase, T., & Ganeshan, R. (Eds.), *New Directions in Supply Chain Management: Technology, Strategy and Implementation* (pp. 3–23). New York: American Management Association.

Jarvenpaa, S. L., Shaw, T. R., & Staples, D. S. (2004). Toward contextualized theories of trust: The role of trust in global virtual teams. *Information Systems Research, 15*(3), 250–267. doi:10.1287/isre.1040.0028

Jarvenpaa, S. L., & Staples, D. S. (2000). The Use of Collaborative Electronic Media for Information Sharing: An Exploratory Study of Determinants. *The Journal of Strategic Information Systems, 9*, 129–154. doi:10.1016/S0963-8687(00)00042-1

Jayaswal, B. K., & Patton, P. C. (2006). *Design for trustworthy software: Tools, techniques, and methodology of developing robust software.* Upper Saddle River, NJ: Prentice Hall.

Jeon, B., Han, K., & Lee, M. (2006). Determining Factors for the Adoption of E-Business: The Case of SMEs in Korea. *Applied Economics, 38*, 1905–1916. doi:10.1080/00036840500427262

Jin, M., Wu, S. D., & Erkoc, M. (2006). Multiple unit auctions with economy/ diseconomy of scale. *European Journal of Operational Research, 174*(2), 816–834. doi:10.1016/j.ejor.2005.02.075

Joe, C., & Yoong, P. (2004). Harnessing the Knowledge Assets of Older Workers: A Work in Progress Report.in *Proceedings of the 2004 DSS Conference*, Prato, Italy.

Johnson, P., Heimann, V., & O'Neill, K. (2001). The "wonderland" of virtual teams. *Journal of Workplace Learning, 13*(1), 24–29. doi:10.1108/13665620110364745

Johnson, G. & Scholes, K. (1997). *Exploring Corporate Strategy.* Hertfordshire: Prentice Hall Europe.

Jukic, N., Sharma, A., Jukic, B., & Parameswaran, M. (2009). M-Commerce: Analysis of Impact on Marketing Orientation. *Loyola University Chicago research series.* Retrieved August 10, 2009, from sba.luc.edu/research/wpapers/011020.pdf.

Kafka, S. (2000).e-Marketplaces Boost B2B Trade, Forrester Report.

Kai-Uwe Brock, J. (2000). Information and communication technology in the small firm. In Carter, S., & Dylan-Jones, D. (Eds.), *Enterprise and the Small Business* (pp. 384–408). Upper Saddle River, NJ: Financial Times/Prentice Hall.

Kalakota, R., & Robinson, M. (1999), *e-Business: Roadmap for Success.* Reading, MA: Addison-Wesley.

Kaplan, S. M., & Carroll, A. M. (1992). Supporting Collaborative Processes with ConversationBuilder. *Computer Communications, 15*(8), 489–501. doi:10.1016/0140-3664(92)90028-D

Kaplan, R. S., & Norton, D. P. (1997). *A Estratégia em Ação – Balanced Scorecard.* 9 ed. Rio de Janeiro: Campus.

Kaplan, S, Sawhney, M. (1999). *The Emerging Landscape of Business to Business E-Commerce.* Business 2.0 Magazine.

Katz, E. (1961). The Social Itinerary of Technical Change: Two Studies in the Diffusion of Innovation. *Human Organization, 20*, 70–82.

Katz, E., Levin, M. L., & Hamilton, H. (1963). Traditions of Research on the Diffusion of Innovation. *American Sociological Review, 28*, 237–252. doi:10.2307/2090611

Kayworth, T. R., & Leidner, D. E. (2000). The global virtual manager: A prescription for success. *European Management Journal, 18*(2), 183–194. doi:10.1016/S0263-2373(99)00090-0

Kayworth, T., & Leidner, D. (2004). Organizational Culture as a Knowledge Resource. In Holsapple, C. W. (Ed.), *Handbook of Knowledge Management* (*Vol. 1*, pp. 235–252). Berlin: Verlanger.

Kelley, H. H. (1992). Lewin, situations, and interdependence. *The Journal of Social Issues*, *47*, 211–233. doi:10.1111/j.1540-4560.1991.tb00297.x

Kelly, K. (1998). *The new rules of the New Economy*. New York: Penguin Books Ltd.

Kieselbach, T. (2009). Health in restructuring: Empirical evidence and policy recommendations. In Hrast, A., & Mulej, M. (Eds.), *Delo – most za sodelovanje/4. mednarodna konferenca Družbena odgovornost in izzivi časa 2009. Maribor: IRDO – Inštitut za razvoj družbene odgovornosti, 58.*

Kim, J., Kim, Y., Kwon, J., Hong, S., Song, C., & Baik, D. (2005). An enter-p rise architecture framework based on a common information technology domain (EAFIT) for improving interoperability among heterogeneous information systems. *Proceedings of the 2005 Third ACIS Int'l Conference on Software Engineering Research.*

Kirkman, B. L., & Rosen, B. (2000). Powering up teams. *Organizational Dynamics*, *28*(3), 48–66. doi:10.1016/S0090-2616(00)88449-1

Kirkman, B. L., Rosen, B., Tesluk, P. E., & Gibson, C. B. (2004). The impact of team empowerment on virtual team performance: The moderating role of face-to-face interaction. *Academy of Management Journal*, *47*(2), 175–192. doi:10.2307/20159571

Kitts, B., & Leblanc, B. (2004). Optimal Bidding on Keyword Auctions. *Electronic Markets*, *14*(3), 186–201. doi:10.1080/1019678042000245119

Klein, N. (2009). *Doktrina šoka: razmah uničevalnega kapitalizma*. Ljubljana: Mladinska knjiga.

Klen, E., Pereira-Klen, A., & Gesser, C. (2009). Towards the sustainability of virtual organisation Management. In *APENDICE XII – ARTIGO ANEXO AO QUESTIONARIO VALIDACAO ETAPA 2.*

Knez Riedl, J. (2007a). Kako DOP povečuje konkurenčnost. In *Projekt CSR – Code to Smart Reality*, Maribor: GZS-OZ.

Knez-Riedl, J. (2003a). Corporate social responsibility and communication with external community = Korporacijska društvena odgovornost i komuniciranje sa vanjskim okruženjem. *Informatologia*, *36*(3), 166–172.

Knez-Riedl, J., Mulej, M., & Dyck, R. G. (2006b). Corporate Social Responsibility from the Viewpoint of Systems Thinking. *Kybernetes*, *35*(3/4), 441–460. doi:10.1108/03684920610653737

Knez-Riedl, J. (2004). Slovenian SMEs: from the environmental responsibility to corporate social responsibility. In Sharma, S. K. (Ed.), *An enterprise odyssey: building competitive advantage* (pp. 127–139). Zagreb: Zagreb International Review of Economics & Business.

Knez-Riedl, J. (2002). Družbena odgovornost malih in srednje velikih podjetij. In M. Rebernik (Ed.) *Slovenski podjetniški observatorij 2002*, (pp 91 – 112), 2nd part.

Knez-Riedl, J. (2003b). Social responsibility of a family business. *MER, Rev. manag. razvoj, 5*(2), 90-99.

Knez-Riedl, J. (2003c). Corporate social responsibility and holistic analysis. In G. Chroust in Ch. Hofer (Ed.), *IDIMT-2003: Proceedings, (Schriftenreihe Informatik, Bd 9)*, Linz: Universitätsverlag R. Trauner, 187-198.

Knez-Riedl, J. (2006c). *Družbena odgovornost in univerza*. In A., Hrast et al. (2006), referenced here.

Knez-Riedl, J. (2007b). Družbena odgovornost podjetja in evropski strateški dokumenti, *Projekt CSR – Code to Smart Reality*. Maribor: GZS OZ Maribor.

Knez-Riedl, J. (2007c). Obvladovanje celovite (družbene) odgovornosti. *Razgledi MBA*, 12 [i.e. 13],(1/2), 37-43.

Knez-Riedl, J., & Hrast, A. (2006a). Managing corporate social responsibility (CSR): a case of multiple benefits of socially responsible behaviour of a firm. In R. Trappl (Ed.), *Cybernetics and systems 2006: proceedings of the Eighteenth European Meeting on Cybernetics and Systems Research*. (pp 405-409). Vienna: Austrian Society for Cybernetic Studies.

Knight, K. E. (1967). A Descriptive Model of the Intra-Firm Innovation Process. *The Journal of Business*, *40*, 478–496. doi:10.1086/295013

Korolova, A., Kenthapadi, K., Mishra, N., & Ntoulas, A. (2009). Releasing Search Queries and Clicks Privately. *Proceedings of the WWW, 2009*, 171–180. doi:10.1145/1526709.1526733

Kotler. P.(1998). *Princípios de Marketing*. Rio de Janeiro: Pretince-Hall.

Kowalkiewicz, M. (2004). *From traditional markets to electronic markets for learning – opportunities an threats*. Poznan University of Economics.

Kraaijenbrink, J., Faran, D., & Hauptman, A. (2006). Knowledge Integration by SMEs – Framework. In Jetter, A., Kraaijenbrink, J. Schroder, H., Wijnhoven, F., (eds). *Knowledge Integration: The Practice of Knowledge Management in Small to Medium Sized Enterprises*, pp. 17-28 New York: Springer

Kreiner, K. (2002). Tacit knowledge management: the role of artefacts. *Journal of Knowledge Management, 6*(2), 112–123. doi:10.1108/13673270210424648

Krishna, V. (2002). *Auction Theory*. San Diego, CA: Academic Press.

Kulpa, M. K., & Johnson, K. A. (2008). *Interpreting the CMMI: A process improvement approach* (2 Ed.). Boca Raton, FL: Auerbach Publications.

Kumar, S., & Chang, C. W. (2007). Reverse Auctions: How much total supply chain cost savings are there? – A conceptual overview. *Journal of Revenue and Pricing Management, 6*(3), 229–240. doi:10.1057/palgrave.rpm.5160088

Kung, H., Tung, H., & Case, T. (2007). Managing E-Government Application Evolution: A State Government Case. *International Journal of Cases on Electronic Commerce, 3*(2), 36–53.

Künzle, V., & Reichert, M. (2009). Towards object-aware process management systems: issues, challenges, benefits. In *Lecture Notes in Business Information Processing, 29* (pp. 197–210). New York: Springer.

Kuo, Y.-F., & Yu, C.-W. (2005). 3G telecommunication operators' challenges and roles: A perspective of mobile commerce value chain. *Science Direct*. Retrieved August 3, 2009, from http://www.sciencedirect.com/science?_ob=ArticleURL&_udi=B6V8B-4H99JC0-2&_user=778200&_rdoc=1&_fmt=&_orig=search&_sort=d&_docanchor=&view=c&_searchStrId=979257359&_rerunOrigin=google&_acct=C000043160&_version=1&_urlVersion=0&_userid=778200&md5=a04f3e5c0e758f5c3aa042dc7459d6fb

Lahovnik, M. (2008). Družbena odgovornost ko dejavnik korporacijskega upravljanja podjetij v Sloveniji. *Naše gospodarstvo, 54* (5/6): 10-21.

Lamoreaux, M., Bush, D., Strovink, E., Beuc, M., Degasperi, A. (2008), *The E-Sourcing Handbook – A Modern Guide to Supply and Spend Management Success*. Carmel, IN: Iasta Publishing.

Lamsweerde, A. v. (2001, August 27). *Goal-oriented requirements engineering: A guided tour*. Paper presented at the 5th IEEE International Symposium on Requirements Engineering, Toronto, Canada.

Lamsweerde, A. v. (2004, September 6). *Goal-oriented requirements engineering: A roundtrip from research to practice*. Paper presented at the 12th IEEE International Requirements Engineering Conference, Kyoto, Japan.

Landry, R., Amara, N., & Lamari, M. (2002). Does Social Capital Determine Innovation? To What Extent? *Technological Forecasting and Social Change, 69*, 681–701. doi:10.1016/S0040-1625(01)00170-6

Langford, B. E., Schoenfeld, G., & Izzo, G. (2002). Nominal grouping sessions vs focus groups. *Qualitative Market Research: An International Journal, 5*(1), 58–70. doi:10.1108/13522750210414517

Laudon, K., & Laudon, J. (2004). *Management Information Systems: Managing the Digital Firm*. Upper Saddle River, NJ: Prentice-Hall.

Lawless, W. F., Bergman, M., Louçã, J., Kriegel, N. N., & Feltovich, N. (2007). A quantum metric of organizational performance: Terrorism and counterterrorism. *Computational & Mathematical Organization Theory, 13*, 241–281. doi:10.1007/s10588-006-9005-4

Lawless, W. F., Castelao, T., & Ballas, J. A. (2000). Virtual knowledge: Bistable reality and the solution of ill-defined problems. *IEEE Systems Man, and Cybernetics*, *30*(1), 119–126. doi:10.1109/5326.827482

Lawless, W. F., Whitton, J., & Poppeliers, C. (2008). Case studies from the UK and US of stakeholder decision-making on radioactive waste management. *Practice Periodical of Hazardous, Toxic, and Radioactive Waste Management*, *12*(2), 70–78. doi:10.1061/(ASCE)1090-025X(2008)12:2(70)

Lawless, W. F., Sofge, D. A., & Goranson, H. T. (2009). Conservation of Information: A New Approach To Organizing Human-Machine-Robotic Agents Under Uncertainty. In P. Bruza, Sofge, D.A., Lawless, W.F., Van Rijsbergen, K., & Klusch, M.(eds). *Quantum Interaction. Third International Symposium, QI-2009*. Berlin:Springer-Verlag.

Layard, R. (2005). *Happiness: lessons from a new science*. London: Allen Lane, Penguin Grou.

Lee, G. L., & Oakes, I. (1995). The 'pros' and 'cons' of total quality management for smaller firms in manufacturing: some experiences down the supply chain. *Total Quality Management*, *6*(4), 413–426. doi:10.1080/09544129550035341

Lee, E., White, M., & Austrian, B. (2000). *B2B e-Markets & Trading Hub Primer*. San Francisco: Bank of America Securities.

Lehlokoe, D., & Malema, F. (2000). *A Green Paper on Electronic Commerce for South Africa – for public discussion 2001*. Retrieved August 17, 2009, from www.polity.org.za/polity/.../green_papers/greenpaper/execsum.PDF

Lehtonen, R., & Pahkinen, E. (2004). *Practical methods for design and analysis of complex surveys* (2 Ed.). Hoboken, NJ: John Wiley & Sons.

Leist, S., & Zellner, G. (2006). Evaluation of Current Architecture Frameworks. *ACM Symposium on Applied Computing* (pp. 1547-1553). Dijon, France: ACM.

Leonard, D., & Senipser, S. (1998). The role of tacit knowledge in group innovation. *California Management Review*, *40*(3), 112–132.

Leonard-Barton, D. (1995). *Wellsprings of knowledge: building and sustaining the sources of innovation*. Boston: Harvard Business School Press.

Lesar, I. (2002). *Med iskanjem smisla in izbiro smisla*. Ljubljana: Inštitut za psihologijo osebnosti.

Leuf, B., & Cunningham, W. (2001). *The Wiki way: quick collaboration on the web*. Reading, MA: Addison-Wesley.

Levy, M., & Powell, P. (2003). Exploring SME Internet Adoption: Towards a Contingent Model. *Electronic Markets*, *13*(2), 173–181. doi:10.1080/1019678032000067163

Lewin, K. (2005). *A Dynamic Theory of Personality – Selected Papers*. Read Books.

Li, Y., Vanhaverbeke, W., & Schoenmakers, W. (2008). Exploration and exploitation in innovation: Reframing the interpretation. *Creativity and Innovation Management*, *17*(2), 107–126. doi:10.1111/j.1467-8691.2008.00477.x

Lichtenthaler, U. (2008). Open innovation in practice: an analysis of strategic approaches to technology transactions. *IEEE Transactions on Engineering Management*, *55*(1), 148–157. doi:10.1109/TEM.2007.912932

Lief, V. (1999). *Net Marketplaces Grow Up*. Cambridge, UK: Forrester Research.

Lin, A., & Patterson, D. (2007). An investigation into the barriers to introducing virtual enterprise networks. In Wang, Y.C., Heng, M.S.H., Chau, P.Y.K. (ed.) (2006). *Supply chain management: Issues in the new era of collaboration and competition*, pp.23-44. Hershey, PA: Idea Group.

Linley, A., & Joseph, S. (Eds.). (2004). *Positive Psychology in Practice*. Newspaper of the National Association of School Psychologists, Retrieved May 25, 2009, from http://people.hofstra.edu/Jeffrey_J_Froh/Froh_Review.pdfSeligman, M.E. [2.2.2009].

Linley, A., Joseph, S., Maltby, J., Harrington, S., & Wood, A. M. (2009). Positive Psychology Applications. In C. R. Snyder & S. J. Lopez (Ed.) 2002. *Oxford Handbook of Positive Psychology*. New York: Oxford University Press.

Linstone, H. A., & Turoff, M. (2002). *The Delphi method techniques and applications*. Reading, MA: Addison Wesley.

Liyanage, J. P., & Langeland, T. (2007). Smart assets through digital capabilities. In Khosrow-Pour, M. (Ed.), *Encyclopaedia of Information Science and Technology.* Hershey, PA: Idea Group.

Liyanage, J. P. (2008b). Integrated eOperations-eMaintenance: Applications in North Sea Offshore assets. In Kobbacy, K. A. H., & Murthy, D. N. P. (Eds.), *Complex systems maintenance handbook* (pp. 585–610). New York: Springer. doi:10.1007/978-1-84800-011-7_24

Liyanage, J. P., & Herbert, M. (2008). Collaborative dynamic networks (CDNs) and Virtual support enterprises (VSEs). In Putnik, G. D., & Cunha, M. M. (Eds.), *Encyclopaedia of Networked and Virtual Organizations* (pp. 237–243). Hershey, PA: IGI-Global.

Liyanage, J. P., Herbert, M., & Harestad, J. (2006). Smart integrated e-operations for high-risk and technologically complex assets: Operational networks and collaborative partnerships in the digital environment. In Wang, Y. C. (Eds.), *Supply chain management: Issues in the new era of collaboration and competition* (pp. 387–414). Hershey, PA: Idea Group.

Liyanage, J. P. (2008a) Rapid virtual enterprising to manage complex and high-risk assets. In Zemliansky, P., St. Amant, K., (ed.), *Handbook of Research on Virtual Workplaces and the New Nature of Business Practice*, pp 702-709. Hershey, PA: IGI Global.

Liyanage, J.P., & Bjerkebæk, E., (2007). Key note paper: Use of advanced technologies and information solutions for North sea offshore assets: Ambitious changes and socio-technical dimensions. *Journal of International Technology and Information Management (JITIM)*, 1-10. International Information Management Association (IIMA).

Locket, N., & Brown, D. (2003). *Innovations Affecting SMEs and E-Business with Reference to Strategic Networks, Aggregation and Intermediaries.* Lancaster University Managament School – Working Paper. Retrieved September 10, 2009 from http://www.lums.lancs.ac.uk

Longman. (1992). *Longman of English Language and Culture.* New York: Longman Dictionaries.

Lopes, J., Filho, J. F. R., & Pederneiras, M. (2008). *Educação Contábil.* Análise das metodologias e técnicas de pesquisa adotadas nos estudos brasileiros sobre *Balanced Scorecard:* um estudo dos artigos publicados do período de 1999 a 2006. Ed. São Paulo: Atlas.

Lopez, S. J., & Gallagher, M. W. (2009). A Case for Positive Psychology. In C. R. Snyder & S. J. Lopez (Ed.) 2002. *Oxford Handbook of Positive Psychology.* New York: Oxford University Press.

Love, P., Irani, Z., Standing, C., Lin, C., & Burn, J. (2005). The Enigma of Evaluation: Benefits, Costs and Risks of IT in Australian Small Medium-Sized Enterprises. *Information & Management, 42*(7), 947–964. doi:10.1016/j.im.2004.10.004

Lucas, R. E., Clark, A. E., Georgellis, Y., & Diener, E. (2003). Re-examining adaptation and the set point model of happiness: Reactions to changes in marital status. *Journal of Personality and Social Psychology, 84*, 527–539. doi:10.1037/0022-3514.84.3.527

Lucas, R. E., Diener, E., & Suh, E. (1996). Discriminant validity of well-being measures. *Journal of Personality and Social Psychology, 71*, 616–618. doi:10.1037/0022-3514.71.3.616

Luce, R. D., & Raiffa, H. (1967). *Games and decision.* New York: Wiley.

Lurey, J., & Raisinghani, M. (2001). An empirical study of best practices in virtual teams. *Information & Management, 38*, 523–544. doi:10.1016/S0378-7206(01)00074-X

MacGregor, R., & Vrazalic, L. (2005). A basic model of electronic commerce adoption barriers. A study of regional small businesses in Sweden and Australia. *Journal of Small Business and Enterprise Development, 12*(4), 510–527. doi:10.1108/14626000510628199

MacGregor, R., & Vrazalic, L. (2008). *SMEs and Electronic Commerce: An Overview of Our Current Knowledge.* Hershey, PA: IGI Global. Retrieved September 10, 2009 from http://www.igi-global.com

Machado, J. (1981). *Grande Dicionário da Língua Portuguesa* (Machado, J., Ed.). *Vol. 1*). Amigos do Livro.

Maguire, S., & Koh, S. (2004). Identifying the Adoption of E-Business and Knowledge Management within SMEs. *Journal of Small Business and Enterprise Development, 11*(3), 338–348. doi:10.1108/14626000410551591

Maguire, S., Koh, S., & Magrys, A. (2007). The Adoption of E-Business and Knowledge Management in SMEs. *Benchmarking: An International Journal, 14*(1), 37–58. doi:10.1108/14635770710730928

Mahadevan, B. (2000). Business Models for Internet based E-Commerce: An Anatomy. *California Management Review, 42.*

Majumdar, S. K. (1995). The Determinants of Investment in New Technology: An Examination of Alternative Hypothesis. *Technological Forecasting and Social Change, 50,* 235–247. doi:10.1016/0040-1625(95)90095-0

Manchanda, P., Dubé, J.-P., Goh, K. Y., & Chintagunta, P. K. (2006, February). The effect of banner advertising on internet purchasing. *JMR, Journal of Marketing Research, 43*(1), 98–108. doi:10.1509/jmkr.43.1.98

Marasini, R., Ions, K., & Ahmad, M. (2008). Assessment of E-Business Adoption in SMEs: A Study of Manufacturing Industry in the UK North East Region. *Journal of Manufacturing Technology Management, 19*(5), 627–644. doi:10.1108/17410380810877294

March, J.G., Sproull, L.S. e Tamuz, Michal, (1999), Learning from samples of one or fewer, The Pursuit of Organizational Intelligence. Thousand Oaks, CA: Sage Publications.

Marks, G. N., & Flemming, N. (1999). Influences and consequences of well-being among Australian young people: 1980-1995. *Social Indicators Research, 46,* 301–323. doi:10.1023/A:1006928507272

Martin, J. (2001). *Organizational Behaviour.* London: Thompson Learning.

Martin, L., & Matlay, H. (2001). "Blanket" Approaches to Promoting ICT in Small Firms: Some Lessons from the DTI Adoption Model in the UK. *Internet Research: Electronic Networking Applications and Policy, 11*(5), 399–410. doi:10.1108/EUM0000000006118

Martin, (2005). *Making Happy People: the nature of happiness and its origins in childhood.* Fourth Estate pubs.

Maslow, A. H. (1954). *Motivation and Personality.* New York: Harper&Row.

Mautner, T. (1995). *A dictionary of philosophy.* Oxford: Blackwell Publishers Ltd.

Mayer, R. C., Davis, J. H., & Schoorman, F. D. (1995). An integrative model of organizational trust. *Academy of Management Review, 20*(3), 709–734. doi:10.2307/258792

McAfee, R. P., & McMillan, J. (1987). Auctions and Bidding. *Journal of Economic Literature (American Economic Association), 25* (2), 699–738, June 1987. Retrieved from http://www.jstor.org/stable/2726107, on 2009-11-16.

McAllister, F. (2005). *Wellbeing Concepts and Challenges. Discussion Paper Prepared by Fiona McAllister for the Sustainable Development Research Network (SDRN).* Retrieved May 1, 2009, from http://www.sd-research.org.uk/wellbeing/documents/SDRNwellbeingpaper-Final_000.pdf.

MCcann. A. Omdal, S. Nyberg, R. K. & Mydland, Ø, (2004), *Statoil's First Onshore Support Center: The Result of New Work Processes and Technology Developed to Exploit Real-Time Data,* Society of Petroleum Engineers (SPE), 90367.

McDaniel, C. D., & Gates, R. H. (2000). *Contemporary Marketing Research* (4th ed.). Cincinnati, OH: Southwestern College Publishing.

Meckel, M., Walters, D., Greenwood, A., & Baugh, P. (2004). A taxonomy of e-business adoption and strategies in small and medium sized enterprises. *Strategic Change, 13*(5), 259–269. doi:10.1002/jsc.682

Medina-Mora, R., Winograd, T., Flores, R., & Flores, F. (1992). The Action Workflow approach to workflow management technology. In J. Turner & R. Kraut (Eds.), *4th Conference on Computer Supported Cooperative Work.* New York: ACM.

Mehrtens, J., Cragg, P., & Mills, A. (2001). A model of Internet adoption by SMEs. *Information & Management, 39*(3), 165–176. doi:10.1016/S0378-7206(01)00086-6

Mendelson, H., & Pillai, R. R. (1999). Information age organizations, dynamics and performance. *Journal of Economic Behavior & Organization, 38*(3), 253–281. doi:10.1016/S0167-2681(99)00010-4

Meneklis, B., Kaliontzoglou, A., Douligeris, C., & Polemi, D. (2005). *Engineering and Technology Aspects of an e-Government Architecture Based on Web Services, Proceedings of the Third European Conference on Web Services.*

Mensah, A. O., Bahta, A., & Mhlang, S. (2002). *E-Commerce challenges in Africa: issues, constraints, opportunities*. ECA briefing paper. World Summit on the Information Society, Geneva 2003, Tunis 2005

Meyer, J. (Ed.). (2000). *Jahrbuch der KMU-Forschung.* München. 1f Meyer, J. (Ed.). (2001). *Flensburger Forschungsbeiträge zur kleinen und mittleren Unternehmen.* Koln. 1ff

Miles, M. B., & Huberman, A. M. (1994). *Qualitative data analysis: An expanded Sourcebook.* Thousand Oaks, CA: Sage.

Miles, R. E., Snow, C. C., & Miles, G. (2000). The Future. org. *Long Range Planning, 33,* 300–321. doi:10.1016/S0024-6301(00)00032-7

Milutinovič, Ž., & Patricelli, F. (2002). *E-business and e-challenges.* Amsterdam: IOS Press.

Mintzberg, H. & Q., J. (2001). *O processo da estratégia.* 3. ed. Porto Alegre: Bookmam.

Mirvis, P. H., Sales, A. L., & Hackett, E. J. (1991). The Implementation and Adoption of New Technology in Organizations: The Impact on Work, People and Culture. *Human Resource Management, 30,* 113–139. doi:10.1002/hrm.3930300107

Mohr, L. B. (1969). Determinants of Innovation in Organizations. *The American Political Science Review, 63,* 111–126. doi:10.2307/1954288

Mooradian, T., Renzl, B., & Matzler, K. (2006). Who Trusts? Personality, trust and knowledge sharing. *Management Learning, 37*(4), 523–540. doi:10.1177/1350507606073424

Moutella. C.(2002). *Fidelização de clientes como Diferencial Competitivo.* Fonte www.portaldomarketing.com.br, acesso em 20/11/2008.

Mulej, M. (1979). *Ustvarjalno delo in dialektična teorija sistemov. Razvojni center.* Celje.

Mulej, M., & Kajzer, S. (1998a). Tehnološki razvoj in etika soodvisnosti. *Raziskovalec, 28,* 1.

Mulej, M. (2009). Lack of requisitely holistic thinking and action – a reason for products to not become winners. In Rebernik, (Eds.), *PODIM 2009. University of Maribor.* Faculty of Economics and Business, Institute for Entrepreneurship and Small Business Management.

Mulej, M. (1974). Dialektična teorija sistemov in ljudski reki. *Naše gospodarstvo,* 21 (3-4): 207-212.

Mulej, M. (1975). *Osnove dialektične teorije sistemov.* Lecture notes. Univerza v Ljubljani, Fak. za telesno kulturo, Ljubljana.

Mulej, M. et al. (2000). *Dialektična in druge mehkosistemske teorije: (podlage za celovitost in uspeh managementa).* Maribor: Ekonomsko-poslovna fakulteta.

Mulej, M., & Hrast, A. (2008). Družbena odgovornost podjetij. V: *Skupaj smo močnejši, Zbornik 2. konference nevladnih organizacij Podravja* (pp 41-52). Regionalno stičišče Podravja.

Mulej, M., & Kajzer, S. (1998b). Ethic of interdependence and the law of requisite holism. In M. Rebernik & M. Mulej (Ed.) *STIQE '98* (pp 56-67). Maribor: ISRUM.

Mulej, M., Božičnik, S., Ženko, Z., & Potočan, V. (2009). Nujnost in zapletenost ustvarjalnega sodelovanja za inoviranje in pot iz krize 2008. In Hrast, A. & Mulej, M. (Ed.). *Delo – most za sodelovanje/4. mednarodna konferenca Družbena odgovornost in izzivi časa 2009.* Maribor: IRDO – Inštitut za razvoj družbene odgovornosti, Musek, J. & Avsec, A. (2002). Pozitivna psihologija: subjektivni (emocionalni) blagor in zadovoljstvo z življenjem. *Anthropos,* 34, (1/3), 41-68.

Musek, J., & Avsec, A. (2006). Osebnost, samopodoba in psihično zdravje. *Anthropos, 38*(1/2), 51–75.

Musek, J., Tušak, M., & Zalokar Divjak, Z. (1999). *Osebnost in zdravje.* Ljubljana: EDUCY.

Musek, J. (1998). *Človek celostno bitje.* Educy: Ljubljana: Inštitut za psihologijo osebnosti.

Musek, J. (2005). *Psihološke in kognitivne študije osebnosti.* Ljubljana: Znanstveni inštitut Filozofske fakultete.

Musek, J., & Avsec, A. (2002). Pozitivna psihologija: subjektivni (emocionalni) blagor in zadovoljstvo z življenjem. *Anthropos*, [online]. *34*(1/3), 41-68. Dostopno na: http://www.educy.com/jmusek/Teksti/Pozitivna%20 psihologija.pdf. [16.2.2009].

Mutafelija, B., & Stromberg, H. (2009). *Process improvement with CMMI v1.2 and ISO standards*. Boca Raton, FL: Auerbach Publications.

Mutula, S., & Brakel, P. (2006). E-readiness of SMEs in the ICT Sector in Botswana with Respect to Information Access. *The Electronic Library*, *24*(3), 402–417. doi:10.1108/02640470610671240

Ndlovu, R. (2009). *ICT guide – Zimbabwe*. Retrieved August 5, 2009, from www.kubatana.net/docs/inftec/ndlovu_ict_guide_zimbabwe.doc

Negroponte, N. (1995). *Being Digital*. New York: Knopf Doubleday Publishing G.

Nelson, S., & Bayrak C. (2009). Categorizing Web Queries. *SIGSOFT Software Engineering Notes. March 2009 34(2)*.

Nette, D. (2005). *Happiness: the Science behind you smile*. Oxford, UK: OU

Neumann, G., & Erol, S. (2009). From a social wiki to a social workflow system. In *Lecture Notes in Business Information Processing, 17* (pp. 698–708). New York: Springer.

Neumann, E. (2001). *Ustvarjalni človek*. Ljubljana: Študentska založba.

Nevo, S., Wade, M. R., & Cook, W. D. (2007). An examination of the trade off between internal and external IT capabilities. *The Journal of Strategic Information Systems*, *16*, 5–23. doi:10.1016/j.jsis.2006.10.002

Nickels, W. G., & Burk Wood, M. (1997). *Marketing: Relationships, Quality, Value*. New York: Worth Publishers Inc.

NJM European. (2000). *A Study and Analysis of Management Training~Techniques for the Heads of SMEs, particularly Using the Information and Communication Technologies (ICTs): Report for the Directorate-General for Enterprise of the European Commission* under contract DGENT 99/C/A3/31 S12.128934

Nonaka, I. (1991). The Knowledge Creating Company. *Harvard Business Review*, November-December, 69, pp. 96-104.

Nordström. Kjell A. & Ridderstråle, J. (2001). *Ta nori posel – Funky business, ko zaigra talent, kapital pleše*. Ljubljana: GV založba.

Oakland, J. S. (2000). *Total Quality Management: Text with Cases*. Boston: Butterworth Heinemann.

OASIS. (2007*). Web Services Business Process Execution Language, V.2.0*. Retrieved September 18, 2009, from http://docs.oasis-open.org/wsbpel/2.0/wsbpel-v2.0.pdf.

O'Dell, C., & Grayson, C. J. J. (1998). *If Only We Knew What We Know: The Transfer of Internal Knowledge and Best Practice*. New York: The Free Press.

OECD. (2008). *Internet Selling and Purchasing by Industry (2), 2008*. OECD Key ICT Indicators in Excel table format. Retrieved November, 30, 2009 from http://www.oecd.org/dataoecd/20/22/34083121.xls.

OLF (Oljeindustriens landsforening / Norwegian Oil Industry Association), (2003), *eDrift for norsk sokkel: det tredje effektiviseringsspranget* (eOperations in the Norwegian continental shelf: The third efficiency leap), OLF (www.olf.no). (*in Norwegian*)

OLF (Oljeindustriens landsforening / Norwegian Oil Industry Association), (2007), *Oppdatert verdipotensiale for Integrerte operasjoner på norsk sokkel* (Updated value potential for Integrated operations on Norwegian shelf), OLF (www.olf.no). (*in Norwegian*)

Olson, G. M., & Olson, J. S. (2000). Distance Matters. *Human-Computer Interaction*, *15*, 139–178. doi:10.1207/S15327051HCI1523_4

OMB (Office of Management and Budget). (2006). *FEA Practice Guidance*. Retrieved June 30, 2006, http://www.whitehouse.gov/omb/egov/documents/FEA_Practice_Guidance.pdf

OMG. (2005). *UML 2.0 OCL Specification*. Retrieved September 18, 2009, from http://www.omg.org/docs/ptc/ 05-06-06.pdf.

OMG. (2007). *Unified Modeling Language: Superstructure, V.2.1.1*. Retrieved September 18, 2009, from http://www.omg.org/docs/formal/07-02-03.pdf.

OMG. (2008). *Business Process Modeling Notation, V.1.1*. Retrieved September 18, 2009, from http://www.bpmn.org.

Ongori, H. (2009). Role of Information Communication Technologies Adoption in SMEs: Evidence from Botswana. *Research Journal of Information Technology, 1*(2), 79–85. doi:10.3923/rjit.2009.79.85

Ordanini, A., Micelli, S., & Di Maria, E. (2004). Failure and success of B-to-B Exchange Business Models: A Contingent analysis of their performance. *European Management Journal, 22*(3), 281–289. doi:10.1016/j.emj.2004.04.013

Ordanini, A. (2006). *Information Technology and Small Businesses: Antecedents and Consequences of Technology Adoption*. Northampton, MA: Edward Elgar.

Orlikowski, W., & Hofman, J. (1997). An Improvisational Model of Change Management: The Case of Groupware Technologies. *Sloan Management Review, 38*(2), 11–21.

Ould, M. (2005). *Business Process Management: a rigorous approach*. The British Computer Society.

Pais, C. (2003). *As representações da Liderança Eficaz no contexto empresarial do Norte de Portugal. Dissertação de Mestrado em Psicologia Social e das Organizações*. Porto: Universidade Fernando Pessoa.

Pandya, A., & Dholakia, N. (2002). *B2C Crash as an Innovation Failure: Organization Learning from the Dotcom Debris*. Working paper, University of Chicago. Retrieved April 24, 2002 from http://ritim.eba.uri.edu/wp2003/pdf_format/JECO-B2C-Innovation-Failure-v01.pdf

Parker, C., & Castleman, T. (2009). Small firm eBusiness adoption: a critical analysis of theory. *Journal of Enterprise Information Management, 22*(1/2), 167–182. doi:10.1108/17410390910932812

Parkes, D. C., & Kalagnanam, J. (2005). Models for iterative multiattribute Vickrey auctions. *Management Science, 51*(3), 435–451. doi:10.1287/mnsc.1040.0340

Patton, M. (1990). *Qualitative Evaluation and Research Methods*. Newbury Park, CA: Sage Publications.

Paul, C. L. (2008). A modified Delphi approach to a new card sorting methodology. *Journal of Usability Studies, 4*(1), 7–30.

Pavic, S., Koh, S., Simpson, M., & Padmore, J. (2007). Could E-Business Create a Competitive Advantage in UK SMEs? *Benchmarking: An International Journal, 14*(3), 320–351. doi:10.1108/14635770710753112

Pavot, W. in E. Diener. (2004). The subjective evaluation of well-being in adulthood: Findings and implications. *Ageing International, 29*(2), 113–135. doi:10.1007/s12126-004-1013-4

Pearsall, J. (2001). *Oxford Dictionary of English* (Pearsall, J., Ed.). Oxford, UK: Oxford University Press.

Pehrson, B., & Ngwira, M. (2006). *Optical Fibre for Education and Research Networks in Eastern and Southern Africa*. Retrieved August 8, 2009, from www.ubuntunet.ssvl.kth.se/.../Sarua-fibre-final-report-draft-2006-03-04.pdf

Pentland, B. (1995). Information systems and organizational learning: the social epistemology of organizational knowledge systems. *Accounting. Management and Information Technologies, 5*(1), 1–21. doi:10.1016/0959-8022(95)90011-X

Peppers, D., & Rogers, M. (1997). [– *Instrumentos para Competir na Era da Interatividade*. Rio de Janiro: Campus.]. *EMPRESA, 1*, 1.

Peppers, D., Rogers, M., & Dorf, B. (2001). *Marketing One to One – Ferramentas para implementação de Programas de Marketing Direto One to One*. São Paulo: Makron Books.

Perrone, G., Bruccoleri, M., & Renna, P. (2005). *Designing and Evaluating value added services in Manufacturing e-marketplaces. Netherlands*. Netherlands: Springer. doi:10.1007/1-4020-3152-1

Pichler, J. (2009). SME-SPECIFIC "PROFILES", STRATEGIC POTENTIALS AND ATTITUDES TOWARD INTERNATIONALIZATION IN THE ENLARGED EU.

Podolny, J. M., & Stuart, T. E. (1995). A Role-Based Ecology of Technological Change. *American Journal of Sociology, 100*, 1224–1260. doi:10.1086/230637

Poon, S., & Swatman, P. (1999). An Exploratory Study of Small Business Internet Commerce Issues. *Information & Management, 35*(1), 9–18. doi:10.1016/S0378-7206(98)00079-2

Porter, M. E. (2008). The five competitive forces that shape strategy. *Harvard Business Review, 86*(1), 78–93.

Porter, M. E., & Ketels, C. (2003). *UK competitiveness: Moving to the next stage Economic Papers.* ESRC.

Porter, M. (1985). *Competitive advantage, creating and sustaining superior performance.* Washington, DC: First Free Press Edition.

Porter, M. E. (1990). *Vantagem competitiva. Trad. Elizabeth M. P. Braga. RJ.* Campus.

Powell, W. W. (1987). Review Essay: Explaining Technological Change. *American Journal of Sociology, 93,* 185–197. doi:10.1086/228714

Prosenak, D., Mulej, M., & Snoj, B. (2008). A requisitely holistic approach to marketing in terms of social well-being. *Kybernetes, 37*(9/10), 1508–1529. doi:10.1108/03684920810907832

Prosenak, D. & Mulej, M. (2008). O celovitosti in uporabnosti obstoječega koncepta družbene odgovornosti poslovanja = About holism and applicability of the existing concept of corporate social responsibility (CSR). *Naše gospodarstvo, 54* (3/4), 10-21.

Prosenak, D., & Mulej, M. (2007). How can marketing contribute to increase of well-being in transitional (and other) societies? In B. Snoj & B. Milfelner (Ed.), *1st International Scientific Marketing Theory Challenges in Transitional Societies Conference* (pp 127-133). Maribor: University of Maribor, Faculty of Economics and Business.

Purao, S., & Campbell, B. (1998). Critical Concerns for Small Business Electronic Commerce: Some Reflections Based on Interviews of Small Business Owners. In *Proceedings of the Association of Information Systems Americas Conference,* Baltimore. *MD Medical Newsmagazine, 14-16*(August), 325–327.

Quayle, M. (2004). E-commerce the challenge for UK SMEs in the Twenty-First Century. *Journal of Operations and Production Management, 22*(10), 1148–1161. doi:10.1108/01443570210446351

Rahmati, N. (2008). National Culture and Adoption of Mobile Commerce: An Overview. *European and Mediterranean Conference on Information Systems 2008* (EMCIS2008). May 25-26 2008, Dubai

Raiffa, H. (1996). *Lectures on negotiation analysis.* Cambridge, MA: PON.

Raisch, W. (2001). *The E-Marketplace- Strategies for Success in B2B Ecommerce.* New York: McGraw Hill.

Ramsey, E., & McCole, P. (2005). E-Business in Professional SMEs: The Case of New Zealand. *Journal of Small Business and Enterprise Development, 12*(4), 528–544. doi:10.1108/14626000510628207

Rappa, M. A. (2004). The utility business model and the future of computing services. *IBM Systems Journal, 43*(1), 32–42. doi:10.1147/sj.431.0032

Rayens, M. K., & Hahn, E. J. (2000). Building consensus using the policy Delphi method. *Policy, Politics & Nursing Practice, 1*(4), 308–315. doi:10.1177/152715440000100409

Raymond, L., Bergeron, F., & Blili, S. (2005). The Assimilation of E-Business in Manufacturing SMEs: Determinants and Effects on Growth and Internationalization. *Electronic Markets, 15*(2), 106–118. doi:10.1080/10196780500083761

Raymond, L., & Bergeron, F. (2008). Enabling the business strategy of SMEs through e-business capabilities: A strategic alignment perspective. *Industrial Management & Data Systems, 108*(5), 577–595. .doi:10.1108/02635570810876723

Rayport, J. F., & Jaworski, B. J. (2003). *Introduction to e-commerce* (2 Ed.). New York: McGraw Hill.

Reilly, G. (2000). *E-Commerce Revenue Models: Don`t be Just One Horse.* Gartner Group Strategic Analysis Report.

Reimenscheider, C., & McKinney, V. (2001). Assessing Beliefs in Small Business Adopters and Non-Adopters of Web-Based E-Commerce. *Journal of Computer Information Systems, 42*(2), 101–107.

Renna, P. (2009). A multi-agent system architecture for business-to-business applications. *International Journal of Services and Operations Management, 5*(3), 375–401. doi:10.1504/IJSOM.2009.024152

Report, I. T. U. (2009). *Measuring the Information Society –The ICT Development Index.* Retrieved July 15, 2009, from www.itu.int/ITU-D/ict/publications/idi/2009/.../ IDI2009_w5.pdf

Report, U. N. (2009). The Millennium Development Goals. Retrieved August 2, 2009, from www.un.org/millenniumgoals/.../MDG%20Report%202009%20ENG.pdf

Revkin, A. C. (2005). A New Measure of Well-Being from a Happy Little Kingdom. *The New York Times*, 4. 10. Retriven May 25, 2009, from http://www.nytimes.com/2005/10/04/science/04haphtml?ex=1171947600&en=5a41a93522961d05&ei=5070.

Rezgui, Y. (2007). Exploring virtual team-working effectiveness in the construction sector. *Interacting with Computers*, *19*, 96–112. doi:10.1016/j.intcom.2006.07.002

Rieffel, E. G. (2007). Certainty and uncertainty in quantum information processing. *Quantum Interaction: AAAI Spring Symposium*, Stanford University:AAAI Press.

Riquelme, H. (2002). Commercial Internet Adoption in China: Comparing the Experience of Small, Medium and Large Business. *Internet research. Electronic Networking Applications and Policy*, *12*(3), 276–286. doi:10.1108/10662240210430946

Riss, U. V., Rickayzen, A., Maus, H., & van der Aalst, W. M. P. (2005). Challenges for business process and task management. *Journal of Universal Knowledge Management*, *0*(2), 77–100.

Rocha, M. P., Macara, J. C., & Sousa, F. V. (2008). *A Contratação Pública Electrónica e o Guia dos Contractos Públicos. Edition*. Semanário Económico, Diário Económico & Academia Vortal.

Rogers, E. M. (2003). *Diffusion of Innovations* (5th ed.). New York: The Free Press of Glencoe. (Original work published 1962)

Rosen, B., Furst, S. A., & Blackburn, R. S. (2007). Overcoming Barriers to Knowledge Sharing in Virtual Teams. *Organizational Dynamics*, *36*(3), 259–273. doi:10.1016/j.orgdyn.2007.04.007

Rosson, P. (2000). Electronic Trading Hubs: Review and Research Questions. 16th. Schmid, B. (1993). *Electronic Markets. Electronic Markets*, 3.

Rozman, R., & Kovač, J. (Eds.). (2006). *Družbena odgovornost in etika v organizacijah. Proceedings of the 7th scientific conference on organisation. (In Slovenian).*, Kranj: Univerza v Mariboru, Fakulteta za organizacijske vede in Zveza organizatorjev Slovenije; Ljubljana: Univerza v Ljubljani, Ekonomska fakulteta.

Rutz, O., & Bucklin, R. (2008). *From Generic to Branded: A Model of Spillover in Paid Search Advertising*. Retrieved from http://ssrn.com/abstract=1024766.

Rutz, O., & Bucklin, R. (2009). *A Shrinkage-based Approach to Measuring Keyword Conversion Rates in Paid Search*. Under first round review at Quantitative Marketing and Economics.

Ryan, B., & Gross, N. C. (1943). The Diffusion of Hybrid Seed Corn in Two Iowa Communities. *Rural Sociology*, *8*, 15–24.

Ryan, R. M., & Deci, E. L. (2001). On Happiness and Human Potentials: A Review of Research on Hedonic and Eudaimonic Well-Being. In s Fiske (Ed) *Annual Review of Psychology* (Annual Reviews Inc, Paolo Alto California).

Ryynänen, V. J., Karvonen, M., & Kässi, T. (2008). The Delphi method as a tool for analysing technology evolution: Case open source thin computing. *Proceedings of the 2008 IEEE ICMIT* (pp. 1476-1481): IEEE.

Sabbaghi, A., & Vaidyanathan, G. (2007). Integration of global supply chain management with small and medium suppliers. In Wang, Y.C., Heng, M.S.H., Chau, P.Y.K. (ed.) (2006). *Supply chain management: Issues in the new era of collaboration and competition*, pp 127-164. Hershey, PA: Idea Group.

SADC. (2002). *SADC e-Readiness Review and Strategy*. Recommendations of the SADC e-Readiness Task Force. Retrieved July 17, 2009 from www.schoolnetafrica.org/fileadmin/resources/SADC_report.pdf

Samuelson, P. (1996). Intellectual Property Rights and the Global Information Economy. *Communications of the ACM*, *39*(1), 23–28. doi:10.1145/234173.234176

Sapolsky, H. M. (1967). Organizational Structure and Innovation. *The Journal of Business*, *40*, 497–510. doi:10.1086/295014

Schmidt, K., & Simone, C. (1996). Coordination mechanisms: towards conceptual foundation of CSCW systems design. *Computer Supported Cooperative Work*, *5*, 155–200. doi:10.1007/BF00133655

Schmiemann, M. (2008). *Enterprises by Size Class – Overview of SMEs in the EU*. Eurostat. Retrieved September 10, 2009 from http://epp.eurostat.ec.europa.eu.

Schneider, B. (2004). *The Successful Management of Small and Middle-sized Enterprises in a Specific Sector – with a Practical Analysis.* München in Mering. Reiner Hampp Verlag.

Schwab Entrepreneur. (2003). *ASAFE: Strategic Challenges for E-Commerce Promotion in Central Africa.* Retrieved August 4, 2009, from www.weforum.org/pdf/.../CaseStudy_ASAFE_Yitamben.pdf

Schwartz, S. M., & Caroll, A. B. (2003). *Corporate social responsibility: A three domain approach.* New York: Business Ethics Quarterly.

Science and Technology Minister (2001). *Electronic Acquisition of things, materials and services by the Public administration.*

Sculley, A. (1999). *B2B Exchanges. The Killer Applications in the Business-to-Business Internet Revolution. New York: ISI Publications.* W.: Woods.

Seligman, M. E. (2002). *Authentic happiness: Using the new positive psychology to realize your potential for lasting fullfillment.* New York: Free Press.

Seligman, M. E., & Csikszentmihalyi, M. (2000). Positive psychology: An Introduction. *The American Psychologist, 55*(1), 5–14. doi:10.1037/0003-066X.55.1.5

Seligman, M. E. (2002). Positive Psychology, Positive Prevention, and Positive Therapy. In C. R. Snyder & S. J. Lopez (Ed.) (2002). *Handbook of positive psychology.* New York: Oxford University Press, page: 3-13.

Seligman, M. E., Steen, T. A., Park, N., & Peterson, C. (2005). Positive Psychology Progress, Empirical Validation of Interventions. *American Psychologist* 60(5), 410-421. Retriven March 13, 2009. http://pq.2004.tripod.com/apa_positive_psychology_progress_july_august_2005.pdf., [12.6.2009].

Sen, R., Bandyopadhyay, S., Hess, J. D., & Jaisingh, J. (2008). Pricing Paid Placements on Search Engines. *Journal of Electronic Commerce Research, 9*(1), 33–50.

Sheldon, K. M., & King, L. (2001). Why positive psychology is necessary. *The American Psychologist, 56*(3), 216–217. doi:10.1037/0003-066X.56.3.216

Sheldon, K., Frederickson, B., Rathunde, K., & Csikszentmihalyi, M. in J. Haidt. (2000). *Positive psychology manifesto (Rev. ed.),* [online]. Dostopno na: Retriven June 22, 2000, from http://www.positivepsychology.org/akumalmanifesto.html [22.6.2000].

Shepard, H. A. (1967). Innovation-Resisting and Innovation-Producing Organizations. *The Journal of Business, 40,* 470–477. doi:10.1086/295012

Siegelmann, H., Avital, O, (1996). Electronic Commerce.

Simchi-Levi, D., Kaminsky, P., & Simchi-Levi, E. (2003). *Designing & Managing the Supply Chain* (2nd ed.). New York: McGraw Hill.

Simpson, M., & Docherty, A. (2004). E-commerce adoption support and advice for UK SMEs. *Journal of Small Business and Enterprise Development, 11*(3), 315–328. doi:10.1108/14626000410551573

Singh, M. (2003). Innovation and Change Management. In *M. Singh M. & D. Waddell. (2003). E-business innovation and change management.* Hershey, PA: Idea Group Publishing.

Singh, M., & Waddell, D. (2003). *E-business innovation and change management.* Hershey, PA: Idea Group Publishing.

Singh, M. (1997). *Effective implementation of new technologies in the Australian manufacturing industries.* PhD Thesis, Monash University, Melbourne, Australia.

Singh, M. (2000). Electronic Commerce in Australia: Opportunities and factors critical for success. *Proceedings of the 1st World Congress on the Management of Electronic Commerce (CD-ROM),* Hamilton, Ontario, January, 19-21.

Smits, R. (2002). Innovation Studies in the 21st Century: Questions from a User's Perspective. *Technological Forecasting and Social Change, 69,* 861–883. doi:10.1016/S0040-1625(01)00181-0

Snyder, C. R., & Lopez, S. J. (Eds.). (2002). *Handbook of positive psychology.* New York: Oxford University Press.

Soriano, D., Roig, S., Sanchis, J., & Torcal, R. (2002). The Role of Consultants in SMEs. *International Small Business Journal, 20*(1), 95–103. doi:10.1177/0266242602201007

Sparrow, J. (2000). Knowledge Features in Small Firms. *Operations Research Society KMAC Conference,* University of Aston, 17-18 July.

Sruk, V. (1995). *Filozofija.* Ljubljana: Cankarjeva založba.

Standish Group. (2001). *Extreme chaos.* Retrieved May 30, 2006, http://www.standishgroup.com/ sample_research/ PDFpages/extreme_chaos.pdf

Steiner, G. A., & Steiner, J. F. (2003). *Business, Government and Society: A Managerial Perspective, Text and Cases* (10th ed.). New York: McGraw-Hill.

Štoka Debevec, M. (2008). Pregled dogajanj na področju družbene odgovornosti v Evropski uniji. In Hrast, A. (Eds.), *Prispevki družbene odgovornosti k dolgoročni uspešnosti vseh udeležencev na trgu. Maribor. Referenced here.*

Storey David John. (1994). *Understanding the Small Business Sector.* Thompson.

Straub, D. (2002). *Foundations of Net-Enhanced Organizations.* New York: Wiley.

Strohmaier, M., & Kröll, M. (2009). Studying databases of intentions: do search query logs capture knowledge about common. *fifth international conference on Knowledge capture,* 89-96.

Suchman, L. A. (1987). *Plans and situated actions: the problem of human-machine communication.* Cambridge, UK: Cambridge University Press.

Sustainable Development Research Network. (2006). *Wellbeing Concepts and Challenges.* Online Available: Retrieved June 26, 2009, from http://www.sd-research. org.uk/wellbeing/documents/FinalWellbeingPolicyBriefing.pdf.

Sviokla, J., & Rayport, J. (1995). *Exploiting the Virtual Value Chain.* Boston: Harvard Business School Review, Nov-Dec.

Szulanksi, G. (1996). Exploring Internal Stickiness: Impediments to the Transfer of Best Practice within the Firm. *Strategic Management Journal, 17,* 27–43.

Tai, J. C. F., Wang, E. T. G., et al. (2007), Virtual integration: Antecedents and role in governing supply chain integration. In Wang, Y.C., Heng, M.S.H., Chau, P.Y.K. (ed.) (2006). *Supply chain management: Issues in the new era of collaboration and competition,* pp 63-104. Hershey, PA: Idea Group.

Tampere. (2006). *Finnish Survey on Collegiate Entrepreneurship.* Tampere University of Technology

Tan, J., Fischer, E., Mitcherll, R., & Phan, P. (2009). At the Center of the Action: Innovation and Technology Strategy Research in the Small Business Setting. *Journal of Small Business Management, 47*(3), 233–262. doi:10.1111/j.1540-627X.2009.00270.x

Tascomi Services (2000-2004). *E-Sourcing cost benefits factors –Issues and Opportunities within local government.*

Taylor, M., & Murphy, A. (2004). SMEs and E-Business. *Journal of Small Business and Enterprise Development, 11*(3), 280–289. doi:10.1108/14626000410551546

Thom, L. H., Reichert, M., & Iochpe, C. (2009). Activity patterns in Process-Aware Information Systems: basic concepts and empirical evidence. *International Journal of Business Process Integration and Management, 4*(2), 93–110. doi:10.1504/IJBPIM.2009.027778

Thompson, K. (2009). *The Networked Enterprise: Competing for the future through virtual enterprise networks.* Tampa, FL: Meghan-Kiffer Press.

Thorelli, H. (1986). Networks: Between Markets and Hierarchies. *Strategic Management Journal, 7.*

Tidd, J. (Ed.). (2001). *From knowledge management to strategic competence: measuring technological, market and organizational innovation.* New York: Imperial College Press.

Tidd, J. (2001). Innovation management in context: environment, organization and performance. *International Journal of Management Reviews, 3*(3), 169–183. doi:10.1111/1468-2370.00062

Timmers, P. (1999). *Electronic Commerce, Strategies and Models for Business-to-Business Trading.* London: John Wiley & Sons, Ltd.

Timo, S., Markku, T., & Anne, T. (2005). *Managing business in multi-channel world: Success factors for E-business.* Hershey, PA: Idea Group Pub.

Toth, G. (2008). *Resnično odgovorno podjetje.* Ljubljana: GV Založba.

Townsend, A., DeMarie, S., & Hendrickson, A. (1998). Virtual Teams: Technology and the workplace of the future. *The Academy of Management Executive, 12*(3), 17–29.

Treasury, H. M. (2005). *Cox Review of Creativity in Business: building on the UK's strengths* Retrieved from http://www.hm-treasury.gov.uk./independent_reviews/cox_review/coxreview_index.cfm (accessed 10/12/09).

Treasury, H. M. (2006). *Prosperity for All in the Global Economy-World Class Skills: Final Report* ('The Leitch Report'), Retrieved from http://www.dcsf.gov.uk/furthereducation/uploads/documents/2006-12%20leitchreview1.pdf (accessed 10/12/09).

Trepp, L. (2000). *Valuing the new industrial model: B2B Internet Exchanges.* Electronic Market Center, Inc, Philadelphia; Turban, E., King, D., Lee, J., Warkentin, M. & Chung, H. (2002). *Electronic Commerce 2002 – A Managerial Perspective.* International Edition; Weiber, R., Kollmann, T., (1998). *Competitive advantages in virtual markets - perspectives of "information-based marketing" in cyberspace.* Germany: University of Trier.

Treven, S. (2005, sept.). in & Mulej, M. (2005a). Sistemski pristop k obvladovanju raznolikosti zaposlenih v globalnem okolju. *Organizacija, 38*(7), 321–329.

Treven, S. in & Mulej, M. (2005b). Teorija sistemov, inovativna družba in management stresa v delovnem okolju. *Naše gospodarstvo,* 51(3/4), 56-63.

Tse, T., & Soufani, K. (2003). Business Strategies for Small Firms in the New Economy. *Journal of Small Business and Enterprise Development, 10*(3), 306–320. doi:10.1108/14626000310489781

Turban, E., King, D., Lee, J., & Viehland, D. (2004). *Electronic Commerce - A Managerial Perspective.* Upper Saddle River, NJ: Prentice Hall.

Turban, E., Lee, J. K., Lee, J. K., & Chung, M. (2006). *Electronic commerce: A managerial perspective* (4 Ed.). Upper Saddle River, NJ: Prentice Hall.

Turowski, K. (2002). Agent-based e-commerce in case of mass customization. *International Journal of Production Economics, 75,* 69–81. doi:10.1016/S0925-5273(01)00182-7

UN & ASPA. (2002). *Bench-marking e-government: A global perspective.* Retrieved May 30, 2006, http://unpan1.un.org/intradoc/groups/public/ documents/UN/UNPAN021547.pdf

Van Akkeren, J., & Cavaye, A. (1999), Factors affecting entry-level Internet adoption by SMEs: an empirical study In *Proceedings of the Australasian Conference in Information Systems,* 2, Brisbane, 1999, pp. 1716-1728.

Van Beveren, J., & Thompson, H. (2002). The use of electronic commerce by SMEs in Victoria, Australia. *Journal of Small Business Management, 40*(3), 250–253. doi:10.1111/1540-627X.00054

Van de Vrandea, V., de Jongb, J. P. J., Wim Vanhaverbekec, W., & de Rochemontd, M. (2009). Open innovation in SMEs: Trends, motives and management challenges. *Technovation, 29*(6-7), 423–437. doi:10.1016/j.technovation.2008.10.001

van der Aalst, W. M. P., Weske, M., & Grünbauer, D. (2005). Case handling: a new paradigm for business process support. *Data & Knowledge Engineering, 53*(2), 129–162. doi:10.1016/j.datak.2004.07.003

VanWeele, A. (2002). *Purchasing and Supply Chain Management – Analysis, Planning and Practice.* London: Thomson Learning.

Vara, J. L. D. l., & Sánchez, J. (2007, June 11). *Business process-driven requirements engineering: A goal-based approach.* Paper presented at the 8th Workshop on Business Process Modeling, Development, and Support (BPMDS'07), Trondheim, Norway.

Veenhoven, R. (1997). Advances in the Understanding of Happiness, publishing in French in. *Revue Québécoise de Psychologie, 18,* 29–74.

Vega, A., Chiasson, M., & Brown, D. (2008). Extending the research agenda on diffusion: the case of public program interventions for the adoption of e-business systems in SMEs. *Journal of Information Technology, 23*(2), 109–117. doi:10.1057/palgrave.jit.2000135

Venkatraman, N. (1991). ICT-Induced Business Reconfiguration. In Scott Morton, M. (Ed.), *The Corporation of the 1990s. Information Technology and Organizational Transformation* (pp. 122–157). Oxford, UK: Oxford University Press.

Verbo. (2001). *Dicionário da Língua Portuguesa Contemporânea da Academia das Ciências de Lisboa* (Vol. 1): Verbo.

Vickery Auction. (n.d.). http://en.wikipedia.org/wiki/Vickrey_auction, Wikipedia Website, Accessed on November 16, 2009.

Vickery, G., Sakai, K., Lee, I., & Sim, H. (2004). *ICT, e-business and SMEs* (No. DSTI/IND/PME (2004)7). Paris, France: Organisation for Economic Co-operation and Development.

Waddock, S., & Bodwell, C. C. (2007). *Total Responsibility Management*. Sheffield: Greenleaf Publishing Limited.

Wagner, B., Fillis, I., & Johansson, U. (2003). E-Business and E-Supply in Small and Medium Sized Businesses. *Supply Chain Management: An International Journal, 8*(4), 343–354. doi:10.1108/13598540310490107

Wang, Y. C., Heng, M. S. H., & Chau, P. Y. K. (Eds.). (2006). *Supply chain management: Issues in the new era of collaboration and competition*. Hershey, PA: Idea Group.

Wang, W. Y. C., Heng, M. S. H., et al. (2007), Implementing supply chain management in the new era: A replenishment framework for the supply chain operations reference model. In Wang, Y.C., Heng, M.S.H., Chau, P.Y.K. (ed.) (2006). *Supply chain management: Issues in the new era of collaboration and competition*, pp 1-22. Hershey, PA: Idea Group.

Warkentin, M., Bapna, R., & Sugumaran, V. (2001). E-knowledge networks for inter-organizational collaborative e-business. *Logistics Information Management, 14*(1), 148–163. doi:10.1108/09576050110363040

Wasko, M., & Faraj, S. (2000). It is what one does: Why people participate and help others in electronic communities of practice. *The Journal of Strategic Information Systems, 9*(2-3), 155–173. doi:10.1016/S0963-8687(00)00045-7

Watson, D., Clark, L. A., & Tellegen, A., A. (1988). Develpoment and validation of a brief measure of positive and negative affect: The PANAS scales. *Journal of Personality and Social Psychology, 54,* 1063–1070. doi:10.1037/0022-3514.54.6.1063

Watson, R., Berthon, P., Pitt, L., & Kinkhan, G. (2000). *Electronic Commerce: The Strategic Perspective*. Orlando, FL: Dryden Press.

Weigand, H. (2006). Two decades of the Language-Action Perspective: introduction. *Communications of the ACM, 49*(5), 44–46. doi:10.1145/1125944.1125973

Weill, P., & Vitale, M. R. (2001). *Place to space: Migrating to ebusiness models*. Boston, MA: Harvard Business School Press.

Wejnert, B. (2002). Integrating Models of Diffusion of Innovations: A Conceptual Framework. *Annual Review of Sociology, 28,* 297–326. doi:10.1146/annurev.soc.28.110601.141051

Wellman, B. (2001). Computer Networks as Social Networks. *Science, 293,* 2031–2034. doi:10.1126/science.1065547

Wellman, B., & Wortley, S. (1990). Different Strokes for Different Folks: Community Ties and Social Support. *American Journal of Sociology, 95,* 558–588. doi:10.1086/229572

Wellman, B. (1983). Network Analysis: Some Basic Principles. In Randall, C. (Ed.), *Sociological Theory* (pp. 155–200). San Francisco: Jossey-Bass, Inc.

Welsh, J., & White, J. (1981). A small business is not a little big business. *Harvard Business Review,* (July-August): 18–32.

Wenger, E., & Lave, J. (1991). *Situated Learning: Legitimate Peripheral Participation*. Cambridge, UK: Cambridge University Press.

Westhead, P., & Storey, D. (1996). Management Training and Small Firm Performance: Why is the Link so Weak? *International Small Business Journal, 14*(4), 13–24. doi:10.1177/0266242696144001

Whinston, A., Stahl, D., & Choi, S. (1998). *The economics of electronic commerce*. Indianapolis, Indiana: Macmillan Technical Publishing.

Wiig, K. M. (1993). *Knowledge Management Foundations – Thinking About Thinking – How People and Organizations Create, Represent, and Use Knowledge.* Arlington, TX: Schema Press.

Windrum, P., & de Berranger, P. (2003). The adoption of e-business technology by SMEs. In Jones, O., & Tilley, F. (Eds.), *Competitive Advantage in SMEs: Organising for Innovation and Entrepreneurship.* New York: Wiley.

Winograd, T. (1987-1988). A Language/Action Perspective on the design of cooperative work. *Human-Computer Interaction, 3*, 3–30. doi:10.1207/s15327051hci0301_2

WMRO. (2009). *E-Business Adoption in the West Midlands – 2008.* Birmingham, UK: West Midlands Research Observatory.

Wood, J., Tung, H.-L., Marshall-Bradley, T., Sofge, D. A., Grayson, J., & Lawless, W. F. (2009). Applying an Organizational Uncertainty Principle: Semantic Web-Based Metrics. In M. M. Cunha, Eva Oliveira, Antonio Tavares & Luis Ferreira (Eds.). *Handbook of Research on Social Dimensions of Semantic Technologies and Web Services.* Hershey, PA: IGI Global.

Xiang, Y., Wu, X., & Hu, B. (2008). A Strategic Alignment Method Based on Demand Classification of Information Technology *IEEE Symposium on Advanced Management of Information for Globalized Enterprises* (pp. 1-10). Tianjin, China: IEEE.

Yao, S., & Mela, C. F. (2009). Sponsored Search Auctions: Research Opportunities in Marketing. *Foundations and Trends in Marketing, 3*(2), 75–126. doi:10.1561/1700000013

Yap, C., Soh, C., & Raman, K. (1992). Information Systems Success Factors in Small Businesses. *Ómega. International Journal of Management Science, 20*(5), 597–609.

Yin, R. (1984). *Case study research: Design and methods.* Thousand Oaks, CA: Sage Publications.

Yousuf, M. I. (2007). Using experts' opinions through Delphi technique. *Practical Assessment. Research Evaluation, 12*(4), 1–8.

Zaccone, S. (2004). The Yin and Yang of Reverse Auctions and Trust. *Converting Magazine, 22*(5), 34–36.

Zaha, J. M., Dumas, M., ter Hofstede, A. H. M., Barros, A., & Decker, G. (2008). Bridging global and local models of service-oriented systems. *IEEE Transactions on Systems, Man and Cybernetics. Part C, Applications and Reviews, 38*(3), 302–318. doi:10.1109/TSMCC.2008.919193

Zeithaml, V. (1988). Consumer Perceptions of Price, Quality, and Value: A Means-End Model and Synthesis of Evidence. [July.]. *Journal of Marketing, 52*(3), 2–22. doi:10.2307/1251446

Zhang, Z., & Jin, M. (2007). Iterative Multi-AttRibute Multi-Unit Reverse Auctions. *The Engineering Economist, 52*(4), 333–354. doi:10.1080/00137910701675239

Zheng, J., Caldwell, N., Harland, C., Powell, P., Woerndl, M., & Xu, S. (2004). Small Firms and E-Business: Cautiousness, Contingency and Cost-Benefit. *Journal of Purchasing and Supply Management, 10*, 27–39. doi:10.1016/j.pursup.2003.11.004

Zhuang, Y & Lederer, A. (2003). An instrument for measuring the business benefits of e-commerce retailing. *International Journal of Electronic Commerce, 7*(3). New York: Spring.

Zigurs, I. (2003). Leadership in Virtual Teams: Oxymoron or Opportunity? *Organizational Dynamics, 31*(4), 339–351. doi:10.1016/S0090-2616(02)00132-8

About the Contributors

Maria Manuela Cruz-Cunha is currently an Associate Professor in the School of Technology at the Polytechnic Institute of Cavado and Ave, Portugal. She holds a Dipl. Eng. in the field of Systems and Informatics Engineering, an M.Sci. in the field of Information Society and a Dr.Sci in the field of Virtual Enterprises, all from the University of Minho (Portugal). She teaches subjects related with Information Systems, Information Technologies and Organizational Models to undergraduated and post-graduated studies. She supervises several PhD projects in the domain of Virtual Enterprises and Information Systems and Technologies. She regularly publishes in international peer-reviewed journals and participates on international scientific conferences. She serves as a member of Editorial Board and Associate Editor for several International Journals and for several Scientific Committees of International Conferences. She has authored and edited several books and her work appears in more than 70 papers published in journals, book chapters and conference proceedings. She is the co-founder and co-chair of CENTERIS – Conference on ENTERprise Information Systems.

Joao Eduardo Varajão is professor of information systems management and software engineering at the University of Trás-os-Montes e Alto Douro and visiting professor at EGP – University of Porto Business School. He graduated in 1995, received his master degree in Computer Science in 1997 and, in 2003, received his PhD in Technologies and Information Systems, from University of Minho (Portugal). He currently supervises several Msc and PhD thesis in the information systems field. His current research includes information systems management, project management and enterprise information systems. He has over one hundred publications, including books, book chapters, refereed publications, and communications at international conferences. He serves as associate editor and member of editorial board for international journals and has served in several committees of international conferences. He is the co-founder and co-chair of CENTERIS – Conference on ENTERprise Information Systems. He is also a member of AIS, IEICE and APSI.

* * *

Frédéric Adam is Associate Professor in Business Information Systems at University College Cork in Ireland and Visiting Research Fellow in the School of Economics and Management at Lund University (Sweden). He holds PhDs from the National University of Ireland and Université Paris VI (France). His research interests are in the area of decision-making and decision support and in the area of ERP. He has written and edited a number of books and has over 20 journal papers published in international journals including the Journal of Strategic Information Systems, Decision Support Systems, and the

Journal of Information Technology. He is the Editor-in-Chief of the Journal of Decision Systems and has been Vice-Chair of the Working Group 8.3 on DSSs of the International Federation for Information processing (IFIP) since 2004.

Tom Alby as director search, Tom Alby is responsible for search engine optimization and search engine marketing at uniquedigital in Hamburg, Germany. Previous to this role, he was director for the international search products of Ask.com and focussed on web and image search relevance. He was also technical director of search in Europe for Lycos Europe and Hotbot. Tom graduated from the University of Bielefeld, with master degrees in English, German and computer science in 2000, and is a certified Project Management Professional (PMP) by the Project Management Institute, 2004. He has published several books about web technologies and is a lecturer at the Hamburg University of Applied Sciences and the private Business and Information Technology University in Iserlohn.

Pierluigi Argoneto received his Master of Science in Mechanical Engineering, year 2003, obtained summa "cum laude" from the Faculty of Engineering of the University of Basilicata, Italy. From the DTMPIG of the University of Palermo, Italy, he holds a doctoral degree in Production Engineering, year 2007. During and after his Ph.D., thematic concerning the analysis, the design and the negotiation protocol tests for e-procurement applications have been investigated. A second research interest has been the analysis of competitive environment, with a particular focus on the decision support methodologies at strategic level, mainly based on a game theoretic approach. Another research line concerns the formalization and the study of networked enterprises by using Real Options and cooperative games as tools for decisional support systems. Nowadays he works at the Healthcare Department of the Regione Basilicata at the office of strategic investments and management of financial resources of the healthcare system.

Susana Badillo is a Ph.D student at the 'Project and Systems Engineering' program by the Polytechnic University of Catalonia. Degree in Graphic Design. Specialization and Master in Design by the Metropolitan Autonomous University, Mexico. Divisional Coordinator of Virtual Education. Teacher-Researcher in the Department of Research and Knowledge in the Division of Sciences and Arts for Design.

Antonio José Balloni is currently a researcher at the Center for Information Technology Renato Archer , working with MIS (Management of Information Systems) in the GESITI Project, Ph.D. in Experimental Plasma Physics/1988, by the Institute of Physics Gleb Wataghin – University of Campinas and Pos Doctor researcher/1992 at Interuniversity Microelectronics Centrum/Bélgica. Visiting professor at the Institute of Economy, at UNICAMP, lecturing about MIS. Author of the books: "Why GESITI? (Why management of system and information technology towards organizations?", and "Why GESITI? Security, Innovation and Society". Creator and Organizer of the Workshop GESITI, an workshop about MIS towards organizations, editions I to V. Has about 30 articles in international and national magazines. Since February 2008 is Coordinator of the GESITI Network, with about 2300 collaborators.

Constant D. Beugré (Ph. D. Rensselaer Polytechnic Institute) is a professor of management at Delaware State University, College of Business where he teaches courses in organizational behavior and strategic management at the undergraduate level and organizational leadership at the graduate level. Dr. Beugré also served as the chair of the department of business administration and acting associate dean of the college of business. Prior to joining Delaware State University, Dr. Beugré was an assistant professor of management and information systems at Kent State University, Tuscarawas Campus. Dr. Beugré was also a visiting fellow at Harvard University in 1996. His research interests include organizational justice, offshoring and neuroeconomics. Dr. Beugré has published three books and more than 70 refereed journal articles and conference proceedings. His publications have appeared in academic outlets, such as Organizational Behavior and Human Decision Processes, Decision Sciences, International Journal of Human Resource Management, International Journal of Manpower, Journal of Applied Behavioral Science, Journal of Applied Social Psychology, and Research in the Sociology of Organizations.

Marjorie Luísa Biehl has been an accountant and a manager at an automobile automobile dealership in Brazil since 2007. She received her degree in Accounting Sciences at Unisinos University in 2009 where she was honored by the Accounting Regional Council. Her current research focuses on Strategic Information Management.

Giorgio Bruno is an Associate Professor at Politecnico di Torino, Italy, where he teaches courses on software engineering and object-oriented programming. His current interests concern the operational modeling of business processes and collaborative services, and the design of information systems and workflow systems. He has authored two books and over 130 technical papers on the above-mentioned subjects.

Stephen Burgess has research and teaching interests that include the use of ICTs in small businesses (particularly in the tourism field), the strategic use of ICTs, and B2C electronic commerce. He has received a number of competitive research grants in these areas. He has completed several studies related to website features in small businesses and how well websites function over time, including his PhD from Monash University, Australia (completed in 2002). He has authored/ edited three books and special editions of journals in topics related to the use of ICTs in small business and been track chair at the international ISOneWorld, IRMA, Conf-IRM and ACIS conferences in related areas. More recently, Stephen has extended his research interests to include the use of websites by community based organisations. He has published in journals such as the Journal of Information Science, Information Systems Frontiers, the International Journal of Tourism Research and the Journal of Hospitality, Marketing and Management.

Claudia C. Cabal-Cruz is a Lecturer in Finance at the Economic and Management Sciences Department, University of Quindio, Colombia. She is studying a doctorate in Social Economy at the International University of Andalucia, Spain. Her research area is e-marketing and consumer behavior.

Anders Carstensen, holds a Master of Science in Applied Physics and Electrical Engineering from Linköping Institute of Technology since1983. He is currently working as Subject teacher in computer science at Jönköping University since 1998, and is mainly teaching Database Management and Programming Methodology. He is also a Ph.D. student with main research interests in the area of enterprise modeling and interoperability problems in extended enterprises.

Rodrigo Baroni de Carvalho is a professor in the Master in Business Administration of Fumec University, Minas Gerais, Brazil. He has a PhD in Information Science from the Federal University of Minas Gerais (UFMG). Part of his PhD was done at the Faculty of Information Studies, University of Toronto, Canada with the supervision of professor Chun Wei Choo. His master degree was in Information Science and the bachelor degree was in Computer Science both from UFMG. Before being a full-time professor, he has worked for 16 years as system analyst and IT project manager mainly in the financial industry. His main research interests are knowledge management, KM software, ERPs, portals, technology acceptance, software engineering and information science.

Ritesh Chugh lectures in the Faculty of Arts, Business, Informatics and Education at CQUniversity Melbourne, Australia. He teaches to both postgraduate and undergraduate students in the fields of Information Systems (IS) Management and Development, IS Project Management, and Electronic Commerce. Ritesh has been awarded CQUniversity's 2007 Faculty/Pro-Vice-Chancellors' portfolios/ AIC Tier One Award for teaching excellence and the CQUniversity's Melbourne teaching excellence award for 2008. Currently, he is working towards a doctoral degree that will develop a model to enhance tacit knowledge transfer and make knowledge ubiquitous. His range of interests includes project management, knowledge management, electronic commerce and developing varied teaching and learning practices on a formal note and philately and numismatics on a more casual note. Ritesh is a member of the Australian Computer Society, IEEE, and IEEE's Computer Society too.

Lawrence Chung joined The University of Texas at Dallas (UTD) in 1994, and currently is an Associate Professor of Computer Science in the Erik Jonsson School of Engineering and Computer Science. He received his Ph.D. in Computer Science in 1993 from The University of Toronto. Dr. Chung is the principal author of the book Non-Functional Requirements in Software Engineering. Working in the early phases of the software development lifecycle for over 15 years, Dr. Chung has written a collection of book chapters and articles in over 100 journal, conference, workshop, and invited papers, in the areas of requirements engineering and software architecture. His work has been applied by other researchers to projects in performance engineering, project risk management, and organizational modelling. Dr. Chung serves as an editorial board member on the international journal, Requirements Engineering, and ETRI journal.

Fintan Clear developed an academic background in Geography and Communications Policy, and then worked in business communications for GKN, Pitman, the European Space Agency (ESA) and the BBC World Service before moving into systems development with Sainsbury's where he gained extensive experience of the complex needs of large supply chain systems. Moving back into higher education, he then helped set up electronic business degrees and developed a research focus in technology adoption, especially amongst small firms. He has worked on a number of funded research projects including a pan-European project on virtual working and HEIF-sponsored projects looking at ICT adoption and 'Web 2.0' tool use by firms and their role in knowledge transfer and business growth. In ongoing work he is looking at the potential role that theatric devices can play in the knowledge transfer of complex knowledge. He is a member of the Institute of Knowledge Transfer, the British Academy of Management and BRESE (Brunel Research in Enterprise, Innovation, Sustainability and Ethics).

Dalila Coelho works as assistant researcher in Beja's Polytechnic Institute, in the scope of national and international projects, related to education and training, since 2005. She is also a teachers' trainer (future and in-service) in the subjects of Pedagogy, Research, Educational Management, as well as an adult trainer in Personal Development and Project Management. She worked in educational management with the local administration for three years. She is currently working in Mozambique as manager in educational projects in poor areas. She has a degree in Educational Sciences.

Kathryn Cormican (Ph.D.) is a lecturer in the College of Engineering & Informatics at the National University of Ireland Galway. Her research interests lies in the areas of enterprise integration and technology innovation. Kathryn leads a number of European Union and industry funded research projects in this area. She has published over 60 papers at international conferences and peer reviewed journals. Kathryn works closely with many leading organisations and SMEs helping them to diagnose, develop and deploy new processes and systems.

José C. Delgado is an Associate Professor at the Computer Science and Engineering Department of the Instituto Superior Tecnico (Lisbon Technical University), in Lisbon, Portugal, where he earned the Ph.D. degree in 1988. He lectures courses in the areas of Computer Architecture, Information Technology and Service Engineering. He has performed several management roles in his faculty, namely Director of the Taguspark campus, near Lisbon, and Coordinator of the B.Sc. and M.Sc. in Computer Science and Engineering at that campus. He has been the coordinator of and researcher in several research projects, both national and European. As an author, his publications include one book and more than 40 papers in international refereed conferences and journals.

Keith Dickson is currently Deputy Head (Research) & Professor of Technology Management at Brunel Business School, Brunel University, UK. Previous academic posts at Kingston University, Technical Change Centre (London), and Aston University. He co-founded BRESE, Brunel Research in Enterprise, Innovation, Sustainability and Ethics, at Brunel in 2001. In the last 15 years he has secured (with partners from UK, France, Germany, Hungary, Italy and Finland) six major research grants from ESRC, HEFCE, European Commission, and the Anglo-German Foundation on such topics as 'Use of IT in SMEs', 'Teleworking in SMEs', 'Intellectual Property Protection in the Textiles Industry', 'Social Capital in SMEs', and 'New Product Development Networks'. His numerous research articles have been published in such journals as Research Policy, Journal of Economic Asymmetries, New Technology Work and Employment, and the International Journal of Technology Management.

Caroline Dominguez is a Professor at the University of Trás-os-Montes e Alto Douro in Portugal, where she lectures business management. Her main research interest lies in development issues, project and quality management. Before pursuing an academic career, she was the head manager of organizations dealing with development issues in Peru and Portugal, where she developed and implemented various international funded projects.

Gerhard Doppler is working in project management and consulting. After studies in telecommunication, informatics and business sciences, he has collected sound experience in giving training, in software development and in the conception and creation of e-learning content. During this time he gained several business market qualifications and certifications like Microsoft Certified Trainer, Sun Certified Web Component Developer and Master in Microsoft Dynamics CRM. Development of educational programs based on Blended Learning methodology is one of his major fields since 2001. He has been working in international projects since 2006, geographically covering Europe and some African countries.

Eduardo Escofet got his B.Sc. from the Central University of Las Villas, Cuba in Computer Sciences Specialized in Artificial Intelligence in 1994. He obtained a M.Sc. degree in business information technology specialized in business executive decision making in 1997 from the University of Holguín, Cuba. He has lectured at several universities, developed multiple software products and advised various theses and software projects. He is now a Ph.D. candidate in the department of Software Engineering and Languages at the University of Granada, Spain. His areas of interest are application framework development, service-oriented architecture integration, business intelligence engineering, Web-based business strategies and software quality improvement methods.

Joaquín Fernández is a PhD in Computer Science by the Polytechnic University of Catalonia and Bachelor of Fine Arts by the University of Barcelona. Professor in the Department of Graphical Expression of Engineering, UPC. Has been Director of Design Superior Degree of UPC and Director of Laboratory of Multimedia Applications (LAM) of UPC. Research activity focuses in innovation in ICT applications in the fields of health and learning. Participating and directing several projects involving the application of multimedia and Internet technology.

Mário Pedro Ferreira is a lecturer at UCP - Porto (since 1999) and Braga (2008) teaching undergraduate and postgraduate courses to Management and Economics Degrees and Msc's in Economics and Marketing in the areas of International Economics, European Economics, Economic Integration, International Business, Project and E-Business. Holds a PhD in Economics from Reading University and a MBA from Cardiff Business School. Researcher at CEGE (Center of Management and Economics Studies) and member of EURAM. His main publications and research interests are in the areas of E-Business, Microfinance, International Business and Finance. Took part in two pioneer projects about the assessment of microfinance in Portugal: one for the OEFP and another for the Aga Khan Foundation.

Marco Ferruzca is a Professor at the Faculty of Design and Arts (Metropolitan Autonomus University) in Mexico City. Industrial Designer. Master in Hypermedia. He obtained in 2008 a Ph.D. degree at the Polytechnic University of Catalonia. His professional experience is focused on Applications, Products and Services of Web-based Systems. His research activity is related to collaborative design and knowledge management.

José Figueiredo, Professor in the Engineering and Management Department of IST – Lisbon Institute of Technology – Technical University of Lisbon, is an Electronic Engineer with an MBA in Information Management and a PhD in Industrial Engineering. Always being involved in the university teaching he started two small companies in the information technologies sector. He currently teaches Project Management and Information Management. He is currently the Vice-President of the research unity of the Engineering and Management Department in IST and the coordinator of the department's master course in industrial management (MEGI). He published several papers in international journals, book chapters, and conference proceedings.

María José Rodríguez Fórtiz received her Ph.D. in Computer Science from University of Granada, Spain, in 2000. She is an Associate Professor in the Department of Computer Languages and Systems at the same University and chairs an accredited research group consisting of 18 researchers since 2001. She had been a member in program committees and referee of several conferences and journals. She has been the main researcher of several national projects related to software engineering, software evolution, cooperative systems modelling, adaptive hypermedia systems, and assistive technology for people with special needs (cognitive and mobility impairments).

Garyfallos Fragidis is Lecturer of Business Information Systems in the Department of Business Administration of the Technological Education Institute of Serres in Greece. He holds a M.B.A. from the University of Macedonia in Thessaloniki, Greece. His research is mostly related with the strategic and organizational aspects of electronic business. His current research interest focuses on the development of customer- centric business models. In the past he was engaged in research related to e-business models, service models, business ecosystems, e-government and knowledge management. He has working experience in information technology projects and participated in the implementation of several EU-sponsored research projects.

Burkhardt Funk is full professor for Information Systems Research at the Leuphana University Lüneburg. After studying physics and computer science he worked as a consultant for McKinsey&Company in banking and E-Commerce. Burkhardt has an entrepreneurial background and is co-founder of unique-digital, one of the Top 10 German Online-Media Agencies, where he developed methods and tools for managing Search Engine Marketing campaigns. His research interests encompass analytical modelling of managerial decision problems in E-Business, the integration of Enterprise Resource Planning (ERP) and Environmental Management Information Systems (EMIS), and patterns in software architecture. He has published several research articles in these fields and consulted leading companies.

Luís Ganhão have a degree in Physics by Faculdade de Ciências de Lisboa, but developed is career in Information & Technology. In his more than 10 years of experience in IT he managed Projects in several countries (Portugal, Italy, Egypt, Saudi Arabia, Dubai) mainly in Extreme Performance. Since 2007 he Manages Oracle Portugal Solutions & Architecture Team. Luís Ganhão his an active lecturer in the most important IT events in Portugal.

José Luis Garrido is currently an Associate Professor in the Department of Computer Languages and Systems at the University of Granada (Spain). He obtained his PhD in Computer Science from the same university in 2003. He had been a member in program committees and referee of several conferences, journals and books. He has also been a co-chair of the International Workshop on System/Software Architectures in the series 2007-09, and guest editor for several conference proceedings and special journal issues. His articles and research interests focus on requirements and software engineering, system/software architectures, coordination models and languages, groupware applications, ubiquitous computing, conceptual models, and notations for specification and modelling of distributed, interactive and cooperative systems.

Juan C. Gázquez-Abad (PhD. University of Almería) is Profesor of Marketing at the University of Almería (Spain). Moreover, he has been visiting professor at the University of Ghent (Department of Marketing), Belgium. His research program focus on issues related to retail management, brand management and consumer choice behaviour. Prof. Gázquez-Abad has published in the major Spanish Marketing Journals, as well as other international journals such as The Services Industries Journal, Managing Service Quality, Agribusiness and has presented papers in several conferences (e.g. EMAC, ICORIA, EAERCD, EIRASS).

Sıtkı Gözlü is a professor of production and operations management in the Faculty of Management at Istanbul Technical University. He holds a B.S. in Chemical Engineering from Bogazici University (June 1969), a M.A. in Management from Istanbul University (June 1981), and a Ph.D. in Management Engineering from Istanbul Technical University (June 1986). He became Associate Professor in October 1990 and full Professor in December 1996. He worked as a researcher for two years and as a plant and technical service engineer for more than four years. He lectures on Quality Management, Production Management, Technology Management, and Project Management. His research interests are in the areas of technology transfer and quality management. His works have been published in international and national journals and conference proceedings. He is a member of Turkish Chamber of Chemical Engineers, Production and Operations Management Society (U.S.A.), European Operations Management Association, and American Society for Quality.

Pramila Gupta has research and teaching interests in Information Modelling, Database Management Systems and e-business. Pramila started her academic career at CQUniversity Melbourne, Australia as a lecturer in 1998 and has progressed to be an Associate Professor providing academic leadership to a large team of about 100 academics at the university's Melbourne campus. Pramila's long tenure at the campus has helped her in acquiring sound knowledge about University's academic policies and processes and contributing to the efficient and positive support systems for students and staff at the Melbourne campus. Pramila has had substantial professional and industrial experience in India with major manufacturing and prestigious development corporations. Pramila is a member of the Australian Computer Society (MACS).

Aura Haidimoschi graduated Economics, International cooperation and trade. Experience in training for adult education and human resources management. Attended training courses focused on international trade, international marketing and business management. Post graduated courses for european project management. Project managemer for projects financed by Lifelong Learning Program and Structural Funds. Head of the CCIB Training Unit and Vicepresident of the Pact for Social Inclusion and Social Protection for Bucharest Ilfov Region.

Ciara Heavin is a College Lecturer in Business Information Systems at University College Cork, Ireland. She holds a BSc and MSc in Information Systems from UCC and has recently submitted a PhD in the area of knowledge management. Her main research interests include the development of the ICT industry, primarily focusing on Ireland's software industry and knowledge management in software SMEs.

Eduardo Huerta is a Ph.D student at the 'Project and Systems Engineering' program by the Polytechnic University of Catalonia. Master in Interactive Systems by the Escola de Disseny ESDI, Barcelona. Professional designer by the Technological Metropolitan University, Chile. Doctoral thesis focuses on methods and processes of collaborative design for ICT artifacts and information systems in the fields of e-health and e-learning.

Ioannis Ignatiadis obtained a PhD degree in Information Systems from the University of Bath, School of Management, UK. He also holds Masters degrees in Information Technology and Technology Management from Imperial College and UMIST, UK. He worked in the industry as a software consultant in information technology projects for large European multinationals in UK, Germany and Greece. He also worked as an Information Systems researcher in the implementation of European Union-sponsored Information Society Technologies (IST) projects. His research interests evolve around the social, business and organizational aspects of Information Systems and E-business development and use. He is the author of a number of research publications in these areas.

George Leal Jamil is a professor in the Master in Business Administration of Fumec University, Minas Gerais, Brazil. He has a PhD in Information Science from the Federal University of Minas Gerais (UFMG). His master degree was in Computer Science (UFMG) and his graduate area was Electric Engineering (UFMG). He wrote 14 books in the information technology and strategic management areas. Yearly, he manages the doctoral consortium of the International Conference on Information Systems and Technology Management at the University of Sao Paulo (USP). His main research interests are information systems management, strategy, knowledge management, software engineering, marketing and IT adoption in business contexts.

Susan M. Jones is a professor of Business Administration at Southwest Minnesota State University (SMSU) in Marshall, Minnesota, where she has taught for the past 15 years. She holds a Bachelor of Science degree from SMSU in business administration and a Master of Business Administration (M.B.A.) degree from the University of Minnesota. She was employed for ten years as a Financial Analyst and Financial Analyst Manager at the Schwan Food Company in Marshall, Minnesota. She then earned a doctorate degree in sociology from South Dakota State University, with concentrations in social organization and demography. She has presented at academic conferences and belongs to several academic organizations, including the Rural Sociological Society and the Midwest Sociological Society. She has three times been named to the Faculty Honor Roll by the students at SMSU.

Bwalya Kelvin Joseph is currently a lecturer and Researcher at the University of Botswana. He holds a Bachelors of Science and Technology in Electrical Engineering (Moscow Power Engineering Tech. University) and a Masters in Computer Science (Korea Advanced Institute of Science and Technology). He is also currently pursuing PhD in Information Systems (Univ. of Johannesburg). He started his carrier in 2003 as a Research Assistant at Samsung's Image and Video Systems lab in Taejon, South Korea. During this time, he wrote and presented several research papers at international fora. In 2007, he headed a IDRC – sponsored project in Zambia. He is also currently, IT Team Leader at the Tertiary Education Council of Botswana. His research interests include e-Government, business information systems, database management, distributed systems and business process modeling.

Stamatia-Ann Katriou is a MSc student in Software Engineering at the University of Glasgow and holds an honors degree in Informatics from the Alexandreio Technological Institute (ATEI) of Thessaloniki. After working as a developer for a year on the EU-funded e-business PANDA project at the Research Programmes Division of ALTEC S.A. in Thessaloniki, Greece., she led ALTEC's development for the OneStopGov, SemantivGov and SCUBE-ICT EU-funded projects. Her research interests are in the fields of business computing, the semantic web and software engineering practices. She has traveled extensively concerning her collaborative work and research interests and also contributes at International Conferences.

Hillevi Koivusalo is a director of the service sector, at Hyria Education, in Finland. Her main interests are SME consultations, management, teaching and education, computing and software.

Adamantios Koumpis heads the Research Programmes Division of ALTEC S.A., which he founded at 1996 (then as independent division of Unisoft S.A.). His previous job position was at the Institute of Computer Science, FORTH, at Heraklio, Crete, where he worked at the Rehabilitation Tele-Informatics and Human-Computer Interaction Group on several EC RTD projects (RACE, ACTS and TAP). He is author of research papers, technical reports and Project deliverables and has successfully lead many industrial and European research projects in the areas of E-Commerce, the public sector and business enterprise re-organisation and information logistics, concerning linking of data/information repositories with knowledge management and business engineering models. Adamantios holds a PhD degree from the University of Kingston, UK and a Bachelor degree from the University of Crete, Greece. Together with Androklis Mavridis they have created the PACE toolkit and are responsible for this research activity in ALTEC.

Hsiang-Jui Kung is an associate professor of information systems in the College of Information Technology at Georgia Southern University. He earned his BS degree in Naval Science from Chinese Naval Academy, his MS degree in Computer Science from Northwestern University, and his Ph.D. in Information Systems from Rensselaer Polytechnic Institute. His research interests include information systems education, systems analysis & design, e-government, e-commerce, and database. He has published extensively in journals such as International Journal of Cases on Electronic commerce, Journal of Information Systems Education, Journal of Business Ethics, Journal of Computing Sciences in Colleges, International Journal of Information Technology Education, and Journal of Informatics Education Research.

Erja Lakanen has its Master in Education from Helsinki University. Further education in management, human resources and organizational development and consultancy. Pedagogical qualifications for adult education. Trainer (management), expert services and pojects for SME's and larger organization at Hyria Education Oy from 2006. Twelve years as human resources manager in research centres (VTT, Geology Survey of Finland) and telecom company. Ten years in commercial and administrative work in different service companies and sectors: banking and financial, media and advertising, hotel and restaurant sectors.

Bojan Lalic, dipl ing during the course of working life over ten years spent working on projects at strategic and operational level in companies such as TESA SCG modeler Ltd., Beohemija Belgrade, Hotel Danube, Serbian Chamber of Commerce, etc. Currently, Manager of the International Graduate School of Engineering and Management, University of Novi Sad and an Institute Program Manager of Cisco Entrepreneur Institute Training Center Serbia. At the university teaches courses: Operations Management, E-Commercial, Strategic Project Management, Intelligent Enterprising and Effective Management. He is working on his doctoral dissertation on "Contribution to the development of conditions for the development of intelligent enterprises in Novi Sad, Maribor and New York". Dissertation is based on a set of real case studies.

Desiree Lawless has 17 years of manufacturing experience; 10 of these in plant management and 7 in supply chain. Ms. Lawless is a graduate of the Georgia institute of Technology with a bachelor's degree in Industrial Systems Engineering. She also has a Master's degree in Textile Science from the Institute of Textile Technology. Additionally, Ms. Lawless is a longtime triathlete and a 2009 Ironman Canada Finisher.

William F. Lawless is a Professor of Mathematics and Psychology. He has a PhD in Social Psychology that was granted in 1992 from Virginia Tech, and a Masters Degree in Mechanical Engineering (LSU, 1977). He is a Professional Engineer with a rating in Nuclear Waste Management and he is a Senior member of IEEE. His research interests are in organizational theory, organizational performance and metrics, and in mathematical models of organizations. He has published over 36 articles and book chapters, over 110 peer-reviewed proceedings and abstracts, and he has received about $1.4 million in research grants. He was a founding member of Department of Energy's Savannah River Site Citizens Advisory Board (1994-2000; 2003-2007) where he authored or coauthored over 100 sets of recommendations. He is also a past member of the European Trustnet hazardous decisions group.

Tatiana Levashova, PhD, received her ME degree at St.Petersburg State Electrical Engineering University, Russia, in 1986 and her PhD in computer science at SPIIRAS in 2009. She is a researcher at Computer Aided Integrated Systems Laboratory of SPIIRAS. Her current research is devoted to knowledge-related problems such as knowledge representation, ontology management, and context management.

Brandon Link is a recent graduate of The University of Kansas School of Business in the United States where he studied Management & Leadership, International Business and Geography. His current studies focus on Retail Management and Inventory Control Systems.

Jayantha P. Liyanage specializes in Asset operations, Maintenance technology, and Asset management at the University of Stavanger (UiS), Norway. He is also the Chair and a Project advisor of Centre Industrial Asset Management (CIAM). He was recently appointed to the Board of Directors of Society of Petroleum Engineers (Stavanger chapter) and serves as the Chair of scholarships. Dr. Liyanage is a Co-organiser and coordinator of the European Network for Strategic Engineering Asset Management (EURENSEAM) involving approx. 15 European countries. Furthermore, he was appointed to a special Working Group (WG) on Advanced maintenance engineering, Services, and Technology of IFAC (International Federation for Automatic Control). He was also honoured as a Founding Fellow of the ISEAM (International Society of Engineering Asset Management), and Honorary Fellow of IFRIM (International Foundation for Research in Maintenance). Dr. Liyanage has earned B.Sc. in Production engineering (First Class Honours), M.Sc. in Human factors (Distinction), and PhD in Offshore engineering specializing in Operations & Maintenance. He is actively involved in joint industry projects both at advisory and managerial capacities, and also currently serves as the principal and external advisor for a number of PhD projects. He has published more than 75 publications in various books, international journals and conferences over the last few years. He is active as a member of a number of International societies and Networks. He also serves as an editorial reviewer and a member of international editorial boards of a number of international journals (inclusive of; IJTHI, ISJ, IJDS, JIITO, IJIKM, and an invited reviewer of JQME, and RASS), and actively involves in national and international conferences as a member of International steering committees and program chair. For his performance he has received a number of prestigious awards inclusive of University of Peradeniya Award for the Best Performance in Engineering (1995), Colombo Dockyard Award for the Best Performance in Production Engineering (1995), The Overall Best in Masters (1999), Lyse Energy Research Award for Excellent Research and Academic Contributions (2001), Society of Petroleum Engineers Best PhD Award (2003), Emerald Literati Club Award for Excellence (2004).

Uglješa Marjanovic, MBA during the course of working life over five years spent working on projects at strategic and operational level in companies such as Bloomsburg Maintenance and Construction, University of Pennsylvania, Flat Rate Moving Systems in New York, Center for Competitiveness and Cluster Development, Faculty of Technical Sciences in Novi Sad. Currently, an assistant manager and facilitator at the Cisco Entrepreneur Institute, Training Center Serbia. At the Institute teaches course iExec Enterprise Essentials. Training iExec Ugljesa has performed in Belgrade, Novi Sad, Leskovac, and Kragujevac for over 120 participants with a positive response to the presented subject matter. Worked as a Teaching/Research Assistant during the course of pursuit of MBA at Bloomsburg University of Pennsylvania. He is working on his magister's thesis at the Faculty of Technical Sciences in Novi Sad where he teaches course E-Commerce

Matjaž Mulej, born on Jan., 20, 1941, in Maribor, Slovenia; married, two adult children; healthy; living in Maribor, Slovenia. M.A. in Development Economics, Doctorates in Systems Theory and in Management. Retired from University of Maribor, Faculty of Economics & Business, Maribor, as Professor Emeritus of Systems and Innovation Theory. +1.400 publications in +40 countries (see: IZUM – Cobiss, 08082). Visiting professor abroad for15 semesters. Author of the Dialectical Systems Theory (see: François, 2004, International Encyclopedia ..) and Innovative Business Paradigm for catching-up countries. Member of New York Academy of Sciences (1996), European Academy of Sciences and Arts, Salzburg, European Academy of sciences and Humanities, Paris, president of IFSR (International Federation for Systems Research with 37 member associations). Many Who is Who entries, including Hall of Fame for Distinguished Accomplishments, ABI, Raleigh, NC.

Josep Maria Monguet, coordinator of the 'Project and Systems Engineering' Ph.D program (UPC). Has been: Vice Chancellor of Polytechnic University of Catalonia (UPC), Director of Design Superior Degree of UPC and Director of Laboratory of Multimedia Applications (LAM) of UPC. Director of the Audiovisual Department in the Education Sciences Institute, UPC. Since 1987, professor at the Industrial Engineering School of Barcelona. Businessman. Research activity focuses on innovation in ICT applications in the fields of health and learning. Since 1982, participating and directing several projects involving the application of multimedia and Internet technology.

Elisabete Paulo Morais is Professor of Computer Science in the Department of Informatics and Communications, in the Polytechnic Institute of Bragança. He received his PhD in Computer Science from Trás-os-Montes e Alto Douro University, Portugal. His current research focuses on electronic business and maturity models. It is a member of several scientific committees. Has several papers published in journals and proceeding of conferences.

Leonel Morgado is a Professor at the University of Trás-os-Montes e Alto Douro, in Portugal, where he lectures on programming and the use of virtual worlds. His main research interest is the use of virtual worlds as tools for learning and business. Before pursuing an academic career, he was terminologist for a MS Office 97 localization team, a manager of Web-development and software-deployment teams, a business technical manager, and a programmer. Publications: http://home.utad.pt/~leonelm/ and http://www.degois.pt/visualizador/cv.jsp?key=5033201325101998.

Valentina Ndou, PhD is an assistant professor at eBusiness Management School, ISUFI, University of Salento. After graduating in 'Business Administration' at University of Scutari, she attended a master in marketing and development of territorial systems at ISUFI, eBusiness Management School. Then, she followed the PhD studies focusing her research on virtual networks applied to tourism enterprises and destinations. Her research specializes in analyzing the effectiveness of information systems for SME and their evolution over time, with particular emphasis on new solutions and approaches for business management, eBusiness models, internetworking approaches for SME, virtual clusters and training mechanisms.

Zlatko Nedelko, born 1983, is a researcher at Faculty of Economics and Business with the Department of Organization and Informatics, University of Maribor, Slovenia. He is also PhD student at same faculty. He published his papers at several scientific conferences, many of them abroad. He is also a member of scientific committees of several international conferences abroad. The fields of his research interests are organization and management. Recently he is involved heavily in researching personal values of managers.

José Adriano Pires is Ph.D. in the technology and information systems field from the University of Minho. Professor Coordinator in the Department of Informatics and Communications, in the Polytechnic Institute of Bragança, where he served as director between 2001-2006. Currently, is Pro-President of IPB to the entrepreneurship area. It is a member of several scientific committees, guiding two PhD projects and has participated in several panels of the Master and Doctoral degree. Has several papers published in journals and minutes of meetings. Was coordinated of four projects resulting in the registration of two marks.

José Porfírio is Director of the Social Sciences and Management Department at Universidade Aberta in Portugal. He has a Phd in Strategic Management, a Master in Operational Research and a Degree in Management. He is currently responsible for the PhD in Management of Universidade Aberta. He is a professor in the MBA course of Universidade Aberta, which he coordinated until September 2009, being responsible for the scientific area of Strategy. Their research activities are mainly being done in the domain of Corporate Strategy, the role of Strategic Tools and MIS for the Strategic Management of Companies, and also in the area of Rural and Regional Development.

Vojko Potocan, born 1962, is an Associate Professor of organization and management on the Faculty of Economics and Business (FEB), Department of Organization and Informatics, University of Maribor, Slovenia. He teaches (on the graduate level, on the undergraduate level, and in doctoral program) in three universities in Slovenia and in three universities abroad (Germany, Croatia and Czech Republic).

He takes part in different foreign scientific conferences and realized a number of study visits on abroad (University of Gent, Belgium; University of Greenwich, London, UK; University of Economics, Vienna, Austria). He was 3 times a visiting professor abroad and gave about eight further seminars at foreign universities. He has published +450 texts (+350 in foreign languages in 32 countries), including 8 books, and edited proceedings and textbooks. His research interests include Organization and Management.

Paolo Renna is an Assistant Professor at Department of Environmental Engineering and Physics in the Engineering Faculty of Basilicata University (Italy). He took Ph.D. degree at Polytechnic of Bari in Advanced Production Systems. His academic researches principally deal with the development of innovative negotiation and production planning in distributed environments and manufacturing scheduling in dynamic environment. Several contributions have been presented on design Multi Agent Architecture and test by discrete event simulation in Business to Business environment. Among the contributions, he is co-author of two research books about e-marketplaces and production planning in production networks. Moreover, he has developed coordination approaches in multi-plant production planning environment and innovative scheduling approaches in flexible and reconfigurable manufacturing systems.

Clara Rodrigues has a degree in Sciences of Education, from the University of Coimbra. Since 2005, she is been working in research project management within International Programmes in different Education fields such as: evaluation, staff development, adult learning and organisational management. She delivers training for trainers and other professionals in the topics of pedagogy, project management, competence' evaluation and research methodology. In parallel she has been working as consultant for companies and associations on Project planning and financing.

Inma Rodríguez-Ardura is an Associate Professor of Marketing in the Economic and Business Department of the Open University of Catalonia (Universitat Oberta de Catalunya or UOC), Spain. Currently she is serving as Director of the Doctoral Programme at the Internet Interdisciplinary Institute (IN3-UOC). She holds a doctorate in Economics and Business Studies from the University of Barcelona. Her research interests include e-commerce, consumer behaviour on the Internet, and marketing e-learning interfaces. She is the author of several books and articles on these areas.

Nezha Sadguy has collaborated with eBusiness Management Section working in projects related to eBusiness models for SME of Agrifood sector. After her graduation in Business Administration in Al Akhawayn University, Morocco - Major: Finance, Minor: International business, she followed the master ISUFI in Business Innovation Leadership. Her fields of research have been mainly concentrated in: Analysis and study of e-marketplace for Agrifood: e-business services, processes and attributes; supply chain management; Business Intelligence for e-Business Application in the Food Sector; Design and development of E-learning modules for Agrifood firms.

Luís Rebordão Sampaio, born in 1980 in Lisbon (Portugal), graduated in Industrial Engineering in 2005 at Instituto Superior Técnico, Lisbon. In 2004 joined Iberdata Equipamentos S.A dealing with customers, in 2005 moved into the logistics department, mainly through new warehouse layouts and definition of purchasing order policies. In April of 2007 entered in the Logistics Departments of PT. In May 2008 joined Vortal S.A. R&D Department.

Chiara Sancin has a degree in "Physics" from the University of Trieste. She has specialisations in the fields of Economics and Management of Industrial Innovation, journalism and science communication, multimedia communications. From March 1998 to August 2005 she worked at ICS-UNIDO, as responsible of the Managing Director's office. Her experience is in institutional activities, management of international projects, organisation, communication, conferences in training education and scientific matter and in the research activities especially connected to the innovative training applied to the ICT. She is currently involved in the field of international projects and tenders. In addition she has experience in international project management.

Kurt Sandkuhl, received his MSc and his PhD in computer science from Berlin University of Technology in Germany and his postdoctoral lecturing qualification from Linköping University in Sweden. He is full professor of information engineering in the School of Engineering at Jönköping University in Sweden. Before joining Jönköping University in 2002, he was department and division manager at Fraunhofer-Institute for Software and Systems Engineering in Berlin. His current research interests are in enterprise knowledge modeling, computer-supported collaborative work, information logistics and ontology engineering.

Gustavo Schneider is a graduation student in Business at Unisinos University. He is collaborator on IT researches at the University with Dr. Adolfo Alberto Vanti since 2007, having contributed in some papers. Nowadays he also is intern at a Brazilian bank.

Nikolay Shilov, PhD, received his ME at St.Petersburg State Technical University, Russia, in 1998 and his PhD in computer science at SPIIRAS in 2005. He is a senior researcher at the Computer Aided Integrated Systems Laboratory of SPIIRAS. His current research interests belong to areas of virtual enterprise configuration, supply chain management, knowledge management, ontology engineering and Web-services.

Alexander Smirnov received his ME, his PhD and D.Sc. degrees at St.Petersburg, Russia, in 1979, 1984, and 1994 respectively. He is a Deputy Director for Research and a Head of Computer Aided Integrated Systems Laboratory at St.Petersburg Institute for Informatics and Automation of the Russian Academy of Sciences (SPIIRAS). He is a full professor of St.Petersburg State Electrical Engineering University. His current research interests belong to areas of corporate knowledge management, Web-services, group decision support systems, virtual enterprises, and supply chain management.

Ronald G. Stover is professor of Rural Sociology at South Dakota State University where he has been employed since 1983. Born and raised in Georgia, USA, he attended the University of Georgia, earning undergraduate, masters and doctorate degrees in Sociology. After being awarded his doctorate in 1975, he taught at Clemson University before moving to South Dakota State University. He has published numerous chapters in books and articles in professional journals. In 1993, he published Marriage, Family, and Intimate Relations with Dr. Christine A. Hope and in 1999, he published Industrial Societies: An Evolutionary Perspective with Dr. Melodie L. Lichty and Ms. Penny W. Stover. He has several times been voted Teacher of the Year by students at South Dakota State University and last year was awarded the university's most prestigious teaching award.

Evangelos Tolias is a programmer and web developer interested in Semantic Web technologies, Web Services, Enterprise Application Integration and Evolutionary algorithms. He was born on 15 April 1985 and is completing a software engineering degree at the Alexandreio Technological Educational Institution (ATEI) of Thessaloniki. He has been working in the Research Programmes Division of AL-TEC S.A since July 2008. He participated in the SemanticGov (Providing Integrated Public Services to Citizens at the National and Pan-European level with the use of Emerging Semantic Web Technologies), OneStopGov (A life-event oriented framework and platform for one-stop government), T-Seniority and SCUBE (Strategic Cooperation in Ukraine, Belarus and EU in Information and Communication Technologies) European Union projects.

Sonja Treven was born in 1956 in Ljubljana. She is employed as an associate professor at the Faculty of Economics and Business, University of Maribor in the field of Human Resource Management. She obtained her doctorate at the Faculty of Economics, University of Zagreb. With contributions participated in more than sixty national and international conferences (Las Vegas, Varanasi, Samos, Puerto Vallarta, Kuala Lumpur, Cancun, Vienna, Caracas, Manali, Jaipur, Orlando, Wollongong, Zadov, Baden Baden, Varaždin, Portorož, ...), is the author of three books (Management of human resources, organizational behavior and Mendarodno Coping with stress) and co-author of several books and more than eighty scientific or technical works.

Hui Lien Tung is an Assistant Professor of Mathematics and Computer Science at Paine College. She has a Masters Degree in Information Science (State University of New York-Albany, 2000) and a Masters Degree in Education (National-Louis University, IL, 1990). Her research interests are in MIS, metrics of organizational information systems and performance, e-Government, IT in eHealth, Systems Analysis and Design and database. She has published several Journal articles, book chapters, peer-reviewed proceedings and conference papers.

Adolfo Alberto Vanti has been a full professor in IT Management at Unisinos University in Brazil since 1998. He received his PhD in Business Administration at Deusto University in Spain. His current research focuses on Strategic Information Management, Business Intelligence and Fuzzy Logic Applications.

George Velegrakis is an Electrical and Computer Engineer, graduate of the National Technical University of Athens. He holds a M.Sc. in Environmental Policies and Development, from the Rural and Surveying School of the National Technical University of Athens. Since 2008 he works for the private company IDEC S.A. as project manager. He speaks fluently Greek, English and German.

Adrian Woods PhD FRSA, Foundation Chair in Management, Assistant Head of School, Brunel University, Business School. Professor Woods has worked extensively as a consultant both in the private and public sector in the U.K. and in the European Community. His consultancy has included labour market analysis, skills shortages, technological diffusion and business conditions. His research has encompassed strategy formation, graduates in small firms, international MBAs and entrepreneurial attitudes in the public sector. More recently he has worked on social enterprises and their strategic development.

Muammer Zerenler was born in 1975, in Konya. He earned his Bachelor of Science (B.Sc.) degree in 1996, his Master of Science (M. Sc.) degree in 1998, and PhD degree in 2003 from Selcuk University in Konya, Turkey. His doctoral thesis is titled "The Effect of Process Flexibility on the Businesses' Performance during the Crisis Period". He is Associate Professor of Production and Operations Management since 2009. He lectures courses such as Modern Production Systems, Strategic Production Management, and Electronic Commerce. He has published three books and co-authored many national and international articles and papers in the areas of Production Systems, Information Systems, and Electronic Commerce.

Simona Šarotar Žižek, MSc., born 01.02.1973 in Murska Sobota, graduated from the Faculty of Economics and Business, University of Maribor. She finished M.Sc. studies in Economic and Business Sciences at the same faculty in 2000. She complemented up her theoretical knowledge permanently by the practical work. In 1998 she was employed with the company Mura d.d. as an assistant of the director in the department of Total Quality Management. In September 2004 she became secretary of the Board of the company Mura d.d.; later on she expanded her frame of work by undertaking the tasks of the Head of Strategic Development. She has been employed at the Faculty of Economics and Business in Maribor since 2007 asenior lecturer in HRM. She is author or co-author of articles in several international and Slovenian journals and on scientific and expert conferences..

Index

Breinigsville, PA USA
07 February 2011
255035BV00002B/1-78/P